MAGI AND *MAGGIDIM*

THE KABBALAH IN BRITISH OCCULTISM,
1860-1940

MAGI AND *MAGGIDIM*

THE KABBALAH IN BRITISH OCCULTISM, 1860–1940

Liz Greene

SOPHIA CENTRE PRESS

Sophia Centre Press
University of Wales, Trinity Saint David
Ceredigion, Wales SA48 7AD, United Kingdom
www.sophiacentrepress.com

ISBN 978-1-907767-02-9

British Library Cataloguing in Publication Data.
A catalogue card for this book is available from the British
Library.

Printed and bound by CPI Group (UK) Ltd, Croydon, CR0
4Y

ACKNOWLEDGEMENTS

I would like to express my gratitude to my doctoral supervisor at the University of Bristol, Professor Ronald Hutton, for his insights and continuous support in the research and writing of the PhD dissertation which formed the original basis for this book. I would also like to thank Nick Campion for his confidence and encouragement, Jennifer Zahrt for her meticulous and inspired help in editing the manuscript, and the staff of the British Library, the British Museum, the Warburg Institute Library, the Wellcome Institute Historical Medical Library, the University College London Library, the London Grand Lodge Library and Museum of Freemasonry, and the Bibliothèque Nationale for their courteous assistance in locating research materials and granting permission for the use of many of the images.

Finally, I would like to thank John Daniel for his constant companionship, interest, and encouragement.

TABLE OF CONTENTS

List of Abbreviations

Periodicals and Encyclopedias

AC: Anthropology of Consciousness
AHR: The American Historical Review
AJ: Ashkenazi Judaism
AJP: American Journal of Philology
AJS: American Journal of Sociology
AJS Review: Association for Jewish Studies Review
AP: Annual of Psychoanalysis
AQC: Ars Quatuor Coronatorum
AS: Annals of Science
ASP: Arabic Sciences and Philosophy
BAAAS: Bulletin of the American Academy of Arts and Sciences
BHM: Bulletin of the History of Medicine
BJC: British Journal of Criminology
BJP: British Journal of Psychiatry
BMJ: The British Medical Journal
CJ: Contemporary Jewry
CL: Comparative Literature
CMP: Culture, Medicine and Psychiatry
CR: The Critical Review, or, Annals of literature
DR: Drama Review
EAJSN: European Association for Jewish Studies Newsletter
EC: Essays in Criticism
EEJA: Eastern European Jewish Affairs
EHQ: European Historical Quarterly
EHR: The English Historical Review
EJ: Encyclopaedia Judaica
ER: Eclectic Review
ES: English Studies
FHS: French Historical Studies
FR: Fortnightly Review
FS: Feminist Studies
GM: The Gentleman's Magazine
HJ: The Historical Journal
HJB: Hispania Judaica Bulletin
HLQ: The Huntington Library Quarterly
HP: History of Psychology
HR: History of Religions
HT: History and Theory
HTR: Harvard Theological Review
HUCA: Hebrew Union College Annual

HWJ: History Workshop Journal
IESHR: Indian Economic and Social History Review
IJP: International Journal of Psychoanalysis
IJPR: International Journal for the Psychology of Religion
ILJ: Inner Light Journal
ILM: Inner Light Magazine
IRP: International Review of Psycho-analysis
JAAR: Journal of the American Academy of Religion
JAF: Journal of American Folklore
JAP: Journal of Analytical Psychology
JAR: Journal of Anthropological Research
JASM: Journal for the Academic Study of Magic
JBS: Journal of British Studies
JC: The Jewish Chronicle
JCR: Journal of Contemporary Religions
JCS: Journal of Consciousness Studies
JE: Jewish Encyclopedia
JGS: Journal of Gender Studies
JH: Jewish History
JHBS: Journal of the History of Behavioral Sciences
JHI: Journal of the History of Ideas
JIH: Journal of Interdisciplinary History
JJS: The Journal of Jewish Studies
JJTP: Journal of Jungian Thought and Practice
JLS: Journal of Literature and Science
JMH: Journal of Modern History
JMJS: Journal of Modern Jewish Studies
JML: Journal of Modern Literature
JMS: Journal of Mental Science
JPJ: Journal of Psychology and Judaism
JQR: The Jewish Quarterly Review
JR: The Journal of Religion
JRAS: Journal of the Royal Asiatic Society
JRS: Journal of Roman Studies
JSH: Journal of Social History
JSJ: Journal for the Study of Judaism
JSP: Journal for the Study of the Pseudepigrapha
JSQ: Jewish Studies Quarterly
JSRI: Journal for the Study of Religions and Ideologies
JSS: Jewish Social Studies
JSSMJ: Journal for the Study of Sephardic and Mizrahi Jewry
JSSR: Journal for the Scientific Study of Religion
JVC: Journal of Victorian Culture
JWCI: Journal of the Warburg and Courtauld Institutes

LT: *Literature and Theology*
ME: *Medieval Encounters*
MIH: *Modern Intellectual History*
MJ: *Modern Judaism*
MLN: *Modern Language Notes*
MM: *Mathematics Magazine*
MP: *Modern Philology*
MRW: *Magic, Ritual, and Witchcraft*
NDT: *Neuropsychiatric Disease and Treatment*
NGC: *New German Critique*
OR: *The Occult Review*
PAAJR: *Proceedings of the American Academy for Jewish Research*
PH: *Psychoanalysis and History*
PM: *Philosophia Mathematica*
PP: *Past and Present*
PR: *Psychoanalytic Review*
PSBA: *Proceedings of the Society of Biblical Archaeology*
PT: *Poetics Today*
REE: *Religion in Eastern Europe*
REJ: *Revue des Études Juives*
RES: *Review of English Studies*
RQ: *Renaissance Quarterly*
RR: *The Russian Review*
RRJ: *Review of Rabbinic Judaism*
SA: *Sociological Analysis*
SC: *Science in Context*
SCJ: *Sixteenth Century Journal*
SEEJ: *Slavic and Eastern European Journal*
SJ: *Studia Judaica*
SMN: *Societas Magica Newsletter*
SR: *Sociology of Religion*
SSHM: *The Society for the Social History of Medicine*
TDR: *The Drama Review*
TH: *Theosophical History*
TM: *Theosophy Magazine*
TR: *The Theosophical Review*
TS: *Theosophical Siftings*
VC: *Visual Communication*
VLC: *Victorian Literature and Culture*
VP: *Victorian Poetry*
VS: *Victorian Studies*
WF: *Western Folklore*
YFS: *Yale French Studies*

COLLECTED WORKS OF SPECIFIC AUTHORS

The Collected Works of C. G. Jung: each volume is cited by volume number and paragraph (e.g. Jung, CW10, ¶382) or page (e.g. Jung, CW6, 244); see the Bibliography for full publishing details of each volume.

The Standard Edition of the Works of Sigmund Freud: each volume is cited by volume number and page (e.g. Freud, SE18, 26–31); see the Bibliography for full publishing details of each volume.

The Collected Writings of H. P. Blavatsky: each volume is cited by volume number and page (*e.g.* Blavatsky, CW6, 241–43); see the Bibliography for full publishing details of each volume.

List of Illustrations

...So let us learn, by all means, why the voices wailed that Pan was dead. Let us learn – the answers are simple enough – why Moses had horns, and why the Israelites worshipped a golden calf; why Jesus was a fish, and why a man with a water-jug on his shoulder directed the Apostles – the Twelve – to an upper room. But let us not think that in such explorations we have disposed of or robbed of significance the story these figures tell. The story remains; if it changes, and it does, it is because our human nature is not fixed; there is more than one history of the world. But when we believe that we have proved there is no story, that history is just one damned thing after another, that can only be because we have ceased to recognize ourselves.

– John Crowley, Ægypt (1987)

You say I took the Name in vain
I don't even know the Name
But if I did, well really, what's it to you?
There's a blaze of light in every word
It doesn't matter which you heard
The holy or the broken Hallelujah...

– Leonard Cohen, Hallelujah (1984)

CHAPTER ONE

INTRODUCTION

It is intensely interesting to follow season after season the rapid evolution and change of public thought in the direction of the mystical....The ugly caterpillar is writhing in the agonies of death, under the powerful efforts of the psychic butterfly to escape from its science-built prison.[1]
– H. P. Blavatsky (1887)

The theory of evolution is increasingly conquering the world at this time, and, more so than all other philosophical theories, conforms to the kabbalistic secrets of the world. Evolution, which proceeds on a path of ascendancy, provides an optimistic foundation for the world....When we penetrate the inner meaning of ascending evolution, we find in it the divine element shining with absolute brilliance.[2]
– Rabbi Abraham Isaac Kook (*c.* 1915)

THE CASE OF THE MISSING KABBALAH

On the eve of the Great War, the essayist and bibliophile George Holbrook Jackson (1874–1948), discussing the remarkable creative vigour of the last decade of the nineteenth century, declared that it was

> ...the decade of a thousand 'movements'. People...were convinced that they were passing not only from one social system to another, but from one morality to another, from one culture to another, and from one religion to a dozen or none.[3]

---

[1] H. P. Blavatsky, 'The Signs of the Times', *Lucifer* 1:2 (1887), 83–89, on p. 83.

[2] R. Abraham Isaac Kook, *Orot ha-Qodesh*, 4 vols. (*c.* 1915–1920, published posthumously, Jerusalem: Mossad Harav Kook, 1963), 2:537; cited in Shai Cherry, 'Three Twentieth-Century Jewish Responses to Evolutionary Theory,' *Aleph* 3 (2003), 247–90, on pp. 252–53.

[3] George Holbrook Jackson, *The Eighteen Nineties: A Review of Art and Ideas at the Close of the Nineteenth Century* (London: Grant Richards, 1913; repr. London: Penguin/Pelican, 1939), 27.

One of the most important 'movements' that came to flower in Britain at the *fin-de-siècle* is now referred to as the occult revival. Emerging in the second half of the nineteenth century, this cultural current generated a proliferation of societies dedicated to the study and practice of abstruse forms of mysticism and magic.[4] These groups, often disparate in terms of religious orientation, were united by an optimistic belief in a dawning new age in which science and religion, perceived as hypostatised entities engaged in an increasingly irreconcilable conflict, might achieve a new and glorious synthesis through the spiritual empowerment of the individual.[5] Until recent decades, the occult revival enjoyed little serious research, largely because scholarly interest in esoteric thought was shaped almost entirely by the evolutionist approach of E. B. Tylor and James Frazer which emerged simultaneously with the very current it sought to dismiss as superstition.[6] This school of thought, sometimes known as the 'religion as primitive error' school, espoused the idea that magic, when it grows up, matures first into religion and then, illuminated by the light of modern reason, transforms into science.[7] However, the emergence, persistence, and increasing social, economic, and religious

---

[4] For the use of terms such as 'mysticism' and 'magic' in this book, see below, 'Definitions of Terms'.

[5] For intellectual currents in the 1890s, see Jackson, *Eighteen Nineties*, 25–26, 132–33. For science and religion as hypostatised entities, see Owen Chadwick, *The Secularization of the European Mind in the 19th Century* (Cambridge: Cambridge University Press, 1975), 161–88. For the science-versus-religion debate, see Mike Jay and Michael Neve (eds.), *1900: A Fin-de-siècle Reader* (London: Penguin, 1999). For self-consciousness and self-empowerment as central aspects of modernity, see Alex Owen, *The Place of Enchantment: British Occultism and the Culture of the Modern* (Chicago, IL: University of Chicago Press, 2004), 118–20; Alex Owen, 'Occultism and the "Modern Self" in Fin-de-Siècle Britain', in Martin Daunton and Bernhard Rieger (eds.), *Meanings of Modernity: Britain from the Late-Victorian Era to World War II* (Oxford: Berg, 2001), 71–96.

[6] See Edward Burnett Tylor, *Primitive Culture: Researches into the Development of Mythology, Philosophy, Religion, Language, Art and Custom*, 2 vols. (London: John Murray, 1871); James Frazer, *The Golden Bough: A Study in Comparative Religion*, 12 vols. (London: Macmillan, 1890–1915).

[7] For an overview of Tylor and Frazer, see James Thrower, *Religion: The Classical Theories* (Edinburgh: Edinburgh University Press, 1999), 99–125.

impact of what are now known as 'contemporary spiritualities' in the late twentieth and early twenty-first centuries,[8] many of which derive their most important doctrines and practices from the occult revival of the *fin-de-siècle*, have raised serious questions about the validity of such a perception of the diverse historical expressions of the human religious imagination. This has resulted in several recent works, discussed later in this chapter, which explore the occult revival not as a reactive throwback to pre-Enlightenment superstition, but as the product of complex historical and social processes involved in the integration of older religious traditions with new social and scientific paradigms in the modern era.

The Kabbalah is central to these older traditions. The term 'Kabbalah' describes an extensive and varied body of Jewish literature, oral traditions, and ritual practices, developed over many centuries and first appearing in textual form in Provence in the late twelfth century. Encompassing theosophical doctrines, esoteric interpretations of Biblical texts, and a wide spectrum of magical rituals, the Kabbalah was believed to contain the secret wisdom tradition given directly by God to Moses as the hidden 'key' to the five books of the Torah.[9] But despite its importance in Western esoteric currents from the medieval period to the twenty-first century, there is as yet no substantial research into the ways in which this Jewish lore was acquired, understood, and utilised in the occult revival. The impact of the Kabbalah on nineteenth-century poets and novelists from Baudelaire to Yeats has long been recognised by scholars of modern

---

[8] For 'contemporary spiritualities', see Eileen Barker and Margit Warburg (eds.), *New Religions and New Religiosity* (Aarhus: Aarhus University Press, 1998); Edward A. Tiryakian, 'Toward the Sociology of Esoteric Culture', *AJS* 78:3 (1972), 491–512; Paul Heelas, *The New Age Movement: the Celebration of the Self and the Sacralization of Modernity* (Oxford: Blackwell, 1996); Steven Sutcliffe and Marion Bowman (eds.), *Beyond New Age: Exploring Alternative Spirituality* (Edinburgh: Edinburgh University Press, 2000).
[9] For introductions to the subject, see Gershom Scholem, *Major Trends in Jewish Mysticism* (New York: Schocken Books, 1961); Moshe Idel, *Kabbalah: New Perspectives* (New Haven, CT: Yale University Press, 1988); Joseph Dan, *Kabbalah: A Very Short Introduction* (Oxford: Oxford University Press, 2006); Elliot R. Wolfson, *Through a Speculum That Shines: Vision and Imagination in Medieval Jewish Mysticism* (Princeton, NJ: Princeton University Press, 1994).

literature.[10] But a more thorough investigation needs to be made into the nature of this so-called 'occultist' Kabbalah. The Kabbalah is accorded primary importance in the writings of virtually every practitioner of the occult revival, from Éliphas Lévi's declaration in the 1850s that 'all truly doctrinal religions have emerged from the Kabbalah and return there' to Dion Fortune's statement in the 1930s that 'the mysticism of Israel supplies the foundation of modern Western occultism'.[11] Present-day groups involved in ceremonial magic continue to accord it the same importance.[12] Yet in most of the contemporary scholarly works addressing the British occult revival, the

---

[10] For the influence of the Kabbalah on nineteenth-century literature, see Denis Saurat, 'Baudelaire, Rimbaud, la Cabale', *Nouvelle revue française* 46:2 (1936), 258–61; Claude Pichois, 'Baudelaire en 1847', *Revue des sciences humaines* (January–March 1958), 121–38; Jean Richer, *L'Alchimie du verbe de Rimbaud ou les jeux de Jean-Arthur* (Paris: Didier, 1972); Françoise Meltzer, 'On Rimbaud's "Voyelles"', *MP* 76:4 (1979), 344–54; George Mills Harper, *Yeats's Golden Dawn: The Influence of the Hermetic Order of the Golden Dawn on the Life and Art of W. B. Yeats* (London: Macmillan, 1974). For the general influence of occultism on nineteenth-century literature, see Lynn Wilkinson, *The Dream of an Absolute Language: Emanuel Swedenborg and French Literary Culture* (Albany, NY: State University of New York Press, 1996), 19–54; Frank Paul Bowman, *Eliphas Lévi, visionnaire romantique* (Paris: Presses Universitaires de France, 1969), 5–61; Maria Carlson, 'Fashionable Occultism: Spiritualism, Theosophy, Freemasonry, and Hermeticism in Fin-de-Siècle Russia', in Bernice Glatzer Rosenthal (ed.), *The Occult in Russian and Soviet Culture* (Ithaca, NY: Cornell University Press, 1997), 135–52.
[11] Éliphas Lévi, *Dogme et rituel de la haute magie*, 2 vols. (Paris: Germer Baillière, 1855–56; repr. as *Dogme et rituel de la haute magie: Édition complète en un volume avec 24 figures dans le texte*, Paris: Éditions Niclaus, 1972), 50; Dion Fortune, *The Mystical Qabalah* (London: Ernest Benn, 1935), 2. All translations of Lévi's original French are mine unless indicated otherwise.
[12] For the importance of the Kabbalah in contemporary spiritualities, see Adrian Ivakhiv, 'The Resurgence of Magical Religion as a Response to the Crisis of Modernity: A Postmodern Depth Psychological Perspective', in James R. Lewis (ed.), *Magical Religion and Modern Witchcraft* (Albany, NY: State University of New York Press, 1996), 237–65; Susan Greenwood, *Magic, Witchcraft and the Otherworld: An Anthropology* (Oxford: Berg, 2000), 68–74; T. M. Luhrmann, *Persuasions of the Witch's Craft: Ritual Magic in Contemporary England* (Cambridge, MA: Harvard University Press, 1989), 60–63, 78–80, 196–200, 236–38; Boaz Huss, 'All You Need Is LAV: Madonna and Postmodern Kabbalah', *JQR* 95:4 (2005), 611–24.

predominance of the Kabbalah is either attenuated, generalised as a modern 'occultist' system of 'programmatic syncretism' disconnected from its Jewish roots, or simply not mentioned.[13]

The Hebrew word *qbl* means 'reception' or 'received tradition'. Emerging in the medieval period but rooted in oral traditions and texts from late antiquity or earlier, the Kabbalah has never been a homogenous entity.[14] However, certain themes repeatedly weave their way through its loose amalgamation of oral and written doctrines and practices: the internal structure of deity, the dynamic relationship between human and divine realms, and the methods by which direct knowledge of and participation in the godhead can be achieved. Also common to the various Kabbalistic 'schools' is the idea that sacred texts may be read on multiple levels, the deepest being accessible only through complex forms of linguistic hermeneutics and ritual exercises designed to induce revelatory experiences. Kabbalistic thought encourages speculation, a constant re-evaluation of ideas, and an open-ended sequence of commentaries which, because of the infinite interpretations of texts, nature, and historical events deemed permissible through Kabbalistic hermeneutics, each successive generation reformulates according to individual predisposition and cultural context. Paradoxically, Kabbalah presents itself as a tradition while simultaneously reflecting unending creative innovation. As Elliot R. Wolfson suggests:

> The notion of the infinity of the text engenders a proliferation of interpretations unfolding in time, an idea that, *prima facie*, would seem to accord with...the rejection of one unequivocal

---

[13] 'Programmatic syncretism' is from Egil Asprem, '*Kabbalah Recreata*: Reception and Adaptation of Kabbalah in Modern Occultism', *Pomegranate* 9:2 (2007), 132–53.

[14] For the emergence of the early Kabbalah, see Gershom Scholem, *Origins of the Kabbalah*, trans. Allan Arkush, ed. R. J. Zwi Werblowsky (Princeton, NJ: Princeton University Press, 1990); Gershom Scholem, *Kabbalah* (New York: Keter Publishing House, 1974), 8–86; Joseph Dan (ed.), *The Early Kabbalah* (Mahwah, NJ: Paulist Press, 1986). For the sources of early Kabbalah, see Peter Schäfer, *The Hidden and Manifest God: Some Major Themes in Early Jewish Mysticism*, trans. Aubrey Pomerance (Albany, NY: State University of New York Press, 1992); Gershom Scholem, *Jewish Gnosticism, Merkabah Mysticism, and Talmudic Tradition* (New York: Jewish Theological Seminary of America, 1960).

meaning in favor of the belief in an ongoing dispersal of meanings; the text, on this accord, changes with each new reading....The expansion of the tradition is itself part of the perpetuation of the tradition, just as the perpetuation of the tradition is part of its expansion.[15]

Discussing this 'pluralistic hermeneutic', Eitan B. Fishbane observes:

Meaning under the expansive rubric of kabbalistic reception, may be characterized as a fluid pluralism, owing to the fact that no single interpretation is to be given priority over another and no single view is to be rejected in favor of another.[16]

Judaism itself has never been a homogenous entity, despite efforts by certain Jewish scholars of the late nineteenth-century German-based academic current called *Wissenschaft des Judentums* ('the scientific study of Judaism') to present it as a rational religion whose magical and pantheistic elements are dubious 'foreign imports'.[17] Tensions as well as syntheses

---

[15] Elliot R. Wolfson, 'Structure, Innovation, and Diremptive Temporality: The Use of Models to Study Continuity and Discontinuity in Kabbalistic Tradition', *JSRI* 6:18 (2007), 143–67, on pp. 149 and 159. See also Elliot R. Wolfson, 'Beyond the Spoken Word: Oral Tradition and Written Transmission in Medieval Jewish Mysticism', in Yaakov Elman and Israel Gershoni (eds.), *Transmitting Jewish Traditions: Orality, Textuality and Cultural Diffusion* (New Haven, CT: Yale University Press, 2000), 167–224, esp. pp. 189–92.
[16] Eitan P. Fishbane, 'Authority, Tradition, and the Creation of Meaning in Medieval Kabbalah: Isaac of Acre's *Illumination of the Eyes*', *JAAR* 72:1 (2004), 59–95, on p. 72. For the infinities of interpretive possibilities in Kabbalistic hermeneutics, see Moshe Idel, *Absorbing Perfections: Kabbalah and Interpretation* (New Haven, CT: Yale University Press, 2002), 80–110; Philip Beitchman, *Alchemy of the Word: Cabala of the Renaissance* (Albany, NY: State University of New York Press, 1998), 57–60.
[17] See, for example, Heinrich Graetz, *History of the Jews*, 5 vols., ed. and trans. Bella Löwy (London: Jewish Chronicle Office, 1901), 3:565; Louis Ginzberg and Kaufmann Kohler, 'Cabala', in *JE* (1901–06), <http://www.jewishencyclopedia.com/view.jsp?artid=1&letter=C>. For arguments against this approach, see Moshe Idel, *Hasidism: Between Ecstasy and Magic* (Albany, NY: State University of New York Press, 1995), 1–30 and 45–102; Moshe Idel, 'Rabbinism Versus Kabbalism: On G. Scholem's Phenomenology of Judaism', *MJ* 11:3

between philosophical, theosophical, mystical, and magical currents have characterised the Kabbalah from the time of its origins, themselves still hotly contested in both academic and religious circles.[18]

Despite the insistence by Gershom Scholem (1897–1982), the initiator of modern Kabbalistic scholarship, that belief in the Torah as divine revelation is an essential aspect of genuine Jewish Kabbalah,[19] Kabbalistic doctrines and practices in their more extreme forms, such as the 'ecstatic' Kabbalah of Abraham Abulafia and those forms promulgated in the Sabbatian and Frankist messianic movements of the seventeenth and eighteenth centuries, are often anomian or even antinomian, and are sometimes disengaged from the formal structures of Jewish belief and ritual.[20] This has allowed the smooth adoption of Kabbalistic

---

(1991), 281–96; Boaz Huss, 'Ask No Questions: Gershom Scholem and the Study of Contemporary Jewish Mysticism', *MJ* 25:2 (May 2005), 141–58. For the *Wissenschaft des Judentums*, see David Myers, 'The Fall and Rise of Jewish Historicism: The Evolution of the *Akademie für die Wissenschaft des Judentums*', *HUCA* 63 (1992), 107–44; Michael A. Meyer, 'The Emergence of Jewish Historiography: Motives and Motifs', *HT* 27:4 (1988), 160–75; Michael A. Meyer, 'Two Persistent Tensions Within *Wissenschaft des Judentums*', *MJ* 24:2 (2004), 105–19; Michael Brenner, 'Gnosis and History: Polemics of German-Jewish Identity from Graetz to Scholem', *New German Critique* 77 (1999), 45–60.

[18] For conflicting views on the origins of the Kabbalah, see Joseph Dan, 'Gershom Scholem's Reconstruction of Early Kabbalah', *MJ* 5:1 (1985), 39–66; Isaiah Tishby, 'General Introduction', in Isaiah Tishby (ed.), *The Wisdom of the Zohar: An Anthology of Texts*, 3 vols., trans. David Goldstein (Portland, OR: Littman Library of Jewish Civilization/Oxford University Press, 1989), 1:1–126. For the different 'strata' in early Kabbalistic literature, see Ronit Meroz, 'The Middle Eastern Origins of Kabbalah', *JSSMJ* 1:1 (2007), 39–56.

[19] See Gershom Scholem, *On the Possibility of Jewish Mysticism in Our Time and Other Essays*, ed. Avraham Shapira, trans. Jonathan Chipman (Philadelphia, PA: Jewish Publication Society, 1997), 14. For Scholem's importance in Kabbalistic scholarship, see Joseph Dan, *Gershom Scholem and the Mystical Dimension of Jewish History* (New York: New York University Press, 1987); Moshe Idel, *Old Worlds, New Mirrors: On Jewish Mysticism and Twentieth-Century Thought* (Philadelphia, PA: University of Pennsylvania Press, 2010), 83–153.

[20] See Moshe Idel, 'Inner Peace through Inner Struggle in Abraham Abulafia's Ecstatic Kabbalah', *JSSMJ* 2:2 (2009), 62–96, p. 76 and n. 31, where Idel suggests that Abulafia's Kabbalah 'has very little to

themes by practitioners of varying religious persuasions. Although it has been suggested that such a 'universalist' approach to Kabbalah is unique to the modern era and arises from 'non-Jewish roots',[21] the Jewish communities of the diaspora, however orthodox, were never entirely isolated from the broader cultures in which they participated, and discourse on the Kabbalah between Jews and Christians was vigorous and mutually fertile from the thirteenth century onward.[22] This interchange between Jews and their neighbours began occurring in antiquity, resulting in recognisable traces of Neoplatonic, Neoaristotelian, Orphic, Stoic, Pythagorean, and Hermetic influences on Jewish esoteric lore. As Idel suggests: 'No scholar of Jewish mysticism will deny the existence of many speculative elements stemming from Greek and Hellenistic thought in some Kabbalistic and even Hasidic writings'.[23] If these Jewish Kabbalists had not believed their Kabbalah was compatible with other religious and philosophical approaches, they would hardly have engaged in such discourse with 'gentiles'.[24] Those directly involved in such exchanges often

---

do, if anything, at all, with the Rabbinic emphasis on the performance of the commandments'. For the Kabbalahs of Sabbatai Zevi and Jacob Frank, see Chapter Five.

[21] See Wouter J. Hanegraaff, 'The Beginnings of Occultist Kabbalah', in Boaz Huss, Marco Pasi, and Kocku von Stuckrad (eds.), *Kabbalah and Modernity: Interpretations, Transformations, Adaptations* (Leiden: Brill, 2010), 107–28, on p. 110.

[22] See Harvey J. Hames, *The Art of Conversion: Christianity and Kabbalah in the Thirteenth Century* (Leiden: Brill, 2000); Richard H. Popkin and Gordon M. Weiner (eds.), *Jewish Christians and Christian Jews: From the Renaissance to the Enlightenment* (Dordrecht: Kluwer Academic Publishers, 1994); Jeremy Cohen (ed.), *Essential Papers on Judaism and Christianity in Conflict: From Late Antiquity to the Reformation* (New York: New York University Press, 1991); Joseph Dan, 'Medieval Jewish Influences on Renaissance Concepts of "Harmonia Mundi"', *Aries* 1:2 (2001), 135–52. See also Kenneth Austin, *From Judaism to Calvinism: The Life and Writings of Immanuel Tremellius (c. 1510–1580)* (Aldershot: Ashgate, 2007) for a nuanced discussion of the scholarly interchange between Christians and Jews in the early modern period.

[23] Moshe Idel, 'On European Cultural Renaissances and Jewish Mysticism', in Daniel Abrams and Avraham Elqayam (eds.), *Kabbalah: Journal for the Study of Jewish Mystical Texts*, Vol. 13 (Los Angeles, CA: Cherub Press, 2005), 43–78, on p. 43.

[24] The reasons for such a conviction vary according to culture, epoch, and individual, but they have often been linked with the

invoked hostility from their own communities, and the practitioners of the British occult revival, fascinated by Kabbalistic texts but antagonistic or, at best, indifferent toward the Jewish communities around them, rarely credited living Jewish sources in their published work. But their private correspondence indicates the continuing vigour of the discourse.[25]

---

idea of a dawning messianic or eschatological revelation encompassing all faiths. For example, Abraham Abulafia's efforts in the late thirteenth century to disseminate the Kabbalah among Jews, Christians, and Muslims were motivated largely by his belief that, as he was living in the age of messianic redemption, he was permitted to reveal secrets; see Idel, 'On European Cultural Renaissances', 63. In the case of Philip Berg's Kabbalah Center (discussed in Chapter Seven), universalising the Kabbalah in the twenty-first century reflects Berg's belief that the world is now reaching 'the complete and final stage in the revelation of kabbalistic mysteries'; see Jonathan Meir, 'The Boundaries of the Kabbalah: R. Yaakov Moshe Hillel and the Kabbalah in Jerusalem', in Boaz Huss (ed.), *Kabbalah and Contemporary Spiritual Revival* (Beer-Sheva: Ben-Gurion University of the Negev Press, 2011), 163–80. Further individual examples are discussed in Chapter Four.

[25] There are numerous textual examples of hostility incurred through Kabbalistic discourse between Christians and Jews. For the sixteenth-century controversy over Reuchlin's 'Judaising', see Erika Rummel, *The Case Against Johann Reuchlin: Social and Religious Controversy in Sixteenth-Century Germany* (Toronto: University of Toronto Press, 2002), and Reuchlin's own response in Johann Reuchlin, *Recommendation Whether to Confiscate, Destroy, and Burn All Jewish Books*, ed. and trans. Peter Wortman (Mahwah, NJ: Paulist Press, 2000). See also David H. Price, 'Christian Humanism and the Representation of Judaism: Johannes Reuchlin and the Discovery of Hebrew', *Arthuriana* 19:3 (2009), 80–96. For a seventeenth-century example, see Knorr von Rosenroth's 'letter' in the *Kabbala denudata* regarding keeping the name of his Jewish teacher secret 'on account of the hatred of his relatives', cited in Alison P. Coudert, *The Impact of the Kabbalah in the Seventeenth Century: The Life and Thought of Francis Mercury van Helmont (1614–1698)* (Leiden: Brill, 1999), 106–07. For the anger directed at the Jewish lawyer and Kabbalistic scholar Adolphe Franck by the French Jewish press for his 'secularised' attitudes, see Michael Graetz, *The Jews in Nineteenth-Century France: From the French Revolution to the Alliance Israélite Universelle* (Stanford, CA: Stanford University Press, 1996), 57. Franck was pilloried by both sides; he was also accused of 'pantheism' by the ultramontane Catholics. See Jay R. Berkovitz, *The Shaping of Jewish Identity in Nineteenth-century France* (Detroit, MI: Wayne State University Press, 1989), 233. For more on Franck and

Thus it is not a simple matter to clarify how 'Christian' or 'occultist' Kabbalah differs from 'Jewish' Kabbalah, other than that it is studied, practised, and sometimes – but not invariably – given a Christian 'gloss' by non-Jews.[26] The discrete category of 'Christian' Kabbalah (frequently spelled 'Cabala' due to the Latinisation of the Hebrew word, since the Latin alphabet does not contain a k or a q) is often assumed in scholarly works by both Jewish and non-Jewish scholars, although convincing explanations of how this category differs in its fundamentals from Jewish Kabbalah are difficult to find. Although these Christian practitioners of the Kabbalah often attempted to enlist their interpretations of Jewish esoteric lore to convert Jews to Christianity, this does not magically transform the Kabbalistic texts they used into

his relationship with French occultists, see Chapter Two. For the animosity expressed toward the Jewish scholar Joshua Abelson by his own community because of his involvement with Theosophical groups in the early twentieth century, see Chapter Six. My use in this book of the word 'antisemitic' with reference to particular British occultists is not anachronistic. For the appearance of the term in the mid-nineteenth century, see Stefan Arvidsson, 'Aryan Mythology As Science and Ideology', *JAAR* 67:2 (1999), 327–54.

[26] For the 'Christian' Kabbalah, see Gershom Scholem, 'The beginnings of the Christian Kabbalah', in Joseph Dan (ed.), *The Christian Kabbalah: Jewish Mystical Books and Their Christian Interpreters*, 17–51; Joseph Dan, 'Christian Kabbalah: From Mysticism to Esotericism', in Antoine Faivre and Wouter J. Hanegraaff (eds.), *Western Esotericism and the Science of Religion* (Leuven: Peeters, 1998), 131–44; Joseph Leon Blau, *The Christian Interpretation of the Cabala in the Renaissance* (New York: Columbia University Press, 1944); Ernst Benz, *Christian Kabbalah: Neglected Child of Theology*, trans. Kenneth W. Wesche (St. Paul, MN: Grailstone Press, 2004); Beitchman, *Alchemy of the Word*; Chaim Wirszubski, *Pico della Mirandola's Encounter with Jewish Mysticism* (Cambridge, MA: Harvard University Press, 1989); G. Mallary Masters, 'Renaissance Kabbalah', in Antoine Faivre and Jacob Needleman (eds.), *Modern Esoteric Spirituality* (New York: Crossroad, 1992), 132–53; François Secret, *Les Kabbalistes Chrétiens de la Renaissance* (La Haye-Paris: Mouton et Cie, 1964); Moshe Idel, 'The Magical and Neoplatonic Interpretations of the Kabbalah in the Renaissance', in Bernard Dov Cooperman (ed.), *Jewish Thought in the Sixteenth Century* (Cambridge, MA: Harvard University Press, 1983), 186–242; Saverio Campanini, 'Recent Literature on Christian Kabbalah', *European Association for Jewish Studies Newsletter* 11 (October 2001–March 2002), <http://www.lzz.uni-halle.de/publikationen/essays/nl11_campanini.pdf>.

Christian texts. What is Christian about the 'Christian' Kabbalah is the intent of its adherents, rather than the Kabbalah itself. The German humanist Johann Reuchlin (1455–1522), one of the most important Hebraists in the early modern period, was aware of the problem, and criticised his fellow Christians' repudiation of the 'Jewishness' of the Kabbalah:

> All the Jewish traditions and discoveries have been popularized by non-Jewish plagiarists, first in Greek and then in Latin; there is nothing in our philosophy that was not first developed by the Jews, although by this time they do not get the recognition they deserve.[27]

Moshe Idel, discussing Reuchlin's 'Christian' Kabbalah in contrast to Jewish Kabbalah, suggests that divergent understandings of theurgy are fundamental to differentiating between the two:[28] Christian Kabbalah seeks to provide a contemplative means through which the soul can ascend to higher spheres, while Jewish Kabbalah seeks through its ritual practices to directly influence the godhead itself.[29] However, this assumes that Christian Kabbalah, like Jewish Kabbalah, is a homogenous entity with theoretical goals and practical applications that remain consistently discrete – an assumption which contradicts the warning of Idel himself against imposing 'a totalizing attitude upon diverging semiotic strategies characteristic of Kabbalistic corpora which

---

[27] Johann Reuchlin, *On the Art of the Kabbalah (De arte cabalistica libri tres)*, trans. Martin and Sarah Goodman (Lincoln, NE: University of Nebraska Press, 1993), 131.

[28] Theurgy (Greek *theurgeia*, or 'god-work') is a term derived from the Neoplatonic milieu of late antiquity, and is associated with magic embedded in a religious framework, or magic aimed toward spiritual rather than material goals. There is an extensive body of work dealing with the concept in pagan, Jewish, and Christian contexts and its apparent differentiation from 'lower' magic (*goetia*); see, *inter alia*, E. R. Dodds, 'Theurgy and its Relationship to Neoplatonism', *JRS* 37 (1947), 55–69; Hans Lewy, *The Chaldean Oracles and Theurgy: Mysticism, Magic, and Platonism in the Later Roman Empire*, ed. Michael Tardieu (Paris: Études Augustiniennes, 1978); Gregory Shaw, *Theurgy and the Soul: The Neoplatonism of Iamblichus* (University Park, PA: Penn State Press, 1971); and further references below in Chapters Four and Five.

[29] See Moshe Idel, 'Johannes Reuchlin: Kabbalah, Pythagorean Philosophy and Modern Scholarship', *SJ* 16 (2008), 30–55, esp. 46–47 and n. 67.

differ from each other'.[30] The assumption also implies a categorisation of theurgy as 'Jewish' rather than 'Christian' because some form of magical manipulation of supernal entities is involved in an effort to transform the godhead itself, which, presumably, Christian Kabbalists, frightened of accusations of trafficking with demons, eschewed in favour of a purely contemplative pursuit of the *unio mystica*. But as Elliot Wolfson has demonstrated, many Christian interpreters of Kabbalah, including Reuchlin, did not reject its theurgic dimension;[31] and some, like Cardinal Egidio da Viterbo (1469–1532), who received his instruction from Jewish Kabbalists, fully embraced its magical aspects.[32] The Kabbalah of the occult revival is based as much on this theurgic form of Kabbalistic praxis as it is on a quest for higher spiritual consciousness.

Gershom Scholem defines 'Christian' Kabbalah as 'the interpretation of kabbalistic texts in the interests of Christianity', implying that the chief difference lies in the use of the Kabbalah to convert Jews rather than in the Kabbalah itself.[33] Joseph Dan states that the use of Kabbalistic texts by Christians such as Reuchlin in the early modern period had an impact on their understanding of Christianity itself, reflecting the realisation that 'there is more truth in Jewish

---

[30] Idel, 'Johannes Reuchlin', 50.
[31] For an illuminating discussion of Reuchlin's 'Christianised' Kabbalah and his faithfulness to Jewish Kabbalistic theory and praxis, see Elliot R. Wolfson, 'Language, Secrecy, and the Mysteries of the Law: Theurgy and the Christian Kabbalah of Johannes Reuchlin', in Abrams and Elqayam (eds.), *Kabbalah*, 7–41.
[32] For Egidio da Viterbo's involvement with the Kabbalah, see François Secret, *I Cabbalisti Cristiani del Rinascimento* (Rome: Arkeios Edizioni, 2001), 114–29; R. J. Wilkinson, *Orientalism, Aramaic and Kabbalah in the Catholic Reformation: The First Printing of the Syriac New Testament* (Leiden: Brill, 2007), 29–62; Adolfo Tura, 'Un Codice Ebraico di Cabala Appartenuto a Egidio da Viterbo', *Bibliothèque d'Humanisme et Renaissance* 68:3 (2006), 535–43. For the Jewish Kabbalist Elias Levita, Cardinal Egidio's most important teacher, see Sophie Kessler Mesguich, 'Early Christian Hebraists', in Magne Saebø (ed.), *Hebrew Bible/Old Testament: The History of Its Interpretation, Vol. 2: From the Renaissance to the Enlightenment* (Göttingen: Vandenhoek & Ruprecht, 2008), 254–75, on pp. 272–75.
[33] Scholem, 'Beginnings', 17.

traditions than was supposed before'.[34] And as Allison Coudert has demonstrated, the Christianity of individual 'Christian' Kabbalists, as a result of this impact, took some surprising forms. In the late seventeenth century, Christian Knorr von Rosenroth (1631–1689) and Francis Mercury van Helmont (1614–1699) produced a massive three-volume compilation of commentaries and Latin translations of Hebrew Kabbalistic texts called the *Kabbala denudata*, in which an interpretation of Lutheran Christianity is offered that is, according to Coudert, closer to the religious perspectives of the sixteenth-century Jewish Kabbalist Isaac Luria than to Catholicism, Lutheranism, or Calvinism.[35] One of Knorr's collaborators, Johann Peter Späth (*c.* 1640–1701), converted to Judaism as a direct result of working on the *Kabbala denudata*, afterward calling himself Moses Germanus.[36] Kabbalistic discourse between Jews and non-Jews in the late-nineteenth-century occult revival, evident in the personal correspondence of both occultists and Jewish Kabbalistic scholars and practitioners, clearly influenced the religious attitudes of both, yet this aspect of the development of the Kabbalah in the British occult milieu has been entirely ignored in current research.

---

[34] Joseph Dan, 'The Kabbalah of Johannes Reuchlin and Its Historical Significance', in Dan (ed.), *Christian Kabbalah*, 55–95, on pp. 56–57.

[35] Christian Knorr von Rosenroth, *Kabbala denudata*, 3 vols. (Sulzbach/Frankfurt: Abraham Lichtenthal, 1677–1684); Allison P. Coudert, 'Five Seventeenth-Century Christian Hebraists', in Allison P. Coudert and Jeffrey S. Shoulson (eds.), *Hebraica Veritas? Christian Hebraists and the Study of Judaism in Early Modern Europe* (Philadelphia, PA: University of Pennsylvania Press, 2004), 286–308, on p. 294. For Knorr's Judaised version of Lutheran Christianity, see also Allison P. Coudert, 'The Kabbala Denudata: Converting Jews or Seducing Christians', in Popkin and Weiner (eds.), *Jewish Christians*, 73–96; Coudert, *Impact of the Kabbalah*; Adam Sutcliffe, *Judaism and Enlightenment* (Cambridge: Cambridge University Press, 2003), 148–64. For the texts in the Kabbala denudata, see Don Karr, 'The Study of Christian Cabala in English: Addenda' (1995–2006), <http://www.digital-brilliance.com/kab/karr/ccineb.pdf>. For van Helmont, see also Stuart Brown, 'F. M. van Helmont: His Philosophical Connections and the Reception of His Later Cabbalistic Philosophy', in M. A. Stewart (ed.), *Studies in Seventeenth-Century European Philosophy* (Oxford: Clarendon Press, 1997), 2:97–116.

[36] For Späth, see Coudert, *Impact of the Kabbalah*, 343–46; Coudert, 'Kabbala Denudata', 90; Popkin, 'Christian Jews', 69.

Kocku von Stuckrad has observed that existing typologies of Western esotericism are essentially 'Christian esotericism in the early modern period', and points out that the 'enormous influence' of Jewish traditions is being marginalised or entirely overlooked.[37] Western esotericism is thus seen as a reaction to normative Christianity, in the same way that the occult revival is often seen as a reaction to the Enlightenment and the rise of 'scientism'.[38] Wouter J. Hanegraaff, one of the most influential scholars writing about the history of Western esotericism, categorically declares that the Kabbalah of the occult revival has 'only the most superficial of connections to original Jewish kabbalah'.[39] In a paper on the appropriate methodology for the study of Western esotericism, Hanegraaff states: 'Western esotericism emerged as a syncretistic type of religiosity in a Christian context'.[40] Antoine Faivre, another major contributor to this field, asserts that modern Western esotericism, which he views as spanning the period from the early Renaissance to the present, includes spiritual alchemy, neo-Alexandrian Hermeticism, 'Christian' Kabbalah, theosophy, Rosi-crucianism, and 'a number of initiation societies'.[41] The Jewish Kabbalah is firmly excluded, despite the fact that its

---

[37] Kocku von Stuckrad, 'Western esotericism: Towards an integrative model of interpretation', *Religion* 35 (2005), 83. See also Kocku von Stuckrad, *Western Esotericism: A Brief History of Secret Knowledge* (London: Equinox, 2005), 31.

[38] For 'scientism', see Gregory R. Peterson, 'Demarcation and the Scientistic Fallacy', *Zygon* 38:4 (2003), 751–61; Olav Hammer, *Claiming Knowledge: Strategies of Epistemology from Theosophy to the New Age* (Leiden: Brill, 2004), 205–08.

[39] Wouter J. Hanegraaff, 'Jewish Influences V: Occultist Kabbalah', in Wouter J. Hanegraaff (ed.), *Dictionary of Gnosis and Western Esotericism* (Leiden: Brill, 2006), 644.

[40] Wouter J. Hanegraaff, 'The Study of Western Esotericism: New Approaches to Christian and Secular Culture', in Peter Antes, Armin W. Geertz, and Randi R. Warne (eds.), *New Approaches to the Study of Religion, Vol. 1: Regional, Critical, and Historical Approaches* (Berlin/New York: Walter de Gruyter, 2004), 489–519, on p. 496. See also Wouter J. Hanegraaff, *Esotericism and the Academy: Rejected Knowledge in Western Culture* (Cambridge: Cambridge University Press, 2011), 5–76, where this argument is developed more fully.

[41] Antoine Faivre, 'The Notions of Concealment and Secrecy in Modern Esoteric Currents since the Renaissance (A Methodological Approach)', in Elliot R. Wolfson (ed.), *Rending the Veil: Concealment and Secrecy in the History of Religions* (New York: Seven Bridges Press, 1999), 155–76, on p. 155.

two seminal texts – *Sefer ha-Bahir* and *Sefer ha-Zohar* – originated in Western Europe in Jewish communities that had lived in Spain and southern France for many centuries, was practiced from the thirteenth century onward by both Christians and Jews (often in collaboration) in various centres throughout Italy, France, Germany, Britain, Spain, and the Netherlands, and fulfils all six categories Faivre lists as defining an 'esoteric' current or text.[42] Faivre considers the first four categories given below as 'essential'; the last two categories may or may not be present in a text or current, but their inclusion strengthens the case for its being considered 'esoteric'.[43] Jewish Kabbalistic texts from Europe, despite Faivre's refusal to include them, usually incorporate all six.

1.   *Correspondences*   'are   symbolic   and/or   real correspondences between all parts of the visible or invisible universe...The entire universe is a great theater of mirrors, a set of hieroglyphs to decipher'. There is virtually no Kabbalistic text that does not emphasise the unity of, and the correspondences between, 'above' and 'below' as well as the mirroring of the divine infrastructure in the individual human soul and body.

2. *Living nature* is concerned with the mirroring of higher realms in material form: 'From the idea of correspondences we begin to see that the cosmos is complex, plural, hierarchical. Therefore Nature occupies an essential place within it. Multilayered, rich in potential revelations of all kinds, it must be read as one reads a book'. The idea of Nature reflecting and revealing the infrastructure of a complex and pluralistic divinity is implicit and often explicit in many Kabbalistic texts, and is particularly evident in the Lurianic Kabbalah, discussed below in Chapter Two.

3. *Imagination and mediation* concern the imagination as the 'organ of the soul', through which the world of divine intermediaries can be accessed: 'Mystics – in the most classic sense – aspire to a more or less complete suppression of images and intermediaries...In contrast, esotericists seem more interested in intermediaries revealed to their interior gaze, by virtue of their creative imagination'. Kabbalistic literature teems with intermediaries – astral, angelic,

---

[42] For these categories, see Antoine Faivre, 'Introduction 1', in Faivre and Jacob Needleman (eds.), *Modern Esoteric Spirituality*, xi–xxii; Antoine Faivre and Karen-Clare Voss, 'Western Esotericism and the Science of Religion', *Numen* 42:1 (1995), 48–77.

[43] All quotations following are from Faivre, 'Introduction 1', xv–xx.

demonic, and linguistic, as discussed in Chapters Two and Four – and the Tree of Life is the most ubiquitous symbol of the mediation of the ten *sefirot* as the infrastructure and active agents within both the godhead and the manifest universe.[44] British occultists did not invent the idea of such intermediaries but appropriated it from a number of sources, partly Neoplatonic and Greco-Egyptian, but primarily through Jewish magical texts and the thinly Christianised grimoires based on them.

4. *'Transmutation'* is a term appropriated from early modern alchemy. 'If one wishes lead to become silver or gold,' Faivre explains, 'one must not separate knowledge (gnosis) from interior experience, or intellectual activity from active imagination. This illuminated knowledge, which promotes a "second birth"...is often called "gnosis" in the general and modern sense of the term'. The process of spiritual transmutation is fully represented in late antique Jewish *heikhalot* literature as well as in medieval and early modern Kabbalah and the practices of modern Hasidism. As discussed throughout this book, the transmutation of the human being and the acquisition of magical powers through the experience of *devekut* ('cleaving' or direct encounter with deity) are fundamental to a number of Jewish esoteric texts, many centuries earlier than the Renaissance idea of the magus as a human transmuted and transformed through magic.

5. *The practice of concordance* involves the establishing of common denominators 'between two different traditions or even more, among all traditions, in the hope of obtaining an illumination, a gnosis, of superior quality'. Faivre states that this practice 'marks most particularly the beginning of modern times...to reappear at the end of the nineteenth century in a different and triumphant form'. While there can be no argument about the 'triumphant' expression of concordances in the British occult revival, it appears in Jewish literature from late antiquity and is particularly marked in medieval Kabbalistic texts. As I have discussed below in Chapters Two, Three, and Four, late antique Jewish esoteric literature reveals explicit concordances between Jewish, Greek, and Egyptian traditions, and medieval and

---

[44] For a seminal discussion of the imagination as the organ of reception of the divine in Jewish esoteric literature, see Wolfson, *Through a Speculum That Shines*.

early modern Kabbalists regularly related their own traditions to Hermetic, Aristotelian, Neoplatonic, and Pythagorean ideas. The *prisca theologia* of Ficino and Pico has its counterpart in the Jewish *prisca theologia*: a revealed knowledge first given to Adam and later shared by Enoch-Hermes, Enoch-Moses, and Plato and Pythagoras as the recipients of ancient Jewish esoteric secrets.

6. *Transmission* is the basis for the word 'Kabbalah' itself: *qbl*, 'received tradition', whether the revelation has been transmitted by a *maggid* (an angelic entity) such as Metatron or Raziel, a disincarnate sage such as Elijah or Shimon ben Yochai, an earlier Kabbalistic authority, or the 'initiation' of a disciple by a rabbi. 'To emphasize "transmission"', states Faivre, 'implies that an esoteric teaching can or ought to be transmitted from master to disciple following a channel already dug, abiding by a course already charted. Two ideas are related to this: (a) the validity of knowledge transmitted by a filiation whose authenticity or "regularity" leaves no room for doubt; and (b) initiation, which generally is effected within a master-disciple relationship'. In Jewish esoteric lore, the *Sefer ha-Raziel* was believed to have been transmitted to Adam by the angel Raziel; Moses was believed to have received a secret 'oral' Torah along with the written one; and the sixteenth-century Kabbalist Isaac Luria claimed that many of his doctrines were received from his *maggid*, Elijah.[45]

Since the medieval Kabbalah not only entirely fulfils every one of Faivre's categories but has clearly influenced the development of these themes in Western esotericism in obvious and seminal ways, it might even be suggested that the Jewish Kabbalah stands at the inception of, and is one of the dominant components of, that current of religiosity which Faivre calls Western esotericism. Consequently, Western esotericism might be said to have begun, not in the Florentine Renaissance, but in the Western European Renaissance of the late twelfth to early thirteenth centuries with the first textual appearances of the Jewish Kabbalah in Europe.[46] Faivre justifies the exclusion of Jewish Kabbalah

---

[45] For the theme of oral, textual, and maggidic transmission in Kabbalistic texts, see Wolfson, 'Beyond the Spoken Word'; Moshe Idel, 'Transmission in Thirteenth-Century Kabbalah', in Elman and Gershoni (eds.), *Transmitting Jewish Traditions*, 138–65.

[46] For the interrelationships of the rise of Kabbalah, the translation of Arabic and Hebrew texts into Latin, the twelfth-century Western European Renaissance, and the Alfonsinian Renaissance of the late

from Western esotericism with an extraordinary statement unsupported by any historical sources:

> 'Western' indicates here a West 'visited' by some Jewish, Islamic, or even far-Eastern religious traditions, with which it has coexisted but does not mingle.[47]

One of the hypotheses I am presenting in the following chapters is that the definition of Western esotericism as an exclusively Christian cultural phenomenon, and assumptions that the Kabbalah of this cultural current (including its manifestations in the British occult revival) is a discrete entity entirely separate from the Jewish Kabbalah, are seriously challenged by the historical evidence and may need to be entirely reformulated.

The various doctrines and practices comprising modern occultism are viewed by these scholars as new inventions or recreations of older traditions, generated as a kind of neo-Romantic response to post-Enlightenment secularisation and

---

thirteenth century, see Idel, 'On European Cultural Renaissances', 46–64

[47] '"Occidental" désigne ici un Occident "visité" par des traditions religieuses juives, musulmanes, voire extrême-orientales avec lesquelles il a cohabité mais qui ne se confondent pas avec lui': Antoine Faivre, *L'esoterisme* (Paris: Presses Universitaires de France, 2007), 8. There have recently been some scholarly challenges to this point of view, although perhaps not enough. See von Stuckrad, *Western Esotericism*, 3–5; Marco Pasi, 'Oriental Kabbalah and the Parting of East and West in the Early Theosophical Society', in Huss, Pasi, and von Stuckrad (eds.), *Kabbalah and Modernity*, 151–66. Pasi appears to excuse Faivre's statement as having been based on an effort to 'avoid universalist concepts of esotericism' (p. 152). See also Christopher I. Lehrich, *The Language of Angels and Demons: Cornelius Agrippa's Occult Philosophy* (Leiden: Brill, 2003), 209, who suggests that Agrippa was in fact the only practitioner of a genuine 'Christian' Kabbalah, and that the Kabbalah of the occult revival as reflected in the work of Éliphas Lévi and his followers is primarily an adaptation of Jewish Kabbalah. See also Anthony J. Elia, 'An Historical Assessment of the Narrative Uses of the Words "Kabbalah", "Cabala", and "Qabala/h": Discerning the Differences for Theological Libraries', *Theological Librarianship* 2:2 (2009), 11–23, in which Elia discusses the various orthographies of the term 'Kabbalah' and, like Lehrich, suggests that a genuine 'Christian Cabala', originating with Pico and reaching its flowering in Agrippa, Reuchlin, Kircher, and von Rosenroth, disappears after the seventeenth century.

'disenchantment'.[48] In an effort to 're-enchant' their world, occultists are seen as employing the 'esoteric method': the 'perennialist' belief in a universal secret tradition passed down through the ages, and the assignment of spurious ancient sources and chains of transmission to newly created cultural forms which are then justified by 'the sanctity of immemorial traditions and the legitimacy of those exercising authority under them'.[49] A second hypothesis presented in this book is that, although the 'esoteric method' is certainly evident in many occultist works, the Kabbalah of the occult revival may be an exception to this tendency, and may necessitate a re-evaluation of the assumption that any occultist claim to tradition is solely a strategy of

---

[48] For Max Weber's influential theory of the 'disenchantment of the world' (*Entzauberung*), see Max Weber, 'Science as a Vocation', in H. H. Gerth and C. Wright Mills (eds. and trans.), *From Max Weber: Essays in Sociology* (Oxford: Oxford University Press, 1958), 129–56; Max Weber, *The Protestant Ethic and the Spirit of Capitalism*, trans. Talcott Parsons (New York: Charles Scribner & Sons, 1958); Max Weber, *The Sociology of Religion*, trans. Ephraim Fischoff (Boston, MA: Beacon Press, 1963). For more recent discussions of the theory, see Patrick Curry, 'Magic vs. Enchantment', *JCR* 14:3 (1999), 401–12; William H. Swatos, 'Enchantment and Disenchantment in Modernity: The Significance of "Religion" as a Sociological Category', *SA* 44:4 (1983), 321–37; Robert W. Scribner, 'The Reformation, Popular Magic, and the "Disenchantment of the World"', *JIH* 23:3 (1993), 475–94; Alkis Kontos, 'The World Disenchanted, and the Return of Gods and Demons', in Asher Horowitz and Terry Maley (eds.), *The Barbarism of Reason: Max Weber and the Twilight of Enlightenment* (Toronto: University of Toronto Press, 1994), 223–47; Roy Willis and Patrick Curry, *Astrology, Science and Culture: Pulling Down the Moon* (Oxford: Berg, 2004), 77–92.

[49] Max Weber, *Economy and Society: An Outline of Interpretive Sociology*, ed. Guenther Roth and Claus Witich, trans. Ephraim Fischoff (Berkeley, CA: University of California Press, 1978), 215. For the 'esoteric method', see Pierre A. Riffard, 'The Esoteric Method', in Faivre and Hanegraaff (eds.), *Western Esotericism and the Science of Religion*, 63–74; Pierre A. Riffard, *L'Ésotérisme: Qu'est-ce que l'ésotérisme? Anthologie de l'ésotérisme occidental* (Paris: Robert Laffont, 1990); Wouter J. Hanegraaff, 'On the Construction of "Esoteric Traditions"', in Faivre and Hanegraaff (eds.), *Western Esotericism and the Science of Religion*, 11–62; Titus Hjelm, 'Tradition as Legitimation in New Religious Movements', in Steven Engler and Gregory P. Grieve (eds.), *Historicizing "Tradition" in the Study of Religion* (Berlin/New York: Walter de Gruyter, 2005), 109–23.

legitimisation. From its earliest textual appearances, the Kabbalah has expressed perspectives deemed essential to modernity.[50] As Eric Jacobson suggests, 'Kabbalah has a clandestine affinity with modernity',[51] and this may be reflected in the continuing vigour of Kabbalistic oral as well as written traditions into the twenty-first century.[52] 'The language of the modern self', asserts Alex Owen in a paper on modern occultism, 'is a language of interiority'.[53] Owen further suggests that the idea of a 'fragmented or multiple self' is an aspect of the modern perception of human consciousness.[54] But interiority and the awareness of a multiplicity of 'selves' is, as demonstrated in the following chapters, a central characteristic of the religious anthropology expressed in Jewish Kabbalistic texts. 'Modernity', from the perspective of the Kabbalah, may need to be understood as a state of mind rather than a specific historical period. According to both Owen and Hanegraaff, one of the 'modern' perspectives that characterise Western esotericism in general and the occult revival in particular is the internalisation of deity and the recognition of divine powers as natural attributes in both the world and the individual human soul. However, the medieval Kabbalistic idea of a cosmos unified by a divine primal substance, emanating through every level from supernal to material, implies an identity between deity and the psychic and

---

[50] For the elements that comprise the 'modernity' of modern occultism, see Wouter J. Hanegraaff, *New Age Religion and Western Culture: Esotericism in the Mirror of Secular Thought* (Leiden: Brill, 1996), 411–513; Wouter J. Hanegraaff, 'New Age Religion and Secularization', *Numen* 47:3 (2000), 288–312; Owen, *Place of Enchantment*, 114–47. For an incisive discussion of 'modernity' and religion, see Gustavo Benavides, 'Modernity', in Mark C. Taylor (ed.), *Critical Terms for Religious Studies* (Chicago, IL: University of Chicago Press, 1998), 186–204.

[51] Eric Jacobson, 'The Future of the Kabbalah: On the Dislocation of Past Primacy, the Problem of Evil, and the Future of Illusions', in Huss, Pasi, and von Stuckrad (eds.), *Kabbalah and Modernity*, 47–75, on p. 47.

[52] For a contemporary Kabbalistic group originating in the eighteenth century and incorporating much older oral and written Kabbalistic traditions, see Pinchas Giller, *Shalom Shar'abi and the Kabbalists of Beit El* (Oxford: Oxford University Press, 2008).

[53] Owen, 'Occultism', 71.

[54] Owen, *Place of Enchantment*, 115–47. For a similar hypothesis, see Hanegraaff, *New Age Religion*, 245–52.

physical life of the world and all its forms. The sixteenth-century Kabbalist Moshe Cordovero describes this identity succinctly:

> The essence of divinity is found in every single thing – nothing but it exists...Do not attribute duality to God...Do not say 'This is a stone and not God'. God forbid! Rather, all existence is God, and the stone is a thing pervaded by divinity.[55]

Humans are thus simultaneously divine and natural, and the individual's capacity to develop inherent 'higher' powers is the chief focus of the doctrines and practices of the 'ecstatic' Kabbalistic current of the late thirteenth century.[56]

Judaism in its various forms, forcibly torn from its primary physical locus of worship in the first century CE and lacking a central religious authority of the kind that the Vatican hierarchy has provided for Catholicism over the centuries, may be seen as what Jonathan Z. Smith calls a 'religion of anywhere'.[57] The precocious modernity of the Kabbalah, evident in European Kabbalistic texts long before the modern period, may be related to the historical phenomenon of a culture in diaspora: a people whose geographical sacred centre was destroyed in the first century CE and who, during the subsequent twelve centuries, recreated that centre and its access in ritualised imaginal forms.[58] Exile does not always take the form of a literal

---

[55] Moshe Cordovero, *Shi'ur Qomah*, Modena MS 206b, cited in Daniel Matt, *The Essential Kabbalah: The Heart of Jewish Mysticism* (Edison, NJ: Castle Books, 1997), 24.

[56] For 'ecstatic' Kabbalah and the work of Abraham Abulafia, its chief exponent, see Moshe Idel, *The Mystical Experience in Abraham Abulafia*, trans. Jonathan Chipman (Albany, NY: State University of New York Press, 1988); Moshe Idel, *Language, Torah, and Hermeneutics in Abraham Abulafia* (Albany, NY: State University of New York Press, 1989); Moshe Idel, *Studies in Ecstatic Kabbalah* (Albany, NY: State University of New York Press, 1988); Idel, *Kabbalah*, 35–59; Elliot R. Wolfson, *Abraham Abulafia – Kabbalist and Prophet: Hermeneutics, Theosophy and Theurgy* (Los Angeles, CA: Cherub Press, 2000).

[57] Jonathan Z. Smith, 'Here, There, and Anywhere', in Scott Noegel, Joel Walker, and Brannon Wheeler (eds.), *Prayer, Magic, and the Stars in the Ancient and Late Antique World* (University Park, PA: Pennsylvania State University Press, 2003), 21–36.

[58] For the interiorisation of Temple rituals, see Maureen Bloom, *Jewish Mysticism and Magic: An Anthropological Perspective* (London:

physical expulsion: it may sometimes be subtler, reflecting the confusion and distress of a culture (or a group of individuals) alienated from previously entrenched and cherished views of reality through economic, social, religious, industrial, or scientific upheaval. Eric Jacobson uses the term 'dislocation' to describe this condition applied to the modern world:

> What serves as a greater signifier of the experience of modernity than the contemporary experience of dislocation, witnessed in the rapid transformation of the most basic experiences of living, residing, consuming, communicating and convening with others?[59]

At the dawn of the twentieth century, the ritualised imaginal forms of the Jewish Kabbalah proved peculiarly attractive to esoterically inclined individuals and groups disturbed by the increasing alienation and religious dislocation of a society in which, as the poet and occultist William Butler Yeats put it, 'Things fall apart; the centre cannot hold'.[60] Jonathan Ray, discussing modern diaspora communities, suggests that one of the most striking characteristics of these communities is that exile 'helps to produce a new and unifying identity that had hitherto not existed among their members prior to emigration from their homeland'.[61] For some elements in the Jewish diaspora, this 'new and unifying identity' emerged in the medieval period as the Kabbalah, in specific theosophical and practical forms that already contained the substance of what has recently been described as a 'modern' approach to spirituality. The locus of the divine within the human psyche, and the emphasis on individual and group magical practices to achieve self- and world-transformation, are characteristic of what Hanegraaff calls the post-Enlightenment 'psychologization of the sacred'.[62] But these

---

Routledge, 2007); Martha Himmelfarb, *Ascent to Heaven in Jewish and Christian Apocalypses* (Oxford: Oxford University Press, 1993), 29–46; Marsha Keith Schuchard, *Restoring the Temple of Vision: Cabalistic Freemasonry and Stuart Culture* (Leiden: Brill, 2002), 9–27.

[59] Jacobson, 'The Future of the Kabbalah', 49.

[60] William Butler Yeats, *The Second Coming* (1921), in *Collected Poems of W. B. Yeats* (London: Macmillan, 1933), 211.

[61] Jonathan Ray, 'New Approaches to the Jewish Diaspora: The Sephardim as a Sub-Ethnic Group', *JSS* 15:1 (2008), 10–31, on p. 18.

[62] On 'the psychologization of the sacred', see Hanegraaff, *New Age Religion*, 224–55 and 482–513; Owen, *Place of Enchantment*, 148–85.

perspectives are also a feature of the earliest Kabbalistic texts. The Jewish Kabbalah did not have to be recreated for the modern era in order to accommodate a new, interiorised perception of the relationship between human and divine. As Eric Hobsbawm suggests:

> The strength and adaptability of genuine traditions is not to be confused with the 'invention of tradition'. Where the old ways are alive, traditions need be neither revived nor invented.[63]

METHODOLOGIES, METHODOLATRIES, AND METANARRATIVES

Current scholarly research into the Kabbalah of the occult revival, while providing an inspiring basis for new explorations, tends to be hampered by its insistence on one specific methodology, referred to by its adherents as 'empirical' or 'analytic'. This methodology, which Hanegraaff refers to as a 'paradigm',[64] sometimes seems perilously close to crystallising as a doctrine. The comprehensive and ground-breaking work of Faivre, Hanegraaff, and their colleagues and students deserves full credit for the establishing of the history of Western esotericism as a legitimate academic discipline, and has provided an invaluable resource for any researcher wishing to explore this important and previously neglected current in the history of Western religious thought. However, this body of work sets theoretical parameters which may sometimes be unnecessarily rigid and at times seem to reflect the need to tailor historical evidence to fit an overriding metanarrative.[65] Christopher Lehrich, in his monograph on Henry Cornelius Agrippa's great sixteenth-century compendium of magic, *De*

---

[63] Eric Hobsbawm, 'Inventing Traditions', in Eric Hobsbawm and Terence Ranger (eds.), *The Invention of Tradition* (Cambridge: Cambridge University Press, 1983), 1–14, on p. 8.
[64] Wouter J. Hanegraaff, 'The Study of Western Esotericism', in Peter Antes, Armin W. Geertz, and Randi R. Warne (eds.), *New Approaches to the Study of Religion, Vol. 1: Regional, Critical, and Historical Approaches* (Berlin: Walter de Gruyter, 2004), 489–519, on pp. 507–08.
[65] For the dangers of metanarratives, see Charlotte Aull Davies, *Reflexive Ethnography: A Guide to Researching Selves and Others* (London: Routledge, 1999), 4–5.

occulta philosophia, is one of the few historians who directly challenges the metanarrative, suggesting that this methodology 'falls into the trap of exclusivity', that a 'pure' empirical approach is an impossibility for any researcher, and that the claim to 'empirical research without ideological apriori' may itself mask a concealed agenda.[66] The determined exclusion of the Jewish Kabbalah from what is now understood as Western esotericism might be construed as reflecting such an agenda.

The 'insider-outsider' debate in the study of religions has strongly influenced this approach to the study of Western esotericism, as has the methodology of the natural sciences.[67] A stark divide is promulgated between 'religionist' and 'empiricist' perspectives, valorising only the latter. Olav Hammer asserts that the 'empiricist' or 'analytic' approach, which he identifies with the 'etic' or outsider's perspective, is the only valid method to explore religious traditions because all religious phenomena are '*entirely* dependent on social and historical context' and their claims are ultimately 'human constructions'.[68] Unfortunately this statement is no more empirically demonstrable than Plato's declaration in the *Timaeus* that God 'put intelligence in soul and soul in body'.[69] Hammer continues his argument by stating that the 'synthesizing spokesperson' who is determined to find a perennial philosophy underlying divergent traditions will apply the strategy of 'reductionism': attending only to common denominators while ignoring cultural differences.[70] Boaz Huss is equally insistent on the necessity of focusing exclusively on contextualism and abandoning comparative and phenomenological methodologies in the exploration of 'mystical' or 'esoteric' currents such as Kabbalah or New Age spiritualities, viewing such methodologies as supportive of 'essentialism'.[71] These scholars might be seen as defining

---

[66] Lehrich, *Demons and Angels*, 161–63.

[67] For the 'insider-outsider' debate, see Russell T. McCutcheon (ed.), *The Insider/Outsider Problem in the Study of Religion: A Reader* (London: Cassell, 1999).

[68] Hammer, *Claiming Knowledge*, xiv–xv. Italic emphasis is mine.

[69] Plato, *Timaeus*, 30b, trans. Benjamin Jowett, in Edith Hamilton and Huntington Cairns (eds.), *Plato: Collected Dialogues* (Princeton: Princeton University Press, 1961), 1163.

[70] Hammer, *Claiming Knowledge*, 160.

[71] Boaz Huss, 'The Mystification of the Kabbalah and the Modern Construction of Jewish Mysticism', trans. Elana Lutsky, *Ben Gurion*

what they deem to be a single acceptable research method which itself presents a metanarrative that, taken to its extreme, may become as inflexible and exclusive as any religionist insistence on a universal sacred doctrine. The implications of inflexibility and exclusivity have aroused a vigorous counter-argument in some scholarly circles, as demonstrated by an online statement by a group of academics comprising the recently formed Phoenix Rising Academy:

> This perspective disregards a defining constituent of the object of study [Western esotericism], namely, the symbolic perception which might also be termed imaginal epistemology. Pejoratively termed 'religionism', carrying connotations of inadequate scholarship, this formative element of esoteric thought has become the new pariah of the academic study of the field broadly termed Western Esotericism in its current form.[72]

Although this statement might be viewed as an extreme response to an exaggerated threat, espousing an academic paradigm as though it were a biblical truth may not always serve scholarship in helpful ways. Methodology can too easily become methodolatry, a term which the Christian theologian Mary Daly coined in 1973 as the 'worship of method' – the process by which the methodology itself determines which problems can be addressed[73] – and which Larry Dossey, discussing it in the context of mind-body medicine, defines as 'the obsession with a particular method of investigation and the willingness to disfigure a therapy to preserve the sanctity of the method of inquiry'.[74] My

---

University of the Negev Review (Summer 2008), at <http://web.bgu.ac.il/Eng/Centers/review/summer2008/Mysticism.htm>. This paper was originally published in Hebrew in *Pe`anim* 110 (2007), 9–30.
[72] See < http://www.phoenixrising.org.gr/en/2582/call-for-papers-demons-in-the-academy-rejecting-rejected-knowledge-again/>.
[73] Mary Daly, *Beyond God the Father: Toward a Philosophy of Women's Liberation* (Boston: Beacon Press, 1973), 11–12.
[74] Larry Dossey, 'Mind-Body Medicine: Whose Mind and Whose Body?', at <http://www.heartmdinstitute.com/heart-healthy-lifestyles/mindbody-connection/whose-mind-body>. See also Harris Friedman, 'Methodolatry and Graphicacy', *American*

approach in this book emphasises the importance of social and historical context; for this reason the occultists discussed in the following chapters are viewed within the specific cultural background within which they worked and the ways in which this background influenced their divergent interpretations of the Kabbalah. But structural similarities between their formulations of the Kabbalah and Jewish Kabbalistic texts, and the surprising continuity of ancient Jewish magical practices within the occult revival, suggest that more than one methodological approach may be needed to achieve a more balanced perspective. Recognition of continuity does not automatically indicate 'perennialism', nor does it invariably support a 'religionist' stance with ontological assumptions on the part of the scholar.[75] Elliot Wolfson addresses this question directly in a paper discussing continuity and discontinuity in Kabbalistic traditions: 'Must we assume that multivocality and essentialism are mutually exclusive? Are polymorphism and monochromatism methodological paradigms that are necessarily oppositional?'[76]

During the eighty years covered by this book, radical changes in religious, social, and sexual attitudes, new scientific discoveries and archaeological finds, the translation of previously inaccessible texts, and the impact of the Great War all left their mark on the reception of the Kabbalah

---

Psychologist 58:10 (2003), 817–18; Patrick Curry, 'Nature Post-Nature', *New Formations* 64 (April 2008), 51–64.

[75] For 'perennialism' or 'traditionalism', see Wouter J. Hanegraaff, 'Tradition', in Hanegraaff (ed.), *Dictionary of Gnosis*, 1132–34; Hanegraaff, 'Construction of "Esoteric Traditions"'; Antoine Faivre, 'Histoire de la notion moderne de tradition dans ses rapports avec les courants ésotériques (XVe–XX3 siècles)', in Antoine Faivre, *Symboles et Mythes dans les mouvements initiatiques et ésotériques (XVIIIe–XXe siècles): Filiations et emprunts* (Paris: Archè/La Table d'Émeraude, 1999), 9–12; Martin Sedgwick, *Against the Modern World: Traditonalism and the Secret Intellectual History of the Twentieth Century* (Oxford: Oxford University Press, 2004). For René Guénon (1886–1951), one of the chief exponents of 'perennialism', see Brannon Ingram, 'René Guénon and the Traditionalist Polemic', in Olav Hammer and Kocku von Stuckrad (eds.), *Polemical Encounters: Esoteric Discourse and Its Others* (Leiden: Brill, 2007), 201–26; Jean Borella, 'René Guénon and the Traditionalist School', in Faivre and Needleman (eds.), *Modern Esoteric Spirituality*, 330–58.

[76] Wolfson, 'Structure, Innovation, and Diremptive Temporality', 150.

within occultist circles. So too did the varying fortunes of British Jews who, like their medieval and early modern counterparts, willingly exchanged ideas about the Kabbalah with their non-Jewish colleagues. The intensely messianic Kabbalah of late-fifteenth-century Spain reflects the imminent expulsion of the Jews from that country, while the Kabbalah of the Sabbatian movement of the seventeenth century in turn mirrors a widespread European expectation of the eschaton which was not limited solely to Jewish communities; and the Kabbalah of the early twentieth century can comfortably cohabit with Darwin, as Rabbi Abraham Isaac Kook demonstrated in the statement quoted at the beginning of this chapter. Events occurring in the lives of the Jews of the diaspora have influenced their Kabbalistic works, just as events in Britain between 1860 and 1940 influenced not only the texts written by occult practitioners, but also the works written by Jewish scholars about their own esoteric traditions.[77]

Moreover, it may be important – although sometimes overlooked in more sociologically inclined scholarly literature – to consider the individual who stands behind any given text. No culture, however cohesive, produces identical individuals, and each individual will respond to external events in highly individual ways. Even if we know little about such individuals, or nothing at all in the case of older pseudepigraphic works, we must still acknowledge that a particular human being produced a specific work or portion of a work, which will bear the stamp of a specific life, world-view, and fund of experience. The infinity of textual interpretations found in the Kabbalah reflects the infinity of individual human possibilities. Yet certain conflicts and aspirations, arising in part from common biological experiences such as birth, puberty, sexual union, parenting, and death, seem to be important to humans regardless of

---

[77] See, for example, the late-nineteenth-century emergence of 'cultural Zionism' in Paul Mendes-Flohr, *Divided Passions: Jewish Intellectuals and the Experience of Modernity* (Detroit, MI: Wayne State University Press, 1991), 84–94. For the romanticising of Hasidism arising from 'cultural Zionism', see Boaz Huss, 'Martin Buber's Introduction to *The Tales of Rabbi Nachman* and the Early 20th Century Construction of 'Jewish Mysticism' (2008), Ben-Gurion University of the Negev, <http://hsf.bgu.ac.il/cjt/files/electures/Buber1.htm>; Joseph Dan, 'A Bow to Frumkinian Hasidism', *MJ* 11:2 (1991), 175–94.

cultural context; and although the reductive perspectives offered by cognitive psychological approaches exhibit their own ontological assumptions, nevertheless cognitive research has convincingly demonstrated that the human religious imagination, while reflecting immense cultural variety, is nevertheless repetitive in terms of the underlying structures of its narratives and imagery.[78] The problematic aspects of 'essentialism' have largely been dispelled by the more culture-specific approach currently advocated in the academy. But the 'esoteric method', which supports the idea of an 'essential' esoteric tradition, is not identical with the recognition that the Kabbalah of medieval Spain, the Kabbalah of seventeenth-century Eastern Europe, and the Kabbalah of *fin-de-siècle* British occultism display unmistakable family resemblances.[79] The questions raised by the enduring attractiveness of certain core themes running through this diversity of Kabbalistic perspectives are as relevant as the differing cultural constructions that have given these themes specific shapes within particular historical contexts.

An effort has been made in this book to incorporate what the religious historian Ninian Smart described as 'methodological agnosticism'. the attempt to reproduce as faithfully as possible the world-view of the occultists themselves.[80] Arthur Versluis, in an effort to find a middle ground between 'religionist' and 'empiric' approaches to Western esotericism, suggests a 'sympathetic empiricist perspective' that allows the researcher to 'understand one's subject...from the inside out'. In this way it is possible to appreciate the subject's 'metaphysical and cosmological self-

---

[78] See, for example, the papers included in Jensene Andresen (ed.), *Religion in Mind: Cognitive Perspectives on Religious Belief, Ritual, and Experience* (Cambridge: Cambridge University Press, 2001).

[79] For 'family resemblances' (*Familienähnlichkeit*) – overlapping similarities rather than one essential common feature – see Ludwig Wittgenstein, *Philosophical Investigations*, trans. G. E. M. Anscombe (London: Blackwell, 2001).

[80] For 'methodological agnosticism', see Ninian Smart, *The Science of Religion and the Sociology of Knowledge* (Princeton, NJ: Princeton University Press, 1973); McCutcheon (ed.), *Insider/Outsider Problem*, 216–17; James L. Cox, 'Religion Without God: Methodological Agnosticism and the Future of Religious Studies', <http://www.thehibberttrust.org.uk/documents/hibbert_lecture_2003.pdf>.

understanding'.[81] No judgement is made here about the ontological veracity or falsity of any of the claims made by either occultists or Jewish Kabbalists; attempting to demonstrate that Kabbalistic theosophy and practice are genuine divine revelations is no more appropriate than attempting to demonstrate that the appearance of such ideas in British *fin-de-siècle* occultism is nothing more than a deluded neo-Romantic attempt to restore enchantment to a disenchanted world. Languages such as those of modern science and psychology can be newly invented, and the practitioners of the British occult revival enthusiastically embraced these new languages. But I have persistently questioned in each of the following chapters whether the ideas communicated through such languages are themselves genuinely new, or might instead reflect a continuity that challenges the reification of constructed categories such as 'pre-modern', 'modern', and 'post-modern'.

In order to explore the 'metaphysical and cosmological self-understanding' of the practitioners of the British occult revival, I have employed the qualitative methodology of the multiple case study to examine the work of six occultists and their perceptions of the Kabbalah.[82] The first, Éliphas Lévi, inaugurated a Kabbalistic system in mid-nineteenth-century France which shaped the later Kabbalistic exegeses of William Wynn Westcott, Samuel Liddell MacGregor Mathers, Arthur Edward Waite, Aleister Crowley, and Dion Fortune. These six individuals were chosen because they are all authors of definitive works on the Kabbalah which dominated the occult revival and enjoy continuing popularity in contemporary spiritualities in the twenty-first century. All of them, with the exception of Lévi, also founded occult groups that are still extant today. Although these individuals, being deceased, are unlikely to respond to

---

[81] Arthur Versluis, 'What is Esoteric? Methods in the Study of Western Esotericism', *Esoterica* 4 (2000), 1–15, on p. 4. For Hanegraaff's labelling of Versluis as the perpetrator of 'an explicit religionist agenda', see Wouter J. Hanegraff, 'Kabbalah in *Gnosis* Magazine (1985–1999)', in Huss (ed.), *Kabbalah and Contemporary Spiritual Revival*, 251–66, on p. 258.

[82] For the use of case studies in qualitative research, see Alan Bryman, *Quantity and Quality in Social Research* (London: Routledge, 1988), 87–91; William Braud and Rosemarie Anderson, *Transpersonal Research Methods for the Social Sciences: Honoring Human Experience* (London: Sage Publications, 1998), 280.

requests for unstructured interviews, questions have been asked of their written work – published literature, letters, diaries, unpublished papers, and the recorded comments of their colleagues – and the responses are explored individually and in relation to each other, as well as in comparison with Jewish Kabbalistic literature and the interpretations of this literature provided by contemporary Kabbalistic scholars.

One of the reasons for this approach is that, just as Jewish Kabbalists across the centuries have expressed highly individual interpretations of this esoteric lore, so too did occultists working in the late nineteenth and early twentieth centuries. There is no single, uniform 'occultist' Kabbalah. The practitioners of the occult revival reflect not only the social, political, and religious currents of the years in which they were writing and working, but also their own predilections and temperamental biases. Just as 'Neo-platonism' is a construct developed by scholars in the late nineteenth century for their own convenience rather than a self-descriptive category devised by the followers of Plato in late antiquity, the current division of the Kabbalah into 'Jewish', 'Christian', and 'Hermetic' or 'occultist' could be viewed as an anachronistic imposition which may serve multiple agendas but does not facilitate an authentic picture of the Kabbalah of the occult revival. What emerges from the use of the case study approach is a richly textured Kabbalah as varied as that presented in medieval and early modern Jewish texts, which nevertheless revolves around particular core themes common to both the Jewish Kabbalah and the Kabbalah of British occultism.

The results of my research strongly suggest that the Kabbalah of the occult revival may not, after all, be an 'occultist' Kabbalah divorced from its Jewish roots, but instead displays a surprising fidelity to the complex currents of the Jewish Kabbalah, interpreted creatively by non-Jews according to the centuries-old tradition of innovation and hermeneutic flexibility promulgated by Jewish Kabbalists themselves. Moshe Idel, one of the most important and prolific living Kabbalistic scholars, advocates an approach of 'methodological eclecticism' in the study of the Kabbalah: a broad perspective that includes phenomenology, psychology, the comparative study of religions, and cultural history.[83] Although Idel has addressed the varying expressions and interpretations of Jewish mysticism in the context of the modern world, he does not explore the forms of Kabbalah developed by British occultists;[84] but his approach is relevant, particularly as an antidote to the limitations of the single methodology advocated in much of the current research in Western esotericism. Idel emphasises the remarkable resilience displayed by particular ideas in Jewish Kabbalistic literature over the centuries, and the ways in which these ideas transform within specific cultural contexts:

> We must be aware of the paradoxical situation of the existence of both a stable core, or cores, or 'minimum-essence' (or even models)...and fluid aspects of the same religious structures.[85]

This same group of ideas has demonstrated its resilience as well as its fluidity in the British occult revival. Recent theories in cognitive psychology suggest that the continuity of certain ideas is as important as their culture-specific differences, and the terms 'intertextuality' and 'cultural representations' are utilised as a means of explaining this continuity through models other than the 'monomyth' approach advocated by earlier twentieth-century historians of religion such as Mircea Eliade.[86] The Kabbalah of the

---

[83] See Idel, *Hasidism*, 28; Moshe Idel, *Ascensions on High in Jewish Mysticism: Pillars, Lines, Ladders* (Budapest: Central European University Press, 2005), 1.

[84] See Idel, *Old Worlds, New Mirrors*.

[85] Idel, *Hasidism*, 19. For the use of 'models' to explore continuity in Kabbalistic literature, see also Wolfson, 'Structure, Innovation, and Diremptive Temporality'.

[86] For 'intertextuality', see Ioan Couliano, *The Tree of Gnosis: Gnostic Mythology from Early Christianity to Modern Nihilism* (New York: HarperCollins, 1992), 28; Julia Kristeva, *Desire in Language: A Semiotic Approach to Literature and Art*, ed. Léon Roudiez, trans. Alice Jardine, Thomas Gora, and Léon Roudiez (New York: Columbia University Press, 1980); Mary Orr, *Intertextuality: Debates and Contexts* (London: Wiley-Blackwell, 2003). For 'cultural representations', see Pascal Boyer (ed.), *Cognitive Aspects of Religious Symbolism* (Cambridge: Cambridge University Press, 1993); Andresen (ed.), *Religion in Mind*; Dan Sperber, 'Anthropology and psychology: towards an epidemiology of representations', *Man* 20 (1985), 73–89.

occult revival may be neither a newly invented 'modern' Kabbalah nor evidence of a perennialist *prisca theologia*, but may represent the emergence in modern times of a particular group of religious ideas, originating in the syncretic milieu of late antique Judaism, that has enjoyed considerable longevity, articulated in languages appropriate to the religious, scientific, and social contexts of late Victorian, Edwardian, and inter-war Britain but retaining a remarkable degree of structural stability and continuity with late antique, medieval, early modern, and modern Jewish esoteric lore.

SOURCES AND EXISTING LITERATURE

My primary sources in the following chapters are the published and unpublished writings of the practitioners of the occult revival, as well as the journals and newspapers of the period and the materials utilised by the occultists in developing their ideas. In addition to these sources, numerous secondary works have been consulted. These may be roughly divided into seven general categories.

1. *Published scholarly work on the Kabbalah of the occult revival*
Until quite recently there has been little published literature in English dedicated to the development and use of the Kabbalah in the British occult revival. Two volumes involving scholars associated with the University of Amsterdam programme in Western esotericism have recently been published which include a number of papers relevant to the Kabbalah in British occultism: *Kabbalah and Modernity* (2010) and *Kabbalah and Contemporary Spiritual Revival* (2011).[87] The Norwegian scholar Egil Asprem has published two papers on Aleister Crowley's use of the Kabbalah, examined in greater detail in Chapter Five.[88]

---

[87] See, in particular, Wouter J. Hanegraaff, 'The Beginnings of Occultist Kabbalah: Adolphe Franck and Eliphas Lévi', and Marco Pasi, 'Oriental Kabbalah and the Parting of East and West in the Early Theosophical Society', both in Huss, Pasi, and von Stuckrad (eds.), *Kabbalah and Modernity*; Hanegraaff, 'Kabbalah in *Gnosis* Magazine', in Huss (ed.), *Kabbalah and Contemporary Spiritual Revival*.
[88] Asprem, *'Kabbalah Recreata'*; Egil Asprem, 'Magic Naturalized? Negotiating Science and Occult Experience in Aleister Crowley's Scientific Illuminism', *Aries* 8 (2008), 139–65. Asprem is currently a

Asprem assumes that the Kabbalah of the occult revival is a secularised, post-Enlightenment reinvention, a form of 'programmatic syncretism' entirely divorced from its original Jewish matrix; the same basic assumptions discussed earlier concerning the non-Jewish nature of Western esotericism and the modern nature of 'occultist' Kabbalah are evident in these papers. More material is available in German. Andreas Kilcher has authored a number of papers and one book that relate, directly or indirectly, to the Kabbalah of the occult revival.[89] 'Verhüllung und Enthüllung des Gehimnisses', for example, examines the importance of the *Kabbala denudata* in the development of French and British occultism.[90] Kilcher's underlying assumption is that the Kabbalah of the occult revival is a 'new' Kabbalah originating in the early modern period and reinvented for the twentieth century. Apart from this highly focused output, which will no doubt continue in the future and which reflects a particular methodology and socio-historical perspective promulgated by a specific group of scholars, recent work on the British occult revival has been focused primarily on its social context, and the role of the Kabbalah has been minimised or bypassed in favour of larger cultural themes.

2. Published scholarly work on the British occult revival and on specific occultists

These works involve comprehensive examinations of the various historical and social currents involved in the emergence and development of the occult revival, but their concerns preclude any in-depth exploration of the Kabbalah. Joscelyn Godwin's *The Theosophical Enlightenment* remains a seminal text on occult currents in the English-speaking world

---

research assistant at the Center for the History of Hermetic Philosophy and Related Currents at the University of Amsterdam.

[89] See, for example, Andreas B. Kilcher, *Die Sprachtheorie der Kabbala als ästhetisches Paradigma: die Konstruktion einer ästhetischen Kabbala seit der frühen Neuzeit* (Stuttgart: Metzler, 1998); Andreas B. Kilcher, 'Kabbala und Moderne: Gershom Scholems Geschichte und Metaphysik des Judentums', in Joachim Valentin and Saskia Wendel (eds.), *Jüdische Traditionen in der Philosophie des 20. Jahrhunderts* (Darmstadt: Primus Verlag, 2000), 86–99.

[90] Andreas B. Kilcher, 'Verhüllung und Enthüllung des Gehimnisses: Die *Kabbala Denudata* im Okkultismus der Moderne', in Andreas B. Kilcher (ed.), *Morgen-Glantz: Zeitschrift der Christian Knorr von Rosenroth-Gesellschaft* 16 (2006), 343–83.

from the early Romantic period to the early twentieth century.[91] Various works on spiritualism and Theosophy in the mid- to late nineteenth century, such as Janet Oppenheim's *The Other World* and Alex Owen's *The Darkened Room*, present incisive investigations into the history and cultural context of these movements, but they do not deal with the Kabbalah of the occult revival.[92] One of the most thorough recent treatments of the British occult revival is *The Place of Enchantment* by the American scholar Alex Owen. Owen rarely mentions the Kabbalah, and when she does, it is described as a branch of 'Western Hermeticism'.[93] Joshua Gunn's recent work, *Modern Occult Rhetoric*, explores the occult revival as an example of the repeated historical emergence of a cultural idiom concerned with language and secrecy; the Kabbalah (which Gunn spells as 'Qabalah' in accord with contemporary 'emic' distinctions between Jewish and 'occultist' Kabbalah) is discussed only in passing as a 'mathematical vocabulary' entirely removed from its Jewish context.[94] Alison Butler's recent work, *Victorian Occultism and the Making of Modern Magic*,[95] is a comprehensive and perceptive discussion of British occultism at the *fin-de-siècle* which repeatedly mentions the inclusion of 'cabala' in the occultists' rituals, but does not explore which Kabbalah has been utilised or in what ways; nor does it investigate any

---

[91] Joscelyn Godwin, *The Theosophical Enlightenment* (Albany, NY: State University of New York Press, 1994).

[92] Janet Oppenheim, *The Other World: Spiritualism and Psychical Research in England, 1850–1914* (Cambridge: Cambridge University Press, 1985); Alex Owen, *The Darkened Room: Women, Power, and Spiritualism in Late Victorian England* (Chicago, IL: University of Chicago Press, 1989).

[93] Owen, *Place of Enchantment*, 55.

[94] Joshua Gunn, *Modern Occult Rhetoric: Mass Media and the Drama of Secrecy in the Twentieth Century* (Tuscaloosa, AL: University of Alabama Press, 2005), 127. For more on the diverse spellings of Kabbalah in accord with various scholarly and 'emic' agendas, see Chapter Seven.

[95] Alison Butler, *Victorian Occultism and the Making of Modern Magic: Invoking Tradition* (Basingstoke: Palgrave Macmillan, 2011). See also Nevill Drury, *Stealing Fire from Heaven: The Rise of Modern Western Magic* (Oxford: Oxford University Press, 2011); this work, like Butler's, offers a thorough examination of the magical practices of the Golden Dawn and mentions various elements from the Kabbalah, but does not examine the Jewish sources for these elements or the ways in which they were acquired.

Jewish sources, textual or living, which might have contributed to the formulation of the magical rituals of 'Victorian occultism'.

Masonic scholars of the British occult revival, in particular R. A. Gilbert and Ellic Howe, have published lively histories of the personalities and internal conflicts of the Hermetic Order of the Golden Dawn, the most important British magical group of the *fin-de-siécle*,[96] and selections of edited papers by Golden Dawn adepts have been produced with comprehensive introductions by other Masonic scholars from the Quatuor Coronati Lodge.[97] These works are concerned with the history of the magical orders rather than with their theoretical frameworks and the sources from which these were derived. An ongoing debate within Masonic scholarly circles about the relevance of Kabbalistic symbols in both normative and 'fringe' Masonic rituals has generated considerable interest in the history of Jewish involvement in Freemasonry,[98] but no publications on the use of the Kabbalah in the Masonic currents of the occult revival have appeared from this group of scholars. Wouter J. Hanegraaff's impressive and influential work, *New Age Religion and Western Esotericism*, devotes little attention to the Kabbalah except as one of many antecedents for the reinvention of older esoteric traditions in 'New Age' cultural contexts. Ronald Hutton's intensive examination of the roots of the modern British Wicca movement, *The Triumph of the Moon*, devotes an important section to Aleister Crowley and Dion Fortune, and he includes further material on British occultists in other published works;[99] but these are not intended as

---

[96] R. A. Gilbert, *The Golden Dawn Scrapbook: The Rise and Fall of a Magical Order* (Slough: Quantum, 1997); Ellic Howe, *The Magicians of the Golden Dawn: A Documentary History of a Magical Order 1887–1923* (London: Routledge & Kegan Paul, 1972).

[97] See, for example, John Hamill (ed.), *The Rosicrucian Seer: Magical Writings of Frederick Hockley* (Wellingborough: Aquarian Press, 1986); Edward Dunning (ed.), *A. E. Waite: Selected Masonic Papers* (Wellingborough: Aquarian Press, 1988).

[98] See, for example, John M. Shaftesley, 'Jews in English Freemasonry in the 18th and 19th Centuries', *AQC* 92 (1979), 25–81; Jacob Katz, *Jews and Freemasons in Europe 1723–1939*, trans. Leonard Oschry (Cambridge, MA: Harvard University Press, 1970); and further references given in Chapter Three.

[99] Ronald Hutton, *The Triumph of the Moon: A History of Modern Pagan Witchcraft* (Oxford: Oxford University Press, 1999), 171–88; Ronald Hutton, *Witches, Druids and King Arthur* (London:

explorations of Kabbalistic currents within the occult revival. Numerous biographies have been published on the occultists discussed in this book, but these works rarely discuss the Kabbalah. An exception is Robert Uzzel's *Éliphas Lévi and the Kabbalah* but, despite its title, this work devotes only a brief section to the primacy of the Kabbalah in Lévi's writings and does not explore the complex sources of Lévi's Kabbalistic system.[100]

3. *Histories of magic*

A few older surveys of modern ritual magic, such as Francis King's *Ritual Magic in England* and E. M. Butler's trilogy – *The Myth of the Magus, Ritual Magic,* and *The Fortunes of Faust* – offer discussions on the ritual practices of the British occult revival.[101] However, these works do not examine the occultists' incorporation of Jewish materials in their ceremonies. As magic is central to most Jewish Kabbalistic works, an extensive examination of magic and its much-contested definitions, in both translated primary sources and secondary works, has been necessary in researching this book, including investigations into ancient Jewish magic, the Greco-Egyptian magical papyri, and the medieval grimoires, as well as translations of and commentaries on Hebrew magical texts such as the late antique *Sefer ha-Razim* ('Book of Secrets') and *Harba de Moshe* ('Sword of Moses'), the early medieval repository of magical materials known as the Solomonic cycle, the early modern *Sefer ha-Raziel* ('Book of [the angel] Raziel'), early modern works such as Agrippa's *De occulta philosophia* and the angelic adjurations of John Dee and Thomas Rudd, and Francis Barrett's influential early-nineteenth-century work, *The*

Hambledon Continuum, 2003), 128–31; Ronald Hutton, 'Modern Pagan Witchcraft', in William de Blécourt, Ronald Hutton, and Jean la Fontaine, *The Athlone History of Witchcraft and Magic in Europe, Vol. 6: The Twentieth Century* (London: Athlone Press, 1999), 1–79, on pp. 8–13, 38–42.
[100] Robert L. Uzzel, *Éliphas Lévi and the Kabbalah: The Masonic and French Connection of the American Mystery Tradition* (Lafayette, LA: Cornerstone, 2006), 17–26.
[101] Francis King, *Modern Ritual Magic: The Rise of Western Occultism* (Bridport: Prism Press, 1989); Elizabeth M. Butler, *The Myth of the Magus* (Cambridge: Cambridge University Press, 1948); Elizabeth M. Butler, *Ritual Magic* (Cambridge: Cambridge University Press, 1949); Elizabeth M. Butler, *The Fortunes of Faust* (Cambridge: Cambridge University Press, 1952).

Magus.[102] There is, as yet, no scholarly work focusing specifically on the use of magic in the Jewish Kabbalah, nor any work relating the Jewish magical tradition to the magic of the British occult revival, although the latter theme comprises an important aspect of my own research.

4. *Published scholarly work on the Jewish Kabbalah*

Considerable use has been made in this book of the large and growing body of work generated by Jewish Kabbalistic scholars, as well as their translations of Kabbalistic texts. A few Hebrew words, transliterated into the Roman alphabet, have been included in the following chapters because they are terms used by British occultists themselves or they appear in the titles of cited Jewish Kabbalistic texts. I make no claim to any expertise in reading medieval Hebrew manuscripts; Kabbalistic texts are cited in their English translations. The practitioners of the British occult revival were neither accomplished Hebraists nor Kabbalistic scholars, but they adopted the ancient Jewish tradition of the magical efficacy of the Hebrew letters and the Divine Names, and were thus familiar with the Hebrew alphabet and, to a greater or lesser extent, with certain Hebrew words and phrases they deemed essential to their magical work.

The development of modern Kabbalistic scholarship is usually credited to Gershom Scholem in the mid-twentieth century, although a favourable academic interest in the Kabbalah first appeared among the tutors of Jews College, University of London, in the late nineteenth century.[103] One of the most important Kabbalistic scholars writing today is Moshe Idel (1947–), Max Cooper Professor of Jewish Thought at the Hebrew University of Jerusalem, whose extensive body of work has both developed and challenged Scholem's research. Idel's work, along with numerous books and papers by other authors such as Elliot Wolfson, Joseph Dan, Daniel Matt, Arthur Green, Mark Verman, Rachel Elior, and Isaiah Tishby, is referenced throughout this book. These researchers do not discuss the Kabbalah of the occult revival. This may be due in part to Scholem's assertion that occultists such as Lévi and Crowley were 'charlatans' who developed

---

[102] The works of Agrippa, Dee, Rudd, and Barrett, as well as the *Sefer ha-Razim,* the *Harbe de Moshe,* the Solomonic literature, and other Jewish magical texts, are discussed in Chapters Three and Four.

[103] These Jewish scholars are discussed in Chapter Four.

ideas about the Kabbalah that are 'highly coloured humbug';[104] this statement has been taken at face value ever since Scholem's *Major Trends in Jewish Mysticism* was first published in 1941. The sensitive issue of Jewish religious identity, and the pervasive presence in occult literature of the notorious Aryan-Semitic discourse that emerged in the mid-nineteenth century and generated such horrific consequences in the twentieth, may also contribute to the tensions surrounding research into 'occultist' Kabbalah.[105] This discourse is still subtly perpetuated in 'emic' magical circles; some contemporary occultists refuse to acknowledge the Jewish sources of their 'Hermetic Qabalah', claiming a Platonic or Greco-Egyptian origin instead.[106] Heated debates continue within academic circles about whether it is possible for the Kabbalah to be extracted from its Jewish socio-historical setting and opened to individual reinterpretation as a transcultural spirituality while still retaining its integrity as a Jewish esoteric lore. Boaz Huss, a Kabbalistic scholar who is critical of the more conservative stance of some of his colleagues, suggests that the polemics of modern Jewish scholarship against 'New Age' Kabbalah is 'an expression of their claim to be the "authorized guardians" of Kabbalah in the modern world'.[107]

The repudiation of the Kabbalah by the scholars of the late-nineteenth-century *Wissenschaft des Judentums*, who attempted to present Judaism as a 'rational' religion compatible with acculturation in a country that had rejected the integration of its Jewish communities for many centuries, resulted in an 'open field' where the Kabbalah could be easily appropriated by sometimes flagrantly antisemitic occult practitioners. Yet paradoxically, it may be partly

---

[104] Scholem, *Major Trends*, 2.

[105] For the Aryan-Semitic racial discourse, see Léon Poliakov, *The Aryan Myth: A History of Racist and Nationalist Ideas in Europe*, trans. Edmund Howard (New York: Basic Books, 1971), including an extensive bibliography of French and British nineteenth-century works on the subject; see also Arvidsson, 'Aryan Mythology'.

[106] For an example, see Colin Low, 'Emanation and Ascent in Hermetic Kabbalah', at <http://www.digital-brilliance.com/kab/essays/Emanation%20Ascent.pdf>. See also Chapter Seven.

[107] Boaz Huss, '"Authorized Guardians": The Polemics of Academic Scholars of Jewish Mysticism Against Kabbalah Practitioners', in von Stuckrad and Hammer (eds.), *Polemical Encounters*, 81–103, on p. 81.

through the work of the occultists that the Kabbalah once again began to attract the attention of Jewish scholars. That Scholem was familiar with an extensive range of occultist literature on the Kabbalah is evident not only in his published comments about Lévi and Crowley, but also in his *Bibliographia kabbalistica*, a listing of Kabbalistic works beginning with the twelfth-century *Sefer ha-Bahir* and including all of Lévi's books as well as those of the Golden Dawn adept A. E. Waite and the Theosophist G. R. S. Mead.[108] Scholem's work is strongly coloured by the academic paradigms of the mid-twentieth century as well as by his personal predilections, and elements within Kabbalistic literature which might have generated opposition to his research in the broader academic community are attenuated.[109] However, as subsequent generations of scholars question some of Scholem's premises, areas of the Kabbalah which were previously neglected – particularly the 'practical' or magical Kabbalah – are beginning to be recognised as fundamental to Kabbalistic doctrines and practices. Some of the most important Kabbalistic texts dealing with these themes, such as the late fifteenth-century *Sefer ha-Meshiv*, bear remarkably close family resemblances to the material found in British occult literature.[110]

5. *Published scholarly work on modern Western esotericism, Rosicrucianism, and alchemy*

The researchers of the Centre for the History of Hermetic Philosophy and Related Currents at the University of

---

[108] Gershom Scholem, *Bibliographia Kabbalistica: Verzeichnis der Gedruckten; die jüdische Mystik (Gnosis, Kabbala, Sabbatianismus, Frankismus, Chassidismus) behandelnden Bücher und Aufsätze von Reuchlin bis zur Gegenwart* (Leipzig: W. Drugulin, 1927). For Waite, see Chapter Five. For Mead, see Chapter Four.

[109] For discussions on Scholem's approach to the Kabbalah, see Daniel Abrams, 'Presenting and Representing Gershom Scholem: A Review Essay', *MJ* 20:2 (2000), 226–43; David Biale, *Gershom Scholem: Kabbalah and Counter-History* (Cambridge, MA: Harvard University Press, 1979); Dan, *Gershom Scholem*; Joseph Dan, 'Scholem's View of Jewish Messianism', *MJ* 12:2 (1992), 117–28; Huss, 'Ask No Questions'; Peter Schäfer and Joseph Dan (eds.), *Gershom Scholem's Major Trends in Jewish Mysticism 50 Years After* (Tübingen: Mohr-Siebeck, 1993). See also the discussion of Scholem's antipathy toward 'magical Kabbalah' in Lehrich, *Demons and Angels*, 149–51.

[110] For the *Sefer ha-Meshiv* and its resemblance to Golden Dawn ritual practices, see Chapters Four and Five.

Amsterdam have generated a growing range of publications that explore Western esoteric currents from the early modern period to contemporary 'New Age' spiritualities. As discussed above, these works approach Western esotericism as a religious current which demands a specifically 'empiricist' methodology. When they deal with the Kabbalah of the occult revival, it is usually viewed homogenously as a modern and non-Jewish 'syncretic system'.[111] Numerous works on the history of Rosicrucian-Masonic and alchemical currents in the early modern and modern periods have been produced outside the academic construct of 'Western esotericism'. These include Christopher McIntosh's *The Rosicrucians* and *The Rose Cross and the Age of Reason*, Frances A. Yates' *The Rosicrucian Enlightenment*, Marsha Keith Schuchard's *Restoring the Temple of Vision*, and a large number of books and papers on the history of 'spiritual' or 'Hermetic' alchemy.[112] The Kabbalah is acknowledged as a dominant factor in the development of these currents in the early modern period, and McIntosh examines Rosicrucian elements in the Golden Dawn and its offshoots, but he does not explore the ways in which Jewish Kabbalistic materials were utilised by British occultists in their own 'Rosicrucian-Hermetic' doctrines.[113]

6. *Unpublished doctoral dissertations on the occult revival*

In recent years, a number of unpublished doctoral dissertations submitted to universities in Britain, the U.S.A., and South Africa have been dedicated to specific aspects of the British occult revival.[114] These works either do not discuss the Kabbalah or, following Faivre and Hanegraaff, accept unquestioningly the sharp demarcation between the Jewish Kabbalah and 'Hermetic' or 'occultist' Kabbalah. For

---

[111] Alfred Vitale, '"The Method of Science, The Aim of Religion": A Systematic Model for the Academic Study of Modern Western Occultism', *Esoterica* 6 (2004), 39–67, on p. 40.

[112] Christopher McIntosh, *The Rosicrucians: The History, Mythology, and Rituals of an Esoteric Order* (York Beach, ME: Weiser Books, 1998); Christopher McIntosh, *The Rose Cross and the Age of Reason: Eighteenth-Century Rosicrucianism in Central Europe and its Relationship to the Enlightenment* (Leiden: Brill, 1992); Frances A. Yates, *The Rosicrucian Enlightenment* (London: Routledge & Kegan Paul, 1972); Schuchard, *Restoring the Temple*.

[113] For this theme with full references, see Chapter Three.

[114] These are referenced in the appropriate chapters.

example, Lloyd Kenton Keane summarises the important texts of the Jewish Kabbalah in relation to C. G. Jung's use of Kabbalistic material in his psychological writings, but follows the current paradigm that 'Hermetic' Kabbalah is entirely different from the Jewish Kabbalah.[115] John Selby, discussing Dion Fortune's 'inner plane contacts', devotes considerable attention to her use of the Kabbalistic Tree of Life and the various historical perceptions of this important symbol.[116] Selby likewise accepts the assumption that 'Western esoteric' Kabbalah is entirely different from the Jewish Kabbalah; he also uses the different spellings of the word common among contemporary occult practitioners – Kabbalah for the Jewish, Cabala for the Christian, and Qabalah for the 'Hermetic' or 'occultist'[117] – to indicate three discrete entities, the latter two developing independently of the Jewish Kabbalah.[118] While these dissertations offer useful insights into various aspects of the occult revival, they do not examine the ways in which Jewish Kabbalistic doctrines and practices were developed by the occultists of the time.

7. Contemporary 'emic' works and websites related to the British occult revival

The Kabbalah of the occult revival is still alive and well in contemporary spiritualities. Among these currents are the present-day incarnations of groups founded in the late nineteenth and early twentieth centuries, including Dion Fortune's Society of the Inner Light, Aleister Crowley's Ordo Templi Orientis, and the Hermetic Order of the Golden

---

[115] Lloyd Kenton Keane, *Routes of Wholeness: Jungian and Post-Jungian Dialogues with the Western Esoteric Tradition* (unpublished PhD dissertation, Centre for Psychoanalytic Studies, University of Essex, 2007).

[116] John Selby, *Dion Fortune and her Inner Plane Contacts: Intermediaries in the Western Esoteric Tradition* (unpublished PhD dissertation, Department of Theology, University of Exeter, 2008).

[117] For examples of the 'emic' use of these three spellings, see the various articles on the 'Hermetic' Kabbalah at <http://digital-brilliance.com/kab/index.htm>.

[118] The various orthographies of Kabbalah have posed a problem not only for scholars but also for cataloguing and reference services attempting to locate the correct place to index English-language works on the Kabbalah. For a trenchant discussion about the confusion caused by the diverse and inconsistent applications of 'Kabbalah', 'Cabala', and 'Qabalah', see Elia, 'An Historical Assessment'.

Dawn founded by William Wynn Westcott and Samuel Liddell MacGregor Mathers. These groups all enjoy a presence on the internet and offer access to recently written articles and books as well as texts by the practitioners of the occult revival. I have utilised the material offered by these contemporary occult orders through their archives, journals, bibliographies, and personal correspondence as an important research resource.

DEFINITIONS OF TERMS

Certain terms used throughout this book – 'magic', 'mysticism', 'esotericism', and 'occultism' – are the subject of ongoing scholarly debate, and the manner in which they are employed in the following chapters needs to be clarified. Current academic definitions may not always accord with the ways in which the practitioners of the British occult revival used the words, and the term 'mysticism' does not exist in Jewish Kabbalistic texts. Moreover, occultists from the same cultural milieu do not always agree with each other's definitions. As no consensus has been reached about these terms, they are applied here as heuristic devices to clarify the research and its conclusions. Brief descriptions are given below and the terms are also discussed in the appropriate chapters.

1. *Esotericism*

Antoine Faivre defines esotericism as 'an ensemble of spiritual currents' in modern Western history which 'share a certain *air de famille*, as well as the form of thought which is its common denominator'.[119] Faivre's list of the features that define this 'ensemble' is given above. In a more general sense, 'esoteric' can imply secret or arcane teachings reserved for initiates. Moshe Halbertal, discussing esotericism in

---

[119] Antoine Faivre, 'Questions of Terminology Proper to the Study of Esoteric Currents in Modern and Contemporary Europe', in Faivre and Hanegraaff (eds.), *Western Esotericism and the Science of Religion*, 1–10, on p. 2. See also Olav Hammer and Kocku von Stuckrad, 'Introduction: Western Esotericism and Polemics', in Hammer and von Stuckrad (eds.), *Polemical Encounters*, vi–xxii, on p. vii, n. 1, where Western esotericism is described as 'a historically related set of currents that include various blendings of Christian teachings with the Jewish kabbalah, Hermeticism, and...astrology, alchemy, and magic'.

Jewish mysticism, suggests that it 'reflects a consciousness of the existence of something concealed and hidden, whose knowledge or experience is of decisive or even redemptive import'.[120] Halbertal identifies a tractate of the Babylonian Talmud from the second century CE as the foundation text for a current of secret knowledge within Jewish tradition. This seed-text, rooted in older rabbinic sources, produced its flowers and fruit in Western Europe in the twelfth and thirteenth centuries in the form of the Kabbalah.[121] Judaism, in Halbertal's view, thus included an esoteric dimension long before the emergence of the Kabbalah, but the twelfth and thirteenth centuries represent the 'age of esotericism' in Jewish thought.[122]

'Esotericism' can also be understood in a socio-political context, as the deliberate effort to conceal teachings, doctrines, or beliefs that are felt to be the proper domain of an elite group of initiates. Harvey J. Hames, discussing the emergence of the Kabbalah in textual form in France and Spain in the thirteenth century, suggests that the movement from oral teachings to written texts – in other words, from esoteric to exoteric – was part of a wider cultural shift both within Judaism and in the broader Christian environment of western Europe, reflecting an urgent concern with the reform of existing religious structures in the face of burgeoning apocalyptic expectations. 'The appearance of Kabbalah on the historical stage', declares Hames, 'can only be understood as an exoteric phenomenon', and could only come about 'where there is a real need for what Kabbalah has to offer'.[123] The Kabbalists of the thirteenth century – and, it might be argued, the occultists of the late nineteenth century – 'try to use the power of revealing what was secret to force political, social and religious change, and by doing so, create a platform for communal reform and deliverance from exile'.[124]

---

[120] Moshe Halbertal, *Concealment and Revelation: Esotericism in Jewish Thought and Its Philosophical Implications* (Princeton, NJ: Princeton University Press, 2007), 1.

[121] Halbertal, *Concealment*, 4. The text is the Mishnah in the tractate *Hagiga* 2:1.

[122] Halbertal, *Concealment*, 5. For esotericism in the Kabbalah, see also Harvey J. Hames, 'Exotericism and Esotericism in Thirteenth Century Kabbalah', *Esoterica*, 6 (2004), 102–12.

[123] Hames, 'Exotericism and Esotericism', 106.

[124] Hames, 'Exotericism and Esotericism', 109.

I have used the terms 'esotericism' and 'esoteric' in both Faivre's and Halbertal's senses. Esotericism as a mode of perception (as in Halbertal) is meant when the term is applied in a general sense (e.g. 'Jewish esoteric lore'), and esotericism as an academically constructed category of currents of thought (as in Faivre) is indicated when the phrase 'Western esotericism' is used. While these two meanings of the word often overlap, they can also diverge radically. The 'esoteric' level of sacred texts, and the forms of hermeneutics believed to reveal its meaning, are often discussed in medieval Jewish literature. This does not necessarily involve the categories stipulated by Faivre as definitive of 'Western esotericism', although Arthur Versluis, who includes the Jewish Kabbalah under the rubric of 'Western esoteric traditions', notes the overlap of the two definitions in the Kabbalah, which he describes as esoteric in both senses.[125] The late twelfth-century philosopher Maimonides' *The Guide of the Perplexed*, for example, relates Aristotelian philosophy to Jewish theology in an effort to rationalise Judaism; and while this work promises to reveal esoteric truths, it cannot be considered an esoteric work in Faivre's sense.[126] 'Esoteric', in *Guide of the Perplexed*, means teachings which must be concealed from those incapable of understanding them or who might, as a result of understanding them without deeper comprehension, lose their faith:

> All these are obscure matters. In fact, they are truly the mysteries of the Torah and the secrets constantly mentioned in the books of the prophets and in the dicta of the sages....These are the matters that ought not to be spoken of except in chapter headings, as we have mentioned, and only with an individual such as has been described.[127]

The 'individual such as has been described' is not one who espouses Faivre's categories, but rather, one who is willing to study the Aristotelian scientific and philosophical literature

---

[125] Arthur Versluis, *Restoring Paradise: Western Esotericism, Literature, Art, and Consciousness* (Albany, NY: State University of New York Press, 2004), 46–54.
[126] Moses Maimonides, *The Guide of the Perplexed*, trans. Shlomo Pines, 2 vols. (Chicago, IL: University of Chicago Press, 1963).
[127] Maimonides, *Guide of the Perplexed*, 1.35, pp. 80–81.

in order to comprehend that all apparently supernatural phenomena – whether prophetic or miraculous – must be 'understood in light of the impersonal operation of the natural order'.[128]

2. *Occultism*

Modern usage of the term 'occultism' is usually credited to Éliphas Lévi, whose Kabbalistic system is discussed in the next chapter. Faivre, equating occultism with modern ceremonial magic, defines it as 'the attempt to reconcile modern science and gnosis', and insists that the term is applicable only to Western esoteric currents from Lévi onward.[129] Faivre also cautions against confusing occultism with esotericism: the former comprises a group of practices, while the latter provides the theories which make these practices possible.[130] Hanegraaff, like Faivre, asserts that occultism is modern, and distinguishes it from the three traditional 'occult sciences' – magic, alchemy, and astrology – incorporated in Agrippa's *De occulta philosophia*.[131] I have used the term 'occultism' partly in Faivre's sense: to describe the application of esoteric systems of thought to magical practices. However, although Faivre and Hanegraaff view occultism as a modern creation, many aspects of the medieval Jewish Kabbalah may be considered 'occultist' because they involve the practical application of Kabbalistic theosophy to magic, incorporate the latest scientific perspectives of their time, and encompass a world-view which includes a belief in the spark of divinity hidden in the human soul and the possibility of developing that spark to achieve individual transformation and magical power over nature.

---

[128] Howard Kreisel, 'Esotericism to Exotericism: From Maimonides to Gersonides', in Howard Kreisel (ed.), *Study and Knowledge in Jewish Thought, Vol. 1* (Beer Sheva: Ben Gurion University of the Negev Press, 2006), 165–83, on p. 182. For the ongoing debate about what constitutes 'esotericism' in Maimonides, see the discussion and references in Kreisel's paper; see also the idea of the 'interpretive riddle' in Sara Klein-Braslavy, 'Maimonides' Exoteric and Esoteric Biblical Interpretations in the Guide of the Perplexed', in Kreisel (ed.), *Study and Knowledge*, 137–64.

[129] Faivre, 'Terminology', 8–9.

[130] Antoine Faivre, 'What is Occultism?', in Lawrence E. Sullivan (ed.), *Hidden Truths: Magic, Alchemy, and the Occult* (New York/London: Macmillan & Collier, 1987), 3–9, on p. 3.

[131] Hanegraaff, 'Construction of "Esoteric Traditions"', 15–16.

3. *Mysticism*

A full discussion of the problems surrounding 'mysticism' as an independent religious category, and the use of the word by British occultists, is given in Chapter Five. 'Mysticism' has largely vanished as a core term in religious studies,[132] and the older understanding of mystical experience as a universal phenomenon has been challenged by many contemporary scholars.[133] Boaz Huss suggests that the term 'Jewish mysticism' should be abandoned within the academy because it is derived from Christian theology;[134] the word 'mysticism' does not exist in the Hebrew language.[135] Attempts to differentiate between 'mysticism' and 'magic' may also be misleading in the context of both British occultism and the Jewish Kabbalah. Moshe Idel has demonstrated in his studies on modern Hasidism and medieval 'ecstatic' Kabbalah that magical rituals may serve as instruments to achieve mystical union, which in turn is seen as a conduit for the acquisition of magical powers.[136] I have used the term 'mystical' to describe the longing for a direct experience of transhuman realms, an inclination which implies no 'essential' qualities other than humanness and whose pursuit is not always easily disentangled from magic. In heuristic terms, mysticism connotes an aspiration, while magic, as utilised in the British occult revival, connotes a praxis aimed at achieving that aspiration. Both, according to Ithamar Gruenwald, involve efforts to achieve altered states of consciousness in order to 'break the gravitational power

---

[132] See William R. LaFleur, 'Body', in Taylor (ed.), *Critical Terms for Religious Studies*, 36–54, on p. 36.

[133] For critiques of universalist assumptions in modern academic definitions of mysticism, see Chapter Five.

[134] Boaz Huss, 'Jewish Mysticism in the University: Academic Study or Theological Practice?' (lecture given as part of the programme, 'The Academy and Spirituality: Can They Go Together?', Van Leer Institute, Jerusalem (30 May 2006), <http://www.zeek.net/712academy>.

[135] See Joseph Dan, 'In Quest of a Historical Definition of Mysticism: The Contingental Approach', in Joseph Dan, *Jewish Mysticism: The Modern Period* (Northvale, NJ: Jason Aronson, 1999), 1–46, on p. 6.

[136] See the discussion of 'mystical', 'magical-talismanic', and 'magico-mystical' models in Idel, *Hasidism*, 53–102. See also Ithamar Gruenwald, 'When Magical Techniques and Mystical Practices Become Neighbors: Methodological Considerations', in Gideon Bohak, Yuval Harari, and Shaul Shaked (eds.), *Continuity and Innovation in the Magical Tradition* (Leiden: Brill, 2011), 159–86.

that normally prevents matter from losing its bonds with the laws that govern the physical world'.[137]

4. *Magic*

A full discussion of the problematic term 'magic' is included in Chapter Four. Because of the complexity of the academic debate, 'magic' is used throughout this book as a heuristic device to identify particular themes common to both British occultism and Jewish ritual practice which, adapting Rachel Elior's broad definition, are specifically concerned with developing and maintaining, through the application of human intent, 'the system of bonds and relationships between the revealed and concealed worlds'.[138]

---

[137] Gruenwald, 'When Magical Techniques and Mystical Practices Become Neighbors', 170.
[138] Rachel Elior, 'Mysticism, Magic, and Angelology: The Perception of Angels in Hekhalot Literature', *JQR* 1 (1993), 3–53, on p. 16.

CHAPTER TWO

THE 'GREAT SECRET':
ÉLIPHAS LÉVI AND THE HEBREW ROOTS OF THE
VICTORIAN OCCULT REVIVAL

There is no science that confirms to us the divinity of Christ
more than magic and the Kabbalah.
— Giovanni Pico della Mirandola (1486)[1]

When I read that a stone consisted of trillions of molecules
constantly in motion and that these molecules consisted of
atoms and that these atoms were in themselves complicated
systems, whirls of energy, I said to myself, 'That's the cabala
after all!'
— Isaac Bashevis Singer (1984)[2]

A VISIT TO A MAGUS

In the first week of December 1861, Kenneth Mackenzie, a
brilliant, ambitious, and hard-drinking twenty-eight-year-old
antiquarian scholar with a history of involvement in occult
and spiritualist pursuits, journeyed to Paris to visit his
father.[3] While there, Mackenzie paid two calls on a French
magus called Alphonse-Louis Constant, known to his
disciples as Éliphas Lévi.[4] Lévi was already familiar to a

---

[1] Giovanni Pico della Mirandola, 'Twenty-Six Magical Conclusions',
9>9, British Library IB18857, cited in S. A. Farmer, *Syncretism in the
West: Pico's 900 Theses (1486)* (Tempe, AR: Medieval & Renaissance
Texts & Studies, 1998), 498–99.
[2] Isaac Bashevis Singer, *Love and Exile* (New York: Doubleday, 1984),
16.
[3] For biographical information on Kenneth Mackenzie, see Ellic
Howe, 'Fringe Masonry in England, 1870–85', *AQC* 85 (1972), 242–
80, on p. 242; Howe, *Magicians*, 27–33; Godwin, *Theosophical
Enlightenment*, 185–86, 213–16, 218–19.
[4] See Kenneth Mackenzie, 'An account of what passed between
Eliphas Lévi Zahed (Abbé Constant), Occult Philosopher, and
Baphometus (Kenneth R. Mackenzie), Astrologer and Spiritualist, in
the City of Paris, December 1861', G.D. MSS V12, Yorke Collection,

small circle of British occultists through a recently published trilogy of works on magic, although none of these books had yet been translated into English.[5] One of Mackenzie's chief interests was the Tarot, and Lévi's work was replete with innovative interpretations of these mysterious cards, which had been well known in European esoteric circles since the late eighteenth century but had not yet been transplanted to English soil.[6] Mackenzie was particularly interested in discovering whether Lévi, an artist as well as an occultist, intended to issue his own hand-drawn set of Tarot cards, of which three examples had so far appeared in his published works.[7]

Warburg Institute NS68(2), repr. as 'Philosophical and Cabbalistic Magic', *The Rosicrucian and Red Cross* 2 (April 1873), 28–34; repr. in King, *Modern Ritual Magic*, 28–38, and in Christopher McIntosh, *Eliphas Lévi and the French Occult Revival* (London: Rider, 1972), 117–22.

[5] Lévi, *Dogme*; Éliphas Lévi, *Histoire de la magie, avec une exposition claire et précise de ses procédés, de ses rites et de ses mystères* (Paris: Germer Baillière, 1860); Éliphas Lévi, *La clef des grand mystères, suivant Hénoch, Abraham, Hermès Trismégiste et Salomon* (Paris: Germer Baillière, 1861). Selected excerpts from Lévi's work began appearing in English in various Theosophical journals from 1882 onward, and the Theosophical Society published an English version of his *Les Paradoxes de la haute science: paradoxes magiques* in India in 1883 in *Theosophical Miscellany*. The first translation of a major portion of Lévi's work published in Britain was *Mysteries of Magic: A Digest of the Writings of Eliphas Lévi*, translated and edited by A. E. Waite (London: George Redway, 1886).

[6] For Mackenzie's interest in the Tarot, see Kenneth Mackenzie, 'Philosophical and Cabbalistic Magic', cited in King, *Ritual Magic*, 31; Ronald Decker and Michael Dummett, *A History of the Occult Tarot 1870–1970* (London: Duckworth, 2002), 46–47; Howe, *Magicians*, 29–30; Godwin, *Theosophical Enlightenment*, 216. For the history of the cards in Europe, see Ronald Decker, Thierry Depaulis, and Michael Dummett, *A Wicked Pack of Cards: The Origins of the Occult Tarot* (London: Duckworth, 1996).

[7] No other images of Lévi's Tarot have been found. For Mackenzie's reference to the 'lost cards of Eliphaz Levi', see his letter to William Wynn Westcott, dated 7 August 1879, in Howe, *Magicians*, 30. See Paul Chacornac, *Éliphas Lévi: Rénovateur de l'occultisme en France (1810–1875)* (Paris: Chacornac Frères, 1926), 291, n. 2, for mention of an unpublished MS by Lévi entitled *Le livre d'Hermès*, which purportedly contained designs for a complete Tarot deck. A posthumously published work by Lévi called *Clefs majeures et clavicules de Salomon* (MS dated 1860; Paris: L. Chamuel, 1895), described by Mackenzie as 'a little volume', presents the Major

*Fig. 1: Lévi's three published Tarot cards. Top left, 'Bouc de Sabbat'
('The Devil'); top right, 'Le Chariot d'Hermès' ('The Chariot');
bottom, 'Le grand agent magique' ('The Wheel of Fortune').*[8]

Arcana not as Tarot images but as the Hebrew letters which Lévi
believed corresponded with them. In this work, the ten numbered
cards of each suit of the Minor Arcana are related to the ten *sefirot* of
the Kabbalah, while the four suits are equated with the four
elements and the four letters of the holiest of the Divine Names, the
Tetragrammaton. This equation of elements with the
Tetragrammaton is not Lévi's invention, but was first presented in
the late thirteenth century by Shem Tov ibn Shem Tov in his
commentary on the *Sefer Yetsirah*; see Daphne Freedman, 'Shem Tov
ibn Shem Tov on "Sefer Yetsirah"', *JJS* 58:2 (2007), 303–13. *Clef
majeures* draws directly on ideas found in early Jewish sources, a
fact neglected by his biographers.
[8] 'Bouc du Sabbat', Lévi, *Dogme*, 180; 'Le Chariot d'Hermès:
Septième clef du Tarot', Lévi, *Dogme*, 338; 'Le grand agent magique:
Dixième clef du Tarot', Lévi, *Clef*, 97.

On the front door of Lévi's apartment, located in one of the poorest quarters of Paris, was a small card on which his full pseudonym – Éliphas Lévi Zahed – was inscribed in Hebrew. Lévi, a 'short, burly man' with 'piercing eyes twinkling with good humour', was an amiable host, although he could only converse with Mackenzie in French. The tiny apartment was bedecked as a shrine to the Jewish Kabbalah. On the wall hung a large 'cabbalistical diagram' of which, Lévi informed his guest, only one hundred impressions had been taken; around the room were displayed various engravings and paintings 'having reference to the Cabbala'. Against one wall stood an altar, at the centre of which lay 'a Hebrew roll of the Law'. On the adjacent wall hung a picture of a woman with hands clasped to her bosom, adoring the Tetragrammaton or sacred four-letter Divine Name, יהוה (YHVH); Lévi informed Mackenzie that she represented 'the Holy Cabbala'. Whatever topic Mackenzie raised – and their conversation ranged from the prophecies of Paracelsus to the art of physiognomy – his host kept returning to the theme of the Kabbalah. Lévi even criticised Edward Bulwer-Lytton, whom he had met during a brief visit to London, as 'a gentleman of versatile talents, but of little real knowledge in relation to the Cabbala'.[9] Although Mackenzie secretly considered his host 'an utter materialist' in matters concerning spiritualism, against which the French magus had expressed strong opinions,[10] accusations of materialism are common expressions of rivalry among occultists in the late nineteenth century, and do not reflect the importance and impact of an individual's work.[11] An unstintingly admiring eulogy penned by Mackenzie appeared two years after Lévi's death:

> A man more unaffected in his manners, or less inflated by his superior attainments, could not be found....When he died,

---

[9] For more on Lord Lytton, see Chapter Six.

[10] For Lévi's negative views on spiritualism, see Lévi, *Dogme*, 130–36; A. E. Waite, 'Biographical and Critical Essay', in A. E. Waite (ed. and trans.), *Mysteries of Magic* (London: George Redway, 1886), 1–41, on p. 9.

[11] For Lévi's view of Mackenzie as a materialist, see Lévi, *Cours*, XXII. For Henry Steel Olcott's view of Lévi as a materialist, see Henry Steel Olcott, 'German Experiences', *Old Diary Leaves, Third Series, 1883–1887* (London: Theosophical Publishing House, 1895), 172.

some two years ago, the Holy Kabbalah lost one of its most learned expositors.[12]

Mackenzie's meetings with Lévi represent the first direct encounter between Lévi's Kabbalistic system and the British occult groups upon which it would exercise a decisive influence in the ensuing decades. Lévi's understanding of the Kabbalah was derived from Hebrew texts transmitted through fifteenth-, sixteenth-, and seventeenth-century Christian Hebraists and alchemists, medieval redactions of late antique Jewish magical texts, late-eighteenth-century French illuminists and mesmerists, and living French and Polish Jewish Kabbalists whom he included in his extensive network of friends. Lévi viewed himself as a Kabbalist – his pseudonym no less than his writings are testimony to this – and believed it was his destiny to reveal to the modern age the lost keys of 'the great Hebrew doctrines of occult theology'.[13] Lévi was also perceived as a Kabbalist by the British occultists who followed him, as Mackenzie's eulogy demonstrates. It is only in current scholarly literature that his lifelong commitment to the Kabbalah has been attenuated and his ideas have been subsumed under the general heading of 'occultism'.[14] All the varied themes he welds together in his work – ritual magic, pagan myth, Hermetic alchemy and Pythagorean philosophy, mesmerism, prophecy, necromancy, the Tarot, the universality of all religions, and the Romantic vision of a reformed Church in a transformed and utopian society – are included in his overarching concept of the Kabbalah; and it is this concept that forms the basis for most of the major developments in British occultism in the ensuing decades. Whatever modern scholars might call Lévi's unique syncretic system, it is his own understanding and application of it that is the chief focus of this chapter, and he defines that system as the Kabbalah.

---

[12] Kenneth Mackenzie, *The Royal Masonic Cyclopaedia of History, Rites, Symbolism and Biography* (London: John Hogg, 1877), 450.
[13] Lévi, *Clef*, 9.
[14] See, for example, Alison Butler, 'Magical Beginnings: The Intellectual Origins of the Victorian Occult Revival', *Limina* 9 (2003), 78–95; Owen, *Place of Enchantment*, 44, 53.

'*LE PETIT ROMANTIQUE*'

Details of Lévi's life are given in various biographies, beginning with Paul Chacornac's definitive eulogy to the magus, published in 1926.[15] Chacornac relied uncritically on the autobiographical preface in Lévi's early apocalyptic work, *L'Assomption de la femme*, published in 1841 under the name Alphonse-Louis Constant,[16] as well as on some

---

[15] Chacornac, *Éliphas Lévi*. A biography of Lévi by Louis Chamaud had been promised at the end of the nineteenth century by Papus, head of the Neo-Martinist order based on Lévi's work, but this biography never materialised. For later biographies in English, largely based on Chacornac, see McIntosh, *Éliphas Lévi*; Thomas A. Williams, *Eliphas Lévi: Master of the Cabala, the Tarot and the Secret Doctrines* (Tuscaloosa, AL: University of Alabama Press, 1975); Uzzel, *Éliphas Lévi*, and the PhD dissertation on which Uzzel's book is based: Robert L. Uzzel, *The Kabbalistic Thought of Eliphas Lévi and Its Influence on Modern Occultism in America* (PhD dissertation, Baylor University, 1995). For Waite's biographical essays on Lévi, see Waite, 'Biographical and Critical Essay'; A. E. Waite, 'Biographical Preface', in Éliphas Lévi, *Transcendental Magic*, trans. A. E. Waite (London: Rider, 1896), xix–xxxi; A. E. Waite, *The Holy Kabbalah* (London: Williams & Norgate, 1929), 487–94. See also Evelyn Underhill, 'A Defence of Magic', *FR* 82:491 (1907), 754–65, repr. in Dana Greene (ed.), *Evelyn Underhill: Modern Guide to the Ancient Quest for the Holy* (Albany, NY: State University of New York Press, 1988), 33–46. For chapters devoted to Lévi in other works, see Jean-Pierre Laurant, 'Eliphas Lévi', in Hanegraaff (ed.), *Dictionary of Gnosis*, 19–54; Decker *et al.*, *Wicked Pack*, 166–93. For modern biographies in French, see Bowman, *Eliphas Lévi*; Alain Mercier, *Eliphas Lévi et la pensée magique* (Paris: Seghers, 1974); Christiane Buisset, *Eliphas Lévi: Sa vie, son oeuvre, ses pensées* (Paris: Guy Trédaniel/Éditions de la Maisnie, 1984). A German biography of Lévi was published before Chacornac's work, but achieved no recognition outside German esoteric circles: R. H. Laarss, *Eliphas Lévi: Der Grosse Kabbalist und Seine Magischen Werke* (Vienna/Berlin: Rikola Verlag, 1922). For early overviews of occultism in nineteenth-century France, see Alexander Erdan, *La France mystique*, 2 vols. (Amsterdam: R. C. Meyer, 1858); Auguste Viatte, *Les Sources occultes du Romantisme: Illuminisme et Théosophie (1770–1820)*, 2 vols. (Paris: Librairie Ancienne Honoré Champion, 1928). For further material on Lévi, see Hanegraaff, *New Age Religion*, 384–85; James Webb, *The Flight from Reason* (London: Macdonald, 1971), 164–87; Hutton, *Triumph of the Moon*, 70–72.

[16] Alphonse-Louis Constant, *L'Assomption de la femme* (Paris: Le Gallois, 1841).

personal correspondence;[17] but most of Lévi's private papers have vanished.[18] A few details relevant to the development of Lévi's Kabbalistic system are worth noting: that the young Alphonse-Louis Constant, born in 1810 to a poor Parisian shoemaker and his wife, trained for the Catholic priesthood but stopped short of taking holy orders, partly because of his heterodox religious views and partly because he fell in love; that most of the early period of his life was spent involved in and writing about revolutionary politics; and that in 1853, at the age of forty-three, he abruptly abandoned the name Alphonse-Louis Constant and began to publish his unique synthesis of the Kabbalah, the Tarot, and ritual magic under the pseudo-Hebrew pseudonym of Éliphas Lévi Zahed. This is usually assumed to be a Hebrew translation of Alphonse-Louis Constant, but the first two names are simply the closest phonetic match to his French names. 'Zahed', which bears no relationship to 'Constant' either phonetically or in terms of meaning, is an Arabic rather than a Hebrew word, meaning

---

[17] Chacornac had access to selected letters from the French magus to his Italian disciple Baron Spedalieri, which were published as Éliphas Lévi, *Cour de philosophie occulte: Lettres au baron Spédalieri, de la Kabbale et de la science des nombres* (Paris: Chacornac Frères, 1932–33). In the English translation of this work, *Letters to a Disciple: Letters from Eliphas Lévi Zahed to Baron Nicolas-Joseph Spedalieri on magic, numerology and the Tarot* (Wellingborough: Aquarian Press, 1980), the word 'Kabbalah' has been dropped from the title, although the entire work revolves around the Kabbalah. Miscellaneous letters from this collection were translated into English by the Theosophists in their various journals during the 1880s; see, for example, Éliphas Lévi, 'A Suicide's After-State', originally published in *Theosophist* 2 (July 1881), 212, and later included as 'A Posthumous Publication' in H. P. Blavatsky, *Kabalah and Kabalism* (Los Angeles, CA: The Theosophy Company, 1912), 44–48.

[18] When, and from whom, Lévi learned the basics of the Kabbalah is still unclear. Material that might have revealed this information with certainty, such as the correspondence between Lévi and his close friend, the occultist Alphonse Esquiros, has disappeared entirely. Anthony Zielonka, in his edited collection of Esquiros' letters, *Alphonse Esquiros (1812–1876): Choix de lettres: Textes réunis, présentés et annotés par Anthony Zielonka* (Paris: Champion-Slatkine, 1990), 3, ruefully complains that there is no trace of any letters between Esquiros and the Abbé Alphonse-Louis Constant, and concludes: 'Certain archives, certain collections, no doubt still guard their secrets'.

'ascetic'. It is a title of respect given to a Sufi initiate.[19]

Post-Revolution France, wracked by political, social, and religious instability in the first decades of the nineteenth century, was a fertile breeding ground for revolutionary millenarianism with its accompanying train of prophets and messiahs, and the fragmentation of structures on every level of society, combined with particular mystical themes unique to Catholic religious thought, made France the ideal soil for the seeding of the occult revival in Europe in the mid-nineteenth century.[20] French Catholics, unlike their Protestant cousins across the Channel, could look back longingly to a 'pure' pre-Reformation past, and those more receptive to new scientific paradigms easily amalgamated this vision of progress with the Romantic belief in a vanished age when human beings enjoyed a knowledge of the occult sciences that was subsequently lost but might be reclaimed.[21] Mesmerism, born in 1778 as a new contribution to medical science, had transformed in the next century to become a popular belief-system that united science and spiritualism, joining hands with the redemptive doctrines of Martinism and the spread of 'irregular' Scottish Freemasonry and its even more irregular cousin, the Rectified Scottish Rite with its thinly disguised Kabbalistic rituals.[22] In 1830, a flood of

---

[19] For this definition, see the online dictionaries at <http://www.economicexpert.com/a/Zahed.html> and <http://en.wiktionary.org/wiki/Transwiki:Zahed>.

[20] For prophets and seers during and after the Revolution, see McIntosh, *Éliphas Lévi*, 17–69. For 'revolutionary millenarianism', see Norman Cohn, *The Pursuit of the Millennium: Revolutionary Millenarians and Mystical Anarchists of the Middle Ages* (London: Secker and Warburg, 1957), 281–86. For the compatibility of Catholic doctrines with the Kabbalah, see Yvonne Petrie, *Gender, Kabbalah and the Reformation: The Mystical Theology of Guillaume Postel* (Leiden: Brill, 2004), 81–86.

[21] For Catholic responses to the 'abyss of Pantheism, Materialism, and Atheism', see Webb, *Flight from Reason*, 80–93.

[22] For mesmerism as science, mysticism, and political philosophy, see Robert Darnton, *Mesmerism and the End of the Enlightenment in France* (Cambridge, MA: Harvard University Press, 1968). For mesmerism as 'magical and talismanic medicine', see Marsha Keith Schuchard, *Why Mrs. Blake Cried: William Blake and the Erotic Imagination* (London: Century, 2006), 208–09. For Martinism and mesmerism, see Darnton, *Mesmerism*, 68–69. For the Kabbalistic inclinations of 'irregular' Scottish Freemasonry, see Schuchard, *Restoring the Temple*. For the Rectified Scottish Rite and its links with

around 12,000 Polish refugees arrived in Paris following an abortive uprising against the partitioning of Poland by the Russians, Prussians, and Austrians, and many thousands more converged on the capitol after a second failed uprising in 1848.[23] This 'Great Emigration' included large numbers of Hasidic Jews as well as mystically inclined Polish Catholic aristocrats, who brought with them a potent injection of Kabbalistic and messianic doctrines that were quickly wedded to French Romantic socialism.[24] Mystical socialists like Lévi quickly embraced the Romantic theories of historical evolution promulgated by German Idealist philosophers, and believed that a divinely impelled transformation of society was imminent.[25]

Martinism and the Lurianic Kabbalah, see Antoine Faivre, *Access to Western Esotericism* (Albany, NY: State University of New York Press, 1994), 147–62; René le Forestier, *La Franc-Maçonnerie Templière et Occultiste aux XVIIIe et XIXe Siècles* (Paris: Aubier-Montaigne, 1970), 533–706; M. L. Danilewicz, '"The King of the New Israel": Thaddeus Grabianka (1740–1807)', in Robert Auty and J. L. I. Fennell (eds.), *Oxford Slavonic Papers*, New Series, Vol. 1 (Oxford: Clarendon Press, 1968), 49–73; Webb, *Flight from Reason*, 146–47, 157–59.

[23] See Mark Brown, 'The Comité Franco-Polonais and the French reaction to the Polish uprising of November 1830', *EHR* 93:369 (1978), 774–93; Edmond Marek, *Quand toute la France devant polonaise: l'insurrection de novembre 1830 et l'opinion française* (Lille: Club Polonia-Nord, 1994); Abraham G. Duker, 'The Polish Political Emigrés and the Jews in 1848', *PAAJR* 24 (1955), 69–102.

[24] For the impact of the Polish messianists on French occultism, see Webb, *Flight from Reason*, 155–68; Samuel Scheps, *Adam Mickiewicz: Ses affinités juifs* (Paris: Les Éditions Nagel, 1964). For Kabbalistic currents in Hasidic Judaism, see Idel, *Hasidism*, 33–43, 149–52; Joseph Weiss, *Studies in Eastern European Jewish Mysticism*, ed. David Goldstein (Oxford: Oxford University Press, 1985), 95–125; Rachel Elior, *The Mystical Origins of Hasidism* (Oxford: The Littman Library of Jewish Civilization, 2006), 97–99.

[25] For the influence of Kabbalah on German Romantic philosophy, see Ernst Benz, *The Mystical Sources of German Romantic Philosophy*, trans. Blair R. Reynolds and Eunice M. Paul (Eugene, OR: Pickwick Publications, 1983), 47–58. For Friedrich Schelling's influence on French Romantic socialism, see Warren Breckman, 'Politics in a Symbolic Key: Pierre Laroux, Romantic Socialism, and the Schelling Affair', *MIH* 2:1 (2005), 61–86; Dietrich von Engelhardt, 'Natural Science in the Age of Romanticism', in Faivre and Needleman (eds.), *Modern Esoteric Spirituality*, 101–31; Pierre Deghaye, 'Jacob Boehme and His Followers', in Faivre and Needleman (eds.), *Modern Esoteric Spirituality*, 210–47. For Schelling as a Kabbalist, see Werner J.

Of the many esoteric currents swelling the stream of the French Romantic imagination, Lévi favoured the Kabbalah because he believed it had generated all the others. As a self-professed Kabbalist, Lévi has been criticised for his poor knowledge of Hebrew; there is no original translation of any Hebrew work in any of his writings, only French renderings of Latin translations of Hebrew texts.[26] Even his efforts to use the Hebrew alphabet appear to involve serious blunders, as A. E. Waite acidly observed: 'He gives the three mother-letters of the Hebrew alphabet inaccurately, which for an accredited student of *Sepher Yetzirah* is almost as inexcusable as if an English author erred in enumerating the vowels of our own language'.[27] He was, in Frank Paul Bowman's words, a *petit romantique*: an artist and a poet whose work faithfully reflects the dominant ideas of the French Romantic movement of the first half of the nineteenth century.[28] These 'esoteric' ideas, all of which can also be found in Jewish Kabbalistic literature, include correspondences between divine and human realms; an unknowable deity from whom the cosmos emanates but whose immanence can be perceived in nature and the purposeful unfolding of history; various forms of numerological mysticism; and the belief in a universal primal revelation, gradually corrupted over the centuries but still secretly embedded in language, symbols, and myths.[29] But despite his clumsiness with Hebrew, Lévi's

Cahnmann, 'Schelling and the New Thinking of Judaism', *PAAJR* 48 (1981), 1–56; Benz, *German Romantic Philosophy*, 50–58.

[26] For Lévi's claim to being a Hebraist, see 'Confession de l'auteur' in Alphonse-Louis Constant [Éliphas Lévi], *L'Assomption de la femme* (Paris: Le Gallois, 1841), xviii; Lévi, *Dogme*, 50–51.

[27] Waite, *Holy Kabbalah*, 490. See also the discussion of Lévi's linguistic incompetence in François Secret, 'Eliphas Lévi et la Kabbale', *Charis: Archives de l'Unicorne* 1 (Milan: Archè, 1988), 81–89.

[28] Bowman, *Eliphas Lévi*, 6.

[29] See Frank Paul Bowman, *French Romanticism: Intertextual and Interdisciplinary Readings* (Baltimore, MD: Johns Hopkins University Press, 1990), 125–54. For the Romantic current in popular French literature during Lévi's lifetime, see James Smith Allen, *Popular French Romanticism: Authors, Readers, and Books in the 19th Century* (Syracuse, NY: Syracuse University Press, 1981). For the relationship between the Romantic movement and Western esotericism, see Arthur McCalla, 'Romanticism', in Hanegraaff (ed.), *Dictionary of Gnosis*, 1000–1007; Arthur McCalla, '"Eternal Sun/Black Sun": Illuminism and Disenchanted Romanticism', *Aries* 7 (2007), 3–19; Frank Paul Bowman, 'Illuminism, Utopia, Mythology', in D. G.

understanding of Jewish Kabbalistic doctrines may be deeper than his critics have acknowledged; and his hermeneutics, although applied in innovative ways that reflect the social and scientific paradigms of his time, display a surprising loyalty to those of the medieval Jewish Kabbalah.

Lévi's Kabbalah is sometimes presented as a theosophical exposition of the internal dynamics of the cosmic structure, in the visionary tradition of Jacob Böhme and Emanuel Swedenborg with their emphasis on the direct experience of revealed spiritual truths, the immanence of the divine in nature, and the close relationship between God-knowledge and self-knowledge.[30] Lynn Wilkinson suggests that Lévi acquired his idea of correspondences between upper and lower worlds from Swedenborg, whose work enjoyed great popularity in France in the first half of the nineteenth century.[31] But the concept of correspondences is an idea of great antiquity, and Lévi would have encountered it in many sources, including Gnostic, Neoplatonic, Neopythagorean, and Hermetic texts, with which Lévi states he became familiar in 1839, before his discovery of Swedenborg's work.[32] Moreover, Swedenborg himself seems to have been steeped in Kabbalistic ideas,[33] among which the theme of

---

Charlton (ed.), *The French Romantics*, 2 vols. (Cambridge: Cambridge University Press, 1984), 1:76–112; Hanegraaff, *New Age Religion*, 415–21. For a classic overview of the development of the Romantic movement, see Arthur O. Lovejoy, *The Great Chain of Being: A Study of the History of an Idea* (Cambridge, MA: Harvard University Press, 1936), 288–314.

[30] For these ideas in early modern theosophy, see Antoine Faivre, *Theosophy, Imagination, Tradition: Studies in Western Esotericism*, trans. Christine Rhone (Albany, NY: State University of New York Press, 2000), 1–48, 137–52; Faivre, *Access*, 71–73; Deghaye, 'Jacob Boehme'.

[31] Wilkinson, *Dream of an Absolute Language*, 19–54.

[32] See Constant, *L'Assomption*, xix–xxi, and Chacornac, *Éliphas Lévi*, 41–43. For correspondences as one of the components of Western esotericism, see Chapter 1.

[33] For Swedenborg's idea of correspondences, see Emanuel Swedenborg, *An Hieroglyphic Key to Natural and Spiritual Mysteries by Way of Representations and Correspondences*, ed. and trans. Robert Hindmarsh (London: Thomas Goyder, 1826). For scholarly debates on Swedenborg and the Kabbalah, see Marsha Keith Schuchard, *Freemasonry, Secret Societies, and the Continuity of the Occult Tradition in English Literature* (unpublished PhD Dissertation, University of Texas at Austin, 1975); Marsha Keith Schuchard, 'Yeats and the "Unknown Superiors": Swedenborg, Falk and Cagliostro', in Marie Mulvey Roberts and Hugh Ormsby-Lennon (eds.), *Secret Texts: The*

correspondences is central and reflects a panentheistic perception of the cosmos, described succinctly in a thirteenth-century text by the Spanish Kabbalist Moshe de Léon:

> Everything is catenated in its mystery, caught in its oneness....The entire chain is one. Down to the last link, everything is linked with everything else, so divine essence is below as well as above, in heavenand earth. There is nothing else.[34]

On the theory of correspondences, Lévi also cites early modern alchemical writers such as Heinrich Khunrath, whom he understands, with considerable justification, to have been a Kabbalist; Khunrath's alchemical androgyne, the union of the principles of sulphur and mercury, is equated with the union of the polarised *sefirot* of *Hesed* and *Geburah*,[35] and Lévi refers to Khunrath's *Amphitheatrum sapientiae*,

---

Literature of Secret Societies (New York: AMS Press, 1995), 114–68; Marsha Keith Schuchard, 'Why Mrs. Blake Cried: Swedenborg, Blake, and the Sexual Basis of Spiritual Vision', *Esoterica* 2 (2000), 45–93; Schuchard, *Why Mrs. Blake Cried*, 59–68; Marsha Keith Schuchard, 'Emanuel Swedenborg: Deciphering the Codes of a Terrestrial and Celestial Intelligencer', in Wolfson (ed.), *Rending the Veil*, 177–207; Wouter J. Hanegraaff, 'Emanuel Swedenborg, the Jews, and Jewish Traditions', in Peter Schäfer and Irina Wandrey (eds.), *Reuchlin und Seine Erben* (Ostfildern: Jan Thorbecke Verlag, 2005), 135–54; Gershom Scholem, *On the Mystical Shape of the Godhead: Basic Concepts in the Kabbalah*, trans. Joachim Neugroschel, ed. Jonathan Chipman (New York: Schocken Books, 1991), 228–29; Moshe Idel, 'The World of Angels in Human Shape', in Joseph Dan and J. Hacker (eds.), *Jewish Mysticism, Philosophy and Ethical Literature* (Jerusalem: Magnes Press, 1986), 1–66; Godwin, *Theosophical Enlightenment*, 95–103. For Lévi's view of Swedenborg as a Kabbalist, see Lévi, *Dogme*, 19; Lévi, *Histoire*, 413.

[34] Moshe de Léon, *Sefer ha-Rimmon* ('Book of the Pomegranate'), ed. Elliot R. Wolfson (Atlanta, GA: Scholars Press, 1988), 181–82, cited in Matt (ed.), *Essential Kabbalah*, 26. For more on correspondences in medieval Kabbalah, see Dov Schwartz, *Studies on Astral Magic in Medieval Jewish Thought* (Leiden: Brill, 2005), 205–33; Moshe Idel, *Kabbalah and Eros* (New Haven, CT: Yale University Press, 2005), 43, 153–54; Idel, *Hasidism*, 107–08.

[35] See Lévi, *Dogme*, 282. For Khunrath's Kabbalistic proclivities, see Chapter Three.

published in 1609, as a Kabbalistic-Hermetic text.[36]

For Lévi, the law of correspondences provides the basis for his entire system:

> That which is in visible Nature, as we already know following the sole dogma of the Kabbalah, reveals that which is in the domain of invisible Nature.[37]

The cosmos, according to Lévi, is a unity emanating from an unknowable divine source and reflecting the substance of deity on all its levels from supernal to material. History unfolds through the dynamic interplay of opposites, the twin attributes of Mercy and Judgement, which Lévi envisages as male and female. For him, as for medieval Kabbalists, the achievement of equilibrium between these opposites is the purpose of 'high' magic. Applying this theosophy to social concerns, Lévi informs us:

> In God...one must recognise two properties necessary one to another – stability and movement, necessity and liberty, rational order and volitional autonomy, justice and love, and consequently also severity and mercy. And these are the two attributes that the Jewish Kabbalists personified...under the names of Geburah and Chesed.[38]

This description of dual forces closely mirrors the late-thirteenth-century Kabbalistic work called *Sha'are Orah* ('Gates of Light') by Rabbi Joseph Gikatilla (1248–1305), translated into Latin in the sixteenth century as *Portae lucis* and included among the texts of the important compilation of Latin translations of Hebrew texts known as *Kabbala*

---

[36] See Lévi, *Histoire*, 366–69. For an overview of the alchemical/Rosicrucian/Kabbalistic current in Western esoteric thought, see Chapter Three. See also McIntosh, *Rose Cross*, 23–37; Godwin, *Theosophical Enlightenment*, 115–30, 247–75; Faivre, *Theosophy*, 5–15, 171–90; Yates, *Rosicrucian Enlightenment*; Didier Kahn, 'The Rosicrucian Hoax in France', in William R. Newman and Anthony Grafton (eds.), *Secrets of Nature: Astrology and Alchemy in Early Modern Europe* (Cambridge, MA: MIT Press, 2001), 235–344. For the appropriation of Khunrath by British occultists, see Chapters Three and Four.

[37] Lévi, *Dogme*, 77.

[38] Lévi, *Dogme*, 111.

denudata a century later.[39] Gikatilla may have been a member of the circle from which the *Zohar*, the great classic of the

---

[39] *Kabbala denudata* 1.1.660ff. For another Latin translation to which Lévi had access, see Johann Pistorius (ed.), *Artis cabalisticae hoc est reconditae theologiae et philosophiae scriptoum* (Basel, 1587), referred to in Lévi, *Dogme*, 50, and Lévi, *Cours*, V. For an English translation of *Sha'are Orah*, see Rabbi Joseph Gikatilla, *Gates of Light: Sha'are Orah*, trans. Avi Weinstein, Bronfman Library of Jewish Classics (New York/Oxford: Rowan & Littlefield, 1994). The mid-sixteenth-century Safed Kabbalist Moshe Cordovero, whose work precedes that of Isaac Luria, is also represented in the *Kabbala denudata*. Cordovero was Luria's teacher and, although they differ in their theosophical speculations in important respects – particularly in the contrast between Luria's more mythic and Cordovero's more philosophical approaches – there is also a close relationship between many of their doctrines. For discussions on Cordovero, see Fine (ed. and trans.), *Safed Spirituality*; Fine, *Physician*, 59–61, 80–82; Johann Maier, 'The Significance of Philosophy for the Kabbalah of Moshe Cordovero and Its Impact', *EAJS* 13 (2003), at www.lzz.uni-halle.de/publikationen/essays/n/13_maier.pdf; Werblowsky, 'Mystical and Magical Contemplation'. A number of Cordovero's works have recently been translated into English: Moshe Cordovero, *The Palm Tree of Devorah*, trans. R. Moshe Miller (Southfield, MI: Targum Press, 1993); Ira Robinson (trans.), *Moses Cordovero's Introduction to Kabbalah: An Annotated Translation of His Or Ne'erav* (Hoboken, NJ: Ktav Publishing, 1994); Moshe Cordovero, *Pardes Rimonim: Orchard of Pomegranates, Parts 1–4*, trans. Elyakim Getz (Monfalcone: Providence University/ULC-Italia, 2007). A section of *Pardes Rimonim* can be found as 'Tractatus de Anima R. Moscheh Korduero Pardes' in *Kabbala denudata*, 1.2.7, 100–49. The Lurianic texts in the *Kabbala denudata* also include a number of works by Luria's chief disciple, Hayyim Vital: commentaries on sections of the *Zohar*, an exposition of Luria's views on reincarnation called *Sefer HaGilgulim* ('Book of Transmigrations'), fragments of his own main work, *Etz Hayyim* ('Tree of Life'), and *Sefer ha-Derushim* ('Book of Dissertations'). Later Lurianic exegeses are represented in the *Kabbala denudata* by Abraham Cohen de Herrera's *Puerta del Cielo* ('Gate of Heaven'), a work influenced by Platonic philosophy, and Napthali Herz Bacharach's magical and alchemical *Sefer Emek ha-Melekh* ('Book of the Valley of the King'). Luria himself left virtually no written work. *Puerta del Cielo* has recently been translated into English from the original Spanish: Abraham Cohen de Herrera, *Gate of Heaven*, trans. Kenneth Krabbenhoft (Leiden: Brill, 2002). For *Emek ha-Melekh*, see the references in Chapter Three.

medieval Kabbalah, emerged in thirteenth-century Spain.[40]
Sha'are Orah is one of the few texts in Knorr von Rosenroth's
compilation that is not related to the late-sixteenth-century
Safedian Kabbalistic current, discussed in greater detail
below, and its inclusion serves as a kind of 'skeleton key' to
illuminate not only the three sections of the *Zohar* included in
the *Kabbala denudata* but also the later, more abstruse material
written by Moshe Cordovero and Isaac Luria's disciples.[41]
Gikatilla, drawing on much older rabbinic sources, declares
that the ten *sefirot* or emanations of deity, basic to all
theosophical Kabbalistic texts, are not equal in weight as
primary creative forces, but are permutations of two central
divine attributes, Mercy (*Chesed*) and Severity (*Geburah*), male
and female respectively and identified with God's right and
left hands.[42] Equilibrium between them is found on the
central 'trunk' of the Kabbalistic diagram known as the Tree
of Life, in the divine emanation called Beauty (*Tiferet*), which
Gikatilla describes as 'the One that brings the Spheres
together'.[43]

---

[40] For the authorship of the *Zohar* and Gikatilla's involvement in its
'redaction', see Yehudah Liebes, 'How the Zohar Was Written', in
Yehudah Liebes, *Studies in the Zohar*, trans. Arnold Schwartz,
Stephanie Nakache, and Penina Peli (Albany, NY: State University
of New York Press, 1993), 85–138; Stephen G. Wald, *The Doctrine of
the Divine Name: An Introduction to Classical Kabbalistic Theology*
(Atlanta, GA: Scholars Press, 1988), 3–31.
[41] For the historical importance of the *Sha'are Orah*, see Moshe Idel,
'Historical Introduction', in Gikatilla, *Sha'are Orah*, xxiii–xxxi;
Scholem, *Major Trends*, 212; Wald, *Doctrine of the Divine Name*, 17.
[42] For the source of this concept in the Babylonian Talmud, see
Wald, *Doctrine of the Divine Name*, 27–30; Scholem, *Origins*, 144.
[43] Gikatilla, *Sha'are Orah*, 147. For *Chesed*, *Geburah*, and *Tiferet*, see
Gikatilla, *Sha'are Orah*, 223–25. The sefirotic Tree or 'Tree of Life' is
first mentioned in the twelfth-century *Sefer ha-Bahir*; see Scholem,
Origins, 75–77. Gikatilla presents his diagram of it in *Sha'are Orah*,
229. A total of sixteen Lurianic versions of the Tree are published in
the *Kabbala denudata*; for these versions, see Christopher Atton and
Stephen Dziklewicz, *Kabbalistic Diagrams of Rosenroth* (London: The
Hermetic Research Trust, 1987); Scholem, *Kabbalah*, 417. Many
Kabbalists in subsequent centuries, including those of the British
occult revival, have used one form or another of this diagrammatic
structure. Lévi, in contrast, rarely includes a diagram of the Tree in
his published work, although he frequently discusses it. However, a
series of diagrams applying the Tree to various aspects of biological,

Lévi asserts that human beings can only know deity through its manifestations in Nature and in society; these manifestations inevitably embody the divine polarity of Mercy and Judgement, and the internal dynamics of the godhead can therefore be perceived – and transformed – through the use of the human will. God-knowledge is equated with self-knowledge, and changing the cosmos depends upon changing oneself. The successful magician must 'equilibriate' the tension between the two great *sefirot*:

> The alternate use of contrary forces, heat after cold, gentleness after severity, love after anger...is the secret of perpetual motion and of the prolongation of power...Thus, in magic, it is necessary to temper works of anger or severity with works of beneficence and love.[44]

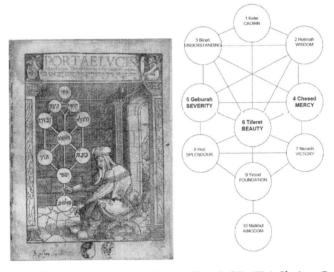

Fig. 2: *Left, cover of a Latin translation of Joseph Gikatilla's* Sha'are Orah *showing the Tree of Life.*[45] *Right, the Tree with the* sefirot *Geburah, Chesed, and* Tiferet *highlighted.*

Lévi's use of Gikatilla's trinity of Mercy, Severity, and Beauty is evident in an early poem called *Les correspondances*, first

---

social, and spiritual life can be found in Lévi, *Cours*, CLXXIV–CLXXIX.

[44] Lévi, *Dogme*, 206–07.

[45] Joseph Gikatilla, *Portae lucis haec est porta tetragrammaton [Sha'are Orah]*, translated into Latin by Paolo Ricci (Augsburg, 1516).

published in 1845.[46] This poem is divided into ten verses of
ten lines each, echoing Pico della Mirandola's injunction in
the fifteenth century that writings about divine matters
should be arranged numerologically 'just as God, the
almighty artificer, arranged them in themselves', so that the
written work structurally reproduces the 'exact image' of the
sacred theme.[47] Lévi himself informs his readers that ten is
'the absolute number of the Kabbalah and the key to the
Sefirot',[48] and the ten verses of *Les correspondences* are
probably intended to reflect the ten *sefirot* and the various
'worlds' or levels of reality with which they correspond. The
fourth verse presents Gikatilla's trinity of *sefirot* under the
names of love, fear, and glory:[49]

> Formed of visible words,
> This world is the dream of God;
> His Name determines its symbols,
> His spirit fills them with fire.
> It is this living writing
> Of love, glory and fear
> That Jesus rediscovered for us;
> For all hidden sciences
> Are nothing more than a letter
> Taken from the sacred name of Jehovah.

When Lévi presents the Kabbalah as a theosophy, it is a
nineteenth-century paraphrase of Gikatilla: the vision of a
unified but dynamically polarised cosmos endlessly
generating forms on multiple levels, from the supernal to the
material, through the endlessly shifting interactions of the
great male and female forces called Mercy and Severity,
harmonised in Beauty. There is nothing newly 'occultist' in

---

[46] Alphonse-Louis Constant [Éliphas Lévi], 'Les correspondences', in
Les trois harmonies: chansons et poésies (Paris: Fellens et Dufour, 1845),
297–301.
[47] Giovanni Pico della Mirandola, *Heptaplus*, in *On the Dignity of
Man, On Being and the One, Heptaplus*, trans. Charles Glenn Wallis,
Paul J. W. Miller, and Douglas Carmichael (New York: Macmillan,
1985), 79. For Lévi's familiarity with Pico's work, see Lévi, *Dogme*,
50, 290. For Pico's use of Kabbalistic numerology, see Wirszubski,
Pico, 77–83; Farmer, *Syncretism*, 30 and n. 81.
[48] Lévi, *Clef*, 44.
[49] For fear and love as Kabbalistic opposites, see Pico, Conclusions
28.38 and 28.39, in Farmer, *Syncretism*, 360–61. For 'fear' as a
synonym for *Geburah*, see Reuchlin, *De arte cabalistica*, III, 291.

this conception, and it is certainly not Lévi's invention. Its syncretic roots draw on Hebraic, Platonic, Empedoclean, Gnostic, and Hermetic doctrines from antiquity, but it is most clearly formulated in the thirteenth-century Kabbalah of Joseph Gikatilla, made available to Lévi through the *Kabbala denudata*.

RESCUING THE 'DIVINE SPARKS': THE KABBALAH OF ISAAC LURIA

Most of the materials in the *Kabbala denudata* are related to a specific current from a particular cultural milieu: the Kabbalah of Rabbi Isaac Luria (1534–1572), which first emerged in the city of Safed in Palestine and eventually became one of the dominant influences in both Hasidic Judaism and the Kabbalah of the Victorian occult revival.[50] Knorr and van Helmont seem to have favoured Kabbalistic texts with intensely messianic and millennarian themes, and the Lurianic corpus satisfied this requirement.[51] Gershom Scholem suggests that Luria's Kabbalah introduced the

---

[50] For the dissemination of the Lurianic Kabbalah in Hasidic currents in Eastern Europe, see Moshe Idel, '"One from a Town, Two from a Clan" – The Diffusion of Lurianic Kabbala and Sabbateanism: A Re-Examination', *JH* 7:2 (1993), 79–104; Moshe Idel, *Messianic Mystics* (New Haven, CT: Yale University Press, 1998), 175–78. The contents of the *Kabbala denudata* can be found online in Don Karr's 'Study of Christian Cabala in English: Addenda', at <http:www.digital-brilliance.com/kab/karr/ccineb/pdf>, and the complete text scanned from the Latin edition of 1684 is available at <http://www.billheidrick.com/Orpd/KRKD/index.htm>.   An original edition of the work (Frankfurt: J. D. Zunner 1677–1684) is held at the Wellcome Institute Library, London, B12841055. Three sections of the *Zohar* are included in Latin versions: *Sifra Dzeniuta* ('Book of Mysteries') in *Zohar* II, and the two *Idrot* ('assemblies'), *Idra Rabba* ('Great Assembly') and *Idra Suta* ('Lesser Assembly') in *Zohar* III (*Kabbala denudata* 2.2.1–3, 347–598). These three works were translated into English in the late nineteenth century: S. L. MacGregor Mathers (trans.), *The Kabbalah Unveiled. Containing the following Books of the Zohar: The Book of Concealed Mystery, The Greater Holy Assembly, The Lesser Holy Assembly, Translated into English from the Latin version of Knorr von Rosenroth, and collated with the original Chaldee and Hebrew text* (London: George Redway, 1887).
[51] For the millennarian and Rosicrucian predilections of Knorr and van Helmont, see Coudert, *Impact of the Kabbalah*, 147–52, 348–49.

concept of messianism into Kabbalistic thought, and arose directly from the catastrophe of the expulsion of the Jews from Spain in 1492.[52] Other scholars argue that the Lurianic Kabbalah cannot be viewed solely as the result of one historical cause, but represents 'natural developments' arising from earlier Jewish religious currents that came to flower in Lurianic messianism.[53]

Certain themes distinguish this remarkable Kabbalistic current. These include a complex cosmogony emerging from a primal light ('or kadmon), out of which the various levels of the universe emanate; a cosmic 'accident' during the process of emanation, resulting in the entrapment of divine 'sparks' in the dense realm of matter; an emphasis on exile and alienation, both human and divine; the transmigration and gradual evolution of souls, individually and in groups; the redemptive power of the feminine face of the godhead; the belief that all creation contains a 'spark' of the primal light and will ultimately be reintegrated into the divine harmony (tikkun); and finally, the correspondence between the macrocosmic spiritual man, called Adam Kadmon or 'primal Adam',[54] and the microcosmic individual, resulting in an inherent godlike power in humans which, if developed, can rescue the 'sparks', restore the damaged cosmos, and usher in the messianic age.[55] Allison Coudert describes the most

---

[52] See Gershom Scholem, 'Isaac Luria: A Central Figure in Jewish Mysticism', *BAAAS* 29:8 (1976), 8–13; Gershom Scholem, *The Messianic Idea in Judaism and Other Essays on Jewish Spirituality* (New York: Schocken Books, 1971), 43–48; Scholem, *Major Trends*, 244–86; Dan, 'Scholem's View'; Harris Lenowitz, *The Jewish Messiahs: From the Galilee to Crown Heights* (Oxford: Oxford University Press, 1998), 125–47; Dan, *Gershom Scholem*, 244–80.

[53] For Idel's argument see Idel, *Hasidism*, 1–30; Idel, *Messianic Mystics*, 162–82. See also Biale, *Gershom Scholem*, 71–93.

[54] For the derivation of the term 'Adam Kadmon', meaning 'primal earth' or 'primal substance', see Leland Ryken, Jim Wilhoit, and Tremper Longman (eds.), *Dictionary of Biblical Imagery* (Westmont, IL: InterVarsity Press, 1998), 9; David Noel Freedman, Allen C Meyers, and Astrid B. Beck (eds.), *Eerdmans Dictionary of the Bible* (Grand Rapids, MI: Eerdmans Publishing, 2000), 19; Mark Verman, *The Books of Contemplation: Medieval Jewish Mystical Sources* (Albany, NY: State University of New York Press, 1992), 147.

[55] For Luria's Kabbalah and its offshoots, see Lawrence Fine, *Physician of the Soul, Healer of the Cosmos: Isaac Luria and His Kabbalistic Fellowship* (Stanford, CA: Stanford University Press, 2003); Lawrence Fine, 'The Art of Metoposcopy: A Study in Isaac

revolutionary aspect of the Lurianic Kabbalah as the role of human beings in the cosmic restoration: 'People are given a central role in this process, for it is only through human actions that the souls, trapped among the shards of the broken vessels, can be reunited with the divine light'.[56] Jonathan Z. Smith concurs with this understanding of the most significant feature of the Lurianic Kabbalah: 'It is man's awesome responsibility to rescue his deity and, in so doing, to rescue himself'.[57] As well as dominating the *Kabbala denudata*, Lurianic doctrines and practices were adopted in France in the late eighteenth century by the Jewish esotericist Martinès de Pasqually and his Catholic disciple, Louis-Claude de Saint-Martin.[58] The Martinist currents arising from

---

Luria's "Charismatic Knowledge"', *AJSR* 11:1 (1986), 79–101; Louis Jacobs, 'Uplifting the Sparks in Later Jewish Mysticism', in Arthur Green (ed.), *Jewish Spirituality, Vol. 2: From the Sixteenth Century Revival to the Present* (New York: Crossroad, 1987), 99–126; Scholem, *Kabbalah*, 128–44, 420–28, 443–48; Idel, *Hasidism*, 33–43; R. J. Zvi Werblowsky, 'Mystical and Magical Contemplation: The Kabbalists in Sixteenth-Century Safed', *HR* 1:1 (1961), 9–36; Shaul Magid, 'From Theosophy to Midrash: Lurianic Exegesis and the Garden of Eden', *AJSR* 22:1 (1997), 37–75; Don Karr, 'Notes on the Study of Later Kabbalah in English: The Safed Period and Lurianic Kabbalah', in Don Karr, *Collected Articles on the Kabbalah*, Vol. 2 (Ithaca, NY: KoM, No. 6, 1985), 23–31. For English translations of Lurianic works, see Morris M. Faierstein (trans.), *Jewish Mystical Autobiographies: Book of Visions and Book of Secrets* (Mahwah, NJ: Paulist Press, 1999); Donald Wilder Menzi and Zwe Padeh (trans.), *The Tree of Life: Chayyim Vital's Introduction to the Kabbalah of Isaac Luria, Vol. 1: The Palace of Adam Kadmon* (Northvale, NJ: Jason Aronson, 1999); Eliahu Klein (ed. and trans.), *Kabbalah of Creation: Isaac Luria's Earlier Mysticism* (Northvale, NJ: Jason Aronson, 2000); Yitzchak Bar Chaim (trans.), *Shaar HaGilgulim: The Gates of Reincarnation by Rabbi Isaac Luria and Rabbi Chaim Vital* (Malibu, CA: Thirty Seven Books Publishing, 2003); Rabbi Philip S. Berg and Rabbi Yehuda Ashlag (eds. and trans.), *Ten Luminous Emanations*, 2 vols. (Jerusalem: Research Centre of Kabbalah, 1969–73); Chayyim Vital, *Window of the Soul: The Kabbalah of Rabbi Isaac Luria (1534–1572)*, ed. David Sunn, trans. Nathan Snyder (San Francisco, CA: Red Wheel/Weiser, 2008).
[56] Allison Coudert, 'Isaac Luria and the Lurianic Kabbalah', in Richard H. Popkin (ed.), *The Columbia History of Western Philosophy* (New York: Columbia University Press, 1995), 213.
[57] Jonathan Z. Smith, 'Earth and Gods', *JR* 49:2 (1969), 122.
[58] For the only published text by Pasqually, see Martinès de Pasqually, *Traité de la réintégration des êtres dans leur premières propriétés, vertus et puissances spirituelles et divines* (Paris:

the work of these men exercised a major influence on 'irregular' Masonic orders in France, Poland, and Russia in the nineteenth century, as well as on the development of Lévi's ideas.[59] Through Lévi, Lurianic themes are found in abundance, in various adapted forms, in the literature of the British occult revival.[60]

Bibliothèque Chacornac, 1899; repr. Paris: Éditions Traditionelles, 1988). For Pasqually's rituals, see Le Forestier, *La Franc-Maçonnerie*, 290–313; Martinès de Pasqually, 'Discours d'instruction à un nouveau reçu sur les trois grades d'apprenti compagnon et maître symboliques', Bibliothèque municipale de Lyon, Fonds Willermoz, MS 5919–12, <http://www.Philosophe-inconnu.com> (2006). For Pasqually's Jewish Marrano background and Lurianic predilections, see Adolphe Franck, *La philosophie mystique en France à la fin du XVIII-e siècle: Saint-Martin et son maître Martinez Pasqualis* (Paris: Germer Baillière, 1866; repr. Paris: Elibron Classics, 2005), 1–26; Steven M. Wasserstrom, *Religion After Religion: Gershom Scholem, Mircea Eliade, and Henry Corbin at Eranos* (Princeton, NJ: Princeton University Press, 1999), 38–39, 44–47; Scholem, *Kabbalah*, 200–01. For a comprehensive biography of Pasqually, see Gérard van Rijnberk, *Un thaumaturge au 18e siècle, Martinès de Pasqually, sa vie, son œuvre, son ordre*, 2 vols. (Lyon: Derain et Raclet, 1938).

[59] For the influence of Martinism on Lévi, see David Allen Harvey, 'Beyond Enlightenment: Occultism, Politics, and Culture in France from the Old Regime to the *Fin-de-Siècle*', *Historian* 65:3 (2003), 665–94; David Allen Harvey, *Beyond Enlightenment: Occultism and Politics in Modern France* (Dekalb, IL: Northern Illinois University Press, 2005), 199–204. For Saint-Martin and Martinism, see Franck, *Philosophie mystique*; A. E. Waite, *The Life of Louis Claude de Saint-Martin* (London: Philip Wellby, 1901); A. E. Waite, *St. Martin: The French Mystic and the Story of Modern Martinism* (London: William Rider & Son, 1922); David Bates, 'The Mystery of Truth: Louis-Claude de Saint-Martin's Enlightened Mysticism', *JHI* 61:4 (2000), 635–55. For Martinism in Polish and Russian Freemasonry, see Konstantin Burmistrov and Maria Endel, 'The Place of Kabbalah in the Doctrine of Russian Freemasons', *Aries* 4:1 (2004), 27–68.

[60] For specific references to Luria in British occult literature, see William Wynn Westcott, *An Introduction to the Study of the Kabbalah* (London: Watkins, 1910), 5; Samuel Liddell MacGregor Mathers, *The Kabbalah Unveiled* (London: George Redway, 1887; revised edition, London: Routledge & Kegan Paul, 1926; repr. York Beach, ME: WeiserBooks, 1970), 15; Waite, *Holy Kabbalah*, 412–20; H. P. Blavatsky, 'Madame Blavatsky on Indian Metaphysics', *The Spiritualist* (22 March 1878), 140–41. See also Kilcher, 'Verhüllung', for an exploration of the impact of Lurianic themes on *fin-de-siècle* occultists. Discussions of the appropriation of specific Lurianic ideas by British occultists can be found throughout this dissertation.

Although the messianic idea has always been one of the core themes of Judaism, it is given a peculiarly modern colouration in the Lurianic Kabbalah because it emphasises the power of individuals, through inner work, to transform not only themselves but also the damaged structure of the godhead. The Lurianic messiah may thus be understood as both a succession of spiritual avatars and a process of individual and collective transformation, psychological and spiritual as well as social.[61] Lurianic texts challenge Cartesian dualism by presenting spirit and matter as aspects of a single continuum, and nature as pregnant with spiritual value:[62]

> The body of this world is the ground and its minerals....The ground possesses all vegetation and it is the vessel of the breath, the soul. Animals possess the higher soul.[63]

As Lawrence Fine points out, the natural world, for Luria, was 'a means by which to encounter the divine'.[64] This harmonising of Kabbalistic theosophy and science opened the Kabbalah to innovative interpretive approaches easily adaptable to Lévi's 'modern' occultism.

Lévi cites a vast range of sources which British occultists would later use as a bibliography: Kabbalists, alchemists, illuminists, mesmerists and Catholic theologians of his own time, and medieval Christianised grimoires based on older Hebrew magical texts. However, the Lurianic Kabbalah acquired from the *Kabbala denudata* informed some of Lévi's most important ideas. He seems to have discovered the *Kabbala denudata* during a stay at the Benedictine Abbey at Solesmes in 1839, while he was struggling with his decision

---

[61] For the interiorisation of the messiah in Lurianic Kabbalah, and thirteenth-century precedents for this perspective, see Idel, *Hasidism*, 227–38.

[62] For Lurianic Kabbalah and Cartesian dualism, see Coudert, *Impact of the Kabbalah*, 124. For the scientific orientation of Lurianic Kabbalah, see Ira Robinson, 'Kabbala and Science in "Sefer Ha-Berit": A Modernization Strategy for Orthodox Jews', *MJ* 9:3 (1989), 275–88. For the empirical study of nature in Lurianic currents in Italy, see David B. Ruderman, *Kabbalah, Magic, and Science: The Cultural Universe of a Sixteenth-Century Jewish Physician* (Cambridge, MA: Harvard University Press, 1988).

[63] Hayyim Vital, *Peri Ez Hayyim* 7:48, cited in Dunn (ed.), *Window of the Soul*, 153–54.

[64] Fine, *Physician*, 356.

to leave the priesthood.[65] Because of the triune structure of the sefirotic Tree – the ten *sefirot* are arranged in three descending groups of three each, with the tenth *sefira*, *Malkuth* (Kingdom) standing apart at the base and equated with the material world – Hebrew Kabbalistic texts had been utilised by Catholic writers as demonstrations of the truth of the Christian trinity since the thirteenth century. The three 'upper' *sefirot* of the Tree of Life – *Keter*, *Hokmah*, and *Binah* (Crown, Wisdom, and Understanding) – were associated by Christian Hebraists with the Father, the Son, and the Holy Spirit,[66] and Latin commentaries on the Kabbalah were therefore often included in Catholic libraries. The climate of Catholic intellectualism in post-Revolution France was often unorthodox,[67] and even an eminent cleric such as Hugues-Felicité de Lamennais, during his ultramontane Catholic period, cites the *Zohar* in the old argument that the messiahship of Jesus is foretold in Jewish esoteric literature.[68]

One of the most influential of the Lurianic ideas Lévi appropriated is the feminine aspect of the godhead, first presented in the twelfth-century *Sefer ha-Bahir* but developed most fully and dramatically by Luria and his disciples.[69]

---

[65] Constant, *L'Assomption*, xix–xxii.

[66] For the Christian use of the Kabbalistic triads, see Hames, *Art of Conversion*, 190–245; Bernard McGinn, 'Cabalists and Christians: Reflections on Cabala in Medieval and Renaissance Thought', in Popkin and Weiner (eds.), *Jewish Christians*, 11–34; Coudert, *Impact of the Kabbalah*, 115–16.

[67] For esoteric currents among the Catholic intelligentsia, see Harry W. Paul, 'In Quest of Kerygma: Catholic Intellectual Life in Nineteenth-Century France', *AHR* 75:2 (1969), 387–423; Bernard Reardon, *Liberalism and Tradition: Aspects of Catholic Thought in Nineteenth-Century France* (Cambridge: Cambridge University Press, 1975). For Lévi's first seminary tutor as an example of post-Revolution clerical heterodoxy, see Constant, *L'Assomption*, iv–vii; Chacornac, *Lévi*, 7–8.

[68] See Hugues-Felicité de Lamennais, *Essai sur l'indifférence en matière de religion*, 4 vols. (1817–1823), in *Oeuvres complètes* (Brussels, 1839), 1.399, cited in Arnold Ages, 'Lamennais and the Jews', *JQR* 63:2 (1972), 163. See also Yves Le Hir, *Lamennais écrivain* (Paris: P. A. Colin, 1948), 225; Nicholas V. Riasanovsky, 'On Lamennais, Chaadaev, and the Romantic Revolt in France and Russia', *AHR* 82:5 (1977), 1168.

[69] For the *Shekhinah* in the *Sefer ha-Bahir*, see Scholem, *Origins*, 162–80; Scholem, *Mystical Shape*, 140–96. For English translations of the *Bahir*, see Aryeh Kaplan (ed. and trans.), *The Bahir* (York Beach, ME:

Lévi's extraordinary apocalyptic epic, *La Mère de Dieu*,[70] is a visionary treatise self-consciously modelled on the *Apocalypse*, which Lévi believed to be a Kabbalistic work because he understood its twenty-two chapters to correspond to the twenty-two Hebrew letters.[71] *La Mère de Dieu* is redolent with Lurianic ideas about the restitution of the world through a divine feminine power, once 'a queen elevated upon a throne of gold' but now in exile, who for Lévi is simultaneously the Kabbalistic *Shekhinah*, Mary, and the 'true' primal Church before its corruption. Lévi describes the union of Mary with God in the 'solitude of the Temple' by using a paraphrase of the *Song of Songs*, a favourite Kabbalistic metaphor for the sacred union of the male and female aspects of the godhead that results in cosmic restitution.[72] The image of the erotic union of God with his

---

Red Wheel/Weiser, 1979); Saverio Campanini (ed. and trans.), *The Book of Bahir: Flavius Mithridates' Latin Translation, the Hebrew Text, and an English Variation* (Torino: Nino Aragno Editore, 2005).

[70] Alphonse-Louis Constant [Éliphas Lévi], *La Mère de Dieu, épopée religieuse et humanitaire* (Paris: Charles Gosselin, 1844; repr. Paris: Elibron Classics, 2006). For an overview of this work, see Léon Cellier, *L'Epopée Romantique* (Paris: Presses Universitaires de France, 1954), 209–20.

[71] For Lévi's view of the *Apocalypse* as a Kabbalistic work, see Éliphas Lévi, *Les mystères de la Kabbale, ou l'harmonie occulte des deux Testaments contenus dans la prophétie d'Ézéchiel et l'Apocalypse de Saint-Jean, d'après le manuscrit autographie d'Éliphas Lévi, 1861* (Paris: Émile Nourry, 1920).

[72] For the juxtaposition of the *Shekhinah* and Mary, see Lévi, *Cours*, LXVIII. For the exile of the *Shekhinah* in Lurianic Kabbalah, see Fine, *Physician*, 59–60. For the return of the Shekhinah to the Temple and her union with the King, see Gikatilla, *Sha'areh Orah*, 11–54; see also the translation of a portion of that chapter cited in Elliot R. Wolfson, *Language, Eros, Being: Kabbalistic Hermeneutics and Poetic Imagination* (New York: Fordham University Press, 2005), 63. For the theurgic practice of drawing down the *Shekhinah* into the Temple, see Idel, *Kabbalah*, 166–69. For the *Shekhinah* as the 'beautiful wife of the King' and mother of the people of Israel who, because of the sins of her children, must go into exile, see Kaplan (trans.), *Bahir* 76, p. 28, and the same passage cited in Peter Schäfer, *Mirror of His Beauty: Feminine Images of God From the Bible to the Early Kabbalah* (Princeton: Princeton University Press, 2002), 132, with Schäfer's comments, 128. See also Peter Schäfer, 'Daughter, Sister, Bride, and Mother: Images of the Femininity of God in the Early Kabbala', *JAAR* 68:2 (2000), 221–42; Fine, *Physician*, 224–25; Idel, *Kabbalah and Eros*, 104–52. For the *Song of Songs* as the favoured Kabbalistic metaphor for

Shekhinah is central to Lurianic thought,[73] and Lévi's elevation of the feminine, usually discussed in the context of his Romantic socialism,[74] seems to be rooted in this amalgamation of the Virgin with the Kabbalistic *Shekhinah* – an idea which he acquired not only from the *Kabbala denudata* but also from the writings of Guillaume Postel (1510–1581), translator of the *Sefer Yetsirah* and the *Sefer ha-Bahir* into Latin

---

the interplay of male and female potencies within the godhead, see Arthur Green, 'Shekhinah, the Virgin Mary, and the *Song of Songs*: Reflections on a Kabbalistic Symbol in Its Historical Context', *AJSR* 26:1 (2002), 1–52, esp. 16–17: 'The Song of Songs is an epithelamium written by King Solomon, the mystic hierophant, to celebrate the marriage of male and female within God, blessed Holy One and *shekhinah*'. For the theme of God's androgyny, see Moshe Idel, 'Androgyny and Equality in the Theosophico-Theurgical Kabbalah', *Diogenes* 208 (2005), 27–38. Many other Lurianic themes appear in *La Mère de Dieu*. For Lévi's appropriation of the Lurianic idea of the redemption of evil, see also Lévi, *Dogme*, 227. For the redemption of evil in the Lurianic Kabbalah, when 'all the forces will be transformed' in the great cosmic restitution, see Coudert, '*Kabbala Denudata*', 82–83; Scholem, *Major Trends*, 245–48. For the doctrine of the redemption of Satan in Martinism, see Harvey, *Beyond Enlightenment*, 16–17. For Lévi's rejection of the idea of eternal damnation, see Lévi, *Grand arcane*, 20–22 and 252–76; for the same theme in Kabbalistic doctrines, see Alexander Altmann, 'Eternality of Punishment: A Theological Controversy', in Fine (ed.), *Essential Papers on Kabbalah*, 270–87. See also the extract from Corodovero's *Tomer Devorah* in Dan (ed.), *Heart and the Fountain*, 198–201; R. J. Zvi Werblowsky, *Joseph Karo: Lawyer and Mystic* (Philadelphia, PA: The Jewish Publication Society of America/Oxford University Press), 148–49.
[73] For translations of Luria's erotic descriptions of the 'divine coupling', see Klein (ed. and trans.), *Kabbalah of Creation*, 98–99. Luria's quotations from the *Song of Songs* appear on pp. 36 and 206. See also Yoram Jacobson, 'The Aspect of the "Feminine" in the Lurianic Kabbalah', in Schäfer and Dan (eds.), *Gershom Scholem's Major Trends*, 239–55.
[74] For Lévi's 'feminism', see Bowman, *Éliphas Lévi*, 29–30; Naomi J. Andrews, '"La Mère Humanité": Femininity in the Romantic Socialism of Pierre Leroux and the Abbé A.-L. Constant', *JHI* 63:4 (2002), 697–716; Naomi J. Andrews, 'Utopian Androgyny: Romantic Socialists Confront Individualism in July Monarchy France', *FHS* 26:3 (2003), 437–57. For the 'feminist' current in French utopian socialism, see Margaret Talbot, 'An Emancipated Voice: Flora Tristan and Utopian Allegory', *FS* 17:2 (1991), 219–39; Naomi J. Andrews, *Socialism's Muse: Gender in the Intellectual Landscape of French Romantic Socialism* (Lanham, MD: Lexington Books, 2006).

and one of the most important of the early modern Christian expositors of the Kabbalah.[75]

La Mère de Dieu was inspired by a vision Lévi experienced while incarcerated in prison for his revolutionary political sentiments.[76] The sequential stages of the vision – entering a state of grief over his own fate and that of France, falling asleep while weeping, and then entering a prophetic dream-state – mirrors a specific Kabbalistic magical practice known as 'mystical weeping'. This technique emerged in antiquity in the form of ritual mourning for the destruction of the Temple at Jerusalem, developed as a magical practice in the *Zohar*, and was taught by Luria and other Safed Kabbalists to provoke the visionary appearance of the *Shekhinah* as a beautiful woman who, despite the misery of her exile in the dark realm of material reality, offers consolation to – and is herself consoled by – those who identify with her suffering.[77] The experience is understood as both an initiation and a participation in the suffering and redemption of the female aspect of the godhead. Lévi presents the chief revelation of

---

[75] See Guillaume Postel, *Abrahami Patriarchae liber Jezirah sive formationis mundi* (Paris, 1552). Postel's translation of the *Bahir* was never published. For Postel's merging of Mary with the *Shekhinah*, see Petrie, *Gender*, 74–75, 91–93, 118–19; William J. Bouwsma, 'Postel and the Significance of Renaissance Cabalism', *JHI* 15:2 (1954), 218–32.

[76] For a description of the vision, see Constant, *Mère de Dieu*, 169. For details of Lévi's trial and sentencing, see Chacornac, *Éliphas Lévi*, 161–62.

[77] For Luria's use of 'mystical weeping', see Hayyim Vital, *Sefer ha-Hezyonot*, ed. A. Z. Aeschcoli (Jerusalem, 1954), 42, cited in Idel, *Kabbalah*, 81. For mystical weeping in the *Zohar*, see Eitan Fishbane, 'Tears of Disclosure: The Role of Weeping in Zoharic Narrative', *Journal of Jewish Thought and Philosophy* 11:1 (2002), 25–47. For a discussion of the technique, see Idel, *Kabbalah*, 75–88; Elliot R. Wolfson, 'Weeping, Death, and Spiritual Ascent in Sixteenth-Century Jewish Mysticism', in John J. Collins and Michael Fishbane (eds.), *Death, Ecstasy, and Other Worldly Journeys* (Albany, NY: State University of New York Press, 1995), 209–47. For similar visionary experiences, see A. Yaari, *'Iggrot 'Eres Yisrael* (Ramat Gan, 1971), 205–06, cited in Lawrence Fine (ed. and trans.), *Safed Spirituality: Rules of Mystical Piety, The Beginning of Wisdom* (Mahwah, NJ: Paulist Press, 1984), 49; R. Isaac Yehudah Yehiel Safrin, *Megillat Setarim*, ed. Naftali ben Menahem (Jerusalem, 1944), 19, cited in Idel, *Kabbalah*, 83. For Luria's identification with the *Shekhinah's* suffering, see Werblowsky, 'Mystical and Magical Contemplation', 18.

his vision as the 'Great Secret': a realisation of the identity between human and divine.[78]

> A light then burst upon my mind, and I realized that humanity, considered in the individuals who compose it, is, so to speak, the analysis of God, and that the idea of God is nothing more than the synthesis of humanity. I thus decided to seek men in God and to find God in men.[79]

This statement echoes Luria's understanding of the messianic advent as the transformation of humanity, and expresses that interiorised locus of the divine in the human which became one of the hallmarks of the magical philosophy of the British occult revival but was articulated in Safed three centuries earlier:[80]

> The coming of the Messiah does not mean that we must wait for some individual to ride through the gate of Mercy in the Eastern Wall of the city of Jerusalem....Rather, the presence of goodwill towards men and peace on earth...is the Messiah. The Messiah is nothing more than the symbol of world harmony.[81]

This observation, made by Luria to his disciples in the early 1570s, might have been written by Lévi himself.

The Lurianic Kabbalah incorporates a range of magical linguistic techniques involving the combining of the Hebrew letters according to certain systematic rules.[82] The three main

---

[78] For Lévi's exposition of the 'Great Secret', see Éliphas Lévi, *Le grand arcane, ou l'occultisme dévoilé* (Paris: Chamuel, 1898; repr. Paris: Elibron Classics, 2005).

[79] Constant, *Mère de Dieu*, 273.

[80] See, for example, Fortune, *Mystical Qabalah*, 306. For the identification of God with the inner self as a unique feature of contemporary spiritualities, see Hanegraaff, *New Age Religion*, 204–29.

[81] Hayyim Vital quoting Isaac Luria in *Sefer ha-Derushim* ('Book of Discourses'), cited in Berg and Ashlag (eds. and trans.), *Ten Luminous Emanations*, 1:152. *Sefer ha-Derushim* can be found in *Kabbala denudata* 1.2.4, 28–61 as 'Tractus I. Libri Druschim, seu Introductio Metaphysica ad Cabbalam Autore R. Jizchak Loriense'.

[82] For Luria's appropriation of linguistic techniques from the *Sefer Yetsirah*, see Fine, *Physician*, 154–55, 180–86. For discussions of *gematria*, see Scholem, *Kabbalah*, 337–43; Idel, *Absorbing Perfection*, 256–62; S. A. Horodezky, 'Gematria', in *EJ* VII:170–79. For the appearance of *gematria* in early rabbinic literature, see Idel,

techniques for extracting hidden meanings from sacred texts
are *gematria, temurah,* and *notarikon. Gematria* is based on the
equivalence of Hebrew letters with numbers: any letter,
word, or phrase can be replaced by a letter, word, or phrase
with the equivalent numerical value, producing entirely new
and infinitely variable interpretations of a sacred text.
Temurah is a more complex system, rather like a code, with
three distinct variations. *Atbash* involves substituting the first
letter of the Hebrew alphabet with the last letter, the second
letter with the next-to-last letter, the third letter with the
third-from-last letter, and so on. *Albam* involves replacing the
first letter of the Hebrew alphabet with the twelfth letter, the
second letter of the alphabet with the thirteenth letter, and so
on. *Avgad* involves replacing each letter in the Hebrew
alphabet with the one succeeding it. Not surprisingly, Lévi
avoids any use of *temurah* in his Kabbalistic exegeses.
Notarikon is similar to the creation of acronyms and involves
using the first and last letters of a word – and sometimes the
middle letters – to create a new word, facilitated by the fact
that vowels in these texts are either not indicated, or
indicated only by 'points' which can represent more than one
vowel, so that the letters used in the various combinations
are solely consonants. Lévi probably derived his
understanding of the techniques not only from the texts of
the *Kabbala denudata* – Gikatilla is particularly fluent in his
use of them – but also from Pico and Reuchlin, who referred
to them as *ars combinatoria*: the art of combinations.[83]

'Defining Kabbalah'; Idel, *Mystical Experience*, 14–15. For a
discussion of *temurah*, see Idel, *Absorbing Perfections*, 265–69. For a
general discussion on the various linguistic techniques, see Daniel
Abrams, 'From Germany to Spain: Numerology as a Mystical
Technique', *JJS* 47 (1996), 85–101; Idel, *Kabbalah*, 210–18; Wirszubski,
Pico, 77–83; Adam Afterman, 'Letter Permutation Techniques,
Kavannah and Prayer in Jewish Mysticism', *JSRI* 6:18 (2007), 52–78.
For the linguo-theosophy forming the basis of Kabbalistic
hermeneutics, see below.
[83] Pico in turn acquired his knowledge of the techniques from
Abraham Abulafia's thirteenth-century expositions of the
application of linguistic hermeneutics to the Divine Names,
translated into Latin by a Jewish convert to Christianity called
Shmuel ben Nissim ben Shabbatai Abu al Faraj (1450–1483), known
under the pseudonym of Flavius Mithridates. For Pico's reliance on
Abulafia, see Brian P. Copenhaver, 'The Secret of Pico's *Oration*:
Cabala and Renaissance Philosophy', *Midwest Studies in Philosophy*
26 (2002), 56–81. For Pico's acquisition and understanding of

Redemption, in the context of the Lurianic Kabbalah, depends on understanding the magical relationship between the godhead and the Hebrew language, described by Eitan P. Fishbane as 'phonetic mysticism'.[84] The structure of reality and the Hebrew letters are deemed to be two expressions of the same thing, and the different levels of the universe reveal the divine source through the different permutations of the letters that both embody and generate them. Utilising the magical power of language can thus transform the cosmos itself.[85] Lévi concurs with this magical potency of the word:

The word...is the veil of being and the characteristic sign of

---

gematria, temurah, and notarikon as 'Kabbalistic magic', see Wirszubski, Pico, 77–83 and 133–52. For Reuchlin's exposition of the techniques, see Reuchlin, On the Art of the Kabbalah, especially Book III, 235–357; Charles Zika, 'Reuchlin's De Verbo Mirifico and the Magic Debate of the Late Fifteenth Century', JWCI 39 (1976), 104–38; Dan, 'Kabbalah of Johannes Reuchlin', 55–95. For Flavius Mithridates, see Marion Leathers Kuntz, 'Review of Saverio Campanini, The Book of Bahir', RQ 60:1 (2007), 140–42. The Kabbalistic ars combinatoria was associated by Pico with the thirteenth-century work of Ramon Lull, primarily due to a pseudepigraphic work attributed to Lull called De auditu kabbalistico, which impelled Pico to write about the ars combinatoria as 'like the Lullian art'. Lévi adopted Pico's ideas about Lull's Kabbalistic skills; see Lévi, Histoire, 329–41. For De auditu kabbalistico and Lull as a Kabbalist, see Wirszubski, Pico, 259–60; Blau, Christian Interpretation, 117–18; Paul Oskar Kristeller, 'Giovanni Pico della Mirandola and His Sources', in L'Opera e il Pensiero di Giovanni Pico della Mirandola nella Storia dell'Umanesimo, Vol. 1 (Firenze: Istituto Nazionale di Studi sul Rinascimento, 1965), 35–142, on p. 75; Moshe Idel, 'Ramon Lull and Ecstatic Kabbalah: A Preliminary Observation', JWCI 51 (1988), 170–74. Although Lull did not present himself as a Kabbalist, he seems to have been exposed to Kabbalistic ideas that contributed to the creation of his complex system of ars combinatoria, reflected primarily in his 'Attributes of God' as creative primordial causes (related to the Kabbalistic sefirot) and his practice of combining the letters on circles or wheels as representations of categories of knowledge. For Lull's system, see Frances A. Yates, Lull and Bruno: Collected Essays, Vol. 1 (London: Routledge & Kegan Paul, 1982), 3–125.
[84] See Eitan P. Fishbane, 'The Speech of Being, the Voice of God: Phonetic Mysticism in the Kabbalah of Asher ben David and His Contemporaries', JQR 98:4 (2008), 485–521.
[85] See Fine, Physician, 211. For Kabbalistic 'linguo-theosophy', see Moshe Idel, Enchanted Chains: Techniques and Rituals in Jewish Mysticism (Los Angeles, CA: Cherub Press, 2005).

life. Every form is the veil of a word, because the idea that is the mother of the word is the sole reason for the existence of forms. Every figure is a character, every character emerges from and returns to its word.[86]

The human being as a magus whose trained will can influence the divine order has been perceived as an idea that arose in the Christian world of the Italian Renaissance and heralded the spirit of early modern science.[87] But this theme also abounds in Jewish esoteric texts from late antiquity onward,[88] and is particularly emphasised in Kabbalistic literature. According to Moshe Idel,

---

[86] Lévi, *Dogme*, 60.

[87] For the Renaissance idea of the human being as magus, see Giovanni Pico della Mirandola, *On the Dignity of Man*, trans. Charles Glenn Wallis, in Pico, *On the Dignity of Man*, 3. For Pico's sources for the 'angelicising' of the human being, see Copenhaver, 'The Secret of Pico's *Oration*'. For further discussions, see Frances A. Yates, *Giordano Bruno and the Hermetic Tradition* (London: Routledge & Kegan Paul, 1964); Karen Johannisson, 'Magic, Science, and Institutionalization in the Seventeenth and Eighteenth Centuries', in Ingrid Merkel and Allen G. Debus (eds.), *Hermeticism and the Renaissance: Intellectual History and the Occult in Early Modern Europe* (London: Associated University Presses, 1988), 251–61; Brian Vickers (ed.), *Occult and Scientific Mentalities in the Renaissance* (Cambridge: Cambridge University Press, 1984); Jacob Neusner, Ernest S. Frerichs, and Paul Virgil McCracken Flesher (eds.), *Religion, Science, and Magic: In Concert and in Conflict* (Oxford: Oxford University Press, 1989); Frank L. Borchardt, 'The Magus as Renaissance Man', *SCJ* 21:1 (1990), 57–76. For changes in the perception of the self during the Renaissance period, see Owen, *Place of Enchantment*, 115.

[88] For the human being as magus in Jewish esoteric literature from late antiquity onward, see Schäfer, *Hidden and Manifest God*, 165; Rebecca Macy Lesses, *Ritual Practices to Gain Power: Angels, Incantations, and Revelation in Early Jewish Mysticism* (Harrisburg, PA: Trinity Press International, 1998); Rebecca Macy Lesses, 'Speaking with Angels: Jewish and Greco-Egyptian Revelatory Adjurations', *HTR* 89:1 (1996), 41–60. See also the legend of the fifteenth-century Kabbalist Joseph della Reina in Joseph Dan (ed. and trans.), *The Heart and the Fountain: An Anthology of Jewish Mystical Experiences* (Oxford: Oxford University Press, 2002), 181–94. See also Yohannan Alemanno, *Collectanaea*, MS Oxford 2234, fol. 164a, cited in Idel, *Absorbing Perfections*, 148. For Alemanno's view of man as magus and his influence on Pico, see Moshe Idel, 'The Anthropology of Yohanan Alemanno: Sources and Influences', *Topoi* 7 (1988), 201–20; Idel, *Kabbalah*, 173–99; Copenhaver, 'The Secret of Pico's *Oration*', 70.

> The theurgical Kabbalist does not need external help or grace; his way of operating...enables him to be independent; he looks not so much for salvation by the intervention of God as for God's redemption by human intervention.[89]

This idea is starkly expressed by Lévi when he declares: 'Do you wish to reign over yourselves and others? Learn how to will.'[90]

Lévi understands the Kabbalah as simultaneously a science, a religious revelation, and a doctrine of 'high' magic. It is also the great reconciler: the most sublime Western formulation of the 'perennial' revelation transmitted from initiate to initiate over the centuries, through which all opposites and all conflicting traditions can be harmonised, and through which a new age, led by a transformed Church and a reinvigorated French republic, can finally dawn.[91] Although various primal revelations were promulgated among French Romantics in the early nineteenth century,[92]

---

[89] Idel, *Kabbalah*, 179.

[90] Lévi, *Dogme*, 199.

[91] See Lévi, *Dogme*, 39; Lévi, *Grand arcane*, 178. For the Kabbalah as the great reconciler in Pico and Postel, see Petrie, *Gender*, 78–93. For the Kabbalah as the great reconciler in the *Kabbala denudata*, see Coudert, *Impact of the Kabbalah*, 137–52.

[92] For eighteenth-century expositors of a primal ur-religion, see Antoine Court de Gébelin, *Monde primitif*, 9 vols. (Paris, M. Robinet, 1772–83), 8:xviii–xix; Antoine Fabre d'Olivet, *Lettres à Sophie sur l'histoire*, 2 vols. (Paris: Lavillette et Cie, 1801); Antoine Fabre d'Olivet, *La langue hébraïque réstitué* (Paris: private publication, 1815). Court de Gébelin (1728–1784) provided, in his *Monde primitif*, a catalyst for Lévi's belief that the Major Arcana of the Tarot were based on the letters of the Hebrew alphabet. Fabre d'Olivet (1767–1825) was a prolific creator of esoteric 'metahistories' in which the ideas of a primal religion, a primal civilisation, and a primal language are all fused and form the basis of the esoteric currents in all subsequent religions and cultures. In *La langue hébraïque réstitué*, d'Olivet claims that the real secrets of the Book of Genesis, grossly distorted by poor translations, can be read at three different levels corresponding to body, soul, and spirit; in *Lettres à Sophie*, d'Olivet presents the Atlanteans as the original inventors of science – an idea enthusiastically appropriated by Blavatsky and, through her, by Golden Dawn occultists such as Dion Fortune. For scholarly discussions on the theme of 'metahistories', see Hayden White, *Metahistory: The Historical Imagination in Nineteenth-Century Europe* (Baltimore, MD: Johns Hopkins University Press, 1973); Harvey, *Beyond Enlightenment*, 35–61; Riffard, 'The Esoteric Method'; Arthur

Lévi sees its purest expression in the Kabbalah:

> All that is grand or scientific in the religious dreams of the
> illuminés, Jacob Böhme, Swedenborg, Saint-Martin...is
> borrowed from the Kabbalah; all Masonic associations owe
> their secrets and their symbols to it. The Kabbalah alone
> consecrates the alliance of universal reason and the Divine
> Word...it has the keys of the present, the past and the future![93]

Lévi's belief in the Kabbalah as a bridge between religion and
science was shared by important figures in the French Jewish
community, with whom he seems to have enjoyed direct
links. Adolphe Franck (1809–1893), an Alsace-born lawyer,
university lecturer, and the respected author of the only
scholarly work on the Kabbalah available in French in the
mid-nineteenth century,[94] declares: 'It is in the province of
Judaism...to reconcile science with God.'[95] In 1870, Rabbi
Eliyahu Soloweyczyk, one of Lévi's many contacts among the
Polish emigrés living in Paris and also one of Franck's
protegés, published a two-volume exegesis on the Gospels of
Matthew and Mark in which he presents the possibility of the
reconciliation of Judaism and Christianity through an
understanding of the Kabbalah, and portrays Jesus as a
Jewish magus who performed his miracles through
Kabbalistic linguistic magic.[96]

McCalla, 'Illuminism and French Romantic Philosophies of History',
in Faivre and Hanegraaff (eds.), *Western Esotericism and the Science of
Religion*, 253–68.
[93] Lévi, *Dogme*, 50.
[94] Adolphe Franck, *La Kabbale, ou la philosophie religieuse des Hébreux*
(Paris: Librairie de I. Hachette, 1843). For the first English
translation of Franck's *La Kabbale*, see Adolphe Franck, *The Kabbalah:
The Religious Philosophy of the Hebrews*, trans. I. Sossnitz (New York:
The Kabbalah Publishing Co., 1926).
[95] Adolphe Franck, *Société des études juives, Annuaire* 2 (1883), 39,
cited in Salo W. Baron, 'The Revolution of 1848 and Jewish
Scholarship', *PAAJR* 18 (1948–49), 1–66, on p. 16.
[96] Elie [Eliyahu] Soloweyczyk, *Kol Kore (Vox Clamantis): La Bible, le
Talmud et l'Évangile*, 2 vols., trans. Lazare Wogue (Vol. 1, Paris:
Imprimèrie de E. Brière, 1870; Vol. 2, Paris: *Les Archives Israélites*),
2:135. For Lévi's first encounter with R. Soloweyczyk, see
Chacornac, *Éliphas Lévi*, 259–60. For Franck's financial support of
Soloweyczyk, see *Kol Kore*, 1:2 and 2:vii.

By the latter part of his life, Lévi had lost his appetite for revolutionary politics.[97] But he still hoped that a divinely impelled regeneration of society might soon occur. This literal form of millenarianism was not retained by the British occultists who adopted his work. By the last decades of the nineteenth century, Darwinian evolutionary theories, with which Lévi was only superficially acquainted and which he seems to have disliked, had been transformed by the Theosophists into a form of spiritual evolutionism, 'teleological rather than mechanical', which presented a more leisurely unfolding of divine intent.[98] Lévi's socially focused messianism became progressively interiorised and individualised in the work of the British occultists. Nevertheless, even after the devastation of the First World War and the looming shadow of the Second, Dion Fortune could still write about the adept's capability of transforming the 'mind of the race' through Kabbalistic ritual magic.[99] By Fortune's time, as discussed more fully in Chapter Six, Lévi's vision had found a new formulation through the language of the emerging psychologies, reflecting Freud's ideas about dualistic forces of the *id* and Jung's theories about the unity of the collective unconscious and the androgynous nature of the psyche.[100] But the Lurianic themes of exile and restitution, like the sacred union of the divine male and female

---

[97] See, for example, the disillusionment expressed in Lévi, *Grand arcane*, 25–26.

[98] For Darwin's influence on Theosophical doctrines, see Hanegraaff, *New Age Religion*, 466, 470–82; for the doctrines themselves, see H. P. Blavatsky, *The Secret Doctrine: The Synthesis of Science, Religion, and Philosophy*, 2 vols. (London: The Theosophical Publishing Company, 1888). For Lévi's equation of Darwin's idea of natural selection with the power of the strong to oppress the weak, see Éliphas Lévi, *Paradoxes of the Highest Science, In Which the Most Advanced Truths of Occultism Are For the First Time Revealed (In Order to Reconcile the Future Developments of Science and Philosophy With the Eternal Religion)*, trans. 'A Master of the Wisdom', in *Theosophical Miscellany* (Calcutta: Calcutta Central Press Co., 1883; reissued, Adyar: Madras Theosophical Publishing House, 1922), 165. Darwin's *On the Origin of Species*, published in Britain in 1859, was not translated into French until 1873 (*L'origine des espèces au moyen de la sélection naturelle*, Paris: C. Reinwald, 1873).

[99] See, for example, Dion Fortune, *Moon Magic* (Wellingborough: Aquarian Press, 1956), 46.

[100] See Chapter Six.

principles, remain intact in Fortune's own creative interpretation of the 'mystical Qabalah'.

LÉVI'S KABBALAH AND THE ALCHEMICAL *OPUS*

Lévi's Kabbalistic magic is concerned with the cultivation of the divinity in human beings, resulting in dominion over the various levels of creation:

> The Great Work is, before all things, the creation of man by himself, that is to say, the full and entire conquest that he makes of his faculties and his future.[101]

As the 'Great Work', his Kabbalah is also synonymous with alchemy, and the Kabbalist can produce alchemical gold at will.[102] Lévi was familiar with a seventeenth-century Hebrew Kabbalistic-alchemical treatise known as the *Aesch Mezareph* ('Purifying Fire'), included in a Latin translation in the *Kabbala denudata*, which affirmed to him that the Kabbalah and the 'Great Work' are identical in their goals.[103] A. E. Waite believed that Lévi had translated the *Aesch Mezareph*

---

[101] Lévi, *Dogme*, 126. See also Lévi, *Grand arcane*, 61 and 362.

[102] See Lévi, *Clef*, 167–68. For the equation of alchemy with Kabbalistic linguistic magic, see Lévi, *Dogme*, 283. For further examples of Lévi's views on alchemy, see Lévi, *Dogme*, 126–29 and 259–63; Lévi, *Histoire*, 342–58.

[103] *Kabbala denudata*, 'Compendium Libra Cabbalistico-Chymici, Aesch Mezareph dicti, de Lapide Philosophico', as part of 'Apparatus in Librum Sohar Pars Prima', 1.1.740. The *Aesch Mezareph* ('Refiner's Fire') was first translated into English in 1714 in *A Short Enquiry Concerning the Hermetic Art*, by an anonymous author calling himself 'The Lover of Philalethes'. This translation was later included in William Wynn Westcott (ed.), *Collectanea Hermetica*, Vol. 4 (London: Theosophical Publishing Society, 1894). In the preface to the work, Westcott states that copies of the *Aesch Mezareph* in Hebrew 'still exist in concealment', hinting that these copies are in the possession of none other than H. P. Blavatsky. No such copy has ever surfaced. A more recent translation of the *Aesch Mezareph* appears in Patai, *Jewish Alchemists*, 322–35. For the earliest evidence of the Hebrew version of the *Aesch Mezareph*, see Scholem, *Alchemy and Kabbalah*, 64–65. See also Waite, *Holy Kabbalah*, 425, for a dating of the text to the early seventeenth century, based on the fact that it quotes the *Pardes Rimonim* of Moshe Cordovero, published in the mid-sixteenth century and, like the *Aesch Mezareph*, included in the *Kabbala denudata*.

into French in 1841 under the title *Le livre rouge* and the pseudonym Hortensius Flamel, although there is no direct evidence of the truth of this assertion.[104] Whether or not Lévi was indeed Hortensius Flamel, he is nevertheless dismissive of the materialistic emphasis of alchemical gold-making, emphasising instead alchemy's role as a means of spiritual transformation.[105] Jean-Pierre Brach asserts that the blending of Kabbalah and alchemy only occurs from the seventeenth century onward, based on the 'natural magic' of Pico, Reuchlin, and Agrippa, and later forming one of the cornerstones of the 'nature mysticism' or *Naturphilosophie* of early modernity within Paracelsian and Rosicrucian discourses.[106] However, both Gershom Scholem and Raphael

---

[104] For Lévi's purported translation of the *Aesch Mezareph* into French under the title *Le livre rouge*, see Hortensius Flamel, *Le livre rouge. Resumé du magisme, des sciences occultes et de la philosophie hermétique d'après Hermes Trismegiste, Pytagore, Cléopatre, Artephins, Marie-l'Egyptienne, Albert-le-Grand, Paracelse, Cornelius Agrippa, Cardan, Mesmer, Charles Fourrier, etc.* (Paris: Lavigne, 1841). See also Patai, *Jewish Alchemists*, 321. For Hortensius Flamel as a pseudonymn for Alphonse-Louis Constant, see Waite, 'Biographical Preface', in Lévi, *Transcendental Magic*, xxii, n. 1: 'There is reason for believing that he was the compiler of *Le livre rouge*, 1841, under the pseudonym of Hortensius Flamel.' Also see Waite's exegesis of the *Aesch Mezareph* in *Holy Kabbalah*, 424–28, in which he notes with scorn Lévi's purported 'discovery' of the fragments. For Lévi's 'discovery' of the *Aesch Mezareph*, see also Scholem, *Alchemy and Kabbalah*, 79–80. François Secret argues in favour of Lévi's authorship of *Le livre rouge* in Secret, 'Éliphas Lévi', 84–85. Lévi included a French adaptation of the *Aesch Mezareph* as a supplement to the first edition of *Clef des grands mystères* (490–98), but this adaptation, which bears little resemblance to either *Le livre rouge* or the *Aesch Mezareph* of the *Kabbala denudata*, was dropped from later editions as well as from Crowley's English version of *Clef*: Éliphas Lévi, *The Key of the Mysteries*, trans. Aleister Crowley (London: Rider & Co., 1959).

[105] See, for example, Lévi, *Dogme*, 126.

[106] See Jean-Pierre Brach, 'Magic IV: Renaissance – 17th Century', in Hanegraaff (ed.), *Dictionary of Gnosis*, 733. For 'natural magic' and *Naturphilosophie*, see Pico, *On the Dignity of Man*; Pico, 'Twenty-Six Magical Conclusions According to My Own Opinion', in *900 Conclusions*, cited in Farmer, *Syncretism*, 495–503. See also Farmer, *Syncretism*, 115–32; Yates, *Giordano Bruno*, 84–116; Frances A. Yates, 'Giovanni Pico della Mirandola and magic', in *L'opera e il pensiero di Giovanni Pico della Mirandola nella storia dell'umanismo*, Vol. 1 (Firenze: Istituto Nazionale di Studi sul Rinascimento, 1965), 159–

Patai offer numerous examples of the amalgamation of Kabbalah and alchemy from the twelfth century onward.[107] The perception of this 'Hermetic' Kabbalah as both a science and a mode of spiritual development was taken up enthusiastically by British occultists, as discussed more fully in the next chapter.

According to Lévi, Kabbalistic magic signifies knowledge of and power over the hidden forces of nature:

> Magical operations...are the result of a science and a practice which exalt human will beyond its normal limits. The supernatural is nothing but the extraordinary natural, or the exalted natural.[108]

This perception of magic is one of the core themes of the Romantic movement: the world is held together by occult forces which operate through chains of correspondences linked by a mysterious primal substance.[109] On this understanding of magic, Wouter Hanegraaff bases his thesis of the modernity of late-nineteenth-century occultism: magic, forced to adapt to changing worldviews in the early modern period, gradually took new, secularised forms, including a psychologisation of ritual and a replacement of the ancient ideas of angelic hierarchies and celestial effluences with that of 'subtle matter' as the intermediary between the human

---

204; D. P. Walker, *Spiritual and Demonic Magic: From Ficino to Campanella* (London: University of Notre Dame Press, 1975), 54–59. For natural magic and Kabbalah in Trithemius, another of Lévi's favourite sources, see Noel L. Brann, *Trithemius and Magical Theology* (Albany, NY: State University of New York Press, 1999). For *Naturphilosophie* see Charles Webster, 'Paracelsus, Paracelsianism, and the Secularization of the Worldview', *SC* 15:1 (2002), 9–27; Allen G. Debus, 'Alchemy in an Age of Reason: The Chemical Philosophers in Early Eighteenth-Century France', in Merkel and Debus (eds.), *Hermeticism and the Renaissance*, 231–50.

[107] For extensive discussions of this amalgamation, see Gershom Scholem, *Alchemy and Kabbalah*, trans. Klaus Ottman (Putnam, CT: Spring Publications, 2006); Raphael Patai, *The Jewish Alchemists: A History and Source Book* (Princeton, NJ: Princeton University Press, 1994). See Chapter Three for the incorporation of the amalgamation into British occultism.

[108] Lévi, *Dogme*, 198.

[109] See Von Engelhardt, 'Natural Science', 101–31; Von Stuckrad, *Western Esotericism*, 62–104; Faivre, *Access*, 10–15, 74–77.

being and the cosmos.[110] Hanegraaff asserts that this kind of magic could not have existed in the pre-Enlightenment period because it is a reaction to the post-Enlightenment 'disenchantment of the world', and 'will no longer be the same magic that could be found in periods prior to the process of disenchantment'.[111] Thus Lévi's Kabbalistic magic is a new magic, aimed at re-enchanting an increasingly secularised world.[112]

Just as Fortune's Kabbalah is presented in the language of the emerging psychologies of Freud and Jung, Lévi's Kabbalah is presented in the language of one of the main scientific discourses of his own day: Franz Anton Mesmer's late- eighteenth-century concept of the 'universal fluid'.[113] Mesmer's idea, itself derived from earlier alchemical speculation about the 'light of nature',[114] is transformed in

---

[110] Wouter J. Hanegraaff, 'Magic V: 18th – 20th Century', in Hanegraaff (ed.), *Dictionary of Gnosis*, 738–44. See also Hanegraaff, *New Age Religion*, 411–513; Wouter J. Hanegraaff, 'How magic survived the disenchantment of the world', *Religion* 33 (2003), 357–80.

[111] Hanegraaff, 'How magic survived', 359–60; Hanegraaff, 'Magic V', 741.

[112] For the 'modern enchanted self' in the occult revival, see Owen, *Place of Enchantment*, 114–47.

[113] For Lévi's debt to Mesmer's 'universal fluid', see McIntosh, *Éliphas Lévi*, 149. For an English translation of Mesmer's works, see *Mesmerism: A Translation of the Original Medical and Scientific Writings of F. A. Mesmer, M. D.*, ed. and trans. George J. Bloch (Los Altos, CA: William Kaufmann, 1980). For the spread of mesmerism in pre- and post-Revolution France, see Darnton, *Mesmerism*; Henri Ellenberger, *The Discovery of the Unconscious* (New York: Basic Books, 1970), 74–83; Faivre, *Access*, 76–77. For one of Lévi's many references to Mesmer, see Lévi, *Dogme*, 33.

[114] For Mesmer's debt to Paracelsus, see Margaret Goldsmith, *Franz Anton Mesmer: The History of an Idea* (London: Arthur Barker, 1934), 18–25; Ellenberger, *Discovery*, 66. For Paracelsus' *lumen naturae* and interrelated ideas, see Paracelsus, *Selected Writings*, ed. Jolande Jacobi, trans. Norbert Guterman, Bollingen Series XXVIII (New York: Pantheon, 1958), esp. *Astronomia magna* (1537–38), 496–97. See also Jung, CW13, 111–32; Walter Pagel, 'Paracelsus and the Neoplatonic and Gnostic Traditions', in Allen G. Debus (ed.), *Alchemy and Early Modern Chemistry: Papers from Ambix* (London: Jeremy Mills/Society for the History of Alchemy and Chemistry, 2004), 101–42; Allen G. Debus, *The Chemical Philosophy: Paracelsian Science and Medicine in the Sixteenth and Seventeenth Centuries* (Newton Abbot: David & Charles, 1977), 229–30; C. G. Jung, 'The

Lévi's work into the 'astral light', the pervasive universal substance or 'Great Magical Agent' through which the trained will of the magus, working through the imaginative faculty, can accomplish miracles. Lévi embeds the astral light in the framework of Gikatilla's Kabbalistic theosophy: the 'Great Magical Agent' or primal light of creation, emanating as 'worlds' or 'planes' through the different levels of the universe, is in constant flux between the two great poles of Mercy and Severity, and is responsible for all the phenomena of spiritualism, mesmerism, and magic.[115] This important concept has dominated occultist doctrines to the present day, initially through its appropriation by Helena Petrovna Blavatsky, founder of the Theosophical Society and one of the most influential figures in late-nineteenth-century occultism.[116] In Lévi's use of scientific language, he may

---

Two Sources of Knowledge: the Light of Nature and the Light of Revelation', in Jung, CW13, 111–32.

[115] Among Lévi's many references to the 'astral light', see especially Lévi, *Dogme*, 102–07.

[116] For Blavatsky's appropriation of the 'astral light', see, for example, H. P. Blavatsky, *Isis Unveiled*, 2 vols. (London: Theosophical Publishing Co., 1875), 1:xxv–xxvii and 1:125–26; Blavatsky, *Secret Doctrine*, 1:76–77. For Blavatsky's choice of a Hindu name (*akasa*) for the astral light, see Mark Bevir, 'The West Turns East: Madame Blavatsky and the Transformation of the Occult Tradition', *JAAR* 62:3 (1994), 747–67; Hanegraaff, *New Age Religion*, 454–55. For further Theosophical borrowings from Lévi's astral light, see Nizida [Louise Off], *The Astral Light: An Attempted Exposition of Certain Occult Principles in Nature With Some Remarks Upon Modern Spiritism* (London: Theosophical Publishing Co., 1889); around half of this work is comprised of quotes from Lévi's *Dogme*. Alex Owen, acknowedging the British occultsts' debt to Lévi, refers to the astral light as 'the great web of otherworldly planes or orders of existence that interpenetrate the world of earthly perceptions, and that can be accessed by those trained in the higher occult arts' (Owen, *Place of Enchantment*, 127–28, n. 39). The Theosophists were fond of claiming Sir Oliver Lodge, the celebrated electromagnetic theorist who made the first public demonstration of wireless telegraphy in 1894, as 'one of us' because they could identify Lodge's ether – which he believed to be the universal primordial medium through which all spiritualist phenomena were manifested – with the astral light; see Annie Besant, *Theosophy and the New Psychology* (London/Benares: Theosophical Publishing Society, 1904), 11; C. W. Leadbeater, *Life After Death* (Adyar: Theosophical Publishing House, 1912), 5. Mathers, in *Kabbalah Unveiled*, 2, likewise invokes Lodge for scientific validation. For Lodge's

certainly be considered modern. His modernity was already recognised in the late nineteenth century by A. E. Waite, who comments: 'He is actually the spirit of modern thought forcing an answer for the times from the old oracles.'[117] However, as Thomas Laqueur observes, 'Every age, and not just the modern age, has felt the need to make its religious beliefs comport somehow with the best scientific and philosophical learning of its day.'[118] The question remains whether Lévi's modernity is truly modern, or whether it is a thin linguistic layer spread over an intact older tradition.

The idea of a primal substance that permeates the whole of creation, animates different forms at different levels, and responds to the power of the human will through the medium of the imagination, is not the invention of Mesmer, nor of the alchemists of the sixteenth and seventeenth centuries. Common to Platonic, Neoplatonic, Hermetic, and Gnostic doctrines from late antiquity, the primal substance as both formless 'subtle' matter and light is also the major theme of the creation process in Genesis, and can be found in Kabbalistic literature from the *Sefer ha-Bahir* onward.[119] Gershom Scholem suggests a Neoplatonic influence for the 'first-created light that represents the primordial spiritual substance of creation'.[120] It is well represented in the Lurianic Kabbalah:

---

spiritualist proclivities, see Courtenay Grean Raia, 'From Ether Theory to Ether Theology: Oliver Lodge and the Physics of Immortality', *JHBS* 43:1 (2007), 19–43.

[117] Waite, 'Biographical Preface' in Lévi, *Transcendental Magic*, xxiii–xxiv.

[118] Thomas Laqueur, 'Why the Margins Matter: Occultism and the Making of Modernity', *MIH* 3:1 (2006), 119.

[119] For the primal light in Jewish late antique and Kabbalistic literature, see Scholem, *Origins*, 62; Gershom Scholem, *On the Kabbalah and Its Symbolism*, trans. Ralph Manheim (New York: Schocken Books, 1969), 35–36; Gershom Scholem, 'The Name of God and the Linguistic Theory of the Kabbala', Part 2, *Diogenes* 20:80 (1972), 165–66. For the primal light as formless matter, see Daniel C. Matt, '*Ayin*: the Concept of Nothingness in Jewish Mysticism', in Lawrence Fine (ed.), *Essential Papers on Kabbalah* (New York: New York University Press, 1995), 67–108.

[120] Scholem, *Origins*, 62. For the primordial ether and light-mysticism in twelfth- and thirteenth-century Provençal Kabbalistic texts and early rabbinic sources, see Scholem, *Origins*, 73–74 and 331–47. See also the partial English translation of *Shekel-ha-Kodesh* in Moshe de Léon, 'From *The Doctrine of Ether*', trans. George

> Before the emanations were emanated and the creatures were created, the upper simple Light had filled entire existence, and there was no empty space whatsoever....There was neither beginning nor end, for everything was simple...in one likeness or affinity, and that is called the Endless Light.[121]

Luria seems to have acquired his ideas about the primal light from the *Zohar*, the *Sefer ha-Bahir*, and other medieval Hebrew texts.[122] In these works, the primal light, identical to

---

Margoliouth, in David Meltzer (ed.), *The Secret Garden: An Anthology of the Kabbalah* (New York: Seabury Press, 1976), 156–63, and the commentary on this text by Margoliouth. For a biographical sketch and summary of de Léon's literary corpus, see Elliot R. Wolfson, *The Book of the Pomegranate: Moses De Leon's Sefer Ha-Rimmon* (Atlanta, GA: Scholars Press, 1988), 3–9. The primal substance is related to Platonic and Neoplatonic ideas of the World Soul; see, for example, Plato, *Timaeus*, 30b–c and 34b; Plotinus, *The Enneads*, trans. Stephen MacKenna (Burdett, NY: Larson Publications, 1992), III.2–3 and IV.9; John Dillon, *The Middle Platonists: A Study of Platonism, 80 B.C. to A.D. 220* (London: Duckworth, 1977), 45–46. Plotinus seems to be an important source for the idea of the primal substance as the carrier of both light/good and darkness/evil, an idea also present in the Lurianic Kabbalah and in Lévi's understanding of the astral light. There is a large body of scholarly literature on the interpenetration of ideas between Platonic, Neoplatonic, Gnostic, Hermetic, and Jewish currents in late antiquity; see, for example, Roelof van den Broek and M. J. Vermaseren (eds.), *Studies in Gnosticism and Hellenistic Religions* (Leiden: Brill, 1981); Birger A. Pearson, *Gnosticism, Judaism, and Egyptian Christianity* (Minneapolis, MN: Fortress Press, 1990); Roelof van den Broek and Cis van Heertum (eds.), *From Poimandres to Jacob Böhme: Gnosis, Hermetism and the Christian Tradition* (Amsterdam: Im de Pelikaan, 2000); Scholem, *Jewish Gnosticism*. For the nexus of primal light/primal substance/imagination in Neoplatonic, Gnostic, and Hermetic sources, see Jean Pépin, 'Theories of Procession in Plotinus and the Gnostics', in Richard T. Wallis and Jay Bregman (eds.), *Neoplatonism and Gnosticism* (Albany, NY: State University of New York Press, 1992), 297–336; John M. Dillon, 'Solomon Ibn Gabirol's Doctrine of Intelligible Matter', in Lenn E. Goodman (ed.), *Neoplatonism and Jewish Thought* (Albany, NY: State University of New York Press, 1992), 43–59; Garth Fowden, *The Egyptian Hermes: A Historical Approach to the Late Pagan Mind* (Cambridge: Cambridge University Press, 1986), 77–78.

[121] Hayyim Vital, *Etz Hayyim*, 1.1, cited in Berg and Ashlag (eds. and trans.), *Ten Luminous Emanations*, 1:3 and 1:9.

[122] See, for example, *Zohar* II.166b–167a, in Isaiah Tishby and David Goldstein (eds. and trans.), *The Wisdom of the Zohar: An Anthology of Texts*, 3 vols. (Portland, OR: Littman Library of Jewish

the primal ether, is the first comprehensible form of the unknown godhead.[123] Six centuries later, Lévi echoes these Hebrew texts and presents the astral light as a primordial emanation which is 'neither a fluid nor a vibration':

> The light...is the first substance, real and living, having within itself the principle of its motion....God is the raison d'être of the light; the light is the external manifestation of the eternal Word of God.[124]

The *Idra Suta* ('Lesser Assembly'), one of the three sections of the *Zohar* found in the *Kabbala denudata*,[125] presents the divine act of creation as the streaming of the primal light from its unknown source into the cosmic structure of the ten *sefirot*:

> The Aged of the Aged, the Unknown of the Unknown, has a form and yet has no form....When He first assumed the form [of the first sefira], He caused nine splendid lights to emanate from it, which, shining through it, diffused a bright light in all directions....So is the Holy Aged an absolute light....We can only comprehend him through those luminous emanations [the ten sefirot] which again are partly visible and partly concealed.[126]

The Hebraic scholar George Margoliouth, in a paper written in 1908 for *The Jewish Quarterly Review*, discusses the exciting new 'ether theory' of Sir Oliver Lodge and notes with satisfaction: 'The Jewish Kabbalah has by a series of centuries anticipated one of the most essential ideas embodied in the latest scientific theory regarding the constitution of matter': a

---

Civilization/Oxford University Press, 1989), 1:442; *Zohar* I.15a, in Daniel C. Matt (trans.), *The Zohar: Pritzker Edition*, Vol. 1 (Stanford, CA: Stanford University Press, 2004), 108.

[123] For the Kabbalistic idea of the primal ether as the first of all created things and the source of all images, see Wolfson, *Through a Speculum*, 195–214.

[124] Lévi, *Cours*, XV.

[125] *Kabbala denudata*, 2.2.3, 521–98: 'Tractatus Tertius: Idra Suta...Synodus Minor'.

[126] *Idra Suta, Zohar* 3.288a, cited in Christian Ginsburg, *The Kabbalah: Its Doctrines, Development and Literature* (London: Longman Green, 1863), 96. For an alternative translation of this passage, see Roy A. Rosenberg (trans.), *The Anatomy of God: The Book of Concealment, the Great Holy Assembly and the Lesser Holy Assembly of the Zohar with the Assembly of the Tabernacle* (New York: Ktav Publishing House, 1973), 135.

single primal substance 'which fills the infinity of space in an unbroken continuity'.[127]

THE 'PSYCHOLOGISATION OF THE SACRED'

Kabbalistic texts comprise a wide range of magical techniques,[128] from the preparation of protective amulets to the invocation of supernal powers through the vocalisation of the Divine Names; and Lévi seems to have availed himself of virtually all of them. For many centuries the Christian world viewed Jewish magic as peculiarly potent because, unlike ordinary sorcery, it was perceived as drawing power from the supernal realms and was therefore divinely sanctioned.[129] The Lurianic practice of invoking a disincarnate sage or angelic *maggid* for the purpose of acquiring knowledge of the divine world has enjoyed currency in some Jewish Kabbalistic circles into the twenty-first century; Lévi attempted it with the spirit of the great first-century Pythagorean magus Apollonius of Tyana,[130] and the *maggid* may be one of the prototypes for Blavatsky's disincarnate 'Masters'.[131] *Maggidim* may be angels, demons,

---

[127] George Margoliouth, 'The Doctrine of the Ether in the Kabbalah', *JQR* 20:4 (1908), 825–61, on p. 828.

[128] For a discussion on the various scholarly definitions of the term 'magic', see Chapter Four.

[129] For the perception of Jews as magicians and sorcerers, see Joshua Trachtenberg, *Jewish Magic and Superstition* (New York: Behrman's Jewish Book House, 1939; repr. Philadelphia, PA: University of Pennsylvania Press, 2004), 1–24; Joshua Trachtenberg, *The Devil and the Jews: The Medieval Conception of the Jew and Its Relation to Modern Antisemitism* (New Haven, CT: Yale University Press, 1943); John G. Gager, *Moses in Greco-Roman Paganism* (Atlanta, GA: Society of Biblical Literature, 1972), 134–61; Pablo A. Torijano, *Solomon the Esoteric King: From King to Magus, Development of a Tradition* (Leiden: Brill, 2002), 192–224; Andreas Kilcher, 'The Moses of Sinai and the Moses of Egypt: Moses as Magician in Jewish Literature and Western Esotericism', *Aries* 4:2 (2004), 148–70.

[130] Lévi, *Dogme*, 132–36.

[131] For Luria's invocation of Elijah as his *maggid*, see Fine, *Physician*, 96–98. For a basic definition of a *maggid*, see Joseph Dan, 'Maggid', in *EJ* 11:698–701. For a discussion of the development of Blavatsky's concept of disincarnate 'Masters', which does not mention possible Kabbalistic sources, see K. Paul Johnson, *The Masters Revealed: Madame Blavatsky and the Myth of the Great White Lodge* (Albany, NY: State University of New York Press, 1994). For the popularity of

or the souls of disincarnate prophets or sages, and they are perceived as spiritual guides and revealers of supernal secrets.[132] Amulets and seals intended to attract these supernal entities figure high on Levi's list of magical priorities, acquired from a variety of sources ranging from Agrippa's *De occulta philosophia* to any medieval grimoire Lévi could lay his hands on.

Lévi considered any grimoire that incorporated Hebrew letters and claimed to be authored by Solomon a genuine 'old Hebrew Grimoire'.[133] The grimoires comprise the main literature of Western ceremonial magic, and generally involve instructions for astral talismans and the ritual invocation of demonic and/or angelic entities. Lévi would have been familiar with sixteenth- to eighteenth-century redactions of earlier medieval versions,[134] which in turn rely

---

Elijah as a *maggid*, see Idel, *Absorbing Perfections*, 143–45. For the absorption of the *maggid* Elijah into Rosicrucian and Masonic currents as the messianic, revelatory figure of 'Elie Artiste', see Antoine Faivre, 'Elie Artiste, ou le Messie des Philosophes de la Nature', Part 1, *Aries* 2:2 (2002), 120–52; Part 2, *Aries* 3:1 (2003), 25–54; Walter Pagel, 'The Paracelsian Elias Artista and the Alchemical Tradition', *Medizinhistorisches Journal* 16 (1981), 6–19. The Rosicrucian/Masonic current in Western esotericism is the most likely channel through which Blavatsky would have encountered the idea of the disincarnate spiritual guide, as she could not read Hebrew.

[132] For seventeenth-century instructions on how to invoke a *maggid*, see the revelation of Rabbi Joseph Taitazak in Dan (ed.), *Heart and the Fountain*, 175–80. For a description of the experience of a *maggid*, see Louis Jacobs, 'The *Maggid* of Rabbi Moses Hayyim Luzzato', in Louis Jacobs (ed. and trans.), *The Jewish Mystics* (London: Kyle Cathie, 1990), 136–47. For further scholarly discussions on the *maggid*, see Werblowsky, *Joseph Karo*, 257–86; Yoram Bilu, 'Dybbuk and Maggid: Two Cultural Patterns of Altered Consciousness in Judaism', *AJSR* 21:2 (1996), 341–66. For *maggidim* and Jewish ritual exorcism, see Yohanan Petrovsky-Shtem, 'The Master of an Evil Name: Hillel Ba'al Shem and His *Sefer ha-Heshek*', *AJSR* 28:2 (2004), 217–48; Nigal, *Magic, Mysticism, and Hasidism*, 67–134.

[133] Lévi, *Histoire*, 217.

[134] For a comprehensive overview of the grimoires, see Owen Davies, *Grimoires: A History of Magic Books* (Oxford: Oxford University Press, 2009); for the use of the grimoires in the occult revival, see Davies, *History of Magic Books*, 168–88. For a survey of English translations of the grimoires, see Owen Davies, *Popular Magic: Cunning-folk in English History* (London: Hambledon Continuum, 2003), 119–45. For a detailed but hostile discussion of

heavily on late antique Jewish magical literature such as the Solomonic texts and the most important early Jewish compilation of magic, the third-century CE *Sefer ha-Razim*.[135] The astral magic presented in these texts is intended to draw down the celestial effluence from the planetary angels and demons through the correspondences between supernal and material substance, godhead and humanity, and the divine nature of language.[136] Although the second part of *Dogme et*

---

the main texts, including those Lévi favoured, see A. E. Waite, *The Book of Black Magic: Including the Rites and Mysteries of Goëtic Theurgy, Sorcery, and Infernal Necromancy* (London: George Redway, 1886). For Mathers' use of these texts, see Chapter Four. For the development of the Jewish Solomonic texts into medieval Christian grimoires, see Lynn Thorndike, *A History of Magic and Experimental Science During the First Thirteen Centuries of Our Era* (New York: Columbia University Press, 1923), IV:279–89; Torijano, *Solomon the Esoteric King*; Todd E. Klutz, *Rewriting the Testament of Solomon: Tradition, Conflict and Identity in a Late Antique Pseudepigraphon* (London: T & T Clark International, 2005); Jesse Rainbow, 'The Song of Songs and the *Testament of Solomon*: Solomon's Love Poetry and Christian Magic', *HTR* 100:3 (2007), 249–74; Sarah Iles Johnston 'The Testament of Solomon: from Late Antiquity to the Renaissance', in Jan N. Bremmer and Jan R. Veenstra (eds.), *The Metamorphosis of Magic: from Late Antiquity to the Early Modern Period* (Leuven: Peeters, 2002), 35–49. For a bibliography of Solomonic texts in English and commentaries on them, see Don Karr, 'The Study of Solomonic Magic in English' (2007), <http://www.digital-brilliance.com/kab/karr/tssmie.pdf>. For a useful contemporary 'emic' survey of the grimoires, see Aaron Leitch, *Secrets of the Magical Grimoires: The Classical Texts of Magick Deciphered* (Woodbury, MN: Llewellyn Publications, 2005).

[135] For an English translation of the *Sefer ha-Razim*, see Michael A. Morgan (trans.), *Sepher ha-Razim: The Book of the Mysteries* (Chico, CA: Scholars Press, 1983). For English translations of the *Sefer ha-Raziel*, see Steve Savedow (ed. and trans.), *Sepher Rezial Hemelach: The Book of the Angel Rezial* (York Beach, ME: Samuel Weiser, 2000); Avraham Yaakov Finkel (ed. and trans.), *Kabbalah: Selections from Classic Kabbalistic Works from Raziel HaMalach to the Present Day* (Southfield, MI: Targum Press, 2002), 23–30. For more on these works, see Chapter Four.

[136] See Schwartz, *Astral Magic*, ix–xiv; Bloom, *Jewish Mysticism*, 165–88; Torijano, *Solomon*, 192–224; Peter Schäfer, 'Jewish Magic Literature in Late Antiquity and the Early Middle Ages', *JJS* 41:1 (1990), 75–91. For astral amulets, see Joseph Naveh and Shaul Shaked, *Amulets and Magic Bowls: Aramaic Incantations of Late Antiquity* (Leiden: Brill, 1985); Michael D. Swartz, 'Scribal Magic and Its Rhetoric: Formal Patterns in Medieval Hebrew and Aramaic

rituel is largely devoted to this art, Lévi reveals his apparent modernity in his insistence that the implements of ritual magic are mere tools to focus the mind of the magus:

> I recognise the relative efficacy of spells, herbs, and talismans. But these are only minor means which are linked with minor mysteries. I am speaking to you now about great moral forces and not of material instruments.[137]

The 'relative efficacy' of the implements notwithstanding, magical rituals in Lévi's Kabbalistic system are perceived as an interior process aimed at moral and spiritual perfection, and the 'entities' such rituals invoke are aspects of the mind of the adept reflected in the fluctuating currents of the astral light. After completing the narrative of his attempted invocation of Apollonius, Lévi informs his readers:

> Will I conclude from this that I really evoked, saw and touched the great Apollonius of Tyana? I am neither so hallucinated as to believe it, or so unserious as to affirm it. The effect of the preparations, the perfumes, the mirrors, the pentacles, is a true drunkenness of the imagination, which must act strongly on a person otherwise nervous and impressionable.[138]

Current scholarly perspectives view the interiorisation of the magical process in late-nineteenth-century occultism as an undertaking focused specifically on the development of individual consciousness: in the modern era, the supernal powers, once addressed with submissiveness and the hope of grace, began to be seen as a powerful inner resource that could be directed by the human will. Wouter Hanegraaff comments that 'the single most important innovation in magic since the late 19th century' is its transformation into 'a series of spiritual techniques for "self-development"'.[139] Alex Owen describes the 'renegotiation of self' involved in this new understanding of magic as 'an accommodation with a unifying and transcendental spirituality even as it underscored the self's multiplicity and contingency'[140] – a

---

Incantation Texts from the Cairo Genizah', *HTR* 83:2 (1990), 163–80. See Chapter Four for a discussion of the Jewish magical tradition.
[137] Lévi, *Grand arcane*, 62–63.
[138] Lévi, *Dogme*, 135.
[139] Hanegraaff, 'Magic V', 743.
[140] Owen, *Place of Enchantment*, 116.

recognition of the multiple layers of the mind, influenced by new medical and psychological theories, that differs radically from the Catholic and Protestant practices of 'pious introspection' belonging to earlier historical periods. The new 'discourse of self' presented in the work of Lévi and his British followers reflects a sense of the fluid nature of human consciousness as well as the existence of a higher or 'permanent' Self, and interprets magical powers as an expression of the 'little-understood powers of the mind'. The goal of occult practices is thus a dialogue and a negotiation, rather than solely a union, between the personality and the Higher Self.[141]

As Owen herself indicates, these observations rely on Christian models of selfhood and the radical shift that occurs in these models in the late nineteenth century. She does not explore the understanding of magical powers presented in medieval Jewish Kabbalistic literature, which found its way, largely by way of Lévi, into the currents of British occultism. Moshe Idel, discussing the thirteenth-century Kabbalist Abraham Abulafia,[142] states that a central element in Abulafia's understanding of prophecy is his perception of the mystical experience as 'the supreme realization of the capacities of human consciousness'.[143]

> His [Abulafia's] visions confirm his metaphysical approach, since in them the intellect, the imagination and the Active Intellect are transformed from theoretical concepts...into a component of the spiritual life of the mystic himself.[144]

Abulafia represents an important current in the medieval Kabbalah: a precociously 'modern' understanding of the complexity and fluidity of the human personality, the interior locus of the godhead, and the importance of magical work to achieve full human potential. The Hebrew letters and the Divine Names are perceived as a symbolic focus, and

---

[141] Owen, *Place of Enchantment*, 121–23. For late-nineteenth-century metaphysical and 'self-help' movements, see Hanegraaff, *New Age Religion*, 203–55 and 482–96.

[142] For this important Kabbalist, see the references in Chapter One, n. 42. For Abulafia's influence on the Lurianic Kabbalah and Pico, see Fine, *Physician*, 292–93; Wirszubski, *Pico*, 60–64, 100–04, 134–38, 151–52.

[143] Idel, *Mystical Experience*, 137.

[144] Idel, *Mystical Experience*, 137.

even angelic guides offering prophetic visions are understood as projected reflections of the mind of the adept as it joins with the divine mind. Rabbi Judah ibn Malka, a contemporary of Abulafia, comments:

> I have seen with my own eyes a man who saw a power in the form of an angel while he was awake, and he spoke with him and told him future things....Know that he sees nothing other than himself, for he sees himself front and back, as one who sees himself in a mirror...and it appears as if it were something separate from your body.[145]

The projected image of the adept's 'Higher Self' as an angelic figure can reveal divine mysteries, as an anonymous disciple of Abulafia affirms:[146]

> Know that the fullness of the secret of prophecy...is that suddenly he will see his own form standing before him...and speaking with him and telling him the future. Of this secret the sages said, 'Great is the power of the prophets, for they make the form similar to the creator.'[147]

The idea that the Kabbalistic adept ritually creates or invokes an image of himself, a 'magical personality' that allows access to supernal secrets, is described by Owen as the modern occult expression of 'a disembodied or otherly-bodied consciousness that can reach far beyond the plane of temporal existence'.[148] It appears without significant alteration from its thirteenth-century Kabbalistic representations in the invocation of the 'Holy Guardian Angel' developed by S. L. MacGregor Mathers for his Hermetic Order of the Golden Dawn.[149] The 'psycho-

---

[145] R. Judah ibn Malka, *Kitab Uns we-Tafsir*, 22–23 and 26, cited in Idel, *Mystical Experience*, 91.

[146] For this figure in other Kabbalistic texts, see Scholem, *Mystical Shape*, 251–73.

[147] Anon., *Shoshan Sodot*, Fol. 69b, MS Oxford 1655, cited in Idel, *Mystical Experience*, 91–92.

[148] Owen, *Place of Enchantment*, 127–28. For a cognitive analysis of Abulafia's interiorised *maggid*, see Shahar Arzy, Moshe Idel, Theodor Landis, and Olaf Blanke, 'Speaking With One's Self: Autoscopic Phenomena in Writings from the Ecstatic Kabbalah', *JCS* 12:11 (2005), 4–30.

[149] For Mathers' source, see S. L. MacGregor Mathers (trans.), *The Book of the Sacred Magic of Abramelin the Mage* (London: John M.

logization of the sacred' described by Hanegraaff and Owen may not always reflect late-nineteenth-century secularisation and disenchantment; it is represented in this surprisingly 'modern' element in the medieval Kabbalah, perhaps constituting one of its great attractions to the practitioners of the Victorian occult revival.

THE POWER OF THE LETTERS

The manipulation of the Hebrew alphabet in Kabbalistic literature is a form of hermeneutics based on the idea that the letters are expressions of the creative power of the godhead. As a magical practice, it is intended to extract the hidden wisdom from sacred texts, invoke mystical states, command angels and demons, and draw down power through which the magus can perform godlike feats. The three most popular linguistic techniques – *gematria*, *temurah*, and *notarikon* – were known collectively in Renaissance Kabbalistic circles as the *ars combinatoria* or 'art of combinations'. Lévi discusses these techniques with diffidence,[150] but he displays great enthusiasm for a fourth and much simpler technique, called *hokhmat ha-tseruf* or 'knowledge of combination', which he derived directly from Latin translations of a Hebrew text called *Sefer Yetsirah* ('Book of Creation'), dated to some time between the third and ninth centuries, and which he uses to great effect in the development of his Tarot system.[151] In 1861,

---

Watkins, 1900). For the use of this text by Crowley, see Chapter Five.

[150] Lévi, *Dogme*, 212–14.

[151] For the *Sefer Yetsirah*, see Scholem, *Major Trends*, 84; Scholem, *Kabbalah*, 28; Moshe Idel, *Golem: Jewish Magical and Mystical Traditions On the Artificial Anthropoid* (Albany, NY: State University of New York Press, 1990), 75. For the problems of dating the text, see Steven M. Wasserstrom, 'Further Thoughts on the Origins of "Sefer Yesirah"', *Aleph* 2 (2002), 201–21. For the various redactions, see Joseph Dan, *Jewish Mysticism, Vol. 1: Late Antiquity* (Northvale, NJ: Jason Aronson, 1998), 155–87. For linguistic magic in the *Sefer Yetsirah*, see Idel, *Absorbing Perfections*, 34–40; Elliot R. Wolfson, *Circle in the Square: Studies in the Use of Gender in Kabbalistic Symbolism* (Albany, NY: State University of New York Press, 1995), 55–56. For recent English translations, see A. Peter Hayman (ed. and trans.), *Sefer Yesira: Edition, Translation and Text-Critical Commentary* (Tübingen: Mohr Siebeck, 2004); Aryeh Kaplan (ed. and trans.), *Sefer Yetzirah: The Book of Creation, in Theory and Practice* (York Beach, ME: Samuel Weiser, Inc., 1997). For a bibliography of English

Lévi informed Kenneth Mackenzie that he had arrived at his various inductions about the Tarot 'by means of the combinations presented by the twenty-two cards of the Tarot', referring to the *Sefer Yetsirah* as a 'venerated primeval book' and a 'ladder of truth', written, according to tradition, by the patriarch Abraham himself.[152] The linguistic cosmology presented in the *Sefer Yetsirah* inspired him with the idea of interpreting the twenty-two Major Arcana or 'Trumps' of the Tarot as synonymous with the twenty-two letters of the Hebrew alphabet, and working with them in a magical art of combinations that could imitate God's creative power.[153]

Lévi was not the first person to see potent recipes for magical manifestations in the *Sefer Yetsirah*, nor would he be the last. This work was a favourite subject for Kabbalistic commentaries, and had served as a source for Jewish magical rituals from the eleventh century onward.[154] It later

translations of the *Sefer Yetsirah*, see Don Karr, 'Notes on Editions of *Sefer Yetzirah* in English' (2001–7), <http://www.digital-brilliance.com/kab/karr/syie.pdf>. For Lévi's use of Postel's translation, see Lévi, *Histoire*, 253.

[152] See Mackenzie, 'Account', 38, and Lévi's statement to Baron Spedalieri in *Cours*, VII: 'The explicative text of talismans, letters, numbers, and the Tarot is the *Sefer Yetsirah*'. Several Latin translations of the *Sefer Yetsirah* were available to Lévi, including Guillaume Postel's; see A. E. Waite's comment on Lévi's use of this version in Éliphas Lévi, *The History of Magic*, trans. A. E. Waite (London: William Rider & Son, 1913; repr. York Beach, ME: Samuel Weiser, Inc., 2001), 82, n. 2. Other Latin translations available to Lévi were one attributed to a Jewish convert to Christianity, Paolo Ricci, and included in Johann Pistorius' *Artis cabalisticae scriptores* (Basel, 1587), which Lévi seems to have favoured; and one by another Jewish convert to Christianity, Johannes Stephanus Rittangelius: *Id est Liber Jezirah qui Abrahamo patriarchae adscribitur* (Amsterdam: Jodocus and Johannes Janssonius, 1642), which was later used by William Wynn Westcott as a basis for his English translation of the work. For Westcott's use of Rittangelius, see A. E. Waite, 'Introduction', in Knut Stenring (trans.), *The Book of Formation (Sepher Yetzirah) by Rabbi Akiba ben Joseph* (Philadelphia, PA: David McKay, 1923), 3–14.
[153] For Lévi's equation of cards and Hebrew letters, see Lévi, *Clefs majeures*, 63–86.
[154] The *Sefer Yetsirah* inspired commentaries from the early medieval period onward. One of the earliest known exegeses is by Sa'adiya Gaon of Fayum in the ninth century; another is by Sabbatai Donnolo in the tenth century. One of the interpretations of the work that was

fascinated British occultists such as William Wynn Westcott, who produced an English translation of the text in 1887.[155] The *Sefer Yetsirah* presents the 'knowledge of combination' in a simple but enigmatic style:

> The twenty-two letters are the foundation: three primary letters, seven double (letters), and twelve simple (letters)[156] ...Twenty-two letters: he [God] carved them out, he hewed them, he weighed them, he exchanged them, he combined them and formed with them the life of all creation and the life of all that would be formed. How did he weigh and exchange them? – Aleph with them all, and them all with Aleph; Bet with them all, and them all with Bet. And they all rotate in turn....The result is that all creation and all speech go out by one name.[157]

The main theme in this terse prose is that the Hebrew letters, which are also numbers, divine attributes, and manifestations of the Divine Name, are the instruments and the

---

favoured by some Kabbalists was the idea of the creation of a *golem*, an artificial anthropoid. For the utilisation of the *Sefer Yetsirah* in the creation of a *golem*, see Idel, *Golem*; Moshe Idel, 'The Golem in Jewish Magic and Mysticism', in Emily D. Bilski (ed.), *Golem! Danger, Deliverance and Art* (New York: The Jewish Museum, 1988), 15–35; Scholem, *On the Kabbalah*, 158–204. For the longevity of the *golem* myth and its appearance in eighteenth- and nineteenth-century Hasidism, see Scholem, *Major Trends*, 99; Hillel J. Kieval, 'Pursuing the Golem of Prague: Jewish Culture and the Invention of a Tradition', *MJ* 17 (1997), 1–23. For an early-twentieth-century occultist's literary rendition of the myth of the *golem*, see Gustav Meyrink, *Der Golem* (original publication serialised in *Die weissen Blätter*, 1913–14; published in complete form, Leipzig: Kurt Wolff, 1915). Meyrink (1868–1932) was involved in Theosophical and occult circles, and through his own publishing company, Rikola, issued the first biography of Lévi (Laarss, *Eliphas Lévi: Der Grosse Kabbalist*). A bilingual English-Hebrew version of the *Sefer Yetsirah* was published in America a decade earlier than Westcott's: Isidore Kalisch, *Sepher Yezirah. A Book on Creation; or, the Jewish Metaphysics of Remote Antiquity* (New York: L. H. Frank, 1877). A copy of Kalisch's book was in Westcott's library, heavily annotated (London, Yorke Archives NS67, Warburg Institute); he clearly relied on it to help his own translation, which was based not only on Rittangelius but also on the Hebrew text.
[155] William Wynn Westcott, *Sepher Yetzirah: The Book of Formation and the Thirty-Two Paths of Wisdom* (Bath: Robert H. Fryar, 1887).
[156] Hayman, *Sefer Yesirah* 9, 79.
[157] Hayman, *Sefer Yesirah* 19a–b, 100–01.

substance by which creation is accomplished, through the dynamic relationships they form with each other in rotation. The sacredness of the letters is not based solely on the idea that Hebrew was the original language spoken by God to Moses; it resides in the nature of the letters themselves, which emanate from deity and provide the impetus as well as the vessels through which the primal light is disseminated. If utilised correctly by a 'Master of the Name',[158] the 'knowledge of combination' was believed to activate the godlike creative potency within the individual. Lévi returns to this theme repeatedly, and it later dominates the lectures given to neophytes in the Golden Dawn.[159]

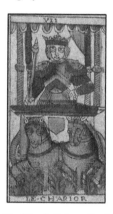 

Fig. 3: Left, 'Le Chariot' from the Marseilles-type Tarot deck of Jean Dodal, c. 1701.[160] Right, Lévi's 'Le Chariot d'Hermès', showing his transformation of the horses into Egyptian sphinxes and his addition of the Hebrew letter ז (zayin) on the left of the image.[161]

---

[158] For the magical powers of the 'Master of the Name' (*ba'al shem*), see Scholem, *Major Trends*, 98–103; Idel, *Hasidism*, 189–207; Gedalyah Nigal, *Magic, Mysticism, and Hasidism: The Supernatural in Jewish Thought* (Northvale, NJ: Jason Aronson, 1994), 1–31; Weiss, *Eastern European Jewish Mysticism*, 183–93; Ada Rapoport-Albert, 'God and the Zaddik as the Two Focal Points of Hasidic Worship', *HR* 18:4 (1979), 296–325; Arthur Green, 'The Zaddiq as Axis Mundi in Later Judaism', in Fine (ed.), *Essential Papers on Kabbalah*, 291–314.

[159] See, for example, the Golden Dawn lecture cited in Pat Zalewski, *Kabbalah of the Golden Dawn* (St. Paul, MN: Llewellyn, 1993), 8–13.

[160] The Jean Dodal Tarot, British Museum 1896, 0501.592-1-78, © The Trustees of the British Museum.

[161] Lévi, 'Le Chariot d'Hermès', *Dogme*, 338. The attribution of *zayin* to 'Le Chariot' is also found in Lévi, *Clefs majeurs*, 71.

Lévi created an ingenious system through which he could practise Kabbalistic hermeneutics in a fashion suited to his visual talents. He based his own Tarot designs on the traditional eighteenth-century French deck type known as the 'Tarot of Marseilles', which he believed to be of ancient Egyptian and Hebrew origin.[162] Lévi begins with 'Le bateleur' ('Juggler' or 'Magician') as the first letter, *aleph*, matches each of the other letters with a specific card, and then applies the *hokhmah ha-tseruf* to all the images.[163] A sacred Name of God comprised of twenty-two letters appears in pre-Kabbalistic Jewish esoteric texts,[164] and it is possible that Lévi encountered this idea and saw it as further confirmation of his theory. He did not generate his system alone: two eighteenth-century Masonic predecessors, Antoine Court de Gébelin and the cartomancer Etteila, pointed the way.[165] Volume Eight of Court de Gébelin's *Monde primitif*, published in 1781, contains an essay in which an association is made in print for the first time between the

---

[162] For the 'Tarot of Marseilles', see Paul Huson, *Mystical Origins of the Tarot: From Ancient Roots to Modern Usage* (Rochester, VT: Destiny Books, 2004), 280; Decker *et al.*, *Wicked Pack*, 36–37, 170–71.

[163] See Lévi, *Dogme*, 114–15.

[164] For this Divine Name, known as Shem Kaf Bet, see Moshe Idel, 'Defining Kabbalah: The Kabbalah of the Divine Names', in R. A. Herrera (ed.), *Mystics of the Book: Themes, Topics and Typologies* (New York: Peter Lang, 1993), 97–122, on p. 101, n. 115; Trachtenberg, *Jewish Magic*, 93; Joseph Dan, 'The Name of God, the Name of the Rose, and the Concept of Language in Jewish Mysticism', *ME* 2:3 (1996), 228–48; Louis Jacobs, *A Jewish Theology* (Springfield, NJ: Behrman House, 1973), 149.

[165] Lévi also seems to have borrowed heavily for his Tarot from the *Oedipus Aegyptiacus* (1652–54) of the Jesuit philologist and Kabbalist Athanasius Kircher, who equates the Hebrew letters with an entire hierarchy of angels, zodiac signs, planets, and elements after the fashion of the *Sefer Yetsirah*; see Lévi, *Dogme*, 50; Lévi, *Histoire*, 81. For Lévi's reliance on Kircher, see Decker *et al.*, *Wicked Pack*; Decker and Dummett, *Occult Tarot*, 16–19. For Kircher, see Joscelyn Godwin, *Athanasius Kircher: A Late Renaissance Philosopher and Scientist* (London: Thames and Hudson, 1979); Paula K. Findlen (ed.), *Athanasius Kircher: The Last Man Who Knew Everything* (London: Routledge, 2004); Daniel Stolzenberg, *Egyptian Oedipus: Antiquarianism, Oriental Studies and Occult Philosophy in the Work of Athanasius Kircher* (unpublished PhD dissertation, Stanford University, 2004).

Major Arcana of the Tarot and the Hebrew letters.[166] Court de Gébelin was associated with 'irregular' quasi-Masonic orders such as Martinès de Pasqually's Order of the Elect Cohens, and the correlation of the twenty-two Major Arcana of the Tarot with the Hebrew letters was probably already current in fringe Masonic circles by the late eighteenth century.[167] From Etteila, Lévi may have borrowed the idea that the ancient Hebrew mysteries were 'written, or rather, drawn, by some wise Kabbalists on ivory, on parchment, on gilt and silvered copper, and, finally, on simple cards', thus providing the origins of the Tarot.[168] But neither Etteila nor Court de Gébelin created a system of explicating the Tarot as refined and complete as Lévi's. His method of combining the cards provides the basis for most divinatory Tarot 'readings' to the present day, although Lévi has left no record of a specific 'spread' or method of laying out the cards.[169] The Tarot, for Lévi, is thus an 'absolute kabalistic alphabet' in the form of images: the twenty-two sacred letters emanated by

---

[166] See Court de Gébelin, *Monde primitif*, Vol. 8, repr. as *Le Tarot, présenté et commenté par Jean-Marie Lhôte* (Paris: Berg International, 1983). The essay referred to is by 'le Comte de Mellet', in Court de Gébelin, *Monde primitif*, 8:155. For Etteila, see Decker *et al.*, *Wicked Pack*, 294.

[167] See Jean-Marie Lhôte, 'Esquisse pour un portrait de Court de Gébelin', in Lhôte, *Le Tarot*, 9–68; Decker *et al.*, *Wicked Pack*, 52–73; Le Forestier, *Franc-Maçonnerie*, 518–19, 734–37; Godwin, *Theosophical Enlightenment*, 8, 29, 32, 152. Where this correlation might have been acquired is unknown, although it is most likely to have developed in Italian esoteric circles in the mid-to-late fifteenth century.

[168] Lévi, *Dogme*, 340. For the assertion that Lévi derived the idea from Etteila, see S. L. MacGregor Mathers, *Fortune Telling Cards: The Tarot, its occult signification, use in fortune telling, and method of play, etc.* (London: George Redway, 1888; repr. in R. A. Gilbert (ed.), *The Sorcerer and His Apprentice: Unknown Hermetic Writings of S. L. MacGregor Mathers and J. W. Brodie-Innes* (Wellingborough: Aquarian Press, 1983), 51–52. Lévi gives considerable credit to the 'science' of Court de Gébelin (see Lévi, *Dogme*, 340–41) but refers to Etteila as an 'illuminated hairdresser' with a 'wearisome, barbarous style' (Lévi, *Histoire*, 327; Lévi, *Dogme*, 174).

[169] Credit for inventing the 'spread' – layouts of a specific number of cards which can be read as entire complexes of ideas – is sometimes given to Etteila; see Decker *et al.*, *Wicked Pack*, 74–75; Huson, *Mystical Origins of the Tarot*, 59. But there appears to be no relationship between Eteilla's 'spreads' and the *ars combinatoria* of the *Sefer Yetsirah*.

God to create the universe, which, if magically combined through ritualistic contemplation[170] – the Juggler with everything and everything with the Juggler – will result in revelation and prophecy.[171]

Those scholars who have explored the Tarot from a historical perspective tend to dismiss as mere coincidence the numerical correlation between the Hebrew alphabet and the Major Arcana of the Tarot.[172] Occultist theories of the Tarot's ancient Hebrew or Egyptian origins certainly seem to provide a flagrant example of the 'esoteric method', and no evidence has yet been found of any ancient Tarot deck. But Lévi's insistence on the link between Tarot trumps and Kabbalistic numerology may be more than a simple manifestation of 'emic historiography'.[173] The first extant set of cards – the Visconti-Sforza deck from mid-fifteenth-century Italy – is a characteristically syncretic Renaissance product whose Major Arcana combine traditional Judaeo-Christian themes with pagan images,[174] and the Sola Busca deck from the late fifteenth century, the first deck to present images on the fifty-six Minor Arcana cards as well as the twenty-two Major, is described by Nadya Q. Chishty-

---

[170] For ritualistic contemplation, called *kavvanah* in Kabbalistic texts, see Scholem, *On the Kabbalah*, 126, 133, 145; Scholem, *Mystical Shape*, 244; Idel, *Enchanted Chains*, 165–204; Fine, *Physician*, 222–28; Lawrence Fine, 'The Contemplative Practice of *Yihudim* in Lurianic Kabbalah', in Arthur Green (ed.), *Jewish Spirituality, Vol. 2: From the Sixteenth-Century Revival to the Present* (New York: Crossroad, 1997), 64–98; Werblowski, 'Mystical and Magical Contemplation'; Aryeh Kaplan, *Meditation and Kabbalah* (York Beach, ME: WeiserBooks, 1982). On the relationship between Lurianic *kavvanah* and the magical practices of Hasidism, see Pinchas Giller, 'Between Poland and Jerusalem: Kabbalistic Prayer in Early Modernity', *MJ* 24:3 (2004), 226–50; Idel, *Hasidism*, 149–70. For magical contemplation of the letters and Divine Names, see Idel, *Ecstatic Kabbalah*, 103–69; Idel, *Mystical Experience*, 13–52; Idel, *Enchanted Chains*, 76–121. For an anonymous early-thirteenth-century text offering instructions in ritual contemplation, see Dan (ed. and trans.), *Heart and the Fountain*, 117–20.
[171] For Lévi's crediting of the *Sefer Yetsirah* for his Tarot system, see Mackenzie, 'Account', 38, and Lévi, *Cours*, VII.
[172] See, for example, Decker *et al.*, *Wicked Pack*, 38; Decker and Dummett, *Occult Tarot*, xii.
[173] For this phrase, see Hammer, *Claiming Knowledge*, 85–200.
[174] The Visconti-Sforza Tarot deck is published by U. S. Games Systems (New York, 1975).

Mujahid, in her discussion of this deck within the context of Western esoteric currents, as 'a *mutus liber* of esoteric ritual initiation'.[175] Given the cultural context of both decks, it is likely that the numerical correspondence of Major Arcana and Hebrew letters is not a coincidence.[176]

Knorr von Rosenroth's *Kabbala denudata*, published in the late seventeenth century, is replete with graphic images of various aspects of the godhead as well as numerous versions of the Tree of Life, and Lévi borrowed some of this visual material for his own work. For example, an image of the Tetragrammaton appears in the *Kabbala denudata* in the magical-messianic Lurianic text called *Sefer Emek ha-Melekh* ('Book of the Valley of the King'):[177]

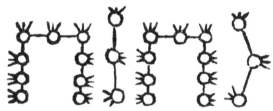

Fig. 4: The Tetragrammaton in Emek ha-Melekh, Kabbala denudata *2.1.212.*

The image presents the four letters that make up the Name (*yod, hé, vau, hé*) highlighted at the 'nodes' with twenty-four 'sparks', each with three rays, yielding a total of seventy-two

---

[175] Nadya Q. Chishty-Mujahid, *An Introduction to Western Esotericism: Essays in the Hidden Meaning of Literature, Groups, and Games* (Lampeter: Edwin Mellen Press, 2008), 115–33, on p. 116. Images of the Sola Busca deck can be found in Chishty-Mjuahid, *Introduction to Western Esotericism*, facing p. 31.

[176] For this form of 'numerological mysticism' as a typical Renaissance preoccupation, see Juliette Wood, 'The Celtic Tarot and the Secret Tradition: A Study in Modern Legend', *Folklore* 109 (1998), 20; Maren-Sofie Röstvig, 'Renaissance Numerology: Acrostics or Criticism?', *EC* 16:1 (1996), 6–21.

[177] Naphtali Herz Bacharach, *Sefer Emek ha-Melekh*, trans. as *Vallem regiam* in *Kabbala denudata* 2.1.151–346. For more on *Emek ha-Melekh*, see Waite, *Holy Kabbalah*, 420–22; Scholem, *Major Trends*, 258; Philipp Theisohn, 'Zur Rezeption von Naphtali Herz Bacharachs *Sefer Emeq ha-Melech* in der *Kabbala Denudata*', in Kilcher (ed.), *Morgen-Glantz*, 221–41. For the alchemical elements in *Emek ha-Melekh*, see Chapter Three.

radiant points – the emanations of each of the letters which comprise the *Shem ha-Mephorasch* or traditional seventy-two-letter Divine Name radiated out through all the levels of creation.[178] Lévi copied this image precisely, along with the interpretations given in both *Emek ha-Melekh* and Cordovero's *Pardes Rimonim* ('Garden of Pomegranates') – part of which is also incorporated in the *Kabbala denudata*[179] – and included it, with minor artistic flourishes, in three of his works.[180]

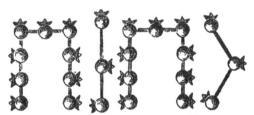

Fig. 5: Lévi's Tetragrammaton.[181]

The *Kabbala denudata* was produced by Christians, and anthropomorphic images of the godhead are therefore permissible. But the Biblical prohibition against the making of 'graven images' would seem to preclude any Jewish involvement in the creation of the Tarot in any historical period, ancient or modern, and warnings against the visual portrayal of deity are frequently found in Kabbalistic texts. For example, Hayyim Vital states firmly that the highly erotic imagery with which he and his master Isaac Luria describe the internal dynamics of the deity is not to be understood pictorially.[182] However, such warnings were not universally

[178] For the *Shem ha-Mephorasch*, see Verman, *Books of Contemplation*, 52, 63, 162, 183; Huss, 'All You Need is LAV', 613–14; Yehudah Berg, *The 72 Names of God: Technology for the Soul* (New York: Kabbalah Research Center, 2003). See also Chapter Four.

[179] *Kabbala denudata* 1.7.100–49.

[180] Lévi, *Dogme*, 113; Lévi, *Cours*, LXV; Lévi, *Clefs majeurs*, 11. For the same image in two Kabbalistic manuscripts from the twelfth and sixteenth centuries, see Giulio Busi, *Qabalah Visiva* (Torino: Einaudi, 2005), 124 and 439. For the source of the image in early Jewish magical alphabets, see Scholem, *Origins*, 328–29.

[181] Lévi, *Dogme*, 113.

[182] Hayyim Vital, *Etz Hayyim*, cited in Steven Louis Goldman, 'On the Interpretation of Symbols and the Christian Origins of Modern Science', *JR* 62:1 (1982), 1–20, on p. 15.

upheld; that Kabbalists were inclined to do the reverse is implied by the very fact that there *are* warnings.[183] Giulio Busi's recent analysis of the visual imagery in unpublished Hebrew Kabbalistic manuscripts reveals a vibrant tradition of figurative portrayals of the divine structure dating from the thirteenth century, most of it diagrammatic but some of it unashamedly anthropomorphic.[184]

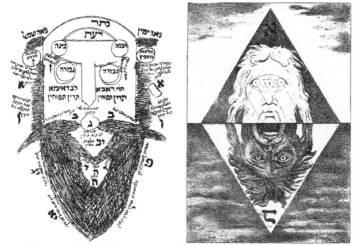

Fig. 6: Left, the head of Arik Anpin *in Sason ben Mordecai Sanduk,* Ilana de-hayye *(Bill Gross Collection MS 151, Tel Aviv). Right, Lévi's 'La tête magique du Sohar'.*[185]

---

[183] For discussions of anthropomorphic imagery and the role of the imagination in Kabbalistic literature, see Wolfson, *Speculum*.

[184] See above, n. 163. For scholars' attenuation of visual presentations in Kabbalistic texts, see Busi, *Qabalah Visiva*, 11–13.

[185] Busi, *Qabalah Visiva*, 435. Busi describes this image as 'a face that concentrates within itself a complex cosmic system'. The image shown in Fig. 5 above is based on the *Zohar*, III.141b, *Idra Rabba* ('Great Assembly'); Arik Anpin or 'long-faced one' is the name given to the 'supernal' *sefira Keter* ('Crown'), the first of the divine emanations out of which all the other *sefirot*, and all creation, flow, and the right and left eyes in Sanduk's image represent the polarised *sefirot Hesed* and *Geburah*. For *Arik Anpin*, see Idel, *Kabbalah*, 134–35; Scholem, *Major Trends*, 270; Scholem, *Mystical Shape*, 50–51. As well as being described in the Latin translation of the *Idra Rabba* included in the *Kabbala denudata* (2.2.386–520), *Arik Anpin*, also known in the *Zohar* as the 'Greater Countenance', is an

Lévi, an inveterate browser of libraries and an avid collector of Hebrew manuscripts,[186] was well acquainted with this imagery, and seems to have made one of his bold imaginative leaps – misguided in terms of an ancient Hebrew origin for the Tarot, but valid in terms of a Jewish tradition of Kabbalistic visual art. Convinced that the Tarot emerged from the lost magical tradition of Egypt and was passed on to Moses, Lévi linked the twenty-two Hebrew letters, the twenty-two Major Arcana of the Tarot, and the suggestive imagery he found in Hebrew manuscripts, and believed that he had discovered proof of the continuity of the ancient *prisca theologia*.[187] He attributed anthropomorphic characteristics to

---

important concept in the Lurianic Kabbalah, where it is called the 'Holy Ancient One'; see Fine, *Physician*, 139–41. Lévi attempted to produce his own drawing of *Arik Anpin*, found in *Histoire*, 41 and entitled 'La tête magique du Sohar'. The drawing is uniquely Lévi's, but it bears some similarities to Sanduk's. The similarities are not sufficient to indicate that Lévi might have had access to Sanduk's manuscript, but the Zoharic description of *Arik Anpin* may have provided inspiration for a number of visually inclined Kabbalists, including Lévi. Lévi attempted a translation of the *Idra Rabba* (which he mistakenly calls the *Idra Suta*) in *Le livre des splendeurs*. In this work Lévi uses the idea of *Arik Anpin* and *Zeir Anpin*, the 'Lesser Countenance' (the complex of six *sefirot* comprising *Hesed, Geburah, Tiferet, Nezach, Hod,* and *Yesod*) as the basis for his concept of the relationship between the invisible and manifest dimensions of creation. Mathers, in *Kabbalah Unveiled*, 24, calls *Arik Anpin* 'the great Father of all things'. See also Mathers' comments on *Arik Anpin* and *Zeir Anpin* in S. L. MacGregor Mathers, 'The Azoth Lecture', official Golden Dawn publication *c.* 1910, repr. in Gilbert (ed.), *Sorcerer and His Apprentice*, 30–39, on p. 33.
[186] For Lévi's penchant for collecting Hebrew manuscripts, see King, *Modern Ritual Magic*, 31.
[187] For the *prisca theologia* or 'perennial philosophy' in the Renaissance, see D. P. Walker, *The Ancient Theology: Studies in Christian Platonism from the Fifteenth to the Eighteenth Century* (London: Duckworth, 1972); D. P. Walker, 'The Prisca Theologia in France', *JWCI* 17:3/4 (1954), 204–59; Charles B. Schmitt, 'Perennial Philosophy: From Agostino Steuco to Leibniz', *JHI* 27:4 (1966), 505–32; Charles B. Schmitt, '*Prisca Theologia e Philosophia Perennis*: due temi del Rinascimento italiano e la loro fortuna', in G. Tarugi (ed.), *Il pensiero italiano del Rinascimento e il tempo nostro* (Firenze: Olschki, 1968), 211–36; Wirszubski, *Pico*, 198–200; Yates, *Giordano Bruno*, 160–65, 427–31; Kocku von Stuckrad, 'Whose Tradition? Conflicting Ideologies in Medieval and Early Modern Esotericism', in Engler and Grieve (eds.), *Historicizing "Tradition"*, 211–26. For the *prisca theologia* in Kabbalistic thought, see Moshe Idel, 'Prisca Theologia in

the Hebrew letters, relating them to the figures of the eighteenth-century Marseilles Tarot deck.[188] About this relationship, Lévi declares:

> The numeric unity or the letter aleph...is represented in the Tarot through the symbol of the Juggler. The figure of this Juggler is the same as that of the letter aleph. [189]

Fig. 7: Left: Jean Dodal Tarot, 'Le bateleur', c. 1701. Right: Lévi's 'Le bateleur' as aleph.[190]

Marsilio Ficino and in Some Jewish Treatments', in Michael J. B. Allen and Valery Rees (eds.), *Marsilio Ficino: His Theology, His Philosophy, His Legacy* (Leiden: Brill, 2002), 137–58; Moshe Idel, 'Major Currents in Italian Kabbalah between 1560 and 1660', in David B. Ruderman (ed.), *Essential Papers on Jewish Culture in Renaissance and Baroque Italy* (New York: New York University Press, 1992), 345–68; Fabrizio Lelli, '"Prisca Philosophia" and "Docta Religio"': The Boundaries of Rational Knowledge in Jewish and Christian Humanist Thought', *JQR* 91:1/2 (2000), 53–99.

[188] See Mathers, *Kabbala Unveiled*, 11, for the continuity of the idea in the Golden Dawn.

[189] Lévi, *Cours*, XI.

[190] The Jean Dodal Tarot, British Museum 1896, 0501.592.1-78, © The Trustees of the British Museum; Lévi, *Clefs majeures*, 65.

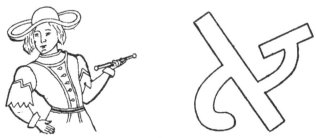

Fig. 8: Lévi's 'Le bateleur' and aleph *in Philosophie occulte, XI.*

There is no evidence of such a correlation in any known Hebrew text. But thirteenth-century Kabbalistic manuscripts portray the letters with animate qualities, and describe them as having 'bodies and souls'.[191]

Fig. 9: Alephs flying heavenward: 'The aleph *of man and of the spirit',
Sefer ha-Orah, mid-thirteenth century.*[192]

Leslie Atzmon, discussing these anthropomorphic attributes, suggests that, interpreted visually, the Hebrew letters 'look and act like living creatures – they are fleshy beings wielding immense creative ability.'[193] It is unlikely that Lévi

---

[191] On the letters having 'bodies and souls', see Scholem, 'Name of God', 168.

[192] Ya'aqov ben Ya'akov ha-Kohen, *Sefer ha-Orah*, in Busi, *Qabalah Visiva*, 113, Figure 13; Milano, Biblioteca Ambrosiana, MS S 13 sup., c. 79ʳ. For a bibliography on this manuscript and its author, see Busi, *Qabalah visiva*, 109, n. 222.

[193] Leslie Atzmon, 'A visual analysis of anthropomorphism in the Kabbalah: dissecting the Hebrew alphabet and Sephirotic diagram',

discovered a lost ancient Hebrew Tarot. But despite his Catholicism and his 'modernity', he is entirely within the tradition of Kabbalistic hermeneutics when he claims that the Hebrew letters have an animate life which can be magically manipulated through the art of combinations.

Although Lévi's original Tarot deck seems to have vanished, his interpretations of the cards did not. Within a few years of the French magus' death, Mackenzie planned his own book on the Tarot, called *The Game of Tarot: Archaeologically and Symbolically Considered*. This work was never published,[194] but Lévi's application of the 'knowledge of combination' to the Major Arcana was enthusiastically adopted, with minor alterations to the order and visual style of the cards, by successive generations of British occultists, who have continued to promulgate Lévi's work into the twenty-first century.[195] As of 1 October 2009, a total of over 20,000,000 entries appears under the word 'Tarot' in Google's on-line search engine, including books, workshops, conferences, information websites, schools, and on-line readings. Every contemporary Tarot practitioner who interprets the cards through the relationships suggested by their combinations rather than the application of fixed divinatory meanings owes a debt to Lévi's understanding of Kabbalistic magic, and through him to the third-century Hebrew *Sefer Yetsirah*. In February 2012 this total had grown to 96,000,000. Karen de Léon-Jones, discussing Giordano Bruno's use of the Kabbalah in the sixteenth century, states:

> Bruno appears to be derivative in his presentation of the Kabbalah....In reality, Bruno is not merely defining or presenting the Kabbalah: he is writing a Kabbalistic text. He is practicing the Kabbalah as hermeneutics.[196]

VC 2:97 (2003), 97. See also Janet Zweig, '*Ars Combinatoria*: Mystical Systems, Procedural Art, and the Computer', *Art Journal* 56:3 (1997), 20–29.

[194] See Decker and Dummett, *Occult Tarot*, 47.

[195] For details of the development of Lévi's Tarot in British occultism, see Chapter Five.

[196] Karen Silvia de Léon-Jones, *Giordano Bruno and the Kabbalah: Prophets, Magicians, and Rabbis* (New Haven, CT: Yale University Press, 1997), 20.

Although he was only a *petit romantique* and not a great
Renaissance magus, this description might also be applied to
Lévi.

LÉVI AND THE JEWS

Jewish emancipation occurred in France in 1791, earlier than
in any other European country.[197] While this provided new
opportunities for Jews to participate in French civic life, it
also worked against them, since their rapid success in
professions from which they had previously been barred
drew a new form of antisemitism from proponents of the
political left, who viewed them as the incarnations of satanic
capitalism.[198] Jews were perceived as amassing indecent
amounts of wealth to which they were not entitled as long as
French   Catholic   citizens   remained   poor.   Another,
particularly virulent form of anti-Jewish feeling had also
begun to develop in France in the mid-nineteenth century:
racial antisemitism, an outgrowth of new discoveries in
linguistics and philology that resulted in an eventually
deadly confusion between the nature of language and the

---

[197] For the emancipation of the French Jews following the
Revolution, see Phillis Cohen Albert, *The Modernization of French
Jewry: Consistory and Community in the Nineteenth Century* (Hanover,
NH: Brandeis University Press, 1977); Berkovitz, *Shaping of Jewish
Identity*; Steven Berkovitz, 'The French Revolution and the Jews:
Assessing the Cultural Impact', *AJS Review* 20:1 (1995), 25–86;
Graetz, *Jews in Nineteenth-Century France*; Arthur Herzberg, *The
French Enlightenment and the Jews: The Origins of Modern Antisemitism*
(New York: Columbia University Press, 1968); Sutcliffe, *Judaism and
Enlightenment*; Jonathan I. Helfland, 'Passports and Piety: Apostasy
in Nineteenth Century France', *JH* 3:2 (1988), 59–83.
[198] For the rapid economic progress of the Jews following their
emancipation, see Zosa Szajkowski, 'Notes on the Occupational
Status of French Jews, 1800–1880', *PAAJR* 46:2 (1979–80), 531–54. For
the emergence of left-wing antisemitism in France, see Eugen
Weber, 'Religion and Superstition in Nineteenth-Century France',
HJ 31:2 (1988), 399–423; Graetz, *Jews in Nineteenth-Century France*,
194–248; Robert S. Wistrich, 'Radical Antisemitism in France and
Germany (1840–1880)', *MJ* 15:2 (1995), 109–35. For comparisons with
older, religious forms of Christian antisemitism, see Marcel Simon,
'Christian Anti-Semitism', in Cohen (ed.), *Judaism and Christianity*,
131–73.

nature of race.[199] In response to these challenges, many French Jewish intellectuals adopted the post-Enlightenment approach of the *Wissenschaft des Judentums*, presenting Judaism as a rational religion, free of 'superstition', which did not interfere with the ordinary duties of a normal French citizen. One of the chief exponents of this approach was Adolphe Franck, author of *La Kabbale*. In company with other notable Jewish academics – in particular, Salomon Munk, a Hebrew and Sanskrit scholar teaching at the Collège de France and curator of the Hebrew manuscript collection at the Bibliothèque Nationale,[200] and Adolphe Crémieux, also a lawyer and a high-ranking Freemason for whom Lévi expresses considerable admiration[201] – Franck was involved

---

[199] For the work which sparked the confusion, see Friedrich Max Müller, *Introduction to the Science of Religion* (London: Longmans, Green & Co., 1873). For racial anti-semitism in the works of Joseph-Arthur Comte de Gobineau (1816–1833) and Ernest Renan (1823–1892), with which Lévi was familiar, see Arvidsson, 'Aryan Mythology', 335–36.

[200] For Munk's published material on the Kabbalah, see Salomon Munk, *Palestine: déscription géographique, historique et archéologique* (Paris: Firmin Didot Frères, 1845), 519–24; Salomon Munk, *Mélanges de philosophie juive et arabe* (Paris: Librairie A. Franck, 1853), 461–511. For Munk's collaboration with Franck, see Jeffrey Haus, 'How much Latin should a rabbi know? State finance and rabbinical education in nineteenth-century France', *JH* 15 (2001), 59–86; Graetz, *Jews in Nineteenth-Century France*, 54–58, 66–70; Berkovitz, *Shaping of Jewish Identity*, 133–34, 145–46, 241–42; Albert, *Modernization*, 167–68, 244–47, 260–63. For Munk's contribution to contemporary Kabbalistic scholarship, see Idel, *Kabbalah*, 9.

[201] French Masonic lodges, unlike those of the Germans, were open to Jews following the Revolution, and Adolphe Crémieux was initiated in 1812. By the end of the 1860s he had become Grand Master of the Scottish Rite in France; see *Les Archives Israélites*, 6 (1869), 187; Posener, *Adolphe Crémieux*, 168–173). For Crémieux's involvement with Freemasonry, see also Katz, *Jews and Freemasons*, 152–53; Howe, 'Fringe Masonry', 7–8. For Crémieux's political activities, see S. Posener, *Adolphe Crémieux (1796–1880)*, 2 vols. (Paris: Félix Alcan, 1933–34). In the posthumously published *Livre des splendeurs* (vi), Lévi speaks admiringly of a 'universal Israelite alliance which welcomes the adhesion of upright men from all religions', which has emerged from Freemasonry as a fusion of 'Kabbalistic Judaism and the Neoplatonic Christianity of St. John', and whose president is Adolphe Crémieux; the study of the Kabbalah promulgated by this alliance 'will unite Israelites and Christians as a single people'. This remark suggests that Lévi may

in a number of organisations and societies, political, educational, and religious, some with a high public profile and some secret, but all dedicated to alleviating the difficult situation of both post-emancipation French Jews and exiled Polish Jews.

In private, however, Franck was not quite the rationalist his public face portrayed. He seems to have shared in the Romantic spirit of the age and, like Lévi, dedicated much of his work to the idea of a reconciliation between religions and between religion and science.[202] In 1886, eleven years after Lévi's death, he demonstrated these beliefs publicly and created the *Ligue nationale contre l'athéisme*, which attracted a wide spectrum of scholars, deists, and spiritualists. In his role as founder and president of the *Ligue*, Franck wielded his considerable public influence on behalf of the occultist and neo-Martinist Papus by declaring that, even if he (Franck) was not a mystic, nevertheless he preferred the 'profound learnedness and deep love of the subject' displayed by Papus over the 'dessication of thought' evidenced in the 'positivism' and 'evolutionism' of the time. These sentiments appear in Franck's 'Letter Preface' to Papus' *Traité méthodique de science occulte*,[203] and were written in response to a positive review given to the new edition of Franck's *La Kabbale* in Papus' journal, *Initiation*, in 1889. In gratitude, Papus dedicated his own work on the Kabbalah, *La Cabbale: tradition secrète de l'occident*, to Franck;[204] the letter of dedication which

---

have been a member of the 'alliance' or, at the least, knew people who were. Lévi also praises Crémieux by declaring that the Kabbalah has opened the hearts of the Jews to charity, a current example being provided by Crémieux in his efforts to obtain political and financial support for the beleagered Christian population of Syria suffering at the hands of their Ottoman rulers (Lévi, *Dogme*, 33). Lévi's assumption that Crémieux was involved with the Kabbalah is interesting in view of the fact that, publicly at least, no such involvement appears to have been noted; this suggests either that Lévi simply believed that any French Jew who was a Freemason and a friend of Adolphe Franck was a Kabbalist, or that Lévi knew Crémieux personally and was aware of aspects of Crémieux' concerns that were not evident in his public life.

[202] For Franck's apparent rationalism, see Baron, 'Revolution of 1848', 16.

[203] Papus [Gérard Encausse], *Traité méthodique de science occulte* (Paris: G. Carré, 1891).

[204] Papus [Gérard Encausse], *La Cabbale: tradition secrète de l'occident* (Paris: G. Carré, 1892).

he sent to Franck appears at the front of the book. Franck's reply to this letter appears immediately after the dedication; in it he states that Papus' *La Cabbale* is 'the most intriguing, the most instructive, the most knowledgeable publication to have so far made its appearance on this obscure subject'. This is a remarkable letter for a Jewish Kabbalistic scholar to write to a Catholic occultist. Papus' *La Cabbale* makes abundantly clear the sources of his understanding of the Kabbalah: along with the predictable credits given to Martinès de Pasqually and Saint-Martin, Fabre d'Olivet and the *Kabbala denudata*, the book contains a series of ten lessons on the Kabbalah delivered by Éliphas Lévi to a disciple, M. Montaut, originally published in *Initiation* in 1891, as well as numerous lengthy quotations from Lévi's *Dogme et rituel de la haute magie, Histoire de la magie,* and *Le clef des grand mysteres.*

As the author of *La Kabbale*, Franck offered to his reading public the complexities of the Kabbalah presented as an enlightened religious philosophy.[205] Lévi, always attentive to

---

[205] Franck's emphasis on the Kabbalah as 'religious philosophy' is not entirely accepted in contemporary academic circles; see Elliot R. Wolfson, 'Hebraic and Hellenic Conceptions of Wisdom in *Sefer ha-Bahir*', *PT* 19:1 (1998), 147–76, on pp. 152–53, n. 10, where Wolfson questions Franck's use of the term 'philosophy' to describe the Kabbalah, thus 'privileging the speculative over the practical or experiential'. Some scholars of Franck's own time considered his work to be 'pantheistic' and akin to the work of Spinoza; see Alessandro Guetta, *Philosophy and Kabbalah: Elijah Benamozegh and the Reconciliation of Western Thought and Jewish Esotericism*, trans. Helena Kahan (Albany, NY: SUNY Press, 2009), 36. For a comprehensive biography and a bibliography of Franck's publications, see Adolphe Franck, *Dictionnaire des science philosophiques* (Paris: Librairie de I. Hachette, 1844–52), at <http://www.textesrares.com/philo19/franck.php>. For Franck's extensive political activities, see Graetz, *Jews in Nineteenth-Century France*, 50–51; Berkovitz, *Shaping of Jewish Identity*, 198–200; Albert, *Modernization*, 244–50. In addition to *La philosophie mystique en France à la fin du XVIII-e siècle: Saint-Martin et son maître Martinez Pasqualis* (Paris: Germer Baillière, 1866), Franck's scholarly work on Pasqually and Saint-Martin, Franck gave a series of lectures on the Kabbalah to the Académie royale des sciences morales et politiques de l'Institut de France from 1839 to 1842; these lectures contained much of the material that later appeared in *La Kabbale*. Franck's interest in the influence of the Kabbalah on Martinism led to several unpublished lectures on Martinès de Pasqually, given to the Académie from 1863 to 1866. Franck also compiled a lengthy entry for his *Dictionnaire des sciences philosophiques* on Henry More, the

the newly emerging ideas of his time, naturally availed himself of *La Kabbale*.[206] That he read and respected it is indicated by the numerous quotations and paraphrases from Franck's book that he includes in the article called 'Cabale' which he wrote for Larousse's *Grand dictionnaire universel* in 1867.[207] Franck, for him, is 'a scholar of the first order'.[208] Although Lévi constantly reminds his readers that he is a loyal Catholic, he often expresses an admiration for the Jews verging on a kind of identification, reflected not only in his choice of a pseudo-Hebrew name but also in many textual references:

---

eighteenth-century British Kabbalist and alchemist associated with Knorr von Rosenroth, who contributed six short treatises to the *Kabbala denudata* (*Kabbala denudata* 1, 2:14–27, 2:62–72, 2:173–224, 2:225–73, 2:274–92, 2:293–312). For More's work, see Noel L. Brann, 'The Conflict Between Reason and Magic in Seventeenth-Century England: A Case Study of the Vaughan-More Debate', *HLQ* 43:2 (1980), 103–26; Allison P. Coudert, 'A Cambridge Platonist's Kabbalist Nightmare', *JHI* 36:4 (1975), 633–52; Coudert, *Impact of the Kabbalah*, 220–40; Brian Copenhaver, 'Jewish Theologies of Space in the Scientific Revolution: Henry More, Joseph Raphson, Isaac Newton and their Predecessors', *AS* 37 (1980), 489–548.

[206] For Lévi's journalistic reporting of new religious, social, political, and scientific ideas, see, for example, Lévi, *Dogme*, 11–36. For his contributions to occultist journals, see Charcornac, *Éliphas Lévi*, 162–63.

[207] Éliphas Lévi, 'Cabale', in Pierre Larousse, *Grand dictionnaire universel du XIXe siècle français*, 17 vols. (Paris: Administration du Grand Dictionnaire Universel, 1866–1890), Vol. 3 (1867), 4–6. See also Lévi, *Cours*, LXXI, for another reference to Franck's *La Kabbale*. Wouter Hanegraaff, working on the assumption that Lévi had little or no contact or even real awareness of the French Jewish community around him, appears to have overlooked these references: 'As far as I have been able to ascertain, the founder of "occultist kabbalah" Eliphas Lévi does not refer even one single time to Franck's famous book on kabbalah'. See Hanegraaff, 'The Beginnings of Occultist Kabbalah', 118.

[208] Lévi, 'Cabale', 3:5. Franck was later highly esteemed by British occultists. H. P. Blavatsky (*Isis*, 2:38) quotes Franck frequently as 'the learned Hebrew scholar of the Institute and translator of the *Kabala*'. William Wynn Westcott, in a paper presented to the Blavatsky Lodge of the Theosophical Society in 1891, declares that Franck's *La Kabbale* 'should be read by every beginner'; see William Wynn Westcott, 'The Kabalah', *Lucifer* 8:48 (1891), 465–69 and 9:49 (1891), 27–32, repr. in Gilbert (ed.), *Magical Mason*, 81–94, on p. 86. Waite uses quotations from Franck's *La Kabbale* throughout *The Holy Kabbalah* to support his own exegesis.

What a strange destiny is that of the Jews! scapegoats, martyrs and saviours of the world! a vital people, a courageous and hardy race, which persecutions have always preserved intact, because it has not yet accomplished its mission![209]

Franck's *La Kabbale* furnished Lévi not only with ideas, but also with handy French translations of many passages of the *Zohar* unavailable from the minimal selection in the *Kabbala denudata*, as well as a French translation of the *Sefer Yetsirah*.[210] Lévi also appropriated Franck's much-contested theory of the Zoroastrian origins of the Kabbalah, although the idea already enjoyed widespread circulation in both scholarly and esoteric circles as a result of new investigations into Persian and Sanskrit literature.[211] Franck's belief in the antiquity of the *Idra Rabba*, one of the three Zoharic selections translated by Knorr for the *Kabbala denudata*, was also taken up by Lévi,[212] and this idea persisted among Golden Dawn adepts into the twentieth century, even in the face of scholarly insistence on the medieval provenance of the text.[213]

It is likely that Lévi and Franck knew each other personally through their mutual Polish contacts. Although

---

[209] Lévi, *Dogme*, 50.

[210] For Franck's translation of the *Sefer Yetsirah*, interspersed with his own comments, see Franck, *La Kabbale*, 103–19.

[211] Franck, *La Kabbale*, 205. For Scholem's dismissal of Franck's Zoroastrian conclusions, see Scholem, *Origins*, 6. For early nineteenth-century German sources for the idea, see Jonathan M. Elukin, 'A New Essenism: Heinrich Graetz and Mysticism', *JHI* 59:1 (1998), 135–48. For the spread of the idea of Zoroastrian and Indian 'ur-religions', see Poliakov, *Aryan Myth*, 183–214. For the nineteenth-century French academic consensus on the Kabbalah's absorption of Zoroastrianism, Gnosticism, and Alexandrian Neoplatonism, see Gedaliahu Stroumsa, 'Gnosis and Judaism in Nineteenth Century Christian Thought', in Eveline Goodman-Thau, Gert Mattenklott, and Christoph Schulte (eds.), *Kabbala und Romantik* (Tübingen: Max Niemeyer Verlag, 1994), 43–57. See Munk, *Mélanges*, 467–69, and Munk, *Palestine*, 519–24, for Munk's belief, contradicting Franck, that the Kabbalah first emerged in late antique Alexandrian Jewish circles.

[212] Franck, *La Kabbale*, 50.

[213] For Mathers' claim of the antiquity of the *Idra Rabba*, see Chapter Four. For Waite's claim that this treatise, in contrast to other sections of the *Zohar*, has an ancient origin, see Chapter Five.

Lévi freely acknowledged the debt he owed, for Hebrew manuscripts as well as financial support, to Polish Catholic aristocrats such as the Counts Braszynsky (Branicki) and Mniszech,[214] and unhesitatingly declared the Polish poet Adam Mickiewicz to be a Kabbalist,[215] the only scholar who has recognised the importance of this group of Polish exiles for the development of Lévi's Kabbalah is James Webb, who refers to this circle as 'Lévi's Polish masters'.[216] However, Webb does not pursue the implications of his research any earlier than 1852, making the usual assumption that Lévi was first initiated into the Kabbalah at that time because he adopted his Hebrew pseudonym in the following year.[217] The

---

[214] For Count Branicki and his sons, see Scheps, *Adam Mickiewicz*, 75; for their relationship with Lévi, see Webb, *Flight from Reason*, 170; Chacornac, *Éliphas Lévi*, 192–94. For Count Mniszech, who provided Lévi with both manuscripts and money, see Lévi's will, dated 26 May 1875 and reproduced in Chacornac, *Éliphas Lévi*, 283.
[215] For Mickiewicz as a Kabbalist, see Lévi, *Dogme*, 32.
[216] On Lévi's 'Polish masters', see Webb, *Flight from Reason*, 181.
[217] Webb, *Flight from Reason*, 169. For the assumption that Lévi learned the Kabbalah in 1852 from the Polish mathematician Józef Maria Hoëné-Wronski (1778–1853), see McIntosh, *Éliphas Lévi*, 96–100; Decker *et al.*, *Wicked Pack*, 183. Wronski, despite his occult proclivities, is still respected by students of differential equations; see D. Bushaw, 'Wronski's Canons of Logarithms', *MM* 56:2 (1983), 91–97, including an extensive bibliography; A. G. Barabashev, 'On the Impact of the World Outlook on Mathematical Creativity', *PM* 2–3:1 (1988), 1–20, on pp. 12–13. In French occult circles, Wronski's work continues to exercise appeal; see, for example, Marie-Louise Herboulet, *La loi de Wronski appliquée à l'astrologie* (Garches: Éditions du Nouvel Humanisme, 1949), 11. Herboulet describes Wronski's 'law' in terms which echo, in a less poetic fashion, Lévi's emphasis on the dynamics of the universe being based on the Kabbalistic polarity of Mercy and Severity, with Love as the central pillar of equilibrium: 'Nothing can exist without its opposite; action emanates from one pole, reaction from the opposite pole. Between these two poles is situated the neutral point. This last is the pivot of the base of the edifice'. However, Lévi had already encountered this doctrine in Gikatilla's *Sha'are Orah*, and it is possible that Wronski learned as much Kabbalah from Lévi as Lévi did from Wronski. For Wronski's messianism, see Webb, *Flight From Reason*, 164–69; Waldemar Chrostowski, 'The Suffering, Chosenness and Mission of the Polish Nation', *REE* 9:4 (1991), 1–14. Lévi, who was acquainted with Wronski for less than a year before the latter's death, expresses considerable ambivalence toward this Polish colleague. In *Dogme*, 75, Lévi credits Wronski with 'an absolute reform of all sciences',

most likely living source who may have provided Lévi with instruction in the Kabbalah earlier than 1852 is Mickiewicz (1798–1855), who was a refugee in Paris during the 1840s.[218] Mickiewicz' Jewish ancestry has been a subject of discomfort for some of his biographers, and the Kabbalistic themes in his work have only recently been acknowledged by scholars of eastern European literature.[219] His enthusiastic participation in Franco-Jewish political circles, his support of Polish-Jewish rapprochement and Jewish emancipation, and his close involvement in Kabbalist and Martinist fringe Masonic orders in Russia has been investigated only in the last few years.[220] The Polish poet's close relationship with a fellow exile – Count Xavier Branicki, who, along with his two sons, Alexander and Constantin, provided Lévi with both money and Hebrew manuscripts – is discussed in Scheps' short biographical work on Mickiewicz' Jewish connections and

---

while in *Histoire*, 477–79, he mocks 'the god Wronski' for trying to sell his occult secrets for 150,000 francs.

[218] For Mickiewicz' involvement with French-Jewish circles, Lévi's with Polish Kabbalist circles, and their overlapping contacts and friends, see Webb, *Flight from Reason*, 155–70; Abraham G. Duker, 'Mickiewicz and the Jewish Problem', in Manfred Kridl (ed.), *Adam Mickiewicz, Poet of Poland* (New York: Columbia University Press, 1951), 108–25. For Mickiewicz' intellectual contacts, see Edmond Marek, *Destinées françaises de l'oeuvre messianique d'Adam Mickiewicz* (Fribourg: Galley et Cie, 1945). For Mickiewicz' messianic proclivities, see Adam Mickiewicz, *Les Slaves: Cours professé au Collège de France (1842–44)* (Paris: Musée Adam Mickiewicz, 1914). For Crémieux' relationship with Mickiewicz, see Adolphe Crémieux, letter to Armand Lévy (20 May 1867), cited in Kridl (ed.), *Adam Mickiewicz*, 208. For Mickiewicz' instruction in the Kabbalah, see Scheps, *Adam Mickiewicz*, 97–100.

[219] For the absence of references to the Jewish and Kabbalistic elements in Mickiewicz' life and work, see W. Lednicki, 'Mickiewicz at the Collège de France, 1840–1940', *Slavonic Year-Book, American Series*, Vol. 1 (1941), 149–72; Manfred Kridl, 'Two Champions of a New Christianity: Lammenais and Mickiewicz', *CL* 4:3 (1952), 239–67. For Kabbalistic themes in Mickiewicz' work, see Stuart Goldberg, 'Konrad and Jacob: A Hypothetical Kabbalistic Subtext in Adam Mickiewicz's *Forefathers' Eve*, Part III', *SEEJ* 45:4 (2001), 695–715; Karen C. Underhill, '*Aux Grand Hommes de la Parole*: On the Verbal Messiah in Adam Mickiewicz's Paris Lectures', *SEEJ* 45:4 (2001), 716–31.

[220] For the Russian Martinist-Masonic orders with which Mickiewicz was involved, see Burmistrov and Endel, 'Place of Kabbalah'.

ancestry.[221]

Franck's involvement with Polish Kabbalists such as Mickiewicz and Soloweyczyk,[222] and the sympathy which both Lévi and Franck evidenced toward the unfortunate fate of Poland after its partition and abortive uprisings in 1830 and 1848, make it probable that they were in direct contact.[223] Franck, who outlived Lévi by nearly a quarter of a century, displayed a surprising public sympathy for the occult society founded by Papus and Stanislas de Guaita in the 1890s and based primarily on Lévi's work. Lévi and Franck also had mutual friends in the world of Romantic socialist literature and politics.[224] Franck was critical of the Lurianic Kabbalah, describing Luria as a man 'of sick mind' and relying almost entirely on the *Zohar* to present his philosophical interpretation of Kabbalistic texts.[225] Lévi would have learned no Lurianic Kabbalah from this particular Jewish source. But the Polish refugees – particularly Mickiewicz – brought with them from their homeland a current of Lurianic Kabbalah tinged with Hasidic magical practices, Polish Catholic messianism, and 'irregular' Masonic rituals.[226] It is unlikely

---

[221] Scheps, *Adam Mickiewicz*, 75. Count Xavier Branicki also published R. Soloweyczyk's *Kol Kore* in Polish in 1879. Although Mickiewicz was dead by the time Soloweyczyk's book appeared in French, the poet's estate is indicated as one of the rabbi's financial supporters.

[222] Franck's link with Mickiewicz appears to have been by way of the Collège de France, where Mickiewicz received his post through Crémieux' influence. Franck and Munk both lectured at the Collège, as did Rabbi Lazare Wogue, who translated Soloweyczyk's *Kol Kore* into French.

[223] See Alphonse-Louis Constant [Éliphas Lévi], *Le deuil de Pologne: protestations de la démocratie française et du socialisme universel* (Paris: Le Gallois, 1847). For French responses to the continuing Polish crisis, including those of Mickiewicz, Franck, Crémieux, and Munk, see Brown, 'Comité Franco-Polonais'; Abraham G. Duker, 'Jewish Emancipation and the Polish Insurrection of 1863: Jan Czynski's Letter of 1862 to Ludwik Królikowski', *PAAJR* 46 (1979–80), 87–103.

[224] For the network of relationships between Franck, Munk, Crémieux, and Romantic socialist writers and editors, see Graetz, *Jews in Nineteenth-Century France*, 194–248.

[225] Franck, *La Kabbale*, 3–4.

[226] For Kabbalistic elements in 'irregular' Eastern European Freemasonry, see Katz, *Jews and Freemasons*, 26–53; McIntosh, *Rose Cross*, 161–78; Burmistrov and Endel, 'Place of Kabbalah'; Le Forestier, *Franc-Maçonnerie*, 936–75; Godwin, *Theosophical*

that Lévi would have ignored the obvious advantages of a personal contact with the respected patron of these living Kabbalistic sources.

HOW THE KABBALAH CROSSED THE CHANNEL

A current of Kabbalistic ideas, symbols, and practices had existed in various streams of British esoteric thought from the thirteenth century onward. This British Kabbalistic current is discussed more fully in the next chapter. But the particular forms in which Lévi utilised Jewish texts transformed the Kabbalah into the primary inspiration of the Victorian occult revival. Kenneth Mackenzie's meetings with Lévi in 1861 acted as a catalyst, focusing the awareness of British occultists on the possibilities of the Kabbalah as an overarching system that could combine Hermetic, Rosicrucian, and Masonic themes with powerful practical magic while remaining firmly within the Judaeo-Christian esoteric tradition. Mackenzie, along with his fellow occultist William Wynn Westcott, later became a member of the Societas Rosicruciana in Anglia, founded in 1865, and it was initially through this quasi-Masonic, quasi-Rosicrucian channel, already replete with Kabbalistic symbolism, that Lévi's Kabbalah began to be circulated before Blavatsky brought it to the attention of her vast reading public.[227]

By the time of his demise in 1875, Lévi's name had become one to conjure with in British occult circles. When

---

Enlightenment, 122–23, 220–22. For Hasidic magical practices, see Idel, *Hasidism*, 171–88; Moshe Idel, 'Jewish Magic from the Renaissance Period to Early Hasidism', in Neusner *et al.* (eds.), *Religion, Science, and Magic*, 82–117, on pp. 100–06. For the spread of the Hasidic movement in Poland, see Rachel Elior, *The Paradoxical Ascent to God: The Kabbalistic Theosophy of Habad Hasidism*, trans. Jeffrey M. Green (Albany, NY: State University of New York Press, 1993), 7–11; Morris M. Faierstein, 'Hasidism: The Last Decade in Research', *MJ* 11:1 (1991), 111–24; Raphael Mahler, *Hasidism and the Jewish Enlightenment: Their Confrontation in Galicia and Poland in the First Half of the Nineteenth Century*, trans. Eugene Orenstein, Aaron Klein, and Jenny Machlowitz Klein (New York: The Jewish Publication Society of America, 1985); Bezalel Safran (ed.), *Hasidism: Continuity or Innovation?* (Cambridge, MA: Harvard University Press, 1988); Adam Teller, 'Hasidism and the Challenge of Geography: The Polish Background to the Spread of the Hasidic Movement', *AJSR* 30:1 (2006), 1–29.

[227] For the SRIA and its Kabbalistic proclivities, see Chapter Three.

Blavatsky's first work, *Isis Unveiled*, was published in the same year as Lévi's death, her critics, much to her annoyance, quickly identified the book as 'a rehash of Éliphas Lévi'.[228] Managing to rise above such 'base diatribes', she continued to refer to Lévi as 'the most learned Kabalist and Occultist of our Age in Europe'.[229] Blavatsky, whose Theosophical Society was responsible for making Lévi's work widely accessible to an English-speaking readership, borrowed some of her most important concepts from him, including the 'astral light' and the seminal doctrine of a gradual spiritual evolution of both individual and group souls through successive incarnations, borrowed almost entirely from Part Two of Lévi's *La science des esprits* – itself a virtual paraphrase of Knorr's translation of the Lurianic *Sefer ha-Gilgulim*, called *De revolutionibus animarum* in the *Kabbala denudata*.[230] British occultists consistently offered Lévi the highest accolades. Waite, who translated Lévi's most important works and was also his most severe critic, nevertheless conceded that Lévi was 'the most fascinating interpreter of occult philosophy in the West'.[231] Westcott, whose Tarot system was heavily indebted to Lévi, called him a 'great Rosicrucian Kabalist'.[232] Mathers,

---

[228] H. P. Blavatsky, 'My Books', *Lucifer* 8:45 (1891), 241–47, on pp. 242–43, repr. in Blavatsky, CW13, 191–202, on p. 194. For Blavatsky's plagiarism of Lévi, see William Emmette Coleman, 'The Sources of Madame Blavatsky's Writings', in Vsevolod Sergyevich Solovyoff, *A Modern Priestess of Isis* (London: Longmans, Green & Co., 1895), 353–66.

[229] H. P. Blavatsky, 'Notice', *Theosophist* 3:1 (1881), 1.

[230] Éliphas Lévi, *La science des esprits: Révelation du dogme secret des Kabbalistes, esprit occulte des évangiles, appréciation des doctrines et des phénomènes spirits* (Paris: Germer-Baillière, 1865; repr. Paris: Elibron Classics, 2005), 124–71. For *gilgul* (transmigration or reincarnation), see Scholem, *Mystical Shape*, 197–250; Joseph Dan, 'Jewish Gnosticism?', *JSQ* 2 (1995), 309–28; and the references below in Chapter Five. For an English translation of the *Sha'ar ga-Gilgulim* ('Gate of Transmigrations'), another version of the same treatise, see Bar Chaim (trans.), *Shaar HaGilgulim*.

[231] A. E. Waite, 'Preface to Second Edition', in *Mysteries*, xiii. For Waite's views on Lévi, see Chapter Five.

[232] William Wynn Westcott, 'The Rosicrucians, Past and Present, at Home and Abroad', in R. A. Gilbert (ed.), *The Magical Mason: Forgotten Hermetic Writings of William Wynn Westcott, Physician and Magus* (Wellingborough: Aquarian Press, 1983), 40–47, on p. 45. For Westcott's debt to Lévi's Tarot, see Decker and Dummett, *Occult Tarot*, 52–56, and below, Chapter Five.

who co-founded the Hermetic Order of the Golden Dawn with Westcott, referred to Lévi as 'that great philosopher and Qabalist of the present century'.[233] And Aleister Crowley, viewing Lévi as a genius of the highest order, paid himself the ultimate compliment by declaring that he was Lévi's reincarnation.[234]

Lévi's work was freely plundered on both sides of the Atlantic, often without acknowledgement.[235] He quickly achieved posthumous mythic status as a 'high initiate' and the purported preceptor of innumerable secret societies, and numerous occult groups claimed him as a member in order to enhance their own status.[236] Although Lévi was no scholar by any contemporary standard, he also received a posthumous scholarly mantle. When Mathers' *The Kabbalah Unveiled* was given a scathing review in *The Jewish Chronicle*, partly because of Mathers' insistence that the *Zohar* had been written in antiquity, Mathers replied angrily that his knowledge of the *Zohar's* history was based on the highest possible scholarly source: Éliphas Lévi.[237] Lévi's books even became protagonists in various works of occult fiction.[238]

---

[233] S. L. MacGregor Mathers, *The Kabbalah Unveiled* (London: George Redway, 1887; repr. York Beach, ME: Weiser Books, 1970), 17. For Mathers' acknowledgement of Lévi, see Mathers, *Kabbalah Unveiled*, 17–18, 35–37.

[234] Aleister Crowley, *The Confessions of Aleister Crowley: An Autohagiography*, ed. John Symonds and Kenneth Grant (Paris: Mandrake Press, 1929; repr. New York: Bantam, 1971), 183; Aleister Crowley, *Magick in Theory and Practice* (Paris: Lecram, 1929; reissued, Secaucus, NJ: Castle Books, 1991), 51–53; John Symonds, *The Great Beast: The Life of Aleister Crowley* (London: Rider & Co., 1951), 61.

[235] See, for example, Albert Pike, *Morals and Dogma of the Ancient and Accepted Scottish Rite Freemasonry*, 2 vols. (self-published, 1871; repr. Charleston, NC: L. H. Jenkins, 1949). For Lévi's influence on Pike, see Uzzel, *Éliphas Lévi*, 68–97.

[236] See, for example, Westcott's insistence that Lévi was 'a Continental Rosicrucian Initiate' in William Wynn Westcott, 'Data of the History of the Rosicrucians', in Gilbert (ed.), *Magical Mason*, 28–39, on p. 35.

[237] The Editor, 'Review of Samuel Liddell MacGregor Mathers, *The Kabbalah Unveiled*', JC (9 Sept. 1887), 12; S. L. MacGregor Mathers, 'Letter to the Editor', JC (22 Sept. 1887), 6.

[238] See J.-K. Huysmans, *Là-bas* (serialised in *L'Echo de Paris* from February 1891; repr. Paris: Garnier-Flammarion, 1978), 95; Algernon Blackwood, 'The Nemesis of Fire', in Algernon Blackwood, *John*

Nearly a century after the publication of his first Kabbalistic works, he was still viewed as a powerful initiate of European secret societies, and Tarot practitioners today continue to accord him this position in their histories of the cards.[239] Lévi's most important work – *Dogme et rituel*, published in English in 1896 as *Transcendental Magic* – has never been out of print, and every new generation of aspiring magicians still turns to it as one of the foundation texts of modern occultism.

Lévi's Catholicism, and his emphasis on Western esoteric traditions, challenged Blavatsky's antipathy toward the Church and her preference for Eastern doctrines. She was also irritated by Lévi's philosemitism, since it collided with her own well-developed antisemitism.[240] Blavatsky presented the Jews as an 'unspiritual people' who were responsible for 'degrading' and 'desecrating' Aryan traditions; they were afflicted by 'gross realism, selfishness, and sensuality'.[241] In order to justify her use of the Kabbalah while denying the Jews any credit for creating it, she applied a method which she had already found efficacious when faced with the Greek provenance of Orphic doctrines: she declared that the Kabbalah was Indian in origin, passed on to the Babylonians and Egyptians and thence to the Jews, who mutilated it.[242]

Silence, Physician Extraordinary (London: Evelyn Nash, 1908, repr. in *The Complete John Silence Stories*, ed. S. T. Joshi, Mineola, NY: Dover, 1997), 84–143, on p. 118; Edward Bulwer-Lytton, *A Strange Story: An Alchemical Novel* (London: George Routledge & Sons, 1861; repr. Berkeley, CA: Shambala, 1973), 386, n. 2.

[239] See, for example, E. Swinburne Clymer, *The Book of Rosicruciae*, 3 vols. (Quakertown, PA: Philosophical Publishing, 1946), 1:xv. For Lévi as a Grand Master of the Rosicrucians, see Christine Payne-Towler, *The Underground Stream: Esoteric Tarot Revealed* (Eugene, OR: Noreah Press, 1999), 6; Christine Payne-Towler, 'The Continental Tarots', <http://www.tarot.com/pdf/continental.pdf>.

[240] For Blavatsky's contribution to Aryan racial theory, see Joan Leopold, 'The Aryan Theory of Race', *IESHR* 7 (1970), 271–97. See also the comprehensive discussion of race theory in *fin-de-siècle* occultism in Peter Staudenmeier, 'Occultism, Race and Politics in German-speaking Europe, 1880–1940: A Survey of the Historical Literature', *EHQ* 39:1 (2009), 47–70.

[241] Blavatsky, *Secret Doctrine*, 2:492–94. See also Blavatsky, *Secret Doctrine*, 1:230, discussed in Chapter Three.

[242] See Blavatsky, CW14, 293, 308. For Blavatsky's claim that the 'real' Kabbalah was misused and subsequently forgotten by the Jews, see Blavatsky, CW14, 194.

Her assessment of Lévi is not, however, entirely lacking in insight:

> Christ was in his [Lévi's] sight more of an ideal than of a living Man-God or an historical personage. Moses and Christ, if real entities, were human initiates into the arcane mysteries in his opinion....The mysticism of the official church, which seeks to absorb the human in the divine nature of Christ, is strongly criticized by her ex-representative. More than anything else Éliphas Lévi is then a Jewish Kabalist.[243]

Lévi's 'occultist' Kabbalah thus remains Jewish in Blavatsky's view, and its paradoxical blend of ancient authority with precocious modernity, psychology with mysticism, and religious devotion with the potency of the human will, seems to have fascinated British occultists seeking a path of equilibrium between the soulless aridity of scientism and the claustrophobic strictures of orthodox faith.

Lévi may have also exercised a special appeal because he founded no school or organisation and his ideas require no allegiance to any esoteric order, thereby allowing British occultists complete freedom to set up their own. Ronald Hutton points out that Lévi 'stripped the secret tradition of identification with any one modern political programme; it now supplied a powerful implicit criticism of orthodox Christianity and an alternative history of Western culture which could be taken up by radicals on both the left and right'.[244] Eclectic and self-contradictory, Lévi's work, like the Kabbalah itself, encourages further speculation rather than obedient discipleship, and his dislike of interference in his private beliefs is reflected in his brief but hostile encounter with 'regular' Freemasonry:

> I ceased to be a Freemason because the Freemasons, excommunicated by the Pope, no longer believe in tolerating Catholicism; I thus separated from them to protect my freedom of conscience and to avoid being associated with their reprisals, perhaps excusable, if not legitimate, but certainly inconsequential, for the essence of Freemasonry is

---

[243] H. P. Blavatsky, 'A Posthumous Publication', *Theosophist* 2:10 (1881), 211–12, repr. in H. P. Blavatsky, *Kabala and Kabalism* (Los Angeles, CA: The Theosophy Company, 1912), 45, repr. in Blavatsky, CW3, 207.

[244] Hutton, *Triumph of the Moon*, 72.

the tolerance of all beliefs.[245]
Despite his loyalty to the Church, albeit a Church largely of his own imagining,[246] his wide circle of friends of various religious and political persuasions reflects a tolerance unusual for his time. Although as a professed Catholic he could hardly be expected to be sympathetic to the Protestant Reformation, he is clearly in harmony with its spirit. In a posthumously published manuscript called *Paradoxes of the Highest Science*, he declares:

> Before the abuses of the Romish Church, protestation is a right and consequently a truth....Catholicity, that is to say Universality, is the character of true religion...but Catholicism is a party and consequently a falsehood....When Catholicity shall have been established throughout the world, there will be no more Catholicism at Rome.[247]

But Lévi's appeal as an individual cannot explain the power that his Kabbalah wielded over the endemically antisemitic social milieu of nineteenth- century British occultism. Four factors may have contributed to this surprising preoccupation among the esoterically inclined Victorian middle classes.[248] The first and most obvious factor is that the Kabbalah, although Jewish, had been perceived by Christian interpreters for many centuries as containing secret allusions to the Christian revelation, and could thus be accommodated to the heterodox but nevertheless broadly Christian sympathies of British occultists; it is not an 'alien'

---

[245] Éliphas Lévi, *Le livre des sages* (Paris: Chacornac Frères, 1912; repr. Le Tremblay: Diffusion Rosicrucienne, 1995), 13. For Lévi's initiatory speech to the Lodge 'Rose du parfait silence', see Éliphas Lévi, *Le livre des splendeurs* (Paris: Chamuel, 1894), 169. For the annoyance the speech caused among the brethren, see Charles Caubet, *Souvenirs 1860–1889* (Paris: Cerf, 1893), 4. For anti-Catholic politics in the 'Rose du parfait silence' at the time of Lévi's initiation, see Philip Nord, 'Republicanism and Utopian Vision: French Freemasonry in the 1860s and 1870s', *JMH* 63:2 (1991), 213–29.

[246] For Lévi's effort to reconcile his Catholicism with his occultism, see Alphonse-Louis Constant [Éliphas Lévi], *Le livre des larmes ou le Christ consolateur: essai de conciliation entre l'église catholique et la philosophie moderne* (Paris: Paulier, 1845).

[247] Lévi, *Paradoxes*, 117.

[248] For the Golden Dawn's 'largely middle class' membership, see Owen, *Place of Enchantment*, 46, 61.

esotericism, but sits firmly within the Western Judaeo-Christian tradition. The second factor is the ongoing myth of the unique efficacy of Jewish magic. This perception of the Jews first appears in Christian literature in texts such as Origen's reply to Celsus, who declares that the Jews 'worship angels and are addicted to sorcery, in which Moses was their instructor'.[249] This myth enjoyed continuing potency in the Christian world, from the medieval adulation of Solomon as 'king of the demons' and hero of the magical grimoires to the fifteenth- and sixteenth-century Kabbalistic exegeses of Pico, Reuchlin, and Agrippa, and the Rosicrucian and Masonic currents of the seventeenth and eighteenth centuries. It even reared its head in the British political climate of the late 1870s, when Disraeli, having offended the Christian clergy by his pragmatic support of the Muslim Turks against Russian ambitions in the Balkans, was denounced as a 'superlative Hebrew conjuror' and a purveyor of 'cabalistic sorcery' who had mysteriously bewitched the British public.[250] The myth of Jewish magical expertise can be seen in the writings of Golden Dawn disciples such as Arthur Machen, who expressed his hope that an 'Aryan' Kabbalah might be formulated that could prove as potent as the 'Semitic' Kabbalah, which 'tells all the hidden secrets of our beginning and our journey and our ending'.[251] Long after the Old Testament was relegated to the realm of literary myth, the

---

[249] Origen, *Against Celsus*, trans. F. Crombie and W. H. Cairns, in *The Anti-Nicene Fathers*, IV, ed. Alexander Roberts and James Donaldson (New York: Charles Scribner's Sons, 1899), 1.28. See also Augustine, *City of God, Books VIII–XVI*, ed. Vernon J. Bourke, trans. Gerald G. Walsh, Demetrius B. Zema, Grace Monohan, and Daniel J. Honan, in *Writings of St. Augustine*, Vol. 7 (Washington, DC: Catholic University of America Press, 1963), 129–30; Gager, *Moses*, 134–61; Jan Assman, *Moses the Egyptian: The Memory of Egypt in Western Monotheism* (Cambridge, MA: Harvard University Press, 1997), 91–143; Kilcher, 'Moses of Sinai'.

[250] Edward Jenkins, *Haverholme, or the Apotheosis of Jingo: A Satire* (London: William Mullan & Son, 1878), 51; Cecil Roth, *Benjamin Disraeli: Earl of Beaconsfield* (New York: Philosophical Library, 1952), 84–85; *Spectator*, 2 November 1878, 1357, cited in Anthony S. Wohl, '"Dizzi-Ben-Dizzi": Disraeli as Alien', *JBS* 34:3 (1995), 375–411, on p. 404. For public perceptions of Disraeli's 'Hebrew' proclivities, see Colin Holmes, *Anti-Semitism in British Society, 1876–1939* (London: Edward Arnold Ltd., 1979), 10–12.

[251] Arthur Machen, *Things Near and Far* (London: Martin Secker, 1926), 23–24.

imagined superiority of Jewish magic has continued to exercise its fascination, reappearing in popular culture in the late twentieth century through the film, *Raiders of the Lost Ark*,[252] and the cult television series, *The X-Files*, in an episode in which a group of Hasidic Jews from Brooklyn creates a *golem* through the linguistic magic of the *Sefer Yetsirah*.[253]

The third factor in the Kabbalah's fascination for British occultists in the late nineteenth century is its messianic message. Alex Owen points out that the occult revival was 'intimately bound up with the desire for an immediate regeneration of society'.[254] The messianic idea, although present in all Kabbalistic literature,[255] is articulated in the Lurianic Kabbalah in a new form that could easily be incorporated into the 'disenchanted' worldview of the late nineteenth century: the responsibility for facilitating the great restitution of cosmic harmony lies on human rather than divine shoulders, and depends on human will rather than divine grace. First engendered by a people who had been severed from their primary religious locus and had lived in diaspora for twelve centuries, the Kabbalah has always presented the themes of homelessness, painful exile, alienation, abandonment of and by God, the fracturing of cosmic harmony, and the yearning for personal and collective redemption. The poetic and mythic properties of the Kabbalah have had an enduring impact on writers from *fin-de-siècle* symbolist poets to postmodern philosophers such as Eco, Derrida, and Ricoeur.[256] The Lurianic Kabbalah,

---

[252] *Raiders of the Lost Ark*, written by Lawrence Kasdan and George Lucas, directed by Steven Spielberg, with Harrison Ford, Karen Allen, and Paul Freeman (Paramount Pictures, 1981).

[253] *The X-Files*: 'Kaddish', written by Howard Gordon, directed by Kim Manners, with David Duchovny, Gillian Anderson, and Justine Miceli (Episode 15, Season 4, 20th Century Fox, 1994).

[254] Owen, *Place of Enchantment*, 24–25.

[255] For the messianic theme in Judaism, see Scholem, *Messianic Idea*; Idel, *Messianic Mystics*; Yehudah Liebes, *Studies in Jewish Myth and Jewish Messianism*, trans. Batya Stein (Albany, NY: State University of New York Press, 1993); R. J. Zvi Werblowsky, 'The Safed Revival and Its Aftermath', in Green (ed.), *Jewish Spirituality, Vol. 2*, 7–33; Stephen Sharot, *Messianism, Mysticism, and Magic: A Sociological Analysis of Jewish Religious Movements* (Chapel Hill, NC: University of North Carolina Press, 1982).

[256] For the Kabbalah's 'literary modernism', see Beitchman, *Alchemy of the Word*, 28; Albert Beguin, 'Poetry and Occultism', trans. Robert G. Cohn, *YFS* 4 (1949), 12–25. See also the computer programmed to

emerging after the expulsion of the Jews from their European homeland in 1492, is particularly rich in these themes of isolation, personal and collective suffering, fragmentation, and the longed-for restitution of a damaged cosmos through the power of the human will. The hope of an imminent transformation of society through the 'universal language' of the Kabbalah – viewed as a 'great reconciler' between religion and science – fired the imagination of the disillusioned Catholic Romantic Éliphas Lévi, inspiring him to envision himself as the prophet of a dawning New Age that would bring peace and harmony to a disillusioned and embittered French people.[257] Two decades later, Lévi's Kabbalah exercised the same spell over British occultists in an epoch dominated by evolutionary theories that ejected humans from their central place in a God-created universe, encouraging Dion Fortune, as late as the 1940s, to believe that the Kabbalistic adept could alter the great collective evolutionary progress of the human race and even help to win the war against Germany.[258]

---

calculate permutations of the Tetragrammaton in Umberto Eco, *Foucault's Pendulum*, trans. William Weaver (New York: Harcourt Brace Jovanovich, 1987). For the relationship between Derrida's thought and Kabbalistic hermeneutics, see Jacques Derrida, *Dissemination*, trans. Barbara Johnson (Chicago, IL: University of Chicago Press, 1981), 344; Elliot R. Wolfson, 'Assaulting the Border: Kabbalistic Traces in the Margins of Derrida', *JAAR* 70:3 (2002), 475–514; Moshe Idel, 'White Letters: From R. Levi Isaac of Berditchev's Views to Postmodern Hermeneutics', *MJ* 26:2 (2006), 169–92; Idel, *Absorbing Perfections*, 77–79, 91, 416–23; Susan A. Handelman, *The Slayers of Moses: The Emergence of Rabbinic Interpretation in Modern Literary Theory* (Albany, NY: State University of New York Press, 1982), 15–25, 116–78, 196, 218; J. Lawton Winslade, 'Techno-Kabbalah: The Performative Language of Magick and the Production of Occult Knowledge', *TDR* 44:2 (2000), 84–100. For Ricoeur's Kabbalistic hermeneutics, see Paul Ricoeur, *The Rule of Metaphor: Multi-Disciplinary Studies of the Creation of Meaning in Language*, trans. Robert Czerny (Toronto: University of Toronto Press, 1977); Idel, 'Rabbinism Versus Kabbalism', 284; Idel, *Kabbalah*, 247; Beitchman, *Alchemy of the Word*, 56–57; Handelman, *Slayers of Moses*, 15–25. For Kabbalah as a model for contemporary literary criticism, see Harold Bloom, *Kabbalah and Criticism* (New York: Seabury Press, 1975).

[257] For Lévi's self-presentation as a prophet, see Lévi, *Dogme*, 334–36.

[258] For Fortune's magical efforts to influence the outcome of the Second World War, see Dion Fortune and Gareth Knight, *The Magical Battle of Britain* (London: SIL Trading, 1993); Alan

The precocious modernity of the Kabbalah, particularly in its Lurianic form, made it an attractive focus for occult concerns in the rapidly changing culture of late nineteenth-century Britain. The Kabbalah was developed in very different ways by British occultists in the years following the publication of Lévi's work, and new scholarly works on Jewish esoteric lore by both Christians and Jews, as well as new translations of Kabbalistic texts into French and English, expanded the 'knowledge base' from which occult practitioners could draw their interpretations. These developments will be explored in depth in the following chapters. But the prevailing understanding of the Kabbalah among British occultists preserves an allegiance to the core themes of Lévi's pioneering vision. These themes are, in turn, integral to the currents of the medieval Jewish Kabbalah, although they are articulated in modern vocabularies that reflect a complex process of adaptation which often obscures their earlier roots. 'Occultist' Kabbalah as it is expressed in Lévi's system would appear to represent the continuity of a particularly vigorous complex of ideas, rather than the reinvention of an older tradition or the creation of a new one.

Richardson, *The Magical Life of Dion Fortune: Priestess of the 20th Century* (Wellingborough: Aquarian Press, 1987), 227–36; Charles Fielding and Carr Collins, *The Story of Dion Fortune* (Loughborough: Thoth Publications, 1998), 106–09; Dave Evans and David Sutton, 'The Magical Battle of Britain: Fighting Hitler's Nazis with Occult Ritual', *Fortean Times* 267 (September 2010), at <http://www.forteantimes.com/features/articles/4435/the_magical_battle_of_britain.html>.

CHAPTER THREE

MASONIC MYSTERIES:
WILLIAM WYNN WESTCOTT
AND HIS 'ROSICRUCIAN' KABBALAH

Masonry has derived its temple symbolism, as it has
almost all its symbolic ideas, from the Hebrew type, and
thus makes the temple the symbol of the lodge.[1]
> – Albert Mackey (1858)

The basis of the Western occultism of medieval Europe is
the Kabalah of the medieval Hebrew Rabbis.[2]
> – William Wynn Westcott (1913)

THE RHIZOME AND THE FLOWER

During the 1860s, while Éliphas Lévi immersed himself in
the mysteries of the Kabbalah in his tiny apartment in the
Avenue de Maine, esoteric groups in Britain had quietly
begun to develop an increasing enthusiasm for obscure
Masonic rituals and a variety of 'higher' Masonic degrees.[3]

---

[1] Albert Mackey, *A Lexicon of Freemasonry* (Philadelphia, PA: Moss,
Brother, 1858), 2:766.
[2] Westcott, 'Rosicrucians, Past and Present', 45.
[3] For the proliferation of Masonic degrees in nineteenth-century
Britain, see Howe, 'Fringe Masonry'; R. A. Gilbert, 'William Wynn
Westcott and the Esoteric School of Masonic Research', *AQC* 100
(1987), 6–20; Henrik Bogdan, *Western Esotericism and Rituals of
Initiation* (Albany, NY: State University of New York Press, 2007),
95–120; Godwin, *Theosophical Enlightenment*, 218–22; Hutton,
Triumph of the Moon, 52–61. For an imaginative *fin-de-siècle* history of
these rituals and degrees, see John Yarker, *The Arcane Schools: A
Review of their Origin and Antiquity* (Belfast: William Tait, 1909). For
the 'higher' degrees, see Owen, *Place of Enchantment*, 53–57; Jan
Snoek, 'On the Creation of Masonic Degrees: A Method and its
Fruits', in Faivre and Hanegraaff (eds.), *Western Esotericism and the
Science of Religion*, 145–90; Jean-Pierre Laurant, 'Esotericism in
Freemasonry: The Example of François-Nicolas Noël's *La Géometrie
du Maçon* (1812)', in Faivre and Hanegraaff (eds.), *Western
Esotericism and the Science of Religion*, 191–200; Edmond Mazet,

This understated but significant return to the 'secret society' propensities of the earlier occultism of the late eighteenth century, although not yet a full-blown 'occult revival', coincided with major shifts in the religious landscape. As Owen Chadwick observes, 'In the [eighteen-]sixties Britain... entered the age of Doubt, in the singular and with a capital D'.[4] The rise of incarnational theology with its emphasis on the immanence of God in the world and the perception of Christ as exemplar rather than saviour,[5] new geological, archaeological, and linguistic discoveries,[6] and the dissemination of Darwin's theories of evolution, severely challenged the authority of the Old Testament and encouraged Christian theologians to understand scripture in a symbolic rather than a literal way. The 'evolutionary paradigm' which first began to emerge in this decade was reflected in both a faith in science as the hallmark of cultural superiority, and a growing belief in spiritual evolution which would later find its apotheosis in the various currents of *fin-de-siècle* occultism.[7]

'Freemasonry and Esotericism', in Faivre and Needleman (eds.), *Modern Esoteric Spirituality*, 248–76.

[4] Chadwick, *Secularization of the European Mind*, 184.

[5] For incarnational theology, see John McLeod Campbell, *The Nature of Atonement and Its Relation to Remission of Sins and Eternal Life* (Cambridge: Macmillan & Co., 1856). For McLeod's life and influence, see Peter Kenneth Stevenson, *God in Our Nature: The Incarnational Theology of John McLeod Campbell* (Chester: Paternoster Press, 1969; repr. Eugene, OR: Wipf & Stock, 2006); George M. Tuttle, *John McLeod Campbell on Christian Atonement: So Rich a Soul* (Edinburgh: Handsel Press, 1986); David Feldman, *Englishmen and Jews: Social Relations and Political Culture, 1840–1914* (New Haven, CT: Yale University Press, 1994), 83–89. For the emergence of philosophical idealism in Britain, linked with this religious current, see Sandra Den Otter, *British Idealism and Social Explanation: A Study in Late Victorian Thought* (Oxford: Clarendon Press, 1996).

[6] For the decipherment of cuneiform, see Lesley Adkins, *Empires of the Plain: Henry Rawlinson and the Lost Languages of Babylon* (London: HarperCollins, 2003); Stanley Casson, *The Discovery of Man* (New York: Harper and Brothers, 1939), 207–08. For the archaeology of the second half of the nineteenth century, see Bruce G. Trigger, *A History of Archaeological Thought* (Cambridge: Cambridge University Press, 1989), 27–72. For Egyptian archaeology during the nineteenth century, see Donald Malcolm Reid, *Whose Pharoahs?: Archaeology, Museums, and Egyptian National Identity from Napoleon to World War I* (Berkeley, CA: University of California Press, 2002), 21–63.

[7] For the 'evolutionary paradigm' see Joy Dixon, *Divine Feminine: Theosophy and Feminism in England* (Baltimore, MD: Johns Hopkins

The spiritualist movement, imported from America in the 1850s, conjoined with a renewed enthusiasm for mesmerism following James Braid's discovery of hypnosis in the 1840s,[8] fostering the growth of one of the dominant themes of the period: the quest for a science of the supernatural.[9] The Theosophical Society as a major cultural phenomenon was inextricably linked with the rise of spiritualism,[10] and it might also be argued that British occultism as it developed in the last decades was equally linked with the rise of Theosophy.

Identifying each of these currents as the 'cause' of the subsequent one may, however, rely too much on what Moshe

---

University Press, 2001), 19; Hanegraaff, 'Study of Western Esotericism', 498; Hanegraaff, *New Age Religion*, 482–513.

[8] See Fred Kaplan, '"Mesmeric Mania": The Early Victorians and Animal Magnetism', *JHI* 35:4 (1974), 691–702; Robin Waterfield, *Hidden Depths: The Story of Hypnosis* (London: Macmillan, 2002), 157–210; James Webb, *The Occult Establishment* (Glasgow: Richard Drew, 1981), 353–54; Ellenberger, *Discovery*, 74–109. For James Braid, see James Braid, *Satanic Agency and Mesmerism* (Manchester: Sims and Dinham, Galt and Anderson, 1842); James Braid, *Magic, Witchcraft, Animal Magnetism, Hypnotism, and Electrobiology* (London: John Churchill, 1852). For Charcot and other 'founding fathers' of modern dynamic psychiatry, see Ellenberger, *Discovery*, 110–81; A. R. G. Owen, *Hysteria, Hypnosis and Healing: The Work of J.-M. Charcot* (London: Dennis Dobson, 1971); Adam Crabtree, *From Mesmer to Freud: Magnetic Sleep and the Roots of Psychological Healing* (New Haven, CT: Yale University Press, 1993); Alan Gauld, *A History of Hypnotism* (Cambridge: Cambridge University Press, 1992).

[9] For the relationship between spiritualism and occultism, see Oppenheim, *Other World*, 159–97. For early twentieth-century works on the spiritualist movement, see Frank Podmore, *Modern Spiritualism: A History and a Criticism*, 2 vols. (London: Methuen, 1902); James Robertson, *Spiritualism: The Open Door to the Unseen Universe. Being Thirty Years of Personal Observation and Experience Concerning Intercourse between the Material and Spiritual Worlds* (London: L. N. Fowler, 1908). For contemporary discussions, see Ruth Brandon, *The Spiritualists: The Passion for the Occult in the Nineteenth and Twentieth Centuries* (London: Weidenfeld and Nicolson, 1983); Logic Barrow, *Independent Spirits: Spiritualism and the English Plebeians, 1850–1910* (London: Routledge & Kegan Paul, 1986); Godwin, *Theosophical Enlightenment*, 187–204; Owen, *Darkened Room*; Oppenheim, *Other World*; Elana Gomel, '"Spirits in the Material World": Spiritualism and Identity in the Fin de Siècle', *VLC* 35 (2007), 189–213.

[10] See Warren Sylvester Smith, *The London Heretics 1870–1914* (New York: Dodd Mead, 1968), 142.

Idel calls a 'proximist' view of history: viewing each significant historical occurence or cultural development as the result of the one immediately preceding it.[11] The esoteric traditions present in Britain from the medieval period onward might equally be seen to have come to flower organically in both the late eighteenth- and late nineteenth-century occult 'revivals' as well as in the Elizabethan age, and particular constellations of social, scientific, political, and religious currents at particular times might be viewed as triggers rather than causes for the emergence of occultism on the public stage at any specific period of history. Spiritualism and Theosophy, while obvious harbingers of an emerging type of religiosity concerned with the accessibility of spiritual dimensions of reality without dependence on clergy, may not necessarily comprise the 'causes' of the occult revival, any more than post-Enlightenment rationalism was the 'cause' of spiritualism, or Maimonidean rationalism in the twelfth century was the 'cause' of the rise of the Kabbalah within Judaism. Such apparently complementary or opposing currents may be seen as arising from the same matrix, and reflect different expressions of a core idea. But whatever paradigm is adopted to explain the remarkable emergence of occultism at the *fin-de-siècle*, its aim was clear, as the spiritualist and historian J. Arthur Hill suggested in 1910: to 'retain our scientific gains, but...extend our vision beyond the material'.[12] The emergence of a new 'occult press', heralded in the 1840s by mesmerist periodicals such as John Elliotson's *The Zoist* and Spencer Hall's *Phreno-Magnet*, catapulted this quest into the public domain. Beginning in the 1850s, a number of spiritualist papers, many of which supported particular organisations, achieved wide circulations.[13] Later occult journals such as *The Occultist*, Aleister Crowley's *The Equinox*, and the various periodicals produced by the Theosophical Society (such as *Lucifer*, *The Theosophist*, *The Theosophical Review*, *The Theosophical Quarterly*, and *The Path*) duly took their place in an already thriving periodical

---

[11] Idel, *Hasidism*, 6–9.
[12] J. Arthur Hill, *Spiritualism, Its History, Phenomena, and Doctrine* (London: Cassell, 1910), 298.
[13] *The Spiritualist Newspaper*, for example, affiliated itself with the British National Association of Spiritualists, while *Light* was associated with the London Spiritualist Alliance. For the spiritualist periodicals, see Owen, *Darkened Room*, 24–25, 46–47; Oppenheim, *Other World*, 46–48.

culture. It was largely through these periodicals that the vogue for occultism was publicly created and sustained, transforming it into a powerful cultural movement rather than a scattering of secret societies pursuing their secret ends.[14]

The land of John Dee, Robert Fludd, and Elias Ashmole', observes Joscelyn Godwin, 'has never lacked practitioners of the occult sciences, even if at times they have lain very low.'[15] Although British occultism had apparently all but vanished in the first half of the nineteenth century, it had never really gone to sleep, and its re-emergence in the 1860s sprang from a vigorous rhizome. The 'silence of the occult sciences' at the turn of the nineteenth century is usually attributed to post-Enlightenment rationalism and the anti-revolutionary fervor that associated occult groups with Jacobite sedition at the end of the previous century,[16] and ceremonial magic was 'more or less in abeyance' in British intellectual circles.[17] But the threads which William Wynn Westcott later wove together with Lévi's Kabbalah to create the Hermetic Order of the Golden Dawn were already deeply embedded in the fabric of British esoteric thought. Many of the Kabbalistic themes appropriated by British occultists in the latter decades of the nineteenth century had enjoyed considerable longevity through Freemasonry and 'Hermetic' Rosicrucianism, and were amalgamated with Lévi's interpretation of the Kabbalah in a manner adapted to the changing currents of the time but nevertheless loyal – structurally, philosophically, and in terms of praxis – to older traditions. The convergence of these currents provides a striking paradigm of the ways in which vigorous ideas can adapt to new cultural contingencies and yet preserve their continuity with the past.

---

[14] For the 'occult press', see Mark S. Morrisson, 'The Periodical Culture of the Occult Revival: Esoteric Wisdom, Modernity and Counter-Public Spheres', *JML* 31:2 (2008), 1–22. The Golden Dawn, as a secret society devoted to practical magic, never produced its own journal, but many of its members were regular contributors to *The Occultist, The Occult Review, The Equinox*, G. R. S. Mead's quarterly journal, *The Quest*, and the numerous Theosophical journals.

[15] Godwin, *Theosophical Enlightenment*, 93.

[16] Godwin, *Theosophical Enlightenment*, 140; Hutton, *Triumph of the Moon*, 69.

[17] Hutton, *Triumph of the Moon*, 69.

A small but persistent trickle of published scholarly literature on the Kabbalah is in evidence in Britain throughout the first half of the nineteenth century, mainly produced by Christian clergymen involved in the widespread evangelical movement to convert Jews to Christianity during a period when Jewish emancipation was a topic of considerable social and political concern.[18] These clergymen were often Freemasons, demonstrating the ongoing concern with the Jewish Kabbalah that quietly occupied British as well as European and Russian Freemasons of both 'regular' and 'irregular' persuasions throughout the nineteenth century.[19] One of the most extraordinary writers of this genre was the Reverend John Oxlee (1779–1854), who in 1815 published the first volume of a trilogy of works quoting extensively from Hebrew Kabbalistic texts which he himself had translated, using the centuries-old argument that the ancient Jewish rabbis were well aware of the doctrine of the Trinity and that this was manifest in the trinitarian nature of Kabbalistic theosophy evidenced in texts such as the *Zohar*.[20]

[18] For Jewish emancipation, see Feldman, *Englishmen and Jews*; Robert Liberles, 'The Origins of the Jewish Reform Movement in England', *AJSR* 1 (1976), 121–50; Steven Singer, 'Jewish Religious Thought in Early Victorian London', *AJSR* 10:2 (1985), 181–210; Steven Singer, 'The Anglo-Jewish Ministry in Early Victorian London', *MJ* 5 (1985), 279–99; Lloyd P. Gartner, 'Emancipation, Social Change, and Communal Reconstruction in Anglo-Jewry, 1789–1881', *PAAJR* 54 (1987), 73–116; Thomas Weber, 'Anti-Semitism and Philo-Semitism among the British and German Elites: Oxford and Heidelberg before the First World War', *EHR* 118 (2003), 86–119; Ursula R. Q. Henriques, 'The Jewish Emancipation Controversy in Nineteenth-Century Britain', *PP* 40 (1968), 126–46; Todd M. Endelman, 'The Checkered Career of "Jew" King: A Study in Anglo-Jewish Social History', *AJSR* 7 (1982), 69–100; Todd M. Endelman, 'The Englishness of Jewish Modernity in England', in Jacob Katz (ed.), *Towards Modernity: The European Jewish Model* (New Brunswick, NJ: Transaction Books, 1987), 225–46; David B. Ruderman, *Jewish Enlightenment in an English Key: Anglo-Jewry's Construction of Modern Jewish Thought* (Oxford: Oxford University Press, 2000); David S. Katz, *The Jews in the History of England, 1485–1850* (Oxford: Oxford University Press, 1997), 323–82.

[19] For Kabbalistic currents in Freemasonry, see Schuchard, *Restoring the Temple*, 796–825; Burmistrov and Endel, 'Russian Freemasons', 27–68.

[20] John Oxlee, *The Christian Doctrines of the Trinity and Incarnation, considered and maintained on the Principles of Judaism*, 3 vols. (London: Hatchards, 1815, 1820, 1850). For early modern examples of the use

Oxlee, an accomplished scholar of Latin, Greek, Hebrew, and Aramaic, was not, however, typical of most writers intent on converting Jews. An ardent philosemite as well as a Freemason,[21] he was a frequent contributor to Jewish newspapers such as *The Jewish Chronicle*, and after his death in 1854 was accused of pantheism by no less eminent a detractor than Samuel Taylor Coleridge.[22] In 1856, *The Eclectic Review* published an article on Oxlee's completed three-volume work. The reviewer informed his readers that 'the secret or Kabbalistic doctrines of the Jews have not ceased to be subject-matter of studious investigation', devoted some fifteen pages to explaining those doctrines in detail, and then declared with something akin to horror that Oxlee, abandoning normative Anglican beliefs, 'has adopted the views of the Kabbalah'.[23]

Oxlee further alienated his fellow clergymen by his refusal to participate in evangelical groups such as the London Society for the Promotion of Christianity Among the Jews.[24] He not only believed such efforts were pointless and demeaning to both Christians and Jews; while he shared the common Christian aspiration that the Jews would eventually come to Jesus, he also fervently hoped that they might still remain Jews.[25] Although Oxlee may seem unusual in the

---

of the Kabbalah to convert Jews, see Wirszubski, *Pico*; Crofton Black, 'From Kabbalah to Psychology: The Allegorizing *Isagoge* of Paulus Riccius, 1509–41', *MRW* 2:2 (2007), 136–73.
[21] For Oxlee's involvement with Freemasonry, see *Freemason* 10 (1877), 115.
[22] See Samuel Taylor Coleridge, *The Complete Works of Samuel Taylor Coleridge, With an Introductory Essay Upon his Philosophical and Theological Opinions*, 7 vols., ed. W. G. T. Shedd (New York: Harper & Brothers, 1884), 5:457.
[23] [Anonymous], Art. IV, 'The Kabbalah', *ER* 11 (February 1856), 141–57.
[24] For this organisation see Brenda Ayres, *Silent Voices: Forgotten Novels by Victorian Women Writers* (Westport, CT: Greenwood Publishing Group, 2003), 3–4. For the messianic prophecies for 1840 which encouraged such groups, see Jonathan Frankel, 'Crisis as a Factor in Modern Jewish Politics, 1840 and 1881–82', in Jehudah Reinharz (ed.), *Living with Antisemitism: Modern Jewish Responses* (Lebanon, NH: Brandeis University Press/University Press of New England, 1987), 42–58.
[25] John Oxlee, *Three Letters, humbly addressed to the Lord Archbishop of Canterbury, on the inexpediency and futility of any attempt to convert the Jews to the Christian Faith, in the way and manner hitherto practised.*

context of both the Anglican evangelical movement and the post-Enlightenment 'rationalism' of the first half of the nineteenth century, he stands as a representative of a particular orientation among learned Protestant clergy which has antecedents in German Lutheran Rosicrucianism, and which would later come to flower in the Reverend William Alexander Ayton and the Reverend A. F. A. Woodford, the Kabbalistically inclined vicars of the Golden Dawn.[26]

THE CREATION OF THE SRIA

The Kabbalistic inclinations of esoterically minded Masonic brethren such as Oxlee eventually bore a remarkable fruit. In 1866, five years after his meeting with Lévi, Kenneth Mackenzie, in collaboration with his friend Robert Wentworth Little (1840–1878), a young clerk working for the Grand Lodge at Freemason's Hall in London, created a new Masonic organisation called the Societas Rosicrucianae in Anglia or SRIA, known familiarly to its members as the 'Soc Ros'.[27] Mackenzie had already generated a sizeable list of exotic quasi-Masonic rites and spurious 'higher' degrees.[28] But the SRIA, unlike Mackenzie's more transient creations, established itself with tenacity, despite Waite's dismissive comment that 'this harmless association deserves a mild sympathy at the hands of the students of occultism'.[29] Ellic Howe refers to the society as an example of 'fringe' rather than 'irregular' Freemasonry: it lacked the power to confer the three Masonic 'Craft' degrees and did not encroach upon

---

Being a General Discussion of the whole Jewish Question (private publication: London, 1842; repr. Philadelphia, PA: Abraham Collins, 1843). For more on Oxlee, see *Oxford Dictionary of National Biography* (2004), <http://www.oxforddnb.com/view/article/21059>.

[26] For the creation of the 'Rosicrucian Manifestos' of the early seventeenth century by a Lutheran parson, Johann Valentin Andreae, see Yates, *Rosicrucian Enlightenment*. See Chapter Four for William Alexander Ayton, and below for A. F. A. Woodford.

[27] For the nickname 'Soc Ros' see A. E. Waite, *The Brotherhood of the Rosy Cross* (London: William Rider & Son, 1924; repr. New Hyde Park, NY: University Books, 1961), 565; William Wynn Westcott, *The History of the Societas Rosicruciana in Anglia* (London: private publication, 1900).

[28] For Mackenzie's Masonic activities, see Waite, *Brotherhood*, 568.

[29] A. E. Waite, *The Real History of the Rosicrucians* (London: George Redway, 1887; repr. Blauvelt, NY: Steinerbooks, 1977), 425.

the preserve of the Grand Lodge and Grand Chapter.[30] The Rules and Ordinances of the SRIA clearly outline the qualifications for would-be aspirants:

> No aspirant shall be admitted into the Society unless he be a Master Mason....He must be...capable of understanding the revelations of philosophy and science; possessing a mind free from prejudice and anxious for instruction. He must be a believer in the fundamental principles of the Christian doctrine, a true philanthropist, and a loyal subject.[31]

The Christian exclusivity of the SRIA seems to be rooted in Rosicrucian doctrines rather than Masonic practices.[32] There was already in existence a Societas Rosicrucianae in Scotia, into which Little had been initiated and from which he had been granted a warrant to form a Society in England.[33] But the SRIA was an entirely different entity from its Scottish parent. Westcott, who entered the order in 1880 and became its Supreme Magus in 1892, refers to this small but immensely influential organization, which under his aegis provided the founders, early recruits, and theoretical matrix for the Order of the Golden Dawn, as an 'English Masonic Rosicrucian Society'.[34] Over the newly created society, like the spirit of God moving over the face of the waters, hovered the irrepressible spirit of Éliphas Lévi, who was still alive when the society was founded and whom Mackenzie, probably without Lévi's knowledge, nominated as an honorary member in April 1873.[35]

Each of the early members of the SRIA was schooled in some form of esoteric expertise. The area they shared in common, apart from their Masonic commitments, was a familiarity with Lévi's works and an interest in the Jewish Kabbalah. Little, who became the SRIA's first Supreme

---

[30] Howe, 'Fringe Masonry', 243.
[31] Rule No. VII, quoted in *Rosicrucian* 1 (July 1868), 7, cited in Waite, *Real History*, 418.
[32] For the eligibility of Jews to enter Masonic lodges and the history of Jewish-Christian relations within British Freemasonry, see Shaftesley, 'Jews in English Freemasonry'; Katz, *Jews and Freemasons*.
[33] For more on the creation of the SRIA, see Hutton, *Triumph of the Moon*, 72–75; Howe, *Magicians*, 26–33; Godwin, *Theosophical Enlightenment*, 216–18.
[34] Westcott, 'Data', 34. All three Golden Dawn founders – Westcott, Mathers, and William Robert Woodman – were SRIA initiates.
[35] See Howe, *Magicians*, 28.

Magus, was 'a student of the works of Eliphas Lévi'.[36] Mackenzie himself, who eschewed any official position in his new society and eventually resigned because he felt it was not 'Rosicrucian' enough, was made an Honorary Magus.[37] William Robert Woodman (1828–1891), a retired physician and another avid disciple of Lévi's work, became the SRIA's first Secretary-General. Westcott describes this unusual man as 'an excellent Hebrew scholar and one of the few English masters of the Hebrew Kabalah'.[38] William Carpenter (1797–1874), another enthusiastic student of Lévi's work, was, like Mackenzie, deeply involved in spiritualist circles.[39] Carpenter does not loom large in scholarly histories of the occult revival, perhaps because he created no florid conflicts and died before the Golden Dawn was created. Yet he was a well-published author of numerous works on scripture, and was the editor of Calmet's *Dictionary of the Bible*.[40] Like Lévi and many Freemasons over the centuries, he was convinced of the Jewish roots of the Craft:

> I know not whether it has struck others as anything remarkable, that so large a number of professing Christians in the United Kingdom...should have adopted a system and united themselves in a body, the foundation of which is obviously and indisputably laid in Judaism....Its traditions, its ceremonies, its ritual, all bear the impress of, and are, in fact rooted in Judaism.[41]

But Carpenter moved far beyond Lévi's assertion that Masonic rituals are 'rooted in Judaism'. In a series of articles first appearing in *The Freemason* in 1872, he attempted to demonstrate through historical and symbolic correspondences that the Anglo-Saxon people are themselves the

---

[36] Howe, *Magicians*, 26. See also Westcott, 'Rosicrucians, Past and Present', 44.
[37] Howe, *Magicians*, 30–31. For Mackenzie's definition of 'Rosicrucian', see Mackenzie, *Masonic Cyclopaedia*, 612–18; for Mackenzie's equation of 'Rosicrucians' with 'Kabbalists', see Mackenzie, *Masonic Cyclopaedia*, 619–33.
[38] Gilbert, *Scrapbook*, 73. For Woodman, see also Howe, *Magicians*, 1–4, 16–21; Hutton, *Triumph of the Moon*, 74–75.
[39] Howe, *Magicians*, 32.
[40] See William Carpenter, *The Israelites Found in the Anglo-Saxons* (London: George Kenning, 1873), which includes a bibliography of his works.
[41] Carpenter, *Israelites*, 1.

remnants of the lost tribes of Israel.[42] The editor of *The Jewish Chronicle*, reviewing Carpenter's book, acknowledged his earnestness, his extensive research, and the implicit flattery of his underlying premise, and then remarked laconically: 'In endeavouring to trace a connection between the Craft and the history of God's ancient people, Mr. Carpenter seems to attempt a little too much.'[43]

In 1869, a West of Anglia Province and College of Bristol branch of the SRIA was created by Major Francis George Irwin (1828–1892), a retired army officer who, like Mackenzie, was an enthusiastic crystal-gazer 'with a passion for Rites and an ambition to add to their number'.[44] Irwin, like his fellow initiates, was a follower of Lévi; he was in Paris the year before Lévi's death, and later, along with Mackenzie, claimed to have been initiated by the French magus into an ancient Kabbalistic Masonic-Rosicrucian order called the Fratres Lucis or 'Brothers of Light'.[45] Frederick

---

[42] For Carpenter's probable source, see John Wilson, *Our Israelitish Origin: Lectures on Ancient Israel, and the Israelitish Origin of the Modern Nations of Europe* (London: James Nisbet, 1840). For the earlier British Israelism of the late eighteenth century, see Tudor Parfitt, *The Lost Tribes of Israel: the History of a Myth* (London: Weidenfeld & Nicolson, 2002), 52–65; O. Michael Friedman, *Origins of the British Israelites: the Lost Tribes* (Lewiston, NY: Edwin Mellen Press, 1993).

[43] The Editor, 'Review of William Carpenter, *The Israelites Found in the Anglo-Saxons*', *JC* (17 January 1873), 587.

[44] Waite, *Brotherhood*, 568.

[45] For Irwin's military and Masonic background, see Waite, *Brotherhood*, 569. The threads comprising the history of the Fratres Lucis are hopelessly tangled. Howe ('Fringe Masonry', 18) quotes a manuscript copy of the 'Ritual of Fratris [*sic*] Lucis or Brethren of the Cross of Light' in Francis George Irwin's handwriting, in which the traditional 'history' of the order states that the brethren used Hebrew in their rituals, and the officers were designated by Hebrew terms as well as being given Hebrew names. The 'history' also claims as early brethren Fludd, Mesmer, Swedenborg, and Martinès de Pasqually; Mackenzie (*Masonic Cyclopaedia*, 453) names Lévi as an initiate. The Fratres Lucis seems to have been re-invented by Mackenzie and Irwin, and later included as members Hockley, Westcott, and William Alexander Ayton. Joscelyn Godwin (*Theosophical Enlightenment*, 121–22) considers that Mackenzie's and Irwin's Fratres Lucis was based on an earlier German-Austrian Masonic group of the same name, also known as the Asiatic Brethren: a 'Kabbalistic-theosophic order' founded in Vienna with the avowed purpose of accepting both Jews and Christians in its

Hockley (1809–1885), a professional astrologer, mesmerist, and crystal-gazer with a vast library and a special interest in the angel magic of the Elizabethan magus John Dee, became a member of Irwin's Bristol College in 1875, the year of the founding of the Theosophical Society and the publication of Blavatsky's *Isis Unveiled*.[46] Hockley too was familiar not only with Lévi's work but with most of Lévi's Latin sources.[47] Many other provincial colleges of the SRIA were created in subsequent years. The SRIA still functions today, and its aims remain precisely as Westcott enumerated them in 1916:

> To afford mutual aid and encouragement in working out the great problems of Life, and in discovering the Secrets of Nature; to facilitate the study of the system of Philosophy

---

ranks. The nineteenth-century Kabbalistic scholar Franz Josef Molitor, a Jewish convert to Catholicism, asserts that the ritual of the Asiatic Brethren was Kabbalistic; see McIntosh, *Rose Cross*, 162. This order was connected with the Jewish Sabbatian messianic movement of the seventeenth century, with which the notorious magician and Kabbalist Rabbi Samuel Falk, the 'Ba'al Shem of London', was later associated; for Falk and the Sabbatians, see Chapter Five. For a comprehensive history of the Asiatic Brethren, see Katz, *Jews and Freemasons*, 26–53. See also Antoine Faivre, 'Asiatic Brethren', in Hanegraaff (ed.), *Dictionary of Gnosis*, 107–09. See also the somewhat less scholarly nineteenth-century work by Charles William Heckethorn, *The Secret Societies of All Ages and Countries* (London: Richard Bentley & Son, 1875), in which Heckethorn asserts that the basis of the Asiatic Brethren was Rosicrucian. Although the Order of the Asiatic Brethren was apparently short-lived, many of its members joined the Masonic 'Judenloge' or 'Jewish Lodge' (also called The Rising Dawn Lodge), a Frankfurt lodge founded by a Jewish Freemason called Sigismund Geisenheimer in 1807 under the aegis of the French Grand Orient. Westcott ('Rosicrucians, Past and Present', 5–6) asserts that Lord Lytton was initiated into this lodge. Waite (*Brotherhood*, 524–28) claims that the Asiatic Brethren drew much of its ritual from the earlier German Order of the Golden and Rosy Cross – the same order that Westcott later insisted had created the Cipher MS he used as the basis of the Golden Dawn, thus completing the circle and furnishing an 'authentic' Jewish Kabbalistic-Rosicrucian lineage for his own order.

[46] For Hockley's experiments in scrying, see Hamill (ed.), *Rosicrucian Seer*. For his astrological interests, see Owen Davies, *Witchcraft, Magic and Culture 1736–1951* (Manchester: Manchester University Press, 1999), 238–39; Patrick Curry, *A Confusion of Prophets: Victorian and Edwardian Astrology* (London: Collins & Brown, 1999), 83.

[47] See Hamill (ed.), *Rosicrucian Seer*, 30–33.

founded upon the Kabalah and the doctrines of Hermes Trismegistus, which was inculcated by the original Fratres Rosae Crucis of Germany, A.D. 1450; and to investigate the meaning and symbolism of all that now remains of the wisdom, art and literature of the ancient world.[48]

The SRIA still presents itself as a society whose members 'believe in the fundamental principles of the Trinitarian Christian faith', and it still concerns itself with the study of the Kabbalah. Moreover, its various branches and colleges in Britain, Canada, and America now enjoy a presence on the internet.[49]

THE KABBALAH AND THE CRAFT

Controversies about the origins of Freemasonry, and whether or not the Kabbalah specifically, or Jewish esoteric lore in general, was a major if not the formative influence in its inception, cannot be addressed here. There is a large body of literature on this theme both within and outside Freemasonry encompassing every possible perspective. Discourse on the Kabbalistic origins of Freemasonry stems from at least the eighteenth century, as expressed by the Viennese Freemason Carl Leonhard Reinhold in 1788:

> I could here appeal to those systems that trace the actual sciences of our Order back to the Hebrews, that try to locate our secrets by means of the thirteen rules of kabbalah in the ancient text of the bible...as a key to all theoretical and practical sciences of nature.[50]

In support of this Hebrew Masonic foundation myth, the Scottish Rite Freemason Dr. Isaac Wise declared in *The Israelite* in 1855:

> Masonry is a Jewish institution whose history, degrees, charges, passwords, and explanations are Jewish from the beginning to the end, with the exception of only one by-degree and a few words in the obligation.[51]

---

[48] Westcott, 'Data', 39.
[49] The Societas Rosicruciana in Anglia is at <http://www.sria.info>.
[50] Carl Leonhard Reinhold ['Bruder Decius'], *Die Hebräischen Mysterien oder die älteste religiöse Freymaurery* (Leipzig, 1788), 211, cited in Kilcher, 'Moses of Sinai', 163.
[51] Cited in Schuchard, *Restoring the Temple*, 9.

A far more extreme view inspired by the Hebrew foundation myth emerged from the wilder forests of conspiracy theory, coupling Freemasons with Jews in a global plot for world domination. This view was exemplified in Britain by Nesta H. Webster's *Secret Societies and Subversive Movements*, one of the most influential antisemitic tracts written in English during the twentieth century.[52] Another notorious work appearing three years after Webster's was a bizarre and distasteful diatribe written by General Erich Friedrich Wilhelm Ludendorff (1865–1937), Germany's chief military strategist during the Great War.[53] Ludendorff's pamphlet, which quickly sold over 100,000 copies, blames the Freemasons for bringing America into the First World War, helped by the Jesuits, the Jewish organisation B'nai B'rith, and the Masonic Grand Lodge of New York. Ludendorff maintained that Freemasonry was essentially a cult-factory that used multi-leveled psychological 'conditioning' to transform German recruits into half-unwitting 'artificial Jews' who thereafter worked for the destruction of the Fatherland, and further claimed that the 'mystery' of Freemasonry 'is everywhere the Jew himself'. He also made a direct link with the Kabbalah: 'We find this Star of David in the Lodges of all the grades. In the lowest grade the six-

---

[52] Nesta H. Webster, *Secret Societies and Subversive Movements* (London: Boswell, 1924). This work is still in print, published by the Christian Book Club of America. Most of Webster's information on the Kabbalah is derived from Ginsburg's *Kabbalah* and Franck's *La Kabbale*, as well as from Lévi and British Masonic sources such as John Yarker and Kenneth Mackenzie. Webster's references to the *Zohar* are from the highly questionable French translation by Jean de Pauly, a Jewish convert to Catholicism: *Moses de Leon. Le livre du Zohar. Pages traduites du Chaldaïque par Jean de Pauly*, 6 vols. (Paris: Lafuma-Giraud, 1906–1911). Scholem (*Major Trends*, 212) refers to this translation as 'faulty and inadequate'. Webster also frequently refers to the work of Henri-Roger Gougenot des Mousseaux (see below), which clearly provided her with a fertile source for her ideas.
[53] Erich Friedrich Wilhelm Ludendorff, *Vernichtung der Freimauerei durch Enthüllung ihrer Geheimnisse* (Munich: self-published, 1927; English translation, *Destruction of Freemasonry Through Revelation of Their Secrets*, Newport Beach, CA: Noontide Press, 1977). Ludendorff is discussed on various Masonic websites; see, for example, 'Why Freemasonry Has Enemies', an anonymous article first published on 27 May 1949, posted as 'The Short Talk Bulletin' (2008), <http://www.freemasoninformation.com>.

pointed star is being replaced by the pentacle, the five-pointed Jewish Soviet star, also a cabalistic symbol'.[54]

The foundation text for such literature, which linked Masons and Jews as sorcerers and allies of Satan, first appeared in France in 1869 in a work by Henri-Roger Gougenot des Mousseaux (1805–1876), a French political writer who believed that the world was falling under the control of a mysterious body of Satan-worshippers whom he called 'kabbalistic Jews'.[55] Although little attention was paid to Gougenot's work at the time of its publication, the myth of a Judeo-Masonic conspiracy began to proliferate during the 1880s in both France and Russia, and erupted with great force and appalling consequences in the early decades of the twentieth century with the anonymously authored *Protocols of the Elders of Zion*.[56] Although the *Protocols*, first published in Russia in 1902, does not specifically mention the Kabbalah or Kabbalistic magic as part of the Judeo-Masonic conspiracy, this connection was soon made in antisemitic circles in France and Russia and subsequently spread throughout Europe.[57] It is still possible to find the sentiments of the *Protocols* alive and well on numerous contemporary Christian

---

[54] Ludendorff, *Destruction of Freemasonry*, 54.

[55] Henri-Roger Gougenot des Mousseaux, *Le Juif, le judaïsme et le judaïsation des peuples chrétiens* (Paris: Plons, 1869). For other works by Gougenot, see Henri-Roger Gougenot des Mousseaux, *La magie au dix-neuvième siècle. Ses agents, ses vérités, ses mensonges* (Paris: Dentu, 1860), in which he quotes Lévi; Henri-Roger Gougenot des Mousseaux, *Les Hauts phénomènes de la magie, précédés du spiritisme antique* (Paris: Plon, 1864). See also Frederick A. Busi, 'Faith and Race: Gougenot des Mousseaux and the Development of Antisemitism in France', in L. Erlich, S. Bolzky, R. Rothstein, M. Schwartz, J. Berkovitz, and J. Young (eds.), *Textures and Meaning: Thirty Years of Judaic Studies at the University of Amherst* (2004), <http://www.umass.edu/judaic/anniversaryvolume/articles/09-B2-Busi.pdf>.

[56] For the first edition of the *Protocols*, see Sergei Nilus, *Velikoe v malom ili Antikhrist kak blizkaia politchkeskaia vozmoshnost (The Great in the Small, or the Antichrist as an Approaching Political Possibility)* (Sergiev Posad, 1902). The seminal scholarly text on the *Protocols* is Norman Cohn, *Warrant for Genocide: The Myth of the Jewish World-Conspiracy and the Protocols of the Elders of Zion* (London: Eyre & Spottiswoode, 1967).

[57] For the contemporary resurgence of the *Protocols* in Russian literature and politics, see Marina Aptekman, 'Kabbalah, Judeo-Masonic Myth, and Post-Soviet Literary Discourse: From Political Tool to Virtual Parody', *RR* 65:4 (2006), 657–81.

fundamentalist web sites.[58]

Many contemporary scholars acknowledge a connection between the Kabbalah and Freemasonry, but there is no consensus about the extent or nature of the relationship.[59] Marsha Keith Schuchard's *Temple of Vision* devotes over eight hundred pages to a careful exploration of the transmission of Jewish esoteric traditions into Rosicrucian currents in Freemasonry. Masonic scholars such as John Shaftesley affirm the centrality of Jewish influence in Masonic rituals and philosophy,[60] while R. A. Gilbert tends to minimise the Jewish contribution and rarely mentions the Kabbalah in his various articles on the Masonic currents in the occult revival.[61] Henrik Bogdan suggests that the Kabbalah is 'specifically connected to the Mason Words', and that 'it becomes fairly safe to assume that we can trace kabbalah as a theme in the legend of Hiram'.[62] Yasha Beresiner, a former Master of the Quatuor Coronati Lodge, discusses the participation of Jews in Freemasonry from the late sixteenth century onward, and asserts: 'There has from the beginning been an affinity between Judaism and Freemasonry', emphasising the inclusion of Hebrew letters and Kabbalistic symbols in the Masonic Coat of Arms.[63]

It might be argued that personal agendas dominate in this discourse. But such an argument is unhelpful in clarifying the kind of impact Kabbalistic doctrines have made on Freemasonry. It may be more appropriate to speak of 'Freemasonries' rather than Freemasonry as a monolithic entity since, despite the existence of charters and regulations, Freemasonry has many branches and offshoots, and each lodge and each Grand Master throughout Masonic history has brought individual and culture-specific ideas and

---

[58] See, for example, <http://www.henrymakow.com/000447.html>; <http://www.sullivan-county.com/id3/dmj.htm>; <http://www.nicenetruth.com/home/2009/05/nwo-front-for-cabalist-jewish-tyranny.html>.

[59] See Lehrich, *Demons and Angels*, 209.

[60] See Shaftesley, 'Jews in English Freemasonry', 25–81

[61] See, for example, R. A. Gilbert, 'Chaos Out of Order: The Rise and Fall of the Swedenborg Rite', *AQC* 1:108 (1995), 122–49, in which the word 'Kabbalah' is never mentioned.

[62] Bogdan, *Western Esotericism*, 89 and 93.

[63] Yasha Beresiner, 'Some Judaic Aspects of Freemasonry: Dermott's *Ahiman Rezon*', first published in *Haboneh Hahofshi* (*The Israeli Freemason*), at *Pietre-Stones Review of Freemasonry*, <http://www.freemasons-freemasonry.com>.

traditions into this centuries-old institution. Ellic Howe emphasises the Kabbalistic focus of the SRIA, while Christopher McIntosh places it under the rubric of 'Masonic Rosicrucianism'.[64] As there is no universally accepted definition of what constitutes Kabbalah even within Jewish scholarly circles, let alone any scholarly consensus on the origins of Freemasonry, it is more relevant here to ask how the Victorian and Edwardian occultists themselves perceived the relationship between the Kabbalah and Freemasonry. The SRIA and the Golden Dawn were created by individuals who were both Freemasons and students of the Kabbalah, and their conjoining of Masonic, Rosicrucian-Hermetic, and Kabbalistic doctrines and practices reflects their own rather than twentieth- and twenty-first-century scholars' understanding of the dynamic interaction between these apparently discrete esoteric currents. Westcott makes his own opinion clear:

> In our Freemasonry may yet be traced allusions and references to that system of esoteric teaching and dogma, which was undeniably the result of the destruction of the exoteric Monotheism of Judea, I mean the Jewish Kabbalah.... The Kabbalah as a system of Theosophy has pre-eminent claims...among all the theistic speculations of mankind which have a bearing on, and have taken part in the formation of, the Masonic Aphanism.[65]

Kabbalistic lore as a central feature of SRIA rituals is demonstrated by an 'in-house' document entitled 'The Symbolism of the 4 Ancients', commissioned by Westcott and written by Mathers.[66] Mathers explains that 'those Four important officers of a College...who are named *Ancients*' represent 'titles applied to God in His innermost and most

---

[64] Howe, *Magicians*, 8; McIntosh, *Rosicrucians*, 122.

[65] William Wynn Westcott, 'The Religion of Freemasonry Illuminated by the Kabbalah', *AQC* 1 (1886–88), 55–58, reprinted in Gilbert (ed.), *Magical Mason*, 114–23, on pp. 117–18. For the Masonic 'aphanism', see Albert G. Mackey, *The Symbolism of Freemasonry, Illustrating and Explaining Its Science and Philosophy, Its Legends, Myths, and Symbols* (New York: Clark & Maynard, 1882), 317.

[66] S. L. MacGregor Mathers, *The Symbolism of the 4 Ancients* (Clavicula II, Societas Rosicruciana in Anglia, 1888); Yorke Collection FDD 805, Warburg Institute; repr. in Gilbert (ed.), *Sorcerer and His Apprentice*, 19–22.

concealed forms'.[67] He then offers his understanding of Kabbalistic linguo-theosophy by stating that 'the Divine Name יהוה, YHVH rushes through the universe, for each letter presides over an element...therefore he who could pronounce it aright would make both heaven and earth totter and quake'.[68] After a brief excursion into corresponding meanings in the Greco-Egyptian mysteries, he reminds the brethren that 'it is not a light thing to thus represent materially the forces of the Ineffable Name'. For Mathers, as for Westcott, the initiatory rituals of the SRIA, and the officers participating in them, are to be understood not only as symbolic but also as magical, in the sense that each officer, each ritual enactment, and each ritual object is an embodiment and a channel of an aspect of the power of the divine infrastructure as illuminated by the Kabbalah.[69]

---

[67] For this dimension of deity, called *En Soph* in Kabbalistic literature, see Scholem, *Kabbalah*, 88–96; Scholemn, *Major Trends*, 214–17, 269–73; Joseph Dan, *Kabbalah*, 39–41; Elliot R. Wolfson, *Alef, Mem, Tau: Kabbalistic Musings on Time, Truth, and Death* (Berkeley, CA: University of California Press, 2006), 73–78. For Westcott's definition, see Westcott, 'Kabalah', 87–89.

[68] The equation of Hebrew letters with elements can be found in the *Sefer Yetsirah*; see Hayman, *Sefer Yesirah* ¶11–13, pp. 82–88.

[69] For an analysis of SRIA rituals, see Jeffrey S. Kupperman, 'Towards a Definition of Initiation: Emic and Etic Views of Initiation in the Western Mystery Tradition', *Esoterica* 6 (2006), 67–80. Kupperman does not mention any Kabbalistic elements as aspects of either the mythic themes or the regalia of the rituals, although the omnipresence of the Divine Name, YHVH, used on virtually all the ritual objects as well as in the rituals themselves, suggests the need for further examination. The first four SRIA rituals contain no specific references to the Kabbalah *per se*; their content is 'Rosicrucian' in the sense that the symbolism is rooted in early seventeenth-century Rosicrucian sources such as *The Chymical Wedding of Christian Rosenkreutz*. Kabbalistic material only appears in the three higher 'teaching' grades – Adeptus Minor, Adeptus Major, and Adeptus Exemptus – with the emphasis on the last of these: the Adeptus Exemptus 'finds the Philosophers' Stone, and studies the Qabalah and Natural Magic'. The ritual for the eighth degree, Magister, makes full use of the Divine Name, YHVH, along with Reuchlin's *verbo mirifico*, YHShVH. For this reformulation of the Tetragrammaton, see Zika, 'Reuchlin's *De Verbo Mirifico*'. For the rituals of the first four SRIA grades, see www.stichtingargus.nl/vrijmetselarij/sria_en.html; www.geocities.com/alex_sumner/sria.pdf. See also A. E. Waite, *Shadows of Life and Thought: A Retrospective Review in the Form of*

Whether the key officers in Masonic rites were intended from the time of the origins of Freemasonry to provide a Kabbalistic magical focus is a question that may never be answered from available sources. Henrik Bogdan offers an extensive discussion of the importance of Kabbalah in Freemasonry as well as initiatory 'fringe' Masonic-Rosicrucian groups, stating: 'Kabbalah is specifically connected to the Mason Words, and it is thus the literary Kabbalah, or gematria, which is seen as compatible with masonry'.[70] Bogdan also asserts that the structure of the initiation rituals, the terminology, and the symbols found in most occult societies 'derive to a large extent from Freemasonry'.[71] This is certainly clear in the SRIA rituals, which, like the rituals of the Golden Dawn, were designed by Freemasons. Christopher McIntosh, in his early work on the history of the Rosicrucians, never mentions Kabbalistic symbolism in relation to Masonic rituals,[72] but in a book written twenty years later he concedes that the eighteenth-century German Gold- und Rosenkreuz order from which Westcott claimed the Golden Dawn had received its charter reveals extensive Kabbalistic references and illustrations, especially of the sefirotic Tree.[73] Masonic symbolism, like Masonic origins, is a

---

Memoirs (London: Selwyn and Blount, 1938), 217–18 and Howe, *Magicians*, 16 for further material. For Mackenzie's version of the grades, see Mackenzie, *Masonic Cyclopaedia*, 616. Mackenzie offers in two elaborate tables the various degrees of the SRIA and their accompanying signs, colours, symbols, numerical equivalents according to *gematria*, and the 'Rosicrucian Significations of the Sephiroth' which are meant to correspond to the degrees. As one of these tables 'has never before been published' and the other 'is not readily accessible to the general student', it is not possible to know whether the elaborate Kabbalistic symbolism presented in Mackenzie's degree tables was an articulated formal aspect of SRIA structure and teachings or simply his own invention.

[70] Bogdan, *Western Esotericism and Rituals of Initiation*, 67–120.

[71] Henrik Bogdan, 'Secret Societies and Western Esotericism', in R. A. Gilbert (ed.), *Seeking the Light: Freemasonry and Initiatic Traditions* (Hersham: Lewis Masonic, 2007), 21–29, on p. 22. See also Hutton, *Triumph of the Moon*, 52–65.

[72] McIntosh, *Rosicrucians*.

[73] McIntosh, *Rose Cross*, 73–74. See also the discussion following John Shaftesley's presentation of 'Jews in English Freemasonry' to the Quatuor Coronati Lodge (48–63), which reflects a spectrum of diverse and conflicting opinions about the extent of Jewish influence on Masonic symbolism and rituals. Roger Dachez ('Freemasonry', in Hanegraaff (ed.), *Dictionary of Gnosis*, 382–88),

scholarly minefield, and it is impossible to know with any
certainty the beliefs of those who created the original
Masonic rituals and those who altered them along the way.
The Kabbalistic proclivities of the founders of the SRIA
suggest that this particular Masonic society had incorporated
Kabbalistic doctrines from its inception. Whatever the
current scholarly concensus on the issue, both Lévi and the
British occultists who followed him understood the meaning
of Masonic rituals to be rooted in Jewish esoteric lore. By the
time Westcott became Supreme Magus of the SRIA, its
orientation was firmly established, and the Ancients were
understood as aspects of a grand magical structure based on
the Jewish Kabbalah.

THE KABBALAH AND THE 'ROSIE CROSS'

British interest in the Kabbalah in the first half of the
nineteenth century is represented not only by John Oxlee's
curious blend of Christian piety, Jewish esotericism, and
Masonic ecumenism, but also by a quietly influential 'occult
underground' which first announced itself in Francis
Barrett's publication of *The Magus* in 1801.[74] This 'occult
underground' links the Kabbalah firmly with the traditions
of German and British Rosicrucianism.[75] *The Magus* is a

---

mentions the Jewish Kabbalah only in relation to the Order of the
Asiatic Brethren, but asserts that in the Ancient and Accepted
Scottish Rite with its higher degrees, a conception of Kabbalah
'often based on misinterpretations and a very vague knowledge of
the sources, became a commonly acknowledged origin of masonic
teachings' (387). Writers in the first decades of the twentieth century
such as Nesta Webster, availing themselves of the rising current of
antisemitism in Europe, were only too pleased to attribute a Jewish
origin of Freemasonry as a reflection of the Jewish 'world
conspiracy' expressed so forcibly in the *Protocols of the Elders of Zion*.
The destruction wrought by this tract and its later derivatives may
account for the reluctance shown by some contemporary scholars to
acknowledge major Kabbalistic elements in Masonic rituals and
history.
[74] Francis Barrett, *The Magus, or Celestial Intelligencer; Being a
Complete System of Occult Philosophy* (London: Lackington, Allen &
Co., 1801; repr. York Beach, ME: WeiserBooks, 2000).
[75] For links between German and British Rosicrucian groups, see
Godwin, *Theosophical Enlightenment*, 119–25; McIntosh, *Rose Cross*,
39–58. The relationship between Freemasonry and Rosicrucianism is
the subject of a curious paper by Thomas de Quincey (the 'Opium

textbook of ritual magic and an ambitious paraphrase of Agrippa's *De occulta philosophia*,[76] with added elements from the pseudepigraphic *Fourth Book of Occult Philosophy* (purportedly by Agrippa) and English translations of medieval grimoires.[77] Although Barrett appears to have been a ritual magician who sometimes used Kabbalistic formulae rather than a Kabbalist in the strict sense, Book Two of *The Magus* is almost entirely devoted to 'Cabalistical Magic'. Barrett's work later proved to be immensely influential in occult circles, but it was inevitably subject to mockery at the time of its publication:

> In vain do we boast of the progress of philosophy; – for, behold! in the beginning of the nineteenth century appears a

---

Eater', 1785–1859), entitled 'Historico-Critical Inquiry Into the Origin of the Rosicrucians and the Free-Masons' and published anonymously in three parts in *The London Magazine* in January, February, and March 1824, 5–13, 140–51, and 256–61. De Quincey writes under the pseudonym 'XYZ'; for his identity, see Tobias Churton, 'The First Rosicrucians', in *Seeking the Light: Freemasonry and Initiatic Traditions* (Hersham: Lewis Masonic, 2007), 72–79, on p. 78. De Quincey compares the 'essential characteristics' of both societies, examines the absence of historical evidence for either order before the early seventeenth century, rejects the idea of an ancient origin for both, and concludes (256) that Freemasonry arose out of the 'Rosicrucian mania' engendered by the Rosicrucian Manifestos published in 1614 and 1615 and was then 'transplanted to England, where it flourished under a new name...For I affirm as the main thesis of my concluding labours, that Free-Masonry is neither more nor less than Rosicrucianism as modified by those who transplanted it into England'.

[76] For Barrett's plagiarism, see Henry Cornelius Agrippa, *Three Books of Occult Philosophy* (*De occulta philosophia*), ed. Donald Tyson, trans. James Freake (St. Paul, MN: Llewellyn Publications, 2004 [1993]), xl. For Frederick Hockley's statement that Barrett plagiarised from Agrippa, see Frederick Hockley, 'On the Ancient Magic Crystal, and its Probable Connexion with Mesmerism', *Zoist*, 8 (1849), 251–66, reprinted in *Theosophical Siftings: A Collection of Essays, 1888–1895*, 7 vols. (London: Theosophical Publishing Society, 1888–95), Vol. 4 (1891–92), 9–22, on p. 10.

[77] Robert Turner (trans.), *Henry Cornelius Agrippa his Fourth Book of Occult Philosophy* (London: John Harrison, 1655; repr. Berwick ME: Ibis Press, 2005). For more on this work and Barrett's borrowings, see Davies, *Popular Magic*, 123, 142–43; Francis King, *The Flying Sorcerer* (Oxford: Mandrake Press, 1986); Alison Butler, 'Beyond Attribution: The Importance of Barrett's Magus', *JASM* 1 (2003), 7–33.

work which ought not to have surpassed the fifteenth.[78]

The Magus contains little to suggest that its author was unduly troubled by the triumph of reason purportedly occurring in post-Enlightenment Britain. But one of the book's most interesting features is Barrett's title page, where he calls himself 'Francis Barrett, F. R. C.': 'Frater Rosae Crucis', a brother of the Rosy Cross. Barrett is believed to have established a school of ritual magic in London which continued to resonate later in the century through such initiates as Frederick Hockley, a Freemason and a member of the SRIA, who exercised a major influence on Mackenzie and Westcott both personally and through his extensive occult library.[79] Godfrey Higgins (1772–1833), another Freemason and antiquarian scholar, declared in 1833 in his massive work, *Anacalypsis,* that a Rosicrucian College existed in England in his time; this statement was taken up by later British occultists as confirmation of the continuity of the order.[80] Whether or not Barrett was indeed a 'Rosicrucian' in the literal sense of belonging to a centuries-old secret order of that name, the Rosicrucian current in Britain from the early seventeenth century onward, closely interwoven with 'fringe' Freemasonry, is one of the chief vehicles by which Kabbalistic ideas and practices embedded in British esotericism reached the attention of Westcott and his Masonic brethren, just at the moment when Lévi's Kabbalah arrived from France.

Literature on the Rosicrucians is vast, ranging from scholarly works such as Frances Yates' *The Rosicrucian Enlightenment*, in which she refers to this current as a

---

[78] [Anon.], 'Review of Francis Barrett, *The Magus, or, Celestial Intelligencer*', Art. VII, *CR* 34 (April 1802), 406.

[79] For Barrett's school, see King, *Modern Ritual Magic*, 21; Godwin, *Theosophical Enlightenment*, 116; Butler, *Ritual Magic*, 257; Butler, *Magus*, 243; Montague Summers, *Witchcraft and Black Magic* (London: Rider, 1946; repr. Mineola, NY: Dover Publications, 2000), 161. For more on Hockley, see below.

[80] Godfrey Higgins, *Anacalypsis: An Attempt to Draw Aside the Veil of the Saitic Isis*, 2 vols. (London: private publication, 1833–36). For more on Higgins, see Godwin, *Theosophical Enlightenment*, 76–91; Hutton, *Triumph of the Moon*, 18–19. For the influence of *Anacalypsis* on Westcott, see Westcott, 'Data', 33. For Higgins' influence on Blavatsky, see Leslie Shepard, 'The *Anacalypsis* of Godfrey Higgins: Precursor of *Isis Unveiled* and *The Secret Doctrine*', *TH* 1:3 (1985), 46–53.

'religious alchemical-Cabalist movement',[81] to 'emic' histories written by late-nineteenth- and early-twentieth-century occultists such as Waite and and members of present-day Rosicrucian organisations such as AMORC.[82] There were many self-professed Rosicrucians in the various currents of British esotericism, the most important being Robert Fludd (1574–1637), whom Yates describes as being 'in the full Renaissance Hermetic Cabalist tradition'.[83] In an early work entitled *Apologia Compendiaria*, written in 1616, Fludd announced himself as a disciple of the Rosicrucians.[84] His *Mosaicall Philosophy* epitomises the amalgamation of Kabbalah, Hermetic alchemy, and Paracelsian medicine understood as 'Rosicrucian' in the British tradition and later appropriated by the adepts of the SRIA.[85] Mackenzie called

---

[81] Yates, *Rosicrucian Enlightenment*, 273.

[82] For scholarly works on the Rosicrucians, see McIntosh, *Rose Cross*; McIntosh, *Rosicrucians*; Godwin, *Theosophical Enlightenment*, 119–30; Roland Edighoffer, 'Rosicrucianism: From the Seventeenth to the Twentieth Century', in Faivre and Needleman (eds.), *Modern Esoteric Spirituality*, 186–209; Roland Edighoffer, 'Hermeticism in Early Rosicrucianism', in Roelof van den Broek and Wouter J. Hanegraaff (eds.), *Gnosis and Hermeticism: From Antiquity to Modern Times* (Albany, NY: State University of New York Press, 1998), 197–215; Roland Edighoffer, 'Rosicrucianism', in Hanegraaff (ed.), *Dictionary of Gnosis*, 1009–20. See also Waite, *Real History*; Waite, *Brotherhood*; A. E Waite, 'The Rosicrucian Brotherhood', *GM* 263 (1887), 598–607; and the various papers in Dunning (ed.), *A. E. Waite* and R. A. Gilbert (ed.), *Hermetic Papers of A. E. Waite: The Unknown Writings of a Modern Mystic* (Wellingborough: Aquarian Press, 1987). For Rudolph Steiner's works on Rosicrucianism, see P. M. Allen (ed.), *A Christian Rosenkreutz Anthology* (Blauvelt, NY: Rudolf Steiner Publications, 1968). For twentieth-century 'emic' Rosicrucian publications, see H. Spencer Lewis, *Rosicrucian Questions and Answers with Complete Answers* (San Jose, CA: Supreme Grand Lodge of AMORC, 1969); R. Swinburne Clymer, *The Rosy Cross, Its Teachings* (Quakertown, PA: Beverly Hall Corporation, 1965); George Winslow Plummer, *Principles and Practice for Rosicrucians* (New York: Society of Rosicrucians, 1947); Max Heindel, *The Rosicrucian Cosmo-Conception* (Oceanside, CA: Rosicrucian Fellowship, 1909).

[83] Frances A. Yates, *The Art of Memory* (London: Routledge & Kegan Paul, 1966), 310.

[84] See William H. Huffman, *Robert Fludd: Essential Readings* (London: Aquarian Press, 1992), 45–56.

[85] Robert Fludd, *The Mosaicall Philosophy. Grounded Upon the Essential Truth or Eternal Sapience* (London: Humphrey Moseley, 1659). See

Fludd 'a prominent member of the Rosicrucian Fraternity' and declared that the English magus 'did more to confirm the existence of the Rosicrucian Society in England than that of any writer before or since'.[86] In 1907, Westcott, an enthusiastic admirer of Fludd, delivered a paper to a group of SRIA brethren assembled at Bearstead in Kent, Fludd's birthplace and the site of his tomb and monument. In this eulogy Westcott describes the 'school of Cabalists and Hermetists' as though it were a single entity, defines Fludd's wisdom as 'Rosicrucian and Cabalistic', and finally declares: 'Our ancient Frater was the real founder of Rosicrucianism in this country'.[87]

Although many present-day Rosicrucians, like the British occultists of the late nineteenth century, accept the historical reality of Christian Rosenkreutz and his medieval order of initiated adepts,[88] there is as yet no scholarly consensus as to whether a 'real' esoteric group calling themselves Rosicrucians existed before the publication of the 'Rosicrucian

---

also William H. Huffman, *Robert Fludd and the End of the Renaissance* (London: Routledge, 1988); Allen G. Debus, *The English Paracelsians* (London: Oldbourne Book Co. Ltd., 1965); Allen G. Debus, *Robert Fludd and His Philosophical Key* (Sagamore Beach, MA. Watson Publishing International, 1979); Joscelyn Godwin, *Robert Fludd: Hermetic Philosopher and Surveyor of Two Worlds* (London: Thames and Hudson, 1979). For Paracelsian medicine, see Debus, *Chemical Philosophy*, 205–93; Walter Pagel, *From Paracelsus to Van Helmont: Studies in Renaissance Medicine and Science* (London: Variorum Reprints, 1986); Webster, 'Paracelsus'; Jole R. Shackelford, *A Philosophical Path for Paracelsian Medicine: The Ideas, Intellectual Context, and Influence of Petrus Severinus (1540–1602)* (Copenhagen: Museum Tusculanum Press, 2004).

[86] Mackenzie, *Masonic Cyclopaedia*, 225.

[87] William Wynn Westcott, 'In Memory of Robert Fludd', address to the members of the SRIA (14 September 1907), repr. in Gilbert (ed.), *Magical Mason*, 48–53.

[88] For the story of Christian Rosenkreutz, see the first of the Rosicrucian 'Manifestos': *Fama Fraternitas, or a Discovery of the Fraternity of the Most Noble Order of the Rosy Cross*, repr. in Yates, *Rosicrucian Enlightenment*, 282–96. For a complete bibliography of the various editions of the 'Manifestos', see Yates, *Rosicrucian Enlightenment*, 279–306. For the authorship of the *Fama*, see Donald R. Dickson, 'Johann Valentin Andreae's Utopian Brotherhoods', *RQ* 49:4 (1996), 760–802. For Rosicrucian works available to Golden Dawn adepts, see Frederick Leigh Gardner, *Bibliotheca Rosicruciana: A Catalogue Raisonné of Works on the Occult Sciences* (London: private publication, 1903).

Manifestos' in Germany in 1614. An examination of these issues is beyond the scope of this book. It is the interchange-ability of the terms 'Rosicrucian' and 'Kabbalistic' in the late-nineteenth-century British occult revival that is of greatest relevance here, and the manner in which 'Rosicrucian' ideas and practices were believed to have originated in the Jewish Kabbalah. Westcott is, as usual, succinct in his opinion:

> Even the Rosicrucian revival of mysticism was but a new development of the vastly older system of the Kabalistic Rabbis....Through the Hebrew Kabalah, we have indeed became possessed of more of the ancient Wisdom than from any other source.[89]

Westcott derived support for his argument from the most important of the 'Rosicrucian Manifestos', the *Fama Fraternitas*, which places the Rosicrucian tradition firmly in the Jewish 'chain of transmission' of the Biblical patriarch-magicians:

> Our Philosophy also is not a new invention, but as Adam after his fall hath received it, and as Moses and Solomon used it.[90]

HERMES AND THE JEWS

Among the brethren of the SRIA, Rosicrucianism was conflated with both Kabbalah and alchemy. There is little scholarly literature devoted to the historical relationship between the Kabbalah and alchemy and the ways in which these two distinctive esoteric currents may have become entwined.[91] There is, however, a growing body of research on the history of alchemy itself, in which debate continues about whether it originated in the Hellenistic period as a physical science or whether its often bizarre mythic language was

---

[89] William Wynn Westcott, 'Historical Lecture for Neophytes', London: unpublished MS, *c.* 1892–1894, repr. in King, *Modern Ritual Magic*, 212–17, and in Israel Regardie, *An Account of the Teachings, Rites and Ceremonies of the Order of the Golden Dawn*, 4 vols. (Chicago, IL: Aries Press, 1937–1940; repr. *The Original Account of the Teachings, Rites and Ceremonies of the Hermetic Order of the Golden Dawn* (St. Paul, MN: Llewellyn, 1989), 15–16.

[90] *Fama Fraternitas*, in Yates, *Rosicrucian Enlightenment*, 295.

[91] For the only scholarly work specifically addressing this subject, see Scholem, *Alchemy and Kabbalah*.

always intended as a symbolic description of the process of spiritual transformation.[92] A surviving work of the third-century Greco-Egyptian alchemist Zosimos includes a series of mystical visions which Dan Merkur understands as allegories of chemical processes;[93] the imagery, in Merkur's view, is meant to describe physical changes involved in the transmutation of actual metals.[94] C. G. Jung, on the other hand, insists that the chemical processes described by Zosimos are allegories of an inner spiritual ascent.[95] Neither perspective can be verified, as there is only the evidence of the text itself, which, to the irritation of scholars, promiscuously mixes both symbolic and literal elements. Erik Hornung dates the earliest forms of Egyptian alchemy to the second millennium BCE, and suggests that this ancient proto-alchemy was based on 'bringing Osiris back to life through decay and putrefaction',[96] implying a magical ritual embedded in a religious framework and enacted through the practical application of metallurgical and chemical knowledge. The Rosicrucian perspective of the early seventeenth century understood the inner process to be reflected in the outer, and did not separate the two levels of interpretation; transmuting base metal into gold was the ritual enactment of

---

[92] For major studies on alchemy, see H. J. Sheppard, 'Gnosticism and Alchemy', *Ambix* 6 (1957), 88–109; Walter Pagel, *Paracelsus: An Introduction to the Philosophical Medicine of the Renaissance* (Basel/New York: S. Karger, 1958); Yates, *Giordano Bruno*; Jack Lindsay, *The Origins of Alchemy in Greco-Roman Egypt* (London: Frederick Muller, 1970); Mircea Eliade, *The Forge and the Crucible: The Origins and Structures of Alchemy*, trans. Stephen Corrin (Chicago, IL: University of Chicago Press, 1956); Fowden, *Egyptian Hermes*; Alison Coudert, *Alchemy: The Philosopher's Stone* (London: Wildwood House, 1980); Stanton J. Linden, *The Alchemy Reader: From Hermes Trismegistus to Isaac Newton* (Cambridge: Cambridge University Press, 2003); Debus (ed.), *Alchemy and Early Modern Chemistry*; Erik Hornung, *The Secret Lore of Egypt: Its Impact on the West*, trans. David Lorton (Ithaca, NY: Cornell University Press, 2001), 34–42.
[93] For this treatise, see F. Sherwood Taylor, 'The Visons of Zosimos: Translation and Prefatory Note', *Ambix* 1:1 (1937), 88–92. For Zosimos, see also Moshe Idel, 'The Origin of Alchemy According to Zosimos and a Hebrew Parallel', *REJ* 145:1–2 (1986), 117–24.
[94] Dan Merkur, *Gnosis: An Esoteric Tradition of Mystical Visions and Unions* (Albany, NY: State University of New York Press, 1993), 89.
[95] Jung, CW13, ¶119–120.
[96] Hornung, *Secret Lore*, 39.

an internal transformation that promised not only material wealth, health, and longevity, but conferred on the adept the power to change the world.[97]

The idea that alchemy has, from the time of its origins, always concerned a transformation of the soul through the transformations of matter was succinctly proposed in the mid-nineteenth century in Mary Anne Atwood's *A Suggestive Inquiry into 'The Hermetic Mystery'*.[98] Ancient alchemical texts which discuss the transmutation of base metals into gold are, according to Atwood, secret allegories of the soul's ascent to spiritual perfection. With Atwood's book, followed in 1857 by Ethan Allen Hitchcock's *Remarks upon Alchemy and the Alchemists*,[99] the conviction crystallised in occult circles that alchemy had always had a soteriological goal.[100] Whatever the intentions of its Hellenistic practitioners, by the sixteenth century alchemy was understood primarily as a spiritual journey, and alchemical authors such as Agrippa and Paracelsus had contributed to occult vocabularies such concepts as the 'shining body': the imaginative faculty as both an aspect of the 'World Soul' and a mediator between the human being and the godhead.[101] These ideas, which seem to be derived in large part from the Kabbalistic lit-

---

[97] See, for example, *Fama Fraternitas*, in Yates, *Rosicrucian Enlightenment*, 296; *Confessio Fraternitas, or The Confession of the Laudable Fraternity of the Most Honorable Order of the Rosy Cross, Written to All the Learned of Europe*, in Yates, *Rosicrucian Enlightenment*, 298.

[98] Mary Anne South Atwood, *A Suggestive Inquiry into 'The Hermetic Mystery', with a Dissertation on the More Celebrated Alchemical Philosophers* (published anonymously: London: Trelawney Saunders, 1850; repr. New York: Julian Press, 1960).

[99] Ethan Allen Hitchcock, *Remarks upon Alchemy and the Alchemists, Indicating a Method Discovering the True Nature of Hermetic Philosophy* (Boston, MA: Crosby, Nichols, 1857; repr. New York: Arno Press, 1976).

[100] For Westcott's reference to Atwood, see Westcott, *Collectanea Hermetica*, 3:5–6.

[101] For the 'shining body', see Agrippa, *Occult Philosophy*, 208; Martin Ruland, *A Lexicon of Alchemy or Alchemical Dictionary, Containing a Full and Plain Explanation of All Obscure Words, Hermetic Subjects, and Arcane Phrases of Paracelsus* (*Lexicon alchemiae sive dictionarium alchemistarum*, Frankfurt: Zachariah Palthenus, 1612), trans. A. E. Waite (London: John Watkins, 1893; repr. York Beach, ME: Samuel Weiser, Inc., 1984), 182. For the absorption of the idea into British occultism, see Blavatsky, *Isis*, 1:xxv–xxvii and 1:125–26; Blavatsky, *Secret Doctrine*, 1:6–77.

erature of the medieval period,[102] were seamlessly incorporated into Rosicrucian doctrines by British alchemists such as
Fludd and Thomas Vaughan (1622–1666),[103] and in the eighteenth century by one of the most enigmatic figures in the
history of magic in Britain, Rabbi Samuel Jacob Hayim Falk
(1710–1782). Falk, a Polish Jewish Kabbalist, Freemason, and
alchemist known as the *Ba'al Shem* of London, was called an
'Eminent Rosicrucian' by Mackenzie and cited by Westcott as
one of the chiefs of the Rosicrucian order he claimed was

---

[102] See above, Chapter Two, and especially Wolfson, *Through a
Speculum That Shines*. For Agrippa's reliance on Hebrew texts, see
Tyson's discussion in Agrippa, *Occult Philosophy*, xvi–xix and 762–
72.
[103] Vaughan was a seventeenth-century Rosicrucian apologist who,
under the pseudonym Eugenius Philalethes, translated the *Fama
Fraternitas* and the *Confessio* into English and published them as *The
Fame and Confession of the Fraternity of R. C. Commonly of the Rosie
Cross* (London: Giles Calvert, 1652). Through this publication the
Rosicrucians became known to a much wider British public.
Westcott, who refers to Vaughan as a 'famous chemist and mystic'
and 'a notable member of the Order', claims that Vaughan was
'probably' initiated into the Brothers of the Rosy Cross in 1641
(Westcott, *History of the SRIA*, 4 and 6). W. J. Hughan, another SRIA
initiate, published Vaughan's translations of the *Fama* and the
Confessio as a series of articles in *The Rosicrucian*, the quarterly
journal of the SRIA, between 1868 and 1872. Vaughan also
produced a work called *Magia Adamica*, in which he states explicitly
that the Kabbalah of the Jews is 'chimicall'. He espoused the
Renaissance idea of the *prisca theologica*, and considered Paracelsus,
Agrippa, Trithemius, and Reuchlin to be his predecessors in
Kabbalistic natural magic. He engaged in a much-publicised dispute
with another philosophical alchemist, Henry More. Although More
believed the Kabbalah was the source of the only true philosophical
theology, he found the Lurianic Kabbalah distasteful because it was
pantheistic, anthropomorphised God, and contradicted his rationalist sensibilities. More was a prolific writer. His best-known work
is *Conjectura Cabbalistica: Or, A conjectural Essay of interpreting the
minde of Moses according to a threefold Cabbala, viz., literal, philosophical,
mystical, or divinely moral* (London, 1653). More does not seem to
have been a Rosicrucian apologist, although Allison Coudert
suggests that his colleagues van Helmont and Knorr von Rosenroth
were 'deeply influenced by Rosicrucianism' (Coudert, *Impact of the
Kabbalah*, 147). For the work of these men and their relationship with
magic and the Kabbalah, see A. M. Guinsberg, 'Henry More,
Thomas Vaughan and the Late Renaissance Magical Tradition',
Ambix 27 (1980), 36–58.

later 'resurrected' as the Golden Dawn.[104] By the 1860s 'Hermetic alchemy' was firmly established among the occultists of the SRIA as 'a path where work upon matter and desire for immortality converge'.[105]

That early modern 'spiritual' alchemy was profoundly influenced by the Jewish Kabbalah is evident, not only in the titles and texts of alchemical works, but also in the extraordinary engravings that illustrate these publications.[106] The two German alchemists most favoured by British occultists – Heinrich Khunrath (c. 1560–1605) and Michael Maier (1568–1622)[107] – were particularly enthusiastic about Kabbalistic theosophy, making full use of the ten *sefirot* and the Tree of Life, the power of the Tetragrammaton, and Lurianic concepts such as Adam Kadmon, and indicating that their knowledge of the Kabbalah was considerably more sophisticated than the mere symbolic ornamentation of a few Hebrew letters. For example, the frontispiece of Khunrath's *Amphitheatrum Sapientiae aeternae* presents not only the Tetragrammaton radiating the primal light at the top of the engraving, but also the two pillars of *Hesed* and *Geburah*, Mercy and Severity, related to the metals according to the traditional Kabbalistic assignment of silver to *Hesed* and gold

---

[104] For Mackenzie's entry on Falk, see Mackenzie, *Masonic Cyclopaedia*, 626–28. For Westcott's references, see William Wynn Westcott, 'A Society of Kabbalists', *Notes and Queries*, 9 February 1889, 116; Westcott, 'Rosicrucians, Past and Present', 43. For full references on Falk and the Sabbatian movement, see Chapter Five.

[105] Françoise Bonardel, 'Alchemical Esotericism and the Hermeneutics of Culture', in Faivre and Needleman (eds.), *Modern Esoteric Spirituality*, 71–100, on p. 74.

[106] For one of the best published collections of alchemical engravings, see Stanislas Klossowski de Rola, *The Golden Game: Alchemical Engravings of the Seventeenth Century* (London: Thames and Hudson, 1988). More engravings are found in Jung, CW12 and CW14, and see also Adam McLean's website, <http://www.levity.com/alchemy>, for another extensive collection. For the word 'Kabbalah' in alchemical titles, see, for example, Steffan Michelspacher, *Cabala, Spiegel der Kunst und Nature: in Alchymia* (Augsburg: David Francken, 1616); for this text, see *Golden Game*, 52.

[107] For Waite's references to Khunrath and Maier, see Waite, *Brotherhood*, 61–70 and 310–39.

to *Geburah*.[108] Emblem 11 in the *Amphitheatrum* portrays concentric circles containing the twenty-two Hebrew letters and the ten *sefirot* arranged around the figure of Christ, who is also the Lurianic Adam Kadmon, the universal androgyne and prototype of both the world and the human being.[109] Emblem 13 displays the ten *sefirot* emanating from the Tetragrammaton as attributes of deity connoted by Latin names.[110] Khunrath's equation of Christ, the Philosopher's Stone or alchemical gold, and Adam Kadmon, the Lurianic divine androgyne, are echoed in Lévi's work and also in the alchemical perspectives described by Westcott and Mathers in their various papers on the 'Hermetic art'.[111] In a similar fashion, in Michael Maier's *Tripus aureus*, published in 1618, Emblem 104 represents the alchemical dyad of Sun and Moon, gold and silver, as *Geburah* and *Hesed* respectively, completed by the central *sefira* of equilibrum, *Tiferet*, as the alchemical 'Mercury of the Wise'.[112]

Yet despite the impact of Kabbalistic thought on early modern alchemy, since Gershom Scholem's classic work *Alchemy and Kabbalah* there has been little discussion of whether late antique and medieval Jewish texts were themselves influenced by alchemical ideas and symbols. Scholem argues that the amalgamation of Kabbalah and alchemy is the product of the Christian theosophists and alchemists of early modern Europe, and that any alchemical 'tendencies' were 'on the whole eliminated from the Kabbalah'.[113] Raphael Patai notes the dramatic contrast between Scholem's extensive knowledge of the links between alchemy and Kabbalah and his attenuation of alchemy in Jewish traditions: 'If they [contemporary Kabbalistic scholars, *e.g.* Scholem] find something that is not to their liking, they

---

[108] Heinrich Khunrath, *Amphitheatrum Sapientiae aeternae* (Hanover: Gulielmus Antonius, 1609). The image is reproduced in de Rola, *Golden Game*, 31.

[109] See de Rola, *Golden Game*, 39. De Rola calls this emblem 'a scheme of Christian Kabbalism'.

[110] De Rola, *Golden Game*, 41. De Rola comments that this emblem portrays the entire process of the formation of the Philosopher's Stone, which Khunrath correlates with the creation of the world through the emanations of the ten *sefirot*.

[111] See also the comments about Khunrath's frontispiece in Patai, *Jewish Alchemists*, 156–57.

[112] Michael Maier, *Tripus aureus* (Frankfurt: Paulus Iacobus, 1618). See de Rola, *Golden Game*, 123.

[113] Scholem, *Alchemy and Kabbalah*, 11, 36.

try to ignore it. And this is precisely what they have done in discussing the Jewish work in alchemy'.[114] Scholem does reluctantly acknowledge that a number of Jewish Kabbalists, including Luria's chief disciple Hayyim ben Joseph Vital (1543–1620), were also alchemists,[115] and concedes that the symbolism of the *Shekhinah*, the female aspect of the godhead manifested in the physical world, 'exhibits close parallels to the alchemical symbolism of the *prima materia*'.[116] In addition to the *Aesch Mezareph*, which provided so much inspiration for Lévi and Westcott, surviving Kabbalistic-alchemical texts such as the mid-seventeenth-century *Emek ha-Melekh* with its detailed alchemical recipes,[117] the late-fifteenth-century *Sefer ha-Meshiv* with its maggidic revelations of the 'secrets of gold and silver',[118] and specific references in the *Zohar* itself,[119]

---

[114] Patai, *Jewish Alchemists*, 8. For Scholem's alchemical interests, see Cis van Heertum, 'The alchemical and kabbalistic correspondence of Walter Pagel and Gershom Scholem' (Amsterdam: Bibliotheca Philosophica Hermetica, 2007):
<http://www.ritmanlibrary.nl/c/p/h/bel_34.html>.

[115] For Vital's large unpublished work containing magical recipes and alchemical operations performed through the use of the Divine Names, see Patai, *Jewish Alchemists*, 340–64 and 519–21; Gerrit Boss, 'Hayyim Vital's *Kabbalah Ma'asit we-Alkhimiyah* (*Practical Kabbalah and Alchemy*): A 17th-Century Book of Secrets', *JJTP* 4 (1994), 55–112.

[116] Scholem, *Alchemy and Kabbalah*, 40.

[117] For *Emek ha-Melekh*, see Scholem, *Alchemy and Kabbalah*, 18–19 and 25, n. 32. See also Waite, *Holy Kabbalah*, 420–22; Scholem, *Kabbalah*, 394–95; Gershom Scholem, *Sabbatai Sevi: The Mystical Messiah*, trans. R. J. Zwi Werblowsky (Princeton, NJ: Princeton University Press, 1973), 87–90; Theisohn, 'Zur Rezeption'.

[118] The late-fifteenth-century *Sefer ha-Meshiv* ('Book of the Responding Entity') identifies itself with the Solomonic magical texts of late antiquity by offering a lengthy discussion of the ten 'lost' books of King Solomon, and asserting that their content will be made available to all with the advent of the Messiah. The work is sometimes known as *Sefer ha-Malakh ha-Meshiv* ('Book of the Responding Angel') because it is presented as a communication from an unnamed high angelic entity or *maggid*. A translation of a large section of the text can be found in Idel, *Enchanted Chains*, 116–18, but the complete work has never been translated into English. For more on the *Sefer ha-Meshiv*, see Moshe Idel, 'L'attitude envers le christianisme du Sefer ha-Mechiv', *Pardes* 76 (1988), 77–93; Moshe Idel, 'Jewish Mysticism in Spain: Some Cultural Observations', *Espacio, Tiempo y Forma* 7 (1994), 289–314; Moshe Idel, 'Magic and Kabbalah in the Book of the Responding Entity', in Mayer I. Gruber (ed.), *The Solomon Goldman Lectures*, 8 vols. (Chicago, IL: Spertus

indicate that relationships between the ten *sefirot*, the seven planets, and the alchemical metals and processes had been postulated since at least the medieval period, and possibly in late antiquity.

A relevant example is a late-fifteenth-century rabbi from Salonika called Joseph Taitazak, one of the first Kabbalists to invoke a *maggid* or angelic guide.[120] Taitazak's *maggid* was

---

College of Judaica Press, 1993), 6:125–38; Idel, *Messianic Mystics*, 126–32 and the references given there on pp. 372–75. The figure of Amon of No, whose name suggests Egyptian origins, is one of the chiefs of the demons in the *Sefer ha-Meshiv*. This entity is also one of the revealers of the 'secrets of gold and silver', and the *Sefer ha-Meshiv* offers rituals by which he can be compelled through magical adjurations to descend and reveal alchemical secrets; see Idel, 'Origin of Alchemy', 119–20. For Amon of No, see also Wout Jac van Bekkum, *A Hebrew Alexander Romance according to MS London, Jews College 145* (Louvain: Peeters, 1992), in which the demon appears as a serpent, and the review of Bekkum's work by Joseph Dan in *JQR* 86:3–4 (1996), 435–38. Dan discusses the appearance of Amon of No in a twelfth-century work called *Sefer Hasidim* by R. Judah ben Samuel 'The Pious' of Regensburg; for this work, see Chapter Five. In *Sefer Hasidim*, Amon of No appears as a dragon-demon, which Dan, like Idel, suggests is a transformation of the ancient Egyptian god Ammon. Other references to the *Sefer ha-Meshiv* can be found in Fine, 'Art of Metoposcopy', and Elisheva Carlebach, 'Two Amens That Delayed the Redemption: Jewish Messianism and Popular Spirituality in the Post-Sabbatian Century', *JQR* 82 (1992), 208–16. The *Sefer ha-Meshiv*, which Idel believes to comprise 'the scant remnants from much larger books', is associated with the Kabbalistic circle of the notorious magician Joseph della Reina, who according to legend attempted to combat the demonic forces through the power of the Divine Names as part of the eschatological struggle perceived in the imminent expulsion of the Jews from Spain. For Joseph della Reina, see Dan (ed.), *Heart and the Fountain*, 181–94; Joseph Dan, 'Joseph della Reina', in *EJ* 10:240–41. An MS of the *Sefer ha-Meshiv* is held in the British Museum, MS 27002 (Margoliouth 766), and another is at Oxford, MS Oxford-Bodleian 1597; it is very likely that Westcott and Mathers had access to these manuscripts and received help in their translation, and that the work influenced some of the rituals created for the Golden Dawn. See, for example, Regardie, *Golden Dawn*, 395–400, where a dragon-demon is invoked in the context of an alchemical ritual.

[119] See, for example, *Zohar* 1.249b–250a; *Zohar* 2.172a.

[120] For Taitazak and his influence on Luria, see Werblowsky, *Joseph Karo*, 97–99, 118–19; Dan, 'Maggid'. See also Dan (ed. and trans.), *Heart and the Fountain*, 175–80, for a translation of a short MS by Taitazak entitled 'Writing Without Pen and Ink'.

versed in alchemy and taught him the secrets of the art:

> And herewith the secret of the upper [mystical] gold and
> silver and the secret of the lower [worldly] gold and silver
> will be revealed to you, as you can bring it forth in actuality
> and in nature out of all seven kinds of metals, and this is the
> true science of nature.[121]

Scholem, discussing Taitazak's unpublished manuscript,
identifies the 'upper gold' as the second *sefira*, *Binah* ('Understanding'), and the alembic of the alchemist is symbolic of the
inner vessel 'in which one attains the mystery of the godhead
in the purification of the holy names'.[122] This is clearly a
spiritual as well as a practical alchemy, leading Scholem to
conclude, contradicting his own statement given earlier, that
Taitazak was the first Kabbalist to identify alchemy with
mystical theology 'even before the Christian humanists pursued this line'.[123] Taitazak's angel magic and use of the
Divine Names place his alchemy firmly within a Jewish
Kabbalistic magical tradition, echoing the angelic *maggid* of
the *Sefer ha-Meshiv*, written in Spain in the same period. It is
unlikely, although not impossible, that an unpublished
manuscript by Taitazak reached the adepts of the British
occult revival. Nevertheless the *maggid* who passes on the
secrets of spiritual alchemy reappears intact in the 'Angel of
the Seventh Sphere' of the SRIA adept Frederick Hockley,
discussed below.

There is evidence that Jewish alchemists, some of whom
were prominent in Hermetic circles, were working in Greco-
Egyptian Alexandria in the first centuries CE.[124] Their doctrines may have influenced the development of Arab
alchemy, which found its way back to Jewish communities
through the Arab-occupied areas of Spain in the medieval
period.[125] Zosimos, the third-century Greco-Egyptian alchem-

---

[121] British Museum MS Margoliouth 766, fol. 107a, cited in Scholem,
Alchemy and Kabbalah, 44. For another translation, see Patai, *Jewish
Alchemists*, 337.
[122] Gershom Scholem, 'The *Maggid* of Joseph Taitazaq', *Sefunot* 9
(1977), 67–112, on p. 87, cited in Patai, *Jewish Alchemists*, 337.
[123] Scholem, *Alchemy and Kabbalah*, 41.
[124] See Gager, *Moses*, 155; Patai, *Jewish Alchemists*, 60–91.
[125] For the transmission of alchemical texts, see Linden, *Alchemy
Reader*, 8; Yates, *Giordano Bruno*, 12–17; Wayne Shumaker, *The Occult
Sciences in the Renaissance* (Berkeley, CA: University of California
Press, 1972), 160–70; Patai, *Jewish Alchemists*, 95–97, 139–40.

ist and Hermetist, cited Moses as one of the great men in the history of alchemy;[126] later alchemists considered Moses and Hermes as co-founders of alchemy, which was also called 'the Mosaico-Hermetic Art';[127] and the eighteenth-century historian of alchemy, Nicolas Lenglet du Fresnoy, declared that Moses was 'trained in all the sciences of the Egyptians, of which the most secret...was that of the transmutation of Metals'.[128] Raphael Patai notes that the identification of Moses and Hermes 'still agitated the minds of not only alchemists but also historians' through the second half of the nineteenth century.[129]

Mackenzie, Westcott, and other nineteenth-century occultists understood early modern alchemists such as Michael Maier to be both Kabbalists and Rosicrucians, and these alchemists, viewing themselves as the inheritors of the ancient Hermetic tradition, in turn understood the *magnum opus* to be a Kabbalistic science.[130] There was also an ample selection of English works on alchemy to convince Westcott and his colleagues that alchemy, Rosicrucianism, and Kabbalah were interchangeable.[131] Westcott refers to a physician called John Heydon (1629–1667), a Kabbalist and self-professed Rosicrucian who seems to have enjoyed the company of a *maggid* or angelic guide in the best Kabbalistic tradition, and who in 1662 produced an impressive work in three parts called *The Holy Guide*.[132] This work, a com-

---

[126] See Patai, *Jewish Alchemists*, 26–29; Torijano, *Solomon*, 88–105. For the Jewish tradition that Hermes was Moses, see Gager, *Moses*, 77; Assman, *Moses the Egyptian*, 36; David Flusser and Shua Amorai-Stark, 'The Goddess Thermutis, Moses, and Artapanus', *JSQ* 1 (1993–94), 217–33, on pp. 225–26.

[127] Patai, *Jewish Alchemists*, 30. For Moses as an alchemist, see Patai, *Jewish Alchemists*, 30–40; Gager, *Moses*, 152–55. For Fludd's incorporation of this idea, see Kilcher, 'Moses of Sinai', 163–65.

[128] Nicolas Lenglet du Fresnoy, *Histoire de la philosophie hermetique*, 3 vols. (1742), 1:18–19, cited in Patai, *Jewish Alchemists*, 38.

[129] Patai, *Jewish Alchemists*, 39.

[130] See, for example, Heinrich Khunrath's declaration that 'in the Cabala is the Union of man...with God', in *Amphitheatrum sapientiae aeternae*, 203, cited in Jung, CW12, ¶427, n. 4.

[131] See, for example, Elias Ashmole, *Theatrum Chemicum Britannicum* (London: Nathaniel Brook, 1652). See also Westcott's *Collectanea Hermetica* for a number of seventeenth-century English alchemical texts.

[132] John Heydon, *The Holy-Guide: Leading the Way to The Golden Treasures of Nature* (London: 'T. M.', 1662; repr. Kila, MT: Kessinger

pendium of alchemical recipes for health, youth, and wisdom, also argues that the Jewish master-masons who built Solomon's Temple were Rosicrucians. 'I shall here tell you what Rosie Crucians are', Heydon informs his readers, 'and that Moses was their Father'.[133]

On the title page of *The Holy Guide*, Heydon promises that the reader will achieve 'Enoch and Elias knowledge of the Mind and Soul'. The reference to Enoch is significant,[134] and reflects a prevailing belief in occult circles that Hermes Trismegistus, the mythical author of the collection of late antique philosophical, astrological, alchemical, and magical treatises known as the *Hermetica*,[135] was the Egyptian name of Enoch, the Biblical prophet and revealer of heavenly secrets, who in *3 Enoch*, a sixth-century CE magical work generally included in the *heikhalot* genre, was taken up to heaven by God and transformed into the angel Metatron.[136] Metatron,

---

Publications, n.d.). For Westcott's view of Heydon, see Westcott, *History of the SRIA*, 4. For Heydon, see also Yates, *Rosicrucian Enlightenment*, 165–66 and 230; Davies, *Popular Magic*, 124; Waite, *Real History*, 315–86.

[133] Heydon, *Holy Guide*, 151.

[134] The reference to Elias (Elijah) is likewise significant; for the alchemical-Rosicrucian incarnation of Elijah in the early modern period, see Faivre, 'Elie Artiste'. For Paracelsus' view of Elijah as an alchemist, see Patai, *Jewish Alchemists*, 29; Walter Pagel, 'The Paracelsian Elias Artista and the Alchemical Tradition', *Medizinhistorisches Journal* 16 (1981), 6–19.

[135] For an exhaustive bibliography on the *Hermetica*, see Brian Copenhaver (ed. and trans.), *Hermetica* (Cambridge: Cambridge University Press, 1992), lxii–lxxxiii.

[136] There is a rich and extensive esoteric literature known under the soubriquet of 'Enoch', spanning a period of a thousand years and inspiring a large body of scholarly work from the nineteenth century onward. Enoch appears first in Genesis 5.18–24, where he is 'taken up' by God, but no angelic transformation occurs. The earliest of the esoteric Enoch texts is known as the *Book of the Heavenly Luminaries*: a section of a compilation known as *1 Enoch* or 'Ethiopic Enoch', in which Enoch traverses the seven heavens and intercedes with God on behalf of the 'Watchers', the fallen angels who pass magical lore to mortal women. This text presents Enoch as the inventor of astrology – echoed in the role of Hermes Trismegistus in the later Hermetic literature – and dates to the second century BCE; a translation by E. Isaac can be found in Charlesworth (ed.), *Old Testament Pseudepigrapha*, 1:5–89. For a *fin-de-siècle* translation of *1 Enoch* available to the occultists of the Golden Dawn, see Robert Henry Charles (ed. and trans.), *The Book of*

also called *Sar ha-Panim* or 'Prince of the Countenance' and sometimes equated with Michael, the angel of the seventh sphere,[137] could be summoned with the appropriate rituals

---

Enoch (Oxford: Clarendon Press, 1893). *1 Enoch* was first translated into English by Richard Laurence in 1821; this translation is reprinted in Elizabeth Clare Prophet, *Fallen Angels and the Origin of Evil* (Corwin Springs, MT: Summit University Press, 2000), 101–259. Laurence's translation was a major factor in arousing the interest of nineteenth-century Christian theologians in the Jewish background out of which Christianity emerged; see Jonas C. Greenfield and Michael E. Stone, 'The Books of Enoch and the Traditions of Enoch', *Numen* 26:1 (1979), 89–103; Annette Yoshiko Reed, 'Heavenly Ascent, Angelic Descent, and the Transmission of Knowledge in *1 Enoch* 6–16', in Ra'anan S. Boustan and Annette Yoshiko Reed (eds.), *Heavenly Realms and Earthly Realities in Late Antique Religions* (Cambridge: Cambridge University Press, 2004), 47–66. For an early twentieth-century translation of *3 Enoch*, see Hugo Odeberg, *The Hebrew Book of Enoch or Third Enoch* (Cambridge: Cambridge University Press, 1928; repr. New York: Ktav Publishing, 1973). For Enoch's transformation as a shamanic initiation, see James R. Davila, 'The Hekhalot Literature and Shamanism', in *Society of Biblical Literature 1994 Seminar Papers*, SBLSP No. 33 (Atlanta, GA: Scholars Press, 1994), 767–89. For the various early traditions concerning Enoch as both prophet and angel, see Greenfield and Stone, 'The Books of Enoch'; Gedaliahu G. Stroumsa, 'Form(s) of God: Some Notes on Metatron and Christ', *HTR* 76:3 (1983), 269–88. For *2 Enoch* ('Slavonic Enoch'), dated to the first century CE and known in Europe by the early middle ages, see D. M. Dumville, 'Biblical Apocrypha and the Early Irish: A Preliminary Investigation', *Proceedings of the Royal Irish Academy* 73:8 (1973), 318–19. For an overview of the Enoch literature in the context of its cultural background, see J. Edward Wright, *The Early History of Heaven* (Oxford: Oxford University Press, 2000), 119–28, 140–42, 174–81. For Enoch's transformation into Metatron, see also Philip S. Alexander (trans.), '3 (Hebrew Apocalypse of) Enoch', in Charlesworth, James H. (ed.), *The Old Testament Pseudepigrapha*, 2 vols. (Garden City, NY: Doubleday, 1983), 1:223–315; Andrei A. Orlov, *The Enoch-Metatron Tradition* (Tübingen: Mohr Siebeck, 2005); Andrei A. Orlov, 'On the Polemical Nature of 2 (*Slavonic) Enoch*', *JSJ* 34:3 (2003), 274–303; Daphna Arbel, '"Seal of Resemblance, Full of Wisdom, and Perfect in Beauty": The Enoch/Metatron Narrative of 3 Enoch and Ezekiel 28', *HTR* 98:2 (2005), 121–42; Naomi Janowitz, *The Poetics of Ascent: Theories of Language in a Rabbinic Ascent Text* (Albany, NY: State University of New York Press, 1989), 22–24; Nathaniel Deutsch, *Guardians of the Gate: Angelic Vice Regency in Late Antiquity* (Leiden: Brill, 1999), 32–35.

[137] See Alexander (trans.), *3 Enoch*, 17:45–48; Swartz, *Scholastic Magic*, 104; Scholem, *Jewish Gnosticism*, 43–55; Philip S. Alexander, 'The

and asked for knowledge of divine secrets and control over demons and spirits.[138] It is from the rich matrix of Enoch literature that John Dee derived the term 'Enochian' for his angel magic. If Hermes and Enoch were the same, then Hermetic alchemy and Jewish Kabbalistic magic and theosophy must also be, as both issued from the same semi-divine intermediary between heaven and earth. This idea was postulated in the West first, however, not by early modern alchemists, or even Renaissance Christian Kabbalists such as Pico (who also espoused the belief), but by the Jews themselves in their own medieval texts.[139]

A legend that there were three Hermes first appears in an early medieval treatise on astrological history called the *Kitab al-Uluf*, written by an important Islamic astrologer and philosopher known as Abu Ma'shar (787–886 CE).[140] According to this treatise, the first all-wise Hermes lived in Egypt before the Flood and is identical with the Biblical Enoch, portrayed in Jewish esoteric literature as a teacher of supernal wisdom and known in Jewish apocalyptic texts as

---

Historical Setting of the Hebrew Book of Enoch', *JJS* 28 (1977), 156–80, on pp. 162–64; Rachel Elior, 'Early Forms of Jewish Mysticism', in Steven T. Katz (ed.), *The Cambridge History of Judaism* (Cambridge: Cambridge University Press, 2006), 4:749–91, on pp. 760–71.

[138] For the adjuration of Metatron in Jewish texts, see Michael D. Swartz, *Scholastic Magic: Ritual and Revelation in Early Jewish Mysticism* (Princeton: Princeton University Press, 1996), 90–91, 120–21, 178–79; Lesses, *Ritual Practices*, 276–78, 345–72; Schäfer, 'Jewish Magic Literature', 79–81. For an early Christian adjuration of Michael-Metatron, see Marvin W. Meyer and Richard Smith (eds.), *Ancient Christian Magic: Coptic Texts of Ritual Power* (Princeton, NJ: Princeton University Press, 1999), 233. For Agrippa's identification of Metatron with the *sefira Keter*, see Agrippa, *Occult Philosophy*, 2:13, 3:10, 3:24.

[139] For the Renaissance equation of Hermes and Enoch, see Wirszubski, *Pico*, 232; François Secret, *Hermétisme et Kabbale* (Napoli: Bibliopolis, 1972). See also Norman Roth, 'The Theft of Philosophy by the Greeks from the Jews', *Classical Folia* 32 (1978), 53–67, esp. 61–65.

[140] See David Pingree, *The Thousands of Abu Ma'shar* (London: Studies of the Warburg Institute No. 30, 1968); Charles S. F. Burnett, 'The Legend of the Three Hermes and Abu Ma'shar's *Kitab al-Uluf* in the Latin Middle Ages', *JWCI* 39 (1976), 231–34. For a mid-twelfth-century Latin version of the *Kitab al-Uluf* by Robert of Chester, see Antoine Faivre, *The Eternal Hermes: From Greek God to Alchemical Magus*, trans. Joscelyn Godwin (Grand Rapids, MI: Phanes Press, 1995), 83.

an angel, his human body having transformed into fire.[141]
The second Hermes lived in Babylon and learned the occult
sciences after the Flood. The third Hermes, like the first, lived
in Egypt, taught alchemy, astrology, and magic to his
disciple Asclepius, and is the author of the *Hermetica*.[142] The
three Hermes were gradually amalgamated, and this
composite 'Thrice-Greatest Hermes' was recognised as
Enoch.[143] Enoch-Hermes seems to have made his way into
Jewish magical traditions in the twelfth century – coincident
(although probably not coincidental) with the emergence of
the first known Kabbalistic text, the *Sefer ha-Bahir* – primarily
through the agency of Abraham ben Me'ir ibn Ezra (*c.* 1089–
1167), a Spanish-born philosopher, mathematician, astrologer, and magician who produced more than fifty books on
astrology and astronomy, who provides an important link
between medieval Arab astrology and magic and Jewish
Kabbalistic texts,[144] and who is likewise a significant

---

[141] Alexander (trans.), 3 *Enoch*, 15:1b–2, ¶19.
[142] Pingree, *Abu Ma'shar*, 14–18; Burnett, 'Three Hermes', 231.
[143] For the conflation of Hermes and Enoch in Arab magic, see
Faivre, *Eternal Hermes*, 19–20.
[144] Ibn Ezra's best known astrological work is *Sefer Reshit Hokmah*
('Book of the Beginning of Wisdom'), written in 1148. Recent
English translations of his three most important astrological works
are available: *The Book of Reasons*, trans. Shlomo Sela (Leiden: Brill,
2007); *The Beginning of Wisdom*, trans. Meira B. Epstein (Reston, VA:
Archive for the Retrieval of Historical Astrological Texts, 1998); *The
Book of Nativities and Revolutions*, trans. Meira B. Epstein (Reston,
VA: Archive for the Retrieval of Historical Astrological Texts, 2008).
In *The Book of Nativities* (61), ibn Ezra quotes 'Enoch' in an explanation of a particular horoscopic configuration, and also refers to the
authority of Enoch as an astrologer several times in *The Book of
Reasons*. It is unclear to which astrological work he refers, as none of
the Enoch literature provides specific horoscopic delineations, but
the interpretation may be derived from the sixth- or seventh-
century Latin translation of the late antique Greek astrological compilation known as *Liber Hermetis*, which was sometimes ascribed to
Enoch; see Robert Zoller's introduction in Robert Zoller (trans.),
Liber Hermetis, Vol. 1, ed. Robert Hand (Berkeley Springs, WV:
Golden Hind Press, 1993), xvii, and Thorndike, *History of Magic*,
2:220–21. For ibn Ezra's astral magic, see Schwartz, *Astral Magic*, 9–
26. For ibn Ezra's mathematics and science, see Tony Lévy and
Charles Burnett, '*Sefer ha-Middot*: A Mid-Twelfth-Century Text on
Arithmetic and Geometry Atrributed to Abraham Ibn Ezra', *Aleph* 6
(2006), 57–238; Shlomo Sela, 'Abraham ibn Ezra's Scientific Corpus:
Basic Constituents and General Characterization', *ASP* 11 (2001),

'junction' between medieval Jewish astrology and magic and the late-nineteenth-century adepts of the Golden Dawn.[145] Connections between the *Hermetica* and late antique Jewish apocalyptic and *heikhalot* literature are already evident in the Hermetic treatise called *Asclepius*, which echoes the story

---

91–149; Shlomo Sela, *Abraham Ibn Ezra and the Rise of Medieval Hebrew Science* (Leiden: Brill, 2003); Carlos Del Valle, 'Abraham Ibn Ezra's Mathematical Speculations on the Divine Name', in R. A. Herrera (ed.), *Mystics of the Book: Themes, Topics and Typologies* (New York: Peter Lang, 1993), 159–76. For ibn Ezra's equation of ten heavenly spheres with the ten *sefirot*, see Y. Tzvi Langermann, 'Cosmology and Cosmogony in *Doresh Reshumoth*, a Thirteenth-Century Commentary on the Torah', *HTR* 97:2 (2004), 199–227. For Mathers' use of the horoscopic 'house division' system used by ibn Ezra, see J. W. Brodie-Innes *et al.*, *Astrology of the Golden Dawn*, ed. Darcy Küntz (Sequim, WA: Holmes Publishing Group, 1996), 44.

[145] Ibn Ezra seems to have provided justification for the synthesising of the Kabbalistic, Enochian, and Hermetic traditions by Golden Dawn members. Ibn Ezra's works appear in Latin translations by Pietro d'Abano in both Westcott's and Frederick Leigh Gardner's libraries. Gardner lists *De luminaribus et Criticis Diebus Tractatus* (Rome, 1544); *Incipit liber Abraham Judei de nativitatibus* (Venice, 1485); and a second edition of *De nativitatibus* (Köln, 1537); see Frederick Leigh Gardner, *Bibliotheca Astrologica: A Catalogue Raisonné of Works on the Occult Sciences, Vol. II: Astrological Books, With a Sketch of the History of Astrology by Dr. William Wynn Westcott*, private publication, 1911, Yorke Collection FAI 25, Warburg Institute, London), 2, and William Wynn Westcott, 'Catalogue of the Westcott Hermetic Library' (unpublished MS, London, 1891, Grand Lodge Library and Museum of Freemasonry MS 1390WES). That ibn Ezra's work was believed by Golden Dawn initiates to be significant for the occult tradition is demonstrated by Mathers, who, in the astrological doctrines taught in the 'Inner Order' of the Golden Dawn, utilises what are now known as 'Porphyry' house cusps: a distinctive Hellenistic method of dividing the horoscope into sectors or 'houses' that differs from the usual Placidus system used by the 'Outer Order' and by virtually all nineteenth-century astrologers, but which is used by ibn Ezra in his own astrological treatises. For Mathers' use of these cusps, which involves dividing each of the four sectors of the horoscope demarcated by the horizon and meridian into three equal 'houses', see Brodie-Innes *et al.*, *Astrology of the Golden Dawn*, 44. For ibn Ezra's description of this system, see *Book of Reasons*, 3.4–6, pp. 63–69. He does not call his system of house division 'Porphyry', but his method is the same: after locating the ascendant-descendant (horizon) axis and the *medium coeli-immum coeli* (meridian) axis, each of the four resulting quadrants of the 360° circle is divided into three equal 'houses'.

from the earlier Jewish Enoch literature of the mating of mortal women with angels who teach them magical secrets.[146] More mystically inclined Jewish thinkers such as ibn Ezra, distrusting the prevailing interest in Aristotelian philosophy that followed the publication of Maimonides' *Guide of the Perplexed* in the twelfth century,[147] looked to pagan traditions for their inspiration, in particular the wisdom of Hermes, whose origins they believed to lie in ancient Jewish sources.[148] They freely imported Hermetic astrological, alchemical, and medical texts from the Arabs, thus introducing Hermetic ideas into medieval Jewish thought. Fabrizio Lelli observes: 'Hermetism was an alternative to Aristotelianism – the likeliest prospect, in fact, for integrating an alien system into their religion'.[149]

Ibn Ezra called the conflated figure of Hermes-Enoch *Hanokh ha-qadmon* ('the primordial Enoch'),[150] and stated that this semi-divine figure 'composed many books on many sciences which are still in existence today', apparently referring to the *Hermetica*.[151] In an important treatise called the *Sefer Hermes*, a Hebrew translation of an anonymous Arabic astrological work,[152] Hermes is clearly identified with Enoch: 'Hermes, the chief of all the wise, who is also said to

---

[146] See *Asclepius* 25, in Copenhaver (trans.), *Hermetica*, 82. The theme also occurs in *Poimandres*, 12–17, in Copenhaver (trans.), *Hermetica*, 3–4. For the Hebrew version, see Alexander (trans.), *3 Enoch*, 6–9. For Jewish influences on the *Hermetica*, see Birger A. Pearson, 'Jewish Elements in *Corpus Hermeticum* I (Poimandres)', in van den Broek and Vermaseren (eds.), *Studies in Gnosticism*, 336–48.

[147] For discussions on Maimonides, including his hostile attitude toward the Kabbalah, see David Hartman, *Maimonides: Torah and Philosophic Quest* (Philadelphia, PA: Jewish Publication Society, 1976); Kenneth Seeskin, *Maimonides on the Origin of the World* (Cambridge: Cambridge University Press, 2005); Menachem Kellner, *Maimonides' Confrontation with Mysticism* (Oxford: Littman Library of Jewish Civilization, 2006); Moshe Idel, 'Maimonides' *Guide of the Perplexed* and the Kabbalah', *JH* 18:2–3 (2004), 197–226; H. S. Lewis, 'Maimonides on Superstition', *JQR* 17:3 (1905), 475–88.

[148] See Fabrizio Lelli, 'Hermes Among the Jews: *Hermetica* as *Hebraica* from Antiquity to the Renaissance', *MRW* 2:2 (2007), 111–35, on p. 116; Schwartz, *Astral Magic*, 26.

[149] Lelli, 'Hermes', 116.

[150] Abraham ibn Ezra, *Sefer ha-'olam* ('Book of the World'), cited in Lelli, 'Hermes', 118.

[151] Cited in Moshe Idel, 'Hermeticism and Judaism', in Merkel and Debus (eds.), *Hermeticism and the Renaissance*, 59–76, on p. 63.

[152] For this work, see Lelli, 'Hermes', 127.

be Enoch'.[153] By the time Pico began receiving instruction from Jewish Kabbalists such as the Neoplatonically inclined Rabbi Yohanan Alemanno, Pico's *magister* or Kabbalistic 'master' for six years,[154] the identification of Hermes and Enoch was firmly embedded in Jewish Kabbalistic circles, Hermetic doctrines were deeply entrenched in Kabbalistic theosophy and magic, the Kabbalah was perceived as an ancient divine revelation received in common by the Jews, the Egyptians, and the Greeks, and Alemanno could authoritatively inform Pico that Solomon's Temple, following the best Hermetic traditions, was in fact an astral talisman built to receive celestial influences:

> Both Solomon's good, and his unseemly, actions indicate that
> his lifelong goal was to cause the descent of spiritual forces to

---

[153] Lelli, 'Hermes', 127, n. 77.

[154] Alemanno was an Ashkenazi Jew who was born in Mantua in 1435. For details of his life and his relationship with Pico, see B. C. Novak, 'Giovanni Pico della Mirandola and Jochanan Alemanno', *JWCI* 45 (1982), 125–47; Idel, 'Magical and Neoplatonic Interpretations'. For Alemanno's magical and Neoplatonic interpretations of the Kabbalah, see Moshe Idel, *Kabbalah in Italy, 1280–1510* (New Haven, CT: Yale University Press, 2011), 177–201, 340–44; Idel, 'Anthropology of Yohanan Alemanno'. For Alemanno's amalgamation of Kabbalah and astrology, see Moshe Idel, *Saturn's Jews: On the Witches' Sabbath and Sabbateanism* (London: Continuum, 2011), 24–28. The importation of late antique Neoplatonic philosophical and magical doctrines into the medieval Kabbalah has been recognised by numerous scholars, but there has been little specific evidence of direct transmission discussed in these investigations. However, in 2007 Yehudah Liebes published a paper called 'Zohar and Iamblichus' (*Journal for the Study of Religions and Ideologies* 6:18 [2007], 95–100) in which he highlights the close similarity of a passage from Iamblichus' *De mysteriis* and a passage in the *Zohar*, thus demonstrating that either the Zoharic authorship used Iamblichus as a source, or that both Iamblichus and the Zoharic authorship borrowed from the same earlier sources. Liebes also points out that Iamblichus' sources were, among others, the *Chaldean Oracles* and the *Hermetica*, both of which he believes exercised influence on the development of the Jewish Kabbalah. The affinities between the *Chaldean Oracles* and the Kabbalah were clear to the Golden Dawn initiate Percy Bullock, who, in the introduction to Westcott's edited version, *The Chaldean Oracles Attributed to Zoroaster* (Vol. VI of *Collectanea Hermetica*, p. 5), asserts that the *Oracles* 'should be studied in the light of the Kabbalah' and then offers a lengthy comparison of the two theosophical-magical systems.

earth...and he made a great dwelling for the Lord his God, in order to bring the *Shekhina* to earth.[155]

Westcott's conflation of the 'art of Hermes' with the Kabbalah thus has considerable justification in Jewish Kabbalistic sources.

For British occultists as well as for Lévi, the inclusion of the *Aesch Mezareph* in the *Kabbala denudata* was clear proof of the Hermetic science of alchemy as 'a Kabbalistic Art of Spiritual Regeneration'.[156] Andreas Kilcher suggests that the *Aesch Mezareph*, following its publication in the *Kabbala denudata*, became the most important document of the new 'Kabbala chymica', in which the *sefirot* represent the order of the supernal world while the seven planetary metals correspond to the manifest world.[157] The *Aesch Mezareph*, which had been translated into English in 1714,[158] does not hint at any links with the Rosicrucians,[159] although it was probably written contemporaneously with the Rosicrucian Manifestos at the beginning of the seventeenth century. But Knorr von Rosenroth seems to have drawn his own conclusions about the relationship between Rosicrucianism and Kabbalah in his declaration that, in the texts of the *Zohar*, the rose symbolises the *Shekhinah*.[160] Alchemists were deemed to be Kabbalists and vice versa, and a knowledge of Kabbalistic theosophy was a necessary correlate to the practice of the *magnum opus*, whether on a physical level (to transform base metals into gold) or a spiritual level (to transform the human adept into a semi-divine magus).[161] Alchemists were

---

[155] Yohanan Alemanno, *Sefer Heshek Shlomo*, Oxford MS 1535, fol. 15r, cited in Idel, 'Magical and Neoplatonic Interpretations', 206.

[156] 'J.K.' [Julius Kohn], 'Introductory', in 'J.K.' (trans.), *Splendor Solis: Alchemical Treatises of Solomon Trismosin, Adept and Teacher of Paracelsus* (London: Kegan Paul, Trench, Trubner & Co., Ltd., 1920), 9.

[157] Kilcher, 'Verhüllung', 350–51.

[158] See Westcott, *Collectanea Hermetica*, 4:iii–vi and 46–60.

[159] But see the invocation of the Rosicrucian 'Elie Artiste' by the anonymous translator of the *Aesch Mezareph*, in Westcott (ed.), *Collectanaea Hermetica*, 9.

[160] See Waite, *Real History*, 435.

[161] For the transformation of the Kabbalistic adept into a semi-divine magus, see Idel, *Hasidism*, 189–207. For the transformation of the Hermetic adept, see *Poimandres*, 26, in Copenhaver (trans.), *Hermetica*, 6; Dan Merkur, 'Stages of Ascension in Hermetic Rebirth', *Esoterica* 1 (1999), 79–96; Hans Dieter Betz, *The "Mithras*

also Rosicrucians, as alchemy was the art *par excellence* of Christian Rosenkreutz and his initiates. Proof of this seemed to be provided by Rosicrucian apologists such as Fludd, Vaughan, and Michael Maier, whose name was familiar to British occultists not least because John Yarker, a contemporary of Mackenzie and another avid initiator of rogue Masonic degrees, states in his monumental 'emic' history, *The Arcane Schools*:

> There exists in the library of the University of Leyden a MS. by Michael Maier which sets forth that in 1570 the Society of the old Magical brethren or Wise Men was revived under the name of the Brethren of the Rosy Cross.[162]

Westcott and his fellow adepts could also find ample evidence for the identity of alchemy and Kabbalah – as well as Kabbalah and Tarot – in the sixteenth-century alchemical work by Salomon Trismosin known as *Splendor Solis*, illustrated with a series of twenty-two exquisite plates portraying the stages of the alchemical *opus*. Trismosin, according to a contemporaneous text called the *Aurum Vellus*,

---

Liturgy": *Text, Translation, and Commentary* (Tübingen, Mohr-Siebeck, 2003), 35; Fowden, *Egyptian Hermes*, 82–87, 168–72. For the transformation of the *heikhalot* adept, see Gilles Quispel, 'Transformation through Vision in Jewish Gnosticism and the Cologne Mani Codex', in van den Broek and van Heertum (eds.), *Poimandres to Jacob Böhme*, 265–69. For the definiton of an 'esoteric school' as one which enables its initiates to transform themselves into magi, see Daniel von Egmond, 'Western Esoteric Schools in the Late Nineteenth and Early Twentieth Centuries', in van den Broek and Hanegraaff (eds.), *Gnosis and Hermeticism*, 311–46, on p. 312.
[162] Yarker, *Arcane Schools*, 212. For more on Michael Maier, see Urszula Szulakowska, *The Alchemy of Light: Geometry and Optics in Late Renaissance Alchemical Illustration* (Leiden: Brill, 2000), 153–66; Hereward Tilton, *The Quest for the Phoenix: Spiritual Alchemy and Rosicrucianism in the Work of Count Michael Maier (1569–1622)* (Berlin/New York: Walter de Gruyter, 2003); Hereward Tilton, '*Regni Christi Frater*: Count Michael Maier and the Fraternity R.C.', *Aries* 2:1 (2002), 3–33; J. B. Craven, *Count Michael Maier* (Kirkwall: William Peace & Son, 1910; repr. Berwick, ME: Ibis Press, 2003); Waite, *Real History*, 217–18; Yates, *Rosicrucian Enlightenment*, 103–26, 243–48. For the engravings in Maier's major alchemical works, see de Rola, *Golden Game*, 59–132. For the German Rosicrucian Order of the Gold and Rosy Cross which Westcott claimed to be the origin of the Cipher MS, see Howe, *Magicians*, 1–25.

learned his art from a Jewish alchemist.[163] *Splendor Solis* was understood by British occultists to be both an alchemical version of the twenty-two Major Arcana of the Tarot and a visual portrayal of the secret meanings of the twenty-two letters of the Hebrew alphabet, which could therefore be equated with the stages of the alchemical work.[164] *Splendor Solis* fascinated Mathers, who is credited with writing a treatise on it; sadly, this work seems to have vanished.[165]

The blurring of boundaries between these distinctive currents – Jewish Kabbalah, Freemasonry, and Christian Rosicrucian-Hermetic alchemy – has prompted some scholars to see the 'concordances' of the occult revival as a typical characteristic of the Western esotericism that first emerged in the early modern period.[166] Late-nineteenth-century occultists themselves did not view their perceptions as 'concordances'; this term is, after all, a late twentieth-century scholarly definition of the 'emic' exploration of affinities between religious motifs through the recognition of 'family resemblances'. British occultists understood that they were rejoining doctrines that had become severed and corrupted over the centuries but were once fully unified in the ancient wisdom teaching of which the Kabbalah was the most eloquent testimony. Medieval Jewish Kabbalists express a similar perception of their own tradition as the original source of Platonic and Pythagorean philosophies – a view that allowed them to integrate philosophical and magical themes from 'outside' sources without any sense of betraying the 'Jewishness' of their beliefs and practices.[167] Moreover,

---

[163] See Kohn (trans.), *Splendor Solis*, 83–84.

[164] For a recent English translation of *Splendor Solis*, see Joscelyn Godwin (trans.), *Salomon Trismosin's Splendor Solis* (Grand Rapids, MI: Phanes Press, 1991). For a psychological approach to *Splendor Solis* as a representation of inner transformation, see Joseph L. Henderson and Dyane N. Sherwood, *Transformation of the Psyche: The Symbolic Alchemy of the Splendor Solis* (London: Routledge, 2003).

[165] See Ithell Colquhoun, *Sword of Wisdom: MacGregor Mathers and "The Golden Dawn"* (New York: G. P. Putnam's Sons, 1975), 104. Mathers' work was evidently published by Frederick Leigh Gardner in 1907, but there is no trace of it in British Library catalogues and no scholar of the occult revival has seen a copy.

[166] For 'concordances', see Faivre, *Access*, 14.

[167] For Kabbalists' attributions of Kabbalistic theosophy and magic to Enoch and Abraham, see Idel, 'Magical and Neoplatonic Interpretations'; Louis Ginzberg, *Legends of the Jews*, 7 vols., trans. Henrietta Szold (Philadelphia, PA: Jewish Publication Society, 1909–

the incorporation of 'alien' elements requires some affinity between a particular culture and the elements it absorbs, as Moshe Idel suggests:

> Without integral magic, there is no incorporation of alien magic. Some forms of magic found in Judaism are similar to others found in the environment, and the affinities between them are one of the clues for the latter's incorporation.[168]

In their application of 'concordances', the British occultists exhibit a traditional Kabbalistic hermeneutic. Late antique and medieval Jewish texts, like the Greco-Egyptian magical papyri and the medieval grimoires, express the same kind of 'concordance' of different magical and mystical traditions. 'Hermetic alchemy' in the first centuries CE was already a syncretic product incorporating Jewish as well as Greco-Egyptian philosophies and practices.[169] Alexandrian Jewish philosophers such as Philo embedded Platonic and Hermetic doctrines within a Jewish religious framework;[170] these Jewish influences seem to have reached 'Middle' Platonists such as Numenius, possibly through Philo, and Numenius in turn passed them on to Plotinus and later Neoplatonists.[171] Jewish esoteric lore echoes a number of concepts, myths, and rituals found in Gnostic currents.[172] And the angel magic of

---

1938; repr. Baltimore, MD: Johns Hopkins University Press, 1998), 1:80.

[168] Moshe Idel, 'On Judaism, Jewish Mysticism and Magic', in Peter Schäfer and Hans G. Kippenberg (eds.), *Envisioning Magic: A Princeton Seminar and Symposium* (Leiden: Brill, 1997), 195–214, on p. 206.

[169] For links between Jewish and Greco-Egyptian alchemy, see Idel, 'Origin of Alchemy'; Patai, *Jewish Alchemists*, 50–91.

[170] For Philo, see Alan F. Segal, *Two Powers in Heaven: Early Rabbinic Reports about Christianity and Gnosticism* (Leiden: Brill, 2002), 159–81; Erwin R. Goodenough, *By Light, Light: The Mystic Gospel of Hellenistic Judaism* (New Haven, CT: Yale University Press, 1935); H. A. Wolfson, *Philo: Foundations of Religious Philosophy in Judaism, Christianity, and Islam*, 2 vols. (Cambridge, MA: Harvard University Press, 1947).

[171] For Numenius' Jewish sources, see Gager, *Moses*, 63–69; Dillon, *Middle Platonists*, 378–79; Flusser and Amorai-Stark, 'Goddess Thermuthis', 225, n. 28.

[172] For Gnostic elements in late antique Judaism, see Scholem, *Jewish Gnosticism*; Scholem, *Origins*, 49–198. Scholem was convinced that Kabbalistic literature, particularly the twelfth-century *Sefer ha-Bahir*, borrowed many themes from Gnostic texts. The affinities between

Jewish *heikhalot* literature shares many ritual practices with Greco-Egyptian magical texts and traditions, which them-selves freely incorporate Jewish angel names and Hebrew letter combinations.[173] The *Sefer ha-Razim*, for example, is a

---

these two currents did not escape the notice of British occultists; nor did they escape the notice of Henry Cornelius Agrippa in the sixteenth century, who in his apparent 'retraction' of magic – *The Vanity of Arts and Sciences* (*De incertitudine et vanitate scientiarum*), trans. Roger L'Estrange (London: Samuel Speed, 1676) – seems to have been the first to suggest that Gnostic texts represent a corrupted form of Kabbalah. According to Agrippa (*Vanity*, 47:125), 'From this Judaical ferment of Cabalistical Superstition, I verily believe the Ophites, Gnosticks, and Valentinians came, Hereticks that with the help of their Disciples invented a Cabala, corrupting the Mysteries of the Christian Faith'. See also G. R. S. Mead, 'Some Notes on the Gnostics', *The Nineteenth Century and After: A Monthly Review* 52:309 (1902), 822–35, in which Mead, the most informed of the British occultists on Gnostic and Hermetic literature, mentions 'a point which is of special interest to students of the Jewish kabalah, and which has not so far been noticed': an untitled Gnostic text known as the Codex Brucianus, dated to the second century CE, which contains 'a full description' of the Macroprosopus or 'Vast Countenance' which appears as the major theme of the *Sefer Dzeniuta* and the two *Idrot* of the *Zohar*. Mead then observes (p. 834). 'This should give the death-blow to the contentions of over-sceptical critics that the kabalah was entirely a medieval invention and had its genesis in the fabricated *Zohar* of Moses de Leon in the thirteenth century'. Although even new discoveries since Mead's time, such as the remarkable Nag Hammadi Library, have not succeeded in giving any 'death-blow' to the academic debate about the age of the Zoharic corpus, but instead have only complicated the issue further, there is increasing interest among scholars in the importance of Judaism in the religious 'common stock' of the late Roman Empire. Of particular interest is Gilles Quispel, 'Hermes Trismegistus and the Origins of Gnosticism', in van den Broek and van Heertum (eds.), *From Poimandres to Jacob Böhme*, 145–66. Quispel demonstrates convincingly in this paper that Mani, long thought to be the chief representative of extreme Iranian dualism in late antiquity, was in fact raised in a Jewish-Christian community. For Jewish influences on Mani's form of Gnostic thought, see Guy G. Stroumsa, *Hidden Wisdom: Esoteric Traditions and the Roots of Christian Mysticism* (Leiden: Brill, 1996), 63–78.

[173] See Morton Smith, 'Observations on Hekhalot Rabbati', in Alexander Altmann (ed.), *Biblical and Other Studies* (Cambridge, MA: Harvard University Press, 1963), 142–60. For Jewish magical practices in Greco-Egyptian texts, see Hans Dieter Betz, 'Jewish Magic in the Greek Magical Papyri (*PGM* VII.260–71)', in Schäfer and Kippenberg (eds.), *Envisioning Magic*, 45–63.

Hebrew work which comfortably combines the ritual use of the letter combinations and Divine Names with adjurations addressing the Greek Sun-god Helios:

> I adjure you, angels that fly through the air of the firmament, by the One who sees but is not seen, by the King who uncovers all hidden things and sees all secret things...Holy Helios who rises in the east, good mariner, trustworthy leader of the sun's rays, reliable (witness), who of old didst establish the mighty wheel (of the heavens)...Lord, Brilliant Leader, King, Soldier.[174]

In many early Jewish magical texts, concordances between deities are acknowledged with the same cheerful abandon that nineteenth century occultists display.[175] This tendency is also evident in an unusual Jewish poetic fragment known as the *Testament of Orpheus*, preserved in various redactions in patristic sources from the fifth century CE onward but dated to possibly the second century BCE, in which Orpheus conflates Moses with his teacher Musaeus and acknowledges Moses' unique status in knowing that all gods are the one God:

> There is one Zeus alone, one Hades, one Helios,
> One Dionysus; and in all things but one God;
> Why should I speak to you of them as separate?[176]

---

[174] Michael A. Morgan (trans.), *Sepher ha-Razim: The Book of the Mysteries* (Chico, CA: Scholars Press, 1983), 70–71.

[175] See Lesses, *Ritual Practices*, 300–10.

[176] Carl R. Holladay (ed. and trans.), *Fragments from Hellenistic Jewish Authors, Vol. 4: Orphica* (Atlanta, GA: Scholars Press, 1996), 107. Holladay (*Orphica*, 69) states that the *Testament* is 'an important testimony to the theology of Greek-speaking Jews in the Graeco-Roman period' and refers to its syncretistic monotheism. In the text, Orpheus also acknowledges Abraham as 'a scion of Chaldean race' who is versed in the secrets of astrology (*Orphica*, 119). Flusser and Amorai-Stark ('Goddess Thermuthis', 225) note that the equation of Musaeus and Moses occurs in the writings of Artapanus, a Jewish writer from Egypt (150–100 BCE), and appears later in the work of the mid-second-century CE Platonist Numenius. The *Testament of Orpheus* seems to predate both these references, suggesting an older tradition linking Moses with Orphic traditions. For the *Testament* as the chief vehicle through which Orphic doctrines entered Christianity in late antiquity, see Miguel Herrero de Jáuregui, *Orphism and Christianity in Late Antiquity* (Berlin: Walter de Gruyter,

Westcott, in asserting the affinities between Jewish esoteric lore and disparate currents such as Hermetic alchemy and astral magic, had behind him a long and respected Jewish tradition of 'concordances' stretching back to antiquity. The ritual practices in antique Jewish *heikhalot* literature and magical texts such as the *Sefer ha-Razim*, the Greco-Egyptian magical papyri, early Christian Coptic magical literature, Gnostic tracts, Aramaic amulets, and Hermetic magic and alchemy all belong to what Rebecca Lesses calls 'a larger complex of practices of adjuration that was widespread in the Greco-Roman world in late antiquity'.[177] This 'larger complex' found its way into the medieval Kabbalah through various channels, many of them traceable, and it is not surprising that Westcott and his fellow adepts recognised family resemblances. They did not have to 'invent' traditions, but perpetuated them while providing a conceptual and linguistic framework appropriate for the time.

The Golden Dawn incorporated not only Masonic rituals, Kabbalistic theosophy, and Rosicrucian 'Hermetic alchemy', but also such diverse themes as astral talismans, astral travel (known as 'path jumping' in Kabbalistic literature), the ascent of the soul through the different levels of the universe, and the angel adjurations of John Dee. These currents, although some are ubiquitous in the ancient Mediterranean world and some appear to be more culture-specific, are nevertheless all included in the translations and redactions of late antique and medieval Jewish esoteric texts available to British occultists in the late nineteenth century.[178] Even the

---

2010), 179–86; John Block Friedman, *Orpheus in the Middle Ages* (Syracuse, NY: Syracuse University Press, 2000), 13–37.

[177] Lesses, *Ritual Practices*, 284. For more amalgamations of Jewish and Greco-Egyptian magical texts, see Gager, *Moses*, 146–52.

[178] For 'path jumping' or astral travel in the Kabbalah, see Mark Verman and Shulamit H. Adler, 'Path Jumping in the Jewish Magical Tradition', *JSQ* 1:2 (1993–94), 131–48. For the ascent of the soul in the *Chaldean Oracles*, see Lewy, *The Chaldaean Oracles and Theurgy*; Sarah Iles Johnston, *Hekate Soteira* (Oxford: Oxford University Press, 2000); Ruth Majercik, *The Chaldean Oracles* (Leiden: Brill, 1989); Hutton, *Witches, Druids*, 118–28. For the appropriation of the *Oracles* in British occultism and their amagamation with Kabbalah, see Percy Bullock ['L. O.'], 'Introduction', in Westcott, (ed.), *Collectanea Hermetica*, 6:7–22, on p. 9. For astral magic in Jewish esoteric lore, see Schwartz, *Astral Magic*; Michael D. Swartz, 'Divination and Its Discontents: Finding and Questioning Meaning in Ancient and Medieval Judaism', in Noegel, Walker, and Wheeler

'Egyptian' magic which Mathers incorporated in the Golden Dawn rituals appears in Jewish esoteric literature since, in the view of some Kabbalists, the Egyptians learned their art from Abraham and then passed it back to Moses.[179] Gerald Yorke asserts that the real creativity of the Golden Dawn, the 'crowning glory of the occult revival', lies in the manner in which its adepts 'synthesized into a coherent whole a vast body of disconnected and widely scattered material and welded it into a practical and effective system'.[180] The synthesis is certainly brilliantly creative, but the material is not as 'widely scattered' as Yorke suggests. The connecting link between the 'disconnected' elements is Jewish esoteric lore from antiquity to the modern era, which the British occultists perceived homogenously as 'Kabbalah'.

JOHN DEE AND HIS JEWISH ANGELS

One of the chief magical practices taken up by Mackenzie and other SRIA adepts, and later incorporated as a major feature in the Golden Dawn repertoire, was scrying, otherwise known as crystallomancy or crystal-gazing. In a 1924 scholarly work on the subject, Theodore Besterman defines scrying as

> a method of bringing into the consciousness of the scryer by means of a speculum through one or more of his senses the content of his subconsciousness...and of bringing into operation a latent and unknown faculty of perception.[181]

(eds.), *Prayer, Magic, and the Stars*, 155–66; Kocku von Stuckrad, 'Astral Magic in Ancient Jewish Discourse: Adoption, Transformation, Differentiation' (paper delivered at the Colloquium on Ancient Astrology, Warburg Institute, London, 16–17 February 2007); Moses Gaster (ed. and trans.), 'The Wisdom of the Chaldeans: An Ancient Hebrew Astrological Text', *PSBA* (20 December 1900), 329–51, repr. in Moses Gaster, *Studies and Texts in Folklore, Magic, Mediaeval Romance, Hebrew Apocrypha, and Samaritan Archaeology*, 3 vols. (London: Maggs Brothers, 1925–1928; repr. New York: Ktav Publishing, 1971), 338–55.

[179] For Mathers' use of 'Egyptian' rituals, see Hutton, *Witches, Druids*, 130 and n. 159. For the 'Bornless Ritual' incorporated into Golden Dawn ceremonies, see Chapter Four.

[180] Gerald Yorke, 'Foreword', in Howe, *Magicians*, ix.

[181] Theodore Besterman, *Crystal-Gazing* (London: Rider, 1924), 160. For works on scrying by British occultists contemporaneous with Besterman, see 'Frater Achad' [Charles Stansfeld-Jones], *Crystal*

Scrying, as utilised by both John Dee and the British occultists of the late nineteenth and early twentieth centuries, has little in common with the spiritualist practices imported from America in the 1850s, other than that both the scryer and the spiritualist medium appear to enter a 'trance', or what cognitive psychologists refer to as an RASC (religiously altered state of consciousness).[182] As a method of contacting transhuman entities to acquire knowledge of occult secrets, scrying can be found in virtually every culture in the ancient world, and its presence in Western esoteric currents has antecedents that vanish into the mists of ancient Mesopotamia.[183] Although this magical practice might seem entirely unrelated to the Kabbalah – it is never considered in that light in scholarly descriptions of the Golden Dawn's practices[184] – scrying with the use of the Divine Names is one of the cornerstones of late antique and medieval Jewish magic, from which John Dee derived his practice of conjuring angels in 'shew-stones' or specially designed and consecrated crystals.[185]

Vision through Crystal Gazing, or The Crystal as a Stepping-Stone to Clear Vision (Chicago: Yogi Publication Society, 1923); 'Sepharial' [Walter Gorn-Old], *How to Read the Crystal; or Crystal and Seer, With a Concise Dictionary of Astrological Terms* (London: Foulsham & Co., 1922).

[182] For the distinction between scrying and spiritual mediumship, see Deborah E. Harkness, *John Dee's Conversations with Angels: Cabala, Alchemy, and the End of Nature* (Cambridge: Cambridge University Press, 1999), 17. For an explanation of RASCs and their relation to Jewish magical practices, see Alan F. Segal, *Life After Death: A History of the Afterlife in Western Religion* (New York: Doubleday, 2004), 322–50.

[183] For scrying as an ancient and widespread method of divination, see Sarah Iles Johnston, 'Introduction: Divining Divination', in Sarah Iles Johnston and Peter T. Struck (eds.), *Mantikê: Studies in Ancient Divination* (Leiden: Brill, 2005), 1–28, on p. 7; Georg Luck, *Arcana Mundi: Magic and the Occult in the Greek and Roman Worlds* (Baltimore, MD: Johns Hopkins University Press, 1985), 254; E. R. Dodds, *The Ancient Concept of Progress and Other Essays on Greek Literature and Belief* (Oxford: Clarendon Press, 1973), 186–88; Thorndike, *History of Magic*, 3:33:774; Keith Thomas, *Religion and the Decline of Magic: Studies in Popular Beliefs in Sixteenth- and Seventeenth-Century England* (London: Weidenfeld & Nicolson, 1971), 230.

[184] See, for example, Owen, *Place of Enchantment*, 196.

[185] For Dee's 'shew-stones' and crystallomancy, see Harkness, *Dee's Conversations*, 116–18 and n. 73; Deborah E. Harkness, 'Shows in the

Scrying can also be performed in a tiny pool of oil, and the earliest Jewish forms, drawn from ancient Assyro-Babylonian magic, often favour this medium. In 1913, Rabbi Samuel Daiches, one of several tutors at Jews' College, London involved in the translation of early Hebrew magical texts at the turn of the twentieth century,[186] published a definitive work on the subject which explores the ancient Jewish practice of scrying in a tiny slick of oil smeared on the thumbnail or at the bottom of a cup.[187] The entities invoked in such rituals and visible on the shining surface of the oil are called 'princes'. The distinction between these entities, understood in Kabbalistic literature as angelic or daimonic and therefore partaking of divinity, and the Christian perception of demons as evil spirits under the dominion of Satan, needs to be emphasised.[188] The entities summoned by traditional Jewish magical invocations are not necessarily viewed as 'evil', although the 'princes of the oil' can sometimes be tricky and badly behaved.[189] But such intermediaries are often high angels from the supernal spheres, and even when they belong to the lower orders of nonhuman entities they are closer to the neutral character of Paracelsus' 'elemental spirits' than to the malevolent Christian demons.[190] Even

---

Showstone: A Theater of Alchemy and Apocalypse in the Angel Conversations of John Dee (1527–1698/9)', *RQ* 49 (1996), 707–37. For scrying involving angelic conjuration in the Talmud, see Swartz, *Scholastic Magic*, 48.

[186] For more on these scholars, see below, Chapter Four.

[187] Samuel Daiches, *Babylonian Oil Magic in the Talmud and in the Later Jewish Literature* (London: Oxford University Press/Jews College, 1913).

[188] For the view of R. Eleazar of Worms that the 'princes' are angels, see Trachtenberg, *Jewish Magic*, 220–22.

[189] See Trachtenberg, *Jewish Magic*, 220–22, for the tendency of the 'princes' to lie.

[190] The Hebrew word for a malevolent demon is *mazik*, while the word for a prince is *sar*, a term that can also mean 'captain'; see Swartz, *Scholastic Magic*, 181–82. *Sar* and *malakh* (angel) are often used interchangeably. For an example of the invocation of a 'prince' who is 'the greatest angel in heaven, second only to God in power and control', the *Sar ha-Panim*, see Rebecca Macy Lesses, 'The Adjuration of the Prince of the Presence: Performative Utterance in a Jewish Ritual', in Marvin Meyer and Paul Mirecki (eds.), *Ancient Magic and Ritual Power* (Leiden: Brill, 2001), 185–206. For other angelic princes, see the description of the angelic entity called *Sar ha-Torah*, the 'Prince of the Torah', in Michael D. Swartz, *Mystical Prayer in Ancient Judaism: An Analysis of Ma'aseh Merkavah*

during the ritual of exorcism, they may suddenly decide to cooperate with the exorcist.[191] Water is sometimes used as a scrying medium, a divinatory technique known as hydromancy that is first mentioned in Genesis 44:5–15.[192] In both late antique and medieval Jewish magic, the entities are summoned by the power of the combinations of the letters, the Divine Names, and, in later texts, the ten *sefirot*, and the invocation often requires the use of a protective circle around the diviner and his medium, usually a child.[193] The entities offer knowledge of supernal secrets, healing remedies, and recipes for the exorcism of evil spirits, and can even help to locate a thief who has made off with one's possessions.[194] Joscelyn Godwin suggests that, when combined with the ritualistic invocation of angels, scrying should be understood as a branch of ceremonial magic in the Judeo-Christian tradi-

---

(Tübingen: Mohr Siebeck, 1992), 10–11, and the ritual for his invocation, 44. This angel, along with the *Sar ha-Panim*, gives instructions to the adept to perform a celestial ascent through the seven heavens. See also the invocation of the *Sar ha-Halom*, the 'Prince of the Dream', in Lesses, *Ritual Practices*, 66–68. The 'princes of the oil' are only minor intermediaries, but they are not always perceived as evil, allowing nineteenth-century occultists the freedom to invoke such entities without feeling they were practising 'black magic'.

[191] See the surprisingly helpful spirit described in Petrovsky-Shtern, 'Master of an Evil Name', 226–31.

[192] For water as a method of scrying (hydromancy) in early Jewish magic, see the *Hygromanteia of Solomon* in Torijano, *Solomon*, 209–24; Moses Gaster (ed. and trans.), *Sword of Moses: An Ancient Book of Magic* (London: D. Nutt, 1896); Geoffrey W. Dennis, 'The Use of Water as a Medium for Altered States of Consciousness in Early Jewish Mysticism: A Cross-Disciplinary Analysis', *AC* 19:1 (2008), 84–106.

[193] For the use of children in scrying practices, see Yoram Bilu, 'Pondering "The Princes of the Oil": New Light on an Old Phenomenon', *JAR* 37:3 (1981), 269–78; Schäfer, 'Jewish Magic Literature', 89–90. For the Jewish tradition of female receptivity to scrying, see J. H. Chajes, 'He Said She Said: Hearing the Voices of Pneumatic Early Modern Jewish Women', *Nashim* 10 (2005), 99–125. For Frederick Hockley's use of a thirteen-year-old female scryer, see R. A. Gilbert, 'Introduction', in Hamill (ed.), *Rosicrucian Seer*, 11–25, on p. 15. See also Mathers' comments on Cagliostro's use of a child-scryer in S. L. MacGregor Mathers (trans.), *The Book of the Sacred Magic of Abramelin the Mage* (London: John M. Watkins, 1900; repr. New York: Dover Publications, 1975), xlii.

[194] See, for example, Text 5 in Daiches, *Oil Magic*, 22.

tion;[195] it is the use of the Divine Names and the adjuration of *maggidim* that gives it its peculiarly Jewish stamp.

The summoning of angels can also be practised with verbal adjurations alone, accompanied by detailed preparatory procedures and ritual actions, and this forms the basis of early Hebrew magical texts such as the *Sefer ha-Razim*, the *Sefer Maphtea Shlomo* ('Book of the Key of Solomon') and the *Harbe de Moshe*, as well as the complex *heikhalot* literature of the third to eighth centuries, with its invocations of angels and recipes for inducing a celestial ascent to achieve a vision of God on his chariot-throne.[196] These texts, acquired by the Jews of Byzantine southern Italy from Babylonian and Palestinian Jewish communities in the ninth and tenth centuries, were appropriated during the eleventh and twelfth centuries by the *Hasidei Ashkenaz* or German Pietists of northern France and the Rhineland.[197] Through the writings of the most important of these *Hasidei*, Eleazar of Worms (d. c. 1230),[198] *heikhalot* texts and practices found their way into Provence and Spain in the mid-twelfth century,[199] and were absorbed into the developing Kabbalistic literature of the time as well as being reformulated with suitable invocations to Christ in the many grimoires that comprise the backbone

---

[195] Godwin, *Theosophical Enlightenment*, 186.

[196] For the ascent in the *heikhalot* literature, see Schäfer, *Hidden and Manifest God*; Peter Schäfer, 'Merkavah Mysticism and Magic', in *Gershom Scholem's* Major Trends, 59–78; Scholem, *Jewish Gnosticism*; Lesses, *Ritual Practices*.

[197] For the transmission of *heikhalot* literature, see Ra'Anan S. Boustan, 'The Study of Heikhalot Literature: Between Mystical Experience and Textual Artifact', *Currents in Biblical Research* 6 (2007), 130–60; Scholem, *Major Trends*, 47; Elliot R. Wolfson, 'The Theosophy of Shabbetai Donnolo, with Special Emphasis on the Doctrine of *Sefirot* in His *Sefer Hakhmoni'*, *JH* 6:1–2 (1992), 281–316.

[198] For Eleazar of Worms and his influence on the development of the Kabbalah, see Scholem, *Major Trends*, 101–04; Wolfson, *Speculum*, 188–269.

[199] For angel magic and scrying with the 'princes' among the German Pietists, see Moshe Idel, 'Some Forlorn Writings of a Forgotten Ashkenazi Prophet', *JQR* 95:1 (2005), 183–96; Swartz, *Scholastic Magic*, 48; Scholem, *Major Trends*, 80–118; Elliot R. Wolfson, 'Metatron and Shi'ur Qomah in the Writings of Haside Ashkenaz', in Karl E. Grözinger and Joseph Dan (eds.), *Mysticism, Magic and Kabbalah in Ashkenazi Judaism* (Berlin: Walter de Gruyter, 1995), 60–92. For scrying among the Hasidim of Poland and Lithuania in the late nineteenth century, see Bilu, 'Pondering "The Princes"', 271–72.

of the medieval Christian magical tradition.[200] *Heikhalot* techniques of angel magic reappear in the sixteenth century in Agrippa's *De occulta philosophia*, with which Dee was familiar.[201] But Dee was a Hebraist and a Kabbalist in his own right, and did not have to rely on Agrippa for his Jewish angel magic; he could go directly to the Hebrew sources, as he undoubtedly did during his stay in Amsterdam in 1548 when he established contact with the large Jewish community living there.[202] One of the texts Dee undoubtedly

---

[200] For the close similarity between Daiches' examples of the 'princes of the oil' and a medieval German magical text, see Richard Kieckhefer, *Forbidden Rites: A Necromancer's Manual of the Fifteenth Century* (University Park, PA: Pennsylvania State University Press, 1997), 115. For more on the relationship between the grimoires and early Jewish magical texts, see Chapter Four.

[201] See Harkness, *Dee's Conversations*, 35; Frances A. Yates, *The Occult Philosophy in the Elizabethan Age* (London: Routledge & Kegan Paul, 1979), 61.

[202] See Harkness, *John Dee's Conversations*, 85–86. Frances Yates states in relation to Dee's major work, the *Monas Hieroglyphica*, published in 1564: 'Above all it is Cabala. It is related to "the stupendous fabric of the Hebrew letters". It is a "Cabalistic grammar"' (Yates, *Occult Philosophy*, 83). Alchemy and Kabbalah form a unity in Dee's work, as they do in the doctrines of Lévi and the practitioners of the British occult revival. For more on Dee's Kabbalistic studies, see Karen de León-Jones, 'John Dee and the Kabbalah', in Stephen Clucas (ed.), *John Dee: Interdisciplinary Studies in Renaissance Thought* (Dordrecht: Kluwer Academic Publishers, 2006), 143–58. For Dee's angel magic, see Meric Casaubon, *A True & Faithful Relation of What passed For Many Yeers Between Dr. John Dee and Some Spirits*, British Museum MSS Cotton Appendix XLVI (London: T. Garthwait, 1659; repr. in facsimile, Berkeley, CA: Golem Media, 2008). For more on Dee, see Nicholas H. Clulee, *John Dee's Natural Philosophy: Between Science and Religion* (London: Routledge, 1988); György E. Szónyi, 'John Dee', in Hanegraaff (ed.), *Dictionary of Gnosis*, 301–09; György E Szónyi, 'Paracelsus, Scrying, and the *Lingua Adamica*: Contexts for John Dee's Angel Magic', in Clucas (ed.), *John Dee: Interdisciplinary Studies*, 207–29; Peter French, *John Dee: The World of an Elizabethan Magus* (London: Routledge, 1972); Geoffrey James, *The Enochian Evocation of Dr. John Dee* (Gillette, NJ: Heptangle Books, 1984); Stephen Skinner and David Rankine, *Practical Angel Magic of Dr. John Dee's Enochian Tables* (London: Golden Hoard Press, 2004); Peter J. Foreshaw, 'The Early Alchemical Reception of John Dee's *Monas Hieroglyphica*', *Ambix* 52:3 (2005), 247–69; Michael T. Walton, 'John Dee's *Monas Hieroglyphica*: Geometrical Cabala', in Debus (ed.), *Alchemy and Early Modern Chemistry*, 178–85; Frances A. Yates,

encountered was the *Sefer ha-Raziel* ('Book of the Angel Raziel'), traditionally attributed to Solomon: a compilation of mystical, cosmological, and magical Hebrew works and portions of works which includes the third-century *Sefer ha-Razim* with its angelic *charactêres*.[203]

Mackenzie learned the practice of scrying from Frederick Hockley in the early 1850s.[204] Hockley, in turn, availed himself of the writings of Agrippa, Dee, and an English alchemist and magician called Dr. Thomas Rudd, who who seems to have been connected with occult circles associated with Dee's son Arthur and who produced a work called *A Treatise on Angel Magic*[205] – although Hockley's predilection

---

The Theatre of the World (Chicago: University of Chicago Press, 1969), 5–19.

[203] For a general introduction to the *Sefer ha-Raziel*, see Joseph Dan, 'Book of Raziel', in *EJ* 13:1591–93. The *Sefer ha-Raziel* was published in Amsterdam in 1701 but contains much older material, including portions of the late antique *heikhalot* literature concerning the conjuration of angels, and portions of works from the twelfth-century German Pietists, particularly Eleazar of Worms. The work also includes sections of pre-Lurianic Kabbalistic literature. The *Sefer ha-Raziel* was circulating in MS long before its publication in 1701, as it is mentioned by Renaissance Christian Kabbalists; see François Secret, 'Sur quelques traductions du Sefer Raziel', *REJ* 128 (1969), 223–45. For Dee's familiarity with this work, see Harkness, *John Dee's Conversations*, 180, n. 101. For an English translation of the *Sefer ha-Raziel*, see Steve Savedow, *Sepher Rezial Hemelach: The Book of the Angel Rezial* (York Beach, ME: WeiserBooks, 2001). Another English translation, Sloane MS 3826, can be found in the British Museum, entitled *Liber Salomonis: Cephar Raziel*. Hockley, Westcott, and Mathers would have had access to this translation as well as other versions in British libraries; see Savedow's Appendix of *Sefer ha-Raziel* manuscripts in Savedow (trans.), *Sepher Rezial Hemelach*, 280–86. For a discussion and transcription of Sloane MS 3826, see Don Karr, *Liber Salomonis: Cephar Raziel*, at www.digital-brilliance.com/kab/karr/Solomon/LibSal.pdf.

[204] Godwin, *Theosophical Enlightenment*, 185.

[205] See Thomas Rudd, *A Treatise on Angel Magic*, ed. Adam McLean (London: Phanes Press, 1989; repr. York Beach, ME: WeiserBooks, 2006); Steven Skinner and David Rankine (eds.), *The Goetia of Dr. Rudd* (London: Golden Hoard Press, 2007); Yates, *Rosicrucian Enlightenment*, 245–46; Egil Asprem, 'False, Lying Spirits and Angels of Light: Ambiguous Mediation in Dr. Rudd's Seventeenth-Century Treatise on Angel Magic', *MRW* (Summer 2008), 54–80. A collection of Rudd's manuscripts comprises the collection MSS Harley 6481–6486, known as 'The Treatises of Dr. Rudd'; these appear to be copies of lost originals, made by Peter Smart in English between

for collecting obscure medieval manuscripts suggests that, like Dee himself, he may also have encountered the tradition in Latin translations of Jewish magical literature.[206] Hockley, who seems to have acquired his enthusiasm for scrying from the remnants of Francis Barrett's occult circle,[207] believed – not without justification – that scrying for the purposes of angelic communication was an ancient Jewish innovation:

> It is to be remembered that divination by the crystal is, more than any other species of modern magic, derived immediately

---

1699 and 1714. Yates, in *Rosicrucian Enlightenment*, 245–46, refers to the Harley manuscripts as 'Rosicrucian' texts, since Harley 6485, which was once attributed to John Dee, is entitled 'The Rosicrucian Secrets', and Harley 6486 is a copy of Foxcroft's English translation of Andreae's *Chymical Wedding of Christian Rosenkreutz*. Rudd's treatises are important because, according to Adam McLean, they are 'an important link in the chain of the transmission of esoteric traditions' (Rudd, *Angel Magic*, 16). They represent a comprehensive compilation of the extant theories and practices of angel magic in the late seventeenth and early eighteenth centuries, and include not only Dee's angel magic, the 'magic squares' offered by Agrippa in *De occulta philosophia* and by the anonymous author of the *Aesch Mezareph*, alchemical and Rosicrucian textual references, and elements from Trithemius' *Steganographia*, but also material from late antique Jewish sources such as *The Wisdom of the Chaldeans*, which gives the same equation of planets, angels, and *sefirot* later used in the Golden Dawn rituals. Although Egil Asprem's paper on Rudd and his sources ('False, Lying Spirits') discusses extensively the currents from which Rudd drew his angel magic, Asprem never mentions Jewish magical texts as possible sources. Rudd's attribution of various angelic names, planets, and sigils is immediately recognisable in Mathers' Golden Dawn papers; see, for example, Samuel Liddell MacGregor Mathers, 'Talismanic Magic: Saturn', in *Lucifer* 2 (March 1888), 10–14, where, as discussed in Chapter Four below, Mathers reproduces the magical squares, seals, and divine and angelic names and sigils for the planet that are found in Rudd's text but are not found in their entirety in Agrippa's *Occult Philosophy*. McLean (Rudd, *Angel Magic*, 13) concludes as a result of his research into Rudd's manuscript: 'Western occultism has been much influenced by the Kabbalistic stream'.
[206] For a list of manuscripts in Hockley's library, see R. A. Gilbert, 'Secret Writing: The Magical Manuscripts of Frederick Hockley', in Hamill (ed.), *Rosicrucian Seer*, 26–33.
[207] Godwin, *Theosophical Enlightenment*, 170. Barrett's references to scrying can be found in Barrett, *Magus*, 2.4.

from the Jews...and their followers, the Cabalists...were diligent investigators of the occult properties of nature.[208]

Hockley appropriated these Jewish magical practices in their entirety, although, like Dee, he preferred *specularii* to a pool of oil. His principal spirit guide, whom Jewish Kabbalists would have recognised immediately as a high *maggid* in the tradition of Taitazak and Luria, was called the Crowned Angel of the Seventh Sphere. This exalted entity, who is clearly related to the late antique Jewish Metatron-Michael, known as the 'angel of the seventh sphere',[209] dictated a work to Hockley entitled *Metaphysical and Spiritual Philosophy*, which Hockley never published.[210] Hockley's *maggid*, like the 'princes', was not entirely beatific, and happily passed on to Hockley rituals to invoke lower demonic entities to do the adept's bidding, in the manner of King Solomon. The angel also opposed Hockley's entering 'regular' Freemasonry, although offering no objection to his initiation into the SRIA in 1872 because 'they are followers of the Rosy Cross'.[211]

Hockley's influence on Mackenzie, Westcott, Mathers, and the Golden Dawn cannot be overestimated. Like Lévi, Hockley was a 'junction', mediating between the British Kabbalistic currents of the sixteenth and seventeenth centuries and the occultism of the late nineteenth century. Mackenzie regarded Hockley as his master in all occult matters, and it was Hockley who transcribed Mackenzie's description of his visit to Éliphas Lévi in Paris in 1861. John Hamill suggests that Hockley should be seen as the 'ultimate source' of the Golden Dawn's angel magic.[212] But the 'ultimate source' for Hockley himself was the long tradition of late antique Jewish magic and medieval Kabbalistic literature, transmitted through the various manuscripts he collected as well as his knowledge of the works of Agrippa, Dee, Rudd, Barrett, and Lévi. From the angel magic transmitted by Hockley, Westcott and Mathers developed a complex amalgamation of Dee's methods, implements, and angelic alphabet (itself derived from early Hebrew magical

---

[208] Hockley, 'Ancient Magic Crystal', 10.
[209] See above, n. 123.
[210] For selections from Hockley's communication with the Crowned Angel, see Hamill (ed.), *Rosicrucian Seer*, 109–29.
[211] Gilbert, 'Introduction', in Hamill (ed.), *Rosicrucian Seer*, 16.
[212] Hamill (ed.), *Rosicrucian Seer*, 29.

alphabets such as that found in the *Sefer ha-Raziel*);[213] the system was known in the Golden Dawn as 'Enochian'. Although it is unlikely that any modern Kabbalistic scholar would view the Golden Dawn's Enochian system as Kabbalah in the strict sense – or even in the broad sense – its practitioners believed it to be exactly that: Jewish practical Kabbalah, whose roots lay in antiquity and which, handed down from one rabbinic initiate to another over the centuries, could be enhanced and expanded according to the tradition of innovation demonstrated in Jewish Kabbalistic texts. Since Hockley declared scrying to be Jewish and Kabbalistic, and eminent Jewish scholars such as Daiches affirmed its continuity in the Jewish magical tradition, British occultists could therefore include scrying as an authentic 'Kabbalistic' technique deserving of incorporation in the rituals of the Golden Dawn.

WESTCOTT AND THE GODDESSES: THE KABBALAHS OF ANNA KINGSFORD AND H. P. BLAVATSKY

In the late spring of 1884, four years before Westcott and Mathers launched their own order, a new occult group called the Hermetic Society was founded in London. It was nominally intended to complement, but in fact challenged, Blavatsky's Theosophical Society. The Hermetic Society was created by a remarkable woman called Anna Bonus Kingsford (1846–1888), whose short, illness-ridden life belies the enormous influence her understanding of the Kabbalah exercised on Westcott, Mathers, and the structure and rituals of the Golden Dawn.[214] Kingsford, who joined the Theosophical Society in 1882, had been President of its London Lodge from the time Blavatsky moved her headquarters to Adyar in 1883 but, in the words of Ellic Howe, 'she could not stomach H.P.B.'s Mahatmas',[215] and asserted her allegiance to a Western 'esoteric Christian'

---

[213] For the magical alphabets, see Chapter Four.
[214] For Kingsford's life, see Godwin, *Theosophical Enlightenment*, 333–46; Dixon, *Divine Feminine*, 29–30, 165–66, 238; Edward Maitland, *Anna Kingsford: Her Life, Letters, Diary and Work* (1895; repr. London, 1913, 2 vols.). See also Amanda Kluveld, 'Anna Bonus Kingsford', in Hanegraaff (ed.), *Dictionary of Gnosis*, 663–65, an article which does not mention the Kabbalah in relation to Kingsford's work.
[215] Howe, *Magicians*, 40.

tradition modelled on Lévi's Kabbalistic theosophy.[216] This led to her removal from the presidency of the London Lodge and the creation of her own society to accommodate those Theosophists who declared their own preference for the 'Western mystery tradition'.

Kingsford, like Blavatsky, was a charismatic figure, and her battle for women's enfranchisement and antivivisection laws places her firmly in what James Webb calls the 'Progressive Underground' of late Victorian Britain.[217] She also stands at the beginning of a line of *fin-de-siècle* female occultists who believed their sex conferred special abilities and sensitivities in the realm of the occult sciences, and who became widely read authors and leaders of esoteric groups.[218] Like Blavatsky, Kingsford had experimented with mediumistic trance-states, but she later grew hostile toward spiritualist practices because the spirits 'are untrustworthy guides'.[219] During the 1870s she encountered Lévi's work as well as the *Kabbala denudata*, Gnostic literature, and the writings of Swedenborg,[220] and began to develop her own Kabbalistic theosophy. Combining belief in the Jewish Kabbalah as the primordial wisdom-teaching with what she called the 'higher' alchemy of Christianised Hermeticism, Kingsford understood Christ as the 'most perfect of initiates': a symbol of the regenerated human being and one of a long series of spiritual avatars, echoing Luria's idea of a succession of human messiahs that appear in every generation.[221] Although the Hermetic Society did not encourage ritual magic, Kingsford studied it during the summer of 1886, two years before the creation of the Golden Dawn. Her tutor was Mathers, 'a notable expert, well-versed in Hermetic and Kabalistic science'.[222] Both Westcott and Mathers lectured on

---

[216] For Kingsford's Christian esotericism, see Oppenheim, *Other World*, 189; Godwin, *Theosophical Enlightenment*, 245.

[217] Webb, *Flight from Reason*, 231.

[218] See Allison P. Coudert, 'Angel in the House or Idol of Perversity?: Women in Nineteenth Century Esotericism', *Esoterica* 9 (2007), 8–48; Dixon, *Divine Feminine*.

[219] Anna Bonus Kingsford and Edward Maitland, *The Perfect Way, Or, The Finding of Christ* (London: Hamilton, Adams & Co., 1881; revised and enlarged, London: Field & Tuer, 1887; repr. New York: Cosimo Classics, 2007), 349.

[220] See Godwin, *Theosophical Enlightenment*, 338.

[221] Anna Bonus Kingsford, *Clothed With the Sun* (London: John M. Watkins, 1889), 71.

[222] See Webb, *Flight from Reason*, 231.

the Kabbalah to Kingsford's society; both were awarded honorary memberships; and Mathers eventually dedicated *The Kabbalah Unveiled* to her and her partner Edward Maitland.[223] Westcott was 'enraptured' by his newfound muse,[224] whom he named as one of the notable Kabbalists in history.[225]

The Lurianic Kabbalah dominates Kingsford's writings through the themes of the primordial anthropos Adam Kadmon, the rescuing of the 'sparks' – which Kingsford, following the early modern alchemists, called 'the redemption of Spirit from Matter'[226] – and, perhaps most important, the androgynous nature of the godhead, comprised of male and female principles which are, 'in their union and cooperation, the life and salvation of the world'.[227] Kingsford also had a *maggid*, which she called her 'genius': an angelic guide who imparted wisdom to her during sleep as well as through visions.[228] She seems to have acquired her Lurianic doctrines from both Lévi and the *Kabbala denudata*. Kingsford, as a committed feminist, took as one of her sources of inspiration Postel's equation of the *Shekhinah* with Mary, which Lévi had also appropriated, and speaks of this female deity as

> ...the heavenly Sophia, or Wisdom, Who encircles and embraces all things....Whose veil is the astral fluid, and Who is, Herself, the substance of all souls....She appears as the Daughter, Mother, and Spouse of God....In Her subsist inherently all the feminine qualities of the Godhead.[229]

Kingsford equated this figure with *Binah*, the third *sefira*, 'the spirit of counsel, in that counsel is wisdom, and love and

---

[223] For Mathers' sympathy with Kingsford's ideals of 'esoteric Christianity', see Moïna Bergson Mathers, 'Preface', in Mathers (ed. and trans.), *Kabbalah Unveiled*, vii–xiii, on pp. xii–xiii.
[224] Gilbert, *Scrapbook*, 5.
[225] Westcott, *Introduction to the Study of the Kabbalah*, 19–20. The list also includes Lévi.
[226] Kingsford and Maitland, *Perfect Way*, 38–44.
[227] Kingsford and Maitland, *Perfect Way*, 272.
[228] For Kingsford's *maggid*, see Kingsford, *Clothed With the Sun*, 36–42; Maitland, *Kingsford*, 1:388–415. For the ability of *maggidim* to teach through dreams as well as spontaneous visions and scrying, see Elliot R. Wolfson, *A Dream Interpreted Within a Dream: Oneiropoiesis and the Prism of Imagination* (New York, NY: Zone, 2011); Dan, 'Maggid', 699; Bilu, 'Dybbuk and Maggid', 349.
[229] Kingsford and Maitland, *Perfect Way*, 55.

wisdom are one'.[230] She was entirely in accord with Lurianic doctrines in her understanding of the *Shekhinah* as the embodiment of God's glory in material manifestation, which she compared with the Egyptian goddess Isis.[231] She summarises her exegesis by declaring, 'The principle of duality is for the Kabbalists...the true God of Hosts',[232] and then launches into a diatribe against the Pauline doctrine of the subjection of women and the necessity of redressing this theological imbalance with a full recognition of the dynamic androgyny of the Kabbalistic godhead.[233]

Kingsford's emphasis on the *Shekhinah*, and on the role of women as her mediators, made a profound impression on Westcott. Although the SRIA, as a Masonic society, was exclusively male, Westcott insisted on the importance of including women in any group dedicated to ritual magic, even to the point of criticising the SRIA for its failure to recognise the value of women in occult work.[234] He discussed the 'baneful result' of the loss of feminine attributes from the idea of deity, pointing out that the female aspect of the godhead 'certainly existed in the oldest forms of the Kabbalah'.[235] With Mathers in full agreement, the Golden Dawn was duly opened to women from the time of its inception; Mathers' wife Mina was its first initiate.[236] Despite

---

[230] Kingsford and Maitland, *Perfect Way*, 55–56.

[231] For references on the *Shekhinah* as 'Nature' in Jewish esoteric literature, see Mark Verman, *The History and Varieties of Jewish Meditation* (Northvale, NJ: Jason Aronson, 1996), 45–65, and further references below in Chapter Six. For the equation of the *Shekhinah* with Isis in eighteenth- and nineteenth-century Masonic-Rosicrucian currents, see Jan Assman, 'The Mosaic Distinction: Israel, Egypt, and the Invention of Paganism', *Representations* 56 (Autumn 1996), 48–67, on p. 60. See also Higgins, *Anacalypsis*, a work whose subtitle – *An Attempt to Draw Aside the Veil of the Saitic Isis* – provided Blavatsky with the inspiration for *Isis Unveiled*. For older traditions equating Isis with 'Nature', see Pierre Hadot, *The Veil of Isis: An Essay on the History of the Idea of Nature*, trans. Michael Chase (Cambridge, MA: Harvard University Press, 2008).

[232] Kingsford and Maitland, *Perfect Way*, 59.

[233] Kingsford and Maitland, *Perfect Way*, 272–93.

[234] Westcott, 'Historical Lecture', 216.

[235] Westcott, 'Religion of Freemasonry', 122.

[236] See Mary K. Greer, *Women of the Golden Dawn: Rebels and Priestesses* (Rochester, VT: Park Street Press, 1995), xvi and 56. See Gilbert, *Scrapbook*, 5, for Kingsford's influence on Westcott's decision to include women in the Golden Dawn.

the order's fragmentation through internecine quarrels, the Golden Dawn demonstrated a striking equality between male and female members at a time when women, despite the efforts of the suffragettes, were still seen as 'angels in the house', fallen prostitutes, or hysterical spiritualist mediums.[237] The Lurianic Kabbalah, as expressed in both the *Kabbala denudata* and the proto-feminist writings of Lévi, provided Kingsford with a theosophical framework in which her feminism could be understood as a spiritual mission. Despite the fact that the study and practice of Kabbalah were not considered appropriate for women within medieval and early modern Judaism, the importance of women in the British occult societies of the late nineteenth and early twentieth centuries nevertheless owes a considerable debt, through Lévi and Kingsford, to the Kabbalah of Isaac Luria.

Westcott was a personal friend of Blavatsky and consistently expressed great admiration for her,[238] although he was inclined to quietly promulgate Jewish Kabbalistic doctrines in the talks he gave to the Theosophical Society.[239] Blavatsky, despite her animosity toward the Jews, made Lévi's work widely accessible, and Kingsford's introduction to the Kabbalah was initially through these Theosophical channels. In *Isis Unveiled*, Blavatsky stated that the ancient Eastern theosophy encapsulated in her teachings could be found in a book of unimaginable antiquity that formed the basis for one of the great works of the Jewish Kabbalah:

> There exists somewhere in this wide world an old Book – so very old that our modern antiquarians might ponder over its pages an indefinite time, and still not quite agree as to the nature of the fabric upon which it is written....The most ancient Hebrew document on occult learning – the *Siphra Dzeniouta* – was compiled from it.[240]

In her introduction to *The Secret Doctrine*, Blavatsky returned once again to a primal source of esoteric wisdom 'scattered

---

[237] See Dixon, *Divine Feminine*; Owen, *Darkened Room*; Owen, *Place of Enchantment*, 85–113; Oppenheim, *Other World*, 185–90.
[238] For Westcott's friendship with Blavatsky, see King, *Modern Ritual Magic*, 48.
[239] See, for example, William Wynn Westcott, 'Death', paper delivered at the Adelphi Theosophical Society Lodge (6 February 1893), repr. in *Theosophical Siftings* 6 (1893), 3–12, in which Westcott refers to reincarnation as a Jewish Kabbalistic idea.
[240] Blavatsky, *Isis*, 1:1.

throughout hundreds and thousands of Sanskrit MSS.'[241] Her readers now learn that this source, unidentified in *Isis Unveiled*, is the *Book of Dzyan*, from which she derived the seven 'Stanzas' she used as the basis for the cosmology of *The Secret Doctrine* – itself a commentary on these verses structured in a fashion similar to Jewish Kabbalistic commentaries on texts such as the *Zohar*. Blavatsky then declared that the 'very old Book' she referred to in *Isis Unveiled* was the source not only of the *Sifra Tzeniuta* but also the *Sefer Yetsirah*. She did not equate this 'very old Book' with the *Book of Dzyan*.[242] However, in 1913, a Jewish Theosophist called L. A. Bosman published a work on the Kabbalah in which he suggested that Blavatsky based *The Secret Doctrine* on the *Sifra Tzeniuta*:

> As one of the Zoharistic works, the Sepher Dzyaniouta must be mentioned, especially for its likeness to the Stanzas of Dzyan of the 'Secret Doctrine'.[243]

There is no recognizable resemblance between the seven stanzas of *The Secret Doctrine* and the *Sifra Tzeniuta*, other than that both present an emanationist cosmology emerging from an unknowable primal deity. Such a cosmology might apply equally to Neoplatonism, Greco-Egyptian Hermetism, and Gnostic doctrines, and Blavatsky replaced the ten *sefirot* of the theosophical Kabbalah with seven powers similar to the Gnostic planetary archons.[244] However, she borrowed the Lurianic idea of Adam Kadmon as the 'heavenly man', the prototype of humanity, and asserted that Stanza VI of the *Book of Dyzan*, concerned with the emanations as rotating wheels, 'is found embodied entirely in the Kabalistic works'.[245] Throughout *The Secret Doctrine*, Blavatsky at-

---

[241] Blavatsky, *Secret Doctrine*, 1:xxii–xxiii.

[242] Blavatsky, *Secret Doctrine*, 1:xliii.

[243] L. A. Bosman, *The Mysteries of the Qabalah* (London: Dharma Press, 1913), 31.

[244] Blavatsky, *Secret Doctrine*, 1:31. For the Gnostic archons, see the various texts in James M. Robinson (ed.), *The Nag Hammadi Library in English* (Leiden: Brill, 1977), esp. *The Hypostasis of the Archons*, NHC 2.4. These texts would not have been accessible to Blavatsky in her lifetime, but descriptions can be found in Christian heresiological literature as well as Plotinus' *Enneads*, translated into English by Thomas Taylor between 1787 and 1834, into French by M. N. Bouillet in 1875, and into German by Herman Friedrich Müller between 1878 and 1880.

[245] Blavatsky, *Secret Doctrine*, 1:199.

tempted to bolster her theories with a liberal peppering of
Kabbalistic ideas, largely derived from Mathers' *Kabbalah
Unveiled* as well as the works of Lévi and Franck[246] –
although she used only those elements that were part of the
common stock of late antiquity and could be easily
amalgamated with her idiosyncratic interpretations of Hindu
and Buddhist thought. Unlike Lévi, she was not interested in
understanding and teaching the Jewish Kabbalah; yet she
could not dismiss it because its influence on Western
esotericism was too pervasive. Her hostility toward the Jews
is as constant throughout *The Secret Doctrine* as are her
references to the Kabbalah: the Jews 'were perfectly
acquainted with sorcery and various maleficent forces' but,
with the exception of the great prophets,

> ...they knew little of, nor would they deal with, the real divine
> Occultism, their national character being averse to anything
> which had no direct bearing upon their own ethnical [*sic*],
> tribal, and individual benefits.[247]

Thus the 'true' Kabbalah, embedded in the *Book of Dzyan*,
must be distinguished from the 'false' Kabbalah developed
by that 'stiff-necked race' of Jewish Kabbalists.[248]

Scholem, who took the time to read not only Lévi,
Blavatsky, and Crowley, but also an obscure author such as
Bosman, accepted the latter's suggestion about the relation-
ship between *The Secret Doctrine* and the *Sifra Tzeniuta*:

> There can be little doubt in my opinion that the famous
> stanzas of the mysterious *Book Dzyan* on which Madame H. P.
> Blavatsky's *magnum opus, The Secret Doctrine*, is based owe
> something, both in title and content, to the pompous pages of
> the Zoharic writing called *Sifra Di-Tseniutha*....The Book
> Dzyan is therefore nothing but an occultistic hypostasy of the
> Zoharic title.[249]

For Blavatsky, the Jewish Kabbalah represented the corruption of a primal Eastern revelation, and she utilised only
those Kabbalistic speculations equally available in Neopla-

---

[246] For Mathers, see Blavatsky, *Secret Doctrine*, 1:242; for Lévi, see
Blavatsky, *Secret Doctrine*, 1:243; for Franck, see Blavatsky, *Secret
Doctrine*, 1:xliii, 1:350, and 2:2.
[247] Blavatsky, *Secret Doctrine*, 1:230.
[248] Blavatsky, *Secret Doctrine*, 1:230.
[249] Scholem, *Major Trends*, 398–99, n. 2.

tonic, Gnostic, Hindu, and Buddhist doctrines. The most important feature of Kabbalistic magic – the linguo-theosophy that supports the ritual use of the Hebrew letters and Divine Names – is absent from her doctrine. For Westcott, in contrast, the Kabbalah represented the most perfect expression of the original wisdom tradition, and he incorporated as much of its theosophy and practice as possible in the rituals of both the SRIA and the Golden Dawn.

THE 'MAGICAL MASON' AND HIS KABBALAH

Westcott was fond of rituals. 'As a Freemason', he declared, 'I prefer the ceremonies and try to limit the banqueting'.[250] Yet he is not remembered as a powerful magician. R. A. Gilbert observes that Westcott was 'cautious, fearful and altogether too respectable'.[251] Ronald Hutton describes him as 'a gentle and kindly scholar, with a taste for theoretical structures and an ability to recognize and promote talent in others';[252] while Westcott provided much of the theory behind the Golden Dawn, it was Mathers who developed its system of rituals.[253] However, like Mary Stewart's fictional portrayal of the young Merlin, Westcott was 'quiet-seeming, but not as quiet as he seems'.[254] Despite the diffidence with which he treated the subject of magic in print, and notwithstanding his efforts to placate Eastern-inclined Theosophists while quietly asserting his allegiance to the Jewish esoteric tradition, Westcott was ultimately responsible for the creation of the Golden Dawn as a vehicle for what Rebecca Lesses calls 'ritual practices to gain power'.[255]

In a privately published paper entitled 'Magic: Does It Exist?', Westcott presented a surprisingly postmodern discussion of the 'various opinions' held by different cultures about 'what powers, causes, and effects should be called

---

[250] Letter to Francis George Irwin (7 March 1875), Library of the United Grand Lodge of England MS, cited in Gilbert, 'Esoteric School of Masonic Research', 3.
[251] R. A. Gilbert, 'Introduction', in Gilbert (ed.), Magical Mason, 7.
[252] Hutton, Triumph of the Moon, 74.
[253] Hutton, 'Modern Pagan Witchcraft', 11.
[254] Mary Stewart, The Hollow Hills (London: Hodder & Stoughton, 1973), 306.
[255] Lesses, Ritual Practices, 55–61.

magical'.[256] After a survey of the use of magic in past civilisations which echoes Lévi's *Histoire de la magie* without the sensationalism, Westcott then reminded his readers of the revival of 'supernatural arts and knowledge' in the last decades of the nineteenth century, and raised the question of whether miraculous events in the Old Testament, such as the battle between Moses and Pharoah's magicians, are parables, miracles, or 'the result of beings, powers, or forces not on the human plane of evolution'.[257] Ultimately he conceded that the latter is the true explanation of magic:

> We must postulate the existence of a series of...conscious, active beings of another plane of creation, who...may and occasionally do interfere with man, and who may possibly on such occasions be the agents of Angelic Beings whose duty it is to supervise mankind.[258]

With this statement, Westcott demonstrated his loyalty to the religious framework of the Jewish magical tradition.

Westcott was capable of offering scientific explanations when his duties as a medical practitioner required it, but he seems to have been a deeply religious man for whom modern scientific paradigms were entirely compatible with esoteric doctrines. Although Janet Oppenheim views the attraction of occultism as 'its antipathy to the strictly rational, empiricist outlook that was increasingly perceived as the hallmark of Victorian thought',[259] Westcott, in accord with the Hasidic *zaddikim*, demonstrated that, in his view, God and the material world are a unity. Although he derided absolute materialism, he nevertheless accommodated the latest scientific innovations in his medical papers, and did not view a hypostatised Science as the enemy. In a privately published paper called 'The Shamir', Westcott discussed the Talmudic legend of the magical insect through whose agency the stones of Solomon's Temple and its cubical porphyry altar were cut and shaped, and concluded: 'No one can doubt

---

[256] William Wynn Westcott, 'Magic: Does It Exist?' (privately published, *c.* 1900, Gerald Yorke Collection FBF135, Warburg Institute, London), 1. For scholarly debates on the term 'magic', see Chapter Four.

[257] Westcott, 'Magic', 3.

[258] Westcott, 'Magic', 6.

[259] Oppenheim, *Other World*, 161–62.

the existence of this species of insect, for the works of God can never be annihilated so long as nature herself exists'.[260]

Born into a medical family in 1848, Westcott qualified as a physician in 1871, and was initiated into Freemasonry in the same year. SRIA sources state that he did not begin his occult studies until 1879, at which time he entered into a two-year 'life of retirement' to study the Kabbalah.[261] He probably encountered the Kabbalah through Masonic circles. In 1880, toward the end of his 'retirement', he was initiated into the SRIA. A year later, he was appointed Deputy Coroner to Central Middlesex and Central London, and in 1894 became His Majesty's Coroner for North-East London, a post he retained until his retirement in 1918 and which, as discussed more fully below, provided him with a unique opportunity for direct interaction with London's Eastern European Ashkenazi Jewish community.[262] Westcott took his coroner's duties seriously, describing his official role as 'a caretaker of the lives of the people'.[263] In 1897, when conflicts within the Golden Dawn forced him to choose between his position as coroner and his involvement with the occult society he had created, he chose the former and withdrew from overt

---

[260] William Wynn Westcott, 'The Shamfer (Shamir) of King Solomon' (unpublished MS, London, 1888; recopied 1910; Grand Lodge Library and Museum of Freemasonry, MS A180WES). The source of the legend is the tractate *Gittin* 68a in the Babylonian Talmud, in which Solomon is said to have required male and female demons to inform him of the whereabouts of an insect which could cut through the sharpest stone, and which he needed to help him build the Temple.

[261] Gilbert (ed.), *Magical Mason*, 7.

[262] For further biographical details on Westcott, see Gilbert, 'Esoteric School of Masonic Research'.

[263] William Wynn Westcott, 'An Address on the Coroner and His Relations with the Medical Practitioner and Death Certification' *BMJ* 2:2188 (1902), 1756–59, on p. 1756. For Westcott's other medical publications, see William Harrison Martindale and William Wynn Westcott, *The Extra Pharmacopoeia of Unofficial Drugs and Chemical and Pharmaceutical Preparations* (London: H. K. Lewis, 1883, repr. London: The Pharmaceutical Press, 2008); William Wynn Westcott, *A Therapeutic Index of Diseases and Symptoms* (London: H. K. Lewis, 1884); William Wynn Westcott, *Suicide, Its History, Literature, Jurisprudence, Causation and Prevention* (London: H. K. Lewis, 1885); William Wynn Westcott, 'Inebriety, Its Causes and Cure', *BJP* 46:195 (1900), 653–73.

involvement in the order.[264] Occasionally his secret Kabbalistic preoccupations overflowed into his professional life,
and his fascination with Jewish lore surfaced in his medical
papers.[265] The themes which preoccupy these medical
writings – suicide, violent death, alcoholism, unofficial drugs
and poisons, esoteric herbology – reveal his ongoing
fascination with the 'night side of nature',[266] although this
blend of occultism and medical practice was not unusual for
the time.[267]

In religiosity, too, Westcott reflected the prevailing
currents of his era. Although he viewed himself as a
Christian, his Christianity reflects the incarnational theology
that dominated Anglican and non-conformist circles from the
1850s onward.[268] The historical Jesus is seen as an 'ideal type'
rather than a saviour, and the 'Christos Spirit' of which he is
the embodiment is not identical to the historical personage.
Westcott was profoundly affected by Kingsford's approach
to Christianity:

> That Jesus was a great prophet, or rather great teacher, no one
> can deny, but alas, like almost every other great master in the
> past, he left no writings of his own....There is no context to
> point us to a vicarious redemption, which by the sacrifice of
> another shall enable us to escape the just penalties of our
> failings.[269]

Westcott published only one slim book of his own: *Numbers:
Their Occult Power and Mystic Virtues*, written a year after he
became Supreme Magus of the SRIA and five years before
the founding of the Golden Dawn.[270] In this work he deferred

---

[264] For this episode, see Howe, *Magicians*, 165–66; Gilbert, *Scrapbook*,
79–92.
[265] See, for example, William Wynn Westcott, 'The Mandrake', *BMJ*
1:1524 (1890), 620–21.
[266] For the phrase 'night side of nature', see Catherine Crowe, *The
Night Side of Nature, Or: Ghosts and Ghost Seers*, 2 vols. (London: T. C.
Newby, 1848).
[267] See Rhodri Hayward, 'Demonology, Neurology, and Medicine in
Edwardian Britain', *BHM* 78 (2004), 37–58.
[268] See, for example, William Wynn Westcott, 'A Lecture to
Enquirers into Theosophy and Practical Occultism', *Theosophical
Siftings* 3 (1891), 5–13, on pp. 8–9.
[269] Westcott, 'Lecture to Enquirers', 7.
[270] William Wynn Westcott, *Numbers: Their Occult Power and Mystic
Virtues* (London: Theosophical Publishing Society, 1890; repr. as *The*

to Lévi, who could offer the reader 'a deeper insight into the analogies between numbers and ideas'.[271] But Westcott's understanding of Kabbalistic hermeneutics far surpassed his French predecessor.[272] By the time the second edition of *Numbers* was published in 1902, he had access to further Kabbalistic works by occultists unknown to Lévi, including a Masonic interpretation of Kabbalistic theosophy, *The Blazing Star and the Jewish Kabbalah*, written by an American esotericist and Freemason called William Bachelder Greene (1819–1878),[273] and William Stirling's *The Canon*, which deals almost exclusively with Kabbalistic *gematria*.[274]

Occult Power of Numbers, North Hollywood, CA: Newcastle Publishing Co., 1984). For the continuing use of this work in contemporary SRIA study programmes, see R. T. L. Hughes, 'The Powers and Properties of Numbers in Rosicrucian Metaphysics', <http://www.bishopwilkins.co.uk/Powers_and_Properties_of_Numbers_in_Rosicrucian_Metaph_.pdf>.

[271] Westcott, *Numbers*, 6.

[272] See the description of Kabbalistic hermeneutics in Westcott, *Numbers*, 25–32.

[273] William Bachelder Greene, *The Blazing Star: With an Appendix Treating of the Jewish Kabbala* (Boston: A. Williams & Co., 1872; repr. as *The Blazing Star and the Jewish Kabbalah*, Berwick, ME: Ibis Press, 2003). Greene had undergone a powerful mystical experience that led him to believe that the Kabbalah was the only true path for achieving the *unio mystica*. He emigrated to Britain after a sojourn in Paris between 1853 and 1859, where he seems to have encountered the works of both Lévi and Franck; *Blazing Star* is laced with the kind of imaginative historical correlations that abound in Lévi's *Histoire de la magie*. R. A. Gilbert, in his thoughtful introduction to Greene's work, suggests that the author may have met Lévi in Paris. Greene's book was not acknowledged in print by any British occultists except A. E. Waite, who mentions it in *Holy Kabbalah*, 33–34 and 217. *Blazing Star* was absent from both the Westcott Hermetic Library and the Golden Dawn's Inner Order Library. This does not mean that Westcott and Mathers were unaware of it, only that, for their own reasons, they did not acknowledge it; this 'curious volume' is mentioned by Francis George Irwin in the April 1877 issue of *The Rosicrucian*, clearly indicating that the brethren of the SRIA were familiar with the work and that it was probably held in their own library, where Westcott would inevitably have encountered it.

[274] William Stirling, *The Canon: An Exposition of the Pagan Mystery Perpetuated in the Cabala as the Rule of All the Arts* (London: Elkin Matthews, 1897). For Stirling, see Cis van Heertum, '"This Mysterious Individual, William Stirling": Unpublished Letters

Westcott's wide range of sources includes not only the early modern Christian Kabbalists who had inspired Lévi, but also British and German Kabbalists and Kabbalistic scholars, both Jewish and Christian, and the impressive Hebrew and Latin manuscript collections of the British Museum and the Bodleian Library. His translation of the *Sefer Yetsirah* and his compilation of alchemical and Kabbalistic texts, published under the title *Collectanea Hermetica*, were invaluable resources for the practitioners of the occult revival, and remain so for students of occultism today. In addition, Westcott ceaselessly generated a vast stream of pamphlets, booklets, and lectures on Kabbalistic, Hermetic, and Rosicrucian themes that were distributed within the SRIA, the Golden Dawn, and the Quatuor Coronati Lodge, and many of which were later published in Theosophical journals such as *Lucifer* and *The Theosophist*. This 'timorous scholar', who at the same time was 'extremely "clubbable"',[275] had a predilection for joining every fringe Masonic-Rosicrucian society he could find, experimenting with various rituals and collecting numerous exotic higher degrees.[276] Although it is unclear how seriously he took these initiations, it is evident from his writings that he believed wholeheartedly in the antiquity of the Kabbalistic doctrines he promulgated with such assiduity.

In 1863 a book appeared which was perfectly tailored to Westcott's requirements: *The Kabbalah: Its Doctrines, Development and Literature*, written by David Ginsburg (1821–1914), a Polish Jewish convert to Christianity who later called himself Christian D. Ginsburg to indicate his shift in theological orientation.[277] Ginsburg first travelled to London

---

Relating to the Author of *The Canon*', *ES* 88:5 (2007), 531–62. For Westcott's familiarity with *The Canon*, see *Numbers*, 31–32.

[275] Godwin, *Theosophical Enlightenment*, 362.

[276] For the various rites and groups that Westcott joined, see Gilbert, 'Chaos Out of Order'; Gilbert, *Scrapbook*, 5–6; Gilbert, 'Esoteric School of Masonic Research'; Howe, 'Fringe Masonry'.

[277] Christian D. Ginsburg, *The Kabbalah: Its Doctrines, Development and Literature* (London: Longmans, Green & Co., 1863). There appears to be some confusion about Ginsburg's year of birth. The *Encyclopaedia Britannica* editions of both 1902 and 1911 give the year of his birth as 1831, as does Waite, and the year of his conversion as 1846, but the correspondence of the Old Testament Revision Company which Ginsburg helped to found gives the year of birth as 1821. It is improbable that he was born in 1831, as his conversion would then have occurred at the age of fifteen and it is unlikely that

under the auspices of the Warsaw mission of the London Society for Promoting Christianity among the Jews, and in 1853 he was appointed a missionary for the Society.[278] He achieved considerable eminence as a Hebrew scholar after the publication of *The Kabbalah*, which A. E. Waite called 'the first clear, simple and methodised account of Kabbalistic doctrine and literature [in English]'.[279] Westcott made full use of Ginsburg's book, and Mathers later pillaged it for *The Kabbalah Unveiled*.[280] Like many other Jewish apostates

---

any rabbinical college, in Poland or elsewhere, would have admitted a student who, in their eyes, was an apostate.

[278] See Christian David Ginsburg, *Letters and photographs of members of the Old Testament Revision Company*, c. 1870–85, Cambridge University Library: British and Foreign Bible Society's Library, GBR/0374/BSMS 651. For Ginsburg's involvement with various programmes aimed at converting Jews, see Juanita S. Carey, *E. W. Bullinger: A Biography* (Grand Rapids, MI: Kregel Christian Books and Resources, 2000), 123. Ginsburg's other publications include a translation of the *Song of Songs* with a historical and critical commentary (1857), *Facsimiles of Manuscripts of the Hebrew Bible* (1897–98), *The Text of the Hebrew Bible in Abbreviations* (1903), and *On the relationship of the so-called Codex Babylonicus of A.D. 916 to the Eastern Recension of the Hebrew Text* (1899). He also contributed numerous articles to reference works such as J. Kitto's *Encyclopedia*, W. Smith's *Dictionary of Christian Biography*, and the *Encyclopaedia Britannica*.

[279] Waite, *Holy Kabbalah*, 494.

[280] For Mathers' appropriation of Ginsburg, see Mathers, *Kabbalah Unveiled*, 4–6, and the review of *Kabbalah Unveiled* in *JC*, mentioned above. Anna Bonus Kingsford was familiar with Ginsburg's *Kabbalah*, published in 1863. Ginsburg in turn was familiar with Kingsford's work and, according to Joscelyn Godwin, paid her the compliment of admiring her knowledge (Godwin, *Theosophical Enlightenment*, 345). As a Jewish convert to Christianity, Ginsburg would have felt particular sympathy with Kingsford's Christianised approach to the Kabbalah. Although he displays his proselytising intentions with subtlety in *The Kabbalah*, Ginsburg repeatedly refers to the triune structures of the sefirotic Tree of Life to demonstrate the correspondences between Jewish mysticism and Christian trinitarian theology. Westcott, ambiguous about this scholarly 'Christianising' of the Kabbalah, states: 'If any desire to refer to the *alleged* reference in the Kabalah to the Trinity, it will be found in the Zohar ii., 43, b.: and an English version of the same in "The Kabbalah" by C. D. Ginsburg' (Westcott, *Introduction to the Study of the Kabalah*, iv; emphasis mine). Some contemporary Theosophists believe that Ginsburg may have 'led two lives', and suggest that he used the pseudonym 'Nurho de Manhar' to become a Golden Dawn

involved with the Kabbalah over the centuries, Ginsburg was a fervent missionary who believed the Kabbalah to be one of the most effective instruments in encouraging Jewish conversion, and he did not hesitate to use his knowledge of Jewish esoteric lore to proselytise:

> It is necessary to advert to the relation between the Kabbalah and Christianity in order to account for the extraordinary part which this theosophy played in the Christian church, especially at the time of the Renaissance. We have already seen that the Sephiric decade, or the archetypal man, like Christ, is considered to be of a double nature, both infinite and finite, perfect and imperfect. More distinct, however, is the doctrine of the Trinity....These and similar statements favouring the doctrines of the New Testament have made many Kabbalists of the highest position in the synagogue embrace the Christian faith, and write elaborate books to win their Jewish brethren over to Christ.[281]

Influenced by the rationalist currents of the *Wissenschaft des Judentums*, Ginsburg did not accept the antiquity of the *Zohar*.[282] Westcott, although he found Ginsburg's work invaluable, insisted on the Kabbalah's ancient provenance. Like Lévi, Westcott had a somewhat eclectic idea of what

---

initiate, as Waite mentions an individual with this name who entered the order in 1888. An English translation of parts of the *Zohar* by Nurho de Manhar appeared in serialised form in E. T. Hargrove's periodical, *The Word*, but the serialisation ended abruptly in March 1914, the date of Ginsburg's death. This work, released in one volume in the late twentieth century – Nurho de Manhar, *The Zohar* (San Diego, CA: Wizards Bookshelf, 1978) – contains numerous references to Blavatsky's *Isis Unveiled* and *The Secret Doctrine*, and includes two articles by Blavatsky formerly published in *The Theosophist* in 1887 and entitled 'Tetragrammaton' and 'The Kabalah and the Kabalists at the Close of the Nineteenth Century' (396–424); the insides of the front and back covers reproduce Ginsburg's article on the Kabbalah for the *Encyclopedia Britannica*, a portion of which is quoted below. For the suggestion that Ginsburg and Nurho de Manhar are the same person, see Blavatsky, CW13, 'General Bibliography with selected bibliographical notes', 383. Given Ginsburg's rather fanatical proselytising tendencies and high public profile, it is unlikely that he would have engaged in such a dangerous venture.

[281] Christian D. Ginsburg, 'Kabbalah', in *Encyclopaedia Britannica* (1902), 15:620–23.

[282] See Ginsburg, *The Kabbalah: Its Doctrines, Development and Literature*, 224–25, 228.

constituted 'Kabbalistic' literature; in addition to the *Sefer Yetsirah* and the *Zohar*, he includes under the rubric of 'Kabbalah' such diverse Hebrew texts as the late antique magical work *Othiyoth de-Rabbi Akiba* ('Alphabet of Rabbi Akiba'),[283] the *Book of Enoch*, and the writings of the Spanish Jewish poet Shelomo ben Yehuda ibn Gabirol (*c*. 1022–1070), known to medieval scholastics as Avicebron.[284]

Westcott discovered ibn Gabirol's doctrines through the work of an American Jewish lawyer, Theosophist, and Freemason called Isaac Myer (1836–1902),[285] whom Westcott believed to be a 'real' Kabbalist like Ginsburg and Franck.[286] Myer, along with many other British and American Jews attracted to the ecumenical spirit of Freemasonry, was a Kabbalist scholar who produced a large quantity of unpublished translations, transcriptions, commentaries, and bibliographies on various Kabbalistic work.[287] Although Myer

---

[283] For the *Othiyoth de-Rabbi Akiba*, see Joel C. Dobbin, *Kabbalistic Astrology: The Sacred Tradition of the Hebrew Sages* (Rochester, VT: Inner Traditions, 1999), 247–50; Scholem, *Origins*, 326; Scholem, *On the Kabbalah*, 62; Idel, *Hasidism*, 336 n. 37, 343 n. 85; Ginsburg, *Kabbalah*, 184; Victoria Durov, 'Codicological Notes on the Text of a Hebrew Magic Manual: A New Perspective?', *SMN* 19 (Spring 2008), 1–7. A Latin translation of the *Othiyoth*, which belongs to the *heikhalot* genre, is found in Athanasius Kircher's *Oedipus Aegyptiacus*, Westcott's most likely source. For this work, see Stolzenberg, *Egyptian Oedipus*.

[284] For ibn Gabirol's poetry, see Peter Cole (trans.), *Selected Poems of Solomon ibn Gabirol* (Princeton, NJ: Princeton University Press, 2001). For ibn Gabirol's philosophy, see Dillon, 'Solomon Ibn Gabirol's Doctrine'; for his Neoplatonic predilections, see Mária Micaninová, 'The Synthetic Thinking of Solomon ibn Gabirol', *Studia Judaica* 11:2 (2008), 215–31. For the 'mystical-masonic interests' of ibn Gabirol and his familiarity with *heikhalot* texts and the *Sefer Yetsirah*, see Schuchard, *Restoring the Temple*, 35–39.

[285] Isaac Myer, *Qabbalah: The Philosophical Writings of Solomon ben Yehudah ibn Gebirol or Avicenbron* (Philadelphia, PA: private publication, 1888; repr. New York: Samuel Weiser, 1970).

[286] William Wynn Westcott, 'The Devil, and Evil Spirits According to the Bible and Ancient Hebrew Rabbis', SRIA, *Transactions of the Metropolitan College* (1902), 17–21, reprinted in Gilbert (ed.) *Magical Mason*, 131–38, on p. 133.

[287] Myer may have been a Jewish convert like Ginsburg, as he exhibits some sympathy for Christian doctrines, but he displays no inclination to proselytise, and it is more likely that he was a heterodox Jew who was tolerant of many religious approaches. Myer's papers and library are currently held at The New York

referred to ibn Gabirol's work as 'Qabbalistic writings',[288] this important medieval philosopher is not generally considered a Kabbalist, as his work was written a century before the *Sefer ha-Bahir* emerged in Provence and two centuries before the *Zohar* was produced; and unlike the Provençal and Spanish Kabbalists of the twelfth and thirteenth centuries, he does not refer to his ideas as *qbl*, 'tradition'. However, ibn Gabirol was deeply involved in Jewish esoteric lore within the framework of the Arab Neoplatonic textual tradition,[289] and Marsha Keith Schuchard suggests that he is one of the key links between early Jewish magical doctrines and the later formulations of esoteric Freemasonry.[290] Myer's *Qabbalah*, although it includes a nominal section on ibn Gabirol's life and philosophy, is primarily an exposition of the theosophy of the *Zohar*, Lurianic teachings, and late antique *heikhalot* texts. Myer was thoroughly familiar not only with the scholars of the *Wissenschaft des Judentums*, but also with the *Kabbala denudata*, Franck's *La Kabbale*, and

---

Public Library Rare Books and Manuscripts Division, No. 86M22, available online at <http://www.nypl.org/research/chss/spe/rbk/faids/myeri.pdf>. His eclectic library includes such diverse materials as the writings of the thirteenth-century Kabbalist Abraham Abulafia, works on demonology, angelology, and Divine Names, German philosophers influenced by the Kabbalah such as Leibniz and Schelling, Shabbatai Donolo's tenth-century commentary on the *Sefer Yetsirah*, Kircher's *Oedipus Aegyptiacus*, German Jewish scholarly works on the Kabbalah (Graetz, Jellinek, Joël), works by Salomon Munk, Ginsburg's *The Kabbalah*, Macrobius, the *Hermetica*, Egyptology, Plutarch's *Isis and Osiris*, the medieval Jewish Aristotelian philosopher Maimonides' *Guide of the Perplexed*, *The Alphabet of Rabbi Akiba*, the work of Philo of Alexandria, the *Upanishads*, Thomas Taylor's English translation of Iamblichus' *De mysteriis*, various Arabic MSS on astrology and magic, Gnostic texts such as *The Testament of Adam*, and, not surprisingly, virtually all the works of Éliphas Lévi. For Jews in the Theosophical Society headquarters in India, see Boaz Huss, '"The Sufi Society from America": Theosophy and Kabbalah in Poona in the Late Nineteenth Century', in Huss, Pasi, and von Stuckrad (eds.), *Kabbalah and Modernity*, 167–93.

[288] Myer, *Qabbalah*, iii.

[289] See Sarah Pessin, 'Jewish Neoplatonism: Being Above Being and Divine Emanations in Solomon ibn Gabirol and Isaac Israeli', in Daniel H. Frank and Oliver Leaman (eds.), *The Cambridge Companion to Medieval Jewish Philosophy* (Cambridge: Cambridge University Press, 2003), 91–110.

[290] See Schuchard, *Restoring the Temple*, 35–39.

Ginsburg's *Kabbalah*, which irritated him because of its rejection of the antiquity of the *Zohar*. Myer's championing of the ancient roots of the Kabbalah, and his sympathy for Theosophical doctrines, endeared him not only to Westcott but also to Blavatsky, who quoted his 'excellent book' extensively in *The Secret Doctrine*.[291]

WESTCOTT AND THE ASHKENAZI

Contrary to Konstantin Burmistrov's statement that late nineteenth- and early twentieth-century occultists 'no longer considered Kabbalah to be an integral part of the Jewish tradition',[292] Westcott was deeply respectful of Jewish culture, and seriously attempted to learn Hebrew rather than simply memorising the alphabet and the Divine Names to use in magical rituals. Despite his allegiance to Theosophy, he declared:

> I was for fifteen years a Kabalist and Hermetist, before I entered upon the Theosophic path, and so my attitude toward the Kabalah is one of love and respect, as that of a pupil to a system which has led him from darkness into light.[293]

In addition to Masonic and Rosicrucian traditions and textual sources such as Lévi, Agrippa, Dee, the *Kabbala denudata*, and the works of Franck, Ginsburg, and Myer, another and equally important inspiration for Westcott's understanding of the Kabbalah was his Jewish contemporaries. Although Eastern European Jews had been arriving in London in small numbers for many decades, the last twenty years of the nineteenth century saw a mass emigration from Russia and the Russian-occupied parts of Poland and Lithuania of many thousands of Ashkenazi Jews fleeing from the pogroms initiated against the Jewish communities after the assassination of Czar Alexander II in 1881, for which the Jews were

---

[291] See Blavatsky, *Secret Doctrine*, 1:374–75, 347–48, 619n; 2:116, 457, 478n.
[292] Konstantin Burmistrov, 'The Interpretation of Kabbalah in Early 20th-Century Russian Philosophy', *EEJA* 37:2 (2007), 157–87, on p. 157.
[293] William Wynn Westcott, 'A Further Glance At the Kabalah', *Lucifer* 12:68–69 (1893), 147–53 and 203–08, repr. in Gilbert (ed.), *Magical Mason*, 95–109, on p. 99.

blamed.[294] This influx of Russian and Eastern European Jewry was not dissimilar to the 'Great Emigration' of Polish Jews into Paris during Lévi's time, although the British immigrants were greater in number, and the impact on the resident Anglo-Jewish community – largely Western European Sephardim, already well-acculturated after their long efforts toward emancipation – was complex and fraught with conflict.[295]

The new wave of immigrants appears to have made an impact on British occultism in a manner similar to that of the Polish Jews on mid-nineteenth-century French occultism: quietly, by way of direct contacts between individual Jews and individual occultists. These Russian, Polish, and Lithuanian Jews, many of whom were extremely poor and unable to speak English, nevertheless brought with them a number of highly educated rabbis, some of them Hasidim steeped in a Kabbalistic lore which amalgamated Lurianic doctrines with the magical practices of the medieval German Pietists – practices which in turn were rooted in the Jewish *heikhalot* literature of late antiquity, itself a syncretic mix of Jewish, Gnostic, Greco-Egyptian, and Neoplatonic magical traditions. As coroner of north London, Westcott's daily work involved him with the deaths, autopsies, funerals, and grieving families of these Jewish refugees, who had settled

---

[294] For the pogroms, see Israel Bartal, *The Jews of Eastern Europe, 1772–1881*, trans. Chaya Naor (Philadelphia, PA: University of Pennsylvania Press, 2002), 3–5; Jonathan Frankel, *Prophecy and Politics: Socialism, Nationalism, and the Russian Jews, 1862–1917* (Cambridge: Cambridge University Press, 1984); Benjamin Nathans, *Beyond the Pale: The Jewish Encounter with Late Imperial Russia* (Berkeley, CA: University of California Press, 2004); John D. Klier and Shlomo Lambroza, *Pogroms: Anti-Jewish Violence in Modern Russian History* (Cambridge: Cambridge University Press, 1992); Irwin Michael Aronson, *Troubled Waters: The Origins of the 1881 Anti-Jewish Pogroms in Russia* (Pittsburgh, PA: University of Pittsburgh Press, 1990).

[295] For the impact of the immigrations on resident Jewish communities, and the historic division of the Jews of the diaspora into Sephardim and Ashkenazi, see above, n. 15; H. J. Zimmels, *Ashkenazim and Sephardim: Their Relations, Differences, and Problems as Reflected in the Rabbinical Responsa* (Oxford: Oxford University Press, 1958); Samantha Baskind, 'Distinguishing the Distinction: Picturing Ashkenazi and Sephardic Jews in Seventeenth- and Eighteenth-Century Amsterdam', *JSSMJ* 1:1 (2007), 1–13.

around Hackney, Bethnal Green, Islington, and London's East End, forming the largest Jewish community in Britain.

Westcott's knowledge of Jewish ritual sometimes exceeded that of his Jewish contacts,[296] suggesting that he learned about the Jewish Kabbalah directly from Jewish teachers as well as from texts. In a talk given to the Theosophical Society, he stated that he had in fact received such instruction from Jewish sources:

> The Kabbalists...are still, in secret, teaching their methods to favoured pupils. I have myself been through a large portion of their tuition.[297]

Westcott's philosemitic inclinations also made him enjoy being perceived as a Jew, once again echoing Lévi, who chose a Jewish pseudonym under which to present his Kabbalistic writings.[298] In March 1914, long after Westcott had withdrawn from the now fragmented Golden Dawn, the editor of *The Jewish Chronicle* noted:

> Dr. Wynn Westcott, the well-known Hackney Coroner, who was telling me the other day that he is frequently mistaken for a Jew – his patriarchal appearance possibly is responsible for the error – is a quite well-known Hebrew scholar....The treasures of his bookcase include many choice volumes on Hebrew lore.[299]

In another paper presented to the Theosophical Society, Westcott referred to the 'practical and wonder-working aspect' of the Kabbalah, and spoke of the magical powers of the Hasidic *zaddikim* of his own time. He praised Luria as 'the greatest of the wonder-working Rabbis', and then stated:

> In Central Europe, parts of Russia, Austria, and Poland, there are even now Jews, known as wonder-working Rabbis, who

---

[296] See, for example, The Editor, 'Cohanim as Jurymen', *JC* (21 September 1900), 15, where Westcott shows off his superior knowledge of Jewish funeral traditions.

[297] Westcott, 'Lecture to Enquirers', 11.

[298] For the occultist practice in the late eighteenth century of using a Jewish pseudonym, see Keleph ben Nathan [Marc Philippe Dutoit-Mambrini], *La philosophie divine, appliquée aux lumières naturelle, magique, astrale, surnaturelle, céleste et divine* (self-published, 1793). On this work, see Faivre, *Theosophy*, 21.

[299] 'One of Them', 'With the "Children of the Ghetto"', *JC* (20 March 1914), 5.

can do strange things they attribute to the Kabalah, and things very difficult to explain have been seen in England, at the hands of students of Kabalistic rites and talismans.[300]

The *zaddikim* to whom Westcott referred were understood to possess extraordinary magical powers based on the ritual use of the Divine Names, and were perceived as intermediaries between the community and God.[301] This tradition is still extant in Hasidic communities in Britain today.[302] It is clear that Westcott, during his work as coroner for the Ashkenazi community, encountered and learned from these important religious leaders.

Westcott persistently introduced Kabbalistic themes into Masonic meetings and publications. He demonstrated his obligation to Blavatsky in declaring that there is 'no sharp line of cleavage between the pure Western mystic doctrines – the Kabalism of the Middle Ages, related to the Egyptian Hermeticism – and the Indian or Tibetan Esoteric Theosophy'.[303] But he insisted, in his polite and diffident fashion, that he favoured a Kabbalistic origin for the Western magical tradition.[304] Unshakeable in this belief that the Kabbalah contains the most authentic source of the ancient mysteries, Westcott declared that his Order of the Golden Dawn 'is formed upon the type of the Decad of the Sephiroth, the Ten Emanations of Deity as figures in the very ancient Qabalah of the Hebrews'.[305] If Mathers was the architect of the ritual magic of the Golden Dawn, Westcott deserves the credit for first drawing together the work of Lévi, Kingsford, and Blavatsky, the British Kabbalistic traditions of John Dee's angel magic and its Jewish sources, Rosicrucian-Hermetic alchemy, the rituals of Freemasonry, new Jewish scholarship on the Kabbalah, and the knowledge of the Ashkenazi Jews of north London, to provide Mathers with a Kabbalistic foundation on which to build the magical core of the Hermetic Order of the Golden Dawn.

---

[300] Westcott, 'Kabalah', 85.

[301] See Dan, 'Bow to Frumkinian Hasidism', 178.

[302] For magical practices among the Hasidim of North London in the 1990s, see Roland Littlewood and Simon Dein, 'The Effectiveness of Words: Religion and Healing Among the Lubavitch of Stamford Hill', *CMP* 19 (1995), 339–83.

[303] Westcott, 'Further Glance', 108.

[304] See the quotation at the beginning of this chapter.

[305] Westcott, 'Historical Lecture', 214–15.

CHAPTER FOUR

IN THE NAME OF YHVH:
MACGREGOR MATHERS
AND THE RITUAL MAGIC OF THE GOLDEN DAWN

> For man stands upon the earth, and his head reaches
> unto the heavens, and the angels of the Lord ascend
> and descend within him.[1]
>
> — Jacob Joseph of Polonnoye (1781)

> To know the Divine Mind is to understand the occult
> laws that rule the universe...His Mind alone rules the
> universe. He is the source of all magic power.[2]
>
> — Julius Kohn (1929)

A MEETING AT THE MUSEUM

1887 was a bumper year for British occultism. Toward the
end of the previous year, Éliphas Lévi's work was unleashed
on a bemused British public through *The Mysteries of Magic*, a
compendium of writings translated by A. E. Waite, which
elicited a predictable hostility from the popular press.[3] But
even scathing reviews of the book reveal a burgeoning public
interest in occultism. The London-based *Graphic* observed:

> We have no doubt that the outcome of Mr. Waite's labours
> will be much appreciated in spiritualist circles, and by those –
> and they are many – for whom the night-side of Nature has a
> charm.[4]

---

[1] Jacob Joseph of Polonnoye, *Ben-Porat Yosef*, fol. 42a[1] (1781), cited in
Elior, 'Angelology', 3.

[2] Julius Kohn, *The Real Black Magic Revealed Without Mystery* (original
typescript, 1929, Wellcome Institute Historical Medical Libary
MS3126), 236.

[3] See, for example, *The Leeds Mercury*, 'Literary Arrivals' (Leeds, 29
August 1887), referring to Lévi's 'wild and hysterical farrago of
blasphemous nonsense'.

[4] *The Graphic* (London, 16 April 1887).

Echoing these sentiments, *The Hampshire Telegraph and Sussex Chronicle* commented:

> Alphonse Louis Constant...has left a sprightly account of how, not many years ago, he called upon the spirit of Apollonius of Tyana in a London drawing room. Ceremonial magic is, without doubt, extensively practised in England at the present time.[5]

The quiet currents that had fostered the creation of the SRIA in 1866 had, in the subsequent two decades, become a full-blown 'occult revival'.[6]

Of equal although less obvious significance was a meeting that occurred in 1887 in the Reading Room of the British Museum in London. Mina Bergson (1865–1928), a twenty-two-year-old graduate of the Slade School of Fine Art, was perusing the volumes on Egyptian antiquities when she encountered an extraordinary individual struggling under the weight of the huge stack of books he was carrying to his reading desk.[7] He was later described by William Butler Yeats, one of the most illustrious adepts of the Golden Dawn, as

> ...a man of thirty-six or thirty-seven, in a brown velveteen coat, with a gaunt resolute face, and an athletic body who seemed...a figure of romance....His studies were two only – magic and the theory of war, for he believed himself a born commander.[8]

---

[5] *The Hampshire Telegraph and Sussex Chronicle* (Portsmouth, 24 January 1891).
[6] Two organisations essential to the growing strength of the occult revival were founded in the two decades after the SRIA was created: the Theosophical Society, born in 1875, and the Society for Psychical Research, born in 1882. Like the Theosophical Society, the Society for Psychical Research is still extant; their website is found at www.spr.ac.uk and their *Journal of the Society for Psychical Research* has been published continuously since 1884. For the SPR, see Renée Haynes, *The Society for Psychical Research 1882–1982: A History* (London: MacDonald, 1982). For the SPR's influence on the occult revival, see Owen, *Place of Enchantment*, 120–21 and 170–71; Owen, *Darkened Room*, 102–04; Webb, *Flight From Reason*, 18–21. For the tense relationship between the two organisations, see Oppenheim, *Other World*, 174–78.
[7] See Greer, *Women*, 45.
[8] William Butler Yeats, *The Autobiography of William Butler Yeats* (New York: Macmillan, 1953), 112–13.

The man was Samuel Liddell MacGregor Mathers (1854–1918), an adept of the SRIA and an aspiring Kabbalistic magus.[9] A. E. Waite offers his own waspish description of Mathers after encountering him at the British Museum:

> I grew curious as to the identity of this strange person, with rather fish-like eyes....The more I saw of him the more eccentric he proved to be...a combination of Don Quixote and Hudibras, but with a vanity all his own.[10]

Ithell Colquhoun suggests that Mathers was 'an ambitious personality with a "disadvantaged" background', and that he represents 'a classic instance of a mother-fixated young man'.[11] Although he avoided the monotony of regular employment, he was firmly committed to what he understood as his 'occult mission'. With Westcott's encouragement and financial support, Mathers had just published his English translation of the three Zoharic treatises from the *Kabbala denudata*, and had, according to the testimony given by Mina Bergson nearly four decades later, already received instructions from his 'occult teachers' to prepare what would eventually become his 'esoteric school': the Hermetic Order of the Golden Dawn.[12] In anticipation of this event, he haunted the British Museum Reading Room every day from early morning until late evening, poring over obscure manuscripts. After their encounter, Mina assured her closest friend, Annie Horniman: 'I won't marry him'. Nevertheless, they did marry in the following year, although both Mina and her husband were pledged to celibacy and Aleister Crowley later insinuated that the marriage had never actually taken place.[13] 1888 marked not only the year of Mina's marriage, but also her entry into the newly created Golden Dawn as its first initiated member.[14] The marriage ceremony was conducted by the Reverend William

---

[9] For biographical references on Mathers, see Colquhoun, *Sword*; Gilbert, *Scrapbook*, 93–113; Greer, *Women*, 49–56; R. A. Gilbert, 'Introduction', in Gilbert (ed.), *Sorcerer and His Apprentice*, 12; Howe, *Magicians*, 37–44.

[10] Waite, 'Obituary for Samuel Liddell MacGregor Mathers', *OR* 29:4 (1919), 196–99, on p. 197.

[11] Colquhoun, *Sword*, 69, 71.

[12] Moïna Mathers, 'Preface', in Mathers (trans.), *Kabbalah Unveiled* (revised edition, London: Routledge & Kegan Paul, 1926), vii.

[13] Colquhoun, *Sword*, 51.

[14] Gilbert, *Scrapbook*, 96.

Alexander Ayton, who had already acquired a reputation as a dedicated alchemist and who would shortly become a Golden Dawn initiate. Ayton, for whom Mina's Jewish background was of special significance, later wrote:

> Some of our Lady Members are the most advanced. One of Jewish extraction is, I think, the most advanced of all....I have told you I have a Jewish learned friend who was very advanced tho' he never would belong to any Order or Society....People in general have no idea of what gifted men, the best of Jews are.[15]

Mathers is generally recognised as the chief architect of the order's ritual magic.[16] Mina's importance is acknowledged by most historians of the order, but she is usually presented as Mathers' adoring acolyte and fierce defender rather than as a creative contributor to the order's Kabbalistic rituals and teachings.[17] It seems that she was both. She served as the scrying medium who 'channelled' most of the knowledge Mathers claimed to have acquired from his *maggidim* or 'Secret Chiefs',[18] and she authored four of the order's Flying Rolls under her magical name, Vestigia Nulla Retrorsum.[19] After Mathers' death in Paris in 1918,

---

[15] Letter from Alexander Ayton to Frederick Leigh Gardner (3 April 1894), in Ellic Howe (ed.), *The Alchemist of the Golden Dawn: The Letters of the Revd. W. A. Ayton to F. L. Gardner and Others 1886–1905* (Wellingborough: Aquarian Press, 1985), 76. The 'Jewish learned friend' is Julius Kohn; for more on Kohn, see below.

[16] See, for example, Gilbert, *Scrapbook*, 107; Hutton, *Triumph of the Moon*, 76–79; Francis King (ed.), *Astral Projection, Ritual Magic, and Alchemy: Golden Dawn Material by S. L. MacGregor Mathers and Others* (Rochester, VT: Destiny Books, 1987), 14; Howe, *Magicians*, 34.

[17] See, for example, Westcott, in a letter to Frederick Leigh Gardner (25 October 1924), cited in Howe, *Magicians*, 64: 'Mrs. Mathers was obsessed by Samuel Liddell M—'. See also Greer, *Women*, 357.

[18] See, for example, Mathers, 'Clairvoyance', 82–83, in which Mathers describes Mina's adjuration of angelic entities by 'vibrating' their Hebrew names. See also Greer, *Women*, 76–79, and the experience recounted by William Butler Yeats, 'Ideas of Good and Evil', in William Butler Yeats, *Essays and Introductions* (New York: Macmillan, 1961), 28–36.

[19] Further material written by Mina can be found in Regardie, *Golden Dawn*: for example, 'On Scrying and Travelling in the Spirit-Vision' (Regardie, *Golden Dawn*, 479–504). It is impossible to know how many of Mathers' Flying Rolls Mina influenced or even authored anonymously. One of her treatises, Flying Roll XXI, 'Know

Mina took over the leadership of the Alpha et Omega, the remnant of the original Inner Order of the Golden Dawn that Mathers had controlled since 1903, demonstrating her capacity for independent authority. In her preface to the revised edition of *The Kabbalah Unveiled*, published in 1926, she makes clear her ongoing devotion to Mathers' life and teachings. But Mathers began his occult career under the wing of William Wynn Westcott, and was supported financially throughout the existence of the original Golden Dawn by Mina's friend and fellow adept, Annie Horniman. Colquhoun's suggestion that Mathers was 'mother-bound' implies that he may have been a far more dependent personality than he cared to admit; Mina was the pillar of strength on which he leaned for both emotional support and, after his alienation from Westcott, knowledge of Jewish magical traditions. Joscelyn Godwin emphasises the fact that Mina's scrying abilities provided the means by which Mathers was able to contact the 'Secret Chiefs' of the order, and that it was her contribution which transformed the 'simple rituals' of the early Golden Dawn into 'a vehicle for effective magical initiations'.[20]

Given the centrality of Jewish magic and Kabbalistic theosophy in Golden Dawn doctrines and practices, it is surprising that Gilbert and Howe, the best-known scholars of the order, never mention the significance of Mina Bergson's Jewish background,[21] nor does Owen in her many references

---

Thyself' (repr. in King [ed.], *Astral Projection*, 151–59), concerns the attainment of 'Knowledge of Divinity', and relies on the *sefirot* as both symbols and stages of spiritual consciousness. The reference to each *sefira* having within it 'its own Ten Sephiroth' reflects Lurianic Kabbalistic conceptions; for the absorption of these Lurianic ideas into Hasidism, see Scholem, *Major Trends*, 327–30; Elior, *Paradoxical Ascent*, 202–05; Elior, *Mystical Origins of Hasidism*, 97–98. The assertion that a vision of the 'God of All' depends on knowing 'the God of yourself' is a Hasidic belief emerging in the eighteenth century, rather than a late nineteenth-century secularised 'psychologization of the sacred'. On this 'psychological' aspect of Hasidic mysticism, see Idel, *Hasidism*, 227–38.

[20] Godwin, *Theosophical Enlightenment*, 224.

[21] Neither Gilbert's *Scrapbook* nor Howe's *Magicians* refers to Mina Bergson's Hasidic background. King, *Modern Ritual Magic*, 49, entirely ignores Mina's family, referring to her only as 'French-born and a sister of Bergson the philosopher'. Godwin, *Theosophical*

to Mina's contributions to the Golden Dawn's magical repertoire.[22] Only two authors comment briefly on the religious upbringing of this Jewish high priestess of British occultism: Ithell Colquhoun in her hagiography of Mathers, and Mary K. Greer, who in her colourful anecdotal portraits of the women of the order calls Mina's family 'orthodox'.[23]

Enlightenment, 224, acknowledges Mina's major contribution to the order but makes no mention of her background.

[22] See Owen, *Place of Enchantment*, 66–67, 71–72, 100–03.

[23] See Colquhoun, *Sword*, 93; Greer, *Women*, 41. Colquhoun attenuates any connection between Mina and her family, suggesting that, although Mina may have been raised as a Jew, she was uninterested in the religion and would have converted to Christianity if Mathers had insisted: 'Moïna would certainly have followed him into the Church as into many more devious paths; being already on chilly terms with her relations, a change of religion would do little to worsen her familial status'. While this may well be true – although no references are given to support the assertion – it in no way diminishes the likelihood that Mina's knowledge of Hasidic literature and Hasidic Kabbalistic practices was fully utilised in the creation of the Golden Dawn rituals. Greer suggests that Mina 'was probably raised in a highly religious, possibly Orthodox, household', and acknowledges the usefulness of Mina's background for the development of the Kabbalah of the Golden Dawn; but she does not explore the ways in which Mina's special knowledge might have been incorporated, nor the fact that the 'orthodoxy' of Mina's family was in fact Hasidic. After Mina's death, all of her private papers were destroyed according to her instructions. In the last decades of her life, growing antisemitic currents in Britain and France would have ensured that she did not publicise her Jewish background. It is thus impossible to know her real attitude toward Judaism, or whether she secretly continued to perceive herself as a Jew, albeit a heterodox one. Her brother Henri Bergson, although he publicly rejected the Hasidism of his family background early in his career and at one point indicated a lively interest in Catholicism, nevertheless affirmed his Jewish roots in later life in the face of growing French antimsemitism and the approaching shadow of German persecution. For Bergson's attitudes toward Judaism, see Ben-Ami Scharfstein, *The Roots of Bergson's Philosophy* (New York: Columbia University Press, 1943), 99–101. Given the sensitivity of the social and political situation for British and European Jews in the late nineteenth and early twentieth centuries, *a priori* assumptions about the private feelings and attitudes of any Jewish occultist may be misleading.

Mina Bergson was not merely 'of Jewish extraction', nor was her family simply 'orthodox'.[24] Her wealthy and influential Polish grandparents were largely responsible for transforming late-eighteenth-century Hasidism from an obscure small-town cultic phenomenon into a thriving mass movement. Mina's paternal grandfather, a merchant called Dov Ber Berek Sonnenberg (1764–1822), was a staunch supporter of the Polish Hasidic movement and, although not one of Westcott's 'wonder-working rabbis' himself, was employed as a painter to produce portraits of them.[25] Sonnenberg inherited a family fortune based on monopolistic leases on state salt, tobacco, and the kosher meat tax, as the Polish government depended on wealthy Jewish merchants and bankers for money and army supplies. He also procured a contract to supply the Prussian army with meat and leather, and at the same time also provided the Polish legions of Napoleon's army with meat. Although he was a 'tycoon' by modern standards, there was no conflict between his religiosity and his extensive financial empire; the Hasidic view that even the most mundane of ventures constitutes an

---

[24] For the distinction between 'orthodox' and Hasidic Jews, see Yaacov Hasdai, 'The Origins of the Conflict Between Hasidim and Mitnagdim', in Safran (ed.), *Hasidism*, 27–45. Both orthodox and Hasidic Jews are deeply loyal to Jewish rabbinic and liturgical traditions. But the former, at the time of the rise of Hasidism, were strongly opposed to the Kabbalah, an antagonism originating in the antinomian appropriation of Kabbalistic ideas in the two failed messianic movements of Sabbatai Zevi and Jacob Frank in the seventeenth and eighteenth centuries, while the latter inherited the magical and mystical traditions of the medieval *Hasidei Ashkenaz* and have built their theosophy and their rituals in part on the Lurianic Kabbalah, the 'ecstatic' Kabbalah of Abraham Abulafia, and the magical practices of late antique *heikhalot* literature. The eighteenth-century Hasidim contemptuously referred to orthodox Jews as *mitnagdim* ('opponents'), although the fierce animosity between the two groups has diminished since the late eighteenth century. Orthodox Jews now comprise the majority of traditionally religious Jews in English-speaking countries, while the Hasidim represent only a small minority. On this theme, see David E. Fishman, *Russia's First Modern Jews: The Jews of Shklov* (New York: New York University Press, 1995), 7–21; Naftali Loewenthal, 'Rabbi Shneur Zalman of Liadi's *Kitzur Likkutei Amarim*, British Library Or 10456', in Joseph Dan and Klaus Herrmann (eds.), *Studies in Jewish Manuscripts* (Tübingen: Mohr Siebeck, 1998), 89–138.
[25] Glenn Dynner, *Men of Silk: The Hasidic Conquest of Polish Jewish Society* (Oxford: Oxford University Press, 2006), 99.

opportunity to serve God allowed the amassing of wealth without any sense of betraying his spirituality.[26] Sonnenberg's service to God was largely responsible for Polish governmental moderation toward the Polish Jewish community as a whole, and he intervened constantly in any government efforts to impose sanctions on Jewish trade or prosecute Jews for the infamous 'blood libel': the accusation, originating in Britain at the end of the thirteenth century, that the Jews used the blood of Christian children for ritual purposes.[27]

Berek Sonnenberg's support of the Hasidic *zaddikim* led them to invoke him frequently in their sermons. He also employed the *zaddikim* as agents in his business enterprises, and used his wealth and influence to promote their powerful religious movement throughout eastern Europe and Russia. As Glenn Dynner points out, 'The zaddikim intervened in heaven...while Berek did his part on earth'.[28] Sonnenberg's wife Temerel, Mina's paternal grandmother, was no less avid a supporter of the movement; a Hasidic hagiography declares that 'all of Berek's good deeds were nothing compared to the good deeds of his famous wife', who 'supported openly and secretly all the zaddikim and

---

[26] For this theme in Hasidism, see Glenn Dynner, 'Merchant Princes and Tsadikim: The Patronage of Polish Hasidism', *JSS* 12:1 (2005), 64–110, on p. 115. For more on Sonnenberg, see Marcin Wodzinski, 'How Modern Is an Antimodernist Movement? The Emergence of Hasidic Politics in Congress Poland', *AJSR* 31:2 (2007), 221–40, on pp. 228–29; Scharfstein, *Bergson's Philosophy*, 100. Scharfstein does not discuss the Hasidic affiliations of the Sonnenberg family, but focuses instead on their financial and political influence. For the spread of the Hasidic movement in Poland, see Adam Teller, 'Hasidism and the Challenge of Geography: The Polish Background to the Spread of the Hasidic Movement', *AJS Review* 30:1 (2006), 1–29.

[27] Blood libel accusations were used as a justification for the expulsion of the Jews from England in 1290. For the blood libel and its history, see Alan Dundes (ed.), *The Blood Libel Legend: A Casebook in Anti-Semitic Folklore* (Madison, WI: University of Wisconsin Press, 1991); Trachtenberg, *Devil and the Jews*, 140–55; Cecil Roth, 'The Medieval Conception of the Jew: A New Interpretation', in Cohen (ed.), *Essential Papers on Judaism and Christianity*, 298–309. Accusations of blood libel were still being made in the Middle East as well as Eastern Europe in the mid-nineteenth century; see Ronald Florence, *Blood Libel: The Damascus Affair of 1840* (Madison, WI: University of Wisconsin Press, 2004).

[28] Dynner, *Men of Silk*, 101.

Hasidim in Poland'.[29] Berek had three sons, Berek-sons or Bergsons, all of whom retained a strong allegiance to the family's religious traditions. The eldest son, Jakob, was a follower of the school founded by the *zaddik* Simcha Bunim of Przysucha, one of the main leaders of Hasidism in Poland. Bunim and other Hasidic leaders were intimates of the Sonnenberg family, 'having ready access to their home',[30] and Mina's father Michael Bergson, as well as his brother Jakob, were exposed to their teachings from an early age. Characteristic Hasidic anecdotes about Simcha Bunim can be found in Martin Buber's *Tales of the Hasidim*, and the following is relevant to the kind of thought in which Mina's father, and Mina herself, were brought up:

> Even now, the world is still in a state of creation. When a craftsman makes a tool and it is finished, it does not require him any longer. Not so with the world! Day after day, instant after instant, the world requires the renewal of the powers of the primordial word through which it was created, and if the power of these powers were withdrawn from it for a single moment, it would lapse into *tohu bohu* [primordial chaos].[31]

Sonnenberg's youngest son, Michael, born in Warsaw in 1818, achieved modest fame in Paris as a composer and an interpreter of Chopin's works. He married Katherine Levinson, born in Yorkshire to an Anglo-Irish Jewish family, and his lifelong loyalty to his religious background ensured that his daughter Mina, like her brother Henri, was brought up in the Hasidic magical and mystical traditions that would later prove invaluable in her contribution to the rituals of the Golden Dawn.[32]

---

[29] Issachar Dov Ber mi-Geza Tsvi, *Meir Eyne ha-Golah*, 17:62, cited in Dynner, *Men of Silk*, 104–05. For more on Temerel Sonnenberg, Mina Mathers' paternal grandmother, see Nahum Sokolów, 'Henri Bergson's Old-Warsaw Lineage', in Lucy Dawidowicz (ed.), *The Golden Tradition: Jewish Life and Thought in Eastern Europe* (New York: Holt, Rinehart and Winston, 1967), 349–59, on p. 353; Dynner, 'Merchant Princes', 64–110. Temerel was referred to by her compatriots as a female *zaddik*, a virtually unheard-of appellation.
[30] Mahler, *Hasidism and the Jewish Enlightenment*, 271–73.
[31] Buber, *Tales of the Hasidim*, 2:259. For more stories about Bunim, see Buber, *Tales of the Hasidim*, 2:239–69.
[32] For Michael Bergson's continuing links with his Hasidic background, see Louis M. Greenberg, 'Bergson and Durkheim as Sons and Assimilators: The Early Years', *FHS* 9:4 (1976), 619–34, on

THE NAME OF THE ROSE

The term 'magic' has been the subject of intense and ongoing scholarly debate for the last two decades, particularly concerning its distinction from, or relationship with, religion, science, and mysticism in different cultural contexts.[33] As Gideon Bohak observes, 'Much ink has been

---

p. 621, fn. 4. For elements of Hasidism in Henri Bergson's philosophy, see Chanan Lehrmann, *Bergsonisme et Judaïsme: Cours professé à l'Université de Lausanne* (Geneva: Editions Union, 1937); Margaret Teboul, 'Bergson, le temps et le judaïsme. Le débat des années 1960', *Archives juives* 38:1 (2005), 56–78. Mary Whiton Calkins, in 'Henri Bergson: Personalist', states: 'Bergson explicitly uses the terms "life" and "vital impulse", in which, most often, he describes the universe, as synonyms for consciousness'. In Bergson's *L'évolution créatrice*, 197, cited in Calkins, 'Henri Bergson: Personalist', 672, Bergson declares: 'Everything happens as if a great current of consciousness had penetrated matter', echoing the immanence of the deity flowing through creation presented in the Lurianic Kabbalah and in Hasidism. See also Michael Vaughan, 'Introduction: Henri Bergson's Creative Evolution', *SubStance* 36:3 (2007), 7–24. Vaughan does not mention Bergson's Hasidic antecedents, but notes the similarity between Bergson's theories of evolution and complexity theory, which is entirely compatible with Kabbalistic conceptions of emerging cosmological patterns. In 1908, the Zionist Max Nordau disparaged Henri Bergson's work by declaring, 'Bergson inherited these fantasies from his ancestors, who were fanatic and fantastic "wonder-rabbis" in Poland' (Sokolów, 'Henri Bergson', 358). For the tradition of 'wonder-working rabbis' in the Talmudic period, see Bohak, *Ancient Jewish Magic*, 402: 'The great thaumaturgical power accumulated by masters of Torah are a topic on which rabbinic literature is always glad to elaborate'.

[33] For one of the most comprehensive discussions on magic, see Hutton, *Witches, Druids*, 98–135. See also Fritz Graf, *Magic in the Ancient World*, trans. Franklin Philip (Cambridge, MA: Harvard University Press, 1997), 8–19; Christopher A. Faraone, *Ancient Greek Love Magic* (Cambridge, MA: Harvard University Press, 1999), 16–18; Christopher A. Faraone and Dirk Obbink (eds.), *Magika Hiera: Ancient Greek Magic and Religion* (Oxford: Oxford University Press, 1991); Alan F. Segal, 'Hellenistic Magic: Some Questions of Definition', in van den Broek and Vermaseren (eds.), *Studies in Gnosticism*, 349–75; H. S. Versnel, 'Some Reflections on the Relationship Magic-Religion', *Numen* 38 (1991), 177–97; Jonathan Z. Smith, 'Trading Places', in Meyer and Mirecki (eds.), *Ancient Magic*, 13–27; Curry, 'Magic vs. Enchantment'; Claire Fanger, 'Medieval Ritual Magic: What It Is and Why We Need to Know More About It', in Claire Fanger (ed.), *Conjuring Spirits: Texts and Traditions of*

spilled in an attempt to define, or eliminate, this term',[34] and it is not my purpose to spill yet more. However, the following discussion of 'Kabbalistic magic' as it was perceived by the adepts of the Golden Dawn requires some clarification of how the term 'magic' is being used in this book. The question of whether there is such a thing as 'Jewish magic' is also relevant and, if so, what distinguishes such magic from the magic of other cultures. This raises the additional question of whether 'Jewish magic' can be understood as a continuous tradition or can only be approached within a particular cultural context. There is as little agreement among scholars about the nature of Jewish magic as there is about magic in general.[35] Because Judaism, like other living forms of religiosity, is a complex entity that has undergone (and is still undergoing) dramatic changes over the centuries, Jewish 'insider' definitions of magic have also altered according to cultural context, exacerbated by the diaspora and the varying degrees of acculturation developed by Jewish communities in response to the levels of hostility, neutrality, or affinity demonstrated by the 'host' culture. These 'emic' definitions vary in their concordance with what a particular modern scholar might define as magic.[36] Jewish magicians, even within the same geographical area in the same period, demonstrate a wide variety of approaches to magic according to local rabbinic authorities, 'outside' cultural influences, shifts from oral to scribal traditions, and

---

Medieval Ritual Magic (University Park, PA: Pennsylvania State University Press, 1998), vii–xviii; Sarah Iles Johnston, John G. Gager, Martha Himmelfarb, Marvin Meyer, Brian Schmidt, David Frankfurter, and Fritz Graf, 'Panel Discussion on *Magic in the Ancient World* by Fritz Graf', *Numen* 46:3 (1999), 291–325; Jan N. Bremmer, 'The Birth of the Term "Magic"', in Bremmer and Veenstra (eds.), *Metamorphosis of Magic*, 1–11.

[34] Gideon Bohak, *Ancient Jewish Magic: A History* (Cambridge: Cambridge University Press, 2008), 3.

[35] For the nature of Jewish magic, see Trachtenberg, *Jewish Magic*; Patai, *Jewish Alchemists*; Bohak, *Ancient Jewish Magic*; Lesses, *Ritual Practices*; Swartz, *Scholastic Magic*; Idel, 'On Judaism'; Idel, 'Jewish Magic'; Elior, 'Angelology', 16; Elliot R. Wolfson, 'Phantasmagoria: The Image of the Image in Jewish Magic from Late Antiquity to the Early Middle Ages', *RRJ* 4:1 (2001), 78–120.

[36] See, for example, Bohak, *Ancient Jewish Magic*, 11–19, on prohibited and permitted practices in rabbinic literature from the first to seventh centuries CE.

individual interpretations of scripture.

Scholars continue to argue about whether or not rabbinic Judaism as presented in the Talmud countenances magic,[37] whether the references to magic in the Torah are unanimously hostile or display a subtler and more

---

[37] For this theme, see Idel, 'On Judaism', 203; Brigitte Kern-Ulmer, 'The Depiction of Magic in Rabbinic Texts: The Rabbinic and the Greek Concept of Magic', *JSJ* 27:3 (1998), 289–303; Mark J. Geller, 'Deconstructing Talmudic Magic', in Charles Burnett and W. F. Ryan (eds.), *Magic and the Classical Tradition* (London/Turin: Warburg Institute/Nino Aragno Editore, 2006), 1–18; L. Mock, 'Oral Law, Oral Magic: Some Observations on Talmudic Magic', *Zutot* 5:1 (2008), 9–14. Mock states (p. 9): 'A closer look at the Talmud shows that magic abounds: in stories on Talmudic figures; in exegesis on biblical themes; in halakhic matters; and in "magical science" in the form of advice on healing, on medicine and with explanations on how nature works'. Éliphas Lévi believed rabbinic literature contained Kabbalistic magical precepts, and the adept must 'enter boldly and courageously into the luminous shadows of the whole doctrinal and allegorical body of the Talmud' (Lévi, *Dogme*, 50). Waite, in his translation of *Dogme* (*Transcendental Magic*, 20, n. 1), ridicules this suggestion: 'A writer who terms the Talmud philosophy – occult or otherwise – has certainly not read the Talmud'. However, it seems that, according to the latest views of scholars of Jewish magic, Lévi was correct in assigning magical elements to the Talmud. Guiseppe Veltri, in 'The Rabbis and Pliny the Elder: Jewish and Greco-Roman Attitudes Toward Magic and Empirical Knowledge', *Poetics Today* 19:1 (1998), 63–89, comments (70) on the rabbinic predilection for talismans and amulets as well as the pragmatism displayed in attitudes toward magic: 'From an analysis of Rabbinic literature it can be inferred that the Rabbis also believed in the power of amulets...The Rabbis allowed the use of all amulets except for those that had traces of idolatry'. In special cases, however, the Rabbinic practice stresses healing as being much higher than the danger of idolatry. According to the Babylonian Talmud, *'Avodah Zarah* 55a, having recourse to idolatrous remedies may be permitted so that the patient does not lose trust in God. In the Middle Ages, rabbinically sanctioned practices of healing permitted not only the use of the Divine Names and *voces magicae*, but even the use of the name 'Jesus' because of its therapeutic value. See also Ephraim Kanarfogel, *'Peering Through the Lattices': Mystical, Magical, and Pietistic Dimensions in the Tosafist Period* (Detroit, MI: Wayne State University Press, 2000), a work which examines the use of magical doctrines and practices among the apparently 'orthodox' Jewish rabbinic scholars of Northern Europe in the medieval period.

ambivalent stance,[38] and whether magic is an inherent dimension of Judaism from ancient times or an 'imported' body of lore alien to the nature of the Jewish religion.[39] Many of these discussions treat Judaism as a monolithic entity rather than a complex interweaving of many different currents from many different cultural milieux over several millennia, and some still preserve the rationalistic stance of the late-nineteenth-century *Wissenschaft des Judentums* in an effort to attenuate or dismiss the magical elements, not only in the Kabbalah but in more traditional Jewish beliefs and practices.[40] The issue is further complicated by the fact that the Jewish magical tradition encompasses a wide spectrum of ritual objectives, from simple spells to injure a hostile neighbour, cure migraine, or protect a pregnant woman, to the sophisticated scribal tradition of 'learned ceremonial magic' and the meditative techniques of thirteenth-century Spanish Kabbalists, which are understood as magical by many modern Kabbalistic scholars.[41]

Rabbinic texts from the Second Temple and late antique periods express, with surprising frequency, an approval of certain kinds of magic which belies the current scholarly assumption that 'magic' is a pejorative reference to ritual practices that oppose the established communal religion.[42] As Gideon Bohak convincingly demonstrates, even Biblical injunctions against various magical applications warn the Jews, not against magic *per se*, but against consulting non-Jewish magicians, who are deemed to be sloppy and

---

[38] For the complexity of attitudes displayed toward magic in the Torah, see Bohak, *Ancient Jewish Magic*, 13–20.
[39] For references on the theory of 'importation', see Chapter Two, n. 28.
[40] See, for example, Joseph Dan, 'Magic', in *EJ*, 11.703–18, Col. 703.
[41] For the ritual objectives of Jewish magic, see Lawrence H. Schiffman and Michael D. Swarz, *Hebrew and Aramaic Incantation Texts from the Cairo Genizah* (Sheffield: Sheffield Academic Press, 1992); Joseph Naveh and Shaul Shaked, *Magic Spells and Formulae: Aramaic Incantations of Late Antiquity* (Jerusalem: Magnes Press, 1993); Joseph Naveh and Shaul Shaked, *Amulets and Magic Bowls: Aramaic Incantations of Late Antiquity* (Jerusalem: Magnes Press, 1985); John G. Gager, *Curse Tablets and Binding Spells from the Ancient World* (Oxford: Oxford University Press, 1992). For scribal magic, see Swartz, 'Scribal Magic'. For Kabbalistic forms of meditation as magic, see the references in Chapter Two.
[42] For this scholarly paradigm, see the discussion and bibliography in Hutton, *Witches, Druids*, 105.

inefficient; the 'right' sort of magic can be found in a more efficacious form at home, and the practitioner rather than the practice is the object of condemnation.[43] The scholarly paradigm of magic as the 'religious Other' may be an entirely inappropriate approach to Jewish magical texts and practices. As Ronald Hutton suggests, magic and religion are 'different points on a single continuum, and could overlap', and certain cultures, such as that of ancient Egypt, viewed them as 'integrated and harmonious'.[44] Although Kabbalistic texts do not usually describe their meditative and linguistic practices as 'magical', it is unlikely that their authors – almost invariably rabbis – were unaware that such practices fell within the parameters of their own definitions of magic.[37] The term 'theurgy', which seems to have arisen in the late antique Neoplatonic milieu and which E. R. Dodds defines as 'magic applied to a religious purpose',[45] is utilised by Moshe Idel to describe the 'mystico-magical' practices of medieval theosophical Kabbalah, which are firmly embedded in the Jewish religious framework.[46]

Peter Schäfer, in a work on the *heikhalot* literature, uses the terms 'magic' and 'theurgy' interchangeably, and contrasts the mystical ecstasy of the celestial ascent described by this literature with its 'magical-theurgic' angelic adjurations.[47] But in a later work, Schäfer asserts that magic 'cannot be distinguished or separated from religion',[48] and for this reason repudiates the use of the word 'theurgy' altogether.[49]

---

[43] Bohak, *Ancient Jewish Magic*, 14–15, 33.

[44] Ronald Hutton, 'Writing the History of Witchcraft: A Personal View', *The Pomegranate* 12:2 (2010), 239–62, on p. 244.

[37] For a biblical list of terms for various types of magicians, see Deuteronomy 18, and the list of magical practices in rabbinic literature in Bohak, *Ancient Jewish Magic*, 15–17 and 357–59.

[45] E. R. Dodds, *The Greeks and the Irrational* (Cambridge: Cambridge University Press, 1951), 291. See also E. R. Dodds, 'Theurgy and its Relationship to Neoplatonism', *JRS* 37 (1947), 55–69.

[46] See Idel, *Kabbalah*, 157. For more on the term 'mystico-magical', see Idel, *Hasidism*, 27, 31, 45–102. See also the discussion of Idel's use of the term 'theurgy' in Lesses, *Ritual Practices*, 48–50.

[47] Schäfer, *Hidden and Manifest God*, 67–69, 143–46.

[48] See Peter Schäfer, 'Merkavah Mysticism and Magic', in Schäfer and Dan (eds.), *Gershom Scholem's Major Trends*, 59–78, on p. 73.

[49] Peter Schäfer, 'Magic and Religion in Ancient Judaism', in Schäfer and Kippenberg (eds.), *Envisioning Magic*, 19–43, esp. pp. 25–26. See also the discussion of Schäfer's methodology in Lesses, *Ritual Practices*, 35–43.

The Jewish magical tradition, from the atropaic spells of the late antique Aramaic bowls to the linguistic magic of Abraham Abulafia and the 'intentional prayer' of the Lurianic and Hasidic Kabbalahs, consistently blurs the boundaries between 'religion' and 'magic' to the point where it is impossible to view them as discrete entities.[50] Magic, when it appears in Jewish texts, is always supported – even if only implicitly, and in what is now called 'aggressive' (rather than 'black') magic – by the sanctity of the Divine Names, the creative power of the Hebrew letters as emanations of deity, and the holiness of God's angels in their myriad ranks and hierarchies. A further complication arises when any effort is made to clarify what is 'Jewish' in the magical texts and practices of late nineteenth-century British occultism. British occultists express definitions of magic which are shaped by the religious, social, and scientific paradigms of their time, by medieval and early modern grimoires, by modern magi such as Barrett and Lévi, and by ancient and medieval Jewish texts as well as living Jewish practitioners. Due to the complexity of the debate, the term 'magic', as stated in Chapter One, is used throughout this book as a heuristic device to identify those themes and practices common to both British occultism and Jewish ritual practice which are specifically concerned with developing and maintaining, through the application of the human will, the system of bonds and relationships between revealed and concealed worlds.

Richard Kieckhefer emphasises the Christian perception of magic as traffic with the satanic realm, while Jewish magic concerns relationships with beings or powers which are aspects of the godhead. The Christian approach is rooted in New Testament ideas about an apocalyptic conflict with demonic forces:

> The life of a Christian might be one of spiritual ascent...but most fundamentally it was a life of conflict with unseen, malevolent spirits. This assumption pervades the New Testament and retained its cogency until the Enlightenment. For writers who conceived the life of the spirit essentially in terms of conflict with demons, magic was the most explicit form of collaboration with the enemy.[51]

---

[50] For the protective magic of the Aramaic bowls, see the references above, n. 34.

[51] Richard Kieckhefer, 'The Specific Rationality of Medieval Magic', *AHR* 99:3 (1994), 813–36, on p. 817.

Joshua Trachtenberg notes that Jewish magic, in contrast,

> ...excluded any such associations, real or fancied, with the
> arch-opponent of God....The primary principle of medieval
> Jewish magic was an implicit reliance upon the Powers of
> Good, which were invoked by calling upon their names, the
> holy Names of God and His angels.[52]

These sentiments are also expressed by the Austrian Jewish
scholar and occultist Julius Kohn, who was closely associated
with early members of the Golden Dawn:[53]

> Adaptation to the Will of the Creator is the way of Magic.
> Opposition to the Divine Will leads to destruction.[54]

Moses Gaster, another Jewish scholar personally involved
with British occultists, affirms the theme:

> For the Kabbalist owed his power to the knowledge which
> was vouchsafed to him through the study of sacred writings,
> whilst the wizard or magician was suspected of some unholy
> compact with the Master of Darkness....Kabbala was never
> associated with evil purposes, nor the Kabbalist with some
> mysterious dark power.[55]

This perception of Jewish magic as dependent on God's will
rather than on the 'powers of darkness' is somewhat
generalised, and does not address the problematic
'aggressive' magic of Jewish texts such as the *Sefer ha-Razim*,
which contains some unashamedly malevolent spells.[56] But
even the most unpleasant of the *Sefer ha-Razim*'s adjurations
are still embedded within the religious framework of the
angelic hierarchies and the Divine Names.

---

[52] Trachtenberg, *Jewish Magic*, 15.
[53] For Julius Kohn's involvement with William Frederick Ayton and
Frederick Leigh Gardner, see below.
[54] Julius Kohn, *Real Black Magic*, 237.
[55] Moses Gaster, 'The Origin of the Kabbala', in *Judith "Montefiore"
College Report for the Year, 1893–1894* (Ramsgate: Judith 'Montefiore'
College, 1894), 15. For Gaster's involvement with British occultists,
see below.
[56] See, for example, Morgan (trans.), *Sefer ha-Razim*, 50. For 'black
magic' in the *Sefer ha-Razim*, see Philip S. Alexander, '*Sefer ha-Razim*
and the Problem of Black Magic in Early Judaism', in Todd E. Klutz
(ed.), *Magic in the Biblical World: From the Rod of Aaron to the Ring of
Solomon* (London: T & T Clark International, 2003), 170–90.

Kieckhefer notes another important dimension of Jewish magic: the intent behind particular magical techniques, which he calls 'fundamental conceptions of spiritual process'.[57] Discussing the notorious fourteenth-century grimoire known as the *Liber Iuratus* or *Sworn Book of Honorius*, which William of Auvergne described as one of the very worst of all the 'execrable' books of magic which he had encountered,[58] Kieckhefer observes that the intent of the ritual instructions in this apparently Christian work – to gain a vision of God – does not belong to any Christian tradition, but is related to the Jewish *heikhalot* literature with its instructions for achieving an ascent of the soul through the seven heavens to the ultimate vision of God in his throne-chariot (*merkavah*), surrounded by his celestial court and ranks of angels.[59] The procedures for achieving the celestial ascent in these remarkable texts from late antiquity, including the ritual purity required of the adept as well as the descriptions of the various palaces or *heikhalot* of the

---

[57] Richard Kieckhefer, 'The Devil's Contemplatives: The *Liber Iuratus*, the *Liber Visionum* and Christian Appropriation of Jewish Occultism', in Fanger (ed.), *Conjuring Spirits*, 250–65, on p. 250.

[58] Robert Mathiesen, 'A Thirteenth-Century Ritual to Attain the Beatific Vision From the Sworn Book of Honorius of Thebes', in Fanger (ed.), *Conjuring Spirits*, 143–62, on p. 146. For more on *Honorius*, see Waite, *Book of Black Magic*, 95–104. Lévi sees *Honorius* as 'a monument of human perversity' which is nevertheless replete with 'the signs and secrets of the Kabbalah' (Lévi, *Histoire*, 307–14). Waite, always eager to criticise Lévi's observations, asserts that 'there was never a magical work which less connected with Kabbalism' (Waite, *Book of Black Magic*, 96). However, Waite ignored the issue of the 'fundamental conceptions of spiritual process', overlooking the fact that the fusion of occultism and contemplation which Kieckhefer feels makes this grimoire exceptional is an integral component of the magical *kavvanah* or 'intentional prayer' of theosophical Kabbalah. Although Kieckhefer dates the *Liber Iuratus* to the fourteenth century, it may have been compiled as early as the first half of the thirteenth century; see Mathiesen, 'A Thirteenth-Century Ritual', 145–47. Although the Spanish Kabbalah was already fully in flower by the fourteenth century, the *Liber Iuratus* demonstrates no knowledge of Kabbalistic theosophy, but relies entirely on earlier *heikhalot* traditions of the celestial ascent. Its author probably derived his materials from the German Jewish Pietists of northern France and Germany, who incorporated these earlier magical texts in their own writings during the twelfth and thirteenth centuries.

[59] See Kieckhefer, 'Devil's Contemplatives', 255.

heavenly realms, reflect on an interior, imaginal level the Temple traditions of early Judaism.[60] The ascent to the *merkavah* has virtually no parallel in any Christian literature except the *Liber Iuratus*,[61] which brazenly appropriates the use of the *Shem ha-Mephorasch* or seventy-two-letter Divine Name as a magical 'seal' to assist in the conjuration of spirits – although Honorius, the purported author of the work, attempted to distance himself from his Jewish sources by declaring that Jewish magicians themselves can never attain the true vision of God because of their 'infidelity'. Kieckhefer concludes that the *Liber Iuratus* is an important example of 'the kind of use Christian magicians might make of Jewish materials in the era before the rise of fully fledged Christian Kabbalah'.[62] It is also an important prototype for the kind of use Mathers made of the medieval grimoires, once he discovered the similarities they share with late antique and medieval Jewish magical literature. Kieckhefer's astute observation can be extended to other grimoires, including the important work called *The Book of the Sacred Magic of*

---

[60] For this theme, see Rachel Elior, 'From Earthly Temple to Heavenly Shrines: Prayer and Sacred Song in the Hekhalot Literature and Its Relations to Temple Traditions', *JSQ* 4:3 (1997), 217–67, and Himmelfarb, *Ascent to Heaven*. According to Elior ('Earthly Temple', 224), 'There is no doubt that *Hekhalot* literature is replete with direct and indirect allusions to the world of the priests and the Levites in the Temple. Its liturgical sections bear the clear imprint of the priestly and Levitical service; its language is strongly influenced by certain aspects of the sacred service and by literary traditions of the Temple Rites.' See also Saul Shaked, '"Peace Be Upon You, Exalted Angels": on Hekhalot, Liturgy and Incantation Bowls', *JSQ* 2:3 (1995), 197–219, where Shaked states (204), 'There is considerable affinity between the Jewish liturgical tradition...and the magic texts. At the same time there was also considerable affinity between those liturgical texts and the *Hekhalot* literature'. For more on ancient Jewish liturgical traditions and their relationship with Jewish magic, see Bloom, *Jewish Mysticism and Magic*, 38–58; Alan Segal, *The Other Judaisms of Late Antiquity* (Atlanta, GA: Scholars Press, 1987), 154–65. See also Vita Daphna Arbel, *Beholders of Divine Secrets: Mysticism and Myth in the Hekhalot and Merkavah Literature* (Albany, NY: State University of New York Press, 2003).

[61] An exception seems to be Paul, 2 Cor. 12:1–12; see Christopher R. A. Morray-Jones, 'Paradise Revisited (2 Cor. 12:1–12): The Jewish Mystical Background of Paul's Apostolate, Part 2: Paul's Heavenly Ascent and Its Significance', *HTR* 86:3 (1993), 265–92.

[62] Kieckhefer, 'Devil's Contemplatives', 256.

Abramelin the Mage, translated by Mathers for his Golden Dawn adepts. This work likewise relies heavily on Jewish antecedents for its 'fundamental conceptions of spiritual process' as well as its magical technology. According to Mathers, the chief object of the ritual magic of *Abramelin* is 'by purity and self-denial to obtain the knowledge of and conversation with one's Guardian Angel, so that thereby and thereafter we may obtain the right of using the Evil Spirits for our servants in all material matters'.[63] Invocation of the 'guardian angel' or *maggid* is a traditional practice in Kabbalistic literature from the fifteenth century onward, but earlier sources are provided by Abraham Abulafia's invocation of the *tselem*, the angelic vision of the adept's own Divine Self.[64]

The *Ars Notoria* or *Notary Art of Solomon*, the most popular of all the medieval grimoires, provides rituals for the acquisition of knowledge through the adjuration of angelic intermediaries.[65] Although the boon requested is appropriate for medieval scholastic Christendom – a knowledge of all the arts and sciences – it bears an unmistakable family resemblance to the adjuration of the *Sar ha-Panim* ('Prince of the Presence'), who is also called the *Sar ha-Torah* and is none other than the angel Metatron, for the purpose of acquiring, through magical means rather than laborious effort, a full knowledge of the Torah.[66] The *Holy Almandal*, a German-French grimoire from the late fifteenth century, betrays its Jewish roots in its ritual invocations of the twelve angels

---

[63] Mathers (trans.), *Abramelin*, xxvi.

[64] For the *tselem*, see Scholem, *Mystical Shape*, 251–73, and Chapter Five. The magical invocation of one's 'personal daimon' is also found in Iamblichus, *De mysteriis*, IX.1–9.

[65] The *Ars Notoria* was translated into English from the Latin by Robert Turner in 1656, and this translation was reissued as a volume in the 'Kabbalistic Grimoire List' of the Holmes Publishing Group. The text, although Christianised, claims to have been written by Apollonius of Tyana, and begins with a statement that this 'most holy Art of Knowledge' was revealed to Solomon by the Holy Angel of the Most High Creator, probably a reference to Metatron, the *Sar ha-Panim*. The reader is then informed, 'There is so great Virtue, Power and Efficacy in certain Names and Words of God, that when you read those very Words, it shall immediately increase and help your Eloquence...and at length attain to the Effects of the powerful Sacred Names of God'.

[66] For translations and a comprehensive discussion of the *Sar ha-Torah* rituals, see Swartz, *Scholastic Magic*.

presiding over the zodiacal signs through the use of the Divine Names. The text of the *Almandal* is ascribed to King Solomon, and the work is related to the astral and angel magic of the *Sefer ha-Razim* and the *Testament of Solomon*, both of which involve angelic adjurations embedded in an astrological framework.[67] Jan R. Veenstra, discussing the *Almandal*, suggests that the 'literary itinerary' of this text has affinity with Kabbalistic doctrines, particularly the idea that the various zodiacal signs are each represented by, or embody, a Divine Name, and the angels associated with the signs are directly linked with the linguo-theosophy of Kabbalistic lore.[68] Veenstra notes that the *Almandal*'s list of names for the zodiacal angels is the same as that presented by at least one of the versions of the *Liber Iuratus* and suggests that both grimoires have drawn on the same sources,[69] although it is also possible that the *Almandal* simply borrowed from the older *Liber Iuratus*. Equally suggestive is the presence in seventeenth-century English redactions of the *Almandal* (but not in French and German versions) of the use of scrying with 'crystal stones' to communicate with the zodiacal angels, suggesting that the

---

[67] For translations of the *Testament of Solomon*, see F. C. Conybeare, 'The Testament of Solomon', *JQR* 11 (1898), 1–45; D. C. Duling, 'Testament of Solomon', in Charlesworth (ed.), *Old Testament Pseudoepigrapha*, 1:935–87. See also Klutz, *Rewriting the Testament of Solomon*, and above, Chapter Two. The *Testament of Solomon* seems to have originated between the first and third centuries CE and bears many resemblances to the *Sefer ha-Razim*. The demons (or angels) whom Solomon confronts and dominates are associated with the planets and zodiacal signs. The earliest known fragments of the *Testament* are in Greek, probably by a Christian redactor, but the work appears to be based on earlier Jewish materials. There have been many debates about the 'Jewishness' as well as the dating of the *Testament*. In 1896, Moses Gaster stated that the Greek text was a translation of an original Hebrew work of an earlier date (see Gaster, 'The Sword of Moses', in Gaster, *Studies and Texts*, 294 and 309), but this assertion is now viewed as untenable. For the difficulties in dating the text, see James Harding and Loveday Alexander, 'Dating the Testament of Solomon', University of St. Andrews School of Divinity, www.st-andrews.ac.uk/divinity/rt/otp/guestlectures/harding/ (28 May 1999).
[68] Jan R. Veenstra, 'The *Holy Almandal*: Angels and the Intellectual Aims of Magic', in Bremmer and Veenstra (eds.), *Metamorphosis of Magic*, 189–215.
[69] Veenstra, '*Holy Almandal*', 203.

English redactors of the *Almandal* were familiar with John Dee's angel magic and incorporated his methods into their texts.[70]

British occultists' definitions of magic vary, not only according to the rapidly shifting landscape of British *fin-de-siècle* culture, but also as reflections of the personal inclinations of individual practitioners. Westcott, although a physician and an enthusiastic participant in the new scientific discoveries of his time, makes it clear that he, like so many Jewish magicians over the centuries, believes the power of magic is derived from the angelic hierarchies.[71] Mathers, a younger man who, despite his wife's religious background, seems to have had less personal affinity with Jewish traditions, was more interested in the use of ritual magic as a route to power and self-transformation, and defines magic as 'the Science of the Control of the Secret Forces of Nature'.[72] Nevertheless, Mathers attributed his rituals to the mysterious 'Secret Chiefs' or *maggidim* whose instructions were channelled through Mina's scrying efforts, and blended older Jewish magical perceptions of supernal powers with emerging late-nineteenth-century views of occult energies operating within the natural world.[73] This curious blend of ancient Jewish religiosity and modern 'scientific' occultism is evident in Mathers' instructions to the adept for achieving clairvoyance, which can be induced

> ...by means of introducing into the Consciousness and by formulating into sound, the highest Divine Names connected therewith; this invocation produces and harmonises currents of spiritual force in sympathy with your object. Then follow with the sacred names of Archangelic and Angelic import, producing them mentally, visually and by voice.[74]

Waite, declaring himself to be 'a professed transcendentalist', defined magic as 'the doctrine of unseen, intelligent powers, with whom it was possible for prepared persons to communicate'. He viewed the 'Kabbalah of the

---

[70] See Veenstra, '*Holy Almandal*', 213–15.
[71] See above, Chapter 3.
[72] Mathers, 'Introduction', in *Abramelin*, xxv.
[73] See Howe, *Magicians*, 127–33 for Mina Mathers' channelling of the 'Secret Chiefs'.
[74] S. L. MacGregor Mathers, 'Clairvoyance', Flying Roll XI, in King (ed.), *Astral Projection*, 75–83, on p. 78.

Jews' as the primary channel for the perpetuation of this ancient mystery tradition.[75] But Waite understood the rituals of what he calls 'Ceremonial Magic', found in grimoires such as the *Liber Iuratus* and the *Almandal*, as a 'travesty' of the sublime symbolism of the Kabbalah, and contemptuously dismissed the 'auto-hypnotic state which much magical ritual would obviously tend to occasion in predisposed persons'.[76] In Waite's view, this type of ritual magic, although purportedly 'Kabbalistic', involves the abuse of power rather than facilitating a channel for the *unio mystica*, and preoccupation with it is thus a form of delusion and even a psychopathology[77] – a view shared not only by late-nineteenth-century scholars such as Frazer, who sharply differentiated magic from religion, but also by some late-twentieth- and early-twenty-first-century psychologists attempting to understand the attraction of ritual magic to contemporary Western seekers.[78] Evelyn Underhill (1845–1941), another Golden Dawn adept who viewed herself as a Christian mystic, followed Lévi's idea that all magic depends on a 'universal agent', which she equated with the 'ground of the soul' of religious mysticism. The 'magical initiation', like the Catholic liturgy, is a 'traditional form of mental discipline, strengthening and focusing the will', and

> ...the true 'magic word' or spell, is untranslatable, because its power resides only partially in that outward sense which is apprehended by the intellect, but chiefly in the rhythm, which is addressed to the subliminal mind.[79]

Later Golden Dawn magicians such as Crowley appear to embrace a thoroughly 'modern' understanding of magic which equates it with science.[80] In the introduction to *Magick*

---

[75] Waite, *Book of Black Magic*, 5, 20, 24.
[76] Waite, *Book of Black Magic*, 5.
[77] For Waite's ambivalent views about magic, see Chapter Five.
[78] For magical and mystical experiences as psychopathology, see Michael A. Thalbourne, 'A Note on the Greeley Measure of Mystical Experience', *IJPR* 14:3 (2004), 215–22; C. Mohr, T. Landis, and P. Brugger, 'Lateralized semantic priming: modulation by levodopa, semantic distance, and participants' magical beliefs', *NDT* 2 (2006), 71–84.
[79] Underhill, 'Defence of Magic', 39.
[80] See Asprem, *'Kabbalah Recreata'*, for Crowley's 'rationalistic' understanding of Kabbalistic magic. See also Alex Owen, 'The Sorcerer and His Apprentice: Aleister Crowley and the Magical

in Theory and Practice, Crowley asserts that 'its fundamental conception is identical with that of modern science',[81] and explains that the Divine Names are 'vibrations calculated to establish general control of the brain'.[82] But Crowley, whose distaste for the Jews was comparable with Blavatsky's,[83] was not averse to using distinctively Jewish magical technologies to invoke a *maggid* or 'Holy Guardian Angel' which he understood as an ontologically autonomous entity.[84] E. J. Langford Garstin, a loyal disciple of Mathers and a member of the Golden Dawn splinter-group known as the Alpha et Omega, defines magic as 'an understanding of the working and application of certain arcane forces of nature', and then proceeds to embed this 'modern' definition within the 'universal language' of the sefirotic Tree and the Kabbalistic tripartite division of the soul.[85]

There is thus no single definition of magic, Jewish or otherwise, offered by Golden Dawn occultists, although it is sometimes difficult to avoid the conclusion that certain ancient ideas with vigorous agency have been dressed up in new, 'modern' clothes to align them with the scientific paradigms of the *fin-de-siècle* while retaining continuity in their structure and intent. There is also no single definition of magic offered by ancient, medieval, or modern Jewish texts, and the metanarrative of a 'new' post-Enlightenment magic transformed through secularisation can begin to sound somewhat specious when one compares the highly sophisticated and surprisingly 'secularised' declaration of the sixteenth-century Kabbalist Moses Isserles – 'on natural elements depends the effectiveness of the various types of magic, all of which consist in bringing out the inner nature of

---

Exploration of Edwardian Subjectivity', *JBS* 36:1 (1997), 99–133. For more on Crowley's views on magic, see Chapter Five.
[81] Crowley, *Magick in Theory and Practice*, ix.
[82] Aleister Crowley, 'The Initiated Interpretations of Ceremonial Magic', in S. L. MacGregor Mathers (trans.), *The Goetia: The Lesser Key of Solomon the King* (London: private publication with Crowley, 1904), 15–20, on p. 17.
[83] For Crowley's antisemitism, see Chapter Five.
[84] For Crowley's invocation of his 'Holy Guardian Angel', see Chapter Five.
[85] E. J. Langford Garstin, *Theurgy or The Hermetic Practice: A Treatise on Spiritual Alchemy* (London: Rider, 1930), 13, 17–24.

things'[86] – with the overtly religious and even 'pre-modern' declaration of Julius Kohn in the early twentieth century that 'God alone is the source of all magical power'.[87]

Hans Dieter Betz concludes that what makes late antique Jewish magic Jewish is its religious framework, which usually involves quotations from Scripture and Jewish hymnic language and theology.[88] Maureen Bloom concurs with this assessment, highlighting the close relationship between the priestly ritual actions and prayers of the ancient Temple service, celestial ascents of the soul as described in the *heikhalot* literature, texts of astral magic such as the *Sefer ha-Razim*, and 'popular' magical praxis. Bloom points out that Jewish magical spells utilise 'core aspects of the orthodox ancient Hebrew sacrificial cult and its prayer ritual'.[89] Talmudic descriptions of these sacred ceremonies were included in the development of standard Jewish prayers, which in turn were appropriated for Jewish magical practices as well as being borrowed by Greco-Egyptian magicians for their own rituals. The magical sword also cuts both ways: Mark Geller and Dan Levene argue that the phrase, 'Blessed be the Name of His glorious Kingdom for ever and ever', routinely recited in everyday Jewish prayer, was originally included in the liturgy precisely because it was perceived as a powerful magical incantation.[90] This idea is supported by Moshe Idel: 'The belief that the performance of the Biblical ritual has dramatic repercussions on the course of nature...is immanently and eminently magical'.[91]

Michael Swartz suggests a phenomenological approach to Jewish magical texts: they regularly exhibit an emphasis on the power of the Divine Names, the intermediacy of the angels, and the application of the Names in ritual practices for the needs of specific individuals.[92] Yuval Harari also focuses on the phenomenology of Jewish magic rather than its social or religious relevance: 'I believe that a Jewish magic text in its clearest and most reduced sense is an adjuration

---

[86] Moses Isserles, *Torat Ha'Olah*, Lemberg, 1858, III.77, cited in Trachtenberg, *Jewish Magic*, 21. See also below, n. 97.
[87] See above, n. 2.
[88] Betz, 'Jewish Magic in the Greek Magical Papyri', 59.
[89] Bloom, *Jewish Mysticism and Magic*, 165.
[90] Mark J. Geller and Dan Levene, 'Magical Texts From the Genizah', *JJS* 49:2 (1998), 334–40, on p. 335.
[91] Idel, 'Jewish Mysticism', 203.
[92] Swartz, *Scholastic Magic*, 20.

text'.[93] The adjuration involves an appeal to (or a coercion of) supernal powers – angels or 'princes', demons, Divine Names, Hebrew letters – to fulfil a specific request, and almost invariably utilises the phrases 'I call' or 'I adjure'.[94] The authors of the grimoires appropriated this characteristic formula for their angelic and demonic adjurations,[95] and these adjurations were in turn appropriated for Golden Dawn rituals.[96] The Divine Names in Jewish esoteric traditions are amenable to infinite permutations according to the rules of letter combinations, yielding many of the adjurational *voces magicae* or *nomina barbara* which permeate Jewish as well as non-Jewish magical literature such as the *PGM* corpus.[97]

Mathers' Golden Dawn rituals are usually adjurations, and they perpetuate the inclusion of Divine Names and characteristic forms of Jewish prayer appropriated from Latin and English translations of late antique and medieval Jewish texts. The *voces magicae* appear as well, although it is not always possible to distinguish whether these have been derived from Jewish, Greco-Egyptian, or medieval and early modern Christian sources.[98] Some may be invented by

---

[93] Yuval Harari, 'What Is a Magical Text? Methodological Reflections Aimed at Redifining Early Jewish Magic', in Shaul Shaked (ed.), *Officina Magica: Essays on the Practice of Magic in Antiquity* (Leiden: Brill, 2005), 91–124, on p. 119.

[94] For the use of these phrases, see Lesses, *Ritual Practices*, 4. For the appropriation of the phrases in medieval grimoires and in Golden Dawn rituals, see below.

[95] See, for example, the adjuration in S. L. MacGregor Mathers (trans.), *Grimoire of Armadel* (York Beach, ME: Samuel Weiser, Inc., 1980; repr. San Francisco, CA: Red Wheel/Weiser, 2001), 18.

[96] See, for example, 'Ritual of Consecration of the Four Elemental Weapons', cited in Regardie, *Golden Dawn*, 325. For the phrases 'I beseech', 'I invoke', and 'I conjure', see William Wynn Westcott, 'Further Rules for Practice', cited in Regardie, *Golden Dawn*, 669.

[97] For the ubiquity of the Jewish Divine Names, angelologies, and *voces magicae* in antiquity, see A. D. Nock, 'Religious Symbols and Symbolism I', *Gnomon*, 27 (1955), 558–72; Gideon Bohak, 'Hebrew, Hebrew Everywhere? Notes on the Interpretation of *Voces Magicae*', in Noegel *et al.* (eds.), *Prayer, Magic, and the Stars*, 69–82.

[98] See, for example, the *voces magicae* in 'Ritual of the Portal', cited in Regardie, *Golden Dawn*, 201; 'Ritual for Invisibility', cited in Regardie, *Golden Dawn*, 423.

Mathers himself, based on his own efforts at *gematria*.[99] In the 'Ritual of the Portal of the Vault of the Adepti', the adept adjures Shaddai el-Chai and Raphael.[100] The latter is one of the chief Jewish archangels; the former is comprised of two Divine Names common in Jewish magical texts, Shaddai ('Almighty'), referred to as 'the seal of the King' and equated with Metatron, and El ('God'). Chai ('living') is an adjective also commonly appended to a Divine Name in Jewish magical texts. The adjuration is thus to 'Almighty Living God'. The 'Ritual for Transformation' opens with a characteristic Jewish formula:

> In the divine name Iao,[101] I invoke Thee thou great and holy Angel Hua.[102] Lay thy hand invisibly upon my head in attestation of this my solemn aspiration to the Light. Aid and guard me, I beseech Thee, and confirm me in this path of truth and rectitude, for the glory of the ineffable Name.[103]

In this ritual the elemental spirits are adjured 'in the name of Shaddai el-Chai and in the name of YHVH', and the deity is addressed as 'almighty and ever living One, blessed be thy Name'. Even in the apparently Christianised 'Adeptus Minor Ritual', intended to be a 'Rosicrucian' ceremony, the Tetragrammaton is invoked along with Reuchlin's Christianised 'secret' derivation, YHShVH.[104]

Joshua Trachtenberg locates the Jewishness of Jewish magic in its reliance on 'a vast, teeming "middle world"',

[99] For Mathers' preoccupation with *gematria*, see Mathers, *Kabbalah Unveiled*, 7–14; Mathers, 'Azoth Lecture'; S. L. MacGregor Mathers, 'Document M', in Regardie, *Golden Dawn*, 479–510.
[100] See Regardie, *Golden Dawn*, 205.
[101] For 'Iao' or Ia(h)ô, the Greek version of YHVH commonly used in Greco-Egyptian texts and in texts written by Greek-speaking Jews, see Hans Dieter Betz, *The Greek Magical Papyri in Translation, Including the Demotic Spells* (Chicago, IL: University of Chicago Press, 1992), xlvii; Bohak, *Ancient Jewish Magic*, 198.
[102] See Crowley, *Confessions*, 1029, for Hua as one of the many titles of the first *sefira*, Kether.
[103] Regardie, *Golden Dawn*, 429–34.
[104] Regardie, *Golden Dawn*, 235–47. For Reuchlin's extraction of the name of Jesus from the Tetragrammaton, unknown in early biblical exegesis, see Zika, 'Reuchlin's *De Verbo Mirifico*'; Price, 'Christian Humanism', 82–83. Price points out (p. 83) that in fact Jesus' name in Hebrew does not contain the roots of the Tetragrammaton; Reuchlin's 'Jehoshua' is based on the verb *yosha* שׁע and does not contain the letters of the Tetragrammaton יהוה.

filled with demons and angels through whose mediation 'the powers of magic were brought into operation.'[105] This 'teeming "middle world"' is not exclusive to Jewish magic; it is shared, like the idea of an emanated universe, by Gnostic and Neoplatonic cosmologies as well as by late-nineteenth-century British occultists. However, the application of the Divine Names to invoke the powers of the 'middle world' is peculiarly Jewish. The sixteenth-century Kabbalist Moses Isserles expresses the 'emic' perspective of a practising Jewish magician of the early modern period:

> The roots of the [magical] arts are three: God, science, and nature....From God comes...the power to invoke the heavenly princes by means of the holy names; the scientific root may be illustrated by astrology...on natural elements depends the effectiveness of the various types of magic, all of which consist in bringing out the inner nature of things.[106]

This statement mirrors the rituals created by Mathers and his wife, which incorporate not only angelic invocations, but also the application of astrology to talismans and divination and the understanding of the 'occult' properties of nature to facilitate inner and outer transformations.[107] Many currents of Jewish magic, from late antiquity onward, are specifically concerned with the possibility of the divinisation of the human being,[108] however temporary, and it is this aspiration toward the transformation of the adept into an angelic being which fuelled Pico's enthusiasm for Kabbalistic magic in the fifteenth century.[109] However 'new' the Golden Dawn magical apparatus is understood to be by modern scholars, and however sophisticated the integration of motifs from Greco-Egyptian, Rosicrucian, and Masonic sources, the traditional Jewish forms of address to the deity, the adjuration of angels, the use of the Divine Names, and the goal of spiritual transformation dominate the corpus of Mathers' ritual magic.

---

[105] Trachtenberg, *Jewish Magic*, 25.
[106] Moses Isserles, *Torat Ha'Olah*, Lemberg, 1858, III.77, cited in Trachtenberg, *Jewish Magic*, 21.
[107] For Mathers' talismanic astral magic, see below.
[108] See Rachel Elior, 'The Concept of God in Hekhalot Literature', in Joseph Dan (ed.), *Binah: Studies in Jewish History, Thought, and Culture*, Vol. 2 (NY: Praeger, 1989), 97–120.
[109] For Kabbalistic divinisation in Pico, see Copenhaver, 'The Secret of Pico's *Oration*'.

MATHERS AND THE GRIMOIRES

The mystery surrounding the 'Cipher Manuscripts' used as the basis for the Golden Dawn's foundation and early rituals has been comprehensively explored elsewhere.[110] Whatever the source of these manuscripts – an invention of Mackenzie, a creation of Westcott, a genuine transmission of older Continental Rosicrucian-Masonic practices, a quiet 'lift' from medieval and early modern grimoires and Jewish magical texts, or a mixture of all of the above – the development of the rituals within both the Outer and Inner Orders of the Golden Dawn in subsequent years was due primarily to the spirited eclecticism of Mathers and the imaginative gifts and knowledge of Jewish esoteric lore of his wife Mina. Many other Golden Dawn members made contributions to the order's 'Flying Rolls' and 'Knowledge Lectures', intended to educate the adepts in various aspects of ritual magic,[111] but the Kabbalistic framework which Westcott and Mathers had established at the beginning remained the firm and unchanging foundation on which were built the ceremonial activities of the order.

In addition to the usual suspects – Agrippa, Dee, Rudd, Barrett, and Lévi – one of the chief literary sources for Mathers' rituals was the large collection of grimoires available to him in the British Library as well as the Bibliothèque de l'Arsenal and the Bibliothèque Nationale in Paris.[112] In the autumn of 1889, a year after his marriage and the foundation of the Golden Dawn, Mathers published the first of his numerous translations of these texts: the *Clavicula Salomonis* or *Key of Solomon the King*.[113] Although the oldest

---

[110] See Howe, *Magicians*, 1–25; King, *Modern Ritual Magic*, 39–46; Gilbert, *Scrapbook*, 21–23; Waite, *Shadows*, 218–19.

[111] For contributions by J. W. Brodie-Innes, see Gilbert (ed.), *Sorcerer and His Apprentice*, 89–224. For contributions by Westcott, Mathers, Mina Mathers, Edward William Berridge, Percy W. Bullock, Elaine Simpson, Annie Horniman, and J. R. Brodie-Innes, see King (ed.), *Astral Projection*.

[112] For Mathers' claim that the rituals for the Inner Order were derived in their entirety from the 'Secret Chiefs', see King, *Modern Ritual Magic*, 45.

[113] S. L. MacGregor Mathers (trans.), *The Key of Solomon the King (Clavicula Salomonis)* (London: George Redway, 1889; repr. San Francisco, CA: Red Wheel/Weiser, 2000). For a careful analysis of the various MS versions of the *Clavicula*, see Robert Mathiesen, 'The Key of Solomon: Toward a Typology of the Manuscripts', *SMN* 17

extant MSS of the *Clavicula* are in French and date to no earlier than the sixteenth century, in 1903 Hermann Gollancz announced his discovery of a Hebrew MS which he believed was much older and based on an original Jewish magical text.[114] Although Gollancz' assumptions are now viewed as

---

(Spring 2007), at <http://brindedcow.umd.edu/socmag>. Mathiesen mentions what he calls the 'Rabbi Abognazar Text-Group', known only from French manuscripts of the eighteenth century; it is the name 'Abognazar' which led Mathers to believe the *Clavicula* had been translated into Latin by Abraham ibn Ezra. Mathiesen also discusses the 'Oldest (Western) Text' group dating to the sixteenth century, which provided another important source for Mathers' translation. See also Adam MacClean's comprehensive list of English library holdings of the *Clavicula* at <http://www.levity.com/alchemy/clav_eng.html>. Mathers would have had access to all these manuscripts as well as those in French libraries. For Lévi's claim to have 'rediscovered' the lost Hebrew version, see Lévi, *Clef*, 9.

[114] Hermann Gollancz, *Clavicula Salomonis: A Hebrew Manuscript* (London: D. Nutt, 1903). In this pamphlet, Gollancz refers to Mathers' translation of the *Clavicula* and the comment that the original Hebrew manuscript had been 'given up as lost', and states that he (Gollancz) had the 'good fortune' to find his Hebrew MS among the books in his late father's library. Gollancz later published the text of the Clavicula with his translation: Hermann Gollancz (trans.), *Sepher Maphtea Shelomoh (Book of the Key of Solomon): An exact facsimile of an original book of magic in Hebrew with illustrations* (Oxford: Oxford University Press, 1914). Gollancz, like Moses Gaster and other Jews working within the British scholarly establishment, was familiar with the Kabbalistic exegeses of the British occultists. Gollancz lists various seventeenth- and eighteenth-century versions of the *Clavicula* and notes: 'A hurried survey of these very MSS. might easily convince one that they are anything but Jewish in character, several of them containing illustrations which, in the eye of the Jewish Law, would be regarded as blasphemous: the human face or more extended form appears in a circle...the face itself in several instances being even supplied with horns and the form with wings'. Gollancz believed that the Hebrew MS in his possession was copied in *c.* 1700 from an older version, and was brought to the West by the followers of the false messiah Sabbatai Zevi at some time during the mid- to late seventeenth century. 'The general impression conveyed by a perusal of the work itself', Gollancz states, 'is that it is perfectly Jewish in tone. The invocations and names contained therein, and the pantheistic spirit underlying the invocations as well as the formulae, are not un-Jewish. The Jewish character of the work as a whole is not affected by the foreign elements and names introduced in the appendices

highly speculative, no concensus has yet been reached about the age and origins of this important magical text. R. A. Gilbert, in his foreward to a recent reprint of this work, calls it 'a crucial text of Western ritual magic'.[115] Waite asserts that the *Clavicula* is the ultimate source of virtually all other magical grimoires.[116] Mathers himself declares the *Clavicula* to be 'the fountain-head and storehouse of Qabalistical Magic',[117] and, like Lévi, assumed that any magical work attributed to Solomon was derived from an authentic ancient Hebrew text actually written by the great biblical king, and therefore belonged to the tradition of 'practical' (magical) Kabbalah:[118] 'I see no reason to doubt the tradition which assigns the authorship of the "Key" to King Solomon'.[119] Waite, although contemptuous of Lévi's and Mathers' assumption of a genuine Solomonic authorship, nevertheless believed the source of the *Clavicula* to be an ancient Jewish work:[120] the *Sefer ha-Raziel*, first published in Hebrew in Amsterdam in 1701 but containing a section of the late antique *Sefer ha-Razim*, 'units' from *heikhalot* literature, and an extract from the *Sode Razaya* ('Secrets of the Mysteries') of Eleazar of Worms, the most influential of the *Hasidei Ashkenaz*, to whom the entire *Sefer ha-Raziel* was traditionally

---

and other parts'. Although acknowledged as a sincere scholarly effort, Gollancz' assumptions are now viewed as highly speculative, although no final consensus has been reached about the age and origins of this important magical text. For more on the *Clavicula*, see the discussions in Butler, *Ritual Magic*, 47–80; Davies, *Grimoires*, 54–56; Waite, *Book of Black Magic*, 67–72.

[115] R. A. Gilbert, 'Foreward', in Mathers (trans.), *Key of Solomon*, v.

[116] See Waite, *Book of Black Magic*, 30–31.

[117] Mathers, 'Preface', in Mathers (trans.), *Key of Solomon*, ix.

[118] For Mathers' division of the Kabbalah into 'literal', 'practical', 'unwritten', and 'dogmatic', see Mathers (trans.), *Kabbalah Unveiled*, 6–7.

[119] Mathers, 'Preface', in *Key of Solomon*, x. See also Lévi, *Dogme*, 337: 'The universal key to the magical arts is the key of all ancient religious doctrines, the key to the Kabbalah and the Bible: the Key of Solomon'; and Lévi, *Clef*, 9: 'There is an occult and sacred alphabet which the Hebrews attributed to Enoch....Solomon represented this alphabet through seventy-two names written on thirty-six talismans, and it is this which the initiates of the East still call...the Key of Solomon'. According to Mathers, the *Clavicula* provided Lévi with the model on which *Dogme* was based; see Mathers, 'Preface', ix.

[120] Waite, *Book of Black Magic*, 33.

credited.[121] Such assumptions of the antiquity of grimoires such as the *Clavicula* cannot be entirely blamed on the 'esoteric method' of claiming a spurious antiquity for modern ideas. The absorption of the terminology and technology of late antique Jewish magical texts such as the *Sefer ha-Razim* into early Kabbalistic speculations led the thirteenth-century Kabbalist Abraham Abulafia to scathingly dismiss these magical practices as the wrong sort of Kabbalah, and the idea of Jewish magic as 'practical' Kabbalah – a term usually attributed to Pico and later Christian Kabbalists – first appears in the works of medieval Jewish authors as *hokhmat ha-shimmush* ('magical knowledge'), a translation of the technical Greek word *praxis* used to denote magical activity.[122]

Much of the adjurational language and structure of the Golden Dawn rituals can be easily recognised as adaptations of grimoires such as the *Clavicula*, and cannot be considered 'Kabbalistic' in the sense that Kabbalah is usually defined by modern scholars. But the technology of the grimoires is itself adapted from the Jewish magical rituals of antiquity, and the use of the Tetragrammaton and the various permutations of

---

[121] See Trachtenberg, *Jewish Magic*, 92; Scholem, *Major Trends*, 373, n. 66. Trachtenberg suggests (*Jewish Magic*, 72, 92, 315) that the *Sefer ha-Raziel* was composed in the thirteenth century, contemporary with Eleazar of Worms, but its material is derived primarily from the Geonic period (*c.* 800–1100 CE). For further references, see Steve Savedow, 'Translator's Introduction' in Savedow (trans.), *Sefer Rezial Hemelach*, 9–20; Secret, 'Sur quelques traductions'.
[122] See Gershom Scholem, 'Practical Kabbalah', *EJ*, 10.632–38. Scholem defines what became known in Jewish circles in the thirteenth century as 'practical' Kabbalah as an 'agglomeration of all the magical practices that developed in Judaism from the Talmudic period down through the Middle Ages'. The distinction between the 'speculative' and 'practical' currents of Kabbalah was thus initially made by Jewish Kabbalists themselves. An anonymous thirteenth-century author of Abulafia's school, in a text once attributed to the Aristotelian Jewish philosopher Maimonides, differentiates between 'rabbinic', 'prophetic', and 'practical' Kabbalah. Other early Spanish Kabbalists also made distinctions between the Kabbalistic doctrine of the *sefirot* and Kabbalistic 'great' and 'lesser' magic (*shimmusha rabba* and *shimmusha zutta*); for this division, see Scholem, 'Practical Kabbalah', 632–33. The magical practices that Mathers understood as 'practical Kabbalah' are thus not a syncretic effort on the part of a modern occultist, but were understood by Jewish Kabbalists themselves as Kabbalah from the medieval period onward.

its letters are an essential aspect of angelic adjuration in the *heikhalot* texts, as described in the treatise known as *Ma'aseh Merkavah*:

> This is the praxis of wisdom and understanding; all who practice it become wise and understanding. In the name of YH YH YH YHW YHW YH[W] YHY YHY HY HY HY HW HW HW 'HW 'HW 'HW 'H YH 'HYH 'HYH 'HYH, Blessed, Blessed, Blessed, Holy, Holy, Holy, Shaddai, Shaddai, Shaddai...He elaborates His name by those forty-two [letters] – for the one who practices it is wise and filled with wisdom.[123]

The late antique work known as the *Harbe de Moshe* ('Sword of Moses'), translated and published by Moses Gaster in 1896, makes plain that the 'sword' is the secret of the Divine Names, knowledge of which can wield enormous magical power.[124] Although the form of the Golden Dawn rituals is based on Masonic prototypes,[125] the kinds of invocation represented by early Jewish magical texts provide the rituals with their adjurational language and intent by way of the wholesale importation of this language into grimoires such as the *Clavicula*:[126]

---

[123] *Ma'aseh Merkavah*, MS NY8128, ¶571, cited in Swartz, *Scholastic Magic*, 109–10.

[124] See above, Chapter Three, n. 75. For a discussion of the linguistic 'sword' tradition in the *Harbe de Moshe*, see Yuval Harari, 'Moses, the Sword, and *The Sword of Moses*: Between Rabbinical and Magical Traditions', *JSQ* 12 (2005), 293–329.

[125] For the Masonic basis of the rituals, see Hutton, 'Pagan Witchcraft', 3–13; Bogdan, *Initiation*, 50–51, 121–44.

[126] The *Lesser Key of Solomon the King*, also known as the *Lemegeton*, contains many invocations similar to those of the *Clavicula*. See, for example, the 'Second Conjuration' (Mathers (trans.), *Goetia*, 82): 'I do invoke, conjure, and command thee, O thou Spirit N...by the name and in the name IAH and VAU, which Adam heard and spake; and by the name of God, AGLA, which Lot heard and was saved with his family; and by the name IOTH, which Iacob heard from the angel wrestling with him...and by the name ZABAOTH, which Moses named and all the rivers were turned to blood'. The references to specific biblical heroes and stories, known as *historiolae*, are unique to late antique Jewish magical texts, revealing the Jewish roots of this grimoire. For *historiolae* in general magical praxis, see David Frankfurter, 'Narrating Power: The Theory and Practice of the Magical *Historiolae* in Ritual Spells', in Meyer and Mirecki, (eds.), *Ancient Magic and Ritual Power*, 457–76. For specific

Adonai, Elohim, El, Eheieh Asher Eheieh, Prince of Princes, Existence of Existences, have mercy upon me...who invokes Thee most devoutedly and supplicates Thee by Thy Holy and tremendous Name Tetragrammaton....O ye Angels and Spirits of the Stars, O all ye Angels and Elementary Spirits...I the Minister and faithful Servant of the Most High conjure ye.[127]

Mathers had an ample range of sources from which to draw the materials for his rituals: Hebrew magical manuscripts, medieval and early modern grimoires, and the invocations of Agrippa, Dee, Rudd, Lévi, and Barrett. It seems he availed himself of all of them. For his translation of the *Clavicula*, he worked primarily from sixteenth- and seventeenth-century Latin and English manuscript versions which he found at the British Museum, as well as a fragment purportedly translated from the 'original' Hebrew by Lévi.[128] Mathers was also convinced that at least one of the Latin versions he worked from was a copy of a translation from the Hebrew by Abraham ibn Ezra in the twelfth century, as the manuscript claimed to be 'translated from the Hebrew into the Latin language by the Rabbi Abognazar',[129] thereby apparently confirming its authenticity as a repository of Hermetic-Kabbalistic magic.

Jewish *historiolae*, see Bohak, *Ancient Jewish Magic*, 312–14; Swartz, 'Divination and Its Discontents, 164; Swartz, *Scholastic Magic*, 65–66 and 215–16. See also Shaul Shaked, 'Form and Purpose in Aramaic Spells: Some Jewish Themes', in Shaked (ed.), *Officina Magica*, 1–30, esp. p. 15: 'The *historiolae* in these spells can be regarded as foundation-myths, giving as they do the mythic precedents for the procedures followed by the spell. Narrating them is part of the spell itself: the narration is supposed to bring about the desired effect'. Golden Dawn rituals use both Jewish and Greco-Egyptian *historiolae*. An example of a characteristically Jewish *historiola* in a Golden Dawn ritual can be found in the 'Ritual of the Portal' (Regardie, *Golden Dawn*, 207), where Isaiah's vision of the six-winged Seraphim is quoted and then 'explained'.
[127] Mathers (trans.), *Key of Solomon*, 1.14.
[128] See Gilbert, 'Foreward' in Mathers (trans.), *Key of Solomon*, vii, for Mathers' use of these manuscripts, and Mathers, 'Preface', in Mathers (trans.), *Key of Solomon*, ix. For Lévi's version, see *Clefs majeures*.
[129] See the heading of the opening paragraph of Mathers (trans.), *Key of Solomon*, 1.

The magical adjurations in the *Clavicula* are characteristic of many grimoires and reveal dominant Jewish influences, if not actual Jewish origins. Jewish influences do not make a grimoire 'Jewish' any more than similar borrowings of Divine Names by pagan magicians make the Greco-Egyptian magical papyri 'Jewish', although in many cases a Jewish origin for the latter is clear. However, even a Jewish origin does not necessarily indicate the existence of an 'original' ancient Hebrew or Aramaic 'book'. Late antique and medieval Jewish magicians, like their Greco-Egyptian colleagues, seem to have utilised traditional magical adjurations as independent literary 'units' in constantly changing larger arrangements and compilations. The origin of the units may lie in oral traditions which do not reflect the existence of a primary source-text. Peter Schäfer describes these units as 'microforms', which change shape and position within 'macroforms': the 'fictive' or 'ideal' text as described in later rescensions and in scholarly literature.[130]

The tendency of Jewish magicians to group such units together in individual creative combinations with new additions seems to continue into the early modern period; an example is the early-eighteenth-century *Sefer ha-Raziel*, which contains units from the *Sefer ha-Razim*, portions of *heikhalot* texts, extracts from the writings of Eleazar of Worms, Kabbalistic sources, and medieval Arab magic squares. This type of grouping is evident not only in grimoires such as the *Clavicula* but also in the Golden Dawn rituals, for which there is also no primary source-text. Regardie's massive compilation, *The Golden Dawn*, may be considered a 'macroform' or later recension of a variegated collection of private papers, transcriptions of oral teachings, and 'official' Flying Rolls.[131] Olav Hammer refers to the 'religious creativity' of modern occultists in their reinterpretation of existing material such as scriptural passages through comparison, cross-referencing, and combinations of materials disembedded from their original contexts.[132] But as Jewish magicians and Kabbalists were applying this form of

---

[130] See Schäfer, *Hidden and Manifest God*, 6–7.

[131] For contemporary examples, see Pat Zalewski, *Inner Order Teachings of the Golden Dawn* (Loughborough: Thoth Publications, 2006); Chic and Sandra Tabatha Cicero (eds.), *The Golden Dawn Journal, Book II; Qabalah: Theory and Magic* (St. Paul, MI: Llewellyn, 1994).

[132] Hammer, *Claiming Knowledge*, 43–44.

'religious creativity' from late antiquity onward, it can hardly be considered unique to modern occultism. The 'practical' Kabbalah of the Golden Dawn and its offshoots remains loyal to the methodology used by Jewish magicians over the centuries in the construction of their literature and praxis.

The Divine Names are used throughout the *Clavicula* to command the angelic and demonic powers, protect the magus against attack, and banish the presences at the end of the ritual:

> Here again I conjure ye and most urgently command ye...by the most mighty and powerful Name of God El...and by all these names: El Shaddai, Elohim, Elohi, Tazabaoth, Elim, Asher Eheieh, Yah, Tetragrammaton, Shaddai...and by His Holy Names, and by the virtue of the Sovereign God, we shall accomplish all our work.[133]

Rituals such as these were clearly adopted in the construction of the Golden Dawn rituals. For example, the 'Philosophus Ritual', representing initiation into the highest grade of the Outer Order, ends with a 'banishing circle' and the adjuration:

> Depart ye in peace unto your habitations. May the blessing of YOD HE VAU HE TZABAOTH be upon ye! Be there peace between us and you, and be ye ready to come when ye are called.[134]

In the 'Ritual of the Pentagram', the adept is instructed to 'vibrate' the traditional Hebrew Divine Names Eheieh, YHVH, Elohim, and Adonai,[135] and in the 'Ritual of the Hexagram' the Names of YHVH Elohim, Elohim Tzabaoth, and El are invoked.[136] While such rituals were primarily intended to protect and guide the Golden Dawn adept through various stages of spiritual transformation, rather than invoking nonhuman entities to catch thieves, curse neighbours, or arouse erotic desire, the invocation of the Divine Names is ubiquitous in virtually all of them. One of

---

[133] Mathers (trans.), *Key of Solomon*, 29–30.

[134] Regardie, *Golden Dawn*, 196. For Sabaôth ('Lord of Hosts'), one of the most common Divine Names in late antique Jewish magical texts, see Bohak, *Ancient Jewish Magic*, 198; Gager, *Moses*, 135; Trachtenberg, *Jewish Magic*, 90–91.

[135] Regardie, *Golden Dawn*, 285–86.

[136] Regardie, *Golden Dawn*, 287–88.

the few exceptions is the 'Ritual of the Rose Cross', described as 'a call to another mode of your consciousness', which utilises only Reuchlin's *verbo mirifico*, YHShVH.[137] But another 'Rosicrucian' ritual, the 'Ceremony for the Consecration of the Rose Cross', once again invokes 'the Divine Name of YHVH' and the two chief Jewish archangels Michael and Raphael, as well as Adonai and Eheieh.[138] In this ritual YHShVH is mentioned at the end, almost as an afterthought.

Although Mathers' occult career began with his publication of *The Kabbala Unveiled* and initially focused on what he had learned from Agrippa, Barrett, Lévi, Westcott, and the *Kabbala denudata*, as time passed the Golden Dawn rituals became peppered with adjurations of many deities – Egyptian, Greek, and even Norse.[139] Mathers, like Barrett before him, may be viewed as a ritual magician who used Kabbalistic formulae along with many other magical components, rather than as a Kabbalist who subordinated everything to the precepts and practices of the Jewish theosophical and magical tradition. Yet while the pagan and Christian divinities come and go in Mathers' rituals, the Hebrew God remains and usually gets the last word. Mathers, like the eclectic ritual magicians of late antiquity, may have been attempting to 'cover his bases'; but he seems to have been firmly bound to the Western Judeo-Christian tradition and, although no philosemite, believed, like Lévi and Westcott, in the special efficacy of Jewish magic.[140] The influence of Mina Bergson's knowledge of Jewish magical lore on these rituals also should not be underestimated. While Mathers was convinced, with considerable justification, that his grimoires owed their content to the Jewish magical tradition and were therefore 'Kabbalistic', he also used English translations of Greco-Egyptian texts such

---

[137] Regardie, *Golden Dawn*, 306–09.

[138] Regardie, *Golden Dawn*, 312–16.

[139] See, for example, 'Official Document' Z.1, 'The Enterer of the Threshold', in Regardie, *Golden Dawn*, 330–62, which enumerates invocations of, *inter alia*, Thoth, YHVH, the ten *sefirot*, YHShVH, Osiris, Horus, Hermes, Moses, Solomon, Thor, Harpocrates, Isis, Nephthys, the planet Saturn, and 'God, the Vast One, the Lord of the Universe'.

[140] See Colqhoun, *Sword*, 108, for F. A. C. Wilson's statement in *W. B. Yeats and the Tradition* (London: Victor Gollancz, 1961) that Mathers was 'a fanatical anti-semite'.

as the 'Bornless Ritual'.[141] But even this ritual depends on Jewish adjurations and conceptions. In addition to the usual Greco-Egyptian incorporation of Hebrew Divine Names such as Sabaôth and Iaô, the 'Bornless Ritual' also makes clear that the 'Bornless One' (or 'Headless One'), although apparently an Egyptian divinity called Osoronophris, is in fact the Hebrew God of Genesis, 'who created earth and heaven, who created night and day, you who created light and darkness...you have made female and male...I call upon you, awesome and invisible god...he is the lord of the gods...he is the one who made all things by the command of his voice'. Affirming the Hebrew identity of the deity, the adept calls himself 'Moses your prophet to whom you have transmitted your mysteries celebrated by Israel'.[142] The obvious family resemblances between Jewish, Greco-Egyptian, and medieval Christian magical traditions confirmed to Mathers, as it did to Lévi and Westcott, the continuity of an ancient tradition which he understood as 'Kabbalah'.

With the exception of Mina Bergson, the Golden Dawn membership appears to have been entirely non-Jewish, and the specific religiosity in which older Jewish magical invocations are embedded – despite their syncretic

---

[141] The 'Bornless Ritual' is included as the 'Preliminary Invocation' in Mathers' translation of the *Lesser Key of Solomon*, and appears in Regardie, *Golden Dawn*, 442–46, as 'The Bornless Ritual for the Invocation of the Higher Genius'. It was first translated into English by Charles Wycliffe Goodwin, *Fragment of a Graeco-Egyptian Work upon Magic* (Cambridge: Cambridge Antiquarian Society, 1852), and seems to have been rewritten by both Mathers and Crowley before 1904, when it was liberally spiced with Rosicrucian references and transformed from an adjuration of the Hebrew god to a less religiously charged invocation of the Holy Guardian Angel. The text of the *Lesser Key of Solomon* itself, which does not include the 'Bornless Ritual', states ('Introduction', 26): 'These Books were first found in the Chaldee and Hebrew Tongues at Jerusalem by a Jewish Rabbi; and by him put into the Greek language and thence into the Latin, as it is said'. The *Lesser Key of Solomon* provides the magical talismans and adjurations for the seventy-two 'spirits' or angels of the *Shem ha-Mephorasch*, and Mathers notes ('Introduction', 69) that the list is the same as that given by Thomas Rudd in his *Treatise on Angel Magic*.

[142] For this translation, see *PGM* 5.96–172, 'The Stele of Jeu the Hieroglyphist in His Letter', in Betz (ed. and trans.), *Greek Magical Papyri*, 103–04, on p. 103. For the probable Jewish origins of the text, see Gager, *Moses*, 142–43.

tendencies – is obviously absent from these late-nineteenth-century occult rituals. Even if the Golden Dawn were comprised entirely of Jewish occultists, the diverse Judaisms of late Victorian Britain, emerging from the long struggle for emancipation and acculturation, necessarily differed in profound ways from the Judaisms of the Greco-Roman, Egyptian, Byzantine, European, and Arab cultural contexts of late antiquity and the Middle Ages.[143] In this sense, the use of late antique Jewish adjurations in British occultism, and even the use of medieval and early modern Kabbalistic practices, cannot be considered a faithful replica of the Jewish magic of earlier epochs. Nevertheless, older Jewish magical technologies have retained their continuity in the Golden Dawn in striking ways, not least in the abiding awe and respect with which the Divine Names are utilised as instruments of ritual power.

THE ASTRAL MAGIC OF THE GOLDEN DAWN

Throughout most of the nineteenth century, astrology in

---

[143] There are many scholarly explorations into the diverse forms of Judaism from late antiquity to modern times. For the Judaism of Hellenistic Alexandria and its absorption of Greco-Egyptian doctrines, see Goodenough, *By Light, Light*; Lee I. Levine, *Judaism and Hellenism in Antiquity: Confict or Confluence?* (Seattle, WA: University of Washington Press, 1998); Alan J.Avery-Peck and Jacob Neusner (eds.), *Judaism in Late Antiquity, Part 4: Death, Life-After-Death, Resurrection and the World-to-Come in the Judaisms of Antiquity* (Leiden: Brill, 2000). For Gnostic influences on early Judaism, see Segal, *The Other Judaisms*; Segal, *Two Powers in Heaven*. For the cultural context of medieval Byzantine Judaism, see Schwartz, *Astral Magic*. For the influence of Sufi doctrines on Jewish communities under Ottoman rule and the absorption of these ideas into the 'ecstatic' current of medieval Kabbalah, see Idel, *Mystical Experience*; Harvey J. Hames, 'A Seal Within a Seal: The Imprint of Sufism in Abraham Abulafia's Teachings', *ME* 12:2 (2006), 153–72. For the impact of the Enlightenment on Judaism, see Sutcliffe, *Judaism and Enlightenment*. For the development of Reform Judaism in late Victorian Britain, see Feldman, *Englishmen and Jews*, 57–59, 63–66, 68–69, 382–83; Liberles, 'The Origins of the Jewish Reform Movement; see also the references in Chapter Three. A useful overview of diversities and constants within Judaism, and the impact of differing cultural contexts – especially Hellenism, the Arab world, the Renaissance, and the Enlightenment – can be found in Raphael Patai, *The Jewish Mind* (New York: Charles Scribner's Sons, 1977).

Britain was more concerned with the prediction of events than with the condition of the soul. Toward the end of the century, this pragmatic application of horoscopic traditions inherited from Ptolemy and the Arab astrologers of the early medieval period was challenged by other perspectives developing within British occultism. Two currents of astrology emerged following the birth of the Theosophical Society in 1875: one a well-publicised perspective which might be viewed as distinctively 'modern', the other a more complex approach not easily categorised as the product of any specific historical epoch. The first current was inaugurated by William Frederick Allan (1860–1917), a former travelling salesman who joined the Theosophical Society in 1890 and published an impressive corpus of astrological works under the name of Alan Leo – this being, as he was fond of informing his reading public, the sign in which both the Sun and the Ascendant were placed at the moment of his birth.[144] Leo's stated goal was to reform the astrology of the past and make it more 'spiritual' in accordance with Theosophy's emphasis on the soul's evolution and the imminent arrival of a New Age in which a more spiritually evolved state of consciousness would transform society. The 'newness' of this astrology lay primarily in its emphasis on the delineation of character in the birth horoscope as a means of achieving spiritual growth.[145] Leo's individualistic focus, which shifted the understanding of astrology from a predictive tool to a map of personal spiritual development, profoundly influenced the currents of twentieth- and twenty-first-century astrological practice. But Leo was still concerned with reading natal horoscopes within the conventional Ptolemaic framework.

---

[144] For biographical material on Alan Leo, see Kim Farnell, *The Astral Tramp* (London: Ascella, 1998); Patrick Curry, *A Confusion of Prophets: Victorian and Edwardian Astrology* (London: Collins & Brown, 1992), 122–59; Nicholas Campion, *A History of Western Astrology, Vol. 2: The Medieval and Modern Worlds* (London: Hambledon Continuum, 2009), 231–34; Bessie Leo, *The Life and Work of Alan Leo, Theosophist-Astrologer-Mason* (London: Fowler, 1919). For Leo's own publications, see, *inter alia*, Alan Leo, *How to Judge a Nativity* (London: Modern Astrology, 1903); Alan Leo, *Astrology for All* (London: Modern Astrology, 1904); Alan Leo, *The Key to Your Own Nativity* (London: Modern Astrology, 1910); Alan Leo, *Esoteric Astrology* (London: Modern Astrology, 1913).
[145] Campion, *History of Western Astrology*, 2:231–33.

The second current of astrology emerged as an alternative to Leo's emphasis on natal horoscopes. Mathers found the characterological and predictive aspects of astrology useful, and the neophytes of the Outer Order of the Golden Dawn learned to cast and interpret their horoscopes in order to achieve knowledge of their strengths and weaknesses as well as assessing the optimum moment for magical work.[146] Although Éliphas Lévi had not concerned himself with the technical complexities of the astrology of his time (although he believed that a 'pure' form once existed as 'one of the branches of the holy Kabbalah'),[147] and Westcott respected horoscopic astrology but questioned its scientific basis,[148] Mathers, in contrast, embraced it wholeheartedly.[149] So eager was he to portray himself as a military strategist that he devised an ingenious method of 'shifting' the components of his horoscope so that he could claim to be born under fiery Aries, the sign of the warrior, rather than under the earthier, more cautious Capricorn, his actual birth-sign.[150] But another, older dimension of astrology appealed to him more, and the adepts of the Inner Order practiced the astral magic of late antique Greco-Egyptian and Jewish magical traditions: a form of astrology which Mathers believed could transform both the individual and the world.

Astrology, in most scholarly literature, is included under the rubric of 'divination', in company with such diverse practices as brontology (divination by thunder) and haruspicy (interpreting animal entrails).[151] The divinatory use of astrology is primarily focused on the prediction of future

---

[146] For the sources of the Golden Dawn teachings on 'mainstream' astrology, see Curry, *Confusion of Prophets*. For the use of astrology in the Outer Order of the Golden Dawn, see J. W. Brodie-Innes et al., *Astrology of the Golden Dawn*, ed. Darcy Küntz (Sequim, WA: Holmes Publishing Group, 1996); Greer, *Women*, 57.

[147] Lévi, *Dogme*, 156.

[148] See William Wynn Westcott, 'The History of Astrology', in Gardner, *Bibliotheca Astrologica*, ix–xx.

[149] See Brodie-Innes et al., *Astrology of the Golden Dawn*.

[150] See Colquhoun, *Sword*, 64. For Mathers' 'shifting' of his horoscope, see Brodie-Innes et al., *Astrology of the Golden Dawn*, 203–05.

[151] See, for example, Johnston, 'Introduction', in Johnston and Struck (eds.), *Mantikê*, 7; David Potter, *Prophets and Emperors: Human and Divine Authority from Augustus to Theodosius* (Cambridge, MA: Harvard University Press, 1994), 17; Tamsyn Barton, *Ancient Astrology* (London: Routledge, 1994), 11.

events, although much of its trajectory from Ptolemy's *Tetrabiblos* onward has also included a belief in celestial influences on individual character as well as individual destiny.[152] However, not all astrology is divinatory or based on an analysis of personality characteristics, and other aspects of this ancient praxis are highlighted by the fluid interchange between astrology, alchemy, and magic – the three 'traditional' sciences of late antiquity – in texts such as Agrippa's *De occulta philosophia* and the works of early modern alchemists such as Khunrath and Maier. Astrology, according to Patrick Curry's brief but useful definition, is 'the practice of relating the heavenly bodies to lives and events on earth, and the tradition that has thus been generated'.[153] Astral magic, which forms an important dimension of this tradition, may be understood as the amalgamation of the tenets of astrological theory with magical praxis, intended not only to 'divine' the right moment to perform a magical ritual or create a talisman, but also to invoke the celestial powers to effect transformations – within the individual as well as in the world, and even in the infrastructure of divinity.[154] 'Astral magic' can be a problematic term, as it might be seen to artificially syncretise two apparently discrete currents of thought and practice. Horoscopic astrology in the West, largely influenced by Arab neo-Aristotelian speculations, had enjoyed a scientific reputation from late antiquity through the early modern period, and many astrologers tended to refer to their work as 'science' or 'divine science' rather than as divination or magic.[155] But

---

[152] See Claudius Ptolemy, *Tetrabiblos*, trans F. E. Robbins (Cambridge, MA: Harvard University Press, 1971), III.13 for Ptolemy's proto-psychological interpretation of character.

[153] Patrick Curry, 'Astrology', in Kelly Boyd (ed.), *The Encyclopedia of Historians and Historical Writing* (London: Fitzroy Dearborn, 1999), 55–57.

[154] See Schwartz, *Astral Magic*, 14.

[155] See, for example, the first-century CE astrologer Dorotheus of Sidon, who refers to his praxis as 'the science of the stars' (Dorotheus Sidonius, *Carmen Astrologicum*, trans. David Pingree [Munich: K. G. Saur, 1976], V.1.1–4); the ninth-century Arab astrologer Al-Kindi, who makes a clear distinction between astral magic and astrology itself, which he considers as 'observing mathematical method and physical laws' (Al-Kindi, *On the Stellar Rays*, trans. Robert Zoller [Berkeley Springs, WV: Golden Hind Press, 1993]; and Ptolemy himself, who presents astrology as a craft with carefully developed rules for conjuncture, not unlike medicine,

some astrologers combined astrological symbolism with practices which they themselves understood as magical: a means of contacting, conjuring, and even coercing planetary and stellar potencies in order to alter astral fate.

John Scott Lucas, in a monograph on astrology in medieval and early modern Catalonia, suggests that astral magic 'makes use of the astrological symbols without the complicated theoretical baggage necessary to compute a horoscope'.[156] While this cruder approach to astrology might apply to a number of the grimoires, which exhibit only a rudimentary understanding of astrological principles, a more sophisticated use of astrological techniques and timing within a religious framework can also be found in many applications of astral magic. In his comprehensive work on astral magic in medieval Jewish thought, Dov Schwartz points out that astrology, in the ordinarily understood sense, is not 'magical'; it only becomes magical when celestial powers are 'drawn down through effigies and other objects (talismans)'.[157] A talisman is usually understood as a physical object bearing an image of magical potency. Its power is based on the assumption that the talisman, and the celestial force it represents, enjoy a secret identity – an expression of the ancient idea of sympathies or correspondences between diverse levels of an interconnected universe. This type of magic is sometimes known as 'astral image magic'.[158] Astral talismans might be represented by the planetary images

---

and calls it 'astronomical prediction' (Ptolemy, *Tetrabiblos*, 1.3). See also the important late-thirteenth-century astrologer Guido Bonatti, who declares that he practices the 'Science of the Judgements of the Stars' (Guido Bonatti, *Liber Astronomiae*, trans. Robert Zoller [Berkeley Springs, WV: Golden Hind Press, 1994], 1.3); Placidus de Titis, who in the mid-seventeenth century understood astrology to be 'a genuine and true science' (Placidus de Titis, *Primum Mobile*, trans. John Cooper [Bromley: Institute for the Study of Cycles in World Affairs, 1983], x); and the seventeenth-century English astrologer William Lilly, who calls astrology a 'divine Science' (William Lilly, 'Introductory Epistle' in William Lilly, *Christian Astrology* (London: John Macock, 1659]).

[156] John Scott Lucas, *Astrology and Numerology in Medieval and Early Modern Catalonia: The Tractat de prenostication de la vida natural dels hòmens* (Leiden: Brill, 2003), 40.

[157] Dov Schwartz, *Studies on Astral Magic in Medieval Jewish Thought* (Leiden: Brill, 2005), 14.

[158] For this classification, see Frank Klaassen, 'Medieval Magic in the Renaissance', *Aries* 3:2 (2003), 166–99.

provided by the eleventh-century Arab magical text, the *Ghayât al-Hakim*, known to the Latin world as *Picatrix*,[159] or by objects such as a Byzantine amulet from the sixth century portraying Christ healing a bleeding woman – not immediately recognisable as astral save for the gemstone from which it is carved: hematite, named after the Greek word for blood and believed by the Romans to be sacred to Mars, offering protection against wounds and bleeding in childbirth.[160] This type of magical astrology relies on the celestial resonances of the substance comprising the talisman, visual representations of the powers being invoked, or both.[161] The influence of medieval Arab astrology is evident in the neo-Aristotelian idea that it is the 'rays' from the planets, acting on the material forms of the sub-lunar world, which are captured in the talisman: an emphasis on the occult properties of substances which avoids any hint of demonic intervention. Astral image magic is also dependent on the appropriate timing of the talisman's creation, a point where magical and divinatory astrology meet. Also known as 'Hermetic' magic, it was understood to originate in Greco-Egyptian texts from late antiquity such as the *Kuranides*, with its detailed lists of healing remedies involving associations between planets, gemstones, animals, plants, and fishes.[162]

Linguistic entities and symbols – particularly the Hebrew letters, Divine and angelic Names, and the strange ring-letters known as *charactêres* found in Greco-Egyptian and late antique Jewish magical texts – may also be understood as talismanic, not only when inscribed on an object, but also

---

[159] See the images in *Picatrix*, Kraków, BJ 793, fol. 190r, Biblioteka Jagiellonska, reproduced in Benedek Láng, *Unlocked Books: Manuscripts of Learned Magic in the Medieval Libraries of Central Europe* (University Park, PA: Penn State University Press, 2008), 99. For more on the *Picatrix*, see David Pingree, 'Some of the Sources of the *Ghayat al-Hakim*', *Journal of the Warburg and Courtauld Institutes* 43 (1980), 1–15.

[160] Metropolitan Museum of Art, 17.190.491. For more on gemstone amulets, see also Patricia Aakhus, 'Astral Magic in the Renaissance', *MRW* (Winter 2008), 185–206, on p. 193.

[161] See Klaassen, 'Medieval Ritual Magic'.

[162] For *Kuranides*, see Brian P. Copenhaver, *Hermetica* (Cambridge: Cambridge University Press, 1992), xxxiv–xxxv; Lynn Thorndike, *History of Magic and Experimental Science* (New York, NY: Columbia University Press, 1923), 3:229–35. For an early modern English translation of *Kuranides*, see *The Magic of Kirani, King of Persia, and of Harpocration* (London: 1655; repr. Renaissance Astrology, 2005).

when uttered in the appropriate ritual. Images, letters, symbols, and colours held in the mind's eye as a focus for meditation or prayer may also be viewed as talismans.[163] Also prominent in Mathers' astral magic are the astrological 'glyphs' and 'sigils', viewed not merely as significators in a horoscope but as powerful magical entities in their own right. This type of magical astrology, blending 'image' and 'ceremonial' types of magic, provides the basis of most of the grimoires or magical books which comprise the backbone of the Western medieval magical tradition. It is sometimes referred to as 'Solomonic' magic, as a number of the grimoires in which it is found are attributed pseud-epigraphically to King Solomon, and involve the invocation of supernal entities – usually perceived as angels, demons, or a mixture of the two – associated with the planets and zodiacal signs. Astral magic does not always pursue noble spiritual goals. *Picatrix*, for example, offers a helpful recipe for an astral talisman that will 'cause discord between any two people',[164] and the *Sefer ha-Razim* ends with a moving blessing glorifying the majesty of the Lord, but also provides a useful invocation of the angels of the third heaven to ensure that one's racehorses 'will be swift as the wind'.[165] But magical astrology has also been utilised over the centuries to induce a direct vision of deity, elicit supernal secrets, and effect psychological and spiritual transformations.[166] It is this latter emphasis that dominates Mathers' magical rituals.

Astral magic is inextricably linked with angelology in early Jewish apocalyptic literature and in texts such as the *Sefer ha-Razim*, where specific groups of angels preside over the seven 'firmaments' or heavens, each associated with a specific planetary sphere;[167] this angelic cosmology is echoed

---

[163] See Elliot R. Wolfson, 'Phantasmagoria: The Image of the Image in Jewish Magic from Late Antiquity to the Early Middle Ages', *RRJ* 4:1 (2001), 78–120; Moshe Idel, 'On Talismanic Magic in Jewish Mysticism', *Diogenes* 43:2 (1995), 23–41.

[164] John Michael Greer and Christopher Warnock (trans.), *The Latin Picatrix, Books I & II* (Raleigh, NC: Renaissance Astrology, 2009), 2:10. This translation is derived from David Pingree (ed.), *The Latin Version of the Ghayat al-hakim* (London: Studies of the Warburg Institute, 1986).

[165] Michael A. Morgan (trans.), *Sepher ha-Razim: The Book of the Mysteries* (Chico, CA: Scholars Press, 1983), 63.

[166] See Schwartz, *Astral Magic*, 14.

[167] For scholarly discussions on the *Sefer ha-Razim*, see Alexander, '*Sefer ha-Razim* and the Problem of Black Magic'; Bernd Roling, 'The

in *3 Enoch*, where each heaven is governed by a specific angel with a group of angelic attendants.[168] In *The Wisdom of the Chaldeans*, a short Hebrew magical compilation dated by Moses Gaster to no later than the eighth century CE, the angels are associated with the days of the week, which are in turn identified with the planets, 'for in each [planetary] sphere there is an angel that moves it'.[169] In the work of the German Pietist Eleazar of Worms, every human being is governed by an angel associated with a specific zodiacal sign, whose image is contained within both angel and human and is in turn an aspect of the godhead:

> Every angel who is an archon of the zodiacal sign (*sar mazzal*) of a person when it is sent below has the image of the person who is under it....And this is the meaning of 'And God created man in his image, in the image of God he created him' (Genesis 1:27). Why is [it written] twice, 'in his image' and 'in the image'? One image refers to the image of man and the other to the image of the angel of the zodiacal sign which is in the image of the man.[170]

Each angel can be invoked by a specific adjuration and a talisman with an image representing the angel's attributes, at an hour governed by the planet with which the angel is associated. In the *Testament of Solomon*, there are thirty-six heavenly 'bodies' or demons, each associated with one of the thirty-six decans or 10° divisions of the zodiac,[171] and each paired with a 'thwarting' angel who can block the demon's malevolent intentions.[172] The demon Ornias, for example,

---

Complete Nature of Christ: Sources and Structures of a Christological Theurgy in the Works of Johannes Reuchlin', in Bremmer and Veenstra (eds.), *Metamorphosis of Magic*, 231–66; Chen Merchavjah, 'Sefer ha-Razim', *EJ*, 13:1594–96.

[168] *3 Enoch*, 17.1–8.

[169] Gaster (trans.), *Wisdom of the Chaldeans*, 348.

[170] Eleazar of Worms, *Ḥokhmat ha-Nefesh* (Benei Beraq, 1987), Ch. 48, p. 80, cited in Elliot R. Wolfson, 'Theosis, Vision, and the Astral Body in Medieval German Pietism and the Spanish Kabbalah', paper delivered at the 'Imagining Astrology' Conference, University of Bristol, 10–11 July 2010.

[171] In the *Testament*, the first demon, Ruax, refers to himself as 'the first decan of the zodiac'; see Duling (trans.), *Testament of Solomon*, 18.5, and Duling's n. f, 978. For the decans, see below, n. 178.

[172] The thirty-six demons, the diseases they inflict on humans, and their 'thwarting' angels are found in Duling (trans.), *Testament of*

announces to Solomon that he 'resides' in Aquarius and is 'thwarted' by the archangel Ouriel, the 'Light of God'.[173]

The astral angels inevitably make their appearance in the grimoires; in the *Armadel*, for example, in the section entitled 'As Regardeth the Planets', seals and adjurations are given for twenty-two angels, one for each Hebrew letter, who must be invoked on specific days at specific hours according to their astrological relevance,[174] while in the *Lemegeton*, the seventy-two angels of the *Shem ha-Mephorasch* are invoked through seven seals made of the appropriate planetary metals associated with the angels connected with that planet.[175] The planetary powers are sometimes personified as demons rather than angels, as represented in a twelfth-century work attributed to Abraham ibn Ezra called *Sefer ha-Atsamim*, which describes demons as stellar forces that can be drawn down into talismans and utilised in order to harm opponents.[176]

The angels of Jewish astral magic are embedded in a cosmology which reflects both Babylonian and Egyptian influences. The thirty-six dyads of angels comprising the seventy-two-letter Divine Name known as the *Shem ha-Mephorasch* are related to the Greco-Egyptian 'decan' system of dividing each of the twelve segments of the heavens with their particular groups of stars into three parts, every one of which is governed by a celestial power; there are thus thirty-six decan 'rulers'.[177] These thirty-six entities appear as

---

Solomon, 18:1–42, where the demons refer to themselves as *hoi kosmokratores tou skotous*, 'world rulers of this age of darkness'.

[173] See Duling (trans.), *Testament of Solomon*, 2:2–4.

[174] Mathers (ed. and trans.), *The Grimoire of Armadel*, 23–45.

[175] Mathers (trans.), *Goetia*, 68.

[176] See Schwartz, *Astral Magic*, 113–22. For older pagan traditions of astral magic resurfacing in the Golden Dawn, see Ronald Hutton, 'Astral Magic: The Acceptable Face of Paganism', in Nicholas Campion, Patrick Curry, and Michael York (eds.), *Astrology and the Academy: Papers from the Inaugural Conference of the Sophia Centre, Bath Spa University College, 13–14 June 2003* (Bristol: Cinnabar Books, 2004), 10–24, on p. 22.

[177] For the thirty-six decans and decan *daimones* in Egyptian astrology from the second millennium BCE to the Hermetic texts of the first centuries CE, see Nicholas Campion, *The Dawn of Astrology: A Cultural History of Western Astrology, Vol. 1: The Ancient and Classical Worlds* (London: Continuum, 2008), 99–100 and 107–08; Fowden, *Egyptian Hermes*, 67; Jack Lindsay, *Origins of Astrology* (London: Frederick Muller, 1971), 156–61. For the decans as

demons in the *Testament of Solomon*, which may have provided a junction between the traditional Jewish angelology of the *Shem ha-Mephorasch* and the thirty-six demonic talismans of the *Lemegeton* or *Lesser Key of Solomon the King*, appropriated in the nineteenth century by Lévi and translated into English by Mathers.[178] The seven heavenly spheres, presented in the *heikhalot* literature as seven heavenly 'palaces', appear to originate in Babylonian cosmology,[179] later finding their way into the large corpus of Hellenistic astrology and the various magical currents represented by the Hermetic literature, the Mithraic rituals, and many Gnostic texts.[180] In late antique Jewish magical exegeses, this astrological angelology is reflected in the angels who govern not only the planets but every hour of every day and every day of every week. Time itself is thus

---

daimones, see Stobaeus, IX.6, cited in G. R. S. Mead (ed. and trans.), *Thrice-Greatest Hermes: Studies in Hellenistic Theosophy and Gnosis*, 3 vols. (London: Theosophical Publishing Society, 1906), 3:49: 'The many call them daimones; but they are not some special class of daimones, for they have not some other kind of bodies made of some special kind of matter, nor are they moved by means of soul, as we [are moved], but they are [simple] operations [or energies] of these Six-and-thirty Gods.' Lindsay also points out (Lindsay, *Origins of Astrology*, 159–60), 'The Egyptian tradition always calls the dekans gods; under the Christians they become malign demons'.

[178] For more on the *Testament*, see Johnston, 'Testament of Solomon'; Klutz, *Rewriting the Testament*; Jesse Rainbow, 'Song of Songs'; Sarah L. Schwartz, 'Reconsidering the Testament of Solomon', *JSP* 16:3 (2007), 203–37.

[179] See Wright, *Early History of Heaven*, 144; Adela Y. Collins, 'The Seven Heavens in Jewish and Christian Apocalypses', in Collins and Fishbane (eds.), *Death, Ecstasy*, 59–93.

[180] For the seven planetary spheres in the *Hermetica*, see Copenhaver, *Hermetica*, CH1.25–26, CHX.16; Merkur, 'Stages of Ascension'. For the planetary spheres in the Mithraic rituals, see Roger Beck, *Planetary Gods and Planetary Orders in the Mysteries of Mithras* (Leiden: Brill, 1988); Roger Beck, *The Religion of the Mithras Cult in the Roman Empire* (Oxford: Oxford University Press, 2006); David Ulansey, *The Origins of the Mithraic Mysteries: Cosmology and Salvation in the Ancient World* (Oxford: Oxford University Press, 1989). For the planetary spheres and archons in Gnostic literature, see Couliano, *Tree of Gnosis*; Hans Jonas, *The Gnostic Religion: The Message of the Alien God and the Beginnings of Christianity* (Boston, MA: Beacon Press, 1963); Roelof van den Broek, 'The Creation of Adam's Psychic Body in the Apocryphon of John', in van den Broek and Vermaseren (eds.), *Studies in Gnosticism*, 38–57.

permeated by, or embodies, the cyclical phases and dynamic internal transformations of deity, and possesses both quantity and quality – represented by the nature of the presiding angel, who can be adjured with the correct formulae to elicit celestial secrets. The correlation of the angels with Hebrew letters, Divine Names, planets, and colours, and the ritual invocation of these 'forces', form an important aspect of Golden Dawn teachings,[181] but such correlations can be found in Jewish texts as early as the *Sefer Yetsirah*,[182] and are articulated with precision in the alchemical-Kabbalistic *Aesch Mezareph*.[183]

The angels of Jewish magic are more ambiguous than their kindlier Christian counterparts, and it is not surprising that they are literally demonised in Christian grimoires. These Jewish potencies resemble the planetary archons of the Gnostic *pleroma*, and they can be hostile and dangerous as well as benign.[184] Although they begin their career in biblical literature as created beings whose function is to serve and adore the divine Throne, they are transformed by late antiquity into powerful sovereign entities sometimes indistinguishable from God; and they can be adjured and even coerced through the use of the Divine Names.[185] Angels in late antique *heikhalot* rituals and medieval Kabbalistic

---

[181] For the correlation of planets with Divine Names and colours in the Golden Dawn, see, for example, the 'Ritual of the Hexagram', in Regardie, *Golden Dawn*, 287–99. For Divine Names and zodiacal signs, see 'Supreme Invoking Ritual of the Pentagram', in Regardie, *Golden Dawn*, 285–86. For further correlations of this kind, see Regardie, *Golden Dawn*, 64, 86, 304.

[182] For correlations in the *Sefer Yetsirah* between the ten primary letters, angelic entities, days of the week, 'gates' in the soul, and the orifices of the human body, see Kaplan, *Sefer Yetsirah* 4:7–14, and Kaplan's comments, 177–84.

[183] See, for example, *Aesch Mezareph*, V:32 and VII:38. For references on colours and the *sefirot* in the Kabbalah, see above, n. 148. For Thomas Rudd's appropriation of the correlations, see Rudd, *Angel Magic*, 90–104.

[184] For the ambiguous nature of the angelic powers, see Deutsch, *Guardians of the Gate*, 16–23; Himmelfarb, *Ascent to Heaven*, 63–69; David Halperin, *The Faces of the Chariot: Early Jewish Responses to Ezekiel's Vision* (Tübingen: Mohr Siebeck, 1988), 439–46; Rachel Elior, *The Three Temples: On the Emergence of Jewish Mysticism*, trans. David Louvish (Oxford: Littman Library of Jewish Civilization, 2004), 246; Schäfer, *Hidden and Manifest God*, 25–26.

[185] See Elior, 'Angelology', 34–39.

magic are the hypostases of specific dimensions of deity, and adjuring an angel is tantamount to adjuring the godhead. Names and angels are made of the same divine substance, and most angelic names, with the notable exception of Metatron, end with the suffix -el, meaning God.[186] Moses Gaster, in his translation of the late antique Hebrew magical text called *The Wisdom of the Chaldeans*, emphasises that -el is included in, or identical to, the names of God's serving or ministering angels, and the first letters of the names of the lesser angels who serve the greater ones are the same as the letters of the name of their chief ruler.[187] Other angelic names are based exclusively on the angel's function. For example, the archangel Ouriel, a favourite in Golden Dawn rituals who also has the power to thwart the demon Ornias in the *Testament of Solomon*, is comprised of *our* ('light') and *el*: Ouriel is thus the 'light of God'.[188] Raziel, the angel who reveals the secrets of God to Adam, is made up of *raz* ('secret') and *el*. The word *raz* has special significance in relation to magic and occultism. According to Rachel Elior, *raz* represents esoteric knowledge: 'the secret of creation, and the power that creates all being...It comprises metaphysical knowledge of the physical world as taught to the mystic by heavenly beings'.[189] In the *heikhalot* literature of late antiquity, *raz* is also concerned with the emergence of an esoteric tradition:

> The divine secrets become magical names, mystical adjurations, speculative subjects. The terrestrial transmission of the names comprising the 'secret'...reflects the conversion of the direct revelationary-mystical experience into a magical-theurgical tradition.[190]

---

[186] Metatron is attributed with multiple names; on this tradition see Joseph Dan, 'The Seventy Names of Metatron', *Proceedings of the Eighth World Congress of Jewish Studies*, Division C (Jerusalem, 1982), 19–23; Idel, 'Some Forlorn Writings', 187–90. For uncertainty about the derivation of 'Metatron', see Elior, 'Angelology', 28.

[187] Gaster (trans.), *Wisdom of the Chaldeans*, 330.

[188] For Ouriel in Golden Dawn rituals, see 'Zelator Ritual', in Regardie, *Golden Dawn*, 143; 'Ritual of Consecration of the Four Elemental Weapons', in Regardie, *Golden Dawn*, 325); 'Evocation Ritual', in Regardie, *Golden Dawn*, 404). For further examples of the functional derivation of angelic names, see Swartz, *Scholastic Magic*, 66; Scholem, *Origins*, 147–48; Trachtenberg, *Jewish Magic*, 99.

[189] Elior, 'Concept of God', 101.

[190] Elior, 'Concept of God', 112.

This angel who communicates the secrets of God is thus that aspect of divinity which both contains and reveals the esoteric mysteries of the supernal realms, embodied in his name.[191]

The infinity of angels or 'princes' reflects the infinity of the Hebrew letter combinations, which in turn mirrors the infinity of the godhead; it is thus deemed acceptable to 'discover' new angelic and demonic names based on letter combinations, as John Dee seems to have done, just as it is acceptable to apply Kabbalistic hermeneutics to generate an endless sequence of new interpretations of sacred texts. In medieval Kabbalistic formulae, these angels are often equated with the ten *sefirot*, which are themselves emanations or aspects of deity.[192] Rachel Elior suggests that the identification of angelic beings with God indicates a radical change in Jewish religious conceptions in late antiquity: an expansion of the idea of deity from a single God to a complex of divine forces, replacing the monotheistic rituals of the earthly Temple with 'a celestial ritual relating to...mythical and visionary polytheism'.[193] This peculiarly Jewish pluralistic cosmology seems to have exercised a special fascination for British occultists seeking a justification for the magical invocation of celestial intermediaries within a nominally monotheistic framework. While the neophytes of the Outer Order of the Golden Dawn occupied themselves with interpreting their personal horoscopes, Mathers and his Inner Order adepts utilised angelic and Divine Names to invoke the supernal powers associated with the planets, elements, and zodiacal signs, as a means of achieving gnosis and enhanced occult power.

Another important feature of the Golden Dawn materials is the use of the strange 'ring-letters' known as *charactêres* for the purpose of creating talismans used in angelic adjurations

---

[191] See Bloom, *Jewish Mysticism and Magic*, 174.
[192] See Idel, *Enchanted Chains*, 54, for Metatron in Kabbalistic literature as both an angel and a *sefira*. See Scholem, *Origins*, 345, and Elior, 'Angelology', 36, for the supreme angel Anafiel as the first *sefira*, *Keter*. For the equation of Metatron and *Keter* in the Golden Dawn, see Regardie, *Golden Dawn*, 64.
[193] Elior, 'Angelology', 34.

and banishing rituals.[194] The *charactêres* as they are employed in Golden Dawn talismans are associated with angels, Divine Names, and the astrological characteristics and animating 'spirits' of the planets.[195] These mysterious symbols are common in late antique Jewish and Greco-Egyptian magical literature and were taken up enthusiastically by medieval and early modern magicians of all religious persuasions.[196] The *charactêres* also appear in Andreae's *Chymical Wedding of Christian Rosenkreutz*, thus associating them with Rosicrucian-alchemical currents in the early seventeenth century.[197] Many futile attempts have been made by scholars over the centuries to decipher their meanings, but no consensus has been reached about whether these magical symbols originated in Greco-Egyptian or Jewish magical

---

[194] See Bohak, *Ancient Jewish Magic*, 272, for possible derivations of the term *charactêre* (*kalaqtiraia* in Aramaic), used by Jewish magicians in late antiquity.

[195] See Regardie, *Golden Dawn*, 479–504.

[196] For a Greco-Egyptian example of the *charactêres*, see *PGM* X.24–35, in Betz, *Greek Magical Papyri*, 149. For an early modern example, see the pseudo-Paracelsian *Archidoxis Magica*, written *c*. 1560. Lévi, assuming the *Archidoxis Magica* to have been written by Paracelsus, asserts (Lévi, *Dogme*, 153) that the study of the *charactêres* was Paracelsus' 'entire life-work', and calls the seals and sigils of the *Archidoxis magica* an 'astral kabbalistic alphabet'. Scholars well into the twentieth century believed the *Archidoxis magica* to have been authored by Paracelsus; Jung, for example, refers to it as evidence that Paracelsus 'designed and used amulets and seals' (Jung, CW13, ¶156). The *Archidoxis magica* was translated into English by Robert Turner and included in Turner's translation of Paracelsus, *Of the Supreme Mysteries of Nature* (London, 1656). For another example of the *charactêres*, see the 'figures of philosophy' found in a fourteenth-century manuscript of the *Ars Notoria* (Bibliothèque Nationale MS lat. 9336, f. 25v and 27v), reproduced in Michael Camille, 'Visual Art in Two Manuscripts of the Ars Notoria', in Fanger (ed.), *Conjuring Spirits*, 110–39, on pp. 130–31. See also Juris G. Lidaka, 'The Book of Angels, Rings, Characters and Images of the Planets*: Attributed to Osbern Bokenham', in Fanger (ed.), *Conjuring Spirits*, 32–75. The *charactêres* in this mid-fifteenth-century work are associated with planetary and angelic powers; Lidaka has reproduced the *charactêres* associated with two particular spells on pp. 60–61.

[197] For the *charactêres* from the *Chymical Wedding*, see Waite's version of the text, cited in its entirety in Waite, *Real History*, 99–196, on pp. 146, 161, 177. For Agrippa's *charactêres*, see *Occult Philosophy*, 3.29–31.

traditions, or who borrowed what from whom.[198] In 1950, Campbell Bonner noted: 'It is possible that we may yet learn something about the characters if some investigator is patient enough to follow up all the leads, but at present they are still undeciphered'.[199] Gideon Bohak observes that Bonner's statement 'remains true even half a century later'.[200] Michael Morgan, in his translation of the *Sefer ha-Razim*, comments that, while the *charactêres* are commonly used in Jewish and Greco-Egyptian magical texts and amulets to designate angels and Divine Names, full magical alphabets made up of *charactêres* (such as those later produced by Agrippa and Dee) only coalesced in the late Middle Ages. Morgan offers a prosaic explanation for the *charactêres*: they are derived from the 'punch-writing' on Greek allotment plates, which were worn in a fashion similar to amulets.[201] In contrast, Giulio Busi suggests that they arise from astrological-cosmological speculations and were originally intended to 'trace groups of stars'.[202] This observation is supported by the *Picatrix*, which declares that the *charactêres* embody the 'rays that reach from one [planet or star] to another, and figures and images are calculated from them'.[203] Given the consistent association of the *charactêres* with astral and angelic adjurations over the centuries, this explanation seems more appropriate.

A perusal of some examples demonstrates that the *charactêres* that Mathers utilised have remained virtually unaltered for many centuries. One of the earliest uses of *charactêres* appears in the *Sefer ha-Razim*, where they are grouped according to the angels presiding over the various levels of the heavens.

---

[198] *Charactêres* can also be found in early Christian magical texts: see Meyer and Smith, *Ancient Christian Magic*, 146 and 223.
[199] Campbell Bonner, *Studies in Magical Amulets, Chiefly Greco-Egyptian* (Ann Arbor: University of Michigan Press, 1950), 12–13.
[200] Bohak, *Ancient Jewish Magic*, 271, n. 125.
[201] Morgan (trans.), *Sefer ha-Razim*, 46, n. 14.
[202] Busi, *Qabalah Visiva*, 32. See also John G. Gager, *Curse Tablets and Binding Spells from the Ancient World* (Oxford: Oxford University Press, 1992), 6–11; Gager likewise attributes an astral origin to the *charactêres*.
[203] John Michael Greer and Christopher Warnock (trans.), *The Latin Picatrix, Books I & II* (Raleigh, NC: Renaissance Astrology, 2009), 2:5.

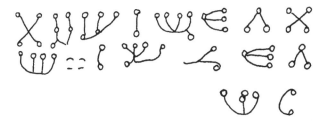

Fig. 10: Charactêres *from* Sefer ha-Razim *signifying the angels of the Second Firmament.*[204]

Another example of a Jewish text with *charactêres* is found in a magical recipe-book from the Cairo Genizah, dated to the early medieval period.[205]

---

[204] Reproduced in Morgan (trans.), *Sefer ha-Razim*, 63. Morgan notes that the *charactêres* differ slightly from one MS to another.

[205] The term *genizah* connotes a secret cache or hiding-place for sacred documents. To date, only a fraction of the texts from the Cairo Genizah has been published. The texts include magical recipes, astrological and alchemical speculations, and various forms of divination such as geomancy, physiognomy, and dream interpretation. Bohak (*Ancient Jewish Magic*, 275) notes that the verso of the Cairo Genizah text from which the photograph reproduced above was taken contains the remains of an Arabic document, suggesting an attempt on the part of Arab magicians to 'decipher' the *charactêres* as letters of the Hebrew alphabet. Bohak observes, 'Such attempts were extremely common in the Middle Ages, among Jews, Christians and Muslims alike'. For surveys of the magical texts from the Cairo Genizah, see Norman Golb, 'Aspects of the Historical Background of Jewish Life in Medieval Egypt', in Alexander Altmann (ed.), *Jewish Medieval and Renaissance Studies* (Cambridge, MA: Harvard University Press, 1967), 1–18; Schäfer, 'Jewish Magic Literature'; Steven M. Wasserstrom, 'The Magical Texts in the Cairo Genizah', in Joshua Blau and Stefan C. Reif (eds.), *Genizah Research after Ninety Years: The Case of Judaeo-Arabic* (Cambridge: Cambridge University Press, 1992), 160–66; Shaul Shaked, 'Medieval Jewish Magic in Relation to Islam: Theoretical Attitudes and Genres', in B. H. Hary, J. L. Hayes, and F. Astern (eds.), *Judaism and Islam: Boundaries, Communication and Interaction* (Leiden: Brill, 2000), 97–109.

Fig. 11. Charactêres *from a magical manuscript of the 10th century, from the Cairo Genizah.*[206]

During the medieval period, the *charactêres* – originally related to angelic and astral adjurations – were developed into full-blown 'angelic' alphabets. The most likely routes of transmission are the *Hasidei Ashkenaz*, the German Jewish Pietists of the eleventh and twelfth centuries, who appropriated earlier *heikhalot* literature and developed a magical cosmology incorporating astral and linguistic magic and angelic adjurations and alphabets which found their way into early Kabbalistic doctrines.[207] The magical text known as

[206] Image reproduced from Moses Gaster, 'Magen David', *Rimon/Milgroim* 3 (1923), 27.

[207] For the transmission of Jewish esoteric traditions, see Elliot R. Wolfson, 'Beyond the Spoken Word: Oral Tradition and Written Transmission in Medieval Jewish Mysticism', in Yaakov Elman and Israel Gershoni (eds.), *Transmitting Jewish Traditions: Orality, Textuality and Cultural Diffusion* (New Haven, CT: Yale University Press, 2000), 167–224; Moshe Idel, 'Transmission in Thirteenth-Century Kabbalah', in Elman and Gershoni (eds.), *Transmitting Jewish Traditions*, 138–65.

Sefer ha-Raziel ('Book of Raziel') or *Sefer ha-Malakh Raziel* ('Book of the Angel Raziel') was first published in Hebrew in Amsterdam in 1701, but it contains much older materials, including a portion of the *Sefer ha-Razim* as well as other treatises on Divine Names, astral and angelic magic, and a full alphabet of *charactêres*. About the *Sefer ha-Raziel*, Sophie Page, in a paper on a Latin translation of this work, observes: 'The most explicit transmission of Jewish magical material into the Christian Latin tradition of magic was the translation of works associated with the name "Raziel"'.[208]

---

[208] Sophie Page, 'Uplifting Souls and Speaking with Spirits: The *Liber de essentia spirituum* and the *Liber Razielis*', paper delivered at the conference 'Magie und Theurgie: Internationales Symposium an der Friedrich-Schiller-Universitäat Jena', 31 January–2 February 2002. An extract from Page's paper is available at <http://digital-brilliance.com/kab/karr/Solomon/LibSal.pdf>. Steve Savedow (*Sefer Rezial Hemelach*, 10) suggests that portions of the *Sefer ha-Raziel* can be dated to the thirteenth century or earlier, and the editor of the 1701 printed edition, Heba'al Hemegieheh, states in his foreword (iv) that he includes in his compilation 'the smaller work of Eleazar, son of the Rabbi Judah, who received the work of Merkabah from the pious Rabbi Judah'. For the attribution of the *Sefer ha-Raziel* to Eleazar of Worms, see Trachtenberg, *Jewish Magic*, 92. The 'pious Rabbi Judah' is probably the much-revered Yehudah ben Shemu'el he-Hasid ('Judah the Hasid', 1150–1217), the author of a theosophical and magical work called *Sefer Hasidim*, which contains instructions for methods of contemplative prayer which are intended to reveal the mysteries contained in the numerical values of the prayer's words and letters. For an English translation of R. Yehudah's *Sefer Hasidim*, see Avraham Yaakov Finkel (trans.), *Sefer Chasidim: The Book of the Pious* (Northvale, NJ: Jason Aronson, 1997). For analyses of this work, see Haym Soloveitchik, 'Three Themes in the "Sefer Hasidim"', *AJSR* 1 (1976), 311–57; Ivan G. Marcus, 'The Recensions and Structure of "Sefer Hasidim"', *PAJR* 45 (1978), 131–53. Trachtenberg (*Jewish Magic*, 92) states that the 'angelic' alphabet of the *Sefer ha-Raziel* is specifically linked to the twenty-two-letter Divine Name, the *Shem Kaf Bet*, discussed in this book in Chapter Five. There are many rescensions of *Sefer ha-Raziel* in Latin and English, each containing a different number of smaller 'books' or 'microforms'. Although Mathers does not mention the *Sefer ha-Raziel* in his published work, it is unlikely that the English rescension of *Raziel* known as *Liber Salomonis* (Sloane MS 3826) escaped his perusals at the British Museum, 'whose enormous collection of Occult Manuscripts I have very thoroughly studied' (Mathers, 'Introduction', in Mathers (trans.), *Abramelin*, xvi).

Fig. 12: An 'angelic' alphabet of charactêres *from the* Sefer ha-Raziel.[209]

A large portion of the *Sefer ha-Raziel* was traditionally attributed to Eleazar of Worms, the most important of the *Hasidei Ashkenaz*. By the early sixteenth century these 'angelic' alphabets, comprised of twenty-two *charactêres*, were firmly associated with Kabbalistic magic, as Agrippa demonstrates in a section of *De occulta philosophia* entitled 'Another manner of making characters, delivered by Cabalists':

> Amongst the Hebrews I find more fashions of characters, whereof one is most ancient, viz. an ancient writing which Moses, and the prophets used....There is also amongst them a writing which they call Celestial, because they show it placed and figured among the stars....There is also a writing which they call Malachim, or Melachim, i.e. Of Angels.[210]

---

[209] From the 1701 Hebrew edition, reproduced in Trachtenberg, *Jewish Magic*, 141.
[210] Agrippa, *Occult Philosophy*, 3.30.

Fig. 13: Agrippa's 'Celestial Writing' and 'Malachim', permutations of the Hebrew letters into charactêres.[211]

Agrippa's alphabets appear in conjunction with a particular technique of magical astrology known as the so-called 'magic squares' of the planets.

ד	ט	ב
ג	ה	ז
ח	א	ו

4	9	2
3	5	7
8	1	6

Fig. 14: Saturn's magic square with Hebrew letters and Arabic numerals. The numbers of any column – horizontal, vertical, or diagonal – always total fifteen.

The squares, which appear in both Jewish and Christian magical texts, were believed to possess talismanic powers because of the peculiar properties of the numbers, interchangeable with the Hebrew letters and therefore amenable to Kabbalistic linguistic hermeneutics. A magic square is a square divided into cells; numbers are inserted into each cell in such a way that if every row, column, and diagonal is added up, they all produce the same total.

---

[211] Agrippa, *Occult Philosophy*, 3.30.439–40.

Because of the peculiar behaviour of numbers in these squares, and the equation of letters with numbers in both Hebrew and Arabic, the magic squares can also produce letter-acrostics and lend themselves to explorations in *gematria*, thus apparently demonstrating to Kabbalistic magicians of various religious persuasions the divinity of the letters of the Hebrew alphabet. The magic squares appear in Hebrew literature only after the Muslim conquest of Egypt and Babylonia, and they seem to have originated in the early medieval Arab magic of the ninth century, rather than in Jewish sources. By the thirteenth century, the squares involving the numbers three to nine became associated with the seven planets and thus with astral magic. In the square of Saturn shown above, each column totals fifteen.[212]

Golden Dawn adepts were enthusiastic about the potency of these figures; Mathers issued instructions for their use on planetary talismans, and cautioned the aspiring neophyte against their dangers, 'for, if left carelessly about, they are very liable to obsess sensitive persons, children, or even animals'.[213] Agrippa, whose alphabets are clearly related to that of the *Sefer ha-Raziel* (which also contains magic squares), and who may have acquired them from early MS versions of this work, also utilises *charactêres* in relation to the specific

---

[212] For Agrippa's use of the magic squares, see Karl Anton Nowotny, 'The Construction of Certain Seals and Characters in the Work of Agrippa of Nettesheim', *JWCI* 12 (1949), 46–57. Gideon Bohak (*Ancient Jewish Magic*, 432) suggests that by the medieval period, the Arab magic squares had become thoroughly 'Judaised'. The squares appear in medieval and early modern Hebrew texts such as the *Aesch Mezareph* (see Westcott (ed.), *Collectanea Hermetica*, 19–41) and the *Sefer ha-Raziel* (see Savedow (trans.), *Sepher Rezial Hemelach*, 168, Fig. 7), and were enthusiastically taken up by Christian Kabbalists such as Agrippa, Trithemius, and Robert Fludd as expressions of 'practical' Kabbalah.

[213] Mathers (trans.), *Abramelin*, xxxviii. Mathers displays an uneasy respect for the magic squares, which he calls 'Qabalistic Squares of Letters'. His efforts to explain the meaning of the letter-acrostic squares through *gematria* (see, for example, Mathers (trans.), *Abramelin*, 59) seem to have impressed at least some of the scholars of his time; J. M. McBryde, Jr., in 'The Sator-Acrostic', *MLN* 22:8 (1907), 245–49, states that Mathers offers 'the most satisfactory explanation I have been able to discover for this perplexing acrostic [the 'SATOR-acrostic']' (248), and concludes from Mathers' discussion that the SATOR-acrostic 'is clearly related to the Jewish Kabbalah' (249).

angelic powers associated with the four elements, the zodiacal signs, and the planets, as demonstrated by the 'seals' and 'sigils' for Saturn:

Fig. 15: Left, Agrippa's 'seal' of Saturn; centre, the 'Intelligence' of Saturn; right, the 'Spirit' of Saturn.[214]

The 'sigils' for the seven planets, which represent the 'Intelligence' (the benign angelic ruler) and 'Spirit' (the malevolent demonic ruler) are derived, like the seal or emblem for the presiding angelic entity ruling the planet, from a complicated method of extracting *charactêres* from the magic squares associated with each planet. Agrippa may have had acquired these seals and sigils from earlier grimoires such as the thirteenth-century *Liber runarum*, which, in the international fashion typical of magical formulae, combines planetary *charactêres* with Scandinavian runes to invoke angels who are called by their traditional Hebrew names.[215]

---

[214] Agrippa, *Occult Philosophy*, 2.22.

[215] For the *Liber runarum*, see Láng, *Unlocked Books*, 109–15, 137–38, 259–60. The grimoires, in turn, seem to have appropriated the squares as a potent form of Kabbalistic magic. The *Clavicula Salomonis*, for example (Figs. 11–12, in Mathers (trans.), *Key of Solomon*, 66), presents the magic squares associated with the planet Saturn using Hebrew letters rather than numbers, and *Abramelin* utilises the squares for angelic names in letter-acrostics throughout Book III (Mathers (trans.), *Abramelin*, 165–247). Dee's Enochian 'Tables' likewise use the magic squares in complex formations for angelic invocations or 'calls'; for examples, see John Dee, *A True & Faithful Relation of what passed for many Yeers Between Dr John Dee...and Some Spirits*, ed. Meric Casaubon (London: 1659; repr. London: Askin Publishers, 1974), 'The Holy Table' (facing p. 1) and 175–79. The Golden Dawn version of Dee's 'Tables', amalgamated with the Minor Arcana of the Tarot, can be found in Regardie, *Golden Dawn*, 624–50. Thomas Rudd includes the more traditional planetary versions with Hebrew letters and numerals in Rudd, *Angel Magic*, 109–21.

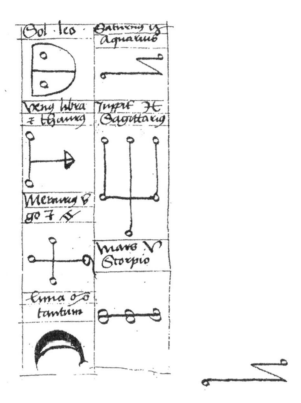

Fig. 16: Left, charactêres *for the 'spirits' of the planets from* Liber runarum.[216] *Right, detail of the 'spirit' of Saturn.*

A sixteenth-century English redaction of the *Liber Iuratus* presents us not only with *charactêres* but with representational images of the planetary angels, wearing helmets and arranged in military formation as befits their Hebrew title of 'prince' or 'captain'. Their planetary associations are designated not only by the text, but by the colours of their robes and wings.

---

[216] *Liber runarum*, Dresden, Sächsische Landesbibliothek N 100, fol. 198r.

Fig. 17: Top, planetary angels of Mars and the Sun in Liber iuratus.
Bottom, detail of charactêres *and planetary glyph for Mars.*[217]

The angels of Mars, at the top of the image, bear wings and
robes of red, and 'cause war, murder, destruction, and
mortality of people and of all earthly things'. First of these
Martial angels, on the far left, is the ancient Jewish prince of
the demons, Samael. Below him are the astrological glyph for
Mars and the planet's *charactêres*; Samael must be invoked on
a Tuesday, the day of Mars.[218] The angels of the Sun, at the
bottom of the image, begin with the archangel Raphael; he
taught Solomon 'Knowledge and Wisdom', and should be

---

[217] *Liber iuratus*, Royal MS 17 A XLII, ff. 68v–69, British Library,
reproduced in Sophie Page, *Magic in Medieval Manuscripts* (London:
British Library, 2004), 46.
[218] Mathers, *Armadel*, 41.

invoked at sunrise on a Sunday.[219] These solar angels bear golden colours, and 'give love and favour and riches to a man and power also to keep him hale'. The *charactêres* and presiding angel of Mars represented in this sixteenth-century redaction of *Liber Iuratus* are in turn faithfully reproduced in a late-eighteenth-century translation of a grimoire known as *The Clavis or Key to the Magic of Solomon* by the astrologer Ebenezer Sibly, transcribed in the mid-nineteenth century by Frederick Hockley.

Fig. 18: Hockley's charactêres *and glyphs for Mars, his angel Samael, and his signs Aries and Scorpio.*[220]

Thomas Rudd, in his *Treatise on Angel Magic*, informs his readers that 'the Magi of old framed certain Tables distributed to the seven planets', and presents *charactêres* and angelic names for Saturn that are identical to Agrippa's.

---

[219] Mathers, *Armadel*, 30. See Trachtenberg, *Jewish Magic*, 251, for the frequency of planetary associations of Raphael and Michael with the Sun. See also Trachtenberg, *Jewish Magic*, 312, fn. 3, for further sources.

[220] Ebenezer Sibly and Frederick Hockley (trans.), *The Clavis or Key to the Magic of Solomon* (Lake Worth, FLA: Ibis Press, 2009), 270.

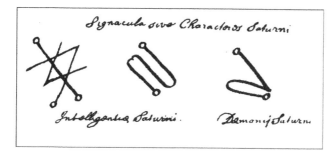

Fig. 19: Thomas Rudd's charactêres *for Saturn.*[221]

Francis Barrett, at the beginning of the nineteenth century, presents a version of the 'Celestial' and 'Malachim' alphabets entirely derived from Agrippa (complete with Agrippa's chapter heading), and incorporates the *charactêres* of the sixteenth-century magus in his own presentation of the 'Intelligences' and 'Spirits' of the planets:

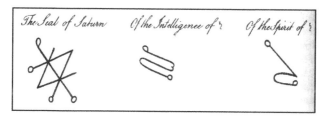

Fig. 20: Frances Barrett's charactêres *for the angelic powers governing the planet Saturn.*[222]

Barrett's magical talisman for Saturn combines the first two *charactêres* with the traditional astrological glyph for Saturn, and he instructs the adept to make the talisman out of the traditional Saturnian metal, lead. It is obvious from which sources Mathers derived his own *charactêres* for a paper on

---

[221] Thomas Rudd, 'Containing the Characters of the 16 Figures of Geomancy, expressed in the great and lesser Squares of Tabula santa; together with an explication of the seven Tables of Enoch, which are charged with Spirits or Genii, both good and bad of several Orders and Hierarchies, which the wise King Solomon made use of', © The British Library Board, MS Harley 6482, fol. 91 verso and fol. 92, Documents of Dr Rudd.

[222] Barrett, *Magus*, 2.26 and 1.2.28.

talismanic magic published in 1888, the year of the creation of the Golden Dawn:

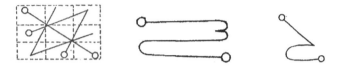

Fig. 21: Left, Mathers' seal of Saturn, formed from a magic square; centre, the sigil of Agiel, the 'Good Spirit' of Saturn; right, the sigil of Zazel, the 'Evil Genius' of Saturn.[223]

A Golden Dawn talisman for Jupiter was consecrated through a direct adjuration of the angels governing the planet, itself referred to throughout as Zedek, its Hebrew name. Zadkiel, the angel of the *sefira Hesed*, is summoned, as both the angel and the *sefira* are associated with Jupiter. Next comes a call to the angel Yohphiel, the 'Intelligence' of Jupiter, who is ordered to inhabit the talisman as his 'dwelling place':

> I command ye to send hither thine Intelligence, the Angel Yohphiel that he may concentrate and bind into this Talisman his life and power. In taking it for his body, let him thereby form a true and wonderful link for me with all those powers of love and wisdom, grace, abundance and benignity which rise rank upon rank to the feet of the Holy Spirit.[224]

The talisman itself is made of silver, the metal of *Hesed* in Jewish esoteric lore, and it displays Jupiter's planetary glyph, his magic square, his Hebrew name, and his *charactêres*. The idea that the talisman provides embodiment for the angelic power associated with the planet reflects the ancient perception of a symbol as both a significator and an imaginal medium through which that which is symbolised can be incarnated in form.

---

[223] S. L. MacGregor Mathers, 'Talismanic Magic: Saturn, The Occult Signification of his Square, Seal, and Sigils', *Lucifer* 2:7 (1888), 9–14, on p. 14. For the same *charactêres* in a contemporary 'emic' text on ritual magic, see John Michael Greer, *Circles of Power: Ritual Magic in the Western Tradition* (St. Paul, MN: Llewellyn Publications, 1997), 106.

[224] Regardie, *Golden Dawn*, 413–22.

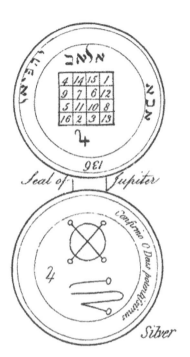

*Fig. 22: Talisman of Jupiter with planetary glyph and magic square, used
in the Golden Dawn ritual 'Consecration Ceremony for Jupiter
Talisman'[225]*

Other sigils related to Divine Names and angelic powers
such as Metatron are also included in Golden Dawn
instructions for the making of talismans,[226] suggesting that
Mathers was not merely using the Jewish Kabbalah as a
convenient resource for 'programmatic syncretism'. He
seems to have been entirely convinced of the reality of the
forces he was attempting to conjure, and found himself in
sympathy with the Jewish conception of a cosmos filled with
divine intermediaries who could be invoked most effectively
through their traditional Hebrew names. Moshe Idel
suggests that the magic of the late-fifteenth-century circle of
Kabbalists responsible for the *Sefer ha-Meshiv* incorporates
the belief that magic is the result of a divine revelation, either

---

[225] Barrett, *Magus*, 2:46.175; Regardie, *Golden Dawn*, 413.
[226] See, for example, Regardie, *Golden Dawn*, 483–85.

from God himself or from an angelic power.[227] Mathers attributed his magical knowledge to the revelations of his transhuman 'Secret Chiefs', for whom Mina acted as a scrying medium. Idel describes the magic of the authors of the *Sefer ha-Meshiv* as embedded within a system which conceived of philosophy, physics, metaphysics, astrology, mathematics, and alchemy as aspects of a single 'knowledge-system'[228] – a view which Mathers wholeheartedly embraced. Idel further explains:

> Even the divine realm is considered as prone to the influence of the magical operations of the elected magician. Therefore, the will of the magician, rather than his contemplation of the divine realm accompanied by the theurgical operations on the divine powers or some ecstatical experiences he may undergo, is the main type of activity.[229]

This is entirely consistent with Mathers' perception of the role of the magician. He repeatedly refers to the angelic intermediaries as 'forces' and, although he also seems to have understood them to be internal in the psychological sense (a perception shared, as discussed above, with medieval and early modern Kabbalists), he also credits them with an independent existence that can be invoked with the appropriate ritual techniques:

> In vibrating the Divine Names, the Operator should first of all rise as high as possible towards the idea of the Divine White Brilliance in KETHER....Formulate the letters of the Name required in your heart, in white, and feel them written there....Pronounce the name as if you were vibrating it through the whole Universe, and as if it did not stop until it reached the further limits.[230]

---

[227] Idel, 'Magic and Kabbalah', 132.

[228] Idel, 'Magic and Kabbalah', 133.

[229] Idel, 'Magic and Kabbalah', 134.

[230] Cited in Regardie, *Golden Dawn*, 486–87. For references on a similar use of colours in Kabbalistic meditation from the thirteenth century onward, see Gershom Scholem, 'Colors and Their Symbolism in Jewish Tradition and Mysticism', trans. Klaus Ottman, *Diogenes* 109 (1980), 69–71; Moshe Idel, 'Kabbalistic Prayer and Color', in David R. Blumenthal (ed.), *Approaches to Judaism in Medieval Times*, Vol. 3 (Chico, CA: Scholar's Press, 1988), 17–28; Moshe Idel, 'An Anonymous Kabbalistic Commentary on *Shir ha-Yihud*', in Grözinger and Dan (eds.), *Mysticism, Magic and Kabbalah*, 139–54, esp. 147–49; Idel, *Kabbalah*, 104–08.

Magic, as Gideon Bohak points out, is 'neither timeless nor ageless', and it is not immune to change;[231] the idea that invocations and spells were faithfully copied because their efficacy depends on meticulous accuracy is belied by evidence not only of scribal sloppiness, but also of the creative inventiveness of magicians freely incorporating new materials from other cultural milieux.[232] The creative eclecticism of the Golden Dawn rituals might be viewed as a new, modern phenomenon, but it is also reflected over the centuries in the many changes and cultural adaptations that have taken place in Jewish magical traditions, including those of the Kabbalah. And although magical technologies reflect particular cultural contexts at different historical periods, some elements have remained extraordinarily stable over the centuries, including the *charactêres* and the astral magic developed by Mathers for his Golden Dawn adepts.

CLOSE ENCOUNTERS OF THE ELEMENTAL KIND

Much of the Jewish magical lore incorporated in the Golden Dawn repertoire can be found in Hasidic folk tales, which were first published in the early decades of the twentieth century but which had been circulating orally and in manuscripts among Ashkenazi Jews since the Middle Ages.[233] In the introduction to his *Ma'aseh Book*,[234] Moses

---

[231] Bohak, *Ancient Jewish Magic*, 432.

[232] See Graf, *Magic in the Ancient World*, 8.

[233] For a collection of these tales from the early seventeenth century, see Moses Gaster, *Ma'aseh Book: Book of Jewish Tales and Legends Translated from the Judeo-German* (Philadelphia, PA: The Jewish Publication Society of America, 1934). See also Martin Buber, *Tales of the Hasidim: The Early Masters* and *Tales of the Hasidim: The Later Masters*, 2 vols. (New York: Schocken Books, 1947). The Babylonian Talmud, *Eruvin* 18b, speaks of Adam's years of banishment after the expulsion from Eden, during which he begat 'spirits, demons, and night-demons', while Eve in her turn was impregnated by male spirits and became the mother of innumerable demon-children who continue to plague humankind. In late antique *heikhalot* literature, the demoness Lilith is presented as the wife of Samael, chief of the demons; she is also Adam's first wife, and texts from the Cairo Genizah describe the demonic progeny of Adam and Lilith (see Scholem, *Origins*, 296 and n. 191). For more on Lilith and the hordes of female demons known as Liliths or *lilins*, see Raphael Patai, 'Lilith', *Journal of American Folkore* 77 (1964), 295–314; Raphael Patai, *The Hebrew Goddess* (New York: Ktav Publishing House, 1967), 180–

Gaster examines the history of the stories, their origins in the Talmudic period of the first centuries CE, their development into a distinctive genre during the Middle Ages, and their popularity among the German- and Yiddish-speaking European Jewish communities in the early modern period. Gaster suggests that these tales, which he calls 'romantic stories of olden times', are meant to be homiletic and to instruct the reader in moral, ethical, and religious precepts. Although only a few of the stories approach the subject of angels and demons, many are unabashedly magical, particularly those about 'wonder-working' rabbis or righteous men who stand as exemplars of the Hasidic *zaddik* or Kabbalistic magus; for example, in a tale entitled 'Honi ha-Me'aggel and His Prayer for Rain', Honi, 'the Drawer of the Circle', adjures God through the use of the Divine Names and invokes a deluge.[235] The word 'magic' is foreign to this story, but Honi is clearly a magician; the use of Honi's phrase, 'I adjure', is common to the *heikhalot* adjurations of angels as well as to medieval Christianised grimoires and Golden Dawn rituals.

Among the themes of these tales is the mating of humans with elemental spirits or demons,[236] a motif which can be found in the late antique Jewish apocalyptic tradition of the mating of the fallen angels with the 'daughters of men'.[237]

---

225. For Greek parallels, see, as one of many examples, the mating of Zeus with the mortal woman Semele, a tale which first appears in *Iliad* 14 and whose development is discussed in Timothy Ganz, *Early Greek Myth: A Guide to Literary and Artistic Sources* (Baltimore, MD: Johns Hopkins University Press, 1993), 472–79. However, the many Greek tales about gods and intermediary beings such as nymphs and satyrs mating with mortals never involve the revelation of forbidden divine secrets, and the progeny of these unions are usually heroes such as Theseus or gods such as Dionysus rather than demonic entities.

[234] Gaster, *Ma'aseh Book*, xvii–xliii.

[235] Gaster, *Ma-aseh Book*, 1:87–91.

[236] See, for example, 'The Proud Prince Who Unwittingly Gave His Daughter in Marriage to a Demon', in Gaster, *Ma'aseh Book*, 2:383–90. For more on Hasidic tales dealing with the mating of humans and demons, see Nigal, *Magic, Mysticism, and Hasidism*, 139–56; Trachtenberg, *Jewish Magic*, 52–53.

[237] For the mating of angels with mortal women and the dissemination of supernal secrets, see 1 Enoch 6–11, in Charlesworth (ed.), *Old Testament Pseudepigrapha*, 1:15–19; Babylonian Talmud, *Eruvin* 18b.

Sexual entanglement with non-human entities is not a subject
included in the Golden Dawn's official documents, and some
adepts, offended by Aleister Crowley's sexual excesses, felt
strongly that the order's teachings should entirely exclude
sexual magic of any kind.[238] However, there are hints in
Golden Dawn papers that have aroused speculation among
scholars about possible teachings regarding matings between
adepts and 'elementals', the non-human entities that preside
over and animate the four Aristotelian elements of earth, air,
water, and fire.[239] Ithell Colquhoun refers to Mathers'
teachings about the 'Elemental spouse', and asserts that both
Mathers and Westcott not only believed in the possibility of
such a union, 'but must have taught methods by which a
partner from praeternatural regions could be attracted'.[240]
Colquhoun further asserts that while Mina Mathers 'disliked
the idea of Elemental mates as much as human ones', she did
not doubt that such a mating could be achieved.[241] It is
unclear what benefits other than pleasure and novelty are
meant to accrue for the human partner in such a union. That
the soulless elemental might gain a human soul is suggested
in the late-seventeenth-century romance known as *Le Comte
de Gabalis*, discussed below; and the human partner, if a
woman, might become pregnant by the elemental and
produce a semi-demonic child with supernatural powers. A
human of either sex might also, following the Jewish
apocalyptic tradition, obtain access to occult secrets known
only to the demonic world. Unfortunately there are no extant
testimonies from British occultists as to whether they
believed they had achieved such a union.

---

[238] See, for example, Garstin, *Theurgy*, 32–33; Colquhoun, *Sword*, 285.
For Crowley's sexual magic, see Chapter Five.

[239] For an occultist exposition on elementals, see H. P. Blavatsky,
'Elementals', *Lucifer* 12:72 (1893), 537–48; *Lucifer* 13:73–74 (1893), 30–
39 and 111–21; repr. in Blavatsky, CW6, 184–201.

[240] Colquhoun, *Sword*, 293–94. For a more sinister description of the
'Elemental Spouse' in a novel written by a Golden Dawn adept, see
Arthur Machen, 'The Great God Pan', in *The Great God Pan and The
Inmost Light* (London: John Lane, 1894), repr. in Arthur Machen,
Tales of Horror and the Supernatural (London: John Baker, 1964), 61–
115.

[241] Colquhoun, *Sword*, 294, referring to a letter from Mina Mathers to
Annie Horniman (31 December 1895) cited in Howe, *Magicians*, 117–
18.

It is probably impossible to locate a single 'original' source for the idea of invoking elementals for sexual purposes. Medieval Jewish philosophers appropriated the Aristotelian elements from the Arabs, relating these four cosmic building-blocks to the angelic rulers of the heavenly bodies; this lore found its way into the work of Eleazar of Worms, who proclaimed that the properties and powers of the heavenly bodies depended on their elemental composition.[242] Jewish literature on matings between humans and non-human entities does not describe the latter as specifically associated with the elements, although particular angels are sometimes related to them.[243] However, Jewish demons are sometimes difficult to distinguish from Jewish angels, as the Talmud suggests:

> They [demons] are like angels in three particulars...Like angels they have wings, are able to fly from one end of the world to the other, and know the future. Whilst, however, the angels have the future revealed to them, they [demons] learn it by listening behind the veil.[244]

As the idea developed in medieval Jewish thought, relations between mortals and demons came to seem both possible and permissible.[245] Joshua Trachtenberg observes:

> The need of the spirits to find completion in the body of man was also utilized to explain the curious belief in sexual relations between man and demon....Just as in antediluvian days 'the sons of God saw the daughters of men that they were fair; and they took them wives, whomsoever they chose'

---

[242] For Aristotle's theories of the elements, see E. S. Forster and D. J. Furley (trans.), *Aristotle III: On Sophistical Refutations; On Coming-to-be and Passing Away; On the Cosmos* (Cambridge, MA: Loeb Classical Library, Harvard University Press, 1955), II.3, 275. See Trachtenberg, *Jewish Magic*, 252, for Jewish appropriation of the astrological associations of the four elements from Arab translations of Ptolemy's *Tetrabiblos*. For Eleazar's use of Aristotelian qualities, see Trachtenberg, *Jewish Magic*, 252.

[243] See, for example, Morgan (trans.), *Sefer ha-Razim*, 2.120–22, 3:20–25, 4:50.

[244] Babylonian Talmud, *Hagigah* 16a, cited in Angelo S. Rappoport, *Myths and Legends of Ancient Israel*, 3 vols. (London: Gresham, 1928; repr. as *Ancient Israel: Myths and Legends*, London: Mystic Press, 1987), 71.

[245] See, for example, *Midrash Tanhuma*, cited in Nigal, *Magic, Mysticism, and Hasidism*, 139; Trachtenberg, *Jewish Magic*, 51.

> (Gen. 6:2), so in the Middle Ages it was not unknown for a lesser order of spirit beings to choose for themselves earthly mates.[246]

Human-demon matings also occur in Kabbalistic literature. The *Zohar* asserts that the propagation of the demonic race is continuous because of the union of men with female spirits in their sleep.[247] Trachtenberg notes the Zoharic doctrine that 'man's nocturnal emissions often result from the efforts of the demons to arouse his passions, and that these provide the seed from which the hybrid offspring are born.'[248] The sexually predatory demons of the *Zohar* are not, however, referred to as 'elementals'.

The concept of elementals is derived from the work of Paracelsus, who does not use the term itself but nevertheless classifies these non-Adamic 'nature-spirits' as ondines (water), sylphs (air), salamanders (fire), and gnomes or pygmies (earth).[249] Agrippa likewise writes of four classes of

---

[246] Trachtenberg, *Jewish Magic*, 51.

[247] See, for example, *Zohar* I, 148a–b; Zohar I, 55a, cited in Tishby, *Wisdom of the Zohar*, 2:541.

[248] Trachtenberg, *Jewish Magic*, 51.

[249] Paracelsus, *Liber de Nymphis, Sylphis, Pygmaeis et Salamandris et de caeteris Spiritibus* (Basel, 1566), ed. Robert Blaser (Bern: A. Francke, 1960), 16–17. Paracelsus, following Jewish traditions, states that the elementals are not descended from Adam, but were created separately. *Genesis Rabba* 7, a *heikhalot* text quoted in Rappoport, *Myths and Legends*, 74 and Nigal, *Magic, Mysticism, and Hasidism*, 136, states: 'The Lord had created their [the demons'] souls, but their bodies were not completed on account of the Sabbath on which the Lord of the Universe rested, and so they remained souls without bodies'. Paracelsus, in *Liber de Nymphis*, 16–17, names the elementals, also calling them Sylvesters, Undines, Gnomes, and Vulcans. See the review of Blaser's edition of Paracelsus by Walter Pagel, 'Book Review', *Isis* 53:4 (1962), 527–30, where Pagel states (529) that *Liber de Nymphis* served as the source of inspiration for a number of later German Romantic writers including Goethe. See also Henry E. Sigerist (ed.), *Paracelsus: Four Treatises*, trans. C. Lilian Temkin, George Rosen, Gregory Zilgoorg, and Henry E. Sigerist (Baltimore, MD: Johns Hopkins University Press, 1996), in which Paracelsus' treatise on the elementals is translated into English as *On Nymphs, Sylphs, Pygmies, and Salamanders*. An earlier translation of the treatise was produced by the American esotericist Manley Palmer Hall in Manley Palmer Hall (ed. and trans.), *Paracelsus: His Mystical and Medical Philosophy* (Los Angeles, CA: Philosophical Research Society, 1964); see an analysis of the two translations by

'spirits' corresponding to the four elements, although he does not give them names.[250] There are antecedents in the work of the late Neoplatonist Proclus (412–484 CE), who divided the *daimones* into those ruling fire, air, water, and earth as well as those belonging to the underworld.[251] Blavatsky relied heavily on these Neoplatonic descriptions and conflated them with both the Paracelsian and Agrippan elementals and the Jewish 'princes' who could be invoked with the appropriate rituals, declaring that, in the Jewish Kabbalah, 'the nature-spirits were known under the general name of *Shedim* and divided into four classes'.[252] Henry Steel Olcott, co-founder of the Theosophical Society, stated that he had discovered the Egyptian priests' ability to invoke 'the spirits of the elements':

> That these so-called elementals or intermediates, or elementary or original spirits were creatures that actually existed, I was convinced through my investigations in Egyptian archaeology....I was led to believe that they formed a series of creatures in a system of evolution running from inanimate nature through the animal kingdom to man, its

---

James F. Ehrman, 'Pragmatics and Translation: the Problem of Presupposition', *TTR: traduction, terminologie, rédaction* 6:1 (1993), 149–70.

[250] Agrippa, *Occult Philosophy*, 3:16.

[251] Proclus, *Commentary on Plato's Timaeus, Vol. 3: Proclus on the World's Body*, ed. and trans. Dirk Baltzly (Cambridge: Cambridge University Press, 2006), III.165.7–20. For the continuation of Proclus' theories in the medieval period, see E. R. Dodds (trans.), *Proclus: The Elements of Theology* (Oxford: Oxford University Press, 1963), 295; Butler, *Ritual Magic*, 35; Kieckhefer, *Forbidden Rites*, 155.

[252] See Blavatsky, *Isis*, 1:311–14. She does not give her source, but it is more likely to be Paracelsus or Agrippa than a Jewish Kabbalistic text. Blavatsky also comments (*Isis*, 1.xxx): 'Éliphas Lévi and some other Kabbalists make little distinction between elementary spirits who have been men, and those beings which people the elements and are the blind forces of nature'. The Theosophist Louise Off, writing under the pseudonym 'Nizida', quotes Paracelsus in her article, 'Nature-Spirits or Elementals', *TS* 1:10 (1888), 1–14, especially Paracelsus' reference to the elementals as 'intermediary beings or composita' (7). Following Blavatsky, Off carefully distinguishes between elementals and 'elementaries', e.g. 'shells' (12), equivalent to the Kabbalistic *qlippot*. 'Elementaries', unlike elementals, derive from the *Sefer ha-Gilgulim* of Isaac Luria and are Kabbalistic in origin, but they are never the object of Golden Dawn adjurations.

highest development; that there were intelligences capable of being more or less perfectly controlled, as able to impress them as being higher or lower in the scale of creation.[253]

The idea that the ancient Egyptian magicians could control the elementals is presented in a story by the Golden Dawn adept Algernon Blackwood, entitled 'The Nemesis of Fire'. Blackwood also wrote a story called 'Smith: An Episode in a Lodging-House', in which a mysterious student lodger in a boarding-house invokes the elementals through 'some system of ancient Hebrew mysticism' represented in 'a very rare Rabbinical treatise'.[254]

Adjuration of the elemental spirits forms a major part of the Golden Dawn magical praxis,[255] and Mathers' understanding of them seems to blend Theosophical ideas with Jewish angelology and folklore and a spicing of Lévi. Another source for the idea was a satirical romance known as *Le Comte de Gabalis*, purportedly written by the Abbé de Villars in the late seventeenth century.[256] The name 'Gabalis' suggests a reference to the Kabbalah, and the Kabbalah is mentioned repeatedly throughout this work; the Count himself is purported to be 'a great nobleman and a great Cabalist, whose lands lie toward the frontiers of Poland'.[257]

---

[253] Henry Steele Olcott, *Old Diary Leaves, First Series, 1874–1878* (London: Theosophical Publishing House, 1895), 117–19.

[254] Algernon Blackwood, 'Smith: An Episode in a Lodging-House', in Algernon Blackwood, *The Empty House and Other Ghost Stories* (London: Evelyn Nash, 1906; repr. in Algernon Blackwood, *Ancient Sorceries and Other Weird Stories*, ed. S. T. Joshi [London: Penguin, 2002], 1–16).

[255] See, for example, 'Fourth Knowledge Lecture', in Regardie, *Golden Dawn*, 69–76, and the Enochian 'Concourse of the Forces', in Regardie, *Golden Dawn*, 671–82.

[256] Abbé Nicolas-Pierre-Henri de Montfaucon de Villars, *Le Comte de Gabalis, ou Entretiens sur les Science Secrètes* (Paris: Claude Barbin, 1670).

[257] Villars, *Comte de Gabalis*, 7. See Bonnie Latimer, 'Alchemies of Satire: A History of the Sylphs in *The Rape of the Lock*', RES 57:232 (2006), 684–700, in which Latimer suggests that Paracelsus transformed the Neoplatonic idea of elemental *daimones* into an aspect of an 'animist-Christian system' (690) and discusses this Paracelsian influence on *Gabalis*, which had first been translated into English in the late seventeenth century as *The Count of Gabalis, or the extravagant Mysteries of the Cabalists*, trans. P. Ayres (London: Cabalistical Society of the Sages, at the Sign of the Rosy-Crucian, 1680). For a scathing opinion of this translation by a late-nineteenth-

Villars, the purported author of *Gabalis* (the work was originally published anonymously), follows Paracelsus in suggesting that elementals have no souls but can marry humans to gain souls.[258] After a new English edition of this work was published in 1886,[259] *Gabalis* inevitably came to the notice of the Golden Dawn adepts, who assumed it was a genuine Rosicrucian-Kabbalistic work because the chief character after whom the book is named is presented as both

---

century Freemason, see Robert Freke Gould, *A History of Freemasonry: Its Antiquities, Symbols, Constitutions, Customs, etc., Embracing an Investigation of the Records of the Fraternity in England, Scotland, Ireland, British Colonies, France, Germany and the United States; Derived from Official Sources*, 3 vols. (London: Caxton, 1884; repr. Edinburgh: Thomas C. Jack, 1887), 2:96.

[258] Villars, *Comte de Gabalis*, 15–16. See Joseph Andriano, *Feminine Demonology in Male Gothic Fiction* (University Park, PA: Pennsylvania State University Press, 1985), 20, where Andriano suggests: 'A controversy over the nature of demons, especially incubi, had been raging since the time of Paracelsus. The latter, as well as the Neoplatonists, did not consider incubi evil; men could benefit themselves by uniting with succubi, which were daemons rather than demons'. Villars's Rosicrucian count in *Gabalis* claims that the Church Fathers mistook the elemental spirits identified by Paracelsus for devils. According to the count, a man should consider himself fortunate to form a sexual union with such creatures, who are sexually superior to mortal women. For more on *Gabalis* and sexual union with elementals, see Nicolas Kiessling, *The Incubus in English Literature: Provenance and Progeny* (Spokane, WA: Washington State University Press, 1977).

[259] *Sub-mundanes: or, the Elementaries of the Cabala: being the history of spirits, reprinted from the text of the abbe de Villars, physio-astro-mystic* (Bath: Robert H. Fryer, 1886). The new translation was privately printed 'for subscribers only' by Robert H. Fryer, the Bath publisher who in 1887 also produced a little work by William Wynn Westcott, *Tabula Bembina sive Mensa Isiaca. The Isiac Tablet of Cardinal Bembo. Its History and Occult Significance* (Bath: Robert H. Fryer, 1887). It is possible that this translation of *Gabalis*, advertised in Fryer's list of 'Bath Occult Reprints' appended at the end of Westcott's *Isiac Tablet*, was issued at the instigation of Westcott himself. A review of this new edition of *Gabalis* appeared in May 1886 in the monthly London journal *Book-lore* (180), in which the reviewer notes, 'The present handsome reprint appears to be intended for the lovers of occult literature, and some portions of the original French have been discreetly left untranslated'. The most significant feature of *Gabalis* for Golden Dawn magical practices is that *Gabalis* merges the theme of sexual encounters with elementals with what the author understands as Kabbalistic magic.

a Rosicrucian and a 'great Kabbalist' who encourages unions between humans and elementals.[260] But despite the work's popularity in the Golden Dawn, there is no suggestion in the published rituals, Knowledge Lectures, or Flying Rolls of any invocation to foster intercourse between a human and an elemental. If Mathers and his wife were indeed engaged in such activity, all documentation has been suppressed.

Because of the intensely erotic imagery found in the *Zohar* and the Lurianic corpus,[261] the issue of sexuality in relation to the Kabbalah was a subject of considerable interest to Golden Dawn initiates.[262] Westcott advised the adept to cultivate moderation rather than asceticism in all matters involving sexual conduct,[263] but the celibate marriage of Mathers and his wife suggests specific beliefs concerning the transmutation of sexual desire into occult power. These ideas seem to be inspired by both the Christian monastic tradition and Victorian concepts of the 'manliness' of celibacy, rather than by any Jewish doctrine, Kabbalistic or otherwise.[264] Ritual purity is emphasised in the *heikhalot* literature in order to achieve the mental and physical perfection required for the ascent to the Divine Chariot-Throne,[265] but in these texts

---

[260] See H. P. Blavatsky, 'Thoughts on the Elementals', *Lucifer* 6:33 (1890), repr. in Blavatsky, CW12, 187–205, for her opinion of this edition of *Gabalis*. See Gardner, *Bibliotheca Rosicruciana*, 92–93, for a list of eight French and English editions of *Gabalis* available to Golden Dawn adepts.

[261] For eroticism in Kabbalistic literature, see Wolfson, *Language, Eros, Being*; Elliot R. Wolfson, 'Murmuring Secrets: Eroticism and Esotericism in Medieval Kabbalah', in *Hidden Intercourse*, 65–109; Moshe Idel, *'Ta'anug*: Erotic Delights from Kabbalah to Hasidism', in Wouter J. Hanegraaff and Jeffrey J. Kripal (eds.), *Hidden Intercourse: Eros and Sexuality in the History of Western Esotericism* (Leiden: Brill, 2008), 111–51.

[262] See, for example, Waite, *Holy Kabbalah*, 377–405, discussed more fully in Chapter Five.

[263] William Wynn Westcott, Flying Roll II, Part 1, 'A Subject for Contemplation', in King (ed.), *Astral Projection*, 55.

[264] For late Victorian doctrines of the 'manliness' of celibacy, see Trev Lynn Broughton, *Men of Letters, Writing Lives: Masculinity and Literary Auto/Biography in the Late Victorian Period* (New York: Routledge, 1999); James Eli Adams, *Dandies and Desert Saints: Styles of Victorian Manhood* (Ithaca, NY: Cornell University Press, 1995).

[265] For purification rituals in *heikhalot* literature, see Michael D. Swartz, '"Like the Ministering Angels": Ritual and Purity in Early Jewish Mysticism and Magic', *AJSR* 19:2 (1994), 135–67; Swartz,

abstinence involves a specific period preceding the ritual, not a lifelong commitment to celibacy. These rituals mirror the older purification procedures demanded of the High Priest who entered the Holy of Holies in the earthly Temple; he was required to guard himself against any defilement by the emission of seminal fluid or contact with impure substances or foods, and in the case of accidental pollution a deputy priest was appointed to take over his duties.[266] Such ancient Jewish ideas of ritual purity reappear in an emphatic form in the Lurianic Kabbalah. But although Luria was preoccupied with the idea of ritual defilement, and devised a series of penitential 'remedies' based on the expiatory rituals of the medieval *Hasidei Ashkenaz*,[267] he did not advocate permanent sexual abstinence, promulgating instead the Zoharic injunction to approach the marital act as an embodiment of cosmic union and a means of augmenting the 'likeness of God' in the world through children.[268]

Ascetic requirements also appear in medieval grimoires such as the *Clavicula*, echoing those in Jewish magical literature:

> Before commencing operations both the Master and his Disciples must abstain with great and thorough continence during the space of nine days from sensual pleasures and from vain and foolish conversation.[269]

Some grimoires, such as the *Lemegeton*, do not include preparatory rituals. This may be due to the fragmentary nature of extant manuscripts rather than a lack of recognition of the importance of such rituals before undertaking magical procedures. The *Ars Notoria* is endearingly lax in its instructions, merely stating: 'Let no man presume to say any of this *Oration* after too much drinking or Luxury'.[270] In contrast, the preparatory rituals presented in *Abramelin* are

---

Scholastic Magic, 153–72; Lesses, *Ritual Practices*, 117–60; Lesses, 'Speaking With Angels'.

[266] See Bloom, *Jewish Mysticism and Magic*, 155.

[267] For Luria's preoccupation with ritual purity, see Fine, *Physician*, 184–85.

[268] Fine, *Physician*, 196–98.

[269] Mathers (trans.), *Key of Solomon*, 15.

[270] Robert Turner (trans.), *Ars Notoria*, ed. Darcy Küntz (London: John Harrison, 1656; repr. Sequim, WA: Holmes Publishing Group, 2006), 18.

painfully arduous, and include six months of solitude, prayer, ablutions, and readings of Scripture.[271] Sexual abstinence is not required in the first two months, but during the remaining four months preceding the ritual, 'ye shall flee sexual intercourse as ye would the Plague'.[272]

The reasons for Mathers' choice of a celibate marriage may reflect both personal predilections and a complex interweaving of various esoteric, religious, and medical currents of the time. In the medical world of Victorian England, Richard von Krafft-Ebing's groundbreaking work on sexual pathology, *Psychopathia Sexualis*, published in 1886, was not translated into English until 1892, four years after Mathers' marriage.[273] But the scientific study of sexuality and its accompanying pathologies was already high on the Victorian intellectual agenda.[274] In the religious sphere, the English Tractarian movement of the mid-nineteenth century, inaugurated by John Henry Newman at Oxford, was still influential in the latter part of the century, and promulgated the idea of celibacy as 'a crucial measure of masculinity'. Mathers' preoccupation with war and military leadership probably rendered him particularly susceptible to such ideas.[275] For the Tractarians and their admirers, 'the degree of

---

[271] See Mathers (trans.), *Abramelin*, 64–80.

[272] Mathers (trans.), *Abramelin*, 66.

[273] Richard von Krafft-Ebing, *Psychopathia Sexualis, With Especial Reference to the Antipathic Sexual Instinct: A Medico-Forensic Study* (London: F. A. Davis, 1892).

[274] See, *inter alia*, Ivan Crozier, 'William Acton and the history of sexuality: the medical and professional context', *JVC* 5:1 (2000), 1–27; Robert Darby, *A Surgical Temptation: The Demonization of the Foreskin and the Rise of Circumcision in Britain* (Chicago: University of Chicago Press, 2005), 128–29, where Darby discusses the panic about masturbation in public schools in the late nineteenth century and highlights the 'insistence on the necessity for sexlessness in children and abstinence in young men'; Frank Mort, *Dangerous Sexualities: Medico-Moral Politics in England since 1830* (London: Routledge & Kegan Paul, 1987); Kelly Hurley, *The Gothic Body: Sexuality, Materialism, and Degeneration at the Fin de Siècle* (Cambridge: Cambridge University Press, 1997).

[275] For the early Victorian ideal of 'muscular celibacy', see Broughton, *Men of Letters*; Adams, *Dandies and Desert Saints*. Adams suggests (103) that celibacy 'could be described, as it had been in early Christian monasticism, as an eminently masculine and martial discipline'. On this theme and Newman's contribution to it, see also Linda C. Dowling, *Hellenism and Homosexuality in Victorian Oxford*

reserve and resolve needed to maintain the celibate life ensures that celibacy is a crucial measure of masculinity'.[276] In the esoteric sphere, the Theosophical Society, to which Mathers belonged, advocated a permanent state of celibacy for the 'higher initiate' because 'for those who wished to make significant occult progress, total abstinence from sexual relations was crucial'.[277] Mathers also had the example of Anna Kingsford, whom he greatly admired, and her celibate partnership with Edward Maitland; Kingsford, following the Theosophical precept, insisted that the adept who aspires to spiritual perfection should practice abstinence.[278] In the Rosicrucian *Fama Fraternitas* of 1614, the eight original followers of Christian Rosenkreutz are 'all batchelors and of vowed virginity',[279] and this esoteric offshoot of the Christian monastic tradition may also have influenced Mathers, who was devoted to Rosicrucian ideas and rituals. Moreover, celibate marriages were not uncommon in the occult milieux of the *fin-de-siècle*. Alan Leo (1860–1917), a Theosophist and one of the foremost astrologers of the early twentieth century, had, according to his wife Bessie, proposed to her with the condition that the marriage be celibate: 'I shall not deceive you, Bessie...I realise that I have a work to do for the world for which celibacy is essential, but I love you with all my heart and soul, and I know you could help me in the work'.[280] The Danish-American Rosicrucian Max Heindel (b. Carl Louis von Grasshof, 1865-1919), who, like Alan Leo, was a great admirer of Blavatsky, likewise practised celibacy within his marriage, asserting: 'It is regarded as a mark of merit when a pupil of the Western Mystery School marries and continues to live a life of chastity'.[281]

For Mina Bergson, the idea of a celibate marriage was directly opposed to the teachings of her Hasidic background. Although Jewish esoteric texts insist on 'ritual purity' before

---

(Ithaca, NY: Cornell University Press, 1994), especially Chapter 2, 'Victorian Manhood and the Warrior Ideal', 32–51; Claudia Nelson, 'Sex and the Single Boy: Ideals of Manliness and Sexuality in Victorian Literature for Boys', *VS* 32:4 (1989), 525–50.

[276] Duc Dau, 'Perfect Chastity: Celibacy and Virgin Marriage in Tractarian Poetry', *VP* 44:1 (2006), 77–92, on p. 78.

[277] Dixon, *Divine Feminine*, 106–07 and 171–73.

[278] Kingsford and Maitland, *Perfect Way*, 8.20, 223.

[279] Cited in Waite, *Real History*, 72.

[280] Leo, *The Life and Work of Alan Leo*, 65.

[281] Heindel, *Rosicrucian Cosmo-Conception*, 690.

any magical operation, celibacy as a lifelong commitment is not usually found in Jewish traditions.[282] The *Zohar* offers many references to the importance of sexual union within marriage as a mystical act, emphasising that Kabbalists 'should give their wives joy, for the sake of the honor due to the celestial union'.[283] Sexual union is also seen as the fulfilment of the commandment to procreate:

> One should engage in procreation, for whoever engages in procreation causes the river to flow continually, so that its waters never cease....Whoever refuses to procreate diminishes, as it were, the image that comprises all images, stops the waters of the river from flowing, and damages the holy covenant on all sides.[284]

In Hasidic literature, sexual union between a *zaddik* and his wife is a magical act performed ritualistically on the Sabbath and intended to invoke the presence of the Shekhinah, bless any offspring of the union, and generate harmony between the male and female principles on the supernal levels.[285] The Zoharic emphasis on conjugal love as a mystical path aroused considerable curiosity among occultists, and Waite devoted an entire chapter to it in *The Holy Kabbalah*.[286] Waite contrasted this Kabbalistic eroticism with the 'failure' of Roman Catholic orthodoxy to recognise that the sexual ideal presented in the *Zohar* 'stands for true and life-long consecration on the highest plane'.[287] While these ideas do

---

[282] See, for example, Swartz, '"Ministering Angels"', 135–67; Swartz, *Scholastic Magic*, 162–65. There are some exceptions to this general rule, possibly influenced by Gnostic and Christian traditions; see Wolfson, *Language, Eros, Being*, 299–332; Idel, *Kabbalah and Eros*, 223–32.

[283] *Zohar* I.49b–50a, cited in Tishby, *Wisdom of the Zohar*, 1398.

[284] *Zohar* I.12b–13a, cited in Tishby, *Wisdom of the Zohar*, 1382. For a discussion of sexual mysticism in the Lurianic Kabbalah, see Fine, *Physician*, 171–80, especially p. 172, where Fine comments: 'For the kabbalists, sexual relations between a wife and her husband represent corresponding dynamic processes within the divine realm. In addition to mirroring the life of God, sexual love is a theurgic rite that stimulates and facilitates love between the *sefirot Tiferet* and *Malkhut*'.

[285] For the mystical significance of sexual intercourse in Hasidism, see Idel, *Hasidism*, 97; for a lengthy discussion of this theme in early and modern Hasidism, see Wolfson, *Language, Eros, Being*, 296–332.

[286] See below, Chapter Five.

[287] Waite, *Holy Kabbalah*, 403–04.

not promulgate either lifelong celibacy or union with elementals, they emphasise the importance of the mystical and even occult dimensions of sexual relations. The Mathers' pledge to celibacy, whatever its sources, is not rooted in Jewish magical and mystical traditions, but it is possible that Jewish ideas of ritual purity, transmitted through the grimoires, combined with the perception of the sexual act as a mystical enactment of the sacred union of the supernal powers, enhanced an already entrenched belief in the efficacy of channelling sexual energies into occult pathways – even those involving close encounters of the elemental kind – rather than the pleasures of the marriage bed.

THE OCCULTISTS AND THE JEWISH SCHOLARS

In the last decade of the nineteenth century, a small group of Anglo-Jewish scholars began translating late antique Jewish magical texts into English. Some of these men had direct links with British occultists, and others indicate their awareness of the occultists' own translations of Kabbalistic and magical texts. Apart from the influence of Mina Bergson, and Westcott's involvement with the Ashkenazi community of north London, evidence of contact between the adepts of the Golden Dawn and Jewish Kabbalists is already apparent in the early years of the order's existence. John William Brodie-Innes (1848–1923), who joined the Golden Dawn in 1890 and wrote some of the order's Flying Rolls under the magical name 'Sub Spe',[288] states in the obituary he wrote for Mathers in 1919 that his first Hebrew teacher was 'a Rabbi and an advanced Kabbalist', to whom he showed Mathers' *Kabbalah Unveiled*. The anonymous rabbi, according to Brodie-Innes, declared that Mathers 'is a true Kabalist. Very few Gentiles know as much, you may follow him safely'.[289] William Alexander Ayton also provides evidence of direct involvement with Jewish Kabbalists. In a letter to Frederick Leigh Gardner written in 1889, he mentions 'Hainau', a rabbi to whom he offered funds to help with the publication of a

---

[288] See, for example, J. W. Brodie-Innes, 'Essay on Clairvoyance and Travelling in the Spirit Vision', Flying Roll XXV, in King (ed.), *Astral Projection*, 85–89; J. W. Brodie-Innes, 'Knowledge Lectures', in Küntz, (ed.), *Astrology of the Golden Dawn* (2005), 7–24.
[289] J. W. Brodie-Innes, 'MacGregor Mathers, some personal reminiscences', *OR* 29:5 (1919), 284–86.

Kabbalistic work.[290] Ayton also casually suggests that Gardner should find a 'Jew Qabalist' to help him with the exorcism of a frisky elemental; enlisting the intervention of 'Jew Qabalists' in difficult rituals was evidently an acceptable activity among Golden Dawn adepts.[291] Equally important is Ayton's long and fruitful relationship with 'my learned Jewish friend', the Austrian Jewish scholar Julius Kohn, who helped Ayton with translations of various alchemical and Kabbalistic texts. Discourse between Jewish scholars and Kabbalists and the adepts of the Golden Dawn and its splinter groups continued well into the twentieth century, as will be explored more fully below. The contributions of living Jewish Kabbalists, rabbis, and academics to late-nineteenth-century Freemasonry and Theosophy, and their sometimes close personal relationships with non-Jewish occult practitioners, are rarely mentioned in scholarly literature, and have never been explored as an important factor in the development of the theoretical and practical dimensions of the Kabbalah in the British occult revival.

Jewish commentaries on the Kabbalah and on late antique Jewish magical texts began appearing in English and American scholarly journals in the last decade of the nineteenth century.[292] This cannot be coincidental, and suggests that the occult revival was not a purely Christian affair. Jewish scholars understood well enough that their religious heritage was being appropriated by non-Jews, and that they needed to begin research into this heritage themselves, rather than following the scholars of the *Wissenschaft des Judentums* in dismissing the Kabbalah and Jewish magic as unworthy of serious study. 'Why should not the Cabbalists be treated with the same respect, with the same deference, by the Jews?' asks Samuel Abraham Hirsch in a paper on Jewish mysticism published in 1890.[293] These

---

[290] See Howe (ed.), *Alchemist*, 43 and 45. The identity of the mysterious 'Rabbi Hainau' and the title of his book remain unknown.

[291] William Alexander Ayton, letter to Frederick Leigh Gardner (30 December 1892), in Howe (ed.), *Alchemist*, 73–74.

[292] See, for example, Samuel Abraham Hirsch, 'Jewish Philosophy of Religion and Samson Raphael Hirsch', *JQR* 2:2 (1890), 109–38; A. Neubauer, 'The *Bahir* and the *Zohar*', *JQR* 4:3 (1892), 357–68.

[293] Hirsch, 'Jewish Philosophy of Religion', 177. See also Samuel Abraham Hirsch, 'Jewish Mystics: An Appreciation', *JQR* 20:1

Anglo-Jewish scholars did not eschew reading occultist literature; Hermann Gollancz, in the introduction to his translation of the *Clavicula*, refers to Mathers' earlier introduction and translation of the work.[294] British occultists also read the papers in journals such as the *Jewish Quarterly Review*.[295] Jewish Theosophists such as Bosman and Myer had been demonstrating an involvement in occultism from the time of the foundation of the Theosophical Society in 1875.[296] The Jewish press invariably reviewed works such as Mathers' *The Kabbalah Unveiled*, although the reviews were not always complimentary; and Westcott's cordial relationship with the editor of the *Jewish Chronicle* emphasises the ongoing exchange between the Jewish community and individual occult practitioners, despite the growing climate of antisemitism in British society at the turn of the century.

Jews who had abandoned the more orthodox elements of their faith joined organisations such as the Theosophical Society and various Masonic lodges, but still considered themselves Jews, and the Kabbalah which they discussed with and taught to non-Jewish occultists was the Jewish Kabbalah. The rise of 'Orientalism' at the end of the nineteenth century the growing interest in all things belonging to 'the East', in which the Holy Land held a place of special distinction – encouraged these Jews to take pride in the mystical and magical elements of their heritage.[297] The

---

(1907), 50–73, where Hirsch emphasises even more strongly the importance and value of the Kabbalistic tradition within Judaism.

[294] Gollancz, *Sepher Maphteah Shelomoh*, ii.

[295] See, for example, Waite, *Holy Kabbalah*, 45, n. 3, on the papers on the *Sefer Yetsirah* published in *JQR* by the American Jewish Hebraist Phineas Mordell. See also Waite, *Shadows*, 235, for his delight when *The Holy Kabbalah* was reviewed favourably by Gershom Scholem in *The Times Literary Supplement* and praised in *The Jewish Chronicle*.

[296] For Bosman and Myer, see Chapter Three. For more on Jewish involvement in Theosophy, see Huss, 'Sufis from America'.

[297] For Orientalism and its impact on European Jews, see Arieh Bruce Saposnik, 'Europe and Its Orients in Zionist Culture Before the First World War', *HJ* 49:4 (2006), 1105–23; Paul Mendes-Flohr, 'Fin de Siècle Orientalism, the *Ostjuden*, and the aesthetics of Jewish self-affirmation', in Mendes-Flohr, *Divided Passions*, 77–132; Edward Said, *Orientalism* (New York: Pantheon, 1978); Richard King, *Orientalism and Religion: Postcolonial Theory, India, and 'The Mystic East'* (London: Routledge, 1999).

importance of this cross-fertilisation between Jewish and non-Jewish occultists and esotericists has been underestimated or entirely ignored in current scholarly literature. The contribution of British Jews as teachers, authors, translators, and commentators on the Kabbalah and the various proto-Kabbalistic currents of Jewish magic from late antiquity demonstrates the serious oversight inherent in any assumption that the development of Western esotericism – and its flowering in the occult revival of the late nineteenth and early twentieth centuries – was ever a purely, or even predominantly, Christian current.

One of the most important scholars involved in translations of Jewish magical literature was Rabbi Moses Gaster (1856–1939), a highly colourful figure in the Jewish scholarly community of the late nineteenth and early twentieth centuries. Born in Roumania, he emigrated to Britain in 1885, and became a lecturer in Slavonic literature at Oxford in the following year. Eugene C. Black notes that Gaster

> ...complained about everything and quarreled with almost everyone. From an institutional perspective, he proved at best a nuisance and at worst a major hazard to those causes into which he flung himself with such abandon. Yet Gaster was English Zionist leadership writ large: substantial talent, excessive ego, and a predilection for quarrelsomeness.[298]

Gaster's public persona was that of a religious Jew who fought fiercely in the cause of political Zionism. However, he revealed his esoteric proclivities early in his career in a paper on the Kabbalah, published in 1894 as an addendum to the annual report for the Judith 'Montefiore' College for rabbinical training at Ramsgate.[299] Gaster's theory that Gnostic doctrines were closely related to the Jewish Kabbalah,[300] postulated first by Agrippa and later by Lévi,[301]

---

[298] Eugene C. Black, 'A Typological Study of English Zionists', *JSS* 9:3 (2003), 20–55, on p. 20. For biographical information on Gaster, see Leon Volovici, 'A Jewish European Modern Intellectual', *EEJA* 28:2 (1998–1999), 109–11; Bruno Schindler (ed.), *Gaster Centenary Publication* (London: Lund Humphries, 1958); Sona Rosa Burstein, 'Moses Gaster and Folklore', *Folklore* 68:1 (1957), 288–90.

[299] See above, n. 48.

[300] Gaster, 'Origin of the Kabbalah', 17, 24, 27–28.

exercised considerable influence on Gershom Scholem three decades later when Scholem first promulgated his theories of Gnostic elements in Jewish mysticism – although Scholem constantly criticises Gaster's methodology and demeans his credibility as a scholar.[302] Gaster's paper also poses a challenge to Scholem's declaration that Jewish scholars in the late nineteenth and early twentieth centuries had 'abandoned' the Kabbalah, leaving the field open for 'all manner of charlatans' such as Lévi and Crowley.[303] Gaster is a fine example of an important late-nineteenth-century scholar who viewed the Kabbalah as a vital aspect of Judaism, and the pamphlet to which his paper is amended demonstrates that the Kabbalah in general, and the *Zohar* in particular, were primary subjects in the courses of study offered for rabbinical training in Britain as early as 1893.

Gaster's essay was published a few years after Westcott produced his first papers on the Kabbalah, and there seems to be no evidence that either Westcott or Mathers ever read the essay, which was an 'in-house' publication prepared for the Judith 'Montefiore' College. But Gaster may well have read works by Westcott and Mathers. In 1896, less than a decade after Mathers began publishing medieval grimoires in English, Gaster produced his first translation of a late antique Jewish magical text: the *Harbe de Moshe*. It is likely that Gaster began to exercise influence on the occult community through this work, long before he became closely involved with the Theosophist G. R. S. Mead (1863–1933) and the Golden Dawn adept E. J. Langford Garstin in the first decades of the twentieth century.[304] It is also likely that

---

[301] For Agrippa's statement, see Agrippa, *Occult Philosophy*, 702. For Lévi's statement, probably inspired by Agrippa, see Lévi, *Histoire*, 217.

[302] For Scholem's hypothesis, see Gershom Scholem, *Das Buch Bahir. Ein Schriftdenkmal aus der Frühzeit der Kabbala auf Grund der kritischen Neuausgabe* (Leipzig: W. Drugulin, 1923); Scholem, *Jewish Gnosticism*, 65–74. For Scholem's criticisms of Gaster, see Scholem, *Major Trends*, 65; 170; 365, n. 90; 390, n. 70.

[303] See Scholem, *Major Trends*, 2.

[304] For further work by Gaster on Jewish magic, see Gaster, 'Wisdom of the Chaldeans'; Moses Gaster, 'Conjurations and the Ancient Mysteries', Presidential Address to The Search Society 1931–32 (London: The Search Publishing Co., 1932); 'The Logos Ebraikos in the Magical Papyrus of Paris, and the Book of Enoch', *JRAS* 33 (1901), 109–17, repr. in Gaster, *Studies and Texts*, 1:356–64.

Gaster's own enthusiasm for publishing texts on Jewish magic was fuelled, at least in part, by the commentaries and English translations of the *Sefer Yetsirah*, the *Zohar*, and the grimoires provided by Westcott and Mathers.

Gaster's involvement with Mead is mentioned briefly by Ithell Colquhoun, who notes the presence of 'Dr. Moses Gaster, the eminent Hebraist' at meetings of Mead's Quest Society, and comments that 'whispers of black magic' were circulating around certain 'unspecified' members of the society who seemed to belong to some other, hidden occult group.[305] Gaster offered frequent lectures to the Quest Society on such themes as 'A Gnostic Text in the *Zohar*',[306] and recommended books to its members such as Westcott's publication of the *Aesch Mezareph* and Mathers' *Kabbalah Unveiled* – 'the kind of thing the initiates studied'.[307] Gaster's relationship with Mead is briefly mentioned by his son Theodore in the introduction to a collection of Gaster's essays published between 1925 and 1928, but Theodore Gaster was clearly embarrassed by his father's relationship with such a peculiar individual and comments dismissively that Mead 'even enveigled my father into attending a couple of séances'.[308] Gaster's private correspondence with Mead contradicts this statement, and reveals that the two men enjoyed a close and mutually admiring friendship for at least a decade.[309] They met regularly to read each other's manuscripts and discuss topics ranging from the Kabbalah and Gnostic doctrines to the philosophy of Henri Bergson and the psychology of C. G. Jung, and they clearly attempted magical work together. In one letter, Mead calls Gaster his 'Magus and Praemonstrator Cabbalae'.[310] Gaster also

---

[305] Colqhoun, *Sword*, 16.

[306] Moses Gaster, 'A Gnostic Text in the *Zohar*', paper given to the Quest Society (8 February 1923), repr. in Gaster, *Studies and Texts*, 1:369–86.

[307] Colquhoun, *Sword*, 18.

[308] Theodore Gaster, 'Prolegomenon', in Gaster, *Studies and Texts*, 1:xv–xxxix, on p. xxxvii.

[309] All letters referred to below are from *The Gaster papers: a collection of letters, documents, etc. of the late Haham Dr. Moses Gaster (1856–1939)*, compiled by Trude Levi (London: The Library, University College London, 1976, 30217017796628). The correspondence between Gaster and Mead covers the period from 1922 to 1932.

[310] Document 36/456, dated 10 February 1928. For more on Mead, see Clare Goodrick-Clarke and Nicholas Goodrick-Clarke (eds.), *G. R. S. Mead and the Gnostic Quest* (Berkeley, CA: North Atlantic

provided financial support, purchasing shares in Mead's short-lived Quest Publishing Company.[311] Through Mead, Gaster met Garstin, a member of the Golden Dawn splinter group known as the Stella Matutina. Garstin was a Kabbalistic scholar and an alchemist who loyally followed Mathers' teachings in his own published works,[312] and Gaster later provided financial as well as intellectual support for Garstin's newly created Search Society, becoming its President in 1931. Gaster, whose commentaries on and translations of early Hebrew magical works are still quoted in scholarly texts,[313] was only one among many Jews involved with the Kabbalistic currents in British occultism. His involvement is demonstrable because his scholarly prominence ensured that his private correspondence was preserved. Some of these Jews, like the mysterious 'Rabbi Hainau' mentioned by Ayton, may never be identified. Some Jewish academics of the period, such as Hirsch, were sympathetically inclined toward the Kabbalah and Jewish magic but have left no record of any discourse with occultists, nor are their names mentioned in the extant correspondence of the occultists themselves. This does not mean there was no discourse, only that no evidence of any discourse has been found.

Other Jews predisposed to occultism have left signs of their involvement in less reputable ways. Julius Kohn, William Alexander Ayton's 'learned Jewish friend',[314]

Books, 2005), which includes a complete bibliography of Mead's published works.
[311] Document 47/439, dated 22 September 1926. Gaster purchased ten '5% non-cumulative preference shares'.
[312] For biographical information on Garstin, see Edward Dunning, 'Foreward', in Garstin, *Theurgy*, v–xvi; Colquhoun, *Sword*, 17–22.
[313] See, for example, Bohak, *Ancient Jewish Magic*, 175, n. 81.
[314] Ayton's first mention of Julius Kohn is in a letter to Frederick Leigh Gardner, 3 April 1894, cited in Howe (ed.), *Alchemist*, 76–77, in which Ayton also comments on Mina Bergson being 'of Jewish extraction'. Ayton eventually introduced Kohn to Gardner, but there seems to be no extant documentation on further contact between these latter two occultists. Ellic Howe (*Alchemist*, 77) states that 'it has not been possible to discover anything about Kohn's life', but he emphasises the 'traffic in manuscripts' between Ayton, Kohn, and Percy Bullock, another Golden Dawn adept, suggesting that Kohn, although not a member of the Golden Dawn, had close communication with several of the order's members. That Gardner himself was from a Jewish background is implied by Howe, who,

appears to have trained with Joseph Wallace, a mesmerist and healer who, like Kohn himself, managed to offend Blavatsky with his 'glaring misconceptions and most ridiculously incorrect statements', thus earning himself one of her vituperative diatribes.[315] Kohn himself spent a brief period in the Theosophical Society and either left abruptly of his own volition or was expelled. In 1881 he began an ongoing battle with Blavatsky through occult journals such as *The Spiritualist*, declaring that Blavatsky was ignorant of the Kabbalah and 'evidently knows nothing of our art'.[316] Blavatsky in turn used her own journal, *The Theosophist*, to attack not only Kohn's views on the Kabbalah but also his character and his Jewishness.[317] Kohn remained bitter toward

---

referring to Ayton's letter about the unnamed female Golden Dawn member who was 'of Jewish extraction', notes that this could not apply to Gardner's wife as she never joined the Golden Dawn, and that the letter therefore must refer to Mina Mathers (Howe, *Magicians*, 77). In October 1886, Gardner joined one of the 'Jewish' Masonic lodges, Montefiore Lodge No. 1017 (see Howe, *Magicians*, 14), which, according to the history provided by the Israeli Montefiore Lodge, was founded by English Jewish Freemasons in 1864; see www.freemasons-freemasonry.com/montef.html.

[315] H. P Blavatsky, 'Mr. Joseph Wallace', *Theosophist* 3 (March 1882), 6–7, repr. in Blavatsky, CW4, 44–48. For Wallace's healing activities, see Owen, *Darkened Room*, 125–27 and 134–37.

[316] Cited in H. P. Blavatsky, 'Editorial', *Theosophist* 4:2 (1882), 43.

[317] See Blavatsky, 'Editorial', *Theosophist* 4:2 (1882), 43. In this article, Blavatsky comments that Kohn's article for the spiritualist journal *Medium and Daybreak* (2 September 1881), entitled 'The Adeptship of Jesus Christ', 'would be received, most likely, with cheerful welcome in those [columns] of a third-class Jewish, Russophobic organ in Germany'. Kohn appears to have not only insulted Theosophy's Indian predilections, but also suggested that the Russian-born Blavatsky had a political agenda which included Russian involvement in India. In 'Western "Adepts" and Eastern Theosophists', *The Theosophist Supplement* 3:2 (1881), 334, Blavatsky declares that 'Mr. Julius Kohn is a very conceited, vain, young gentleman, who, hardly weaned from the A.B.C. of Occultism, puts on the airs of a mysterious grand adept...There is no Kabbalistic organ, and even the third-class London Weeklies, but would throw his articles in the waste basket'. She also describes him (H. P. Blavatsky, 'Stray Thoughts on Death and Satan', *Theosophist* 3:1, 1881, 12) as 'the illustrious Jewish Kabalist who, like a bashful violet, hides his occult learning under two modest initials' (Kohn habitually signed his work 'J.K.'). Her contempt for Kohn fuses with, or is fuelled by, her contempt for the Jews: in yet another

the Theosophical Society long after Blavatsky's death, and in an unpublished satire called *The Secret of Anaxagoras*, he mocks the Theosophical hopes of a new World Teacher and calls the members of the society 'Gymnosophists'.[318] In this work, Kohn shows as much contempt for his less educated Jewish compatriots as he does for the Theosophists, and mocks the Yiddish accents of the East End immigrant Ashkenazi Jews, although he emigrated to Britain from Austria and was probably of Ashkenazi ancestry himself. But despite his disaste toward Theosophy, he exhibits no antagonism toward the Golden Dawn, and was happy to work with Ayton. He seems to have been familiar with Mathers' now vanished treatise on the alchemical work *Splendor Solis*; in his own translation of this work, Kohn refers to the relationship discussed by Mathers between the twenty-two alchemical plates of the *Splendor Solis* and the twenty-two Major Arcana of the Tarot.[319] Kohn represents a particular kind of heterodox Jewish scholar working within the world of British occultism in the late nineteenth century, holding himself aloof from both the academic establishment and the Jewish community but deeply involved in the magical lore of his heritage.

Other Jewish scholars have left documentary evidence of their involvement with occultists. Joshua Abelson (1873–1940), the principal of Aria College at Portsmouth, who wrote the introduction to the English translation of the *Zohar*

---

diatribe published in *The Spiritualist* (12 August 1881), Blavatsky declares: 'J.K. seems to be superbly ignorant even of the enormous difference which exists between a Kabbalist and an Occultist. Is he aware, or not, that the Kabbalist stands, in relation to the Occultist, as a little detached hill at the foot of the Himalayas, to Mount Everest? That what is known as the Jewish Kabbala of Simon Ben Jochai, is already the disfigured version of its primitive source, the Great Chaldean *Book of Numbers?*'

[318] Julius Kohn, *The Secret of Anaxagoras: A Great Mystery, Revealed by J. K.* (unpublished manuscript, no date; Wellcome Institute Historical Medical Library MS 3125), 10–11 and 14. That this diatribe postdates Blavatsky's death is clear from the reference to the new World Teacher, an idea which arose under Blavatsky's successor, Annie Besant.

[319] See above, Chapter Three.

published in 1934,[320] did not enjoy Gaster's academic prestige, but he published several important works on Jewish esoteric lore and contributed regular articles on the subject to *The Jewish Chronicle*.[321] Abelson's *The Immanance of God in Rabbinical Literature* postulates that the rabbis of the Talmudic period adopted a practical mysticism (or a magical world-view) which acknowledges the power of the human soul to commune with an immanent God.[322] Abelson's *Jewish Mysticism*, an exegesis of the Kabbalah, was the third volume of the 'Quest Series' edited by G. R. S. Mead, who wrote the Editor's Preface to the book. The contact between these two men probably occurred through Abelson's involvement with the Theosophical Society (in which Mead served for a time as Blavatsky's secretary), and emphasises not only the willingness of Jewish scholars to concern themselves with occultism, but the willingness of occultists such as Mead to avail themselves of the knowledge of Jewish scholars.

Abelson was closely allied with the Theosophical Society in the early decades of the twentieth century, lecturing frequently to their lodges and contributing papers to their journals.[323] Abelson also wrote a sympathetic review of Dion Fortune's *The Mystical Qabalah* for *The Jewish Chronicle*, declaring that the work 'possesses qualities which will attract

---

[320] Joshua Abelson, 'Introduction', in Harry Sperling and Maurice Simon (trans.), *The Zohar*, 5 vols. (New York/London: Soncino Press, 1934), 1:ix–xxx.

[321] See, for example, Joshua Abelson, *Jewish Mysticism: An Introduction to the Kabbalah* (London: G. Bell & Sons, 1913). Other works by Abelson include 'Jewish Magic', in *The Friday Night Book: A Jewish Miscellany* (London: Soncino Press, 1933), 45–69; 'Occult Thought in Jewish Literature', *The Jewish Chronicle Supplement* (28 January 1921), v–vi; and 'A Garment of Divers Sorts', *The Jewish Chronicle Supplement* (25 August 1922), v–vi, in which Abelson quotes Lévi's definition of magic as 'the exercise of a power which is natural but superior to the ordinary powers of Nature'. Abelson also produced a short essay on Maimonides (Joshua Abelson, 'Maimonides on the Jewish Creed', *JQR* 19:1 (1906), 24–58) which, while presenting clearly and simply the major points of Maimonidean philosophy, tends to endow the thirteenth-century sage with a greater involvement in mysticism than he seems to have possessed.

[322] Joshua Abelson, *The Immance of God in Rabbinical Literature* (London: Macmillan, 1912; repr. New York: Hermon Press, 1969).

[323] See, for example, Joshua Abelson, 'The Talmud and Theosophy', *TR* 37:1 (1905), 9–27.

others besides technical students of the occult', and highlighting her skillful application of the complexities of the *Sefer Yetsirah* to the 'Practical Kabbalah'.[324] In addition to reviewing Fortune's *Mystical Qabalah*, Abelson also reviewed Israel Regardie's influential work, *The Tree of Life: A Study in Magic*.[325] Regardie was then a member of the Golden Dawn splinter group Stella Matutina. Abelson first points out Regardie's predilection for the Lurianic Kabbalah, and then comments: 'But what is most arresting to the Jewish reader is the dominating position assigned to the medieval Cabbalah in the whole variegated and complicated sphere of esoteric thought in all its developments, both medieval and modern'.[326] This statement by an early twentieth-century Jewish scholar challenges directly some current assumptions that the development of Western esoteric thought is a purely Christian affair. Abelson assigned himself the difficult role of mediating between the Jewish community and the world of British occultism at a time when antisemitic feeling was growing in intensity in the decades before and after the First World War.[327] This role earned him the overt hostility of his

---

[324] Joshua Abelson, 'Review of Dion Fortune, *The Mystical Qabalah*', *JC* (24 May 1935), 26.

[325] Israel Regardie, *The Tree of Life: A Study in Magic* (London: Rider, 1932).

[326] Joshua Abelson, 'Review of Israel Regardie, *The Tree of Life*', *The Jewish Chronicle* (12 May 1933), 21.

[327] For an example of antisemitic literature in the early twentieth century, see Joseph Banister, *England under the Jews* (London: private publication, 1901; repr. Boston, MA: Adamant Media Corporation, 2001). Banister was obsessed with the 'alien immigration plague', the encroaching swarm of 'Asiatic invaders', and the 'semitic sewage' spilling into Britain; for more on Banister, see Holmes, *Anti-Semitism*, 39–42. For more on antisemitism during this period, see Paul Knepper, 'British Jews and the Racialisation of Crime in the Age of Empire', *BJC* 47 (2007), 61–79; Feldman, *Englishmen and Jews*, 353–78; Holmes, *Anti-Semitism*, 89–120. A number of complex factors fed the swelling currents of antisemitism in Britain in the first decades of the twentieth century. The British Brothers League, established in 1901, agitated vociferously against Jewish immigration between 1901 and 1905. The agitation of the British Brothers League and its wide and influential circle of followers led directly to the Aliens Act of 1905, brought into force after the general election of January 1906, which restricted the flow of immigrants into Britain and attempted to isolate those who were 'genuine' refugees from those who were simply seeking a better life. The Act, which was motivated largely by the growing numbers of

more orthodox fellows. A journalist writing for *The Jewish Chronicle* under the name 'Mentor' castigates him for taking 'dangerous risks' in lecturing to Theosophical lodges,[328] and declares that the Theosophical Society is 'an institution inimical to Judaism'.[329]

Some Jewish scholars, unlike Abelson, found the occultists' efforts to understand and utilise the Kabbalah entirely distasteful. Phineas Mordell, an American Jewish

---

Jewish refugees attempting to enter Britain following the new pogroms in Russia and Eastern Europe accompanying the Russian counter-revolution, provoked a furious battle in Parliament and in the press. The Act required immigrants to demonstrate that they could support themselves and their dependents 'decently' – a condition often impossible for the poorest immigrant Jews to meet – and allowed asylum only for those seeking to evade persecution because of religious beliefs, excluding those whose property or liberty was endangered for more general reasons. Immigrants could be expelled if they were found living in overcrowded conditions, which was the case in the poorest areas of London's East End. The Aliens Act stimulated already rampant fears of 'alien crime', and the Conservative press drew a frightening picture of a country overrun by dangerous Jewish criminals and political anarchists; on this theme see Knepper, 'British Jews'. The Aliens Defence Committee was organised by East End Jews in 1911 as a response to the general rise in antisemitism, and attempted to lobby the government to counter the threat of new legislation aimed against alien Jews. For the Aliens Act and its causes and consequences, see Feldman, *Englishmen and Jews*, 353–78; Holmes, *Anti-Semitism*, 89–120. The First World War brought its own specific form of nationalism, and antisemitism during this period was fuelled by the fact that many Jewish immigrants had not been naturalised and were still technically German or Russian citizens; and many of those who had become part of the British social fabric were known to have German origins. For antisemitism during the First World War, see Holmes, *Anti-Semitism*, 121–40. For antisemitism between the wars, see Thomas P. Linehan, *British Fascism, 1918–1939: Parties, Ideology and Culture* (Manchester: Manchester University Press, 2000). By the 1920s the *Protocols of the Elders of Zion* had appeared in Britain, and conspiracy theories about Jewish world domination had begun to take root; see the discussion in Chapter Six. It is against this background that Joshua Abelson attempted to create a dialogue between liberal Jews and the non-Jewish esoteric and occult groups with which he was involved, using the Kabbalah as a potential bridge.

[328] 'Mentor', 'Missions to Jews', *JC* (25 March 1927), 13.
[329] 'Mentor', 'Two Matters', *JC* (24 February 1928), 9.

Hebraist of a more rationalist persuasion, reviewed a translation of the *Sefer Yetsirah* produced by Knut Stenring with an introduction by Waite, and damned Stenring's efforts by attacking his poor grasp of Hebrew and contemptuously dismissing his expressed belief in a 'secret' hidden in this enigmatic Hebrew work.[330] While this type of animosity was common enough in Jewish circles influenced by the *Wissenschaft des Judentums*, equally common was a lively interest in, and a willingness to support and supplement, the efforts of British occultists to understand the Jewish Kabbalah and the traditions of Jewish magic.

THE KABBALAH ACCORDING TO S. L. MACGREGOR MATHERS

Mathers' fertile correlations between the *sefirot*, angels, colours, metals, planets, zodiacal signs, Hebrew letters, Divine Names, and Tarot cards appear to support Egil Asprem's assertion that, in the British occult revival, the Kabbalah was divorced from its roots and recreated as a kind of mnemonic grid into which all knowledge could be 'programmatically syncretised' through elaborate chains of correspondences.[331] Mathers certainly utilised the sefirotic Tree as an all-inclusive symbolic system, and incorporated its correspondences in his rituals and in the grades and initiation ceremonies of the Golden Dawn.[332] But his large and fragmented corpus of writing – including his introductory notes for *The Kabbalah Unveiled*, introductions to his translations of the grimoires, Golden Dawn Flying Rolls and Knowledge Lectures, papers given to the occult societies to which he belonged, and contributions to various occult journals – reflects a more complex understanding of the Kabbalah which is closely bound to the theories and practices of late antique and medieval Jewish magic, understood by late Victorian occultists and Renaissance Hermeticists, as

---

[330] Phineas Mordell, 'Review: Notes on the *Sefer Yezirah*', *JQR* 19:1 (1928), 79–80. For other publications by Mordell, see Phineas Mordell, *The Origins of the Letters and Numerals According to the Sefer Yetzirah* (Philadelphia, PA: Dropsie College, 1914; repr. New York: Samuel Weiser Inc., 1975); Phineas Mordell, 'The Beginning and Development of Hebrew Punctuation', *JQR* 24:2 (1933), 137–49.

[331] Asprem, *'Kabbalah Recreata'*, 133, 141–42.

[332] For the Kabbalistic grade structure of the Golden Dawn and its planetary and sefirotic correspondences, see Greer, *Women*, 59.

well as medieval and modern Jews, to constitute 'practical'
Kabbalah.[333] Mathers believed in powers and potencies,
angelic and demonic entities, and an unknowable and all-
encompassing divine being whose emanated manifestations
could be invoked through ritual magic. Although he
understood these supernal beings to be interior, he also
acknowledged their objective existence; and his use of the
scientific jargon of the day, like Westcott's, reflects a blend of
religiosity and science that was not unfamiliar to either
medieval Kabbalists or late antique Jewish magicians.
Although Mathers deemed the Kabbalah to be the best
symbolic exegesis of the hidden unity of the diverse levels of
reality, it was more than a mere classification system; it was
for him, as it had always been for Jewish Kabbalists, a path to
gnosis and a method of self-transformation. The use of its
symbolism as a means of ordering and manipulating the
phenomena of creation is itself an ancient Jewish practice
which can be found in the *Sefer Yetsirah* and later texts such
as the *Aesch Mezareph*. The 'modernity' of Mathers' Kabbalah
and the 'newness' of the magical rituals of the Golden Dawn
may, in the words of Mark Twain, be 'greatly exaggerated'.

In 1903, the Hermetic Order of the Golden Dawn
imploded. After William Robert Woodman, one of its three
founding Chiefs, died in 1891, Westcott and Mathers began
to travel on a collision course which eventually divided the
adepts into violently warring factions.[334] Westcott became
Supreme Magus of the SRIA, while Mathers and his wife
took over the Inner Order of the Golden Dawn and moved to
Paris in the same year that Woodman died. The order
eventually split apart, divided into those few who were loyal
to Mathers and those (the majority of the adepts of the Inner
Order) who either opposed his autocratic behaviour or, like
Waite, wanted less magic and more mysticism.[335] By 1915 a
half-dozen offshoots had formed from the wreckage of the
original order, of which three – Waite's Fellowship of the
Rosy Cross, J. W. Brodie-Innes' Stella Matutina, whose best-

---

[333] See Abelson's praise of Fortune's understanding of 'Practical
Kabbalah' in his review of her book, above, n. 244.
[334] For the progressive deterioration of relations between Westcott
and Mathers, see Howe, *Magicians*, 165–70; Gilbert, *Scrapbook*, 79–92;
Harper, *Yeats's Golden Dawn*, 12.
[335] For Yeats' opposition to Mathers' policies, see Harper, *Yeats's
Golden Dawn*, 259–68. For Waite's opposition to the magical rituals,
see Chapter Five.

known adept was Dion Fortune, and Aleister Crowley's
Ordo Templi Orientis – have continued to exercise a
powerful influence on occult currents in Britain into the
twenty-first century.[336] While Waite pursued the path of what
he understood as 'Christian mysticism',[337] the Stella Matutina
retained the doctrines and spirit of the original order,
complete with its Kabbalistic framework and a corps of
'Secret Chiefs' comprised of disincarnate Arab magicians and
Jewish *maggidim*.[338] Meanwhile, Crowley, who had been
initiated into the Golden Dawn in the autumn of 1898 and
was expelled by Mathers in 1905, established a chapter of the
German-based Ordo Templi Orientis in Britain in 1902, using
his journal, *Equinox*, as its mouthpiece. Crowley's order
positioned itself wildly right of the Stella Matutina and in
bitter opposition to Waite's Fellowship of the Rosy Cross.[339]
The development of the Kabbalah in the occult revival of the
early twentieth century followed the widely diverging paths
of these three important figures – Arthur Edward Waite the
mystic, Aleister Crowley the magician, and Dion Fortune the
psychologist – as it emerged in both new and familiar forms
in the new century.

[336] For the history of these orders, see Chapters Five and Six.
[337] For Waite's Christian mysticism, see Chapter Five.
[338] See Gilbert, *Scrapbook*, 186; R. A. Gilbert, *A. E. Waite: Magician of Many Parts* (Wellingborough: Crucible, 1987), 120–21.
[339] For Crowley and his magical order, see Chapter Five.

CHAPTER FIVE

ARTHWAIT AND THE BEAST:
MYSTICISM AND SEXUAL 'MAGICK'
IN BRITISH OCCULTISM

> In the state of Ecstatic Absorption, man, united to his Spirit, obtains divine knowledge immediately....Herein is the true healing; the man is made one with himself in a celestial harmony.[1]
>
> – A. E. Waite (1893)

> There is a single main definition of the object of all magical Ritual. It is the uniting of the Microcosm with the Macrocosm. The Supreme and Complete Ritual is therefore the Invocation of the Holy Guardian Angel; or, in the language of Mysticism, Union with God.[2]
>
> – Aleister Crowley (1929)

THE MYSTIC AND THE MAGUS

In 1929, as Britain teetered on the edge of the global economic disaster known as the Great Depression, Aleister Crowley (1875–1947) published a wickedly satirical novel about the creation of a child whose body is intended to house an elemental spirit from the realm of the Moon.[3] *Moonchild*

---

[1] A. E. Waite, *Azoth or The Star in the East* (London: Theosophical Publishing Society, 1893; repr. Secaucus, NJ: University Books, 1973), 203.

[2] Crowley, *Magick*, 11.

[3] Aleister Crowley, *Moonchild* (London: Mandrake Press, 1929; repr. New York: Samuel Weiser Inc., 1970). Crowley is probably the most famous figure of the British occult revival, and literature on his life and work is extensive and still growing. For recent biographies, see Booth, *A Magick Life*; Lawrence Sutin, *Do What Thou Wilt: A Life of Aleister Crowley* (New York: St. Martin's Press, 2000); Kaczynski, *Perdurabo*. These works are reviewed with a detailed discussion by Pasi in 'Neverendingly Told Story'. Other biographies include Symonds, *The Great Beast*; Gerald Suster, *The Legacy of the Beast: The Life, Work and Influence of Aleister Crowley* (London: Whallen, 1988); Roger Hutchinson, *Aleister Crowley: The Beast Demystified*

introduces Crowley's readership to an unprepossessing character called Edwin Arthwait, a 'dull and inaccurate pedant without imagination or real magical perception'.[4] An initiate of a lodge of 'black' magicians whom Crowley gleefully modelled on the adepts of the Golden Dawn,[5]

(Edinburgh: Mainstream Publishing, 1998). For papers on Crowley's magic, see Owen, 'Sorcerer and His Apprentice'; Urban, 'Unleashing the Beast'; van Kleeck, 'The Art of the Law'; Asprem, 'Magic Naturalized?'; J. F. Brown, 'Aleister Crowley's "Rites of Eleusis"', *DR* 22:2 (1978), 3–26. A number of scholarly works include chapters or lengthy sections on Crowley; see Hutton, *Triumph of the Moon*, 171–81; Hugh B. Urban, *Magia Sexualis*, 109–39; Urban, 'Yoga of Sex'; Owen, *Place of Enchantment*, 186–220. For Crowley's political persuasions, see Marco Pasi, *Aleister Crowley und die Versuchung der Politik*, trans. Ferdinand Leopold (Graz: Ares Verlag, 2006), and the review of this work by Kocku von Stuckrad in *Pomegranate* 9:2 (2007), 194–96. On Crowley's continuing influence, von Stuckrad comments (194–95): 'Crowley's influence is also felt in the intellectual and religious history of the twentieth century, which makes him an important representative of modern forms of religious expression'. Crowley published his first book of verse in 1898, while still an undergraduate at Trinity College: *Aceldama, A Place to Bury Strangers in* (London: Mandrake Press, 1898). This was followed in the same year by *White Stains* (Amsterdam: Leonard Smithers, 1898), a collection which caused considerable offence and which Crowley states was intended to 'confute' Krafft-Ebing's attribution of 'sexual aberrations' to physiological disease in his *Psychopathia Sexualis* (see Crowley, *Confessions*, 127).

[4] Crowley, *Moonchild*, 151.

[5] Many of the important figures in the Golden Dawn are readily recognisable in *Moonchild* under thinly disguised names. Most of these were deceased by the time Crowley published the novel in 1929; the exception is Waite ('Arthwait'), who was still alive at the time *Moonchild* was written; he died in 1942. The fact that Waite might have been offended by the caricature of 'Arthwait' no doubt provided Crowley with considerable satisfaction. Westcott, who died in 1925, is transformed in *Moonchild* into 'Dr. Victor Vesquit', 'the most famous necromancer of his age', who had 'obtained an appointment as coroner in the most murderous district of London'; there was 'really little harm in the man beyond his extraordinary perversion in the matter of corpses' (Crowley, *Moonchild*, 173). Mathers, who died of influenza in 1918, is identifiable as 'S.R.M.D.', the head of the 'black' magical order: a man 'who called himself the Count Macgregor of Glenlyon' but was in reality 'a Hampshire man, of lowland Scottish extraction, of the name of Douglas'. In the Outer Order of the Golden Dawn, Mathers usually signed his documents with the magical name 'Deo Duce Comite Ferro'

Arthwait is a caricature of Arthur Edward Waite (1857–1942), 'the only comprehensive analyst of the history of occultism in all its many branches',[6] who took control of the Golden Dawn in 1903 and maneuvered it in a direction blatantly inimical to Crowley's own philosophy of magic and of life.

Crowley demonstrated his unrelenting hostility toward Waite in a long succession of publications,[7] making

---

(D.D.C.F.), but in the Inner Order he used a Celtic magical name, 'S' Rhioghail Mo Dhream', from which Crowley appropriated the initials S.R.M.D. for his novel. In *Moonchild*, S.R.M.D. had 'developed an astounding taste and capacity for magic' but had 'chosen the wrong road' (Crowley, *Moonchild*, 122). Not surprisingly, Crowley was himself caricatured in other people's fictional work. H. Russell Wakefield presented a memorable portrait of Crowley as a Satanist and incorrigible womaniser called Oscar Clinton in his short story, 'He Cometh and He Passeth By', in H. Russell Wakefield, *They Return at Evening* (London: Phillip Allen, 1928). Dion Fortune, in *The Winged Bull* (London: Norgate, 1935), used Crowley as the model for the bloated, drug-addicted magician Hugo Astley, who 'looked as if he had been an athlete before time and debauchery had taken toll of him' (Fortune, *Winged Bull*, 80). For more on this characterisation, see Chapter Six; see also R. A. Gilbert, '"Two Circles to Gain and Two Squares to Lose": The Golden Dawn in Popular Fiction', in Roberts and Ormsby-Lennon (eds.), *Secret Texts*, 303–21, on p. 311. W. Somerset Maugham, in *The Magician* (London: William Heinemann, 1908), used a younger Crowley as the prototype for the sinister magus Oliver Haddo, who 'had the look of a very wicked, sensual priest'. Crowley found this literary portrait amusing, and adopted the pseudonym Oliver Haddo for a lengthy piece entitled 'The Herb Dangerous', a discussion of the properties and uses of *cannabis indica*, in *Equinox* 1:2 (1909), 31–89. For Crowley's reaction to Maugham's novel, see Booth, *Magick Life*, 166–67.

[6] Gilbert, *A. E. Waite*, 12.

[7] R. A. Gilbert (*A. E. Waite*, 11–13) states that, throughout the ten issues of *Equinox*, Crowley 'maintained a stream of invective and abuse against A. E. Waite, condemning the man, his works, his friends and all that he stood for', and that the source of this hostility was 'Waite's measured analysis of the futility and wickedness of magic'. Crowley's hatred 'centred on his awareness that Waite had perceived the true nature of magic and pointed to another way – that of the mystic'. Given Crowley's assiduous cultivation of outrage in others and his delight in exercising the power to shock, this seems an unsatisfactory explanation, perhaps coloured by Gilbert's own preconceptions about the intrinsic superiority of mysticism over magic. Gilbert also indicates that Crowley admired Waite's gifts as a poet (Gilbert, *A. E. Waite*, 13); Crowley admits in

abundantly clear the reason why Arthwait despises the hero of *Moonchild*, Cyril Grey, modelled loosely on Crowley himself:

> He hated Cyril Grey as much as he hated any one, because his [Arthwait's] books had been reviewed by that bright spirit, in his most bitterly ironical strain...and Grey had been at particular pains to point out elementary blunders in translation which showed that Arthwait was comically ignorant of the languages in which he boasted scholarship.[8]

Waite returned the hostility but, in public at least, never rose to the bait; there is no mention of Crowley anywhere in the massive corpus of literature he produced, both scholarly and confessional, on a comprehensive range of esoteric subjects.[9] This exercise of a Roman-style *damnatio memoriae* – the punishment of a despised individual by the simple method

---

his 'Campaign against Waite', an unpublished part of his *Confessions*, that 'as a poet his genius was undeniable'. It is more likely that envy of Waite's imaginative gifts, combined with a not entirely unjustified dislike of Waite's hypocrisy, lay at the root of Crowley's venom.

[8] Crowley, *Moonchild*, 151–52. For Crowley's 'bitterly ironical' reviews of Waite's work, see, for example, his opinion of Waite's compilation of poetry, *A Book of Mystery and Vision* (London: Philip Wellby & Son, 1902), which Crowley describes as 'bunkum, bombast, and balderdash' (*Equinox*, 1:3 (1910), 113). Crowley entitled his review of Waite's *Book of Ceremonial Magic* 'My Crapulous Contemporaries: Wisdom While You Waite' (*Equinox*, 1:5 (1911), 133–41). In this review, after declaring that 'Mr. Waite still talks as if his mouth were full of hot potatoes', Crowley makes a highly insightful statement relevant to the antipathy between the two men: 'As to the rituals of ceremonial magic which he [Waite] condemns, he is right. But the Mass itself is a Magical Ceremony, and he does not condemn the Mass. The ceremonies which might be practised by, say, a neophyte of the AA [Astrum Argentum, Crowley's own occult order] would be as sublime as, and less tainted than, the services of the Church. Of such rituals Mr Waite is ignorant...Cannot God deal with a soul even by allowing him to pass through the "Houses of Sin"? Mr Waite blasphemes if he denies it'.

[9] But see Waite's condemnation of self-obsessed magicians in A. E. Waite, *The Book of Ceremonial Magic* (reissue of *The Book of Black Magic*, London: William Rider & Son, 1911), 336–37, probably directed at Crowley.

of refusing to acknowledge their existence[10] – was a fitting retaliation against someone as self-absorbed as Crowley. Both men were adepts of the Golden Dawn at the same time, and both wrote lengthy treatises on the Kabbalah. Waite's championing of Christian mysticism and apparent repudiation of magic,[11] and Crowley's cultivation of pagan 'magick' and apparent disdain for Christian beliefs,[12] might suggest that their respective interpretations of Jewish esoteric lore would produce the kind of distortions by occultists of which Gershom Scholem later complained. Yet the two currents expressed by these fellow adepts – the mystical and the magical – are both fully represented, and often indistinguishable, in Jewish Kabbalistic literature. Even the excesses of Crowley's sexual magic find their prototype in the colourful career of the eighteenth-century Jewish pseudo-messiah Sabbatai Zevi, discussed below; and the full *unio mystica* which Waite believed only Christian mystics could experience is described in a number of Kabbalistic texts.[13]

Waite and Crowley, on more careful examination, emerge as far more alike than either could bear to admit, and they might even be viewed as each other's 'religious Other', exhibiting the kind of mutual 'shadow-projection' of which C. G. Jung speaks in his discussions of the dynamics of

---

[10] On the 'damnation of memory' imposed by the Romans on those who brought discredit to the Empire, see Eric R. Varner, *Mutilation and Transformation: Damnatio Memoriae and Roman Imperial Portraiture* (Leiden: Brill, 2004).

[11] For Waite's view of medieval and early modern magic as a 'degeneration' of the Kabbalah, see, for example, Waite, *Holy Kabbalah*, xxv; A. E. Waite, 'Masonic Tradition and the Royal Arch', *Transactions of the Somerset Masters' Lodge No. 3746* (1921), repr. in *Waite: Selected Masonic Papers*, 19–29, on p. 23.

[12] See Crowley, *Magick*, xii, for the peculiar spelling of the word. For Crowley's view of Christianity as 'historically false, morally infamous, politically contemptible and socially pestilential', see Crowley, *Confessions*, 580. For Crowley's ambiguous religious views, see Hutton, *Triumph of the Moon*, 174–80.

[13] See Moshe Idel, 'Universalization and Integration: Two Conceptions of Mystical Union in Jewish Mysticism', in Moshe Idel and Bernard McGinn (eds.), *Mystical Union and Monotheistic Faith: An Ecumenical Dialogue* (London: Collier Macmillan, 1989), 27–57. For further Kabbalistic descriptions of the *unio mystica*, see Scholem, *Messianic Idea*, 203–27; Elliot R. Wolfson, 'Forms of Visionary Ascent as Ecstatic Experience in the Zoharic Literature', in Schäfer and Dan (eds.), *Gershom Scholem's* Major Trends, 209–35.

fateful relationships.[14] Both men, by the early years of the
twentieth century, were entirely absorbed in Kabbalistic lore,
but both exhibited considerable ambivalence toward Jews;
Waite's antisemitism seems to have taken the 'gentlemanly'
form characteristic of the British establishment in the decades
before the Second World War,[15] while Crowley's antipathy is
more overt.[16] Both relied on Lévi's writings but were also

---

[14] For 'shadow-projection', see Jung, CW10, ¶444–57; Jung, CW9ii,
¶13–19.

[15] Waite never engages in obvious anti-Jewish polemics in his
published work, but expresses his disdain in covert, non-violent
forms such as snobbery and literary stereotypes. For this type of
antisemitism in early-twentieth-century Britain, see Weber, 'Anti-
Semitism and Philo-Semitism'; Todd M. Endelman, 'English Jewish
History', *MJ* 11:1 (1991), 91–109. Waite's low-key contempt toward
Jews is expressed in a letter he wrote in 1936 to an adept of his
Fellowship of the Rosy Cross, in which he comments on Israel
Regardie's attempt to publish the Golden Dawn rituals: 'There are
spurious Temples in existence, and as an illustration of the kind of
persons whom they include it may be mentioned that a Jew is
attempting to find a publisher in America or here...who will risk
capital over the publication of all G.D. Rituals, Knowledge Lectures
and so forth' (cited in Gilbert, *A. E. Waite*, 153). On this letter,
Gilbert comments: 'The implicit anti-Semitism is surprising in one
who had taken great pains in 1921 to condemn Nesta H. Webster's
hysterical account in *The Morning Post* of a Jewish 'occult' peril'.
Waite also displays antisemitic feeling in his efforts to Christianise
the Kabbalistic associations of the Tarot that had been accepted by
British occultists since Lévi's time. In A. E. Waite, 'The Tarot and
Secret Tradition', *OR* 29:3 (1919), 157–61, he states: 'Since the
appearance of *The Pictorial Key* [Waite's own work on the Tarot] I
have inspected a Jewish Tarot which has not, I think, been printed.
It represents the black magic of divination – a most extraordinary
series of designs, carrying messages of evil in every sign and
symbol'. This suggestion that Jewish versions of the Tarot reflect the
practices of 'black' magic is echoed in Waite's belief that the
medieval grimoires are a corrupted form of Jewish Kabbalistic
magic. The implications are clear: the Jews practice 'black' magic,
and the Kabbalah, although a sublime theosophical system, must be
Christianised to be cleansed of its magical taint. No 'Jewish Tarot' as
described by Waite has ever come to light.

[16] For examples of antisemitism in Crowley's writing, see, for
example, Crowley, *Confessions*, 501, where he suggests that the Jew
'really does only too often possess the bad qualities for which he is
disliked'. He then takes an apparently apologetic stance and
suggests that it is the behaviour of others that has made the Jews so
disagreeable: 'No people can show finer specimens of

influenced by Frazer's evolutionist approach to religion; both participated in the new psychological theories emerging at the turn of the century yet retained a belief in the objective reality of the powers they sought to contact through ritual; and both were gifted poets who continued to produce their poetic works in tandem with their occult publications.[17] Astrologically inclined members of the Golden Dawn such as Mathers and Brodie-Innes no doubt found significance in the fact that both Waite and Crowley were born under Libra.[18] Both were driven by a quest for transformative religious experiences, and both used ritual to induce what they understood as union with a higher power. And both men

---

humanity...But the Jew has been persecuted so relentlessly that his survival has depended on the development of his worst qualities: avarice, servility, falseness, cunning, and the rest'. At the same time Crowley expressed such sentiments in print, he was involved in an intense sexual relationship with the Jewish poet Victor Benjamin Neuberg; but this apparent display of tolerance was contradicted by his later explanation for Neuberg's psychological breakdown: 'racial congenital cowardice' (Crowley, *Confessions*, 593). For Crowley's relationship with Neuberg, see Crowley, *Confessions*, 606–10, 620–23, 633–39; Booth, *Magick Life*, 255–69; Owen, 'Sorcerer and His Apprentice'. For Neuberg's Jewish background, see Kaczynski, *Perdurabo*, 133. The 'Jewish problem' to which Crowley refers in the anonymous paper he published in *The English Review* in 1922 is the emigration of many thousands of Jews from Russia and Eastern Europe to Britain in the early decades of the twentieth century, which led to a marked rise in antisemitic feeling. Crowley redefines the problem, not in terms of social and economic pressures, but as 'an irreconcilable antagonism' between Jew and Gentile fuelled by the Jew's eternal quest for a spiritual 'Something' which cannot be fulfilled by the 'Freudian Phantasm' of the Christian Messiah (Crowley, 'Jewish Problem Restated', 32). Crowley's solution is neither Zionism nor repatriation, but a recommendation that the Jews become followers of his own religion: if they were to accept his Law of Thelema, they would induce 'a complementary current in every other racial and religious section of humanity', and would fulfil their destiny. 'Let the Jew lead the way! Let the Jew...assert himself without fear of others, or reference to their ideals and standards..."The word of Sin is Restriction", and the sin of Israel is this, that it has never known itself, or done its will. Love is the law, love under will' (Crowley, 'Jewish Problem Restated', 37).
[17] For Waite's and Crowley's debts to Frazer, their involvement in the new psychologies, and their published poetry, see below.
[18] Waite was born on 2 October 1857; Crowley was born on 12 October 1875.

focused, in very different ways, on the Kabbalistic portrayal of the sexual act as the chief vessel through which the ecstasy of the *unio mystica* might be achieved.

Early in 1891, Waite, a published poet, aspiring historian of the Western mystery tradition, and enthusiastic translator of Lévi's works, was initiated as the ninety-ninth adept of the Golden Dawn.[19] He abandoned his training after only two years, although he requested readmittance in 1893 and finally entered the Inner Order in 1899.[20] Waite was unimpressed by the Golden Dawn's two surviving Chiefs, Westcott and Mathers. 'I knew them sufficiently well,' he declares in his autobiography, 'to loathe their false pretences, their buskined struttings and their abysmal ignorance of the supposititious arcana which they claimed to guard.'[21] Mathers, he notes, was 'like a comic Blackstone of occult lore', while Westcott was 'like a dull owl, hooting dolefully among cypresses over tombs of false adepts'.[22] These observations were made nearly fifty years after Waite's initiation, however, and at first he was enthusiastic enough about the order's promises of secret wisdom to tolerate his mistrust of its Chiefs.

Waite's knowledge of the Kabbalah was initially limited to what he had gleaned from Lévi and from Blavatsky's *Isis Unveiled*, a work which he 'hated' because of its anti-Christian bias.[23] In an early publication entitled *The Occult Sciences*, he expresses cynicism toward Lévi's idealisation of Hebrew esoteric lore; in his own view, the Kabbalah

> ...is simply a series of dogmatic hypotheses; it is not a guide to knowledge; it is a body of positive doctrine, based on a central assumption which is incapable of proof, and enunciated in a singularly barbarous and unintelligible form.[24]

This attitude altered dramatically over the ensuing three

---

[19] For a complete bibliography of Waite's published work, see R. A. Gilbert, *A. E. Waite: A Bibliography* (Wellingborough: Aquarian Press, 1983).

[20] For Waite's reasons for leaving the Golden Dawn, see Waite, *Shadows*, 126; Gilbert, *A. E. Waite*, 111.

[21] Waite, *Shadows*, 99.

[22] Waite, *Shadows*, 124.

[23] Waite, *Shadows*, 68.

[24] A. E. Waite, *The Occult Sciences* (London: Kegan Paul, Trench, Trübner & Co., 1891), 185.

decades, largely through an increasing familiarity with Jewish Kabbalistic sources and the work of Jewish scholars.[25] In *The Doctrine and Literature of the Kabbalah* (1902), he still views the Kabbalah as 'a rationalized system of mystic thought' inferior to the mysticism of the 'Church of Christ'.[26] But *The Secret Doctrine in Israel* (1913) and *The Holy Kabbalah* (1929) reflect an increasing respect for and dependence on Kabbalistic theosophy as the basis for Waite's own activities and aspirations. He insists that the rituals he designed for his Fellowship of the Rosy Cross, created in 1915, are based on a Christian interpretation:

> The tradition and symbolism of the Fellowship are a derivation from the Secret Doctrine of Israel, known as Kabalah and embodied in the Sepher Ha Zohar. The mode of interpretation in respect of Kabalistic Tradition is a Christian Mode.[27]

However, despite this Christian allegiance, he declares in his autobiography:

> The *Zohar* is one of the world's great books....I shall never regret the long years that I have devoted to the Theosophical side of Kabbalistic literature; and were it not that I am called in other directions, I should have been willing to dedicate more.[28]

Although he became increasingly disillusioned with the Catholic faith in which he had been raised,[29] Waite retained a love of its ceremonies, and never abandoned his commitment to what he understood as the Christian mystery tradition[30] –

---

[25] See, for example, Waite, *Holy Kabbalah*, 426, n. 1, for his familiarity with Scholem's early work, 'Alchemie und Kabbala' (*Monatschrift für Geschichte und Wissenschaft des Judentums*, 1925).
[26] A. E. Waite, *The Doctrine and Literature of the Kabbalah* (London: Theosophical Publishing Society, 1902), 486.
[27] 'Constitution and Laws of the Fellowship of the Rosy Cross', cited in Gilbert, *A. E. Waite*, 183–85. See also Thomas Willard, 'Acts of the Companions: A. E. Waite's Fellowship and the Novels of Charles Williams', in Roberts and Ormsby-Lennon (eds.), *Secret Texts*, 269–302, on p. 269.
[28] Waite, *Shadows*, 197.
[29] Details of Waite's life can be found in Gilbert, *A. E. Waite*, and in Waite, *Shadows*.
[30] For Waite's commitment to Christian mysticism, see A. E. Waite, *The Way of Divine Union* (London: William Rider & Son, 1915); A. E.

an esoteric path which he deemed superior to Theosophy's
eastern doctrines.[31] Mathers' Golden Dawn was too eclectic
to support Waite's most cherished beliefs, and he began to
entertain the idea of taking over the order and restructuring
it along what he deemed to be mystical rather than magical
lines. Not all the adepts were in accord. In November 1898,
five years after Waite had rejoined the order, a new and
charismatic star appeared among the ranks of the neophytes:
Edward Alexander Crowley, who had already achieved
notoriety as a poet, a mountaineer, and a libertine.[32]

Ironically, Crowley had been attracted to the Golden
Dawn after reading Waite's *Book of Black Magic*.[33] In later life,
Crowley was no more impressed by Mathers than Waite was;
but initially he viewed Mathers as his master and patron,
allying himself with the older magus in the farcical power-
battle that erupted within the order in 1900.[34] However, this
atypical sojourn as Mathers' loyal acolyte eventually ended
with his expulsion from the order in 1905.[35] Crowley, like
Waite, believed that he was the only person who could

Waite, 'The Interior Life from the Standpoint of the Mystics' and A.
E. Waite, 'On Intimations Concerning the Interior Church in Schools
of Christian Mysticism', both in Gilbert (ed.), *Hermetic Papers of A. E.
Waite*, 195–204 and 215–51.

[31] For Waite's attitude toward the Theosophical Society, see *Shadows*,
86–89 and 196–97.

[32] Crowley's first published collection of poetry was *White Stains*
(Amsterdam, 1898), which appeared under the pseudonymn
'George Archibald Bishop' in the same year that Crowley entered
the Golden Dawn. He self-published most of his early poetry,
written between 1898 and 1902, in three volumes between 1905 and
1907.   See
<www.poemhunter.com/i/ebooks/pdf/aleister_crowley_2004_9.p
df> for a complete collection of Crowley's poetry online.

[33] See Crowley, *Confessions*, 112–13.

[34] For this episode in the history of the Golden Dawn, see King,
Modern Ritual Magic, 66–78; Gilbert, *Scrapbook*, 50–56; Howe,
Magicians, 203–32; Harper, *Yeats's Golden Dawn*, 14–35; Mary K.
Greer and Darcy Küntz, *The Chronology of the Golden Dawn* (Sequim,
WA: Holmes Publishing Group, 1999), 33–37. For Crowley's
version, see *Confessions*, 187–91. See Gilbert, *A. E. Waite*, 114, for
Waite's reactions. For Crowley's poor opinion of Mathers'
Kabbalistic capabilities, see Aleister Crowley, 'The Temple of
Solomon the King', *Equinox* 1:5 (1911), 65–120.

[35] For Crowley's final expulsion, see Richard Kaczynski, *Perdurabo:
The Life of Aleister Crowley* (Tempe, AR: New Falcon Publications,
2002), 104–05.

regenerate the Golden Dawn and restructure it along the 'right' lines. Once he and Mathers had parted ways, Crowley's future path was clear. The founding of his own 'religion', called Thelema, and the promulgation of its teachings through the Ordo Templi Orientis, became the occult revival's strongest statement of magic as a reflection of the godlike potency of the human will, and they remain so to this day.[36]

WAITE'S KABBALISTIC 'MYSTICISM'

An exploration of the Kabbalistic themes in Waite's writing requires an investigation into his use of the term 'Christian mysticism'. 'Mysticism' is currently almost as beleaguered a category in academic study as 'magic', and its 'essentialist illusions', first emerging in mid-nineteenth-century scholarship, have been widely critiqued in the last three decades.[37] Although Waite presents himself as a

---

[36] For the present-day OTO, see <http://www.oto-uk.org> (Grand Lodge of Great Britain and Northern Ireland) and <http://oto-usa.org> (United States Grand Lodge).

[37] For critiques of universalist assumptions in modern academic definitions of mysticism, see Steven T. Katz, 'Language, Epistemology, and Mysticism', in Steven T. Katz (ed.), *Mysticism and Philosophical Analysis* (London: Sheldon Press, 1978), 22–74; Hans H. Penner, 'The Mystical Illusion', in Steven T. Katz (ed.), *Mysticism and Religious Traditions* (Oxford: Oxford University Press, 1983), 89–116; Wayne Proudfoot, *Religious Experience* (Berkeley: University of California Press, 1985), 119–54. For the term 'mystocentrism', the academic inclination to compartmentalise mysticism as an autonomous category in the study of religions, see Wasserstrom, *Religion after Religion*, 239–41. For a comprehensive survey of these academic currents and their antecedents, see Leigh Eric Schmidt, 'The Making of Modern "Mysticism"', *JAAR* 71:2 (2003), 273–302. For various arguments for and against the 'essential' nature of mystical experience, see William James, *The Varieties of Religious Experience: A Study of Human Nature* (New York: Longmans Green, 1902); Rudolf Otto, *Mysticism East and West: A Comparative Analysis of the Nature of Mysticism*, trans. Bertha L. Bracey and Richenda C. Payne (New York: Macmillan, 1932); Walter T. Stace, *Mysticism and Philosophy* (Philadelphia, PA: Lippincott, 1960); Ralph W. Hood, Jr., 'The Construction and Preliminary Validation of a Measure of Reported Mystical Experience', *JSSR* 14 (1975), 29–41; Sallie B. King, 'Two Epistemological Models for the Interpretation of Mysticism', *JAAR* 56:2 (1988), 257–79; F. Samuel Brainard, 'Defining "Mystical Experience"', *JAAR* 64:2 (1996), 359–93.

Christian mystic, he displays a precociously post-modern
sensibility in his awareness of the ambiguity of the term
'mysticism' and his recognition that, although the adjective
'mystical' had been used in Christian exegetical literature
from the second century CE – it appears in the *Stromata* of
Clement of Alexandria as a synonym for 'esoteric' or
'hidden'[38] – the noun 'mysticism' had only come into use as a
universal religious category in the mid-nineteenth century.[39]
'The definitions of Mysticism', Waite declares, 'are
many...the word is a modern word'.[40] The prevailing
classification in earlier centuries was 'mystical theology', a
devotional current in Christianity that recommended a life of
prayer, contemplation, and self-denial.[41] Waite rejected the

---

[38] Clement, *Stromata* 5.6, where Clement speaks of a 'mystical
interpretagtion' of Scripture. For 'mystical' as a synonym for
'esoteric' or 'hidden' in the *Stromata*, see Bernard McGinn, *The
Foundations of Mysticism: Origins to the Fifth Century* (New York:
Crossroad, 1991), 12, quoting Philo in David Winston (trans.), *Philo
of Alexandria* (New York: Paulist Press, 1981), 79. This use of the
term 'mystical' is not the same as the late-nineteenth-century
understanding of 'mysticism' as a generalised religious category
characterised by the quest for union with God; see Louis Bouyer,
'Understanding Mysticism: An Essay on the History of the Word',
in Richard Woods (ed.), *Understanding Mysticism* (Garden City, NY:
Doubleday/Image, 1980), 42–55.
[39] For the term 'mystical' in the second-century work of Clement of
Alexandria, see Clement, *Stromata*, trans. W. L. Alexander, in
Alexander Roberts, James Donaldson, Philip Schaff, and Henry
Wace (eds.), *The Ante-Nicene Fathers: Translations of the Writings of the
Fathers Down to A.D. 325*, 10 vols. (Peabody, MA: Hendrickson,
1994), 2:5:6. Schmidt, in 'Making of Modern Mysticism', 282, notes
that the fundamental shift in the Anglo-American discourse on
mysticism took place in the 1840s and 1850s through entries in the
Encyclopaedia Britannica. Mysticism was taken out of its exclusively
Christian context and applied to a range of experiences from Hindu
to Swedenborgian: 'Mysticism becomes a global species of religious
experience with innumerable subspecies, historical, geographic, and
national: Oriental mysticism, Neo-Platonic mysticism, Greek
mysticism, German mysticism'.
[40] Waite, *Way of Divine Union*, 3.
[41] Schmidt, 'Modern "Mysticism"', 276. Schmidt gives as an example
of this earlier terminology the work of Thomas Blount, who in his
Glossographia, published in 1656, declared: 'Mystical Theology, is
nothing else in general but certain Rules, by the practise whereof, a
vertuous Christian may attain to a nearer, a more familiar, and
beyond all expression comfortable conversation with God'.

term 'mystical theology' as inappropriate for his own quest because there is no 'theological doctrine based on faith' involved in the direct experience of deity;[42] instead, he recommended an 'agnostic standpoint' rather than conventional religious devotion as the necessary 'threshold of mysticism':

> Those persons who admit that the great problems of life are insoluble, and that every attempt to extract some intelligible answers to the eternal questions of the sphinx, ultimately proves to be inadequate, more especially in the case of religious systems which are based upon arbitrary revelation...they are still, it may be, conscious of spiritual aspiration.[43]

Waite had read William James' psychological approach to mystical states in *The Varieties of Religious Experience*, and sympathised with the mystical perception of nature found in the work of the American Transcendentalist Ralph Waldo Emerson (1803–1882).[44] Also contemporaneous with Waite's writings were new hypotheses emerging in German academic circles at the turn of the century concerning the early Iranian 'origin' of Western beliefs in the immortality of the soul and the possibility of a ritually induced ascent or *psychanodia* to achieve mystical union.[45] These 'origin hypotheses' found their way into the British academic circle known as the 'Cambridge Ritualists' through the work of Jane Ellen Harrison (1850–1928), Gilbert Murray (1856–1957), Francis MacDonald Cornford (1873–1943), and Arthur Bernard Cook (1868–1952),[46] and reflected in an academic

---

[42] Waite, *Way of Divine Union*, 5.

[43] Waite, *Azoth*, 13.

[44] For James, see Waite, *Divine Union*, 33, n. 2 and 79, n. 1; for Emerson, see Waite, *Azoth*, 36.

[45] See, for example, Wilhelm Anz, *Zur Frage nach dem Ursprung des Gnostizismus: Ein Religionsgeschichtlicher Versuch* (Leipzig: A. Preis, 1897); Wilhelm Bousset, 'Die Himmelreise der Seele' (Stuttgart: *Archiv für Religionswissenschaft*, 4, 1901), 136–69, 229–73. On these works, see Ioan P. Couliano, *Psychanodia I: A Survey of the Evidence Concerning the Ascension of the Soul and Its Relevance* (Leiden: Brill, 1983).

[46] For the work of the 'Cambridge Ritualists', see Jane Harrison, *Prolegomena to the Study of Greek Religion* (Cambridge: Cambridge University Press, 1903); Jane Harrison, *Themis: A Study of the Social Origins of Greek Religion* (Cambridge: Cambridge University Press,

context a mixture of universalist and evolutionist-anthropological religious perspectives echoed, through more overtly esoteric methodologies, in Waite's idea of a 'Secret Tradition': 'the immemorial knowledge concerning man's way of return whence he came by a method of the inward life'.[47] Waite sometimes referred to the Secret Tradition as the 'Church Mystic', declaring that was made up of 'numerous confraternities to each of which there is assigned...a certain characteristic tissue of symbolism by means of which their peculiar instruction has received an outward shape or vesture'.[48] Ronald Hutton suggests that Harrison's perception of ancient religion seems to be 'an extreme example of that already displayed by Tylor and Frazer', and her reconstruction of a 'putative prehistoric religion' reflects the conflict between her romanticism and her rationalism.[49] The same might be said of Waite's 'Secret Tradition'. Waite's

---

1912); Gilbert Murray, *Four Stages of Greek Religion: Studies Based on a Course of Lectures Delivered in April 1912 at Columbia University* (New York: Columbia University Press, 1912)); Francis M. Cornford, *From Religion to Philosophy: A Study in the Origins of Western Speculation* (Cambridge: Cambridge University Press, 1912); Arthur B. Cook, *Zeus: A Study in Ancient Religion*, 3 vols. (Cambridge: Cambridge University Press, 1914–1925). For Harrison's influence on Crowley, see Justin Scott van Kleeck, 'The Art of the Law: Aleister Crowley's Use of Ritual and Drama', *Esoterica* 5 (2003), 193–218, on p. 194.

[47] A. E Waite, *The Secret Tradition in Freemasonry*, 2 vols. (London: Rebman Ltd., 1911), 2:379.

[48] Waite, 'Spiritual Symbolism of Freemasonry', 153. Waite wrote three works intended to explore the Secret Tradition through the history of three of these 'confraternities' – Freemasonry, the Kabbalah, and alchemy – which he viewed as closely interwoven and even interchangeable: *The Secret Tradition in Freemasonry*, *The Secret Doctrine of Israel: A Study of the Zohar and Its Connections* (London: William Rider & Son, 1913), and *The Secret Tradition in Alchemy* (London: Kegan Paul, 1926). Although the idea of the Secret Tradition was inspired by both Lévi (who believed it was best exemplified by the Kabbalah) and Blavatsky (who believed it was best exemplified by the teachings of the Eastern adepts and appeared in a distorted form in the Kabbalah), and was apparently confirmed 'scientifically' by the 'Cambridge Ritualists' with their focus on Orphic doctrines as a Western mystical proto-religion, Waite developed his own interpretation which emphasised mystical experience rather than occult knowledge, and gave equal weight to the Kabbalah, alchemy, and Rosicrucianism as the primary examples of genuine 'mysticism'.

[49] Hutton, *Triumph of the Moon*, 124.

emphasis on a 'perennialist' mystical tradition is an esoteric version of Harrison's prehistoric ur-religion, although Waite viewed the tradition as one kept deliberately secret over the ages and hidden within 'Instituted Mysteries and cryptic literature'.[50]

Waite's understanding of mysticism also reflects the 'Christian mystical revival', which dominated British theological circles at the beginning of the twentieth century. This 'mystical revival' was expressed most powerfully in the work of William Ralph Inge (1860–1954), an Anglican priest, professor of divinity at Cambridge, Dean of St. Paul's from 1911 to 1934, and spokesman for turn-of-the-century Anglican Modernism with its emphasis on individual experience as the ground of faith.[51] Waite's views also demonstrate his extensive reading of alchemical works: he calls his belief-system a 'qualified Christian Mysticism, expressed...in Hermetic symbolical terms'.[52] Following the ideas presented in Mary Anne Atwood's *A Suggestive Inquiry*,[53] Waite declared alchemy to be the 'physical' form of mysticism; the great alchemists of history, such as Paracelsus, were mystics of a 'Hermetic' persuasion.[54] The new understandings of mysticism as both a universal religious

---

[50] Waite, *Secret Tradition in Freemasonry*, 1:ix.

[51] See William Ralph Inge, *Christian Mysticism* (London: Methuen & Co., 1889); Adam Fox, *Dean Inge (1860–1954)* (London: John Murray, 1960); Robert M. Helm, *The Gloomy Dean: The Thought of William Ralph Inge* (Winston-Salem, NC: John F. Blair, 1962). For the 'Christian mystical revival' as a response to the rise of medical psychiatry, see Dan Merkur, 'Unitive Experiences and the State of Trance', in Idel and McGinn (eds.), *Mystical Union*, 125–53. For Anglican Modernism as an outgrowth of the Christian mystical revival, see Clive Pearson, Allan Davidson, and Peter Lineham, *Scholarship and Fierce Sincerity: Henry D. A. Major, The Face of Anglican Modernism* (Auckland: Polygraphia, 2006); Paul Badham, *The Contemporary Challenge of Modernist Theology* (Cardiff: University of Wales Press, 1998); Alan Stephenson, *The Rise and Decline of English Modernism* (London: SPCK, 1984).

[52] Waite, *Shadows*, 131–32.

[53] On Atwood's work, see Chapter Three. For Waite's debt to Atwood, see A. E. Waite, 'What is Alchemy?', *The Unknown World* 1:1 (1894), 7–11, on p. 11.

[54] For Waite's division of mystics into 'physical' and 'spiritual', see Waite, *Occult Sciences*, 189. For Waite's view of Paracelsus as a Kabbalist who combined both types of mysticism, see Waite, *Occult Sciences*, 193; Waite, *Real History*, 30.

316 Magi and *Maggidim*

category and a historical current with a single cradle of origin, along with alchemical traditions and Lévi's Kabbalistic speculations, supported Waite in his belief that in Kabbalistic and alchemical doctrines he had found the hidden tracks of an ancient Western esoteric tradition in which mysticism as he defines it – 'that it is possible for "the divine in man" to be borne back consciously to "the divine in the universe"'[55] – was the crown and ultimate goal.[56]

Although Waite was familiar with an extensive range of Christian mystical writings from late antiquity to his own time,[57] his most favoured author was Louis-Claude de Saint-Martin, a late-eighteenth-century Christian mystic steeped in Kabbalistic doctrines and rituals.[58] But despite Waite's later equation of the Kabbalah with 'Jewish mysticism',[59] there is

---

[55] Waite, 'What is Alchemy?', 19.

[56] For the 'fundamentals' of Waite's mystical doctrine, see *Azoth*, 11.

[57] For the Christian mystical literature with which Waite was familiar, see Waite, *Divine Union*, 45–89 and 90–110.

[58] See Waite, *Life of Louis Claude de Saint-Martin*; Waite, *St. Martin*; A. E. Waite, 'A Message of Saint-Martin', *The Seeker*, 5:17 (1909), 43–58, repr. in Gilbert (ed.), *Hermetic Papers of A. E. Waite*, 205–14. See Waite, *Shadows*, 163, for Waite's description of Saint-Martin as 'my ever beloved'. Waite acknowledges the Kabbalistic influence on Saint-Martin reluctantly: see, for example, Waite, *Holy Kabbalah*, 486, where he states, 'There is nothing to indicate that he [Saint-Martin] had read any Kabbalistic literature...Some of his lesser doctrines possess notwithstanding a certain Kabbalistic complexion', in particular the doctrine of the Divine Name. Waite was also intrigued by Saint-Martin's master, Martinès de Pasqually, whose eighteenth-century rituals he admits are 'ceremonial magic' but which he understands as redeemed by the fact that their intention is 'communication with the personal Christ Himself'. Pasqually is therefore exonerated as a Christian mystic (see Waite, 'Message of Saint-Martin', 211). In 'A Lodge of Magic', a paper devoted to Pasqually, Waite fails to acknowledge the obvious Kabbalistic elements in Pasqually's rituals, although he attributes Saint-Martin's discourses on angelology to Pasqually's teachings (Waite, *Way of Divine Union*, 180) and concedes that there is a connection between the *Zohar* and Pasqually's *Traité de la réintégration des êtres* (Waite, *Way of Divine Union*, 99). In *The Holy Kabbalah* (487), Waite admits that Pasqually's doctrines were 'derived from a source which retained some filtrations of Kabbalism', but he appears to have rejected Adolphe Franck's identification of Pasqually as a Marrano, a Portuguese Jew who nominally adopted Christianity (see Franck, *La philosophie mystique*, 1–26).

[59] Waite, *Holy Kabbalah*, xxv and xxxiii.

no separate tradition of 'mysticism' within Judaism equivalent to that represented by 'Christian mystical theology', nor does the word 'mysticism' exist in the Hebrew language.[60] Joseph Dan suggests that the Christian mystic 'may feel that he belongs to a certain succession of religious thinkers, and knowingly molds his own expressions according to their earlier terminology and literary genres'.[61] It is in this 'succession of religious thinkers' that Waite placed himself. Like many Christian apologists, Waite perceived Jewish 'mysticism' as inferior because, in his view, the mystical experience for the Jew is a direct revelation of 'the Fatherhood of God and the sonship of all mankind', while the Christian mystic seeks, and experiences, something 'much closer than any filial relation':[62] a full *unio mystica* between the human being and Christ.[63] Referring to a work by the British Jewish scholar Joshua Abelson called *The Immanence of God in Rabbinic Literature*, in which Abelson discusses the mystical experience as 'contact between human spirit and divine spirit',[64] Waite emphasises the 'inadequacy' of the Jewish idea of 'contact' compared with the 'consummation' of the Christian mystical experience.[65] He seems to have been either unaware of, or reluctant to acknowledge, the great variety of metaphors used in Kabbalistic literature to describe the encounter between human and divine. In the work of Abraham Abulafia, for example, the Kabbalist is envisoned as 'the "female" into whom the divine spark is sown and the spiritual son born'; the human being

> ...can link the lower part with the higher one and the lower will ascend to and unite with the supernal and the higher will descend and will kiss the entity ascending toward it, like a bridegroom actually kisses his bride, out of his great and real

---

[60] See Ithamar Gruenwald, 'Reflections on the Nature and Origins of Jewish Mysticism', in Schäfer and Dan (eds.), *Gershom Scholem's Major Trends*, 25–48.

[61] Joseph Dan, 'Historical Definition of Mysticism', 6.

[62] Waite, *Divine Union*, 18–20.

[63] See Waite, *Holy Kabbalah*, 84, for his criticism of the Jewish mystical path, and the critique of Waite's comments by Solomon B. Freehof, 'Review: Jewish Mystic Lore, *The Holy Kabbalah* by A. E. Waite', *JR* 10:2 (1930), 269–70.

[64] Abelson, *Immanence of God*, 340–41.

[65] Waite, *Divine Union*, 19–20.

desire, characteristic of the delight of both, coming from the power of God.[66]

This is a fully realised *unio mystica* described in explicitly erotic terms, in which there are no 'filial' components.[67]

---

[66] Abraham Abulafia, *Or ha-Sekhel*, Ms. Vatican 233, fol. 115, cited in Idel, 'Sexual Metaphors', 200.

[67] Among Kabbalistic scholars a debate is ongoing about the extent to which Jewish mystical texts describe a full *unio mystica*; the argument, like the debate about magic, inevitably depends on how the terms 'mysticism' and 'mystical experience' are defined and in what context they are applied. 'Seeing' or being 'in proximity to' God, rather than union with him, is the object of the *heikhalot* rituals, which are generally termed 'mystical'; see, for example, Joseph Dan, *The Revelation of the Secret of the World: The Beginning of Jewish Mysticism in Late Antiquity* (Providence, RI: Brown University, 1992). Dan ('In Quest of a Historical Definition', 9) raises an important question: 'How can one differentiate between "proximity" or "adherence" to God and "union" with Him?...How can a scholar decide who "really" achieved "union" and not just "proximity", when all he has to depend on is the individual style and selection of words of his source?' Idel (*Hasidism*, 53) considers the celestial ascents of *heikhalot* literature, Abraham Abulafia's 'ecstatic' Kabbalah, and the ecstatic states cultivated in modern Hasidism to represent different expressions of Jewish mystical experience. 'Ecstasy' does not necessarily imply the 'nuptial alliance' of which Waite speaks when he describes Christian mysticism, but equally, it could embrace such an experience. This would depend on the individual mystic rather than whether he/she was Christian or Jewish, and the descriptions of erotic union in the *Zohar* suggest that for some Jewish mystics, 'contact' with God was indeed a 'nuptial alliance'. For the *unio mystica* as 'contact' with God, see Scholem, *Major Trends*, 4–7; Scholem asserts that the attitude of the 'genuine' mystic is determined by 'the fundamental experience of the inner self which enters into immediate contact with God or the metaphysical Reality'. However, the 'essence' of the experience, Scholem suggests, is 'the great riddle which the mystics themselves, no less than the historians, have tried to solve' (4). For further contributions to the debate, see also the five papers presented in Idel and McGinn (eds.), *Mystical Union and Monotheistic Faith*, in particular Louis Dupré, 'Unio mystica: The State and the Experience', 3–23, and Bernard McGinn, 'Love, Knowledge, and *Unio Mystica* in the Western Christian Tradition', 59–86. For a vehement criticism of the use of the term 'mysticism' in academic contexts other than Christian theology, see Huss, 'Jewish Mysticism in the University'. Huss argues that 'mysticism' is a Christian theological term which has been imposed as a universal category on

The Kabbalistic 'Tree of Life', as Waite understands it, is therefore a powerful symbol of the mystical path – perhaps *the* most powerful – but it must be transformed through interpretation 'in the Christian mode' to be fully effective as a means of achieving the longed-for *unio mystica*. Waite's view of magic as a primitive and inferior form of mysticism was probably influenced by Frazer's theories about magic as a primitive form of religion.[68] Frazer's conceptual framework still echoes in scholarly discussions differentiating mysticism from magic, which itself might be viewed as a more specialised branch of the ongoing 'magic versus religion' debate. Marcel Mauss (1872–1950), one of the scholars most influential in shaping this debate, differentiates religious rituals – 'mystical' or otherwise – from magical ones by declaring: 'Magical and religious rites often have different agents; in other words, they are not performed by one and the same person'.[69] This does not apply to Waite, who created rites which were magical and religious at the same time, although he preferred to call these practices 'ceremonial observances' rather than magical rituals.[70] Nor does it apply to the ritual magic of the Golden Dawn, which, derived primarily from Jewish roots, blends magic and religiosity in a seamless unity. If mysticism is characterised by 'a search for and experience of immediacy with God',[71] then the Golden Dawn rituals must be considered mystical, since many of these ceremonies involve an effort to experience the divine directly, whether it is the divinity of Abrahamic monotheism, the Holy Guardian Angel, the Greco-Egyptian pantheon, or

---

the historical and sociological study of the highly individual religious expressions of non-Christian cultures.

[68] See James G. Frazer, *Adonis, Attis, Osiris: Studies in the History of Oriental Religion*, 2 vols. (London, Macmillan, 1906; 3rd edition 1936), 1:3–4. See Waite, *Shadows*, 173, for one of many references to Frazer.

[69] Marcel Mauss, *A General Theory of Magic*, trans. Robert Brain (London: Routledge, 2001), 23.

[70] For the private ritual Waite created for himself and two other members of his Independent and Rectified Rite, see A. E. Waite, 'The Viaticum of Daily Life on the Way of the Homeward Quest' (unpublished MS, 1910), repr. in Gilbert (ed.), *Hermetic Papers of A. E. Waite*, 252–56. See also Waite, *Azoth*, 126–28. For the resemblance between Waite's idea of the mystical ascent and the *heikhalot* ascent, see Waite, *Holy Kabbalah*, 247; Waite, 'Interior Life', 201.

[71] Andrew Louth, *The Origins of the Christian Mystical Tradition: From Plato to Denys* (Oxford: Clarendon Press, 1981), xv.

the elemental powers;[72] and both Waite and Crowley, in their radically different ways, must also be understood as mystics.[73]

Distinguishing between 'Jewish magic' and 'Jewish mysticism' has fuelled an ongoing debate among Kabbalistic scholars, some of whom echo Waite in their insistence that the theosophical Kabbalah, most eloquently expressed in the *Zohar*, is the crown of Jewish mysticism, and any magical elements are 'alien imports'.[74] But Waite had a tendency to practice what he would never have dreamed of preaching to the unenlightened, and the rituals of his Fellowship of the Rosy Cross betray a complex blend of mystical and magical elements characteristic of the 'peculiar version of Kabbalah known as Hasidism'.[75] Moshe Idel, discussing the 'mystico-magical model' in Hasidic thought, states:

> Magic has been conceived of as a phenomenon drastically different from [mystical] ecstasy. However, the founder of eighteenth-century Hasidism has been described as both a mystic and a magician. Rabbi Yisrael ben Eliezer...combines in his praxis these two ways of relating to reality.[76]

Idel argues that the Hasidic *zaddikim* – Westcott's 'wonder-working rabbis' – did not conceive of mystical union as their ultimate goal; they had the additional aim of drawing down the 'divine effluence' for the benefit of the

---

[72] See, for example, 'Adeptus Minor Ritual', in Regardie, *Golden Dawn*, 221–47.

[73] See, for example, Crowley's statement at the beginning of this chapter.

[74] See above, Chapter One.

[75] Idel, *Hasidism*, 27.

[76] Idel, *Hasidism*, 1. For Yisrael ben Eliezer, known as the Ba'al Shem Tov, see also Abraham J. Heschel, *The Circle of the Baal Shem Tov: Studies in Hasidism*, ed. Samuel H. Dresner (Chicago, IL: University of Chicago Press, 1985); Samuel H. Dresner, *The Zaddik: The Doctrine of the Zaddik According to the Writings of Rabbi Yaakov Yosef of Polnoy* (London: Abelard Schuman, 1960); Scholem, *Major Trends*, 325–50; Immanuel Etkes, *The Besht: Magician, Mystic, and Leader* (Waltham, MA: Brandeis University Press, 2005). For the Ba'al Shem Tov's magical and prophetic powers, see Weiss, *Eastern European Jewish Mysticism*, 183–93; Moshe Idel, 'On Prophecy and Early Hasidism', in Alberto Ferreiro and Moshe Sharon (eds.), *Studies in Modern Religions, Religious Movements and the Babi-Baha'i Faiths* (Leiden: Brill, 2004), 41–75.

community.[77] This model differs from the Christian mystical quest because the final object is not the loss of self in the ecstasy of the *unio mystica*. The Hasidic quest, according to Joseph Weiss, is magical because its ultimate purpose is 'intended to change the mundane world', and involves 'a more primary magic, working in stark physical reality'.[78] Hasidic prayer – *kavvanah* or 'prayer with intent' – can be understood as a magical technique; its objectives include both a personal quest for divine union and a process of world-transformation.[79] Naftali Loewenthal suggests that the Hasidic amalgamation of mysticism and magic 'presupposes the capacity of the *Zaddiq* to leave this world by ascending to or by assimilating with the divine'.[80] This 'ascent' involves a transformation of the self through self-effacement and cleaving to the divine. But it is also an activity of the human will through which the damaged godhead is repaired, the 'holy sparks' redeemed, and the earthly world transformed. Waite embraces this Kabbalistic doctrine of human responsibility for the fulfilment of divinity when he declares:

> There is no revelation of God except through us as channels. It is we who go up into heaven to find Him there; it is we who descend into hell on the same research; it is we who take wings in the morning to the uttermost parts of the sea. It is we in fine who still the heart and mind and wait on revelation in the silence....When it speaks within us it is we ourselves who speak: all words are those of Man.[81]

The resemblance between Hasidic magico-mystical practices and Waite's 'modified' Christian mysticism is demonstrated in a work by the early-nineteenth-century Hasid Ephraim of Sedylkov:

> All that belongs to a man, be it his servants and animals, be it even his household effects – they are all of his sparks which belong to the root of his soul....For all these are holy sparks which are held in captivity in very low spheres and need to

---

[77] Idel, *Hasidism*, 107.
[78] Weiss, *Eastern European Jewish Mysticism*, 183.
[79] For *kavvanah*, see Chapter Two, n. 157.
[80] Naftali Loewenthal, *Communicating the Infinite: The Emergence of the Habad School* (Chicago, IL: University of Chicago Press, 1990), 30.
[81] Waite, *Shadows*, 257.

be lifted up.[82]

Although Waite preferred to cast himself in the role of a Christian priest, he more often resembled a Hasidic *zaddik* with his group of hand-picked, initiated disciples,[83] not least because Waite's idea of a spiritually elite 'Holy Assembly', which formed the basis for his Fellowship of the Rosy Cross, is derived, not from Christian models, but from the fellowship of Rabbi Shimon ben Yochai in the *Zohar*. R. A. Gilbert comments: 'It was through the Kabbalah – specifically through the two sections of the *Zohar*...that Waite first discovered the concept of the "Holy Assembly", and having found it he transformed it into a doctrine of his own'.[84] Isaac Luria's own Kabbalistic fellowship was modelled after R. Shimon's mythic Zoharic brotherhood,[85] and such Kabbalistic 'orders' existed in many centres of the diaspora throughout the early modern period.[86] Yehudah Liebes suggests that such a fellowship may have authored the *Zohar* itself, and included Moshe de Leon and Joseph Gikatilia among its members.[87] A late-thirteenth-century Hebrew text called *Meshal ha-Kadmoni* ('Fables of the Ancients'), written by the Castilian Kabbalist Isaac ibn Sahula – possibly also one of the Zoharic authors – portrays, through parables embedded in the literary framework of a rhymed prose narrative, various fellowships that gather to engage in learning with a master, and that specialise in esoteric lore and visionary and prophetic experience.[88] The descriptions of

---

[82] Ephraim of Sedylkov, *Degel Mahane Efrayim* (Koretz, 1810), f. 38a, cited in Scholem, *Messianic Idea*, 189.

[83] For the Hasidic *zaddik* as a priest, see Arthur Green, 'Typologies of Leadership and the Hasidic Zaddiq', in Green (ed.), *Jewish Spirituality*, 127–56.

[84] Gilbert, *A. E. Waite*, 96.

[85] For Luria's efforts to reproduce Shimon ben Yochai's fellowship, see Fine, *Physician*, 300–58. For Waite's use of Kabbalistic structures in the Fellowship of the Rosy Cross, see Gilbert, *A. E. Waite*, 123 and 142–54.

[86] For these Kabbalistic fellowships, see Werblowsky, 'The Safed Revival', 13–14; Jonathan Garb, 'The Cult of the Saints in Lurianic Kabbalah', *JQR* 98:2 (2008), 203–29.

[87] See Yehudah Liebes, *Studies in the Zohar*, trans. Arnold Schwartz, Stephanie Nakache, and Penina Peli (Albany, NY: State University of New York Press, 1993), 5–25.

[88] For the *Meshal ha-Kadmoni*, see Hartley Lachter, 'Spreading Secrets: Kabbalah and Esotericism in Isaac ibn Sahula's *Meshal ha-*

the fellowships in the *Meshal ha-Kadmoni* resemble, in turn, the fellowship of R. Shimon in the *Zohar*.[89] Although Waite accepted Ginsburg's assertion of the medieval provenance of the *Zohar*, he believed that the Zoharic tract called the *Idra Rabba* ('Greater Holy Assembly') had 'the appearance of a much older document' concerned with the 'Mysteries of Initiation', which 'stands alone in the great body of texts, an anonymous revelation, without antecedents or history'.[90] It would seem that Waite not only believed in the historical reality of R. Shimon's brotherhood, but was also determined to recreate it.

The Zoharic *Idra Suta* ('Lesser Holy Assembly') seems to have made an equally strong impression on Waite, because this text reveals the secrets of the androgynous nature of the godhead, the union of the supernal male and female, and what Waite calls 'the Kabbalistic doctrine of the sexes, so much in advance of its time, in whatever Christian century we may elect to place the literature'.[91] The *Idra Suta*, like the *Idra Rabba*, presents a group of mystics gathered under the guidance of R. Shimon to hear and experience the most profound and closely guarded cosmic secrets. R. Shimon refers to these disciples as those who have 'already entered the assembly of the Tabernacle',[92] a reference which Elliot Wolfson understands to represent the *Shekhinah*, the feminine face of deity.[93] In other words, the initiates have already experienced a collective *unio mystica* with the *Shekhinah* and will do so again. Although Mathers' stilted translation of the two *Idras* from Knorr's Latin fails to convey the experiential dimension of these treatises, Waite's access to de Pauly's French translation of the *Zohar* from the original Aramaic may have instilled in him a greater awareness of the ritual

---

kadmoni', *JQR* 100:1 (2010), 111–38; S. M. Stern, 'Rationalists and Kabbalists in Medieval Allegory', *JJS* 6:2 (1956), 73–86. For an English translation, see Raphael Loewe (ed. and trans.), *Meshal ha-kadmoni: Fables from the Distant Past* (Oxford: Littman Library of Jewish Civilization, 2004).

[89] See Ronit Meroz, 'Zoharic Narratives and Their Adaptations', *HJB* 3 (2000), 3–63, on pp. 13–17.

[90] Waite, *Holy Kabbalah*, 139, 141.

[91] Waite, *Holy Kabbalah*, 146.

[92] *Zohar* 3.127b.

[93] See Wolfson, 'Forms of Visionary Ascent', 212–13.

implications of the texts.[94] Waite eventually understood the significance of the sefirotic Tree, not as a 'rationalised system of mystic thought', but as the imaginative portrayal of a direct experience of ascent to a *unio mystica*. In the *Idra Suta*, R. Shimon dies the ecstatic-erotic death of the mystic, the 'death by a kiss', which must have made a great impression on Waite because of its resemblance to similar currents in the Christian mystical tradition.[95] A Holy Assembly of adepts, gathered to experience through ritual contemplation and practice the secret doctrine of the sacrament of sexual union as a 'Mystery of Initiation', describes precisely the object of Waite's Fellowship of the Rosy Cross.

WAITE'S 'MYSTERY OF SEX'

In *The Holy Kabbalah*, Waite includes a section entitled 'The Mystery of Sex'.[96] This part of the work, 'at once most important and difficult', is an exposition of the Zoharic doctrine of the mystical union of God with his *Shekhinah*, with its assertion that human nuptial union is an enactment of this cosmic mating on the earthly plane and is therefore a sacramental ritual. Waite begins his discussion with a reference to the original androgyny of souls,[97] an ancient idea which can be found in Plato's *Symposium* and which appears not only in Kabbalistic texts but also in various currents in the British occult revival.[98] According to Waite, the 'Mystery

---

[94] For Scholem's attenuation of the experiential elements in the *Zohar*, see Scholem, *Major Trends*, 123. For Wolfson's critique of Scholem on this theme, see Wolfson, 'Forms of Visionary Ascent', 214–16.

[95] *Zohar* 3.287b. For the 'mystical kiss' of the *Idra Suta*, see, *inter alia*, Fine, *Physician*, 350–53; Michael Fishbane, *The Kiss of God: Spiritual and Mystical Death in Judaism* (Seattle, WA: University of Washington Press, 1994); Idel, *Mystical Experience*, 180–84; Wirszubski, *Pico*, 153–60.

[96] Waite, *Holy Kabbalah*, 377–405.

[97] See Waite, *Holy Kabbalah*, 379.

[98] Plato, *Symposium*, 189e–193d, trans. Michael Joyce, in *Plato: Collected Dialogues*, 542. For Adam as a primordial androgyne in Kabbalistic literature, see, for example, R. Abraham ben David of Posquieres, *The Secret of Du-parzufim*, cited in Idel, *Kabbalah*, 128–29; Wolfson, *Language, Eros, Being*, 167–68; Scholem, *Origins*, 216–18; Idel, *Kabbalah and Eros*, 73–77. For the prolapsarian state of androgyny in Theosophy, see Blavatsky, *Isis*, 1:303. See Deveney, *Paschal Beverly Randolph*, 305–06, for Blavatsky's reliance on the

of Sex' involves 'the raising of the heart and mind on the part of the Lover and Beloved, to the Most Holy Shekinah, the glory which cohabits and indwells, during the external act.'[99] The sexual act is thus a 'Supreme Mystery' because it symbolises the union of male and female in both the supernal and corporeal worlds, which may also be understood as the union of God and the human soul:

> Marriage for the mystical Jew had become a sacrament, and I care nothing if scholarship – supposing that it were to take up the question – should decide in its wisdom that the Zoharic notion of marriage owes something to the sacramental system of the Catholic Church. I reject the proposition in advance.[100]

Waite ends his discussion of this great secret of the *Zohar* by declaring: 'There is a very secret path in which "the joy of living honourably with his wife" may bring the completed man – male and female – into the spiritual city of joy...wherein is the joy of the Lord'.[101]

There is no explicit mention of sexual magic here, but it is implicit in the phrase 'a very secret path', which suggests a Kabbalistic teaching on the mysteries of sex, passed from rabbi to disciple, which Waite believed to represent the most important dimension of Kabbalistic mysticism and which may have formed part of the ritual activity of his Fellowship of the Rosy Cross.[102] The sexual act as the central symbol of the *unio mystica* is also found in alchemical texts, which are often illustrated with explicitly erotic images of the *coniunctio* as the heart of the alchemical process, sometimes adorned

---

works of the Rosicrucian apologist Hargrave Jennings (1817–1890), from whom, according to Deveney, she acquired the idea of the 'double-sexed and hitherto-inactive Deity' from whom the androgynous primordial Adam first emanates. Jennings, who was steeped in Kabbalistic lore and quotes Christian Ginsburg's *Kabbalah* as a scholarly source, authored a number of bizarre works such as *The Rosicrucians: Their Rites and Mysteries* (London: Chatto and Windus, 1870). Waite was familiar with Jennings' work but dismissed him as a fantasist; see, for example, Waite, *Real History*, 409.

[99] Waite, *Holy Kabbalah*, 381.

[100] Waite, *Holy Kabbalah*, 403.

[101] Waite, *Holy Kabbalah*, 404–05. For this central motif in Kabbalistic texts, see Idel, *Kabbalah and Eros*, 235.

[102] For the 'wholly mystical' nature of Waite's Fellowship, see Gilbert, *A. E. Waite*, 142–54.

with Kabbalistic symbols.[103] This overlap between the Kabbalah and the 'Hermetic art' would hardly have escaped Waite's notice. Although Waite's autobiography reveals no clue about the application of these ideas in his own life, it seems he did not merely theorise about the Kabbalistic mysteries of sex. In 1904, he and his close friend Arthur Machen, newly initiated into Waite's 'Independent and Rectified' Golden Dawn,[104] produced a privately printed work called *The House of the Hidden Light*, an enigmatic text about which R. A. Gilbert comments: 'No work of either author has been the subject of so much eccentric speculation and ill-informed comment as this one'.[105]

At one extreme of the speculation stands Ithell Colquhoun, who suggests that the ritual described in *Hidden Light*, called the 'Veritable, Ancient and Rectified Rite of Lilith', was written for the adepts of the Inner Order of the Golden Dawn and concerns 'sexual congress with praeternatural beings' because, according to Colquhoun, the demoness Lilith, in Kabbalistic traditions, rules over the *qlipot* or 'shells' of the lower realms, 'microcosmically the sphere of sex'.[106] Colquhoun concludes that Waite was

---

[103] See, for example, the *Rosarium Philosophorum*, an anonymous alchemical work published in 1550 but probably composed much earlier, whose frankly erotic images, portraying the 'King' and 'Queen' in the act of copulation, are reprinted in Jung, CW16, ¶402–537, and posted by Adam MacLean, <http://www.levity.com/alchemy/rosarium.html>. See also the images in *Atlanta fugiens* by the Rosicrucian apologist Michael Maier (Oppenheim: Johann Theodor de Bry, 1618), reproduced in de Rola, *Golden Game*, 68–104.

[104] For the lifelong friendship between Waite and Machen, see Waite, *Shadows*, 103–12; Roger Dobson, Godfrey Brangham, and R. A. Gilbert (eds.), *Arthur Machen: Selected Letters* (Wellingborough: Aquarian Press, 1988), 25–81; Marco Pasi, 'Arthur Machen's Panic Fears: Western Esotericism and the Irruption of Negative Epistemology', *Aries* 7:1 (2007), 63–83.

[105] Arthur Machen and Arthur Edward Waite, *The House of the Hidden Light* (London: private publication, 1904; Yorke Collection FBH 904.H58, Warburg Institute, London); Gilbert, *A. E. Waite*, 69. Only three copies of *Hidden Light* were printed.

[106] Colquhoun, *Sword*, 288. For Lilith in Kabbalistic lore, see Joseph Dan, 'Samael, Lilith, and the Concept of Evil in Early Kabbalah', *AJSR*, 5 (1980), 17–40; Patai, 'Lilith'. For the *qlipot* and the 'shells' in the Golden Dawn, see S. L. MacGregor Mathers, 'The Qliphoth of the Qabalah', Golden Dawn Instructional Paper (*c.* 1900), repr. in Gilbert (ed.), *Sorcerer and His Apprentice*, 23–29; Fortune, *Mystical*

dealing not only with sexual magic, but with its '"blacker" side'.[107] As the 'Rite of Lilith' is not fully described in *Hidden Light*, it is impossible to ascertain whether there is any validity in Colquhoun's speculations, although the text itself, taken as a whole, suggests otherwise. Colquhoun probably made the association between *Hidden Light* and the human-elemental sexual encounters rumoured to be part of Golden Dawn Inner Order teachings because Waite, writing as 'Frater Elias Artista', declares:

> At this time also there were given unto them two sisters, daughters of the House of Life, for high priestesses and ministers....These were children of the elements, queens of fire and water, full of inward magic and of outward witchery, full of music and song, radiant with the illusions of Light.[108]

Qabalah, 297–304. For the *qlipot* in the Kabbalah, see Scholem, *Major Trends*, 238–39; Fine, *Physician*, 142–44, 243–44.

[107] Colquhoun, *Sword*, 289. In her claim that Waite's 'Rite of Lilith' concerns sexual magic, Colquhoun (*Sword*, 289) refers to Waite being influenced by the sexual magic of Andrew Jackson Davis. Davis (1826–1909) was an American spiritualist, mesmeric trance healer, and proto-feminist who, in a series of twenty-six major works, blended spiritualist ideas with Swedenborg's cosmological speculations and created a universal system called the 'Harmonial Philosophy'. Waite produced a preface and biographical summary of Davis, known as the 'Seer of Poughkeepsie', for his edited digest of Davis' work: A. E. Waite (ed.), *The Harmonial Philosophy: A Compendium and Digest of the Works of Andrew Jackson Davis, the Seer of Poughkeepsie* (London: William Rider & Son, 1917). For more on Davis, see Robert S. Cox, *Body and Soul: A Sympathetic History of American Spiritualism* (Charlottesville, VA: University of Virginia Press, 2003); Deveney, *Paschal Beverly Randolph*, 14–15; Owen, *Darkened Room*, 36–37; Oppenheim, *Other World*, 101–03. Although Davis can hardly be considered a sexual magician, he opposed Christian doctrines of the sinful nature of the body and, like many American spiritualists of the mid-nineteenth century, advocated a philosophy of 'free love'. On this American esoteric current, see Arthur Versluis, 'Sexual Mysticisms in Nineteenth Century America: John Humphrey Noyes, Thomas Lake Harris, and Alice Bunker Stockham', in Hanegraaff and Kripal (eds.), *Hidden Intercourse*, 333–54. Waite used the pseudonym 'A Doctor of Hermetic Science' for his digest of Davis' work, and Gilbert suggests that by the time the book was ready for publication, Waite had come to dislike Davis's philosophy and wished to distance himself from it (see Gilbert, *Waite: A Bibliography*, 126–27).

[108] Machen and Waite, *Hidden Light*, 12–13.

It is more likely that these descriptions of 'queens of fire and water' are references linking the two women to two of the four queens of the Minor Arcana of the Tarot, since Waite, long preoccupied with the meaning of the cards, suggests that the appearance of these cards in a 'spread' can signify individuals who enter one's life at the time: 'The subject of the divination falls ultimately into the hands of a person represented by that card, and its end depends mainly on him'.[109] The Queen of Wands, associated with the element of fire, is full of 'life and animation', 'friendly, chaste, loving, honourable'.[110] The Queen of Cups, associated with the element of water, is 'beautiful, fair, dreamy – as one who sees visions in a cup'.[111] In *Hidden Light*, the two women are also described as partaking of the qualities of the female *sefirot* *Binah* and *Nezach*.[112]

Gilbert, at the other extreme, dismisses Colquhoun's revelations as 'an entertaining point of view',[113] and suggests that *Hidden Light*, far from being the record of a disreputable immersion in the mud of 'black' sexual magic, is merely a hyperbolic record of Machen's and Waite's escapades with their lady friends during 1900 and 1901, 'recounted in literary form'.[114] The doctrines and practices which form the basis for *Hidden Light* may lie somewhere between these extremes. It is possible that Gilbert's insistence on the dichotomy between mysticism and magic has resulted in a 'whitewashing' of Waite's preoccupation with sex, which is evident in the importance Waite assigns to its role in the *Zohar*. While it is unlikely that Waite was secretly mimicking Crowley's unforgettable blend of scatology and eschatology, *Hidden Light* suggests something more than the hyperbolic record of two enjoyable love-affairs.[115] Waite was inclined to design private rituals for himself and his friends,[116] and he and Machen probably created the 'Rite of Lilith' specifically for themselves and their two female companions. The fact that it was private rather than practiced under the auspices

---

[109] Waite, *Pictorial Key to the Tarot*, 304.
[110] Waite, *Pictorial Key to the Tarot*, 172.
[111] Waite, *Pictorial Key to the Tarot*, 200.
[112] Machen and Waite, *Hidden Light*, 71–72.
[113] Gilbert, *A. E. Waite*, 69.
[114] Gilbert, *Scrapbook*, 172.
[115] For the identity of the women, see Gilbert, *A. E. Waite*, 57–75. Waite's lady-friend was his sister-in-law, Annie Lakeman.
[116] See Waite, 'Viaticum'.

of an organised occult order does not exclude the use of sexual magic, of a kind based specifically on Kabbalistic formulations and blended with themes which Waite understood as belonging to the traditions of both alchemy and Christian mysticism.

The chapter of *Hidden Light* entitled 'The Versicles and Symbols of the Secret Order According to the Mysteries of Love' speaks of the purgation of the vanity of earthly love, a familiar enough theme in the Christian mystical tradition. But the text then insists:

> Even upon the material plane there are high ministries and consolations for mystic love, to whom the earthly object is often restored...palpably transfigured, a high priestess, radiant and immortal, filling the whole world with graciousness and glory.[117]

The 'Rite of Lilith', also referred to as 'The Rite of Hermetic Marriage', is evidently intended to invoke the potencies of the supernal realms in order to transform the participants of the ritual so that they become 'vessels of the sacraments'.[118] This idea is derived directly from the *Zohar*, in which the marital act, performed as a sacred ritual, becomes the earthly embodiment of the sacred union of God and his *Shekhinah*. It is not a Christian concept, as Waite himself acknowledges.[119] Because the rite is intended to transform the participants and alter worldly conditions, it may be considered magical.

'Letter XXVII' presents the Kabbalistic symbolism overtly: 'In the light of which order the world is transfigured, and the Crown is made one with the Kingdom'. The Crown is the first *sefira*, *Keter*, while the Kingdom is *Malkuth*, the last *sefira*, equated with the *Shekhinah*.[120] 'Letter XXX' reveals Lurianic themes through its reference to the 'great day of

---

[117] Waite and Machen, *Hidden Light*, 26–32.
[118] Waite and Machen, *Hidden Light*, 30. See Idel, *Hasidism*, 105, on the 'drawing down of the divine influx from the supernal source'.
[119] See Waite, *Holy Kabbalah*, 403.
[120] For the Crown and the Kingdom, see Arthur Green, *Keter: The Crown of God in Early Jewish Mysticism* (Princeton, NJ: Princeton University Press, 1997); Scholem, *Mystical Shape*, 140–96; Elliot R. Wolfson, *Luminal Darkness: Imaginal Gleanings from Zoharic Literature* (Oxford: Oneworld, 2007), 144–84. For Waite's understanding of the union of *Keter* and *Malkuth*, see Waite, *Holy Kabbalah*, 350.

reintegration'.[121] Kabbalistic references abound throughout *Hidden Light*; the entire document is rooted in Zoharic lore, which seems to have yielded to Waite and Machen a 'most precious secret' which, 'though it have the savour of immortality, is still mixed with mortal elements'.[122] The 'Rite of Lilith' appears to be a serious magical ritual, private rather than embedded in a formal group structure, based firmly on Kabbalistic traditions, and involving the sexual act as a means of achieving a mystical experience through the transformation of the participants into vessels of the divine sefirotic influx. Crowley's portrait of Arthwait as a dull, spiritless pedant 'without imagination or real magical perception' may be somewhat wide of the mark.

THE KABBALAH ACCORDING TO A. E. WAITE

Waite introduced into his writings and rituals a proliferation of themes from the more obscure byways of Rosicrucian and Grail lore.[123] He equates the quest for the Holy Grail with the ascent of the soul through the twenty-two Hebrew letters from *aleph* to *tau* on the pathways of the sefirotic Tree; both symbolic journeys, like the alchemical *opus*, are concerned with the *unio mystica*.[124] Waite did not view himself as a Kabbalist, but as an aspirant following in the footsteps of great Christian mystics such as Louis-Claude de Saint-Martin, who had availed himself of Kabbalistic speculations 'in the Christian mode'. However, the entirety of Waite's work is rooted in the theosophical doctrines of the Jewish Kabbalah. It is virtually impossible to find a text by Waite, whether on the Rosicrucians, alchemy, Freemasonry,

---

[121] For Waite's probable source for the term 'reintegration', describing the Lurianic idea of *tikkun* or restitution of all living beings in the godhead, see Pasqually, *Traité de la réintégration*, discussed in Waite, 'A Lodge of Magic', *OR* 26:6 (1917), 228–34.

[122] Waite and Machen, *Hidden Light*, 121–22.

[123] For Waite's published work on the Grail, see A. E. Waite, *The Hidden Church of the Holy Graal* (London: Rebman Ltd., 1909); A. E. Waite, *The Book of the Holy Graal* (London: Watkins, 1921); A. E. Waite, *The Holy Grail, Its Legends and Symbolism* (London: Rider & Co., 1933); A. E. Waite, 'The Holy Graal in the Light of the Celtic Church', *OR* 5:6 (1907), 334–45; A. E. Waite, 'Mystic Aspects of the Grail Legend', *OR* 6:2 (1907), 35–44; A. E. Waite, 'Notes on the Grail Tradition', *OR* 6:3 (1907), 121–25.

[124] See Waite, *Shadows*, 253.

the Tarot, or the mystical ascent of the soul, which does not use the sefirotic Tree as a symbol of that process of spiritual transformation which forms the core of his aspirations. In *Azoth*, his most intensely devotional work, he offers his vision of the ultimate 'perfection of humanity', when the manifestation of God's love transfigures the world: this manifestation is 'the Shekinah of the Jews, in whose shining, central, circumambient, flame-like glory, God was wont to manifest His presence'.[125] Nor does Waite fail to echo Lévi in referring to Kabbalistic theosophy as the origin of the 'Secret Tradition' in the Western world. In *The Real History of the Rosicrucians*, he informs his readers that the central symbol of that order, the rose itself, is 'the Shecinah [*sic*] of Rabbinical theosophy, the chosen habitation of God'.[126] In his view, the entirety of the Masonic tradition – the great pillars of Jakin and Boaz, the spiritualisation of Solomon's Temple, the Lost Word – derives from the 'Secret Tradition of Israel',[127] and the roots of alchemy lie not only in Egypt but in 'the people of Israel', who are 'accredited with science and wisdom like that of Solomon'.[128]

For Waite, the Kabbalah was neither a method of practical magic nor a mere instrument for 'programmatic syncretism'. Like Lévi, he formulated in considerable detail the debt owed to the Kabbalah by the various currents of the 'Secret Tradition' and, like Westcott, he attributed the origins of Western ceremonial magic to this source. But the sefirotic Tree seems to have provided Waite with an all-embracing symbol of the spiritual journey of humankind. All the manifestations of human aspiration can be related to aspects of the Tree, and his own personal journey was understood as an ascent along its pathways:

As one who ascends the Tree of Life, I have passed upwards

---

[125] Waite, *Azoth*, 80–81.
[126] Waite, *Real History*, 17.
[127] See A. E. Waite, 'Some Deeper Aspects of Masonic Symbolism', *The Builders* (1915), repr. in Dunning (ed.), *Waite: Selected Masonic Papers*, 153–70, on pp. 168–69; A. E. Waite, 'The Spiritual Symbolism of Freemasonry', 'Introduction' in A. E. Waite (trans.), *The Liturgy of the Rite of the Strict Observance* (privately printed, 1934), repr. in Dunning (ed.), *Waite: Selected Masonic Papers*, 123–52, on pp. 130–32.
[128] A. E. Waite, 'Kabalistic Alchemy', *Journal of the Alchemical Society* 2:9 (1914), 43–58, repr. in Gilbert (ed.), *Hermetic Papers of A. E. Waite*, 99–119, on pp. 100–01.

clothed in Symbols and have dwelt amidst a ministry of images.[129]

The poet often overwhelms the scholar, and Waite used the Tree as a grand poetic metaphor that encapsulates the ineffable: the return of the human soul from the alienation of earthly embodiment to its original state of perfection and unity with deity, and the immanence of the divine in a world radiant with signatures and correspondences that reveal the secret identity of God and Nature. These aspects of Kabbalistic theosophy spoke to Waite's imagination in a way that the doctrines of the Catholic Church apparently could not do. Although he intended to use the Kabbalah 'in the Christian mode', in fact Waite used the Kabbalah as Jewish Kabbalists have always done: as a mode of reflection, imagining, and ritual practice which builds a bridge between 'revealed and concealed worlds'.

THE KABBALAH ACCORDING TO ALEISTER CROWLEY

The Kabbalah also provides the central reference point for Crowley's many expositions on magic. But Crowley's Kabbalah emphasises everything in this Jewish esoteric lore that Waite repudiates. In *Liber 777* and other works, it is clear that the Kabbalah served Crowley with what Israel Regardie, who worked as Crowley's personal secretary, calls 'a basic system or method of filing new information on any topic or subject'.[130] In 'An Essay upon Number', Crowley indulges his delight in the linguistic techniques of Kabbalistic hermeneutics, which Waite dismisses as 'solemn follies';[131] and in Crowley's last work, *Magick Without Tears*, he calls the Kabbalah 'The Best Training for Memory' and reveals his fascination with the curious properties of the Hebrew letters:

Now you must learn Qabalah. Learn this Alphabet of Magick. You must take it on trust, as a child does his own alphabet.

---

[129] Waite, *Shadows*, 277.
[130] Israel Regardie, 'Introduction', in Aleister Crowley, *777 and Other Qabalistic Writings of Aleister Crowley*, ed. Israel Regardie (York Beach, ME: Red Wheel/Weiser, 1986), iii.
[131] Aleister Crowley, 'An Essay upon Number', in *777*, 27–50. For Crowley's preoccupation with *gematria*, see Regardie, 'Introduction', iii. For Waite's dismissive view of *gematria*, see Waite, *Holy Kabbalah*, 36.

No one has ever found out why the order of the letters is what it is. Probably there isn't any answer.[132]

For *Liber 777*, Crowley appropriated the detailed tables of correspondences between the *sefirot*, planets, Hebrew letters, angels, magical images, numbers, and Tarot cards provided in Mathers' *Book T*,[133] and embellished this Golden Dawn material by incorporating additional symbolic systems such as the Hexagrams of the *Yi King*.[134] *Liber 777* presents an all-encompassing system of classification which uses the Kabbalah as

> ...an instrument for interpreting symbols whose meaning has become obscure, forgotten, or misunderstood by establishing a necessary connection between the essence of forms, sounds, simple ideas (such as number) and their spiritual, moral, or intellectual equivalents.[135]

It is this aspect of Crowley's Kabbalah that Egil Asprem justifiably identifies as 'programmatic syncretism *par excellence*': a Kabbalah that has been 'disembedded from its cultural context and re-embedded as a *taxonomical device*'.[136] Although Jewish Kabbalists were also fond of enumerating chains of correspondences related to the *sefirot*, they did so within the framework of the Jewish religious matrix. Crowley claimed to have no interest in this matrix:

> I have very little sympathy with Jewish Theology or ritual; but the Qabalah is so handy and congenial that I use it more than almost any [esoteric system] – or all the others together – for daily use and work.[137]

---

[132] Aleister Crowley, *Magick Without Tears*, ed. Karl J. Germer (New York: Ordo Templi Orientis, 1954), reissued by Bill Heidrick for the O.T.O. (1988) at <http://danbartlett.co.uk/AC_MWT.pdf>, Chapter IV: 'The Qabalah: The Best Training for Memory'.

[133] *Book T*, also called *The Book of Correspondences*, is reproduced in Regardie, *Golden Dawn*, 540–65, and in Robert Wang, *An Introduction to the Golden Dawn Tarot* (New York: Samuel Weiser Inc., 1978), 63–143. See also Colquhoun, *Sword*, 104–05.

[134] See Crowley, *777*, 1–155. For Crowley's 'plagiarism' of the Table from Mathers, see Colqhoun, *Sword*, 104–05.

[135] Crowley, *777*, 125.

[136] Asprem, '*Kabbalah Recreata*', 137.

[137] Aleister Crowley, 'Letters Written by the Master Therion to a Student', Letter F (20 August 1943), in Crowley, *Magick Without Tears*.

But Crowley was as inconsistent in his presentations of the Kabbalah as he was when describing his views on religion.[138] In an essay privately published in 1907,[139] he discusses the merits of the Kabbalah from both theoretical and practical perspectives, emphasising the importance of focused meditation as the method of 'true magical ceremonial' and interpreting the paraphernalia of magical rituals – fumigations, purifications, invocations, banishings – as a means of directing the will toward the 'supreme moment', the *unio mystica* with the 'Qabalistic Zero' or *En Soph*.[140] He concludes by declaring:

> True symbols do really awake those macrocosmic forces of which they are the eidola....I therefore definitely affirm the validity of the Qabalistic tradition in its practical part as well as in those exalted regions of thought through which we have so recently, and so hardly, travelled.[141]

In a revealing article entitled 'The Jewish Problem Restated', published anonymously in 1922, Crowley affirms that the true spirit of Israel 'shines in the splendour of its literature, and in such moral qualities as that rigorous sense of Reality which made him [the Jew] the torch-bearer of Science through the Dark Ages'.[142] It is to this spirit, and to the 'practical' Kabbalah presented in Mathers' translation of *Abramelin*,[143] that Crowley attributes his own new religion of Thelema:

---

[138] See Hutton, *Triumph of the Moon*, 174–80, for Crowley's chameleon-like tendencies in religious matters.

[139] Aleister Crowley, בראסית [*Berashit*]: *An Essay in Ontology, by Abhavananda* (Paris: private publication for the Sangha of the West, 1907; Yorke Collection FBH 929 B26 C.1, Warburg Institute, London). Crowley uses the Hebrew letters on both the cover and title page of the work. For the use of *berashit* ('in the beginning') in Kabbalistic texts, see Idel, *Kabbalah*, 183.

[140] Crowley, בראסית, 22.

[141] Crowley, בראסית, 23.

[142] Aleister Crowley, 'The Jewish Problem Restated, by a Gentile', *English Review* (July 1922), 28–37, on p. 37.

[143] *Abramelin* was purportedly written in 1458; Mathers translated this grimoire from a French MS he found at the Bibliothèque de l'Arsenal in Paris. The work claims to be Kabbalistic and, according to Mathers' introduction (xxvi), intends 'by purity and self-denial to obtain the knowledge of and conversation with one's Guardian Angel, so that thereby and thereafter we may obtain the right of using the Evil Spirits for our servants in all material matters'.

It was by means of the secret tradition of the Hebrews that the leader of the new Law [Crowley himself] obtained 'the knowledge and conversation of his Holy Guardian Angel', whose words constitute the whole Law.[144]

This understanding of Kabbalah as both a theosophy and a magical path toward mystical union reflects a sophisticated understanding of Jewish traditions that credits them with nothing less than Crowley's own apotheosis as the prophet of the new Aeon.

SEX, 'MAGICK', AND THE JEWISH MESSIAHS

A number of recent scholarly works discuss Crowley's sexual magic, its place in the context of the larger British fascination with sexuality in the early twentieth century, and its enduring influence on present-day ceremonial magic.[145]

Crowley took this text seriously, and from 1899 onward attempted on numerous occasions to complete the rigorous preparatory stages necessary for the invocation. He felt he had finally achieved his goal in 1904 with the manifestation of Aiwass, the entity who dictated *The Book of the Law*, whom he identified as his Guardian Angel. For Crowley's discussions of the magic of *Abramelin* and its potent effects, see Crowley, *Confessions*, 172, 175–76, 350, 569–72. Although Crowley often used up-to-date modern terminologies to justify his magic as 'scientific illuminism', it seems he nevertheless accepted the ontological reality of the entities described in *Abramelin*: 'I should have liked to deny the whole reality of the Abra-Melin business, but the phenomena were just as patent as the stones of the house' (Crowley, *Confessions*, 375). The 'scientific method' which Crowley developed as his contribution to the occultism of the early twentieth century is unquestionably phrased in new language adapted to the currents of the time, but this suggests that he needs to convince both himself and his readership that he is a 'modern'. The uneasy relationship between Crowley's conceptualisations and his personal responses and beliefs, reflected in his experiences with the *Abramelin* material, appears to be profoundly ambiguous and rests on a conviction of the ontological potency of pre-modern Jewish magic as much as on 'programmatic syncretism'.
[144] Crowley, 'Jewish Problem', 28–29.
[145] For papers dealing specifically with Crowley's sexual magic, see Owen, 'Sorcerer and His Apprentice'; Hugh Urban, 'Unleashing the Beast: Aleister Crowley, Tantra and Sex Magic in Late Victorian England', *Esoterica*, 5 (2003), 138–92; Hugh Urban, 'The Yoga of Sex: Tantra, Orientalism, and Sex Magic in the Ordo Templi Orientis', in Hanegraaff and Kripal (eds.), *Hidden Intercourse*, 401–43.

Crowley's autobiography remains the definitive statement of the flamboyant, self-destructive, and tragic career of this remarkable man,[146] although his veracity regarding his sexual exploits, as with other aspects of his life, is often questionable.[147] Crowley's sexual 'magick' has been viewed by scholars and by later generations of occultists as a derivative of Tantric practices, but Crowley demonstrates little real knowledge of Tantra in his writings.[148] The emphasis on sexual magic within *fin-de-siècle* British occultism, and the particular influences that shaped Crowley's versions of it, are not attributable entirely, or even primarily, to the Western importation of Tantric practices in the late nineteenth century.[149] Marco Pasi suggests that Crowley acquired his knowledge of sexual magic from Theodor Reuss' OTO, which Crowley joined in 1910.[150] But Crowley had begun to experiment with sexual magic at least a year before his encounter with Reuss, and he reveals his knowledge of one of the main principles of Kabbalistic sexual magic when he declares: 'Like the Jews, the wise men of India have a belief that a certain particular Prana, or force, resides in the Bindu, or semen'.[151]

Whether Crowley acquired his knowledge of Jewish sexual magic from the OTO, the Kabbalistic literature

---

[146] For Crowley as a tragic figure, see Hutton, *Triumph of the Moon*, 172; Marco Pasi, 'The Neverendingly Told Story: Recent Biographies of Aleister Crowley', *Aries* 3:2 (2003), 224–45, on p. 229.

[147] For Crowley's economy with the truth, see Pasi, 'Neverendlingly Told Story', 240.

[148] See the discussions in Urban, 'Unleashing the Beast', 150–59; Pasi, 'Neverendlingly Told Story', 234–36.

[149] For the Western appropriation of Tantra, see Urban, 'Unleashing the Beast', 150–55; Urban, 'Yoga of Sex', 410–14.

[150] See Pasi, 'Neverendingly Told Story', 236. For Crowley's description of his first encounter with Reuss, see Crowley, *Confessions*, 775–76. For Crowley's involvement with Reuss' order, see Urban, 'Yoga of Sex', 428–35. For the OTO and its rituals, see Francis King, *The Secret Rituals of the O.T.O.* (York Beach, ME: Samuel Weiser, Inc., 1973); Theodor Reuss and Aleister Crowley, *O.T.O. Rituals and Sex Magick*, ed. Peter-R. Koenig (Thame: I-H-O Books, 1999); Ellic Howe and Helmut Moller, 'Theodor Reuss: Irregular Freemasonry in Germany, 1900–23', *AQC* 91 (1978), at http://freemasonry.bcy.ca/aqc/reuss/reuss/html.

[151] Aleister Crowley, *De Arte Magica: Secundum ritum Gradus Nonae O.T.O.*, XVI, private publication, repr. in Francis King (ed.), *Crowley on Christ* (London: C. W. Daniel, 1974), 213–32, on p. 221.

provided by the Golden Dawn, other occult groups and authors, unnamed living Jewish sources, or a combination of all of these, *Moonchild* demonstrates Crowley's awareness of a belief expressed in one of the most influential Kabbalistic texts from the late thirteenth century, the anonymously authored *Iggeret ha-Kodesh* ('Letter on Holiness'):

> When the husband copulates with his wife, and his thought unites with the supernal entities, that very thought draws the supernal light downward, and it dwells upon the drop [of semen] upon which he directs his intention and thought...that very drop is permanently linked with the brilliant light.[152]

Moshe Idel, discussing this text, acknowledges the affinity of this 'mystical' conception of the sexual act with Tantric practices, but highlights a fundamental difference: in Kabbalistic literature, intercourse as a vehicle for spiritual experience is a preparatory phase leading to procreation, while in Tantra, mystical consciousness is an aim in itself, and is achieved by curtailing the flow of semen. Thus the Kabbalists 'put mystical union in the service of procreation; tantra put fruitless intercourse into the service of mystical consciousness'.[153] The *Zohar*, written at roughly the same time as the *Iggeret ha-Kodesh*, expresses the same idea:

> These are the companions who...abstain from sexual intercourse during the six weekdays while they labor at the Torah, but who on Sabbath eve prepare themselves for intercourse, because they know the exalted mystery concerning the time when the consort is united with the King...and then they are blessed on that night with the fruit of their loins.[154]

In the Lurianic Kabbalah, the more exalted the state of the couple during the sexual act, the higher the soul that is drawn down into incarnation. According to Luria, on the Sabbath eve souls descend from the highest supernal realms, and the child resulting from a sexual union performed with

---

[152] *Iggeret ha-Kodesh*, in Chavel (ed.), *Kitve ha-Ramban* (Jerusalem, 1964), 2:373, cited in Moshe Idel, 'Sexual Metaphors and Praxis in the Kabbalah', in David Kraemer (ed.), *The Jewish Family: Metaphor and Memory* (Oxford: Oxford University Press, 1989), 197–224, on p. 205. For the *Iggeret ha-Kodesh*, see also Fine, *Physician*, 174.
[153] Idel, 'Sexual Metaphors', 205.
[154] *Zohar* II.89a–89b, cited in Tishby, *Wisdom*, 3:1391.

the correct 'mystical intentionality' on this special night will be a holy child.[155] Although it is unlikely that Crowley observed the Jewish Sabbath in his practice of sexual magic, the effort presented in *Moonchild* to create a magical child whose body is inhabited by an elemental spirit of high lineage and power – echoing, despite its overlay of Greco-Egyptian symbolism, the Jewish concept of *ibbur* or impregnation of a human body by a 'higher soul' or supernal entity – reflects Kabbalistic, not Tantric, doctrines.[156]

Sexual magic had been endemic in British occultism for at least a century and a half before it emerged with explosive notoriety in Crowley's work,[157] and the specific forms Crowley chose to pursue reflect Jewish Kabbalistic traditions related to the antinomian doctrines of Sabbatai Zevi (1626–1676), who provoked the largest and most important messianic eruption in Jewish history after Jesus of Nazareth, and whose similarities with Crowley's own messianic apotheosis suggest that Crowley might have been familiar with Zevi's history and found it both attractive and useful.[158] The theories of sexuality circulating in the late-nineteenth-century occult milieu may have been partly inspired by the 'practical Kabbalah' of *Le Comte de Gabalis*, partly by Tantra, and partly by the sexual theories of the Anglo-American spiritualist prophet Thomas Lake Harris (1823–1906), which were circulated informally within the Golden Dawn's Inner Order.[159] Like Waite, Harris appears to have been a Christian

---

[155] Fine, *Physician*, 197.

[156] For the 'ritual of the moon' intended to draw down the lunar spirit, and Crowley's Kabbalistic references to the ritual, see *Moonchild*, 145–49. For *ibbur*, see below.

[157] For the Kabbalistic sexual magic of Rabbi Samuel Falk, see below. See also Godwin, *Theosophical Enlightenment*, 1–25, for the 'worship of the generative powers' in the eighteenth century.

[158] For documentation of Zevi's activities among British millennarians, see Richard H. Popkin, 'Christian Interest and Concerns About Sabbatai Zevi', in Matt Goldish and Richard H. Popkin (eds.), *Millenarianism and Messianism in Early Modern European Culture, Vol. 1: Jewish Messianism in the Early Modern World* (Dordrecht: Kluwer Academic Publishers, 2001), 91–106; Richard H. Popkin, 'Three English Tellings of the Sabbatai Zevi Story', *JH* 8 (1994), 43–54; Michael McKeon, 'Sabbatai Sevi in England', *AJSR* 3 (1977), 131–69.

[159] Harris began receiving his revelations at the age of twenty-seven. In 1861 he founded a commune in Wassaic, New York called the Brotherhood of the New Life; to this esoteric society, which

of a mystical bent who preached the Zoharic doctrine of the sacred nature of the sexual act and the androgynous nature of the godhead. It seems that Harris also involved himself with sexual encounters with elementals; his relationship with a disincarnate being called 'Lily Queen' purportedly resulted in the begetting of astral children.[160] Harris appears to have been an admirer of Blake and a follower of Swedenborg, both of whom seem to have been influenced not only by the Kabbalah but by the Kabbalistic magic of Rabbi Samuel Falk; and much of Harris' vocabulary is derived from the Kabbalah, including his various references to the *Shekhinah*.[161]

---

numbered around 2000 members while at its height, he issued secret doctrines about sexual magic which the community put into practice in an enthusiastic manner reminiscent of Crowley's notorious Abbey of Thelema in Sicily. Colquhoun (*Sword*, 148–49) states that the Golden Dawn adept Edward W. Berridge was an admirer of Harris' 'tantrik' theory of prolonged intercourse without ejaculation, and that Berridge discussed this and other doctrines promulgated by Harris within the Golden Dawn. For a biography of Harris written by one of his disciples, see Arthur A. Cuthbert, *The Life and World-Work of Thomas Lake Harris* (Glasgow: private publication, 1908), from which selected chapters are available at <http://www.spiritwritings.com/LifeThomasHarris.pdf>. Three of Harris' works – *A Lyric of the Morning Land* (New York: Partridge & Brittan, 1854), *An Epic of the Starry Heaven* (New York: Partridge & Brittan, 1855), and *The Song of Theos* (Glasgow: private publication, 1903) – are at <http://onlinebooks.library.upenn.edu/webbin/book/lookupname?key=Harris%2C%20Thomas%20Lake>. See <www.spiritwritings.com/harrisbibliography.html> for a complete bibliography of Harris' works.

[160] See Godwin et al., *Hermetic Brotherhood*, 72 and n. 113.

[161] Harris' biographer Cuthbert, in *Life and World-Work*, declares (17): 'Harris affirmed the absolute Divine and personal supremacy of the Lord Jesus Christ, and the writer of this narrative feels called, in the unity of the Breath, with all who receive it consciously in the life, to affirm the derivative supremacy of the King – the King-Queen, twain-one, from their Heaven in Lilistan – as being, in point of fact, the centre and fountainhead of perfect law for the structural edification both of the individual man and of humane society in the world'. See Kaczynski, *Perdurabo*, 203, for the suggestion that the promulgation of Harris' doctrines within the Golden Dawn influenced Crowley. Arthur Versluis devotes several pages to Harris in his paper, 'Sexual Mysticisms in Nineteenth Century America' and discusses Swedenborg's influence on Harris, but Versluis does not mention any Kabbalistic influences on Harris' doctrines.

But esoteric sources such as Harris provided threads in a complex fabric that later incorporated new explorations into sexuality by Richard von Krafft-Ebing, Havelock Ellis, and Edward Carpenter.[162] In 1898 Crowley published his poetic compilation, *White Stains*, specifically to refute Krafft-Ebing's theory that sexual aberrations were the result of disease,[163] and he defends both Ellis and Carpenter, declaring: 'Havelock Ellis and Edward Carpenter have been treated with the foulest injustice by ignorant and prejudiced people'.[164] Crowley was also acquainted with the work of Henry Maudsley (1835–1918), founder of the Maudsley Hospital in London for the treatment of psychiatric illness, an entrenched opponent of spiritualism and occultism and a vigorous promulgator of the theory of psycho-physical 'degeneration' as the inevitable by-product of too much civilisation.[165] Crowley's response to Maudsley's theory was

---

[162] See von Krafft-Ebing, *Psychopathia Sexualis*; Havelock Ellis and John Addington Symonds, *Sexual Inversion* (London: Wilson & Macmillan, 1897); Edward Carpenter, *The Intermediate Sex* (London: Swan Sonnenschien & Co., 1908). Havelock Ellis (1859–1939), whose theories of narcissism and autoeroticism exercised considerable influence on Freud, produced *Sexual Inversion* in 1897 in collaboration with John Addington Symonds. The book was banned a year later. *Sexual Inversion*, an examination of sexual relationships between men and boys, presented Ellis' idea that homosexuality was neither a disease nor a crime, but was a constitutional fact in certain individuals. Despite its hostile reception, the book was republished four years later (Philadelphia, PA: F. A. Davis, 1901), and *Studies in the Psychology of Sex*, a massive eight-volume work, followed after a nine-year interval (Philadelphia, PA: F. A. Davis, 1910). Alex Owen (*Place of Enchantment*, 108) suggests that both Ellis and Krafft-Ebing 'helped to bring the concept of the homosexual into cultural circulation'. Edward Carpenter (1844–1929), who was a member of Anna Kingsford's Hermetic Society, went further than Ellis, suggesting in *The Intermediate Sex* that homosexuality might be seen as a superior stage in spiritual evolution which could confer special intuitive and psychic powers. For Carpenter's impact on British occult currents, see Owen, *Place of Enchantment*, 108–09; Hutton, *Triumph of the Moon*, 27. For an examination of new currents in 'the science of sexuality' at the turn of the century, see also Urban, *Magia Sexualis*, 57–63.

[163] Crowley, *Confessions*, 127.

[164] Crowley, *Confessions*, 133.

[165] For the theory of 'degeneration', see Bruce Haley, *The Healthy Body and Victorian Culture* (Cambridge: Cambridge University Press, 1978); Hurley, *Gothic Body*; Owen, *Darkened Room*, 183–88. For

predictable: while he did not disagree, he insisted that his own practice of 'magick', especially of the sexual variety, could transform the process of 'degeneration' into 'regeneration' and release the godlike potential in humans.[166] Other psychological currents were more easily adaptable to the occult milieu: the emerging theories on 'unconscious libido' provided by Freud and Jung were welcomed as modern scientific proof of ideas known to initiates since ancient times.[167] Crowley was especially fond of Freud, using the Viennese psychiatrist's ideas to provide a new framework for older practices by identifying the unconscious libido with the highest magical power.[168] The psychological models in which Crowley's sexual theories are embedded are unique to the turn of the twentieth century, and may thus be understood as 'modern'. But it is possible to trace many of Crowley's ideas – particularly the belief that forbidden sexual practices can induce the ultimate magical goal of a *unio mystica* – to the Sabbatian movement of the seventeenth

---

Maudsley's views on spiritualism and occultism, see Henry Maudsley, *Natural Causes and Supernatural Seemings* (London: Kegan Paul & Trench, 1886); Henry Maudsley, 'Lessons of Materialism', in *A Selection of Letters Delivered Before the Sunday Lecture Society, Fourth Selection* (London: Sunday Lecture Society, 1886); Henry Maudsley, 'Materialism and Spiritualism', *JMS* 63:263 (1917), 494–506; John Johnson, 'Henry Maudsley on Swedenborg's Messianic Psychosis', *BJP* 165 (1994), 690–91. For Maudsley's life and published work, see Trevor H. Turner, 'Henry Maudsley: Psychiatrist, Philosopher and Entrepreneur', *Psychological Medicine*, 18 (1988), 551–74; Michael Collie, *Henry Maudsley: Victorian Psychiatrist. A Bibliographical Study* (Winchester: St. Paul's Bibliographies, 1988).

[166] For Crowley's purported meeting with Maudsley, see Crowley, *Confessions*, 386. For his appropriation of Maudsley's ideas, see Justin Sausman, 'Science, Drugs and Occultism: Aleister Crowley, Henry Maudsley and Late-Nineteenth Century Degeneration Theories', *JLS* 1:1 (2007), 40–54. For the theme of regeneration in the occult revival, see Jennifer Walters, *Magical Revival: Occultism and the Culture of Regeneration in Britain, c. 1880–1929* (unpublished PhD dissertation, University of Stirling, 2007).

[167] See, for example, Fortune, *Moon Magic*, 96. For the spread of Freudian theories among occultists, see Mathew Thomson, 'Psychology and the "Consciousness of Modernity" in Early Twentieth-century Britain', in Daunton and Rieger (eds.), *Meanings of Modernity*, 97–115; Owen, 'Occultism and the "Modern Self"', 71–96. For a fuller discussion of Freudian and Jungian theories in British occultism, see Chapter Six.

[168] See Crowley, *Confessions*, 3, 50.

century and its later offshoots.[169]

One of the chief junctions between Sabbatianism and the adepts of the Golden Dawn is the mysterious Samuel Jacob Hayim Falk (1710–1782), a Polish Rosicrucian, Freemason, Kabbalist, alchemist, and 'wonder-working rabbi' whom Westcott claimed as an initiate of the 'original' Golden Dawn. A small body of scholarly literature has been dedicated to Falk, particularly the extensive research of Marsha Keith Schuchard, who refers to him as a secret follower of Zevi's Kabbalistic doctrines.[170] Falk adopted a radical version of Sabbatianism promulgated by Barukhia Russo (d. 1720), a post-Sabbatian messiah who believed that it was necessary to systematically violate the commandments of the 'lower', written Torah, especially those forbidding sexual activities such as incest, adultery, sodomy, and orgiastic practices, in order to reveal the 'higher' Torah which would become the new law in the messianic aeon.[171] Falk's career in London, from his arrival in 1737 to his death in 1782, involved him in a network of subversive political currents within fringe masonic groups all over Europe,[172] but his relevance to Crowley lies in his reputation as Swedenborg's initiator into antinomian Kabbalistic practices such as ritualised masturbation, intended to induce erotic trance-states in which the adept receives visions of the *Shekhinah* and

---

[169] For scholarly works exploring Zevi and the phenomenon of Sabbatianism, see Scholem, *Sabbatai Sevi*; David Halperin, *Sabbatai Zevi: Testimonies to a Fallen Messiah* (Oxford: Littman Library of Jewish Civilization, 2007); Matt Goldish, *The Sabbatean Prophets* (Cambridge, MA: Harvard University Press, 2004); Moshe Idel, *Messianic Mystics* (New Haven, CT: Yale University Press, 1998), 183–211; Lenowitz, *Jewish Messiahs*, 149–66; Sharot, *Messianism, Mysticism, and Magic*, 86–129; Liebes, *Studies in Jewish Myth*, 107–14; Idel, '"One from a Town"'.

[170] Schuchard, 'Dr. Samuel Jacob Falk', 204. See also Hermann Adler, 'Dr. Falk: The Baal Shem from London', *Transactions of the Jewish Historical Society of England, 1902–1905* (London, 1908), 57–60.

[171] For Russo, see Lenowitz, *Jewish Messiahs*, 168–70. For Falk's adherence to Russo's doctrines, see Schuchard, 'Yeats and the "Unknown Superiors"', 140.

[172] For a full discussion of Falk's political activities, see Schuchard, 'Dr. Samuel Jacob Falk'; Schuchard, 'Yeats and the "Unknown Superiors"'. For Falk's possible involvement with the eighteenth-century Masonic-Kabbalistic and post-Sabbatian Order of the Asiatic Brethren, see Scholem, *Alchemy and Kabbalah*, 81–83.

prophetic illumination.[173] Orgiastic behaviour and promiscuous marriage were also associated with Falk's circle;[174] like Zevi, the 'Ba'al Shem of London' married a woman whom his more orthodox opponents referred to as 'the infamous whore'.[175] Although Zevi died nearly a century before Falk pursued his secret activities, the impact of the Sabbatian movement on later developments in Jewish esoteric circles, particularly among the Hasidic *zaddikim*, has continued to reverberate to the present day.[176] It is possible that the impact of Sabbatianism on British occultism likewise reverberated into the early twentieth century, and the pathways of this little-explored terrain lead back to Crowley as the flamboyant exemplar of a seventeenth-century Jewish eschatological vision torn from its orthodox anchors and remade for a new aeon.[177]

Zevi, a precociously brilliant rabbi and Kabbalist born in Ottoman-ruled Izmir in western Turkey, began experiencing divine revelations at the age of fifteen. His messianic movement erupted in Palestine in 1665, publicised not by Zevi himself but by his self-appointed prophet, Nathan of Gaza, 'at once the John the Baptist and the Paul of the new messiah',[178] a follower of the Lurianic Kabbalah who received prophetic inspirations from *maggidim* during trance.[179] By the

---

[173] For Falk's use of these practices, see Michal Oron, 'Dr. Samuel Jacob Falk and the Eibeschütz-Emden Controversy', in Grözinger and Dan (eds.), *Mysticism, Magic and Kabbalah*, 243–56, on p. 254, n. 50; Schuchard, *Why Mrs. Blake Cried*, 92. For Swedenborg's use of the practices, see Emanuel Swedenborg, *Emanuel Swedenborg's Journal of Dreams*, trans. J. J. Garth Wilkinson, ed. W. R. Woofenden (New York: Swedenborg Foundation, 1986); Schuchard, *Why Mrs. Blake Cried*, 99–121; Schuchard, 'Emanuel Swedenborg', 184–86, 200–07. For Kabbalistic references, see Wolfson, *Speculum*, 42. For references on the Hasidic use of *kavvanah* to induce erotic trance-states, see Elijah Schochet, *The Hasidic Movement and the Gaon of Vilna* (Northvale, NJ: Jason Aronson, 1994), 47.

[174] Schuchard, *Why Mrs. Blake Cried*, 113.

[175] Oron, 'Dr. Samuel Jacob Falk', 252.

[176] See Lenowitz, *Jewish Messiahs*, 168 and 200, for the merging of the Sabbatian messiah with the Hasidic *zaddik*.

[177] For the 'unsectarian' nature of the Sabbatian Kabbalah, see Scholem, *Kabbalah*, 304.

[178] Scholem, *Sabbatai Sevi*, 207.

[179] For Nathan's *maggidim*, see Idel, *Messianic Mystics*, 198. For the origins of Nathan's angelic guides in the *Sefer ha-Meshiv*, see Goldish, *Sabbatean Prophets*, 56–88.

following year the startling news of the advent of the
messiah had spread throughout the entire Jewish diaspora
and even aroused excitement among British Christian
millennarians.[180] Zevi's anarchic acts, systematic repudiation
of rabbinic law, and eventual conversion to Islam were
interpreted by Nathan as a divinely ordained journey into
the domain of the evil *qlipot* in order to rescue the 'holy
sparks' trapped in the darkness of the lower realms.[181] Unlike
other messiahs who remain pure while they voyage to the
underworld to rescue sinners,[182] Zevi, according to Nathan,
was required to steep himself in sin and degradation in order
to fulfil his task, deliberately violating every traditional
Jewish taboo *en route*.[183] Gershom Scholem describes this idea
of 'redemption through sin' as the core of Sabbatian
doctrines:

> Just as a grain of wheat must rot in the earth before it can
> sprout, so the deeds of the 'believers' must be truly 'rotten'
> before they can germinate the redemption. This
> metaphor...conveys the whole of sectarian Sabbatian
> psychology in a nutshell.[184]

As the mouthpiece for higher powers, Zevi, like Crowley two
and a half centuries later, believed he could declare all earlier
religious laws superseded, and create his own laws for the
new age.

Radical Sabbatianism is distinguished by three primary
beliefs: the necessary apostasy of the messiah and the
sacramental nature of his descent into the realm of evil; a
'higher' Torah or divine law which can be fulfilled only
through the violation of the 'lower' Torah, especially in
sexual matters; and three hypostases of God, including the

---

[180] For Sabbatianism in Britain, see Popkin, 'Christian Interests';
McKeon, 'Sevi in England'; Halperin, *Sabbatai Zevi*, 3.
[181] For the rescuing of the 'sparks', see Scholem, *Messianic Idea*, 94–
95; Jacobs, 'Uplifting the Sparks'.
[182] For the messianic *katabasis* in antiquity, see Guy [Gedaliah] G.
Stroumsa, 'Mystical Descents', in Collins and Fishbane (eds.), *Death,
Ecstasy*, 139–54. For the *katabasis* in medieval Christian literature, see
Carol Zaleski, *Otherworld Journeys: Accounts of Near-Death
Experiences in Medieval and Modern Times* (Oxford: Oxford University
Press, 1987), 34–42.
[183] See Sharot, *Messianism, Mysticism, and Magic*, 87; Scholem,
Sabbatai Sevi, 671.
[184] Scholem, *Messianic Idea*, 110.

Shekhinah, all of which have been or will be incarnated in human form.[185] Although Crowley does not specifically condemn the Torah, but instead castigates Christian doctrines and the hypocrisy of conventional social norms, all three of these Sabbatian beliefs can be found in Crowley's revelatory text, *The Book of the Law*, and in his subsequent works.[186] Sabbatian doctrines, as presented in the extensive Kabbalistic-Sabbatian literature that continued in a steady stream for nearly a century, reached their most extreme form in the sexual excesses of the last of the post-Sabbatian messiahs, Yakov Frank (1726–1791).[187] These doctrines are not preoccupied with the worldly redemption of the Jewish people, but concern the mythic vision of a cosmic war between good and evil, which can only be won by the good 'with the assistance of a primeval element resembling evil and rooted in it'.[188]

In an epistle that Zevi circulated to the communities of the diaspora, he identifies himself with his own angelic *maggid*.[189] In a similar fashion, Crowley understands Aiwass, the supernal entity who dictated *The Book of the Law*, to be his own Holy Guardian Angel or higher self.[190] Zevi imaged his *maggid* as a 'holy serpent', and signed his documents with the drawing of a twisting snake.[191] Crowley's Aiwass is likewise a serpent in *The Book of the Law*: 'I am the Snake that giveth Knowledge & Delight and bright glory, and stir the

---

[185] See Scholem, *Messianic Idea*, 126.

[186] Aleister Crowley, *The Book of the Law (technically called Liber AL vel Legis Sub Figura CCXX, As Delivered by XCIII = 418 to DCLXVI)*, *Equinox*, 1:7 (1912), repr. London: OTO, 1921. For this work, see below. For Crowley's presentation of the three Aeons, echoing the Sabbatian tripartite unfolding of history, see Crowley, *Confessions*, 420–21.

[187] For Yakov Frank and the Frankist or 'Zoharist' movement, see Scholem, *Kabbalah*, 287–308; Harry Lenowitz, 'The Charlatan at the *Gottes Haus* in Offenbach', in Goldish and Popkin (eds.), *Millenarianism and Messianism*, 189–202; Lenowitz, *Jewish Messiahs*, 167–98. For Yakov Frank's own writings, see Harry Lenowitz (ed. and trans.), *The Collection of the Words of the Lord*, <http://www.languages.utah.edu/kabbalah/protected/dicta_frank_lenowitz.pdf> (2004).

[188] Liebes, *Studies in Jewish Myth*, 102–03.

[189] Sabbatai Zevi, 'Circular Letter', dated 1676, cited in Halperin, *Sabbatai Zevi*, 209–10.

[190] For Aiwass, see below.

[191] Halperin, *Sabbatai Zevi*, 209, fn. 3.

hearts of men with drunkenness'.[192] Both men perceived themselves as Luciferian rebels struggling against the tyrannical God of their respective religions.[193] Through a maggidic dream-revelation, Zevi was persuaded to marry an 'unchaste consort', and took as his bride a young prostitute called Sarah, an orphaned refugee from the bloody Polish pogroms of 1648–49.[194] The resemblance to Crowley's own 'Scarlet Concubine' is striking:

> Now ye shall know that the chosen priest & apostle of infinite space is the prince-priest the Beast; and in his woman called the Scarlet Woman is all power given....Let her work the work of wickedness!...Let her be covered with jewels, and rich garments, and let her be shameless before all men![195]

Zevi was never accused of practising Kabbalistic sexual magic;[196] this charge, apparently with ample justification, was reserved for Yakov Frank, 'one of the most frightening phenomena in the whole of Jewish history'.[197] But Zevi's 'strange acts', initially directed at dietary taboos, rapidly assumed an overtly sexual form.[198] The public outcry against Zevi's 'abominations' provides an interesting parallel with the condemnations of Crowley that appeared in the British press.[199] Like Crowley, Zevi was fond of presenting himself in gorgeous costumes in a theatrically ceremonial style.[200] He

---

[192] Crowley, *Law*, 2.22.

[193] For Zevi's identification with Lucifer, see Halperin, *Sabbatai Zevi*, 4.

[194] For the pogroms, see Halperin, *Sabbatai Zevi*, 5. For Sarah's history, see Goldish, *Sabbatean Prophets*, 89–97; Scholem, *Sabbatai Sevi*, 191–97.

[195] Crowley, *Law*, 1.15 and 3.44.

[196] But see Scholem, *Kabbalah*, 248, for Zevi's use of 'practical' Kabbalah.

[197] Scholem, *Messianic Idea*, 126. For Frank's sexual practices and reputation as a sorcerer, see Scholem, *Kabbalah*, 294, 297, 306.

[198] See Scholem, *Sabbatai Sevi*, 242 and 671–72.

[199] For the media campaign against Crowley, see 'A Wizard of Wickedness', *John Bull*, 17 March 1923; 'The Wickedest Man in the World', *John Bull*, 24 March 1923; 'King of Depravity Arrives', *John Bull*, 11 April 1923; 'A Man We'd Like to Hang', *John Bull*, 19 May 1923. See also Kaczynski, *Perdurabo*, 349–50.

[200] See Zalman Shazar, *The Story of Shabbetay Zevi by R. Lieb ben Ozer* (Amsterdam, 1711–1718), 19–20, cited in Lenowitz, *Jewish Messiahs*, 152–53. For Crowley's theatrical displays, see van Kleeck, 'Art of the Law'.

was a 'lewd person' who enjoyed 'debauches with women and with favorites'.[201] The reference to 'favorites' is especially relevant; according to a follower of Zevi who subsequently returned to the orthodox Jewish faith, the 'accursed Sabbatai', wearing the traditional Jewish *tefillin* (phylacteries) on his head, 'had intercourse with a boy and declared that this was a great [mystical] *tiqqun*'.[202] The discovery that sexual intercourse can open the gates to a *unio mystica*, particularly if performed as a ritual antinomian act, is vividly portrayed by Crowley when he describes his experience of being ritually sodomised by Victor Neuberg in the Algerian desert: 'I sacrificed myself. The fire of the all-seeing sun smote down upon the altar, consuming every particle of my personality'.[203] Alex Owen suggests that it was this experience that first impelled Crowley to believe that 'sex magic was an unrivaled means to great magical power'.[204]

British commentators had been writing about Zevi from 1664 onward, and Crowley, raised in a religious environment redolent with expectations of the messianic advent, could easily have accessed this literature. He would also have known about Falk, who was claimed by Golden Dawn adepts as one of their own. Crowley's animosity toward 'Arthwait' did not preclude reading his rival's work, and Crowley would have encountered the important observation in Waite's *Holy Kabbalah* that 'the history of Abraham Abulafia, of Sabbatai Zevi and the founder of the Hassidim, are typical cases in point which warrant us in saying that the Kabbalah gave spurious Messiahs to Israel.'[205] It seems that the Kabbalah also gave a spurious messiah to the British occult revival. There are, of course, other explanations for the similarities between Crowley and his seventeenth-century Jewish counterpart. The figure of the sexually rampant messiah is not unique to Judaism; abundant examples can be found in Christian millenarian movements throughout the

---

[201] Scholem, *Sabbatai Sevi*, 672.
[202] Cited in Scholem, *Sabbatai Sevi*, 671, n. 227. For *tikkun* as both 'reintegration' and a specific type of ritual practice aimed at cleansing sin and restoring the purity of the soul, see Scholem, *Kabbalah*, 140–44; Scholem, *Major Trends*, 273–78; Fine, *Physician*, 143–44, 167–68, 243–44.
[203] Crowley, *Confessions*, 674.
[204] Owen, 'Sorcerer and His Apprentice', 108.
[205] Waite, *Holy Kabbalah*, 81.

Middle Ages,[206] and they are not unknown today in certain American religious circles,[207] although these more recent messiahs do not usually embed their revelations in a Kabbalistic framework as Zevi and Crowley did. The resemblances between Zevi and Crowley might be seen to spring from similar cultural configurations: the messiah-magus who believes he can only perform his mission through forbidden sexual practices may be the predictable product of religious structures which promulgate the rigorous suppression of sexuality and view it as sin.[208] This persistent archetype emerges in antiquity in the mythic figure of Simon Magus, first described through the perspective of authors such as the Christian heresiologist Irenaeus.[209] But in Crowley's case, the sexual attitudes of the

---

[206] See Cohn, *Pursuit of the Millennium*; Walter L. Wakefield and Austin P. Evans (eds. and trans.), *Heresies of the High Middle Ages* (New York: Columbia University Press, 1969), 258–63.

[207] For contemporary examples such as David Koresh (1959–1993) and Jim Jones (1931–1978), see Carolyn Marvin and David W. Ingle, 'Blood Sacrifice and the Nation: Revisiting Civil Religion', *JAAR* 64:4 (1996), 767–80; David Chidester, *Salvation and Suicide: An Interpretation of Jim Jones, the Peoples Temple, and Jonestown* (Bloomington, IN: Indiana University Press, 2003); James D. Tabor, 'Patterns of the End: Textual Weaving from Qumran to Waco', in Peter Schäfer and Mark R. Cohen (eds.), *Toward the Millennium: Messianic Expectations from the Bible to Waco* (Leiden: Brill, 1998), 409–30.

[208] For sin in Christian theology, see F. R. Tennant, *The Concept of Sin* (Cambridge: Cambridge University Press, 1912); Joseph Pieper, *The Concept of Sin* (South Bend, IN: St. Augustine's Press, 2001). For sin in Islamic theology, see Toshihiko Kzutsu, *The Concept of Belief in Islamic Theology: A Semantic Analysis of Imam and Islam* (Selangor, Malasia: Islamic Book Trust/The Other Press, 2001), 43–70. For Jewish concepts of sin, see Adolph Büchler, *Studies in Sin and Atonement in the Rabbinic Literature of the First Century* (London: Oxford University Press/Jews College, 1928); Nathan A. Perilman, *The Doctrine of Original Sin in Judaism* (unpublished PhD dissertation, Hebrew Union College, 1932); Jonathan Klawans, *Impurity and Sin in Ancient Judaism* (Oxford: Oxford University Press, 2000). For a psychological perspective on sin, see Ralph W. Hood, Jr., 'Sin and Guilt in Faith Traditions: Issues for Self-Esteem', in John F. Schumaker (ed.), *Religion and Mental Health* (Oxford: Oxford University Press, 1992), 110–21.

[209] For Simon Magus, see Acts 8:9–24; Irenaeus, *Adversus Haereses*, in Roberts et al. (eds.), *The Ante-Nicene Fathers*, 1:23:1–5; *Clementine*

late Victorian era into which he was born, although often stereotypically viewed as 'repressed', reflect a more complex range of behaviours encompassing a considerable degree of sexual license; and Crowley's work spanned a fifty-year period during which sexual values altered radically through the social impact of the First World War and the spread of the new psychologies.[210]

Crowley's oppressive upbringing in the claustrophobic embrace of the Plymouth Brethren might be seen to resemble the rigorous religious piety of Zevi's seventeenth-century Jewish world, and Crowley's biographers have been quick to note that his violent rebellion against Christian moral and social norms was linked to his religious background.[211] Efforts have also been made to understand Zevi from a modern psychological perspective. Gershom Scholem explains Zevi's behaviour as a case of 'manic depression';[212] David Halperin suggests that Zevi might have experienced 'sexual trauma' in early life;[213] and Matt Goldish observes that the 'sexual tension' generated by Zevi's youthful piety may have engendered 'unconscious frustration and confusion in a sensitive individual'.[214] But however useful such diagnoses might be in individual terms, they are not

---

Homilies, trans. Philip Schaff, in Roberts et al. (eds.), *The Ante-Nicene Fathers*, 8:2:5–16.

[210] For the ambiguities of Victorian sexuality, see Carol Zisowitz Stearns and Peter N. Stearns, 'Victorian Sexuality: Can Historians Do It Better?', *JSH* 18:4 (1985), 625–34; Michael Mason, *The Making of Victorian Sexuality* (Oxford: Oxford University Press, 1995); Ronald Pearsall, *The Worm in the Bud: The World of Victorian Sexuality* (London: Weidenfeld & Nicholson, 1969); Broughton, *Men of Letters*; Vincent A. Lankewish, 'Love Among the Ruins: the Catacombs, the Closet, and the Victorian "Early Christian Novel"', *VLC* 28:2 (2000), 239–73. For changes in views of sexuality and gender roles at the turn of the century, see Urban, *Magia Sexualis: Sex, Magic, and Liberation in Modern Western Esotericism* (Berkeley, CA: University of California Press, 2006), 57–63.

[211] For pre-Enlightenment Jewish piety, see Alexander Altmann, *Essays in Jewish Intellectual History* (Hanover, NH: University Press of New England, 1981), 190–245. For fanatical piety in Crowley's family background, see Martin Booth, *A Magick Life: A Biography of Aleister Crowley* (London: Hodder & Stoughton, 2000), 6–9; Kaczynski, *Perdurabo*, 20; Symonds, *Great Beast*, 16.

[212] See Scholem, *Sabbatai Sevi*, 126–28; Halperin, *Sabbatai Zevi*, 19.

[213] Halperin, *Sabbatai Zevi*, 3.

[214] Goldish, *Sabbatean Prophets*, 4.

helpful in understanding the enduring influence of the doctrines.[215] Nor are such doctrines attractive only to the poor and the persecuted; Zevi had many wealthy disciples among the rabbinic elite,[216] and Crowley's followers cannot be considered to represent a poor, oppressed, or persecuted 'underclass'.[217]

Sociological and psychological explanations can sometimes fail to explain the longevity of powerful ideas. The pervasive influence of Sabbatianism on currents in British occultism may be related to the Kabbalah's unique synthesis of magic, science, mysticism, messianism, and eroticism, which seems to have appealed to occultists such as Crowley who could not tolerate the segregation of these spheres of human activity in the normative religious and scientific milieux of *fin-de-siècle* Britain. The paradoxical nature of Kabbalistic speculations encompasses apparently irreconcilable opposites, weaving together the mystical yearning for union with deity, the magical power of the focused human will, the science of self-transformation, and the sexual act as a pathway to ecstatic religious experience. This potent mix also incorporates ideas of a fragmented cosmos and an alienated humanity, an eschatological vision of history and, in the case of radical Sabbatianism, a demand for the systematic destruction of all social and religious norms. The paradoxes inherent in the Kabbalah could not be fully expressed by either Waite or Crowley, who, according to their respective temperaments, responded to different aspects of Jewish esoteric lore and polarised against each other. It might even be suggested that the complex of ideas embodied in Kabbalistic doctrines shaped the perspectives of these and other occultists according to their individual natures, rather than that the occultists 'recreated' the Jewish Kabbalah as something 'new'.[218]

---

[215] For a more multifaceted interpretation of Zevi's temperament, see Idel, *Messianic Mystics*, 187–97; Moshe Idel, 'Saturn and Sabbatai Tzevi: A New Approach to Sabbateanism', in Schäfer and Cohen (eds.), *Toward the Millennium*, 173–202

[216] See Halperin, *Sabbatai Zevi*, 16–17.

[217] See Kaczynski, *Perdurabo*, 276–99.

[218] For the term 'idea complex', see Hanegraaff, 'Construction of Esoteric Traditions', 43. For the similar concept of the 'ideal object' in cognitive thought, see Couliano, *Tree of Gnosis*, 28. For ideas with agency that create cultural contexts rather than the reverse, see

THE HERMETIC BROTHERHOOD OF LUXOR

Kabbalistic sexual magic entered British occultism through many channels. Another important junction was provided by the shadowy and highly secretive group known as the Hermetic Brotherhood of Luxor, referred to by its members as the HB of L and created (or re-created) by the elusive Louis Maximilian Bimstein (1847–1927), the son of a Polish Hasidic rabbi, known to his British followers as Max Theon ('Great God') and to his French disciples as Aia Aziz ('The Beloved').[219] Joscelyn Godwin, Christian Chanel, and John Patrick Deveney, in their comprehensive examination of the HB of L, state that Theon 'succeeded in maintaining a personal obscurity verging on invisibility';[220] so carefully did this order guard its secrets that no list of its membership has survived in either Britain or America.[221] However, from 1884 the HB of L's official representative in England, the 'Provincial Grand Master of the South', was none other than the Reverend William Alexander Ayton, the Golden Dawn adept who later officiated at the marriage of Mathers and his wife and who is better known to historians of the occult revival for his alchemical proclivities.[222] Ayton was involved with the HB of L for at least three years before he entered the Golden Dawn, and assiduously recruited potential initiates among the order's members. It would be surprising if he had not recognised Crowley as a likely candidate, and equally

---

James L. Henderson, *A Bridge Across Time: An Assessment of Historical Archetypes* (London: Turnstone Books, 1975).

[219] For Theon's Polish background, see Joscelyn Godwin, Christian Chanel, and John P. Deveney, *The Hermetic Brotherhood of Luxor: Initiatic and Historical Documents of an Order of Practical Occultism* (York Beach, ME: Samuel Weiser, Inc., 1995), 8–9. For Theon's initiation into Hasidic practices, see Godwin et al., *Hermetic Brotherhood*, 11; Allen H. Greenfield, *The Roots of Modern Magick: Glimpses of the Authentic Tradition from 1700 to 2000* (self-published, 2004), 53; Pascal Themanlys, 'Introduction', in Pascal Themanlys (ed. and trans.), *Visions of the Eternal Present: Selections from the Cosmic Works of Max Theon* (Jerusalem: Argaman, 1991). For the Lurianic Kabbalah in Theon's work, see Giovanangelo Dumà, 'Max Théon e il Movimento Cosmique', *Lex Aurea: Libera Rivista di Formazione Esoterica* 19 (2006), 14–18.

[220] Godwin et al., *Luxor*, 13.

[221] Godwin et al., *Luxor*, 3.

[222] For Ayton's involvement with the HB of L, see Godwin *et al.*, *Hermetic Brotherhood*, 4, 35–36, 75–77, 345–48, 352–54, 361–62.

surprising if Crowley did not at least experiment with the HB of L's rituals. Ayton also wrote to Waite about the HB of L, and Waite included a reference to Theon and his organisation in both his *New Encyclopaedia of Freemasonry* and an article published in *The Occult Review*.[223] The HB of L, however secretive, was no secret to the Golden Dawn adepts.

The HB of L encouraged self-initiation rather than formal progression through group rituals, and the order's extant documents indicate that a form of sexual magic based on the Kabbalah was taught to the adepts. While Theon incorporated some Tantric practices,[224] the HB of L 'taught the same principle as is found in the *Zohar*...that the aspirations of the man at the moment of conception can cause a child to be born who possesses from the start the magical powers that define adeptship'.[225] The goal of the order's magic was the development of the individual's spiritual potentials, so that he or she could communicate directly with supernal entities and provide a vehicle for 'blending': the merging of the adept's conscious personality with an exalted being from the supernal realms.

'Blending' is a late nineteenth-century occultist version of the Kabbalistic idea of *ibbur* ('impregnation'), especially favoured by Lurianic Kabbalists but originating in concepts of spirit possession in the late thirteenth-century Spanish Kabbalah: the belief that an individual's body might house not only its own soul, but also that of a higher or more spiritually evolved being, human or angelic.[226] Although *ibburim* could sometimes be malevolent and constitute a form of demonic possession requiring exorcism, Luria and his

---

[223] See A. E. Waite, *A New Encyclopaedia of Freemasonry*, 2 vols. (London: Rider, 1921), 1:349–50; A. E. Waite, 'Periodical Literature', *OR* 41:5 (1925), 326–27. See also Godwin et al., *Hermetic Brotherhood*, 424–27, 436–37.

[224] Godwin et al., *Hermetic Brotherhood*, 12.

[225] Godwin et al., *Hermetic Brotherhood*, 77. See also Johnson, *Masters Revealed*, 45.

[226] For the origin of the idea of *ibbur*, see J. H. Chajes, *Between Worlds: Dybbuks, Exorcists, and Early Modern Judaism* (Philadelphia, PA: University of Pennsylvania Press, 2003), 14–16. For *ibbur* in Lurianic doctrines, see Menachem Kallus, 'Pneumatic Mystical Possession and the Eschatology of the Soul in Lurianic Kabbalah', in Matt Goldish (ed.), *Spirit Possession in Judaism: Cases and Contexts from the Middle Ages to the Present* (Detroit, MI: Wayne State University Press, 2003), 159–85. For *ibburim* as catalysts for awakening the powers of the soul, see Chajes, 'He Said She Said', 100–01.

disciples practiced magical techniques to achieve 'holy *ibbur*', the drawing down into one's own body of the soul of a deceased sage:

> Occasionally a person will happen to perform a particular commandment in an ideal manner. Thereupon a certain soul will be called upon him, a righteous man of old who himself ideally performed that commandment. Because of the similarity between them that was established through this commandment, the soul of the righteous man will impregnate him.[227]

The affinity between the two souls, according to Lurianic doctrines, also depends on the sharing of a particular soul-root; each individual soul-spark is given three or four lifetimes in which to atone for its sins, and other souls from the same soul-root are responsible for helping that soul achieve perfection.[228] Impregnation by an angelic entity or *maggid* rather than the disincarnate soul of a sage is another form of *ibbur* cultivated by Lurianic Kabbalists. J. H. Chajes calls this phenomenon maggidism, 'the most significant and recognized form of positively valued spirit possession in early modern Jewish culture';[229] and it seems that this uniquely Kabbalistic concept and its accompanying rituals found its way into the doctrines of the HB of L through Max Theon and his Hasidic background.

THE 'MAN WITH TWO SOULS'

'Blending' is also a distinctive feature of the teachings of the American spiritualist and abolitionist Paschal Beverly Randolph (1825–1875), the illegitimate son of a wealthy Virginian landowner and a black slave from Madagascar. Randolph, who was raised in the slums of New York but rose to become a well-known trance medium and the creator of a system of sexual magic which would have far-reaching consequences on British occultism, describes himself as 'the

---

[227] Hayyim Vital, *Sha'ar ha-Gilgulim*, 126, cited in Chajes, *Between Worlds*, 24–25.
[228] See Kallus, 'Pneumatic Mystical Possession', 160. On this aspect of *ibbur*, see also Scholem, *Mystical Shape*, 221–23.
[229] Chajes, *Between Worlds*, 28.

man with two souls'.[230] His work closely resembles that of Max Theon and the HB of L.[231] Randolph's ideas also shaped the sexual magic of Theodor Reuss' OTO, from which Crowley purportedly derived many of his rituals.[232] Whether

---

[230] Paschal Beverly Randolph, *P. B. Randolph: The "Learned Pundit" and "Man with Two Souls", His Curious Life, Works, and Career: The Great Free-Love Trial* (Boston, MA: self-published, 1872). For this apologist work, written as a defence against accusations of purveying obscene materials, see Urban, *Magia Sexualis*, 71. Godwin et al. (*Hermetic Brotherhood*, 44) acknowledge that Randolph's links with Max Theon and the HB of L are never explicitly stated: 'Nowhere in the surviving HB of L material is the exact relationship between the Order and Randolph, or between Randolph and Theon, spelled out', although 'the entirety of the HB of L manuscript material...is essentially derived from Randolph'. Randolph published many books in his short lifetime, but one of his most important works in terms of the HB of L seems to have been 'Mysteries of Eulis', privately published in 1873 and circulated among the adepts of his occult society, the Brotherhood of Eulis, founded in 1870.

[231] For Randolph's life and work, see John Patrick Deveney, *Paschal Beverly Randolph: A Nineteenth-Century Black American Spiritualist, Rosicrucian, and Sex Magician* (Albany, NY: State University of New York Press, 1996); John Patrick Deveney, 'Paschal Beverly Randolph and Sexual Magic', in Hanegraaff and Kripal (eds.), *Hidden Intercourse*, 355–68; Godwin et al., *Hermetic Brotherhood*, 40–55; Urban, *Magia Sexualis*, 55–80; Godwin, *Theosophical Enlightenment*, 247–61.

[232] See Godwin, *Theosophical Enlightenment*, 361; Urban, *Magia Sexualis*, 74. Theodor Reuss, who created the Ordo Templi Orientis, acquired most of his ideas from the Austrian industrialist Karl Kellner (1850–1905), who was a member of the HB of L. The two men conceived the idea of a 'masonic academy' incorporating HB of L teachings in 1895; see Godwin, *Theosophical Enlightenment*, 361. Godwin argues that a distinction must be made between Randolph's relatively conservative teachings (his theories of sexual magic were intended solely for married couples) and those of Crowley and the OTO: 'Randolph had a typical nineteenth-century horror of masturbation, and neither he nor Davidson had the slightest tolerance for homosexuality – both integral parts of Crowley's practice'. This distinction is also emphasised by Hugh Urban (*Magia Sexualis*, 74): 'Nothing could be further from the sexual magic later developed by the Ordo Templi Orientis, still less that of Aleister Crowley and his followers'. The distinction is also reflected in the differences between the Zoharic teachings on sex expressed in the Lurianic Kabbalah and the antinomian Kabbalah of Zevi and Frank. However, in all these cases – Randolph, the OTO, and Crowley – the sexual act is understood, as it is in the Kabbalah,

Theon borrowed doctrines from Randolph or Randolph from Theon, it seems that both men drew on the fertile matrix of the Kabbalah as well as Sabbatian ideas about the liberating power and spiritual potential of the sexual act. Randolph makes clear his familiarity with the Kabbalah when he declares:

> The footprints here and there are of mortals, but of those who have beheld the hidden mysteries of Eulis, who are familiars of the Cabbala, who have raised the veil of Isis, and revealed the Chrishna.[233]

His writings also reflect the Zoharic notion of the sacramental nature of the sexual act:

> The ejective moment, therefore, is the most divine and tremendously important one in the human career...for then the mystic Soul swings wide its Golden gates, opens its portals to the whole vast Universe and through them come trooping either Angels of Light or the Grizzly Presence from the dark corners of the Spaces.[234]

Randolph presents three ideas which bear an affinity with concepts found in Kabbalistic texts: the practice of physiognomy as an occult means of determining the

---

as a potential gateway to divine union and individual and worldly transformation.

[233] Paschal Beverly Randolph, *Eulis! The History of Love* (Toledo, OH: Randolph Publishing, 1874), cited in Greenfield, *Roots of Magick*, 41. Randolph does not mention any specific Kabbalistic texts, but claims to have acquired his knowledge of sexual magic during his travels in Egypt, Palestine, and Turkey. He is vague about his sources, referring to them only as 'some dervishes and fakirs' through whom he discovered 'the Elixir of Life, the universal Solvent...and the philosopher's stone' (Randolph, *Eulis!*, 218, cited in Urban, *Magia Sexualis*, 66). John Patrick Deveney (*Paschal Beverly Randolph*, 211) suggests that the 'dervishes and fakirs' are the radical Shi'ite mystical order called the Nusa'iri or Ansairi, persecuted by orthodox Muslims because of their alleged Gnostic rituals and 'antinomian, libertine' practices.
[234] Paschal Beverly Randolph, *The Ansairetic Mystery: A New Revelation Concerning Sex!* (Toledo, OH: privately printed, Toledo Sun, Liberal Printing House, 1874), repr. in Deveney, *Randolph*, 311–326, on p. 317.

condition of the individual soul;[235] 'blending' with angelic entities or *maggidim*; and the belief that reincarnation (called *gilgul* in the *Zohar* and later Kabbalistic works) is not a universal human phenomenon, but is restricted to instances when the individual soul has failed to fulfil specific obligations.[236] The presence of any of these ideas in both Randolph's teachings and the Kabbalah could be explained either by coincidence or by the widespread dissemination of the concept in both Jewish and non-Jewish occult currents. But the presence of all three suggests that Randolph had access to Kabbalistic doctrines, confirmed by his own statement given above.[237]

There is a major difference in the ideas behind the restrictions on reincarnation offered by Randolph and those presented in Kabbalistic literature, but both Randolph and the *Zohar* view transmigration as an exceptional event. The special exceptions which Randolph believes necessitate reincarnation include 'mental defectives', abortions, and those who die before the soul really emerges into being – all cases where the individual is not at fault, but has not had sufficient opportunity to develop a full soul-life.[238] Max Theon agrees that reincarnation is an exception, but does not agree with Randolph's three categories, suggesting instead

---

[235] For Randolph's emphasis on physiognomy, see R. Swynburne Clymer, *Dr. Paschal Beverly Randolph and the Supreme Grand Dome of the Rosicrucians in France* (Quakertown, PA: The Philosophical Publishing Company, 1929), 21–23. For Luria's use of 'metaposcopy', a form of physiognomy, see Fine, 'Art of Metoposcopy'.

[236] For Randolph's views on reincarnation, see Deveney, *Randolph*, 279–80; Godwin et al., *Hermetic Brotherhood*, 41. For ideas of reincarnation in the *Zohar*, see *Zohar* I.66a, I.388.48a, and I.278. For ideas of reincarnation in other Kabbalistic texts, see Waite, *Holy Kabbalah*, 378–79; Scholem, *Mystical Shape*, 209–10, 228–41; Rachel Elior, 'The Doctrine of Transmigration in *Galya Raza*', in Fine (ed.), *Essential Papers on Kabbalah*, 243–69; Fine, *Physician*, 305–14; David M. Wexelman (ed. and trans.), *The Jewish Concept of Reincarnation and Creation: Based on the Writings of Rabbi Chaim Vital* (Northvale, NJ: Jason Aronson, 1999); Dina Ripsman Eylon, *Reincarnation in Jewish Mysticism and Gnosticism* (Lampeter: Edwin Mellen Press, 2003).

[237] See Deveney, 'Paschal Beverly Randolph', where Deveney does not mention the Kabbalah and concludes (365) that 'it is impossible to say where Randolph acquired these ideas'.

[238] See Deveney, *Paschal Beverly Randolph*, 279–80; Godwin et al., *Hermetic Brotherhood*, 41.

that reincarnation is 'impossible except for extremely powerful mentalities (or intelligences) that are already cosmic: those that have already conquered their immortality and which are recalled to earth by the ardent and *legitimate* desire to complete a mission interrupted by death'.[239] The *Zohar* restricts reincarnation to men (and, rarely, women) who by their own choice have ignored the obligation of reproduction and remain childless, and to those who have transgressed one of the commandments of the Torah, particularly those concerning sexual offences. This perspective views reincarnation primarily as a punishment for sin.[240] In Zoharic literature, the number of reincarnations during which the soul may redeem the offence is limited to three. Many post-Zoharic texts abandon these restrictions; in the fourteenth and fifteenth centuries, *gilgul* was gradually understood as a universal human experience except for the righteous sage or *zaddik*, bringing the doctrine more in alignment with Eastern thought and with later Theosophical speculations. The *Galya Raza*, an anonymous mid-sixteenth-century Kabbalistic text, proposes that up to a thousand transmigrations, linked to complex astrological cycles, may be necessary for souls to achieve perfection.[241] In the late sixteenth century, Isaac Luria taught that his own soul and those of his disciples participated in long chains of soul transmigrations reaching back to the origins of humanity, and related reincarnation to 'soul affinities'. He divided souls into various groups, including 'old' and 'new' souls – an idea that Lévi discusses in *Science des esprits* and which was appropriated with certain adaptations by Blavatsky. 'New' souls (those who had not participated in Adam's sin and had never been born before) could perfect themselves in one lifetime through the appropriate meditative practices, but if they failed, they were required to reincarnate. 'Old' souls, who had fallen with Adam and shared in his sin, required a

---

[239] Max Theon, *Revue Cosmique* 1:8 (1902), 505, cited in Godwin et al., *Hermetic Brotherhood*, 187.
[240] See, for example, *Zohar* I.66a, I.388.48a, and I.278, and Waite's comment (Waite, *Holy Kabbalah*, 378–79) that, according to Zoharic doctrines, an unmarried or incomplete person cannot enter Paradise but is forced to reincarnate 'so that the Sacred Name may be completed in all directions'. On this theme, see also Scholem, *Mystical Shape*, 209–10.
[241] See Elior, 'Galya Raza'.

series of transmigrations before they could achieve perfection.[242]

An extensive mythology has grown up around Randolph in occult circles, largely due to the enthusiastic efforts of an American esotericist called R. Swinburne Clymer (1878–1966), who for over forty years served as Grand Master of the Fraternitas Rosae Crucis, one of the main American Rosicrucian groups extant today.[243] Clymer may be questionable as a scholarly source, but his description of Randolph's purported meeting with Lévi in Paris in 1861, although unverified by any documentation, is nevertheless an interesting hypothesis which Clymer uses to identify Randolph as an 'initiate' and to relate his doctrines to the teachings of other, older occult orders such as the Fratres Lucis and the Asiatic Brethren.[244] According to Clymer, Lévi initiated Randolph and taught him occult secrets.[245] It is not necessary to postulate a meeting, let alone an elaborate initiation ritual, between the two occultists; Randolph probably read Lévi's books in French.[246] In *Sexual Magic*, Randolph presents his vision of the polarity of forces underpinning the cosmic structure:

> The entire universe, all living beings...are ruled by the principle of two contrary forces, exercising, one on the other, a power of inescapable attraction. One calls the forces positive and negative, and one rediscovers them in good and bad, emission and reception, life and death, idea and action, man and woman.[247]

---

[242] For these Lurianic doctrines, see Fine, *Physician*, 305–14; Scholem, *Mystical Shape*, 228–41; Wexelman (ed. and trans.), *Jewish Concept of Reincarnation*.
[243] For the Fraternitas Rosae Crucis, see their website at www.soul.org. For Clymer's use of Randolph's teachings, see R. Swinburne Clymer, *Higher Race Development: A Course of Instructions on the Right Use of Sex* (Quakertown, PA: Philosophical Publishing Co., 1950).
[244] For links between the HB of L, the Fratres Lucis, the Hermetic Brothers of Egypt, and Blavatsky's Theosophical Society, see Godwin, *Theosophical Enlightenment*, 277–306; Blavatsky, CW1, 142; Godwin et al., *Hermetic Brotherhood*, 6–7; Deveney, *Randolph*, 283–308.
[245] Clymer, *Dr. Paschal Beverly Randolph*, 14–15.
[246] For Randolph's visits to Paris, see Deveney, *Randolph*, 56–59.
[247] Paschal Beverly Randolph, *Sexual Magic*, ed. and trans. Robert North (New York: Magickal Childe, 1988), 10.

The closeness of this theosophical vision to Lévi's, although shorn of its Kabbalistic terminology, is unmistakable:

> In God, that is, in the first living and active cause, one must recognise two properties necessary one to another – stability and movement, necessity and liberty, rational order and volitional autonomy, justice and love, and consequently also severity and mercy. And these are the two attributes that the Jewish Kabbalists personified…under the names of Geburah and Chesed.[248]

This similarity of doctrines suggests that, whether or not the two men actually met, the long arm of Éliphas Lévi once again exercised its extensive reach.[249]

Hugh Urban, discussing the sources of sexual magic in the British occult revival, does not consider the Kabbalah to be a relevant influence on Crowley because, although Jewish mystical traditions, in company with Gnosticism and Renaissance alchemy, express a close relationship between spiritual power and sexual union, 'in none of them have we seen any trace of orgiastic behavior, immorality, black magic, or the explicit use of sexual intercourse as a means of achieving magical effects'.[250] This statement is challenged by the use of both theosophical and 'practical' Kabbalah in the Sabbatian and Frankist movements. Hasidism likewise appropriated the idea, drawn from the *Zohar* and from Lurianic currents, that the moment of sexual union, supported by the appropriate *kavvanah*, can become a specific technique for achieving mystical ecstasy and the drawing down of supernal power. While this Hasidic form of ritual practice cannot be considered 'orgiastic', 'black', or 'immoral', it may certainly be considered magical. Whatever the truth of the historical chains of transmission between Lévi, Max Theon, Paschal Beverly Randolph, the HB of L, the Golden Dawn, and the OTO, Crowley's sexual magic, like Waite's, may ultimately derive, directly or indirectly, from what Elliot Wolfson calls 'the psychosexual worldview of the kabbalists'.[251]

---

[248] Lévi, *Dogme*, 111.
[249] For the similarities between Lévi's 'astral light' and Randolph's 'Aeth', see Deveney, *Randolph*, 57.
[250] Urban, *Magia Sexualis*, 54.
[251] Wolfson, 'Murmuring Secrets', 100.

CROWLEY'S *MAGGID* AND *THE BOOK OF THE LAW*

The Book of the Law was 'revealed' to Crowley in April 1904 by the angelic being 'Aiwass'.[252] This entity was in turn sent by the Egyptian deity Nuit (Nut), whom Crowley describes as 'the category of unlimited possibility'.[253] Nuit has chosen Crowley as her prophet:

> Now ye shall know that the chosen priest & apostle of infinite space is the prince-priest the Beast; and in his woman called the Scarlet Woman is all power given. They shall gather my children into their fold: they shall bring the glory of the stars into the hearts of men.[254]

The message of the revelation, called the 'threefold book of Law' or 'Thelema', is clear enough: 'The word of Sin is Restriction....There is no law beyond Do what thou wilt'.[255] The text is riddled with references to the Tarot and to Hebrew *gematria*,[256] although the deities are apparently Egyptian and no mention is given to Kabbalistic theosophical concepts such as the *sefirot*.[257] *Law* is an ironic parody of the *Apocalypse* of John, inverted so that the Beast is honoured as the prophet of the revelation. The question of whether the work is a genuine revelation, as Crowley would have his readers believe, or an extremely clever contrivance, has inevitably been raised by Crowley's biographers, and the answer seems to depend on the particular orientation of the researcher.[258] But the question may be irrelevant: the author of the work is Crowley, whether he deliberately concocted a brilliant parody of an apocalyptic revelation, acted as the unwilling medium for his Holy Guardian Angel or, equally

---

[252] For the events leading up to the revelation, see Crowley, *Confessions*, 413–24.

[253] Aleister Crowley, *The Book of Thoth by the Master Therion* (London, self-published, 1944; repr. New York: Samuel Weiser, Inc., 1969), 115.

[254] Crowley, *Law*, I.15

[255] Crowley, *Law*, III.60. 'Thelema' is the English transliteration of the Greek noun θελεμα, 'will', from the verb θελω, 'to will'.

[256] For the Tarot, see, for example, Crowley, *Law*, II.16. For *gematria*, see, for example, Crowley, *Law*, I.24–25.

[257] But see Crowley, *Confessions*, 425, for his declaration that Aiwass 'had shown a knowledge of the Cabbala immeasurably superior to my own'.

[258] See, for example, Booth, *Magick Life*, 187.

pertinent to his own multiple frames of reference, gave voice to the 'libido of the unconscious'.[259]

The sonorous and declamatory style, reminiscent of the Jewish pseudepigraphic literature produced during the Second Temple period (515 BCE–70 CE) known as 'apocalyptic', also bears a close family resemblance to the pronouncements of the late-fifteenth-century *Sefer ha-Meshiv*, the first Jewish Kabbalistic work to be attributed to an angelic *maggid*.[260] Jewish apocalyptic literature is not magical in the limited sense of simply providing recipes for spells and invocations; it often describes mystical visions induced through ritual practices, during which supernal secrets concerning eschatological matters are revealed and magical instructions are given to facilitate the advent of the eschaton.[261] Crowley's *Law* may be understood as an early-

---

[259] See Crowley, *Confessions*, 50, and above, n. 137.

[260] For *maggidim* in the circle who produced the *Sefer ha-Meshiv*, see Goldish, *Sabbatean Prophets*, 63. For the strongly messianic message of the *Sefer ha-Meshiv*, see Idel, *Messianic Mystics*, 126–32; Goldish, *Sabbatean Prophets*, 42.

[261] For Jewish apocalyptic literature, see Himmelfarb, *Ascent to Heaven*; Collins, *Apocalypse*. For translations of the texts, see James H. Charlesworth (ed.), *The Old Testament Pseudepigrapha, Vol. 1: Apocalyptic Literature and Testaments* (New York: Doubleday, 1983), which includes commentaries as well as translations of the 'Testament' Literature, much of which includes apocalyptic sections. See also Gottfried Schimanowski, '"Connecting Heaven and Earth": The Function of the Hymns in Revelation 4–5', in Boustan and Reed (eds.), *Heavenly Realms*, 67–84; Reed, 'Heavenly Ascent'; Collins, 'Seven Heavens'; McGinn, *Foundations of Mysticism*, 9–22. The word 'apocalypse', although the Greek term simply means 'revelation', has come to suggest prophecies of the End of Days, particularly in a Christian context; for examples of this type of literature, see Bernard McGinn (trans.), *Apocalyptic Spirituality: Treatises and Letters of Lactantius, Adso of Montier-en-Der, Joachim of Fiore, the Franciscan Spirituals, Savanarola* (New York: Paulist Press, 1979). There is a direct line of transmission from the Jewish apocalypses to the *heikhalot* literature which followed them in the subsequent five or six centuries; on the understanding of both genres as 'mystical', see Gruenwald, 'Jewish Mysticism'. The late fifteenth-century *Sefer ha-Meshiv*, which fulfils Collins' definition of an apocalyptic text, abounds in instructions, transmitted by an unnamed angel (probably Metatron) on behalf of God, which provide both a historical vision of past ages and magical recipes to destroy the forces of evil and bring about the advent of the messianic age. In this respect, Crowley's *Book of the Law* resembles

twentieth-century apocalypse which fulfils all of the requirements for this unique genre of literature, described by John J. Collins:

> Apocalypse is a genre of revelatory literature with a narrative framework, in which a revelation is mediated by an otherworldly being to a human recipient, describing a transcendent reality which is both temporal, insofar as it envisages eschatological salvation, and spatial insofar as it involves another, supernatural world.[262]

In Kabbalistic contexts, Aiwass would be described as a *maggid*. That this being is the emissary of a female deity is a characteristic Crowleyan reversal of traditional revelations, which are usually conveyed by an angelic mentor on behalf of YHVH or, in the case of Moses and other biblical prophets, by YHVH himself. Martin Booth observes that Crowley uses two spellings of the angel's name, Aiwass in magical work and Aiwaz for mystical visions: 'Both were numerologically important'.[263] The name Aiwass may be constructed through *gematria*, but it may equally be a private pun, the nature of which Crowley deliberately kept to himself. It is interesting to note in passing that there is a noticeable similarity between Aiwass/Aiwaz and Aia Aziz, the pseudonym Max Theon acquired when he established his occult centre at Tlemcen in Algeria in 1888. Although Crowley never mentions Theon in his description of his Algerian adventure or, for that matter, anywhere else, many of his theories of sexual magic, as discussed above, are clearly related to Theon's doctrines, which were common currency in the Golden Dawn's Inner Order. Theon had been firmly ensconced at Tlemcen for six years before *Law* was revealed. Crowley's journey to Algiers and Bou Saada in 1909 occurred five years after his revelation, and it seems unlikely, as he knew everyone in the occult world, that he would have been unaware of Theon's presence in Algeria. Even if he had not acquired the information from any other source, Crowley

---

nothing more closely than the *Sefer ha-Meshiv*, although this work was never translated into either Latin or English and would have been inaccessible to Crowley in its Hebrew form, unless an unknown individual provided him with a translation of the MS available in the British Museum and Bodleian collections.
[262] Collins, *Apocalypse*, 9.
[263] Booth, *Magick Life*, 184.

would have certainly heard about Theon's centre from Ayton. Theon died there in March 1927, at the age of seventy-six.[264] Tlemcen, situated in the northwest corner of the country, is 600 kilometres due west of Algiers but is easily accessed by a major road. Alex Owen suggests that the magical ceremonies Crowley performed at Bou Saada 'prefigured his elaboration of the techniques of sex magic', and it is possible that a direct meeting with Theon prior to or immediately after the ceremonies facilitated that elaboration.[265]

THE BATTLE OF THE TAROTS

The Tarot had been at the centre of Golden Dawn speculation and creative innovation since the inception of the order, largely because of the Kabbalistic framework Lévi had assigned to the cards, and also because the mysterious coded 'Cipher Manuscript' that Westcott and Mathers used as the validation for the order's rituals contained several pages on the Tarot, including an allocation of the cards to the Hebrew letters, the four elements, the planets and zodiacal signs, and the thirty-two 'paths' enumerated in the *Sefer Yetsirah*.[266] Mathers claimed that the Cipher MS had been in Lévi's keeping, and that its correspondences represented the 'secret' system of the French magus, which necessarily differed from what he had publicly offered:

> He [Lévi] probably felt he was not at liberty to divulge to the Outer and uninitiated world the secret and true attribution of the Tarot which was given in the cypher MSS and the attribution which he gave in the *Dogme et Rituel de la Haute Magie*, and which has been accepted among the uninitiated, is very different.[267]

---

[264] See Godwin et al., *Hermetic Brotherhood*, 8–9.
[265] Owen, 'Sorcerer and His Apprentice', 99–100.
[266] For a facsimile of the Cipher MS, see Caroll "Poke" Runyon, *Secrets of the Golden Dawn Cypher Manuscript* (Silverado, CA: Church of the Hermetic Sciences, 2005), 134; K. Frank Jensen, *The Story of the Waite-Smith Tarot* (Melbourne: Association for Tarot Studies, 2006), 85. For a 'deciphering' of the Cipher MS allocations, see Runyon, *Secrets*, 133.
[267] S. L. MacGregor Mathers, 'On the Tarot Trumps', copied from Mathers' MS by J. W. Brodie-Innes in 1910, reproduced in Gilbert (ed.), *Sorcerer and His Apprentice*, 79–80. The order of the Major Arcana and the corresponding Hebrew letters in the Cipher MS

differ from Lévi's allocations primarily in the placement of 'The Fool'; in the Cipher MS this card stands at the beginning, while Lévi locates it nearly at the end, between 'Judgement' and the final card, 'The World'. The Hebrew letters associated with the cards alter accordingly. For Lévi's Major Arcana order, see Éliphas Lévi, *The Magical Ritual of the Sanctum Regnum*, trans. William Wynn Westcott (1896; repr. Sequim, WA: Holmes Publishing, 2006). In 1886, Westcott produced untitled drawings for some of the Major Arcana cards, inscribed with the Hebrew letters following Lévi's allocations; see Jensen, *Waite-Smith Tarot*, 149. Lévi never illustrated the Minor Arcana cards, although he relates the four suits to the four elements and the numbered cards of each suit from Ace to Ten to the ten *sefirot* from *Keter* to *Malkuth* – a system which Mathers also followed and which Waite and Crowley appropriated in their turn. For Lévi's exposition of the Minor Arcana and the court cards, see Lévi, *Clefs majeures*. The elemental correspondences are: wands = fire, swords = air, cups = water, pentacles = earth. These correspondences can be found in drawings from Mathers' personal notebooks, reproduced in Raine, *Yeats, The Tarot and the Golden Dawn*, 24–25. Mathers, in *Book T*, changes the value as well as the gender of some of the court cards of the Minor Arcana from the earlier Marseilles depictions, turning the Knaves into Princesses and conferring the highest value on the Knight rather than the King. Waite did not accept these changes, preserving the masculine nature of the Knaves as Pages and according the King the highest value. Crowley accepted Mathers' alterations, presenting four Princesses in his own deck and honouring the Knight as the leader of each suit. For further variations on Lévi's original system, see Robert Wang's illustrations for the Stella Matutina version of the Tarot in Wang, *Golden Dawn Tarot*. The instructions for Wang's illustrations were provided by Israel Regardie, who apparently followed the drawings first produced *c.* 1912 by R. W. Felkin, the original head of the Stella Matutina; these designs in turn resemble those found in Westcott's papers, apparently drawn by Mina Mathers. Wang (*Golden Dawn Tarot*, 24) believes that this is the 'original' Golden Dawn Tarot conceived by Mathers and illustrated by his wife, exemplified by the instructions given in *Book T*. For a discussion of these designs, see Anthony Fleming, 'Introductory Notes', in Darcy Küntz (ed.), *The Golden Dawn Court Cards as Drawn by William Wynn Westcott and Moïna Mathers* (Sequim, WA: Holmes Publishing Group, 2006), 3–5, on p. 3. They bear little resemblance to Waite's court cards. See Jensen, *Waite-Smith Tarot*, 76–77, for reproductions of some of Felkin's images. Mathers' own drawing for the Major Arcana card 'Temperance', taken from his personal notebooks, is reproduced in Raine, *Yeats*, 53. See also the discussion in Helen Farley, *A Cultural History of the Tarot: From Entertainment to Esotericism* (London: I. B. Tauris, 2009), 121–50.

The idea that Lévi had concealed the 'real' system, rather than simply getting it wrong, persisted in occult circles. Although Waite doubted that Lévi possessed such subtlety, Crowley accepted Mathers' explanation for the disparity and justified his own preference for the Cipher MS allocations without disparaging Lévi's initiatic wisdom:

> Lévi felt himself bound by his original oath of secrecy to the Order of Initiates which had given him the secrets of the Tarot....When the matter is examined, it becomes quite clear that Lévi's wrong attribution of the letters was deliberate; that he knew the right attribution, and considered it his duty to conceal it.[268]

Golden Dawn theories on the Tarot are encapsulated in Mathers' *Book T*, and on the basis of its information adepts were expected to experiment with their own designs for the cards.[269] This was not merely a learning process, but was also intended to provide a ritualistic context in which the adept could begin to experience those altered states of awareness of which the Tarot symbols were a pictorial representation.[270] However, among British occultists only Waite and Crowley, working with artists who acted on their detailed instructions, produced complete new decks which are still in use today. Both men accepted Lévi's affiliation of the cards with the Kabbalah, but their very different understanding of this affiliation reflects the polarisation between Kabbalistic mysticism and Kabbalistic magic that permeates all their work.

Shortly before Christmas in 1909, Waite launched his 'rectified' Tarot on the British public, along with a short book enumerating both the esoteric and divinatory meanings of the cards.[271] He preceded this publication with an article in *The Occult Review*,[272] in which he gives no credit to Lévi

---

[268] Crowley, *Thoth*, 6.

[269] See, for example, the drawings from various unpublished Golden Dawn notebooks in Kathleen Raine, *Yeats, The Tarot and the Golden Dawn* (Dublin: Dolmen Press, 1972).

[270] For the magical import of drawing the Tarot images, see Anke Timmerman, '"Pictures passing before the mind's eye": the Tarot, the Order of the Golden Dawn, and William Butler Yeats's Poetry', *SMN* 15 (Spring 2006), 1–8.

[271] A. E. Waite, *The Key to the Tarot* (London: Rider, 1910).

[272] A. E. Waite, 'The Tarot – A Wheel of Fortune', *OR* 10:12 (1909), 307–17.

despite the fact that Lévi was clearly the chief source of his inspiration; nor does Waite acknowledge Mathers' efforts in *Book T* to produce a coherent system through which the Tarot could be correctly interpreted, although Waite borrowed freely from those efforts.[273] Despite his disparagement of the Marseilles deck,[274] Waite, like Lévi, used its iconography as the basis for his own depictions. Disagreements about the details of the cards – the order of the Major Arcana, the specific allocation of Hebrew letters, gender differences in the Court Cards of the Minor Arcana – were rife in the early years of the Golden Dawn, and continued in the various offshoots of the order after its fragmentation. But no one, including Waite, quarrelled about Lévi's insistence that the Tarot and the Kabbalah are inextricably intertwined, and that the Major Arcana are symbolic depictions of the letters of the Hebrew alphabet.[275]

Fig. 23: Left, Jean Dodal Tarot, c. 1701, 'Le Jugement'.[276]
Right, Waite's 'Judgement', an updated version of the Marseilles card.[277]

---

[273] See Jensen, *Waite-Smith Tarot*, 79.
[274] See Waite, 'Tarot – A Wheel of Fortune', 308.
[275] See, for example, J. W. Brodie-Innes, 'The Tarot Cards', *OR* 29:2 (1919), 90–98.
[276] The Tarot of Jean Dodal, British Museum 1896, 0501.592.1-78, © The Trustees of the British Museum.

Waite did not include in his own designs the overt Kabbalistic associations conveyed by inscribing a Hebrew letter on each Major Arcana card, a practice which Lévi had initiated and which other Golden Dawn adepts such as Westcott followed in their own Tarot designs.[278] Eager to challenge Lévi's authority in all occult matters, Waite appears to be ecumenical in discussing the Tarot's origins, declaring that the cards are 'universal and not particular' and that the Tarot 'is not...a derivative of any one school or literature of occultism'.[279] Nevertheless he reveals his dependence on Kabbalistic concepts when he declares that the 'truest and highest name' of the card of 'The High Priestess' is 'Shekinah',[280] asserts that the female figure in the card of 'The Star' is 'the Great Mother in the Kabalistic Sephira Binah', and describes the central figure in the card of 'The World' as guarded by 'the powers and the graces of the Holy Name, Tetragrammaton, יהוה'.[281] Waite also insists that Lévi's attributions of the Hebrew letters are wrong, and that he himself has discovered the 'right' ones 'by taking the old Yetziratic classification of the Hebrew letters and placing those cards against them which corresponded to their conventional allocations'.[282] He then suggests that, had Lévi 'understood Sephirotic Kabalism better', he would have

> ...established the operation of the Sacred Name in the four Kabalistic worlds and would have exhibited the distinctions and analogies between Shekinah in transcendence and the Shekinah manifested in life and time.[283]

It would seem that Waite's sporadic efforts to de-Judaise the Tarot were motivated more by the need to prove himself more esoterically knowledgeable than Lévi than by any lack of belief in the Kabbalistic meanings of the cards.

Between 1921 and 1923, Waite designed another set of

---

[277] A. E. Waite, *The Pictorial Key to the Tarot* (London: Rider, 1910), 149.
[278] See Jensen, *Waite-Smith Tarot*, 84. For Westcott's designs, see Jensen, *Waite-Smith Tarot*, 75.
[279] Waite, *Key*, 62.
[280] Waite, *Key*, 77.
[281] Waite, *Key*, 79, 139, 30.
[282] A. E. Waite, 'The Great Symbols of the Tarot', *OR* 43:1 (1926), 11–19, on p. 12.
[283] Waite, 'Great Symbols', 17.

Tarot-like images for his Fellowship of the Rosy Cross, which he called 'The Great Symbols of the Paths'.[284] Ronald Decker and Michael Dummett refer to these images as 'Waite's second Tarot',[285] but Waite did not produce any drawings for the Minor Arcana and the designs were probably never intended to be used for ordinary divinatory purposes. The 'Symbols' consist of twenty-two plates, numbered from XI to XXXII, with a twenty-third plate numbered 0 which portrays a bishop offering the Sacrament. No plates exist from I to X, perhaps because these numbers are associated with the ten *sefirot*, for which Waite, following the biblical injunction against 'graven images', would not prescribe designs; the numbers from XI to XXXII reflect the twenty-two pathways between the *sefirot* as enumerated in the *Sefer Yetsirah*.[286] Apart from Plate 0, the images portray primarily angelic figures. Some can be correlated with the Major Arcana of the Tarot, but most cannot. These twenty-two hauntingly beautiful images are not discussed in modern 'emic' handbooks on the Tarot and they have never been satisfactorily explained, although Decker and Dummett attempt to offer correspondences between some of them and the Major Arcana.[287] These authors, despite their valiant efforts, concede that they cannot identify many of the plates 'with any show of plausibility'; nor can they 'fathom the system governing the association of Hebrew letters with trumps'.[288]

---

[284] For the artists responsible for the images, see Jensen, *Waite-Smith Tarot*, 94; Willard, 'Acts of the Companions', 269–302.

[285] Decker and Dummett, *Occult Tarot*, 157.

[286] For Stenring's comments on the '32 Paths of Wisdom' (of which ten are equated with the *sefirot* and twenty-two with the Hebrew letters), see Stenring, *Book of Formation*, 54. For the Paths in the *Sefer Yetsirah*, see Hayman (trans.), *Sefer Yesirah* 1.1. For Kaplan's analysis of the meaning of the Paths, see Kaplan (trans.), *Sefer Yetzirah*, 10–11.

[287] Decker and Dummett, *Occult Tarot*, 157–60. See also Jensen, *Waite-Smith Tarot*, 95.

[288] Decker and Dummett, *Occult Tarot*, 160.

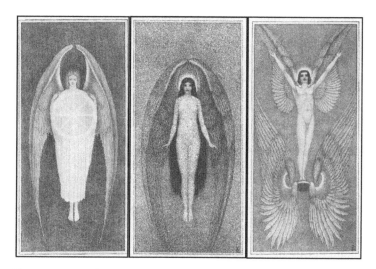

Fig. 24: Waite's 'Great Symbols of the Path'; from left to right, Plates XIII, XV, and XIV.[289]

In 1923, at precisely the time his 'Great Symbols' were created for the Fellowship, Waite dissociated himself in print from Lévi's belief in the correlations between the Major Arcana and the Hebrew alphabet. In his introduction to Knut Stenring's translation of the *Sefer Yetsirah*, he declares: 'I am not to be included among those who are satisfied that there is a valid correspondence between Hebrew letters and Tarot Trump symbols'.[290] If this were indeed the case, Waite would hardly have produced a set of twenty-two Tarot-like images intended to represent the paths between the *sefirot*. Whatever the reasons for his statement, and however disillusioned he eventually became with Lévi, the Golden Dawn, and occultism in general, Waite's 'mysticism' still rested on a firm Kabbalistic base.

The 'Great Symbols' were meant for the private use of the initiates of the Fellowship of the Rosy Cross, and Waite does

[289] British Museum 1973, 0616.21.1-38, *Album of the Great Symbols of the Paths; Illustrations to the Ritual of the Most Holy Order of the Rosy and Golden Cross*, © The Trustrees of the British Museum. The images are also reproduced in Jensen, *Waite-Smith Tarot*, 98–100, and twelve images are reproduced in Decker and Dummett, *Occult Tarot*, 148–49.

[290] A. E. Waite, 'Introduction', in Stenring (trans.), *Book of Formation*, 3–14, on pp. 13–14.

not mention them anywhere in his published writings. It is possible, given the celestial nature of the figures, that they are intended to represent not only the twenty-two paths on the sefirotic Tree, but also the living power of the letters, personified by angels, which comprise the twenty-two-letter Divine Name called *Shem Kaf Bet*, which first appears in the early modern magical compilation *Sefer ha-Raziel* (with which Waite was familiar) and, according to a seventeenth-century Kabbalistic prayer-book, 'comes from the Priestly Blessing, according to the Kabbalistic tradition, by means of many "alphabets"'.[291] If Waite did indeed link this Divine Name with the twenty-two sefirotic paths and the Major Arcana of the Tarot, and utilised the angelic images for meditative and adjurational purposes, he was drawing on one of the oldest and most influential of Kabbalistic traditions, the 'ecstatic' Kabbalah of Abraham Abulafia, one of the dominant elements in the formation of the Hasidic Kabbalism of the eighteenth and nineteenth centuries.[292] It is possible, and even likely, that Waite designed the 'Great Symbols' as part of a series of ritual invocations intended to induce a *unio mystica*. Although the Kabbalah of Waite's Fellowship was interpreted 'in the Christian mode', it seems that Waite remained, at heart, the proponent of an enduring magico-mystical Kabbalistic current which found its modern flowering in the Hasidic Judaism of his own time.

Crowley's more flamboyant Tarot, with its accompanying explanatory book, appeared in 1944, thirty-five years after Waite's 'rectified' deck. The 'wickedest man in the world', who delighted in disagreeing with everyone about everything, nevertheless remained faithful to the conviction of that 'very great Qabalist and scholar' Éliphas Lévi, that the Tarot is 'a pictorial form of the Qabalistic Tree of Life'.[293] Despite his apparent scientific rationalism, Crowley declares that the ultimate source of the cards lies in 'superiors whose mental processes were, or are, pertaining to a higher Dimension'.[294] The details of the images, painted by Lady

---

[291] Cited in Trachtenberg, *Jewish Magic*, 93. For Waite's familiarity with the *Sefer ha-Raziel*, see Waite, *Book of Black Magic*, 31–34. For the *Shem Kaf Bet*, see Dan, 'Name of God'; Louis Jacobs, *A Jewish Theology* (Springfield, NJ: Behrman House, 1973), 149.
[292] For the use of Abulafia's linguistic magic in Hasidism, see Idel, *Hasidism*, 53–65.
[293] Crowley, *Thoth*, 4–5.
[294] Crowley, *Thoth*, 10.

Frieda Harris, a member of Crowley's OTO,[295] draw on symbolic sources very different from Waite's, and contain overt astrological significators as well as detailed allusions to the Egyptian pantheon and Hermetic alchemy. There are few Christian references to be found. But Crowley, even more than Waite, clung to the original Golden Dawn teachings on the Tarot and allocated a Hebrew letter to each of the Major Arcana according to the Cipher MS, with the Fool assigned to the letter *aleph* at the beginning of the deck.[296]

For example, Crowley entirely rejects Waite's Christian image of 'Judgement' and renames the card 'The Aeon', replacing the Christian angel with the figure of the Egyptian goddess Nuit and declaring: 'In this card it has been necessary to depart completely from the tradition of the cards, in order to carry on that tradition'.[297] Where Waite removed Lévi's Hebrew letters from the cards, Crowley instructed his artist to incorporate within the image of each card the shape of the Hebrew letter which he associated with it. The letter which both Crowley and the Cipher MS attribute to 'Judgement' ('The Aeon') is ש (*shin*), which is integrated into the design of the card; it contains three human figures 'arising to partake in the Essence of the new Aeon'.[298]

---

[295] For Frieda Harris, see Kaczynski, *Perdurabo*, 410–32; Booth, *Magick Life*, 473–75; Decker and Dummett, *Occult Tarot*, 153. For Harris' artistic background in Rudolph Steiner's 'Projective Synthetic Geometry', see Olive Whicher, *Projective Geometry: Creative Polarities in Space and Time* (London: Rudolf Steiner Press, 1971); George Adams, *Physical and Ethereal Spaces* (London: Rudolf Steiner Press, 1965); Lawrence Edwards, *Projective Geometry: An Approach to the Secrets of Space From the Standpoint of Artistic and Imaginative Thought* (Phoenixville, PA: Rudolf Steiner Institute, 1985).
[296] For other details peculiar to Crowley's cards, see Crowley, *Thoth*, 9–10; Decker and Dummett, *Occult Tarot*, 153–54.
[297] Crowley, *Thoth*, 115.
[298] Crowley, *Thoth*, 115.

Fig. 25: Left, Waite's 'Judgement'; right, Crowley's 'Aeon'.[299]

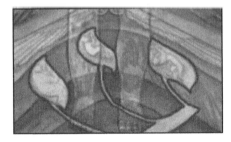

Fig. 26: Detail of Crowley's 'The Aeon' with the Hebrew letter ש (shin) highlighted.

With some cards the Hebrew letter provides the structure for the entire image, as א (*aleph*) does for the figure of 'The Fool'.[300] The importance of the shape of the letters as the foundation of Crowley's designs reflects the Kabbalistic understanding of the letters as divine emanations. Because the letters are viewed not merely as linguistic signs but as

---

[299] Crowley's 'The Aeon', in *Thoth*, 230.
[300] For Crowley's explanation of 'The Fool', see Crowley, *Thoth*, 53–69.

creative agents and embodiments of the supernal powers, they provide the basis for the magical invocation of those powers through vocalisation (as proposed by Abraham Abulafia in the thirteenth century);[301] visualisation with colour (as demonstrated by Moshe Cordovero in the sixteenth century);[302] and prayer with intention (*kavvanah*) as a method of inducing a *unio mystica*, as described by the founder of the modern Hasidic movement, the Ba'al Shem Tov:

> In each and every letter there are worlds and souls and divinity and they ascend and combine and unify with each other and with the Godhead...and the soul will be integrated with them.[303]

Although Crowley's Kabbalah was dismissed by Scholem as mere charlatanry, his use of the Hebrew letters in *The Book of Thoth* reflects a deeper grasp of Kabbalistic magical theory and practice than Scholem was prepared to acknowledge. *Thoth*, produced only three years before Crowley's death, suggests that, despite his presentation of the Jewish Kabbalah as a system of classification, his dislike of Jews and Jewish theology, and his predilection for pagan pantheons, the Kabbalah, for Crowley, represented something far more potent and aligned with ancient Jewish linguo-theosophy than some modern scholars are willing to recognise. Crowley's Tarot is the ripe fruit yielded from Lévi's seeding: a Tarot which is unique in its artistic style, Greco-Egyptian in its iconography, and Kabbalistic in its structure and intention through the use of the Hebrew letters and the complex interrelationships they form on the sefirotic Tree. As the Beast himself declares: 'The whole of the Tarot is based upon the Tree of Life'.[304]

Waite created Tarot cards as tools of divination, instruments of esoteric instruction, and symbolic representations of the eternal human journey from darkness

---

[301] See Abraham Abulafia, *Hayyê ha-'Olam ha-Ba*, MS Oxford 1582, fol. 54a–b, cited in Idel, *Mystical Experience*, 29.

[302] See Moshe Cordovero, *Pardes Rimmonim*, 32:2, cited in Moshe Idel, 'Mystical Techniques', 477.

[303] Baal Shem Tov, *Epistle on the Ascent of the Soul*, in *Shivhei Ha-Bal Shem Tov* (Jerusalem,1982), 235–36, cited in Idel, *Enchanted Chains*, 151.

[304] Crowley, *Thoth*, 54.

to light. His cards are also talismanic, although he would have hotly denied such an accusation, at least in public.[305] Crowley created Tarot cards which were overtly intended as magical talismans, imbued with the power to invoke the 'forces' they represent. The cards present symbols not merely as signifiers, metaphors, social constructs, or forms of communication, but as the embodiment or imaginal vessel of that ineffable potency which is being portrayed.[306] This use of symbols, according to Ernst Gombrich's still relevant analysis, unites 'mystic significance and magic effect'.[307] Both Waite and Crowley anchored their Tarots in Kabbalistic speculations first delineated by Lévi and then adapted and altered by Mathers in *Book T*. But Waite and Crowley polarised, as was their wont, and each articulated only those aspects of the Kabbalah with which he could identify within the apparently irreconcilably opposed domains of 'mysticism' and 'magic'. The battle between the two men is demonstrated nowhere more clearly than in their Tarot cards – not in terms of the structure, which remains consistent with older decks, or the theoretical framework, which remains Kabbalistic in both cases, but in terms of the 'fundamental conceptions of spiritual process' for which the images were designed.

Despite the proliferation of new Tarot designs from the 1980s onward,[308] Waite's Tarot is still accepted by many practitioners as 'definitive', especially within Masonic circles,[309] while Crowley's Tarot, although still popular, was

---

[305] The term 'talismanic' is used here to describe an object, image, structure, or unit of language (such as a Divine Name or a Hebrew letter) which, based on the idea of correspondences, is utilised to summon invisible entities or draw down supernal energies for the magician's purposes. For language as a talisman, see Moshe Idel, 'On Talismanic Language in Jewish Mysticism', *Diogenes* 43:2 (1995), 23–41.

[306] For similar definitions of a symbol, see Dan, 'Name of God'; Dan, 'Gershom Scholem's Reconstruction'.

[307] Ernst H. Gombrich, '*Icones Symbolicae*: The Visual Image in Neo-Platonic Thought', *JWCI* 11 (1948), 163–92, on p. 175.

[308] For a presentation of hundreds of new and old Tarot decks, see <http://www.aeclectic.net/tarot>.

[309] For Masonic approval of Waite's Tarot, see William Steve Burkle, 'Masonic Allusion and Symbolism in the Figures and Interpretations of the Major Arcana of the Tarot by Arthur Edward Waite' (23 September 2008), <http://www.freemasons-freemasonry.com/major_arcana_tarot.html>.

always intended for a small, elite readership, and is favoured primarily by practitioners sympathetic to his system of Thelemic 'magick'.[310] In a similar fashion, the theosophically inclined *Zohar* is generally perceived as the 'definitive' Kabbalah, while the magical dimensions of Kabbalistic literature, found in works such as the *Sefer ha-Meshiv* and understood by both Jewish and non-Jewish occultists as 'practical' Kabbalah, have, until recently, been either ignored by scholars or neutralised under the safer rubric of 'theurgy'. Current scholarship has demonstrated that it is impossible to disentangle mystical and magical threads in the fabric of the Kabbalah, although Waite and Crowley, for reasons personal to themselves, attempted to do so. The more inclusive inheritance of Lévi, who, perhaps influenced by his Polish Jewish contacts, understood the Kabbalah as a unity of mystical theosophy and magic, gradually fell into the hands of warring camps which mirrored the conflicts of the broader backdrop of British religious and scientific currents in the first decades of the twentieth century. It would become the task of the last major practitioner of the occult revival, Violet M. Firth, known to her readers as Dion Fortune, to reunite the opposites and perform, like the Lurianic adepts of the sixteenth century, the necessary *tikkunim* to facilitate the reintegration of the Kabbalah within British occultism, just prior to the disintegration of the Western world in the catastrophe of the Second World War.

---

[310] For contemporary sympathetic efforts to interpret Crowley's Tarot, see, for example, P. C. Tarantino, *Tarot for the New Aeon: A Practical Guide to the Power and Wisdom of the Thoth Tarot* (Pebble Beach, CA: Alternative Insights Publishing, 2007); Maja Mandic, *The Keys of Arcana: Practical Handbook to Crowley's Tarot* (Belgrade: Arkona, 2008); Lon Milo DuQuette, *Understanding Aleister Crowley's Thoth Tarot* (York Beach, ME: Red Wheel/Weiser, 2003); Michael Osiris Snuffin, *The Thoth Companion: The Key to the True Symbolic Meaning of the Thoth Tarot* (St. Paul, MN: Llewellyn Publications, 2007).

CHAPTER SIX

WHEN SHE WAS 'JUNG AND EASILY FREUDENED':[1] DION FORTUNE'S 'PSYCHOLOGICAL' KABBALAH

> With Jungian psychology the ancient Mystery Tradition can join hands....All that is needed is a Rosetta Stone bearing parallel inscriptions in different languages...to enable translation to begin and an immense wealth of data and experience to be made available for both sides of the council table.[2]
>
> – Dion Fortune (1944)

> For a real understanding of the Jewish component in Freud's outlook...this would carry us beyond Jewish orthodoxy into the subterranean workings of Hasidism, and then into the intricacies of the Kabbalah, which still remains unexplored psychologically.[3]
>
> – C. G. Jung (1957)

BETWEEN THE WARS

Piers Brendon, in a review published in *The Guardian* in 2008, observed that the inter-war years in Britain (1919–1939) have been seen as 'a tableau of horrors: industrial graveyards, dole queues, means tests, hunger marches, poverty, inequality, malnutrition, disease and despair'.[4] It might seem that

---

[1] 'Jung and easily freudened', James Joyce, *Finnegans Wake* (London: Faber & Faber, 1939), 115.

[2] Dion Fortune, 'Monthly Letter' (May 1944), cited in Gareth Knight, *Dion Fortune and the Inner Light* (Loughborough: Thoth Publications, 2000), 291.

[3] C. G. Jung, 'Letter to Edith Schröder' (April 1957), in *C. G. Jung Letters*, 2 vols., ed. Gerhard Adler, trans. R. F. C. Hull (London: Routledge & Kegan Paul, 1976), 1:358–359.

[4] Piers Brendon, 'The Devil's Decade': Review of Martin Pugh, *A Social History of Britain Between the Wars*, *The Guardian* (5 July 2008), 9. For the inter-war years, see Keith Laybourn (ed.), *Modern Britain Since 1906 – A Reader* (London: I. B. Tauris, 1999), 105–35; Adrian Bingham, *Gender, Modernity, and the Popular Press in Inter-War Britain*

religious belief, already ailing since the Enlightenment, went into terminal decline during this period, in the face of both the new religion of 'scientism' and the post-Armistice spiritual desert described so disturbingly by T. S. Eliot in his 1922 poem, 'The Waste Land':

> What are the roots that clutch, what branches grow
> Out of this stony rubbish? Son of man,
> You cannot say, or guess, for you know only
> A heap of broken images, where the sun beats,
> And the dead tree gives no shelter, the cricket no relief,
> And the dry stone no sound of water.[5]

It might also seem that the exotic indulgences of late Victorian and Edwardian occultism, with its elaborate rituals, its secret elite, its belief in the divine power of the human will, and its vision of a regenerated society in an imminent New Age, had been rendered redundant if not ridiculous by the grinding realities of a more sombre world. Interest in Jewish esoteric lore might likewise be expected to fade in the face of rising antisemitism, fuelled by the belief that Jewish 'international usury' was responsible for the depressing plight of the ordinary working Englishman. Oswald Moseley, at a rally in Manchester in 1934, gave voice to these sentiments when he declared:

> What they call today the will of the people is nothing but the organized corruption of press, cinema and Parliament, which is called democracy but which is ruled by alien Jewish finance.[6]

'Alien Jewish finance' was not the only target for antisemitic sentiments. Despite the apparent triumph of modernity – or perhaps as one of its unwitting by-products – the medieval spectre of the Jew as the Devil's agent,

---

(Oxford: Oxford University Press, 2004); Roy Hattersley, *Borrowed Time: The Story of Britain Between the Wars* (London: Little, Brown, 2007); Charles Loch Mowat, *Britain Between the Wars, 1918–1940* (Chicago, IL: University of Chicago Press, 1955); John Stevenson and Chris Cook, *Britain in the Depression: Society and Politics, 1929–39* (London: Longman, 1994); Richard Overy, *The Morbid Age: Britain Between the Wars* (London: Allen Lane, 2009).
[5] T. S. Eliot, 'The Waste Land' (1922), in *The Complete Poems and Plays of T. S. Eliot* (London: Faber and Faber, 1978), 59–75, on p. 61.
[6] *The Times* (1 October 1934), cited in Holmes, *Anti-Semitism*, 177.

proficient in Kabbalistic magic and intent on destroying the Christian world, once again materialised from the shadows. An English translation of the *Protocols of the Elders of Zion* appeared in 1920, followed in 1923 by an 'official' translation published by a vociferously antisemitic group called 'The Britons'.[7] Nesta Webster's virulent *Secret Societies and Subversive Movements* came hard on the heels of this translation in 1924, and engendered in its turn a rash of conspiracy-theory publications, including one by the British Army officer John Frederick Charles Fuller (1878–1966), a devoted admirer of Crowley, who fulminated against what he believed to be a Jewish-Masonic conspiracy to destroy Europe through Kabbalistic magic.[8]

Assumptions about an inter-war decline in religiosity in general and occultism in particular may be somewhat simplistic. Callum Brown has convincingly demonstrated that the British were no more irreligious or 'secularised' after the Great War than they had been in the eighteenth and nineteenth centuries.[9] The intolerable losses of the war precipitated a resurgence of interest in spiritualism comparable with its Victorian heyday, inspired by writers such as Arthur Conan Doyle (1859–1930), who announced his conversion to the spiritualist cause in 1916 and produced eleven nonfiction works on the subject between 1918 and his

---

[7] George Shanks, *The Jewish Peril. Protocols of the Learned Elders of Zion* (London: Eyre & Spottiswoode, 1920); Victor E. Marsden (trans.), *Protocols of the Meetings of the Learned Elders of Zion* (London: The Britons Publishing Society, 1923). For 'The Britons', see Webb, *Occult Establishment*, 130–31; William I. Brustein, *Roots of Hate: Anti-Semitism in Europe Before the Holocaust* (Cambridge: Cambridge University Press, 2003), 149–50; Gisela C. Lebzelter, 'Henry Hamilton Beamish and the Britons: Champions of Anti-Semitism', in Kenneth Lunn and Richard C. Thurlow (eds.), *British Fascism: Essays on the Radical Right in Inter-War Britain* (London: Croom Helm, 1980), 41–56.
[8] See J. F. C. Fuller, *The Secret Wisdom of the Qabalah: A Study in Jewish Mystical Thought* (London: Rider, 1937). For Fuller's involvement with British fascist groups, see Linehan, *British Facism*, 193. For Fuller's uncritical analysis of Crowley's works, see J. C. F. Fuller, *The Star in the West: A Critical Essay Upon the Works of Aleister Crowley* (New York, NY: Walter Scott, 1907). For other groups promulgating anti-Jewish sentiment in the inter-war years, see Holmes, *Anti-Semitism*, 203–19; Webb, *Occult Establishment*, 125–36.
[9] Callum Brown, *The Death of Christian Britain: Understanding Secularisation, 1800–2000* (London: Routledge, 2001), 164.

death twelve years later,[10] and Arthur Findlay (1883–1964), president of the London Spiritualist Alliance, whose book, *On the Edge of the Etheric*, was reprinted twenty-five times between November 1931 and June 1932 and which, according to *Psychic News*, sold at the rate of five hundred copies per week.[11] A plethora of reformers emerged after the war with plans to transform the 'materialist' system held responsible for the catastrophe; some of these groups, such as Aubrey Westlake's Order of Woodcraft Chivalry, promulgated a neoromantic pantheism that easily merged with occult theories of the immanence of the divine in Nature.[12] Awareness of the enormous power of the hidden depths of the human psyche was also beginning to capture the attention of a war-ravaged populace. In 1933, speaking on behalf of the new psychologies, C. G. Jung articulated an increasing anxiety about the destructive potential of the unconscious:

> The conscious, modern man, despite his strenuous and dogged efforts to do so, can no longer refrain from acknowledging the might of psychic forces....We can no longer deny that the dark stirrings of the unconscious are effective powers.[13]

Meanwhile, the Theosophical Society had survived schism, scandal, the defection of its long-awaited new 'World Teacher' Jiddu Krishnamurti in 1929, and the death of its most charismatic early-twentieth-century exponent, Annie Besant, in 1933; and although its British membership had diminished, the TS showed no signs of rolling over and

---

[10] For Doyle's conversion to spiritualism, see Owen, *Place of Enchantment*, 221–37. For the rise of spiritualism after the Great War, see also Jenny Hazelgrove, *Spiritualism and British Society Between the Wars* (Manchester: Manchester University Press, 2000).
[11] Arthur Findlay, *On the Edge of the Etheric* (London: Psychic Press, 1931). The text is available online at www.thegreatquestion.com/books/On_the_Edge_of_Etheric.pdf. See also Hazelgrove, *Spiritualism and British Society*, 15.
[12] For the Order of Woodcraft Chivalry and similar groups in the inter-war years, see Webb, *Occult Establishment*, 81–143; Hutton, 'Pagan Witchcraft', 36–38.
[13] C. G. Jung, 'The Spiritual Problem of Modern Man', in C. G. Jung, *Modern Man in Search of a Soul*, trans. W. S. Dell and Cary F. Baynes (London: Kegan Paul, Trench, Trubner & Co., 1933), 226–54, repr. in Jung, CW10, 74–94, ¶161, on p. 80.

dying.[14] Nor did the Victorian magical orders vanish in the wake of Armageddon. The Golden Dawn, despite its fragmentation and the deaths of many of its early members, continued to generate progeny.[15] Not all these groups espoused the Kabbalah as the foundation of their doctrines as the original order had done, and some occultists, such as Fuller and Christina Stoddart, one of the Chiefs of the Stella Matutina during the 1920s,[16] embraced the sentiments of the *Protocols* and took up the burden of warning the world of the great occult conspiracy of Jews, Freemasons, and Bolsheviks.[17]

However, some adepts remained loyal to the original Kabbalistic vision that Lévi had first promulgated in the mid-

---

[14] For these events in the history of the Theosophical Society, see Roland Vernon, *Star in the East: Krishnamurti, the Invention of a Messiah* (Boulder, CO: Sentient Publications, 2002); Bruce F. Campbell, *Ancient Wisdom Revived: A History of the Theosophical Movement* (Berkeley, CA: University of California Press, 1980), 113–46; Josephine Ransom, *A Short History of the Theosophical Society* (London: Theosophical Publishing House, 1992).

[15] For the splinter orders derived from the original Isis-Urania Temple of the Golden Dawn, see Colquhoun, *Sword*, 180, 182–83, 205. These groups span the period from the foundation of the Golden Dawn in 1888 to the late 1960s. Many of them emerged during the Great War, but a number were founded during the interwar years, including the reconstituted Alpha et Omega (1919), the Fraternity of the Inner Light (1922), the Hermanoubis Temple (1930), the Universal Order (1935), and the Order of Coinherence (1935).

[16] The Stella Matutina ('Morning Star') was originally adopted as a title to include all the Golden Dawn members who broke with Mathers after the schism in 1903. For a time this order was run by J. W. Brodie-Innes, but later came under the control of Dr. Robert William Felkin. Felkin retained most of the traditional Kabbalistic elements of the original Golden Dawn, and his Secret Chiefs – the disincarnate 'higher entities' or *maggidim* who were believed to guide the order – were primarily Jewish or Arabic. For more on the Stella Matutina, see Howe, *Magicians*, 252–72. For more on Felkin, see Harper, *Yeats's Golden Dawn*, 124–37; Gilbert, *Scrapbook*, 184–86; Howe, *Magicians*, 273–77; King, *Modern Ritual Magic*, 97–108; Colquhoun, *Sword*, 193–97.

[17] See Christina M. Stoddart [writing under the pseudonym 'Inquire Within'], *Light-Bearers of Darkness* (London: Boswell, 1930); Christina M. Stoddart ['Inquire Within'], *The Trail of the Serpent* (London: Boswell, 1936). For Stoddart, see Owen, *Place of Enchantment*, 225; Harper, *Yeats's Golden Dawn*, 126–45; Gilbert, *Scrapbook*, 186–88; Howe, *Magicians*, 273–84.

nineteenth century, and they quickly recognised that not all modern science was inimical to occultism. Psychology, presenting itself as a new and powerful instrument that could transform human nature by scientific means, still kept its left hand quietly immersed in the occult waters that had given birth to it in the first place.[18] As James Webb observes, 'Psychoanalysis, psychical research, and the more religious aspects of the Occult Revival can by no means be disentangled'.[19] The devastation following the Great War, for many occultists as for many Jews struggling with the growing tide of antisemitic feeling, brought a more direct and profound understanding of the world of the Jewish Kabbalah: a world of suffering, alienation, fragmentation, loss, grief, and homelessness, mitigated only by a vision of the reconciliation of warring opposites through the marriage of psychological theory and Kabbalistic ritual magic.

THE OCCULT PSYCHOLOGIST

In the year after the Armistice, Violet Mary Firth (1890–1946), the twenty-nine-year-old daughter of a middle-class Christian Scientist couple from Sheffield,[20] was initiated into

---

[18] For the roots of modern dynamic psychiatry and psychology in mesmerism and magic in the late eighteenth century, see Ellenberger, *Discovery*, 53–109; Henriette Gezundhajt, 'An Evolution of the Historical Origins of Hypnotism Prior to the Twentieth Century: Between Spirituality and Subconscious', *Contemporary Hypnosis* 24:4 (2007), 178–94. For the occult antecedents of psychoanalysis in the late nineteenth century, see Webb, *Occult Establishment*, 347–81.

[19] Webb, *Occult Establishment*, 347.

[20] Dion Fortune was born in Llandudno, Wales, but her family were Sheffield steel tycoons. Four biographies of Fortune have been published in the last two decades: Fielding and Collins, *Story of Dion Fortune*; Richardson, *Magical Life*; Janine Chapman, *Quest for Dion Fortune* (York Beach, ME: Samuel Weiser, Inc., 1993), and Knight, *Dion Fortune*. The first of these biographies has been severely criticised by Jack Adrian in his introduction to *Taverner*, ix–xi. Adrian feels that Chapman's book is probably the most reliable, although he wrote his conclusions before Knight's biography of Fortune appeared. Ronald Hutton's *Triumph of the Moon*, 180–88, devotes a section to Fortune's influence on modern pagan witchcraft; on this theme see also Hutton, 'Background to Pagan Witchcraft', in *Witchcraft and Magic in Europe*, 38–40, and Chas S. Clifton, 'A Goddess Arrives: The Novels of Dion Fortune and the

the London Temple of the Alpha et Omega, the remnant of the original Inner Order of the Golden Dawn which had remained loyal to Mina Bergson Mathers after her husband's death from influenza in 1918.[21] Following her initiation, Firth took the magical name Deo Non Fortuna ('God not Fortune'), which provided the pseudonym 'Dion Fortune' under which her prodigious literary output on occultism in general, and the Kabbalah in particular, was later published.[22] Fortune became disillusioned with the Alpha et Omega after three years:

> Practical teaching from official sources was conspicuous by its absence....The glory had departed...for most of its original members were dead or withdrawn; it had suffered severely during the war, and was manned mainly by widows and

---

Development of Gardnerian Witchcraft', *Gnosis* 9 (Fall 1988), 20–30. Little scholarly work has been done on Fortune's 'occult' novels, but see Algeo, 'Integrated Alien'. Researchers into Fortune's life have been consistently frustrated by the withholding of her personal documents by the current incarnation of the occult group she founded, the Society (formerly the Fraternity) of the Inner Light, which claims that these documents were all destroyed. The present Society has declared itself to be firmly Christian and attenuates the Kabbalistic magical framework Fortune originally used as the basis of her work, as well as her emphasis on sexual magic. One of Fortune's articles, originally published in *The Occult Review*, is available from the Society's website at http://www.innerlight.org.uk, but Fortune's work is not entirely in accord with the present teachings of the order and researchers attempting to learn more about Fortune's life are blocked from access to further information. For comments by an irritated researcher on the current stance of the Society, see Adrian, 'Introduction', xii.

[21] The Alpha et Omega was initially run by Brodie-Innes, who for a time played both ends of the conflict between Mathers and his rebellious adepts by running the Alpha et Omega and the Stella Matutina simultaneously. Mina Mathers returned to London in 1919, a year after her husband's death in Paris, and set up another Alpha et Omega Temple independent of the one run by Brodie-Innes, although both were understood to be 'official' Golden Dawn temples and were not publicly antagonistic toward each other. Fortune spent a year in Brodie-Innes' Alpha et Omega and then, in 1920, joined the Alpha et Omega of Mina Mathers.

[22] For the derivation of this magical name, see Richardson, *Magical Life*, 17–18.

grey-bearded ancients.[23]

The Great War had not left the Golden Dawn unscathed. But disillusionment alone did not drive Fortune out; a mutual antipathy began to fester between her and Mina Mathers, who eventually decided to expel her trainee.[24] Fortune already had considerable experience of the internecine power-battles within occult groups through her early involvement with the Theosophical Society.[25] Like Mathers, Waite, and Crowley, she was an autocrat with firm ideas about how an occult order should be structured and on what basis its doctrines should be formulated, and she could not tolerate the authority of those she considered less proficient than herself:

> What is required of the neophyte is not a blind obedience but an intelligent comprehension of principles....The request for an oath of obedience does not sound well, for if obedience is required for purposes which would obtain the approval of the pupil, why should not he, as a free man, give his loyalty? And if they are of such a nature as not to command his acceptance, is it right that he should be coerced against his conscience?[26]

Although a declared Christian, Fortune exhibited no interest in Waite's Fellowship of the Rosy Cross, perhaps because Waite had made clear his hostile attitude toward magic and Fortune was not interested in a purely mystical path. Her sentiments are expressed by Hugh Paston, the protagonist in one of her novels:

> He was of too active a nature to be content to sit indefinitely on old Jelkes' broken-down sofa and talk philosophy. He was not interested in occultism from the philosophical side, as the old man was. He wanted phenomena.[27]

In 1922, after a brief sojourn in the Stella Matutina, Fortune created her own occult society, the Fraternity of the

---

[23] Dion Fortune, 'Ceremonial Magic Unveiled', *OR* 57:1 (1933), 13–24, on p. 20.
[24] Fortune, 'Ceremonial Magic', 22.
[25] For Fortune's early experiences in the Theosophical Society, see Richardson, *Magical Life*, 65–71.
[26] Dion Fortune, *The Esoteric Orders and Their Work* (London: Rider & Co., 1928; repr. York Beach, ME: Samuel Weiser, 2000), 98–99.
[27] Dion Fortune, *The Goat-Foot God* (London: Norgate, 1936), 143–44.

Inner Light. Despite her conflicts with other occultists, she had acquired an invaluable resource from her time in the various Golden Dawn orders, which Alan Richardson identifies as the Kabbalah: 'Perhaps the best thing that Dion was ever given by the Golden Dawn on intellectual levels was knowledge of the Qabalah. This philosophy was the basis of everything that Dion believed or taught'.[28] This statement is open to question; Jack Adrian describes Fortune as 'a maze of contradictions',[29] and Ronald Hutton considers her a 'complex thinker' whose interests shifted constantly between ritual magic, paganism, Kabbalah, and mystical Christianity.[30] Fortune's *Avalon of the Heart*, reminiscent of Waite at his most lyrically devotional, presents Glastonbury as an ancient spiritual centre where pagan and Christian mysteries are intertwined.[31] The Kabbalah does not feature in this work. In the introduction to *Mystical Meditations on the Collects*, Fortune states that she 'withdrew successively' from Theosophy, New Thought, and Spiritualism in order to return to Christianity 'with an entirely new concept of its significance'.[32] No hint of Jewish esoteric lore can be found in this book. Another work, *The Cosmic Doctrine* – a posthumously published treatise 'channelled' between 1927 and 1928 by 'higher entities'[33] – relies heavily on the Theosophical cosmology of Blavatsky's *The Secret Doctrine*.[34] But allusions to Kabbalistic concepts are woven like flourescent threads into most of Fortune's works, including *The Cosmic Doctrine*, where she speaks constantly of the Lurianic 'Divine Sparks' and discusses the angelic beings who personify the ten *sefirot*.[35] From the early 1930s onward,

---

[28] Richardson, *Magical Life*, 113.
[29] Jack Adrian, 'Introduction', in Dion Fortune, *The Secrets of Dr. Taverner* (London: Noel Douglas, 1926; repr. Ashcroft, BC: Ash-Tree Press, 2000), ix–xxvi, on p. xiii.
[30] Hutton, *Triumph of the Moon*, 187–88. See also Hutton, 'Pagan Witchcraft', 38–40.
[31] Dion Fortune, *Avalon of the Heart* (London: Muller, 1934).
[32] Dion Fortune, *Mystical Meditations on the Collects* (London: Rider, 1930), 5.
[33] Dion Fortune, *The Cosmic Doctrine* (London: Society of the Inner Light, 1949; repr. York Beach, ME: WeiserBooks, 2000), 1.
[34] See, for example, Fortune, *Cosmic Doctrine*, 196–97, compared with Blavatsky, *Isis*, 1:594–95 and 2:263–76; and Blavatsky, *Secret Doctrine*, 1:xlii and 160, and 2:172.
[35] For the 'Divine Sparks', see Fortune, *Cosmic Doctrine*, 84–89, 193–95. For the sefirotic archangels, see Fortune, *Cosmic Doctrine*, 204–06.

the Kabbalah – laced, in characteristic Golden Dawn fashion, with Greco-Egyptian motifs – seems to have dominated her understanding of magic, and Fortune herself supports Richardson's observation in the opening statement of her foreword to *The Mystical Qabalah*: 'The Tree of Life forms the ground-plan of the Western Esoteric Tradition'.[36]

Fortune first encountered occultism in her mid-twenties during her training and practice as a lay psychotherapist, when she fell under the spell of a charismatic Irish Freemason and occultist called Theodore Moriarty, the figure on whom her fictional 'psychic doctor' John Taverner was partly based. With a background in both esoteric lore and the psychological theories of Freud and Jung, Fortune believed that occultism was the 'real key to psychology',[37] and even suggests that it could be viewed as a form of psychology: 'Occultism is the study of certain little-understood powers of the human mind and of the mind side of Nature'.[38] Through her psychotherapeutic training she was uniquely equipped to interpret occult theory and practice in the language of this new mapping of the human soul – an innovative contribution which has made her work relevant to many contemporary spiritualities.[39] Fortune certainly stands as a prime example of the 'psychologization of the sacred',[40] and everything in her system, from her magical rituals to her elaborations of the sefirotic Tree, is explained in psychological terms. But her understanding of the Kabbalistic 'forces' as an interior psycho-spiritual landscape, and her firm belief in 'self-spirituality' and the accessibility of God-knowledge through self-knowledge,[41] are not evidence of a new, post-Enlightenment internalisation of deity. These perceptions, as discussed in earlier chapters, can be found in Kabbalistic texts from the thirteenth century onward, and are implicit in Isaac Luria's depiction of the androgynous Adam

---

[36] Fortune, *Mystical Qabalah*, v.

[37] Dion Fortune, *Psychic Self-Defence* (London: Rider, 1931), 9.

[38] Dion Fortune, 'Types of Mind Working', in Dion Fortune and Gareth Knight, *An Introduction to Ritual Magic* (Loughborough: Thoth Publications, 1997), 13–23, on p. 13.

[39] For the merging of psychology and occultism in contemporary 'New Age' spiritualities, see Hanegraaff, *New Age Religion*, 224–55, and below.

[40] For this phrase, see above, Chapter One, and Hanegraaff, *New Age Religion*, 224.

[41] 'Self-spirituality' is from Heelas, *New Age Movement*, 19.

Kadmon as the cosmic anthropos, whose organs and limbs, embodied in the ten *sefirot*, correspond to both the human body and the various aspects of the human soul:

> There is one entity that is included in all worlds and places. All worlds develop from it, depend on it and grasp into it. They exit from it and are revealed as separate entities from it. This entity is Adam Kadmon. Adam Kadmon preceded all.[42]

Fortune refers to Adam Kadmon as 'the archetypal man', the link between macrocosm and microcosm, through which the individual is connected to the divine.[43] Jung likewise borrowed the theme of Adam Kadmon to describe the 'Original Man of Jewish gnosis', the invisible centre or higher 'Self' of the individual personality.[44]

Fortune's Kabbalah has not been reduced to a mere psychological map. The ten *sefirot* are ontic powers which 'sum up the objective world on all its levels',[45] while the twenty-two Paths on the Tree, correlated with the Hebrew letters, the signs of the zodiac, and the Major Arcana of the Tarot, are understood as 'the subjective aspect of the Tree as it is applied to consciousness and the powers of the mind'.[46] The Tree is therefore 'a compendium of science, psychology, philosophy, and theology',[47] representing ascending levels of both human and divine consciousness. This highly sophisticated understanding of the subjective nature of the human effort to achieve a psycho-spiritual transformation rooted in an ontically objective higher reality is reflected not only in Jewish Kabbalistic precepts but also in the analytical psychology of Jung, who eventually proved more important than Freud in Fortune's psychological arsenal of conceptual frameworks and who, as discussed more fully below, was, like Freud, strongly influenced by Kabbalistic doctrines and practices. Fortune may be viewed as one of the most creative

---

[42] Dunn (ed.), *Window of the Soul*, 120–21.

[43] Fortune, *Mystical Qabalah*, 189.

[44] Jung, CW14, ¶44, ¶548. For other references to Adam Kadmon in Jung's work, see, *inter alia*, CW11, ¶94; CW13, ¶168; CW14, ¶591–92, ¶594, ¶596, ¶600, ¶606–07, ¶611.

[45] Dion Fortune, 'The Paths Upon the Tree', originally published in *ILM* 9:11 (1936); 9:12 (1936); 10:1 (1936), available from the Societas Rosicruciana in America, <http://www.sria.org/paths_tree.htm>.

[46] Fortune, 'Paths'. See also Dion Fortune, 'The Reality of the Subtle Planes', in Fortune and Knight, *Ritual Magic*, 92–98, on p. 93.

[47] Fortune, *Mystical Qabalah*, 13.

Kabbalistic innovators in the British occult revival, and she has left the legacy of a 'psychological' Kabbalah which, superficially, seems an entirely modern, twentieth-century invention. Yet she is surprisingly loyal to the Kabbalistic doctrines expressed in the Jewish texts of previous centuries, particularly the interiorised Kabbalah of the Hasidic movement that arose in Eastern Europe in the eighteenth century. That the various dimensions of the sefirotic Tree are understood by the Hasidim as aspects of the human psyche is made clear by the *Tanya*, a short but immensely influential eighteenth-century text expressing the most important doctrines of Hasidism, in which the *sefirot* are referred to as 'mind-faculties'.[48]

Making no claim to being a Hebraic scholar as some of her predecessors did,[49] Fortune makes clear her 'modern' position on Jewish traditions:

> The modern Qabalist is the heir of the ancient Qabalist, but he must re-interpret the doctrine and re-formulate method in the light of the present dispensation...I do not claim that the modern Qabalistic teachings as I have learnt them are identical with those of the pre-Christian rabbis, but I claim that they are the legitimate descendants thereof and the natural development theretrom.[50]

Fortune's indifference toward historical continuity has provoked the hostility of scholars such as J. H. Laenen, who attacks the practitioners of the occult revival for their 'distortion' of the Jewish Kabbalah.[51] Lévi, Mathers, Waite, and Crowley are all tarred with the same brush, but Laenen reserves his most vigorous abuse for Fortune, perhaps because, as discussed later in this chapter, she has been so influential in the popularising of the Kabbalah in the late twentieth and early twenty-first centuries. After insisting that anyone wishing to understand the Kabbalah must be thoroughly familiar with 'the ideas of Jewish mysticism',

---

[48] R. Schneur Zalman of Liadi, *Tanya* 2, *Sha'ar haYichud v'haEmunah*, cited in Adin Steinsalz, *Opening the Tanya: Discovering the Moral and Mystical Teachings of a Classic Work of Kabbalah*, trans. R. Yaacov Tauber (San Francisco, CA: Josey-Bass, 2003), 226.

[49] For Fortune's dismissal of the Hebraist pretentions of Westcott and Mathers, see Fortune, 'Ceremonial Magic', 20.

[50] Fortune, *Mystical Qabalah*, 2.

[51] J. H. Laenen, *Jewish Mysticism: An Introduction*, trans. David E. Orton (Louisville, KY: Westminster/John Knox Press, 2001), 265.

Laenen points out that Fortune's belief in an 'unwritten' Kabbalah passed down by initiates 'makes it impossible for anyone to check her statements: even the most arrant nonsense is thereby spared any criticism *a priori*'.[52] Laenen further complains about Fortune's use of astrology, insisting that it, like alchemy, plays only a marginal role in the Jewish Kabbalah.[53] This statement can easily be contested by the astrological content of such works as the *Aesch Mezareph*, the *Emek ha-Melekh*, the *Sefer ha-Meshiv*, and the alchemical and astrological writings of Luria's chief disciple, Hayyim Vital.[54] All of these texts are understood by scholars such as Scholem and Idel to be important Kabbalistic works, and Idel suggests that knowledge of astrology may be necessary for understanding many Kabbalistic texts.[55] Fortune's astrology is not a mere predictive system, but is an integral aspect of the application of Kabbalistic theosophy and magic:

> The Tree of life, astrology, and the Tarot are not three mystical systems, but three aspects of one and the same system, and each is unintelligible without the others....All systems of divination and all systems of practical magic find their principles and philosophy based upon the Tree.[56]

While Fortune's Kabbalah displays no allegiance to traditional rabbinic doctrines, her god is nevertheless the androgynous deity of Kabbalistic theosophy, her Secret Chiefs are unmistakable *maggidim*, and her understanding of the *sefirot* as psychological potencies echoes Abraham Abulafia more than six centuries earlier, when he declares that 'there are ten *sefirot* in man, who is called microcosm',[57]

---

[52] Laenen, *Jewish Mysticism*, 267.

[53] Laenen, *Jewish Mysticism*, 267.

[54] For these works, see Chapters Four and Five.

[55] See Idel, 'Saturn and Sabbatai Tzevi', 202.

[56] Fortune, *Mystical Qabalah*, 6. For Fortune's diagram of the sefirotic Tree with astrological correspondences, see Fortune, *Mystical Qabalah*, 311. For the same system of correspondences in a late-twentieth-century work by a Jewish Kabbalist, see Warren Kenton [Z'ev ben Shimon Halevi], *The Anatomy of Fate: Kabbalistic Astrology* (London: Rider, 1978), 29.

[57] Abraham Abulafia, *Toledot Ya'akov Yosef*, fol. 86a, cited in Moshe Idel, '*Ta'ung*: Erotic Delights from Kabbalah to Hasidism', in Hanegraaff and Kripal (eds.), *Hidden Intercourse*, 111–51, on p. 118.

and that 'man...comprises all the sefirot'.[58] Fortune also understands the *sefirot* as primary matrices through which the divinities of other pantheons can be understood, as though these various deities were culturally distinct manifestations of the ten primary building-blocks of the sefirotic Tree.[59] While this specific type of syncretism does not appear in Jewish Kabbalistic texts, the *sefirot* are perceived as matrices out of which every aspect of creation has emerged.[60] Whether the Kabbalah magically transforms into something 'non-Jewish' when developed and utilised by a non-Jewish practitioner such as Fortune seems to depend on the perspective of the scholar for its answer. Fortune may be viewed as following the paradoxical tradition of innovation proposed by Jewish Kabbalists and reflected in the fourteenth-century 'pluralistic hermeneutic' of Rabbi Isaac ben Samuel of Acre:

> The *maskil* [Kabbalistic adept] will make peace between these different receptions [*qabbalot*], just as it is proper for a wise individual to make peace between the different teachings of sages...and not to completely reject the word of wisdom of one in favor of that of another.[61]

Fortune treated the psychologies of Freud and Jung as valid Kabbalistic 'receptions', clothed in modern language, that could be fitted seamlessly into the sefirotic Tree. Eitan Fishbane observes that the Kabbalistic approach of reconciling disparate meanings through a single model 'rests on an assumption of interpretive *flexibility*...pluralism is possible because a fixed determinate meaning is not'.[62]

---

[58] Abraham Abulafia, *Ve-Zo't li-Yehudah*, MS New York, JTS, 1887, cited in Idel, *Studies in Ecstatic Kabbalah*, 9. See also Abraham Abulafia, *Ve-Zot li-Yihudah*, 16–17, cited in Idel, *Hasidism*, 229, where the individual attributes of the ten *sefirot* are described as human attributes.

[59] See Fortune, *Mystical Qabalah*, 85–91; Chas S. Clifton and Graham Harvey, *The Paganism Reader* (London: Routledge, 2004), 103–04.

[60] For discussions of the *sefirot* as matrices, see Scholem, *Major Trends*, 212–25; Idel, *Kabbalah*, 112–55. For early Jewish magical texts linking pagan divinities with Hebrew angels and Divine Names, see above, Chapter Four.

[61] Isaac ben Samuel of Acre, *Me'irat 'Einayim*, 55, cited in Fishbane, 'Authority', 72.

[62] Fishbane, 'Authority', 73. Emphasis is original.

Fortune was neither a Kabbalistic scholar nor a philosemite.[63] But she seems to have understood instinctively – or was perhaps taught by unrecorded sources – the Kabbalistic doctrine of synthesising diverse forms of wisdom 'so as to reveal the ultimate unity of spiritual *'emet* [truth]'.[64]

FREUD, THE HASIDIM, AND THE LURIANIC KABBALAH

In 1913, Ernest Jones, one of Freud's most energetic disciples, established the London Psycho-Analytical Society in an effort to make his master's theories more palatable to the British medical establishment.[65] In the same year, another group was founded toward which Jones expressed unrelenting hostility,[66] but which offered the first psychoanalytic training in Britain: the Medico-Psychological Clinic, also known as the Brunswick Square Clinic, which, during and after the Great War, treated shell-shocked soldiers as well as a wide range of other psychological disorders.[67] The official literature of the Clinic attempted to reassure the public, the medical profession, and psychoanalysts such as Jones that the Clinic did not dabble in occult pursuits.[68] However, despite this public claim to scientific respectability, somewhat unorthodox practices were quietly pursued by

---

[63] For examples of Fortune's 'gentlemanly antisemitism', see Fortune, *Psychic Self-Defence*, 204–05; Fortune, *Goat-Foot God*, 10.

[64] Fishbane, 'Authority', 74.

[65] For the early history of psychoanalysis in Britain, see Ernest Jones, *Free Associations: Memories of a Psycho-Analyst* (London: Hogarth Press, 1959), 229–40; Ernest Jones, 'Reminiscent Notes on the Early History of Psycho-Analysis in English-Speaking Countries', *IJP* 26 (1945), 8–10; Suzanne Raitt, 'Early British Psychoanalysis and the Medico-Psychological Clinic', *HWJ* 58 (2004), 63–85; Dean Rapp, 'The Early Discovery of Freud by the British General Educated Public, 1912–1919', *SSHM* 3 (August 1990), 217–43; R. D. Hinshelwood, 'Psychoanalysis in Britain: Points of Cultural Access, 1893–1918', *IJP* 76 (February 1995), 135–51.

[66] For Jones' antagonism toward the Medico-Psychological Clinic, see Philippa Martindale, '"Against All Hushing Up and Stamping Down": The Medico-Psychological Clinic of London and the Novelist May Sinclair', *PH* 6:2 (2004), 177–200.

[67] See Raitt, 'Psychoanalysis', 63.

[68] See, for example, the letter from Charles Spearman in *The Lancet* (20 December 1913), 1803, cited in Raitt, 'Psychoanalysis', 67. For the Clinic's reputation for occult practices, see Martindale, '"Hushing Up"', 193.

Clinic members, including mesmerism, spiritual healing, and scrying.[69]

The apparently more orthodox London Psycho-Analytic Society was not immune to such practices. W. H. B. Stoddart, a later member of the Society, published a work on psychoanalytic techniques which was 'perhaps the most widely read text book of psychiatry at the present day'.[70] Stoddart's psychoanalytic techniques include scrying as well as hypnotic experiments and the interpretation of dreams, reflecting the continuity of that eclectic mixture of medicine with occult practices which had characterised Westcott's approach in the last decades of the nineteenth century.[71] Much to the annoyance of Jones and his more orthodox colleagues, the Medico-Psychological Clinic boasted many female doctors and was run on feminist lines.[72] Despite the increasing influence of psychology on the British public as well as on progressive education and the criminal justice system in the decades during and after the Great War, the Medico-Psychological Clinic survived for only nine years, closing in 1922.[73] But its impact has continued to reverberate in circles other than those originally intended. Fortune trained at the Clinic as a lay analyst in the years just after the war,[74] and the experience she acquired there permeates both her theories about the relationship between psychoanalysis and occultism and her 'occult' novels, which reveal a direct knowledge of conditions such as shell-shock and the various

---

[69] See Raitt, 'Psychoanalysis', 78.

[70] W. H. B. Stoddart, *Mind and Its Disorders* (London: H. K. Lewis, 1908); 'E. J.', 'Review of W. H. B. Stoddart, *Mind and Its Disorders*', *IJP* 3 (1922), 84.

[71] For this mixture of scientific and occult medicine, see Hayward, 'Demonology, Neurology, and Medicine'.

[72] For the feminist stance of the Clinic, see Martindale, '"Hushing Up"', 188.

[73] For the permeation of psychological theories into British culture, see Thomson, 'Psychology and the "Consciousness of Modernity"'; Bingham, *Gender*, 102–05; Claire Valiér, 'Psychoanalysis and Crime in Britain During the Inter-war Years', in Jon Vagg and Tim Newburn (eds.), *The British Society of Criminology Conferences: Selected Proceedings, Vol. 1: Emerging Themes in Criminology* (London: British Society of Criminology, 1998), 1–12.

[74] For Fortune's involvement with the Clinic, see Raitt, 'Early British Psychoanalysis', 67; Suzanne Raitt, *May Sinclair: A Modern Victorian* (Oxford: Oxford University Press, 2000), 140, n. 106; Richardson, *Magical Life*, 52; Knight, *Dion Fortune*, 31–32.

stages of obsessional disorders.

The need to supplement psychology with occult theory was evident to Fortune from the outset of her training:

> As soon as I touched the deeper aspects of practical psychology...I realized that there was very much more in the mind than was accounted for by the accepted psychological theories....It was in order to understand the hidden aspects of the mind that I originally took up the study of occultism.[75]

It seems she also felt occult theory needed a psychological framework. In 1922, the year in which she created her Fraternity of the Inner Light, she published under the name Violet M. Firth a little book called *The Machinery of the Mind*, which claims to offer 'certain fundamental concepts' of psychology to 'serve as a basis for future studies'.[76] Although the work is predominantly a mixture of Freudian and Jungian approaches and does not reveal the occult predilections of its author, it was not well received by the psychoanalytic community.[77] But Fortune probably never intended it for this readership. As so much popular literature on the subject was already available at the time, the *raison d'être* for *Machinery of the Mind* may have been an attempt to educate occultists in the language of the psyche, as Fortune recommends it to aspiring students in two of her occult treatises.[78]

Fortune had great respect for Freud and recommends his seminal work, *The Interpretation of Dreams*,[79] as 'occultism on a sound scientific basis'.[80] But she felt Freud had missed the occult understanding of the individual as a 'spiritual being' whose 'mind and body are the garments of his

---

[75] Fortune, *Psychic Self-Defence*, 18–19.

[76] Violet M. Firth [Dion Fortune], *The Machinery of the Mind* (London: George Allen & Unwin, 1922), 11.

[77] See Barbara Low, 'Review of Violet M. Firth, *The Machinery of the Mind*', *IJP* 5 (1924), 388–89.

[78] See Dion Fortune, *Sane Occultism* (London: Rider & Co., 1929), 141; Fortune, *Psychic Self-Defence*, 211.

[79] Sigmund Freud, *The Interpretation of Dreams*, trans. A. A. Brill (London: George Allen & Unwin, 1913; repr. Freud, SE4 and SE5).

[80] See the bibliography in Fortune, *Psychic Self-Defence*, 211, and the recommended reading list in Dion Fortune, 'The Literature of Illuminism', *ILM* (July 1929 to September 1930), repr. in Dion Fortune and Gareth Knight, *Practical Occultism* (Loughborough: Thoth Publications, 2002), 140–74.

manifestation'.[81] As she became more involved with Jung's analytical psychology, her views of Freud increasingly reflected the attitudes of the Swiss psychiatrist toward his former mentor. In Fortune's *Goat-Foot God*, Hugh Paston disparages Freud's materialistic view of the human psyche: 'It was a great pity that the learned doctor had not also had a classical education, and learnt that Priapus and Silenus are gods, and not dirty little boys playing with filth'.[82] By the late 1930s Fortune had become a firm Jungian, and in 1942 she stipulated as required reading for her disciples not only her own *Mystical Qabalah* but also *The Psychology of C. G. Jung*, a newly published work summarising the main principles of analytical psychology by one of Jung's most important disciples.[83] Fortune's concept of the unconscious is not only personal, but also encompasses the domain of the 'Unseen', extending beyond humanity to 'the World soul deep hidden in the most primitive depths of subconsciousness':[84]

> We live in the midst of invisible forces whose effects alone we perceive. We move among invisible forms whose actions we very often do not perceive at all, though we may be profoundly affected by them.[85]

This is the realm of Kabbalistic theosophy, teeming with angels, demons, and sefirotic powers, and animated by the primal light streaming through creation as the organising principle of the universe. Fortune's ideas about the unconscious may certainly be seen as what Olav Hammer calls 'psycho-religion'.[86] But this 'active syncretistic tendency' that merges esoteric and psychological dimensions, and which Hammer considers unique to modern post-Enlightenment Western esotericism,[87] is already present in the medieval Kabbalah and is particularly emphasised in the Kabbalah of the Hasidim, to whom Freud's own family

---

[81] Fortune, *Psychic Self-Defence*, 30.
[82] Fortune, *Goat-Foot God*, 51.
[83] Jolande Jacobi, *The Psychology of C. G. Jung*, trans. K. W. Bash (London: Kegan Paul, Trench, Trubner & Co., 1942). See also Knight, *Dion Fortune*, 290–91.
[84] Fortune, *Mystical Qabalah*, 17.
[85] Fortune, *Psychic Self-Defence*, 25.
[86] See Hammer, *Claiming Knowledge*, 67–73.
[87] Hammer, *Claiming Knowledge*, 6.

belonged.[88]

Freud is not usually thought of as an occultist. In a conversation with Jung, he calls on his disciple to help him form an 'unshakeable bulwark' against 'the black tide...of occultism'.[89] Jung, who believed Freud's insistence on the centrality of sexuality in all the manifestations of the unconscious was 'just as occult' as anything the occultists could offer, understood his teacher's passionate dogmatism as an eruption of 'unconscious religious factors':

> Freud, who had always made much of his irreligiosity, had now constructed a dogma; or rather, in the place of a jealous God whom he had lost, he had substituted another compelling image, that of sexuality.[90]

But as Stanley Schneider and Joseph Berke suggest, there seems to have been a 'concealed Freud' far more familiar with esoteric ideas, including those of the Kabbalah, than he cared to make public.[91] While 'unconscious eruptions' may

---

[88] For the Hasidic psychologisation of the Lurianic Kabbalah, see Arthur Green, *Menahem Nahum of Chernobyl: Upright Practices, The Light of the Eyes* (New York: Paulist Press, 1982); Idel, *Hasidism*, 227–38.

[89] C. G. Jung, *Memories, Dreams, Reflections*, trans. Richard and Clara Winston (London: Routledge & Kegan Paul, 1963; repr. London: HarperCollins/Fontana, 1995), 173.

[90] Jung, *Memories*, 174.

[91] Stanley Schneider and Joseph H. Berke, 'Sigmund Freud and the Lubavitcher Rebbe', *PR* 87 (2000), 39–59, on p. 55. Freud's efforts to present psychoanalysis as a science did not preclude his becoming a Fellow of the Society for Psychical Research, nor did it stop him from producing papers dealing with esoteric themes, such as 'Dreams and Telepathy', published in English in *Imago* 8 (1922), 1–22, trans. C. J. M. Hubback, repr. in Sigmund Freud, *Collected Papers*, 4 vols., trans. C. J. M. Hubback and Joan Riviere (London: Hogarth Press, 1924–1925), 4:408–35. In this paper Freud reveals his willingness to consider the possibility of telepathy but insists that, even if some dreams do display telepathic elements, this is not mutually exclusive of his own method of dream interpretation. See also 'Psychoanalysis and Telepathy' (1921), published posthumously in English in Freud, *SE18*, 177–94. In this paper Freud initially presents occultism as a 'new danger' that threatens the psychoanalytic edifice, but then declares (178–79): 'It is probable that the study of occult phenomena will result in the admission that some of these phenomena are real'. Other papers by Freud on the occult include 'The Occult Significance of Dreams' (1925), published

have played their part, so too did Freud's need to maintain scientific respectability and protect psychoanalysis from 'the danger of becoming a Jewish national affair'.[92]

David Bakan, in the preface to the paperback edition of a controversial work first published in 1958, *Sigmund Freud and the Jewish Mystical Tradition*, describes the personal account of Rabbi Hayyim Bloch, a historian and Kabbalistic scholar who discovered in Freud's library a number of German scholarly works on the Kabbalah as well as Jean de Pauly's French translation of the *Zohar*.[93] In adopting Freud's theories of the unconscious, Fortune was appropriating a psychological system which was itself impregnated by Freud's Hasidic background and the Lurianic and 'ecstatic' Kabbalistic currents that fuelled the Hasidic movement.[94] Bakan asserts

---

in English for the first time in George Devereux (ed.), *Psychoanalysis and the Occult* (New York: International Universities Press, 1953), 87–90; and 'Dreams and the Occult' (1933), in Sigmund Freud, *New Introductory Lectures in Psychoanalysis* (New York: Norton, 1933), 257–75, repr. in Devereux (ed.), *Psychoanalysis and the Occult*, 91–109. The fact that these papers were not included in the *Standard Edition* of Freud's works reveals a good deal about the attitudes of the psychoanalytic community toward Freud's esoteric inclinations. When Ernest Jones pressed Freud about his occult interests, Freud retaliated: 'My acceptance of telepathy is my own affair, like my Judaism and my passion for smoking' (Sigmund Freud to Ernest Jones (7 March 1926), Letter 478, in R. Andrew Paskauskas (ed.), *The Complete Correspondence of Sigmund Freud and Ernest Jones, 1908–1939* (Cambridge, MA: Harvard University Press, 1993), 596–97. For Freud's involvement with Wilhelm Fliess and the 'borderland' between medicine and occultism which Fliess represented, see Webb, *Occult Establishment*, 356–61.
[92] Hilda C. Abraham and Ernst L. Freud (eds. and trans.), *The Letters of Sigmund Freud and Karl Abraham, 1907–1926* (New York, NY: Basic Books, 1965), 34.
[93] David Bakan, *Sigmund Freud and the Jewish Mystical Tradition* (Princeton, NJ: D. Van Nostrand, 1958; repr. Boston: Beacon Press, 1975), xviii.
[94] For the relevance of Freud's Hasidic family background to his psychoanalytic theories, see Willy Aron, 'Notes on Sigmund Freud's Ancestry and Jewish Contacts', *YIVO Annual of Jewish Social Science* 11 (1956–1957), 286–95; Paul Roazen, *Meeting Freud's Family* (Amherst, MA: University of Massachusetts Press, 1993); Emanuel Rice, *Freud and Moses: The Long Journey Home* (Albany, NY: State University of New York Press, 1990); Yosef Hayim Yerushalmi, *Freud's Moses: Judaism Terminable and Interminable* (New Haven, CT: Yale University Press, 1991); Schneider and Berke, 'Sigmund Freud'.

that Freud, 'consciously or unconsciously, secularized Jewish mysticism; and psychoanalysis can intelligently be viewed as such a secularization'.[95] In Fortune's work, a curious uroboric circle may be observed: an early-twentieth-century occultist 'psychologises' esoteric ideas through the use of a psychological system which is itself a 'secularised' expression of those same ideas, and likewise 'sacralises' that psychological system through the framework of the same esoteric ideas that infused it to begin with.

Crowley, who referred to psychoanalysis as 'hashed-up paganism with Semitic sauce',[96] nevertheless recognised the importance of the Kabbalah for Freud's theories, observing tartly that the magical tradition and the Kabbalah were 'the Children's table from which Freud...ate a few crumbs that fell'.[97] But until the 1980s, little scholarly exploration was made into the conceptual structures of psychoanalysis in relation to the Kabbalah, with the exception of Bakan's often-disputed work.[98] This decades-long neglect may be partly due to the antisemitic sentiments evident in many early academic discussions on Freud's Jewishness. Despite Freud's efforts, psychoanalysis was marked from its inception as a 'Jewish' science.[99] Jung, after he had broken with Freud, attempted to bolster the validity of his own psychological theories by joining, for a time, the swelling tide of anti-Jewish feeling during the 1930s and, inadvisedly in the light of subsequent world events, referred to psychoanalysis as 'Jewish psychology':

> It has been a grave error in medical psychology up till now to apply Jewish categories...indiscriminately to Germanic and Slavic Christendom. Because of this the most precious secret of the Germanic peoples – their creative and intuitive depth of soul – has been explained as a morass of banal

---

[95] Bakan, *Freud*, 25.
[96] Crowley, *Confessions*, 45.
[97] Crowley, *Confessions*, 19.
[98] An exception is Harry Trosman, 'Freud's Cultural Background', *AP* 1 (1973), 318–35.
[99] For this theme see Janet Liebman Jacobs, 'Freud as Other: Antisemitism and the Development of Psychoanalysis', in Janet Liebman Jacobs and Donald Capps (eds.), *Religion, Society, and Psychoanalysis: Readings in Contemporary Theory* (Boulder, CO: Westview Press, 1997), 11–22.

infantilism.[100]

More recent scholarly work has tended to focus on Freud's
Jewish roots in a general sense, rather than on the relevance
of the Kabbalah to fundamental Freudian concepts such as
the centrality of sexuality, the linguistic playfulness of the
unconscious, and the hidden meanings underlying the
'manifest content' of dream imagery.[101] Some researchers
have actively opposed Bakan's placement of Freud within
the Jewish esoteric tradition.[102] However, in the last two
decades a number of psychologists and psychoanalysts have
begun examining the relationship between Freud's ideas and
the Kabbalah,[103] and this growing body of work affirms the
centrality of Kabbalistic concepts, particularly those of the
Lurianic Kabbalah, in virtually every aspect of the

---

[100] Jung, CW10,¶354. For Jung's pre-war foray into antisemitism, see
Aryeh Maidenbaum and Stephen A. Martin (eds.), *Lingering
Shadows: Jungians, Freudians, and Anti-Semitism* (Boston: Shambhala,
1991), and Aryeh Maidenbaum (ed.), *Jung and the Shadow of Anti-
Semitism: Collected Essays* (Berwick, ME: Nicolas-Hays, 2002);
Poliakov, *Aryan Myth*, 286–90.
[101] See Miriam Huttler, 'Jewish Origins of Freud's Interpretation of
Dreams', *JPJ* 23:1 (1999), 5–48; D. B. Klein, *Jewish Origins of the
Psychoanalytic Movement* (New York, NY: Praeger, 1981); J. Miller,
'Interpretation of Freud's Jewishness', *JHBS* 17 (1981), 357–74. For
Freud's work on the linguistic playfulness of the unconscious, see
Sigmund Freud, *Jokes in Relation to the Unconscious*, in Freud, SE8.
[102] See Susan Handelman, 'Interpretation as Devotion: Freud's
Relation to Rabbinic Hermeneutics', *PR* 68 (1981), 201–18. For
possible reasons for such opposition, see Dan Merkur, 'Freud and
Hasidism', in Jacobs and Katz (eds.), *Religion, Society, and
Psychoanalysis*, 11–22.
[103] For references more recent and comprehensive than Bakan's
which discuss Freud's knowledge of Kabbalah, see Ana-Maria
Rizzuto, *Why Did Freud Reject God?* (New Haven, CT: Yale
University Press, 1998); Joseph H. Berke and Stanley Schneider,
Centers of Power: The Convergence of Psychoanalysis and Kabbalah (New
York, NY: Jason Aronson, 2008). See also Stanley Schneider and
Joseph H. Berke, 'Freud's Meeting with Rabbi Alexandre Safran',
PH 12:1 (2010), 15–28; Sanford L. Drob, 'This is Gold': Freud,
Psychotherapy and the Lurianic Kabbalah' (1998–2006), at
<http://www.newkabbalah.com>. For other recent papers, see
Joseph H. Berke, 'Psychoanalysis and Kabbalah', *PR* 83 (1996), 849–
63; Stanley Schneider and Joseph H. Berke, 'The Oceanic Feeling,
Mysticism and Kabbalah: Freud's Historical Roots', *PR* 95:1 (2008),
131–56.

psychoanalytic edifice. Lurianic themes also seem to have permeated the theories of Melanie Klein (1882–1960), one of Freud's most important followers and, like him, from an Eastern European Hasidic background.[104] It remains unclear whether the Kabbalah was consciously utilised by Freud or had been absorbed unconsciously from his family background. Karen Starr suggests the latter, stating: 'It is unlikely that Freud consciously incorporated Jewish mystical ideas into his theories. However, it is almost certain that he was exposed to these ideas and influenced by them'.[105] Whether Freud was a conscious or an unconscious Kabbalist, it is not surprising that Dion Fortune, whose maiden voyage into occult waters coincided with her work at the Medico-Psychological Clinic, was quickly attracted to Freud's ideas and felt there was a close relationship between occultism and these new researches into the unknown regions of the human soul.

Freud avoided mentioning the Kabbalah, but he never concealed his interest in numerological and linguistic word-plays as expressions of the unconscious – although he only referred to the source of this preoccupation with *gematria* in a private letter to Jung, calling it 'the specifically Jewish nature

---

[104] See, for example, Harriet Lutzky, 'Reparation and Tikkun: A Comparison of the Kleinian and Kabbalistic Concepts', *IRP* 16 (1989), 449–58; Joseph H. Berke and Stanley Schneider, 'Repairing Worlds: An Exploration of the Psychoanalytical and Kabbalistic Concepts of Reparation and Tikkun', *PR* 90 (2003), 723–49. For more on Klein, an Austrian Jewish psychoanalyst who studied with Sandor Ferenczi in Budapest during the Great War and emigrated to London in 1926, see Hanna Segal, *Introduction to the Works of Melanie Klein* (London: Hogarth Press, 1975); Robert Caper, *Immaterial Facts: Freud's Discovery of Psychic Reality and Klein's Development of His Work* (London: Routledge, 1999). For Klein's most important work on the subject of reparation, see Melanie Klein, *Love, Guilt, and Reparation and Other Works 1921–1945* (London: Hogarth Press/Institute of Psycho-Analysis, 1981). There is no mention of Klein in Fortune's work, although Philippa Martindale ('"Against All Hushing Up"', 179–80) points out that Klein had 'a powerful impact on the development of British psychoanalysis in the late 1920s and 1930s' and her ideas were already circulating at the Medico-Psychological Clinic during the period of Fortune's training.
[105] Karen E. Starr, *Repair of the Soul: Metaphors of Transformation in Jewish Mysticism and Psychoanalysis* (London: Routledge 2008), 18.

of my mysticism'.[106] Such hermeneutics, although utilised in most Kabbalistic texts, are found in older rabbinic sources, and Susan Handelman argues that Freud's method of dream interpretation is therefore based on rabbinic, not Kabbalistic, methods of extracting the hidden meanings from scripture.[107] But it is not only Freud's psychological *gematria* that suggests Kabbalistic influences; the major themes of his work echo the major themes of the Kabbalah. Freud believed that the dream, like the Torah, is a text that must be decoded in order to reveal the secret workings of the psyche:

> There is a psychological technique which makes it possible to interpret dreams, and...if that procedure is employed, every dream reveals itself as a psychical structure which has a meaning....I shall further endeavor to elucidate the process to which the strangeness and obscurity of dreams are due and to deduce from those processes the nature of the psychical forces by whose concurrent or mutually opposing action dreams are generated.[108]

If the phrase 'psychical forces' is replaced by 'ten *sefirot*', Freud might be describing the nature of traditional Kabbalistic hermeneutics. Freud's concept of 'free association' as a means of accessing the depths of the unconscious – 'noting and reporting whatever comes into his [the patient's] head' with a 'completely impartial attitude'[109] – strongly resembles the Kabbalistic 'jumping and skipping' technique advocated in the thirteenth century by Abraham Abulafia to achieve altered states of consciousness.[110] While *gematria* may be rabbinic in origin, it reaches its apotheosis in Kabbalistic speculations about the infrastructure of the godhead. The angelic and Divine Names are the linguistic manifestations of objective powers, as Fortune herself was

---

[106] Sigmund Freud, letter to C. G. Jung (April 1909), in William McGuire (ed.), *The Freud-Jung Letters*, trans. Ralph Manheim and R. F. C. Hull (London: Hogarth Press/Routledge & Kegan Paul, 1977), 219–20.

[107] Handelman, 'Interpretation', 201–18.

[108] Freud, SE4, 57.

[109] Freud, SE, 4, 175. For more on Freud's 'free association', see Sigmund Freud, *The Psychopathology of Everyday Life*, trans. A. A. Brill (London: T. Fisher Unwin, 1914); repr. Freud, SE6.

[110] For Abulafia's 'jumping and skipping' (*dillug* and *kefitsah*), see Bakan, *Freud*, 77–81; Scholem, *Major Trends*, 135–36; Idel, *Mystical Experience*, 13–41.

aware:

> Those profound students of the subtler aspects of existence,
> the Qabbalists, were in the habit of reducing to numerical
> value all potencies with which they worked....If, therefore, we
> are dealing with the names which the Hebrew Qabbalists
> gave to the potencies...we may be sure that...when deciphered
> and reduced in turn to their factors, will tell us a very great
> deal about the potency concerned.[111]

For Freud, as for Lurianic Kabbalists, the most pervasive
'potency' animating human life is *eros*, the sexual urge, which
in the psychoanalytic framework is presented as an
unconscious power permeating, and even dominating, the
whole of human existence. Freud's insistence on 'the
importance of sexuality in all human achievements' echoes
Shaul Magid's suggestion that the entire Lurianic myth is
based on sexual desire, and that in Lurianic Kabbalah 'a
healthy cosmos is a cosmos in the state of erotic desire
leading to sexual union'.[112] In the introduction to the first
English translation of Jung's *Psychology of the Unconscious*[113] –
the edition with which Fortune herself was familiar –
Beatrice Hinkle explained that Freud's concept of sexuality is
'entirely different' from the popular understanding.
According to Hinkle, Freud conceived sexuality as
'practically synonymous with the word *love*....It must also be
borne in mind that Freud strictly emphasises the psychic idea
of sexuality...as well as the somatic expression'.[114] As a
scientist and a true son of the Enlightenment,[115] Freud could
not assign to sexuality the religious significance it enjoys in
Kabbalistic texts. He used the term 'libido' to describe
sexuality as an all-encompassing, compelling life-force,
similar to Henri Bergson's *élan vital*, which itself echoes the

---

[111] Fortune, *Sane Occultism*, 76.

[112] Freud, SE7, 43; Shaul Magid, *From Metaphysics to Midrash: Myth,
History, and the Interpretation of Scripture in Lurianic Kabbalah*
(Bloomington, IN: Indiana University Press, 2008), 31.

[113] C. G. Jung, *The Psychology of the Unconscious*, trans. Beatrice M.
Hinkle (London: Kegan Paul, 1917).

[114] Beatrice M. Hindle, 'Introduction', in Jung, *Psychology of the
Unconscious*, vii–xxviii, on p. xii.

[115] For Freud as a rationalistic atheist, see Peter Gay, *A Godless Jew:
Freud, Atheism, and the Making of Psychoanalysis* (New Haven, CT:
Yale University Press, 1987).

same Hasidic roots.[116] Fortune, on the other hand, exhibited no such shyness in assigning divinity to the libido:

> The esotericist does not use the term 'sex' as we do, he speaks of 'life-force' which he conceives to be...a radiating and magnetising vibratory activity....This force he conceives to radiate from the Great First Cause, and therefore to be divine in its nature.[117]

Following Mathers and Crowley, who followed Lévi, who in turn followed the Kabbalistic theosophy of Joseph Gikatilla and the Lurianic texts of the *Kabbala denudata*, Fortune proposed that this divine life-force is dual in nature, a polarity of cosmic male and female potencies that comprise the twin pillars of the sefirotic Tree. The Tree is 'a scheme of relationships, stresses, and reflections',[118] and its dualism is fundamental to creation: 'There can be no manifestation without differentiation into the Pairs of Opposites'.[119] By 1920, Freud too had moved beyond his original idea of a one-tune psyche, and presented two opposing unconscious forces: the life-drive or *eros*, and the death-drive, referred to by post-Freudians as *thanatos* after the Greek god of death.[120] Where the life-drive seeks to perpetuate life through pleasure and relationship, the death-drive seeks to achieve a return to the primal state of inanimate matter, on both biological and psychological levels. Echoing Zoharic descriptions of the 'evil impulse',[121] Freud associated this urge toward repetition, stasis, and disintegration with a 'daemonic' quality:

> The manifestations of a compulsion to repeat...exhibit to a high degree an instinctual character and, when they act in opposition to the pleasure principle, give the appearance of

---

[116] Freud, SE7, 45. For the influence of Bergson's Hasidic background on his idea of *élan vital*, see Mary Whiton Calkins, 'Henri Bergson: Personalist', *Philosophical Review* 21:6 (1912), 666–75.
[117] Dion Fortune, *The Esoteric Philosophy of Love and Marriage* (London: Rider, 1923), 28. For the term 'life-force', preferred by some practitioners at the Medico-Psychological Clinic, see Martindale, '"Hushing Up"', 181.
[118] Fortune, *Mystical Qabalah*, 43.
[119] Fortune, *Mystical Qabalah*, 45.
[120] See Freud, SE18.
[121] See, for example, *Zohar* 1:165b and *Zohar* 1:179a.

some 'daemonic' force at work.[122]

Fortune, perceiving the Kabbalistic polarity of *Hesed* and *Geburah* in Freud's idea of a dialectic within the unconscious, describes this second, female potency as 'locked up in form'; it embodies the 'disintegrating forces that constantly seek to reduce all specialised substance to its common root'.[123] The interaction of the two powers stands behind all manifestation: 'This fundamental duality extends into all combinations of which the atom is the base'.[124] It is difficult to know whether Fortune derived her ideas from Freud or from the Kabbalah since, for her, the two sources seem to have represented two different languages describing the same creative process on both cosmic and human levels.

Harold Bloom, although he does not claim that Freud consciously borrowed themes from the Kabbalah, points out another aspect of Kabbalistic thought which he believes 'prefigures' Freud's ideas: the *tselem* or 'divine image' in the human psyche, first mentioned in the *Zohar* and later developed by Luria and his disciples, who refer to it as the 'ethereal body'.[125] The *tselem* bears a close family resemblance to the *ochêma pneuma* or 'spirit vehicle' of the Neoplatonists, a quasi-material entity which links body and soul and mediates vital psycho-spiritual energies to the physical form of the individual.[126] The astral vehicle can also be found in Gnostic texts, where each of the seven layers of the vehicle, now described as the carrier of astral fate, is impregnated with the vices of each of the seven planetary archons as the

---

[122] Freud, SE18, 29. For Fortune's understanding of the 'evil influence' and the *qlippot* which represent it, see Fortune, *Mystical Qabalah*, 297–304. For the relationship of Freud's dialectic between *eros* and *thanatos* and various passages in the *Zohar*, see Schneider and Berke, 'Freud's Meeting', 20.

[123] Fortune, *Esoteric Philosophy*, 29.

[124] Fortune, *Cosmic Doctrine*, 36.

[125] Bloom, *Kabbalah and Criticism*, 20–21. For the *tselem*, see Fine, *Physician*, 95–96, 384–85, n. 45; Scholem, *Mystical Shape*, 251–73.

[126] For the Neoplatonic 'spirit vehicle' or astral body, see John F. Finamore, *Iamblichus and the Theory of the Vehicle of the Soul* (Chico, CA: Scholars Press, 1985); D. P. Walker, 'The Astral Body in Renaissance Medicine', *JWCI* 21:1/2 (1958), 119–33; E. R. Dodds, 'The Astral Body in Neoplatonism', in Dodds (trans.), *Proclus: Elements of Theology*, 313–22; Robert Christian Kissling, 'The Ochêma-Pneuma of the Neo-Platonists and the *De Insomniis* of Synesius of Cyrene, *AJP* 43:4 (1922), 318–30.

individual soul descends into worldly incarnation.[127] In the Lurianic Kabbalah, as in Neoplatonic thought, this 'divine image' carries the seeds of the individual personality, and Bloom suggests that Freud's ideas of personality and the emotional responses of the individual reflect this 'enigmatic' intermediary between soul and body.[128] The idea of a multi-layered astral body was enthusiastically taken up by the Theosophists,[129] and the various tiers of this complex vehicle were incorporated into Fortune's system as different levels of 'etheric, astro-mental, and spiritual consciousness'. Fortune explained that the tiers of sefirotic emanations described in Kabbalistic theosophy are reflected in these various levels of individual human consciousness;[130] the *sefirot*, including their planetary correlations, are within the human soul. As Abraham Abulafia explained in the thirteenth century, the human being is

> ...the ultimate composite, which is man, who comprises all the *sefirot*, and whose intellect is the active intellect; and when you will untie its knots, you will be united with it [the active intellect] in a unique union.[131]

FORTUNE'S JUNGIAN ARCHETYPES

Aleister Crowley, demonstrating the same astuteness he displayed in perceiving the Kabbalistic undertones in Freud's

---

[127] See Jonas, *Gnostic Religion*, 160; Couliano, *Tree of Gnosis*, 102–05. For Gnostic texts describing the astral vehicle as *antimimon pneuma* or 'counterfeit spirit', see, *inter alia*, The Apocryphon of John II.1.15, in *Nag Hammadi Library*, 107; *Pistis Sophia*, trans. G. R. S. Mead (London: J. M. Watkins, 1921), 111.283.

[128] Bloom, *Kabbalah and Criticism*, 20.

[129] For the Theosophical astral body, see H. P. Blavatsky, 'Astral Bodies, or Doppelgängers', *Lucifer* 3:16 (1888), 328–33, repr. in Blavatsky, CW10, 217–26; Annie Besant, *Man and His Bodies* (Los Angeles, CA: Theosophical Publishing House, 1914); C. W. Leadbeater, *Man Visible and Invisible* (Wheaten, IL: Theosophical Publishing House, 1902). Blavatsky's sources probably included Thomas Taylor's translations of Neoplatonic texts such as Proclus' *Elements of Theology*, published in 1816, in which Proclus discusses the *ochêma* in Proposition 209, as well as Lévi's *La science des esprits*.

[130] Dion Fortune, *Aspects of Occultism* (Wellingborough: Aquarian Press, 1962), 47–53.

[131] Abraham Abulafia, *Ve Zot Li-Yehudah*, cited in Wolfson, *Abraham Abulafia*, 145–46.

work, recognised Jung's importance for occultists:

> We should all study Jung. His final conclusions are in the
> main correct, even if his rough working is a bit sketchy; and
> we've got to study him, whether we like it or not, for he will
> soon be recognized as the undoubted Autocrat of the 1917
> dinner-table.[132]

B. J. Gibbons suggests that Jung, like Swedenborg in the late
eighteenth century, 'reformed esoteric thought, giving it a
renewed lease of life in the twentieth century'.[133] Fortune
created a Kabbalistic system which might be viewed as an
esotericised version of Jung's analytical psychology, which is
itself interpreted by some scholars as an esoteric system
rather than a legitimate 'empiric' psychology.[134] One of the

---

[132] Aleister Crowley, *The Revival of Magick and Other Essays* (Las
Vegas: Falcon/OTO, 1998), 81. In 1917 the first English translation
of Jung's *The Psychology of the Unconscious* was published.

[133] B. J. Gibbons, *Spirituality and the Occult: From the Renaissance to the
Modern Age* (London: Routledge, 2001), 111.

[134] See Hanegraaff, *New Age Religion*, 496–513, for the rejection of
Jung's work as a 'legitimate' psychology. Hanegraaff asserts that,
although Jung was not an occultist, he was 'essentially a modern
esotericist, who represents a crucial link between traditional (i.e.,
pre-occultist) esoteric worldviews and the New Age Movement'
(Hanegraaff, *New Age Religion*, 497). This is inarguable, and the
parallels which Hanegraaff draws between Jung's thought and
earlier esoteric systems clearly validate this conclusion.
Unfortunately, Hanegraaff eschews methodological neutrality on
the subject of Jung and draws most of his interpretations of Jung
from quotations cited in Richard Noll's aggressively hostile work,
The Jung Cult: Origins of a Charismatic Movement (Princeton:
Princeton University Press, 1994). Based on Noll's conclusions,
Hanegraaff categorically dismisses analytical psychology as a
'religious worldview' which cannot represent a legitimate
psychological theory of links between religious representations in
different historical periods. Assessing the legitimacy of analytical
psychology, whether or not it is also a 'religious worldview',
requires direct experience of its psychological procedures as empiric
evidence, and cannot be either accepted or rejected on the basis of *a
priori* assumptions. Olav Hammer, in *Claiming Knowledge*, 68–70 and
437–41, refers to 'Jungianism' as a current in 'New Age'
spiritualities; he reiterates Hanegraaff's argument that Jung was an
esotericist, but points out the 'highly selective reception' of Jung's
ideas in the 'New Age' milieu and the important differences
between Jung's own ideas and the uses to which they have been put
in these contemporary esoteric currents. This is an important

earliest of Jung's works which Fortune encountered was *The Psychology of the Unconscious*, which heralds Jung's divergence from Freud's psychoanalytic school and which Fortune recommends, like Freud's *Interpretation of Dreams* and her own *Machinery of the Mind*, to the aspiring disciples of the Fraternity of the Inner Light. Many of the concepts Jung introduces in this work – the great antiquity and universality of the unconscious psyche, the mythic images through which it expresses itself in individuals and in collectives, and the importance of comparing these images as they emerge in different cultures in order to elucidate their meaning[135] – were enthusiastically, although selectively, embraced in Fortune's own system:

> The racial past lives on in the subconscious mind of each of us, as the Zürich [Jungian] school of psychology recognizes; but it can be evoked to visible appearance in a manner which no orthodox psychologist is acquainted with. It is this evocation of the racial past which is the key to certain forms of ceremonial magic which have as their aim the evocation of Principalities and Powers.[136]

Jung makes no Kabbalistic references in this early work. His first allusions to the Kabbalah appear in *The Archetypes and the Collective Unconscious*, first published in English in 1959, in which he displays considerable proficiency in Kabbalistic terminologies and quotes extensively from the *Kabbala denudata*.[137] The paper in which these references later

---

distinction which may be applied to Dion Fortune, who was highly selective about what she borrowed from Jung. While 'Jungianism' might or might not represent a 'legitimate psychology', Jung's own work must be judged by more empiric criteria than those presented by Hanegraaff.

[135] See, for example, Jung, *Psychology of the Unconscious*, 57–58, for the manner in which the libido appears spontaneously in different symbolic forms in various religious frameworks. For Fortune's version, see Dion Fortune, 'Psychic Perception', in Fortune and Knight, *Ritual Magic*, 62–69.

[136] Fortune, *Aspects of Occultism*, 5. See also Fortune, *Winged Bull*, 147–61 and 167.

[137] See C. G. Jung, 'A Study in the Process of Individuation', in CW9i, 290–354. Citations from the *Kabbala denudata* appear on p. 314, n. 77; p. 328, n. 115; p. 338, n. 143. A large number of references to Kabbalistic sources appears in Jung's later 'alchemical' volumes (CW12, CW13, CW14) and he clearly availed himself of an extensive range of materials, from the *Zohar* to Adolphe Franck's *La Kabbale*

appear was published in English in 1939 in a volume entitled *The Integration of the Personality*, and, given her predilection for Jung, Fortune probably read this early version.[138] But like *Psychology of the Unconscious*, it is devoid of Kabbalistic references, and was rewritten for its inclusion in *Archetypes* with the Kabbalistic elements added afterward.[139] However, in a series of private seminars on dream interpretation given in Zürich between 1928 and 1930, Jung discusses various aspects of the Kabbalah, including the idea of an androgynous deity.[140] He had clearly encountered the Kabbalah by the late 1920s, possibly through Freud or through alchemical texts.[141] The alchemical writings Jung

---

(in German translation), Waite's *Holy Kabbalah*, Scholem's *Das Buch Bahir* and *Major Trends*, and the work of Siegmund Hurwitz, a Jungian analyst who translated and commented on important Hasidic texts. Jung seems to have been familiar with most of Waite's work. A useful list of Jung's Kabbalistic sources can be found in Keane, *Routes of Wholeness*, 93. References to Waite's *Holy Kabbalah* appear in CW14, ¶18n; Waite's *Lives of Alchemical Philosophers* in CW9ii, ¶204n; Waite's *Real History* in CW14, ¶312n and CW16, ¶500n; Waite's *Secret Tradition in Alchemy* in CW11, ¶165n, CW12, ¶422n and 453, CW16, ¶417n; and A. E. Waite (ed.), *The Works of Thomas Vaughan: Eugenius Philalethes* (London: Theosophical Publishing House, 1919) in CW911, ¶204n and CW14, ¶27n. Apart from G. R. S. Mead, Waite is the only occultist whom Jung mentions – there are no references to Lévi, Westcott, Mathers, Crowley, or Fortune – but the work of Mead was clearly acceptable, perhaps because, like Waite, he was a scholar as much as an occultist. For the many references to Mead, whose writings Jung seems to have read in their entirety, see Jung, CW20, 436. Jung was also familiar with the work of the Theosophists, and describes Blavatsky and Annie Besant as 'sombre celebrities' whose Eastern doctrines represent 'the peaks of submarine mountain-ranges' that could have an incalculable effect on Western spiritual currents (Jung, CW10, ¶176). There is no mention of Moses Gaster, Samuel Daiches, or Hermann Gollancz in Jung's *Collected Works*, although all three scholars translated Jewish magical texts which were relevant to Jung's researches.

[138] C. G. Jung, *The Integration of the Personality*, trans. Stanley Dell (NY: Farrar & Rinehart, 1939; London: Routledge & Kegan Paul, 1940).

[139] See, for example, Jung, CW12, ¶576, n. 114 and 115; ¶588, n. 136.

[140] William C. McGuire (ed.), *Dream Analysis: Notes of the Seminar Given in 1928–1930 by C. G. Jung* (London: Routledge & Kegan Paul, 1984), 504–06.

[141] In the mid-1930s, Jung gave a series of lectures on alchemy at the Eranos conferences, including 'Individual Dream Symbolism in

discusses are underpinned by Kabbalistic themes and symbols, which prompted him to later declare: 'Directly or indirectly, the Cabala was assimilated into alchemy. Relationships must have existed between them at a very early date'.[142] While Fortune would have found no direct allusions to Kabbalistic doctrines in Jung's early work, she did not find them in Freud either; but she perceived close affinities between the psychological systems of both these men and her own understanding of the Kabbalah.

Fortune's magical techniques, although they perpetuate older Jewish and Greco-Egyptian practices as taught in the Golden Dawn, owe more than a little to Jung, in both her development of the techniques and the explanations she offers for why they work. They involve the use of the imagination and the capacity for concentrated visualisation, the primary focus of which is the sefirotic Tree:

> Each symbol upon the Tree represents a cosmic force or factor. When the mind concentrates upon it, it comes into touch with that force...a channel in consciousness has been made between the conscious mind of the individual and a particular factor in the world-soul....This results in a tremendous access of energy to the individual soul; it is this which endows it with magical powers.[143]

Jung, attempting to maintain 'methodological agnosticism' – at least in print – prefers the term 'archetype' to 'cosmic force', and 'collective unconscious' to 'world-soul'.[144] There is

---

Relation to Alchemy', published as 'Dream Symbols of the Process of Individuation' in *Integration of the Personality* (1940). For Jung's probable early acquaintance with the Kabbalah through alchemical texts, see Sanford L. Drob, 'Towards a Kabbalistic Psychology: C. G. Jung and the Jewish Foundations of Alchemy', *JJTP* 5:2 (2003), 77–100. This paper, and a later one published by Drob in the same journal – Sanford L. Drob, 'Jung's Kabbalistic Visions', *JJTP* 7:1 (2005), 33–54 – elicited irritated rejoinders from some analytical psychologists opposing Drob's emphasis on the importance of Jewish mysticism in Jung's theoretical structures; see, for example, Wolfgang Giegerich, 'Response to Sanford Drob', *JJTP* 7:1 (2005), 55–58. The debate is ongoing in Jungian circles. See also Sanford L. Drob, 'Jung and the Kabbalah', *HP* 2:2 (1999), 102–18.

[142] Jung, CW14, ¶19.

[143] Fortune, *Mystical Qabalah*, 18.

[144] For Jung's associations between the *unus mundus* of alchemy, the Platonic world-soul, the Paracelsian *lumen naturae*, and the collective unconscious, see Jung, CW8, ¶393; Jung, CW11, ¶448.

also an important difference in their approaches. Fortune, as a magician, advocates the application of the will in 'building' images;[145] Jung, as a psychotherapist, emphasises the importance of allowing the unconscious to offer its images spontaneously; these images 'must be allowed the freest possible play'.[146] Nevertheless, Fortune also asserts that success in magical operations lies in 'keeping the mind steadily on its plane and subject, but leaving it free within the limits of that subject'.[147] She advises using the 'mighty synthetic glyph' of the Tree as the focus of what Jung terms 'active imagination': an analytic technique which, through meditation on and emotional engagement with images emerging in dreams or spontaneously in waking states, is intended to allow the individual access to the archetypes of the collective unconscious, and can result in the healing of the polarisations that generate psychic distress and suffering.[148] Jung suggests that this technique emerged in early modern alchemy, although the alchemists were unaware of the psychological nature of the visions they experienced.[149]

Dan Merkur notes that a 'measure of mystery' surrounds Jung's practice of active imagination and the sources from which he derived the technique.[150] Jung published his early thoughts on it in 1921,[151] but it is clear from the recently published *Liber Novus*, Jung's private diary – better known as *The Red Book* because of its red leather binding. The term 'active imagination' was first presented in a series of lectures he delivered in English at the Tavistock Clinic in London in 1935, the year in which Fortune's *Mystical Qabalah* was published.[152] Jung insists that psychic energy 'cannot appear

---

[145] See, for example, Fortune, 'Types of Mind Working', 18–19.

[146] Jung, CW8, ¶167.

[147] Fortune, *Sane Occultism*, 39.

[148] For Jung's many discussions on 'active imagination', see Jung, CW6, ¶722 and n. 45; Jung, CW8, ¶166–75; Jung, CW9i, ¶621; Jung, CW14, ¶752–55. See also Joan Chodorow (ed.), *Jung on Active Imagination* (Princeton, NJ: Princeton University Press, 1997); Marie-Louise von Franz, *Alchemical Active Imagination* (Irving, TX: Spring Publications, 1979; repr. New York, NY: Shambhala, 1997); Jeffrey Raff, *Jung and the Alchemical Imagination* (York Beach, ME: Nicolas-Hays, 2000); Merkur, *Gnosis*, 37–54.

[149] See Jung, CW14, ¶446.

[150] Merkur, *Gnosis*, 37.

[151] Jung, CW6, ¶711–22.

[152] The 'Tavistock Lectures' are published in Jung, CW18, 1–182.

in consciousness except in the form of images',[153] and Fortune adopts this view:

> The uninstructed person thinks he is developing psychism when he sees elves, archangels, and elementals with the inner eye. The instructed person knows that he is using a technique of the imagination in order to clothe with visible form intangible things that would otherwise be imperceptible to his consciousness.[154]

This is apparently a 'modern' understanding of such images: they are products of the unconscious, emerging either spontaneously or through deliberate invocation, and they give shape to otherwise incommunicable psycho-spiritual realities. But the practice itself long predates the modern era and forms an important aspect of Kabbalistic magical techniques, particularly in the writings of Moshe Cordovero, whose *Pardes Rimmonim* appears in Latin in the *Kabbala denudata* and was well known to Jung.[155] Although Jung's expositions on active imagination are psychological, they often, albeit covertly, attribute the qualities of divinity to the archetypal realm.

In an interview celebrating his eightieth birthday, Jung finally conceded that esoteric Judaism had foreshadowed his work by a century and a half:

> But do you know who anticipated my entire psychology in the eighteenth century? The Hasidic Rabbi Baer from Meseritz, whom they called the Great Maggid....He was a most impressive man.[156]

Rabbi Dov Ber (1710–1722) was one of the disciples of Israel ben Eliezer (1700–1760), the founder of modern Hasidism,

---

[153] Jung, CW6, ¶722.
[154] Fortune, 'Types of Mind Working', 22.
[155] For Jung's familiarity with Cordovero's *Pardes Rimmonim*, see Jung, *Memories*, 345. For Jewish magical practices involving visualisation, see above, Chapters Four and Five.
[156] C. G. Jung, 'An Eightieth Birthday Interview', in William McGuire and R. F. C. Hull (eds.), *C. G. Jung Speaking: Interviews and Encounters* (Princeton, NJ: Princeton University Press, 1993), 271–72. For the term *maggid* as both an angelic mentor and a Hasidic *zaddik*, see Dan, 'Maggid'.

known as the Ba'al Shem Tov.[157] Dov Ber's interiorised and unashamedly pantheistic doctrines are indeed very close to the main lines of Jung's thought. According to Dan Cohn-Sherbok, the starting-point of Dov Ber's system is 'his conviction that God is present in all things';[158] Gershom Scholem notes that Dov Ber's doctrines 'contain the notion of the unconscious', and observes: 'The *Tzaddikim* make God, if one may phrase it thus, their unconscious'.[159] Steven Joseph suggests that Jung may have encountered Dov Ber's ideas early in his career, and might have been inspired by the Great Maggid's idea of *kadmut ha-sekhel* ('the primordiality of the unconscious') in his own formulation of the collective unconscious.[160] Meditation on the unity of the sefirotic Tree as an interior symbol of divinity is a central aspect of the teachings of Habad Hasidism,[161] and it is a short step from this interiorised godhead to Jung's idea of the role of the Self as a transcendent, unifying dynamic within the human

---

[157] For biographical information on R. Dov Ber, see Jacob Immanuel Schochet, *The Great Maggid: The Life and Teachings of Rabbi Dov Ber of Mezhirech* (New York: Kehot Publication Society, 1974). For an extensive examination into the doctrines of Dov Ber and the Habad current within Hasidism, see Elior, *Paradoxical Ascent*; Weiss, *Studies in Eastern European Jewish Mysticism*, 194–201. According to Cohn-Sherbok (*Fifty Key Jewish Thinkers*, 54), Dov Baer was 'preoccupied with kabbalistic doctrines as propounded by Isaac Luria'. For more on Dov Ber, see Scholem, *Major Trends*, 334–43; Stephen Sharot, 'Hasidism and the Routinization of Charisma', *JSSR* 19:4 (1980), 325–36. Sharot observes (328) that Dov Ber was perceived by his disciples as a magician and 'a man of extraordinary attributes whose every action had divine significance'. For a translation of portions of Dov Ber's works, see Siegmund Hurwitz, 'Psychological Aspects in Early Hasidic Literature', trans. H. Nagel, in James Hillman (ed.), *Timeless Documents of the Soul* (Evanston, IL: Northwestern University Press, 1952/1968), 151–239.

[158] Dan Cohn-Sherbok, *Fifty Key Jewish Thinkers* (London: Routledge, 2007), 54.

[159] Scholem, *Mystical Shape*, 139. See also Wasserstrom, *Religion*, 188–89, for Scholem's understanding of the psychologised doctrines of the Hasidim.

[160] Steven Joseph, 'Jung and Kabbalah: Imaginal and Noetic Aspects', *JAP* 52 (2007), 321–41.

[161] See, for example, Rabbi Hillel of Paritch, *Likkutei Biurim*, fol. 32a, cited in Elior, *Paradoxical Ascent*, 242, n. 5. See also Gustav Dreifuss, 'The Union of Opposites in the Kabbalah', *Journal of Jungian Theory and Practice* 7:1 (2005), 65–71.

psyche.[162] Scholem comments that the distinctive feature of Habad Hasidism is the mixture of a pantheistic perception of the universe with an 'intense preoccupation with the human mind and its impulses'.[163] The same might be said of both Fortune and Jung.

Meditation on the Tree as a means of invoking the divinity within the human being can also be found in medieval Kabbalistic texts. An anonymous Ashkenazi Kabbalist of the fourteenth century envisions the ten *sefirot* existing within the human soul and body, and advises contemplation of 'the Binah in my soul'; during prayer, the adept visualises his ascent on this 'tree of myself'.[164] Despite the obvious cultural disparities, it is difficult to ignore the family resemblance between this approach and Fortune's suggestion that meditation on the Tree represents 'the successive stages of the unfolding of cosmic realisation in human consciousness'.[165] Moshe Idel notes that, according to the anonymous Kabbalist, 'there is a complete Sefirotic system...which constitutes the personal, spiritual, Sefirotic tree'.[166] Such concepts, which present a precociously psychological understanding of Kabbalistic theosophy, found their way into the Hasidic current of the early modern period. Fortune did not 'invent' the interiorisation of the *sefirot* as a dimension of twentieth-century 'psychologised' occultism, although Lloyd Kenton Keane, in his doctoral dissertation on Jung's use of the sefirotic Tree, suggests that she is responsible for initiating this approach.[167] Nor did Fortune derive the idea from Jung; she merely borrowed his language, applying it in an often ingenious way to explain the potency of ritual meditation:

> When our emotion goes out strongly towards an object, we are pouring out a subtle but nevertheless potent form of force...the outpouring force is formulated into a thought-form; the mental picture is ensouled by the outpoured force

[162] See, for example, Jung, CW9ii, ¶68–126 and 347–421; Jung CW10, ¶582–88; and Jung, CW6, ¶789–91, where he states: 'It [the Self] is a transcendental concept...and thus characterizes an entity that can be described only in part but, for the other part, remains at present unknowable and illimitable'.
[163] Scholem, *Major Trends*, 341.
[164] Cited in Idel, *Hasidism*, 232–33.
[165] Fortune, *Mystical Qabalah*, 25.
[166] Idel, *Hasidism*, 233.
[167] Keane, *Routes of Wholeness*, 72.

and becomes an actuality upon the astral.[168]

The Hasidim of the early modern period understood the use of emotion within ritual as a means of drawing down supernal forces and inducing a *unio mystica*.[169] For Jung, emotions cannot be separated from their symbolic representations: 'Emotion and symbol are actually one and the same thing'.[170] The degree of emotional intensity accompanying an image or a ritual act not only provides a clue to the power and importance of the unconscious content; such emotional 'affect' also creates a psychic participation between the individual and the symbol:

> In point of emotional intensity...the most heterogeneous things – rain, storm, fire, the strength of the bull, and the passionate game of dice – can be identical. In emotional intensity, game and gambler coincide.[171]

It is emotion that allows the analytic patient to form a creative relationship with the image arising from the unconscious. While it is unlikely that many analytical psychologists would view their work as magic, Fortune seems to have understood Jung's psychology as a tried and proven pathway to the transformational potential of magical ritual.

THE KABBALAH ACCORDING TO DION FORTUNE

Fortune's appropriation of Jung's theories gave her a new vocabulary in which she could clothe and justify the Kabbalistic magical practices she had inherited from her predecessors in the Golden Dawn. Although she acknowledges the usefulness of the sefirotic Tree as a 'card-index system',[172] Fortune's Kabbalah cannot be considered mere 'programmatic syncretism', and she does not use it

---

[168] Dion Fortune, *Applied Magic* and *Aspects of Occultism* (London: Thorsons/Society of the Inner Light, 1985), 25. See also Dion Fortune, 'The Use of Ritual', in Fortune and Knight, *Ritual Magic*, 48–53, on p. 49.

[169] For the activation of emotion as a magical technique in Hasidic prayer, see Idel, *Hasidism*, 149–70.

[170] Jung, CW18, ¶571.

[171] Jung, CW12, ¶341.

[172] Fortune, *Mystical Qabalah*, 95.

solely as an instrument for categorising a range of symbolic associations. Although syncretism marks the work of all the practitioners of the British occult revival, including Fortune – who states categorically that 'the modern initiate works a synthetic system'[173] – her method of using these correspondences resembles not only Jung's active imagination but also the meditation on the combinations of the Divine Names described by Abraham Abulafia. Abulafia's descriptions of this magical technique would have been difficult for Golden Dawn adepts to access, as his work remained untranslated until the last decades of the twentieth century;[174] but it is possible that Fortune might have received instruction from unnamed sources. In an article produced for the *Inner Light Magazine*, she describes her mode of meditation on the *sefirot* with their accompanying Divine Names, archangels, and planetary spheres:

> I would commence my mental rehearsal of the sacred names, and would suddenly find that I was aware of mental pictures only....I maintained my concentration on the images arising in consciousness, and did not allow it to wander....Out of the sky over the water a vast angelic figure began to form, and I saw

[173] Fortune, *Mystical Qabalah*, 11.
[174] Although Pico relied on Flavius Mithridates' Latin translations of Abulafia for much of his understanding of the Kabbalah, he does not acknowledge his sources, which remained unclear until the late twentieth century; on this subject see Wirszubski's important work, *Pico della Mirandola's Encounter with Jewish Mysticism*. None of Abulafia's work was available in any modern language other than Hebrew until Moshe Idel's publications on this Kabbalist from the 1980s onward. However, Abulafia's techniques were well known to the Hasidim of the eighteenth and nineteenth centuries; see Idel, *Hasidism*, 156–70, and Elior, *Paradoxical Ascent*, 167–72. For Abulafia's method of meditating on the various combinations of Divine Names, see Idel, *Mystical Experience*, 14–41; Idel, *Ecstatic Kabbalah*, 108–12; Idel, *Language, Torah*, 1–28; Idel, 'A Unique Manuscript of an Untitled Treatise of Abraham Abulafia', *Kabbalah: Journal for the Study of Jewish Mystical Texts* 17 (2008), 7–28. For an incisive discussion of the importance of the language and symbolism of the theosophical Kabbalah in Abulafia's work, see Elliot R. Wolfson, *Abraham Abulafia – Kabbalist and Prophet: Hermeneutics, Theosophy, and Theurgy* (Los Angeles, CA: Cherub Press, 2000). Bilingual Hebrew-English editions of three of Abulafia's most important works appeared in 2007, listed in the bibliography.

what I felt to be an archangel bent above me in a vast curve.[175]

Abulafia also describes visitation by an angel, who 'taught me knowledge and related to me the way of understanding'.[176] The result of Fortune's meditations was *The Mystical Qabalah*, which Gareth Knight asserts 'is rooted in practical experience'.[177] Although Fortune repeatedly emphasises her mystical Christianity, she nevertheless declares that the Kabbalah is the 'Yoga of the West',[178] and advises Western adepts to ally themselves to a tradition that belongs to their own history rather than engaging in 'alien initiation' into Eastern esoteric practices.[179] She is supported in this belief by Jung, who emphasises the different archetypal backgrounds behind different cultures and suggests that little psychological insight can be gained through methods 'which have grown up under totally different psychological conditions'.[180] Jung was convinced that the West would one day 'produce its own yoga'.[181] Fortune believed it already had.

Fortune's Kabbalah is simultaneously a comprehensive symbol-system synthesising various esoteric traditions, a set of techniques intended to achieve mystical states and magical powers, and a 'theoretical basis upon which all ceremonial is developed'.[182] This multifaceted understanding of the Kabbalah reflects the complex relationship between 'practical', 'ecstatic', and 'theosophical' Kabbalah expressed in Jewish Kabbalistic texts.[183] Fortune, moving beyond the polarisation of Waite's mysticism and Crowley's magic, seems to have understood the Kabbalah to encompass both these dimensions simultaneously. Nor does she reject the Jewish tradition of the Kabbalah as a 'received' body of wisdom originating in supernal realms. Discussing the 'first Qabalists who built up the whole scheme', she declares:

---

[175] Cited in Knight, *Dion Fortune*, 213–14.
[176] Abraham Abulafia, *Sefer ha Ge'ulah*, MS Jerusalem 8° 1303, fol. 73b, cited in Idel, *Mystical Experience*, 141.
[177] Knight, *Dion Fortune*, 212.
[178] Fortune, *Mystical Qabalah*, 1.
[179] Fortune, *Sane Occultism*, 162.
[180] Jung, CW11, ¶876.
[181] Jung, CW11, ¶876.
[182] Fortune, *Mystical Qabalah*, 2.
[183] See above, Chapter Four. See also Mathers, *Kabbalah Unveiled*, 6–7; Fortune, *Mystical Qabalah*, 21–22.

> The Rabbis are unanimous upon this point, they were angels.
> In other words, it was beings of another order of creation than
> humanity who gave the Chosen People their Qabalah....We
> shall be very foolish if we altogether disregard such a cloud of
> witnesses.[184]

Fortune, who, like Blavatsky and Anna Kingsford, had
trained in trance mediumship, makes clear her reliance on
transhuman 'contacts' for her 'unwritten Qabalah'.[185] Such
relationships with angelic or maggidic sources, although
hardly compatible with normative Christian theological
precepts, are entirely within the tradition of Jewish
Kabbalists such as Luria, and reflect their understanding of
the word 'Kabbalah' as 'reception'.[186]

An extensive examination of Fortune's literary sources is
given by John Selby in his discussion of Fortune's other-
dimensional intermediaries.[187] Fortune appears to be entirely
transparent in naming the Golden Dawn as the source of her
Kabbalistic knowledge, and Gareth Knight, who is familiar
with Fortune's work through his long involvement with the
Society of the Inner Light, suggests that her Kabbalah is
'pretty largely homespun'.[188] But this 'homespun' Kabbalah
may be more than it seems. Fortune gives chief credit to
Mathers and Crowley for her understanding of the Kabbalah,
although, faced with Crowley's growing notoriety during the
inter-war years, she is understandably eager to dissociate
herself from him publicly.[189] Lévi's *Dogme et rituel* and
Histoire de la magie are recommended to aspiring adepts,
along with Westcott's papers on the Kabbalah. Christian
Ginsburg and Adolphe Franck are not mentioned – a
surprising omission, given the high regard accorded to them
by Golden Dawn adepts.[190] In *Mystical Qabalah*, Fortune

---

[184] Fortune, *Mystical Qabalah*, 13–14. See also Dion Fortune, 'The
Inhabitants of the Unseen', in Dion Fortune and Gareth Knight,
Spiritualism and Occultism (Loughborough: Thoth Publications,
1999), 116–27, on p. 119, where Fortune discusses the objective
reality of the angelic hierarchies.

[185] For an in-depth examination of Fortune's 'contacts', see Selby,
Dion Fortune.

[186] For the maggidic tradition in Kabbalah, see Chapter Four.

[187] See Selby, *Dion Fortune*, 416–30.

[188] Gareth Knight, personal email communication (27 May 2009).

[189] See Fortune, *Mystical Qabalah*, vi.

[190] Franck's *La Kabbale* appeared in English in 1926, nine years before
Fortune's *Mystical Qabalah*.

presents the Table of Correspondences as published in Crowley's *Liber 777*, while noting that Crowley's information was derived from Mathers' *Book T*. She also comments that Mathers relied on Dee and Agrippa as well as the *Kabbala denudata*, and that 'the same material' can be found in the works of Westcott, Lévi, Blavatsky, Kingsford, Saint-Martin, and G. R. S. Mead.[191] She mentions the new English translation of the *Zohar*, which appeared a year before her own *Mystical Qabalah*, and she was familiar with Waite's *Holy Kabbalah*, published in 1929, which she calls 'a massive and scholarly standard work'.[192]

If these entirely non-Jewish references represent Fortune's only sources, it is remarkable that she is able to present an understanding of the 'practical' Kabbalah so close to the approaches of both Abulafia and the Hasidic *zaddikim*. There are many possible explanations for this alignment of ideas, ranging from acceptance of the ontic reality of *maggidim*, through Jung's idea of the structural consistency of archetypal patterns, to the cognitive understanding of religious 'representations' and the continuous oral diffusion of the ideas by both Jewish and non-Jewish practitioners through the many currents of Western esoteric thought. Because Fortune's private papers were either destroyed or secreted beyond any researcher's reach, it is impossible to know whether she, like so many of her fellow occultists, sought the help of living Jewish scholars and Kabbalists, directly or through their writings. Fortune's insistence on the Christian bias of her doctrines, as well as the general climate of antisemitism in Britain during the inter-war years, could easily preclude any credit being given to such Jewish sources, and the Society of the Inner Light has continued to assert a firmly Christian focus that minimises any Jewish contribution to its esoteric doctrines. Fortune's reliance on Freud, as well as her friendly relations with Israel Regardie, are notable exceptions to the absence of any acknowledgement of Jewish influence on her work.[193] But

---

[191] Fortune, *Mystical Qabalah*, 104–05.

[192] Fortune, 'Literature of Illuminism', 149.

[193] Francis Israel Regardie (Israel Regudy, 1907–1985) was born in the East End of London to a Polish Jewish immigrant family, but was raised in the United States from the age of thirteen. He joined the American branch of the SRIA in 1926. As this society was and is open only to Christians, Regardie must have nominally converted at some point before the age of nineteen, although his Christianity

Freud was a psychiatrist, not a Kabbalist, and avoided discussing Jewish esoteric speculations; and Regardie, whose youthful membership in the SRIA suggests that he had become at least nominally Christian, endeared himself to non-Jewish occultists with his statement that 'so far as the Qabalah is concerned, it could and should be employed without binding it to the partisan qualities of any one particular religious faith'.[194]

Despite Fortune's claim that the 'mystical Qabalah' was, in her time, almost entirely in the hands of Christian occultists and not Jews, Jewish scholarly literature on the Kabbalah commenced its flowering during the inter-war years. The new translation of the *Zohar* reflected a growing involvement on the part of Jewish researchers in their own esoteric traditions. Moses Gaster continued to produce works on Jewish magic until his death in 1939.[195] Scholem's researches were not available to most English readers until the publication of *Major Trends* in 1941, but his influence was already growing among scholars (and occultists such as Waite) able to understand German, and his comprehensive

---

seems to have been of the broadly heterodox variety espoused by occultists such as Mathers. Regardie became Aleister Crowley's unpaid secretary and travelling companion in 1928. Crowley's influence is evident in Regardie's *The Tree of Life: An Illustrated Study in Magic* (London: Rider, 1932; repr. Woodbury, MN: Llewellyn, 2001), which Fortune declared to be 'quite the best book on magic, in my opinion, not excepting either Crowley or Levi' in a letter to Regardie (1 November 1932) cited in Knight, *Dion Fortune*, 198. Regardie eventually broke from Crowley and joined the Stella Matutina in 1933. He was notorious in occult circles for publishing the Golden Dawn rituals, although Crowley had already done this two decades earlier in various issues of *The Equinox*; but Fortune supported Regardie's venture, as she was opposed to the kind of secrecy espoused by many of her fellow adepts. A number of Fortune's letters to Regardie are printed in Knight, *Dion Fortune*, 197–205. For Regardie, see also Gerald Suster, *Crowley's Apprentice: The Life and Ideas of Israel Regardie* (London: Rider, 1989); King, *Modern Ritual Magic*, 152–55; Chic Cicero and Sandra Tabatha Cicero, 'Introduction to the Third Edition', in Regardie, *Tree of Life*, xxiii–xxxii; Chris Monastre and David Griffin, 'Israel Regardie, The Golden Dawn, and Psychotherapy', *Gnosis* 37 (1995), 37–42.
[194] Israel Regardie, *A Garden of Pomegranates: Scrying on the Tree of Life* (London: Rider, 1932; repr. Woodbury, MN: Llewellyn, 1999), xxi.
[195] For Gaster's publications, including those during the inter-war years, see Chapter Four.

Bibliographia kabbalistica, discussed in Chapter One, represents the first major scholarly effort to list all published works on the Kabbalah from Reuchlin to Scholem's own time.[196] The centuries-old discourse between Jews and Christians that had fuelled the Kabbalah of the Renaissance and later the Kabbalah of the Victorian occult revival also influenced both Jewish writers and occultists during the inter-war years. The Theosophist L. A. Bosman had already published *The Mysteries of the Kabbalah* in 1913, and Joshua Abelson had published his own work on the Kabbalah in the same year.[197] In Abelson's introduction to the new translation of the *Zohar*, he declares that Mathers' *Kabbalah Unveiled* 'contains much valuable material and has proved particularly useful to Christian scholars', and he gives 'grateful reference' to the work of 'the celebrated Scholar, Mr. Arthur Edward Waite'.[198] Like Gaster, Abelson seems to have enjoyed a scholarly exchange with G. R. S. Mead,[199] and favourably reviewed Fortune's *Mystical Qabalah* in *The Jewish Chronicle*.[200]

It is likely that Fortune was familiar with Abelson's work, and she may possibly have known the man himself, since he moved in Theosophical circles. Other occultists were not shy of showing appreciation for Abelson's efforts to present the Kabbalah in terms comprehensible to esoterically inclined Christians, and he is praised as 'the most able and learned of Hebrew exponents of the Kaballa and Talmud' in a work published in 1914 by Holden E. Sampson, an English clergyman with occult predilections and Theosophical connections.[201] Abelson was favourably disposed toward

---

[196] For Scholem's main publications as well as publications written about him, see *Stanford University Encyclopedia of Philosophy* at <http://plato.stanford.edu/entries/scholem/#BooGerSchSel>. See also Gershom Scholem, *Bibliography of the Writings of Gershom G. Scholem Presented to Gershom G. Scholem On the Occasion of his Eightieth Birthday by The Israel Academy of Sciences and Humanities* (Jerusalem: Magnes Press, 1977).

[197] For Bosman, see Chapter Three. For more on Abelson, see Chapter Four.

[198] Abelson, 'Introduction', in *The Zohar*, 1:xxv.

[199] Abelson's *Jewish Mysticism* was first published in a shorter version as *Hebrew Mysticism* by Mead's Quest Society, with which Gaster was also involved.

[200] See above, Chapter Four.

[201] Holden E. Sampson, *The True Mystic: Three Lectures on Mysticism* (London: Rider & Son, 1914), 67. Sampson also wrote articles for

Hasidism as well as occultism, and in *Jewish Mysticism* he lists Lévi's *Livre des Splendeurs* in his recommended bibliography. He also devotes considerable space to an explanation of what he refers to as 'Shechinah mysticism',[202] and, echoing the *Zohar*, emphasises the manner in which, through the meditative work of a fellowship of like-minded adepts, the divine feminine presence of the *Shekhinah* can be 'brought down' into the consciousness of the wider human collective.[203] It is precisely this effort to 'bring down' the feminine aspect of deity and inject the idea into the 'racial consciousness' that is described in detail in Fortune's novels.

FORTUNE'S OCCULT NOVELS

Fortune's decision to use fiction to communicate occult doctrines began in 1925 with her 'Dr. John Taverner' stories. *The Demon Lover*, her first full-length 'occult' novel, appeared in 1927.[204] One of Fortune's most important literary prototypes is Edward George Bulwer-Lytton (1803–1873), whose novels enjoyed considerable influence in the late Victorian occult revival and continued to fascinate adepts well into the twentieth century.[205] Joscelyn Godwin considers Bulwer-Lytton to be the central figure in the development of British occultism in the nineteenth century,[206] and S. B. Liljegren, in an essay exploring Lord Lytton's influence on

---

occult journals; see, for example, 'My Occult Experiences', *OR* 18:5 (1913), 273–79.

[202] See Abelson, *Jewish Mysticism*, 174–75.

[203] See Abelson, *Jewish Mysticism*, 87–97. See also Abelson, *Immanence of God*, 77–149, for the *Shekhinah* as the manifestation of divine immanence.

[204] Dion Fortune, *The Demon Lover* (London: Douglas, 1927).

[205] See Edward Bulwer-Lytton, *Zanoni* (London: Saunders & Otley, 1842); Bulwer-Lytton, *Strange Story*; Edward Bulwer-Lytton, *The Coming Race* (London: William Blackwood & Sons, 1871). For the high regard in which Lord Lytton was still held in Theosophical circles in the twentieth century, see Annie Besant, 'Lord Lytton: A Great Occultist', *TR* 44 (February 1923), 448; C. Nelson Stewart, *Bulwer Lytton as Occultist* (London: Theosophical Publishing House, 1927). For Lord Lytton's brief involvement with the SRIA, see McIntosh, *Éliphas Lévi*, 116; Decker and Dummett, *Occult Tarot*, 43; Howe, *Magicians*, 31–32; Godwin, *Theosophical Enlightenment*, 123–30.

[206] For Godwin's discussions of Lord Lytton's occult pursuits, see Godwin, *Theosophical Enlightenment*, 123–30, 192–96, 215–16.

Blavatsky's doctrines, suggests that the two protagonists in *Zanoni*, adepts of an ancient order far older than the Rosicrucians, provided Blavatsky with her chief inspiration for *Isis Unveiled*.[207] The characters in *Zanoni* may also have contributed to the sequence of paired male initiates, one older and more philosophical, the other younger and craving fuller involvement with life, who inhabit Fortune's novels.[208] Literary models offered by the *Zohar*, translated into English after Fortune's *Demon Lover* but before her other novels, also need to be considered in the context of the dynamic between older and younger male initiates and the ways in which such relationships are utilised as a literary device to convey esoteric truths.[209] The association of literary fiction with occultism, for which Lord Lytton provided such an influential example, was a major feature of the Golden Dawn membership, and many of the order's adepts were published novelists.[210] These works tend to reflect not only the beliefs of the authors and the views of the order's successive Chiefs;[211]

---

[207] S. B. Liljegren, *Bulwer-Lytton's Novels and Isis Unveiled* (Cambridge, MA: Harvard University Press, 1957).

[208] See, for example, T. J. Jelkes and Hugh Paston in *The Goat-Foot God*, and Alick Brangwyn and Ted Murchison in *The Winged Bull*.

[209] For an analysis of the literary dimensions of the *Zohar* and the manner in which the relationships between Shimon ben Yochai and his younger disciples are utilised to convey esoteric truths, see Eitan P. Fishbane, 'The Scent of the Rose: Drama, Fiction, and Narrative Form in the *Zohar*', *Prooftexts* 29 (2009), 324–61; Ellen Haskell, 'Metaphor, Transformation, and Transcendence: Toward an Understanding of Kabbalistic Imagery in *Sefer hazohar*', *Prooftexts* 28 (2008), 335–62.

[210] See, for example, Machen, 'The Great God Pan'; Florence Farr, *The Dancing Faun* (London: Elkin Matthews and John Lane, 1894); Bram Stoker, *Dracula* (London: A. Constable & Co., 1897); J. W. Brodie-Innes, *The Devil's Mistress* (London: William Rider & Son, 1915); Algernon Blackwood, *The Human Chord* (on this novel, see below); Crowley, *Moonchild*; Charles Williams, *The Greater Trumps* (London: Victor Gollancz, 1932).

[211] An example is the fictional work of Charles Williams, much of which bears the stamp of Waite's Fraternity of the Rosy Cross, with which Williams was involved between 1917 and 1930. Williams seems to have been influenced by both Waite's doctrines and his antisemitism. See, for example, Williams, The *Greater Trumps*, which presents the Major Arcana of the Tarot dancing creation in their infinitely varying combinations, manipulated, predictably, by a sinister Jewish magus; and Charles Williams, *All Hallows' Eve* (London: Faber & Faber, 1948), in which another evil Jewish magus

they also mirror the shifting fashions in fictional themes which permeated the British literary circles of the time, discussed in numerous present-day scholarly analyses of the writers of the period.[212] Yet they have an important precedent in the narrative poetics and dramatic forms provided by the *Zohar*.

Fortune was not unique among Golden Dawn adepts in using fiction as a vehicle for Kabbalistic speculations and magical rituals, nor were her tales of John Taverner, the 'psychic doctor', an entirely original creation. Algernon Charles Blackwood (1869–1951), who was initiated into the Golden Dawn in 1900 and followed Waite after the fragmentation of the parent order in 1903, published his own collection of stories about an occultist-physician – *John Silence, Physician Extraordinary* – in 1908. While the Irish occultist Theodore Moriarty might have provided the human model for Fortune's initiated psychic detective, Dr. John Silence preceded Dr. John Taverner by nearly two decades and gave Fortune an important literary model, including the use of the doctor's trusted assistant as narrator – a device originally used by Arthur Conan Doyle in his Sherlock Holmes stories, which first appeared in 1887.[213] In 1910, Blackwood produced *The Human Chord*, a novel based entirely on Kabbalistic themes, which focuses on the power of the Divine Names and the rituals designed to transform

---

uses the power of the Divine Names to manipulate both the living and the dead. For Williams' involvement with Waite, see Humphrey Carpenter, *The Inklings: C.S. Lewis, J.R.R. Tolkien, Charles Williams and their friends* (Boston: Houghton Mifflin, 1979), 80–84; Gavin Ashenden, *Charles Williams: Alchemy and Imagination* (Kent, OH: Kent State University Press, 2008); Willard, 'Acts of the Companions'.

[212] See, for example, Nicholas Freeman, '"Nothing of the Wild Wood"? Pan, Paganism, and Spiritual Confusion in E. F. Benson's "The Man Who Went Too Far"', *LT* 19:1 (2005), 22–33, in which Freeman briefly discusses the work of Fortune, Arthur Machen, and Algernon Blackwood on pp. 23–24. For Machen, see above, Chapter Four. For Blackwood, see below.

[213] The first Sherlock Holmes story appeared as a short novel in *Beeton's Christmas Annual* in 1887; the second, also a short novel, appeared in *Lippincott's Monthly Magazine* in 1890. A further series of stories was published in *The Strand Magazine* in 1891. More short stories and serialised novels continued to appear until 1927.

humans into gods:[214]

> That ancient language [Hebrew] and the magical resources of
> sound are profoundly linked....The secret of this knowledge
> lies in the *psychic values of sound*; for Hebrew, the Hebrew of
> the Bahir, remains in the hierarchy of languages a direct
> channel to the unknown and inscrutable forces; and the
> knowledge of mighty and supersensual things lies locked up
> in the correct utterance of many of its words, letters and
> phrases.[215]

The Human Chord was written while Blackwood was involved
with Waite's order, and may reveal a good deal about the
kind of practices Waite was promulgating:

> For the Name manifests the essential attributes of the Being it
> describes, and in uttering it we shall know mystical union
> with it....We shall be as Gods![216]

Although Fortune recommends many of Blackwood's works
to her students, she surprisingly omits any mention of *The
Human Chord*.

Gareth Knight comments that the distinguishing feature
of Fortune's novels is that she 'fully believed in everything
she wrote'.[217] Fortune's novels are not likely to be
remembered as great literary works, but they are exceptional
in their ability to communicate magical as well as
psychological theory and practice through stories that hold
the reader's interest despite their stylistic failings – perhaps

---

[214] For more on Blackwood, see Howe, *Magicians*, 52; Mike Ashley,
Algernon Blackwood: A Bio-Bibliography (New York, NY: Greenwood
Press, 1987); S. T. Joshti, 'Introduction', in Algernon Blackwood, *The
Complete John Silence Stories* (Mineola, NY: Dover, 1997), v–x; Simon
Clark, 'Introduction', in Algernon Blackwood, *The Lost Valley and
The Wolves of God* (Eureka, CA: Stark House Press, 2003), 7–12; E. F.
Bleiler, 'Introduction', in *Best Ghost Stories of Algernon Blackwood*
(New York, NY: Dover Publications, 1973), v–x. For Blackwood as a
portrayer of literary paganism in the inter-war years, see Nick
Freeman, 'The Shrineless God: Paganism, Literature and Art in
Forties' Britain', *Pomegranate* 6:2 (2004), 157–74.
[215] Blackwood, *Human Chord*, 41.
[216] Blackwood, *Human Chord*, 117.
[217] Gareth Knight, 'The Magical World of Dion Fortune', *ILJ* 24:1
(2003),
<http://www.innerlight.org.uk/journals/Vol24No1/magwrld.pdf
>.

because, as Knight suggests, she believed in what she wrote, or perhaps because, as Fortune herself states, the writing of the books was itself a magical act in which each reader becomes a participant.[218] All of her novels are once again in print, more than seventy years after their first publication during the inter-war years. Despite the fact that Fortune refers to her fictional heroine Lilith Le Fay as 'purely pagan',[219] her readers are informed that the novels, while they can stand alone, reveal their deeper meaning if read as an accompaniment to the study of *The Mystical Qabalah*:

> The 'Mystical Qabalah' gives the theory, but the novels give the practice. Those who read the novels without having studied the 'Qabalah' will get hints and a stimulus to their subconscious. Those who study the 'Qabalah' without reading the novels will get an interesting intellectual jig-saw puzzle to play with; but those who study the 'Mystical Qabalah' with the help of the novels will get the keys of the Temple put into their hands.[220]

The reader unfamiliar with this instruction cannot assume any connection between *The Mystical Qabalah* and Fortune's 'occult' fiction; there are few direct references to Kabbalistic terminology in any of the novels, and the indirect hints depend on *a priori* knowledge on the part of the reader.[221] For example, Hugh Paston, in *The Goat-Foot God*, discovers a mysterious painting on the blank east wall of the church of an abandoned medieval monastery where the monks had been persecuted by the Church authorities for unsavoury practices. The painting portrays

> ...a vast green tree bearing multi-coloured fruit. Ten of them, he counted, in the faded remains of crude primary colours, arranged in stiff triangles, three by three, with the odd one

---

[218] See Fortune, *Moon Magic*, xviii. See also the discussion of Fortune's novels as magical initiations in Versluis, *Restoring Paradise*, 123–26.

[219] Fortune, *Moon Magic*, xvii.

[220] Fortune, *Moon Magic*, v. See also Gareth Knight, *The Occult Fiction of Dion Fortune* (Loughborough: Thoth Publications, 2007), 57.

[221] Even direct references to the Kabbalah are obscure. See, for example, Fortune *Goat-Foot God*, 298. For examples of the Zoharic precedent for this kind of specific symbolic allusion intended solely for the initiated, see Fishbane, 'Scent of the Rose', 346–48; Haskell, 'Metaphor, Transformation, and Transcendence', 343–47.

low down on the trunk at the bottom.[222]

The long-dead monks evidently practiced the same kind of Kabbalistic magic as the adepts of the Golden Dawn, but only a reader acquainted with the symbolism would understand the allusion to the sefirotic Tree.

It would be anachronistic to suggest that Fortune's particular method of using fictional narrative to both conceal and reveal esoteric truths was a deliberate effort to recreate older Jewish traditions; there is no evidence that she knew of such traditions, although she was certainly aware of the English translation of the *Zohar*, and this literary mode of conveying secrets of spiritual import through narrative – along with its enthusiastic interpreters – can also be found in the Greek allegorical tradition.[223] However, as with virtually everything belonging to the realm of 'occultist' Kabbalah, prototypes for Fortune's novels are evident not only in the narrative sequences of the *Zohar*, but also in other Jewish esoteric texts.[224] Using fables and riddles to advocate the cause of morality and inspire religious devotion is hardly unique to Jewish literature, but the use of such narratives to present specifically Kabbalistic themes such as the ten *sefirot*, understood to be inaccessible to rational speculation but communicable as a 'secret wisdom' through the medium of the fictional narrative, are presented in Isaac ibn Sahula's *Meshal ha-Kadmoni*,[225] in which Sahula describes his own effort much as Fortune describes hers, albeit in the specific religious terminology characteristic of Jewish thirteenth-century texts:

---

[222] Fortune, *Goat-Foot God*, 169.

[223] For examples of this type of narrative and its interpreters in Greek literature, see Peter T. Struck, *Birth of the Symbol: Ancient Readers at the Limits of Their Texts* (Princeton, NJ: Princeton University Press, 2004); André Laks and Glenn W. Most, *Studies on the Derveni Papyrus* (Oxford: Clarendon Press, 1997), 4–6, 165–65; Gábor Betegh, *The Derveni Papyrus: Cosmology, Theology and Interpretation* (Cambridge: Cambridge University Press, 2004), 143–45.

[224] For the use of these literary devices in the *Zohar*, see Eitan P. Fishbane, 'The Scent of the Rose: Drama, Fiction, and Narrative Form in the *Zohar*', *Prooftexts* 29:3 (2009), 324–61; Ellen Haskell, 'Metaphor, Transformation, and Transcendence: Toward an Understanding of Kabbalistic Imagery in *Sefer hazohar*', *Prooftexts* 28 (2008), 335–62.

[225] See above, Chapter Five, 192 and n. 88.

...And you shall find that it bears mundane parables, but there is a sequestered allusion and knowing meaning within it, and holy words and instruction are enclosed in its heart, and angels of God ascend and descend upon it.[226]

Sahula, like Fortune, is concerned with demonstrating to his readers that he is familiar with the scientific theories and terminologies of his time; he asserts that science is entirely legitimate, but that it is limited in scope and must be augmented with esoteric knowledge in order to comprehend mysteries such as the relationship between the godhead and the world.[227] This marriage of esotericism and science, which many scholars now assume to be a peculiarly 'modern' phenomenon reflected in the occultism of the nineteenth century, may thus be found in the late thirteenth century in this remarkable Kabbalistic work, along with a literary structure that finds a twentieth-century counterpart in Fortune's novels.

John Algeo, in a paper discussing Fortune's occult fiction, focuses on the characteristic pattern of her plots, although he does not examine these in relation to either *The Mystical Qabalah* or its sources.[228] The stories invariably centre on an alienated human being whose life has become fragmented and meaningless, and who is restored to wholeness through ritual magic and knowledge of the cosmology and psychology which justify its efficacy. Some of Fortune's characters are damaged and at the same time rendered sensitive to hidden forces through their experience of the Great War, such as Ted Murchison in *The Winged Bull* and the

---

[226] Isaac ibn Sahula, *Meshal ha-kadmoni*, vv. 30–67, cited in Lachter, 'Spreading Secrets', 116.

[227] See Lachter, 'Spreading Secrets', 121.

[228] See John Algeo, 'The Integrated Alien: Magic in the Fiction of Dion Fortune', in Olena H. Saciuk (ed.), *The Shape of the Fantastic: Selected Essays from the Seventh International Conference on the Fantastic in the Arts* (New York, NY: Greenwood Press, 1990), 211–18. There is little scholarly exploration of Fortune's novels; but see Clare Fanger, 'Mirror Mask and Anti-self: Forces of Literary Creation in Dion Fortune and W. B. Yeats', in Arthur Versluis, Lee Irwin, John Richards, and Melina Weinstein (eds.), *Esotericism, Art, and Imagination* (East Lansing, MI: Michigan State University Press, 2008), 161–82, in which Fanger examines Fortune's creative activity according to Freudian psychoanalytic models. The Kabbalah is not mentioned in this paper.

pilot Arnold Black in 'The Man Who Sought'.[229] Others, like
Hugh Paston in *The Goat-Foot God* and Rupert Malcolm in
Moon Magic, are tormented because their relationships with
women have proven disastrous; yet these personal failures
reflect what Fortune perceives as an endemic problem of her
times, the loss of knowledge of the dynamic male and female
forces behind manifestation, 'forgotten by modern
civilization which stereotypes and conventionalizes all
things'.[230] Wilfred Maxwell, in *The Sea Priestess*, is rendered
receptive to the invisible realms through illness, but his
asthma, which Fortune presents as psychosomatic in origin,
likewise reflects the endemic collective problem of the
misalignment of sexual energies. Mona Cailey, in 'The Soul
That Would Not Be Born', is damaged because of the
consequences of actions performed in former incarnations,
and these actions, involving the misuse of sexual power,
must be expiated in her present life.[231] Still other characters,
like Diana in 'A Daughter of Pan', are alienated because they
are 'outsiders' who cannot resonate with the values of the
society in which they live.[232] They are, like the Jewish
Kabbalists of the medieval diaspora, strangers in a strange
land: despised, rejected, and persecuted by those who cannot
comprehend the Otherworld to which they are attuned.
Other characters are alienated because of their superior
occult knowledge, such as Justin Lucas in *The Demon Lover*.
Dr. Taverner's assistant Rhodes, in 'A Son of the Night',
reveals that, through his exposure to his employer's occult
knowledge, he 'no longer valued the things that most men
value', and has become an alien in a world to which he once
felt he belonged.[233]

---

[229] Dion Fortune, 'The Man Who Sought', in Fortune, *Taverner*, 29–38.

[230] Fortune, *Sea Priestess*, 101.

[231] Dion Fortune, 'The Soul That Would Not Be Born', in *Taverner*, 39–47.

[232] Dion Fortune, 'A Daugher of Pan', in *Taverner*, 75–91.

[233] Dion Fortune, 'A Son of the Night', in Fortune, *Taverner*, 145–62. 'Son of the Night' appeared after Fortune's death in later editions of *Taverner*, and it has been suggested that it was 'ghosted' by one of Fortune's surviving disciples. Jack Adrian, in a note discussing the authorship of the story, believes that 'Son of the Night' is genuine because 'stylistically, it certainly reads like Fortune's unaided work' (Adrian in Fortune, *Taverner*, 163). Gareth Knight (*Occult Fiction*, 29) states that 'Son of the Night' was first published in *Inner Light Magazine* in 1938, confirming that Fortune was indeed the author of

These fragmented souls are usually men, as Algeo notes, and they represent a collective in a state of alienation and dislocation from its spiritual roots. They are what Freud and Jung would have understood as 'neurotic', but their neurosis reflects a wider spiritual problem – a theme to which Jung addressed much of his own work in the inter-war years,[234] but which was also an important dimension of the ongoing experience of the Jews of the diaspora. Fortune's novels are set in a modern world which has lost both its soul and its understanding of the sacred nature of sexuality, and these fictional works provide a form of social commentary which highlights not the economic or social factors responsible for human suffering, but the spiritual malaise which has created both an ill and hypocritical society and a dislocated godhead in need of human intervention. This perception of a world which depends on the individual's transformation and reconnection for its eventual healing reflects Jung's insistence on the importance of 'individuation' – full integration of the individual self – for the healing of the collective.[235] It is also one of the dominant themes in the Lurianic Kabbalah, and forms the core of the Kabbalah of eighteenth-century Hasidism.[236] The healing of Fortune's alienated protagonists is symbolic of the healing of the 'race'; it is the Kabbalistic *tikkun* or reintegration which must begin with the *zaddik*, the enlightened or 'initiated' individual, but which ultimately restores the androgynous unity of the godhead itself, embodied in the 'collective unconscious'. Taverner's assistant Rhodes, at the climax of 'A Son of the Night', is healed through a recognition of the unity behind diversity:

> In all things there was a profound difference; for to me, they

---

the work, as she was alive at the time and would hardly have countenanced a work which she had not written appearing under her name in the journal of her own occult society.

[234] See, for example, Jung, 'Spiritual Problem of Modern Man'.

[235] For Jung's definition of individuation, see Jung, CW6, ¶757–62. For the relationship between individuation and the fate of the collective, see Jung, CW10, ¶536.

[236] See Fine, *Physician*, 142–44. For the individual *hasid* as the instrument through which the community is healed, see Scholem, *Major Trends*, 325–30. For the *zaddik* as the vessel for collective healing and reintegration, see Dresner, *Zaddik*, 113–41; Idel, *Hasidism*, 189–207; Green, 'Zaddiq as Axis Mundi'. For the *zaddikim* as a 'spiritual elite' with collective responsibilities, see Rapoport-Albert, 'God and the Zaddik'.

had suddenly become alive....I shared in their life, for I was one with them. And then I knew that, isolated though I must always be in the world of men, I had this infinite companionship all about me. I was no longer alone....I had passed over into the Unseen.[237]

This experience of a direct revelation of the unity of all things is reflected in the Hasidic *coincidentia oppositorum*, described succinctly by Rabbi Aharon Halevi in the early nineteenth century:

> He [God] is the perfection of everything, for it is the essence of completeness that even the reversals of opposites will be included in the One.[238]

In Hasidic thought, the dissolving of the illusion of opposites such as good and evil occurs through the perception of *hashvaah* ('equalisation'), an idea echoed in Lévi's concept of 'equilibrium'. Rachel Elior understands *hashvaah* to mean that all aspects of life, however antipathetic they might seem, 'have a single, common root that equalizes them within the infinite'.[239] The idea is also presented by Jung in a precise mirroring of Hasidic doctrines: 'The concept of an all-encompassing God must necessarily include his opposite'.[240] The 'anti-cosmic' dualism which permeates Gnostic texts and much of Christian doctrine, pitting God against Satan and the spirit against the body, is dissolved by a realisation of the illusory nature of these opposites and their secret unity in the godhead. Although Jung suggests that the experience of opposition is essential to psychological development, recognition of the paradoxical unity behind these oppositions allows healing, because in God (or in the collective unconscious, depending on one's frame of reference) there is no division or conflict, and a direct experience of this unity, unmediated by the personal ego, is tantamount to a *unio*

---

[237] Fortune, 'Son of the Night', 161–62.
[238] R. Aharon Halevi, '*Avodat ha-Levi*, Va-Yehi, fol. 74a, cited in Elior, *Paradoxical Ascent*, 64.
[239] Elior, *Paradoxical Ascent*, 67. For Lévi's idea of 'equilibrium', see Chapter Two. For Fortune's 'equilibrium of forces', see Dion Fortune, 'Talismanic Magic', in Fortune and Knight, *Ritual Magic*, 168–73, on p. 169; Fortune, *Mystical Qabalah*, 55–61.
[240] Jung, CW13, ¶256.

mystica.[241] This theme runs consistently through Fortune's work, where it is reflected in the *coniunctio* of the male and female aspects of divinity through the ritualised marriages of her male and female protagonists, and in the declaration that 'all the gods are one god, and all the goddesses are one goddess, and there is one initiator'.[242]

Fortune also uses her novels to express her views of what constitutes 'good' and 'bad' magic, and enlists her fellow occultists as models. Despite the 'sneaking regard' she felt for Crowley,[243] he appears in *The Winged Bull* as Hugo Astley, the quintessential 'black' magician drunk on power and ruined by debauchery. Bradford Verter, in his doctoral dissertation on modern occultism, proposes that this novel reflects Fortune's distaste for Crowley's magical philosophy. Both Crowley and Fortune 'emphasized Kabbalah....Both articulated systems of spiritual alchemy, and placed sexual relations as the center of ritual magic'.[244] However, through the figures of Astley and Alick Brangwyn, the 'white' magician who opposes him, Verter suggests that Fortune deliberately contrasts herself with Crowley through opposing themes such as androgyny, polymorphous sexuality, and miscegenation (Astley=Crowley) versus sexual polarisation, heterosexuality, and Aryan purity (Brangwyn=Fortune).[245] Gareth Knight, taking a different approach, asserts that Fortune's novels are 'Qabalistic works', each of which focuses on a specific *sefira* on the Tree of Life: 'In Dion Fortune's view, each book was...an initiation to a particular Sephirah or a psychoanalysis according to the capacity for response of the reader'.[246] *The Winged Bull*, in Knight's view, is a dramatic portrayal of the *sefira Tiferet*, whose astrological correspondence is the Sun and whose colours and symbolism appear in both the blonde

---

[241] For the *coincidentia oppositorum* as the major dialectic in Hasidism, see Elior, *Paradoxical Ascent*, 13–15.

[242] Fortune, *Goat-Foot God*, 344. See also Dion Fortune, *The Sea Priestess* (London: Inner Light, 1938), 171–73; *Winged Bull*, 322–23.

[243] For Fortune's 'sneaking regard' for Crowley, see her letter to Israel Regardie (16 November 1932), cited in Knight, *Dion Fortune*, 200.

[244] Bradford J. M. Verter, *Dark Star Rising: The Emergence of Modern Occultism, 1800–1950* (unpublished PhD dissertation, Princeton University, 1997), 328.

[245] Verter, *Dark Star*, 325–28.

[246] Knight, *Dion Fortune*, 225.

protagonist Ted Murchison and the ritual of the Sun in which Alick Brangwyn appears robed in pink and gold, 'the colours of Tiphareth'.[247] If Verter and Knight are correct, Fortune, like the authorship of the *Zohar* more than seven centuries earlier, has packed Kabbalistic symbolism into every nook and cranny of her fiction, and these works, like the tales of the sages presented in the *Zohar*, are meant not only to teach but to take the reader through a form of magical initiation. As Ellen Haskell suggests in a paper on the Zoharic narrative: 'Symbolic and metaphoric images serve as cognitive mechanisms that provide experiential understanding of the subjects they signify'.[248]

Another significant feature of Fortune's novels is the role of women in these mythic portrayals of alienation and restitution. Fortune's predilection for goddess-worship, particularly evident in her last two novels, has been emphasised in a number of analyses of her impact on contemporary spiritualities,[249] and Ronald Hutton notes her 'direct and obvious influence' on the various currents of modern pagan witchcraft.[250] But the importance of the Kabbalah in Fortune's formulation of the feminine dimension of deity is often overlooked. Susan Johnston Graf, in a paper on the women in Fortune's novels, perceives Fortune as a feminist who deliberately intended to revive goddess-worship and 'create a spiritual tradition in which a female divinity would be pre-eminent'.[251] Johnston does not mention the fact that Fortune herself links her novels with the Kabbalah, or that this emphasis on 'female divinity' has its roots in Kabbalistic theosophy as well as in the nineteenth-century Romantic vision, inspired by Greek myth, of Nature as a great earth-goddess.[252] Graf also suggests that Fortune's

---

[247] Knight, *Occult Fiction*, 60; Knight, *Dion Fortune*, 223. Fortune also wrote articles about her 'occult fiction' for *ILM*: Dion Fortune, 'The Novels of Dion Fortune' (November 1936) and Dion Fortune, 'The Winged Bull: A Study in Esoteric Psychology' (August–October 1937), discussed in Knight, *Dion Fortune*, 223, and Knight, *Occult Fiction*, 67–68.

[248] Haskell, 'Metaphor, Transformation, and Transcendence', 342.

[249] See, for example, Greenwood, *Magic, Witchcraft*, 152–63.

[250] Hutton, *Triumph of the Moon*, 180–88. See also Hutton, 'Modern Pagan Witchcraft', 38–40.

[251] Susan Johnston Graf, 'The Occult Novels of Dion Fortune', *JGS* 16:1 (2007), 47–56, on p. 47.

[252] For the goddess Nature in nineteenth-century Romantic poetry and the influence of this figure on early twentieth-century writers,

biographers have not recognised the 'radicalism' in this emphasis on 'goddess-centered spiritual practices', and credits Fortune with a new contribution to contemporary neo-pagan and goddess-centred spiritualities.[253] Fortune's influence on contemporary spiritualities is unquestionably important, and her work might be considered innovative in terms of the social climate of her times, although the sexual *mores* of the inter-war years were far more flexible than those of Victorian Britain.[254] But the importance of the feminine dimension of deity is not Fortune's invention, nor did she ally it with a feminist political agenda. The *Shekhinah* had permeated the British occult revival from Anna Kingsford onward, and is a direct outgrowth of Kingsford's involvement with the writings of Lévi, the *Kabbala denudata*, and the alchemical lore of the *coniunctio* derived, in large part, from Kabbalistic cosmology.[255] The amalgamation of the Romantic theme of the goddess Nature and the Kabbalistic *Shekhinah*, who is, according to the *Zohar*, 'dressed in garments on which are drawn all created things',[256] is evident in Fortune's declaration that Isis is 'but another name for Nature', and that 'Nature is God made manifest'.[257] Likewise, the darker aspects of the *Shekhinah*, whose feet, according to the *Zohar*, 'go down to death',[258] and whom Scholem views as symbolizing 'the esoteric interior of the "earth"',[259] are echoed in Fortune's Black Isis, whom she describes as primordial 'elemental force' and equates with the *sefira Binah*.[260]

Fortune's female protagonists – Veronica Mainwaring in *The Demon Lover*, Mona Wilton in *The Goat-Foot God*, Ursula

---

see Hutton, *Triumph of the Moon*, 32–42 and the references given there on pp. 419–21.

[253] Graf, 'Occult Novels', 49.

[254] For changes in sexual attitudes in the inter-war years, see Bingham, *Gender, Modernity*, 145–81.

[255] For Anna Bonus Kingsford and the Lurianic Kabbalah, see above, Chapter Three.

[256] *Tikkunei Zohar* 22, f. 65a, cited in Scholem, *Mystical Shape*, 180.

[257] Fortune, *Moon Magic*, 67. For the Greco-Roman identification of Isis as Nature and its appropriation as a Romantic trope in the eighteenth and nineteenth centuries, see Hadot, *The Veil of Isis*, 233–314. For Fortune's identification of Isis with Nature, see also Hutton, *Triumph of the Moon*, 185–86, and above, n. 252.

[258] *Zohar* 1:148a and 154b.

[259] Scholem, *Mystical Shape*, 190.

[260] Fortune, *Moon Magic*, 44 and 167.

Brangwyn in *The Winged Bull*, and Vivien Le Fay Morgan in *The Sea Priestess* and *Moon Magic* – are all exiles, echoing the *galut ha-Shekhinah* ('exile of the *Shekhinah*') in Lurianic texts.[261] In the first two novels, the women are both materially impoverished and emotionally fragile. Mona Wilton, before her 'restitution', is on the verge of starvation, and dresses in such dull tones that Hugh Paston 'would have had her inlaid with precious stones to brighten her up'.[262] Veronica Mainwaring is likewise in a state of semi-starvation and sees 'grey ghosts about her instead of men and women'.[263] Ursula Brangwyn, although comfortably cocooned by family wealth, is emotionally shattered and unable to protect herself from the evil influence of Hugo Astley, just as the exiled *Shekhinah* is at the mercy of the dark forces of the *qlippot*.[264] Fortune does not present these women as omnipotent powers, but as isolated individuals who, like their male counterparts, suffer from the sexual imbalances inherent in the world around them. Even in the last two novels, where the powerful figure of Vivien Le Fay Morgan, priestess of Isis, is anything but helplessly dependent on a male saviour, it is the *coniunctio* that accomplishes the magic. The goddess requires restitution, but even Vivien, with all the powers of Isis at her disposal, cannot accomplish this task alone; she depends on a ritualised union with a male partner, both precipitating and reflecting the sefirotic union that will heal the cosmos. This is the wedding of *Tiferet* and *Malkuth* which first appears in the *Zohar*,[265] and which Jung, describing the Kabbalistic vision he experienced after a heart attack in 1944, understood to be a symbol of psychological wholeness:

> I myself was, so it seemed, in the Pardes Rimmonim, the garden of pomegranates, and the wedding of Tifereth with Malchuth was taking place....It was the mystic marriage as it appears in the Cabbalistic tradition....My beatitude was that

---

[261] On the exiled *Shekhinah*, see above, Chapter Two; Fine, *Physician*, 59–65; Lawrence Fine, 'Purifying the Body in the Name of the Soul: The Problem of the Body in Sixteenth-Century Kabbalah', in Howard Eilberg-Schwartz (ed.), *People of the Body: Jews and Judaism from an Embodied Perspective* (Albany, NY: State University of New York Press, 1992), 117–42, esp. pp. 122–24.

[262] Fortune, *Goat-Foot God*, 79.

[263] Fortune, *Demon Lover*, 19.

[264] For the *Shekhinah*'s vulnerability to the *qlippot* of the 'Other Side', see Scholem, *Mystical Shape*, 189–91.

[265] *Zohar* 3.107b.

of a blissful wedding.[266]

Graf's assumption of Fortune's 'feminism' may be somewhat anachronistic. If Crowley was an antinomian libertine, Fortune, as Alan Richardson tartly observes, was a prude.[267] Throughout her work she displays an inflexible intolerance toward premarital intercourse, homosexuality, and abortion.[268] Even contraception, although 'better than nervous disease', is inferior to 'the direction of the life-forces into channels in which they can do creative work'.[269] Although the sexual act is 'life flowing into the world direct from God, and human beings as channels for it',[270] Fortune circumscribes this sacralised sexuality with traditional Judeo-Christian rules determining the suitable forms for its enactment. Equilibrium and the union of opposites, rather than female emancipation, seem to lie at the core of Fortune's sexual philosophy, and human intercourse, provided it is enacted within marriage, is the microcosm and vessel for the union of the great male and female forces of the cosmos. Fortune's invariably dark-haired heroines mirror the Kabbalistic association of the *Shekhinah* with the *sefira Malkuth* and the dark, earthy realm of the *qlippot* in which she is imprisoned. By the time *The Sea Priestess* and *Moon Magic* were written, other deities had begun to encrust Fortune's *Shekhinah*-figures, in particular the Egyptian Isis. But even in these late works, Fortune is careful to mention that Isis has her correspondence on the sefirotic Tree:

> She is the matrix of matter; the root-substance of all existence, undifferentiated, pure. She is also Binah, the Supernal Mother, that receiveth Chokmah, the Supernal Father.[271]

Fortune does not present herself as a Kabbalist, nor do her fictional characters. But like Lévi, Mathers, and Crowley before her, she grafts her Egyptian motifs onto a firm Kabbalistic base. She also found an effective means of reconciling her pagan proclivities with her allegiance to 'the

---

[266] Jung, *Memories*, 325.

[267] Richardson, *Fortune*, 150.

[268] See Fortune, *Sane Occultism*, 130–31; Fortune, *Love and Marriage*, 89; Fortune, *Winged Bull*, 322–23.

[269] Fortune, *Love and Marriage*, 88–89.

[270] Fortune, *Winged Bull*, 322.

[271] Fortune, *Sea Priestess*, 170.

Master Jesus' through the unifying symbol of the Kabbalistic Tree, and through Jung's idea of the diversity of images through which he believed archetypal patterns are wont to clothe themselves in individuals and cultures.

FORTUNE'S KABBALISTIC LEGACY

Fortune, although less of a 'household name' than Crowley, may be considered the most influential of the British occultists in terms of the perpetuation of the Kabbalah in the milieux of contemporary spiritualities. Susan Greenwood, in her ethnographic survey of these currents, notes that the Kabbalah is 'the cornerstone of much high magical practice' in twenty-first-century groups involved in the Western esoteric tradition,[272] and demonstrates the ubiquity of Fortune's expositions of the Tree as the basis for an understanding of contemporary Kabbalistic magic.[273] Despite the fact that *The Mystical Qabalah* was published seventy-five years ago, Adrian Ivakhiv observes that the 'most highly touted manuals of practical "Qabalism"' in contemporary magical circles are Fortune's book and *A Practical Guide to Qabalistic Symbolism* by Gareth Knight, who initially derived his understanding of the Kabbalah from his training in the Society of the Inner Light.[274] T. M. Luhrmann, exploring ritual magic in contemporary England, likewise notes Fortune's impact on groups involved with the 'Western Mysteries', highlighting their emphasis on meditation and visualisation – an emphasis drawn directly from Fortune's instructions for the use of the Tree as the focus of ritual work.[275] Luhrmann also comments that, when she first began exploring magic, 'I was directed towards her [Fortune's] novels as the best way to understand the practice'.[276] It is difficult to find a contemporary book on the Kabbalah written by a non-Jewish practitioner that does not rely, directly or indirectly, on Fortune's work for its inspiration.[277]

---

[272] Greenwood, *Magic, Witchcraft*, 68.
[273] Greenwood, *Magic, Witchcraft*, 49–74.
[274] Ivakhiv, 'Resurgence of Magical Religion', 258, n. 10; Gareth Knight, *A Practical Guide to Qabalistic Symbolism* (York Beach, ME: WeiserBooks, 2002).
[275] Luhrmann, *Persuasions of the Witch's Craft*, 56–57.
[276] Luhrmann, *Persuasions of the Witch's Craft*, 87–88.
[277] See, for example, Madonna Compton, 'The Sacred Feminine on the Tree: Mother of Magic and Mystery', in Chic Cicero and Sandra

The Society of the Inner Light, like so many descendants of the original Golden Dawn, continues to maintain a presence in the twenty-first century. Gareth Knight, discussing the fertility of the parent order, observes:

> Just as the work of Dion Fortune had developed out of the pioneering work of others – Barrett, Lytton, Kingsford, Mathers, Moriarty, Brodie-Innes and the like – so did the pioneering work of Dion Fortune and the Fraternity of the Inner Light spawn forth other groups and movements.[278]

The list of groups emerging from Fortune's original Fraternity of the Inner Light is a long one, rivalling the fecundity of the primal ancestor.[279] Although not all these groups place the Kabbalah at the centre of their doctrines, many do, including Knight's own order, founded in 1973.[280] Fortune's influence has also extended into Jewish Kabbalistic circles through authors such as Z'ev ben Shimon Halevi (Warren Kenton), one of the most important contemporary practitioners writing on the Jewish Kabbalah and a frequent contributor to the *Inner Light Journal*, whom John Selby, in an article posted on the Inner Light's website, describes as 'appealing mainly to the esoteric fraternity'.[281] There is nothing 'Christian', 'Hermetic', or 'occultist' about Halevi's Kabbalah, which emphasises theosophy rather than magic and is firmly rooted in the medieval Jewish esoteric traditions of thirteenth-century Spain.[282] Nevertheless Halevi

---

Tabatha Cicero, *The Golden Dawn Journal, Book 2: Qabalah: Theory and Magic* (St. Paul, MN: Llewellyn, 1994), 233–52; John Michael Greer, *Paths of Wisdom* (St. Paul, MN: Llewellyn, 1996).

[278] Knight, *Dion Fortune*, 318.

[279] For a list of these groups and their founders, see Knight, *Dion Fortune*, 318.

[280] See Knight's autobiography, <http://www.angelfire.com/az/garethknight/aboutgk.html>.

[281] John Selby, 'Key Figures in Twentieth Century Esoteric Kabbalah', *ILJ* 23:1 (2005), <http://www.innerlight.org.uk/journals/Vol23No1/keyfig.htm>.

[282] Halevi currently works as Principal Tutor for the eclectic Kabbalah Society, <http://www.kabbalahsociety.org>. See his 'Interview' at <http://www.skyscript.co.uk/kenton.html>. Halevi's works include *Introduction to the Cabala: Tree of Life* (York Beach, ME: Weiserbooks, 1991); *Adam and the Kabbalistic Tree* (York Beach, ME: Weiserbooks, 1990); *Kabbalah and Exodus* (York Beach, ME: Weiserbooks, 1988).

presents a Kabbalistic Tree that mirrors precisely Fortune's planetary-sefirotic correspondences and is explained through psychological concepts which echo Fortune as much as Jung:

> In the exercise based upon the Sephirotic Tree the particular form of the archetypal symbols evoked reveal the present state of the psyche. Take note of any striking element and ponder what it means. Each 'person' is a subpersonality and each 'room' a function of the mind.[283]

Knight suggests that there is a 'massive difference' between the Jewish Kabbalah and Fortune's 'occult Qabalah', 'the first being theistic and based on a mystical approach to God, the latter monist or more or less platonic with the emphasis more on how the inner side of God's creation works'.[284] This perspective is shared by a number of contemporary occult groups.[285] However, many Jewish Kabbalistic sources – particularly Cordovero, the Lurianic corpus, and modern Hasidism – are strongly monist and pantheist in their perception of an immanent deity in a unified creation. The thirteenth-century Kabbalist Moshe de Leon declares:

> Everything is concatenated in its mystery, caught in its oneness....The entire chain is one. Down to the last link, everything is linked with everything else, so divine essence is below as well as above, in heaven and earth. There is nothing else.[286]

Fortune's Kabbalah is as Jewish as it is 'occult', and appears to speak to both Jews and non-Jews with equal authority.

One possible reason for Fortune's ongoing influence in contemporary Western spiritualities is her ability to convey the magical and theosophical aspects of the Jewish Kabbalah in the neutral language of psychology, allowing her readers the freedom to explore this complex Jewish lore without the necessity of specific religious allegiances. Psychological models are certainly a 'new' contribution in terms of

---

[283] Warren Kenton [Z'ev ben Shimon Halevi], 'The House of the Psyche', *ILJ* 24:4 (2004),
<http://www.innerlight.org.uk/journals/Vol24No4/house.pdf>.
[284] Gareth Knight, personal email communication (29 May 2009).
[285] See above, Chapter One, and below, Chapter Seven.
[286] Moshe de Leon, *Sefer ha-Rimmon*, 181–82, cited in Matt, *Essential Kabbalah*, 26.

conceptual formulation, but the 'universality' of the Kabbalah, and its harmonization with the conceptual formulations of Platonic and Aristotelian philosophic currents, is a theme already evident in the Jewish-Christian and Jewish-Muslim discourses of twelfth-century Spain. These philosophical frameworks provided a similar kind of 'neutral ground' in which the apparent conflicts between religions, and the apparent contradictions between religion and science, could be resolved.[287] In some contemporary magical circles, the concepts which Fortune describes are no longer couched in Kabbalistic terminology, often leading to a lack of understanding of one of the most important sources from which Fortune's rituals and 'goddess-worship' spring. Whether Fortune produced a 'secularised' Kabbalah is open to debate, since she asserts the ontic reality of the Kabbalistic worlds while using the neutrality of psychological models to explain them. This same neutrality allowed Jung to convey esoteric ideas as interior human dynamisms while remaining aloof from both the belief-systems of occult and religious doctrines and the reductionism of medical psychiatry.

Wouter Hanegraaff suggests that the 'psychologisation' of magic has severed the pre-modern relationship between a particular symbol and the objective spiritual reality it was once seen to embody. He offers as an example the 'universal filing cabinet' of the sefirotic Tree, which transforms the traditional Jewish Kabalistic framework into 'a convenient way of imposing a symbolic order of one's own personal preference upon outside reality'.[288] Symbolic correspondences have thus become mere tools for training the individual imagination, and psychological models allow occultists to 'legitimate their practice in a disenchanted

---

[287] For the Hasidic interweaving of esotericism and science, including that of R. Abraham Isaac Kook, quoted at the beginning of Chapter One above, see Jonathan Garb, 'The Modernization of Kabbalah: A Case Study', *MJ* 30:1 (2010), 1–22, esp. pp. 7–8. For more on Kook's 'modernism', see also Jonathan Garb, 'Rabbi Kook and his Sources: From Kabbalistic Historiosophy to National Mysticism', in Moshe Sharon (ed.), *Studies in Modern Religions, Religious Movements and the Babi-Bahai Faiths* (Brill: Leiden, 2004), 77–96. In 'Modernization of Kabbalah', Garb adheres to the idea that the psychologisation of Kabbalah 'profoundly increased' from the seventeenth century onward, but does not deny psychological perceptions in earlier Kabbalistic currents.
[288] Hanegraaff, 'How magic survived', 367.

world'.[289] Fortune certainly acknowledges the usefulness of the Tree as a means of classifying esoteric knowledge, and she emphasises the importance of training the imagination for any kind of magical work.[290] However, so too have Jewish Kabbalists from the medieval period onward. Fortune's declaration that the Tree symbolises 'the raw material of the Divine consciousness and of the processes whereby the universe came into being' does not sever the relationship between symbol and symbolised, nor does it secularise the original Jewish conception of the *sefirot*;[291] in fact, this statement expresses complete loyalty to Jewish Kabbalistic theosophy. And legitimation of a body of esoteric knowledge through the scientific paradigms of the day is not unique to the post-Enlightenment world. In the second century CE, Claudius Ptolemy attempted to counter Cicero's influential diatribe against astrological divination by insisting that the practice of astrology was a 'stochastic *techné*': a craft similar to medicine, with carefully developed rules for conjecture.[292] Isaac ibn Sahula's thirteenth-century *Meshal ha-Kadmoni* offers a similar perception of the compatibility of esoteric lore with the science of the day. The quest for legitimation of esoteric revelation through the affirmations of science seems to be a human rather than a secularised post-Enlightenment need.

Although Fortune was no religious agnostic, she appears to have understood the idea of 'methodological agnosticism' long before late-twentieth-century scholars developed their research paradigms. David Katz highlights the importance of this approach for the development of British occultism:

> The wonderful thing about the subliminal is that it provided a space for all sorts of unnatural and supernatural phenomena to occur...we now had a theoretical site in which they could reside. This neutrality regarding the veracity of ideas in the mind made psychology a useful no man's land in late

---

[289] Hanegraaff, 'How magic survived', 378.

[290] See, for example, Fortune, 'Types of Mind Working', and Dion Fortune, 'Mind Training', in Fortune and Knight, *Ritual Magic*, 32–39.

[291] Fortune, *Mystical Qabalah*, 17.

[292] Ptolemy, *Tetrabiblos*, I.1–3. For Ptolemy's 'stochastic *techné*', see Barton, *Ancient Astrology*, 7. For Cicero's attack on astrology, see M. Tullius Cicero, *On Divination*, in M. Tullius Cicero, *Old Age, On Friendship, On Divination*, trans. W. A. Falconer (Cambridge, MA: Harvard University Press, 1970), 223–539, in 2:42–47.

Victorian England where scientists, clergymen and spiritualists could happily meet.[293]

Fortune's Kabbalah, offering a 'theoretical site' in which science and religion could 'happily meet', may require a more complex approach than defining it as the reinvention of a pre-modern esoteric tradition. Instead, her Kabbalah may be viewed as she herself describes it: a legitimate heir of the complex and paradoxical currents of the Jewish Kabbalah, embedded in a language skillfully adapted to the diverse spiritualities of the modern world. If psychoanalysis, as Bakan suggests, is indeed a secularisation of Jewish mysticism, Fortune in turn de-secularised it and, by marrying the conceptual structures of the psychologies of the early twentieth century with a body of much older theosophical and magical approaches, returned the Jewish Kabbalah to its traditional role as a mode of creating, articulating, and maintaining the dynamic relationship between macrocosm and microcosm, and between 'revealed and concealed worlds'.

---

[293] David S. Katz, *The Occult Tradition* (London: Jonathan Cape, 2005), 140.

CHAPTER SEVEN

CONCLUSION

> Students of literature, philosophy and religion who have
> any sympathy with the Occult Sciences may well pay
> some attention to the Kabalah of the Hebrew Rabbis of
> olden times; for whatever faith may be held by the
> enquirer he will gain not only knowledge, but also will
> broaden his views of life and destiny.[1]
>
> – William Wynn Westcott (1910)

> That which was the mark or stigma of a particular group
> becomes a distinction of the human condition in
> general...Whenever, more recently, we have resorted to
> the trope, myth, or ideal of exile...Cabala can loom into
> view.[2]
>
> – Philip Beitchman (1998)

'IS KABBALAH JEWISH?'

In 1922 – the year in which the fiercely nationalist group
called The Britons was preparing its 'official' translation of
the *Protocols of the Elders of Zion*, and the year in which Dion
Fortune created her Fraternity of the Inner Light – a small
Kabbalistic school was formed in Jerusalem by the Polish
Hasidic rabbi Yehuda Lieb ha-Levi Ashlag (1885–1954),
whom Boaz Huss describes as 'the most important and
innovative Kabbalist of the twentieth century'.[3] Ashlag's
group, reinvented as the Kabbalah Center in 1970 and now
grown wealthy and international, is currently run by Rabbi
Philip Berg (1929–), who describes it as 'a spiritual and

---

[1] Westcott, *Introduction to the Study of the Kabalah*, iii.
[2] Beitchman, *Alchemy of the Word*, 34–35.
[3] Huss, 'All You Need is LAV', 615. For an introduction to Ashlag's
teachings, see Rav Yehudah Ashlag, *Kabbalah for the Student*, ed.
Michael Laitman (Toronto: Laitman Kabbalah Publishers, 2008). See
also Mark Cohen and Yedidah Cohen (eds.), *In the Shadow of the
Ladder: Introductions to Kabbalah by Rabbi Yehudah Ashlag* (Safed:
Nehorah Press, 2002). The Kabbalah Center has translated, edited,
and published a number of Ashlag's works, e.g. *Ten Luminous
Emanations*.

educational organization dedicated to bringing the wisdom of Kabbalah to the world'.[4] It is also a magnet for disenchanted celebrities such as Madonna and Britney Spears, who have been largely responsible for the Center's high public profile. Just as some contemporary Rosicrucian groups present themselves as the legitimate descendents of the teachings of the legendary Christian Rosenkreutz,[5] the Kabbalah Center presents itself as the legitimate descendent of the teachings of Isaac Luria and, ultimately, of the legendary Shimon ben Yochai, the great sage of the *Zohar*. Through the Kabbalah Centre, its website informs visitors, 'the practical tools and spiritual teachings of Kabbalah are accessible to everyone for personal change and transformation'.

Berg then poses, and provides his own answer to, a question relevant to the Kabbalah of every occultist discussed in this book: 'Is Kabbalah Jewish'?

> It is quite understandable that Kabbalah could be confused with Judaism. Throughout history, many scholars of Kabbalah have been Jewish. But there have also been many non-Jewish scholars of this wisdom, such as Christian Knorr-von-Rosenroth, Pico Della [*sic*], and Sir Isaac Newton....The startling truth is that Kabbalah was never meant for a specific sect. Rather, it was intended to be used by all humanity to unify the world.

The idea that the Kabbalah is the 'great reconciler', capable of transcending religious boundaries and healing religious conflicts, might appear to belong to what Jody Myers calls 'postmodern religious sensibility',[6] but it is a persistent

---

[4] The Kabbalah Center is at <http://www.kabbalah.com>. All quotations are from <http://www.kabbalah.com/01A.php> or <http://www.kabbalah.com/03.php>. For a comprehensive history of the founders, aims, and philosophy of the Kabbalah Center, see Jody Myers, *Kabbalah and the Spiritual Quest: The Kabbalah Center in America* (Westport, CT: Praeger, 2007). Philip Berg was born Feivel Gruberger in New York; he received a traditional religious education and was ordained as a rabbi at the age of twenty-two.
[5] See, for example, the Rosicrucian Fellowship, <http://www.rosicrucian.com/faq1.htm#q2>, and the Confraternity of the Rosy Cross, <http://www.crcsite.org/rosicrucianism.htm>.
[6] Jody Myers, 'Marriage and Sexual Behavior in the Teachings of the Kabbalah Center', in Pasi and von Stuckrad (eds.), *Kabbalah and*

aspiration expressed in the thirteenth century in the 'spiritual messianism' of Abraham Abulafia,[7] promulgated in the late fifteenth and early sixteenth centuries by Pico and Guillaume Postel, shared by Knorr von Rosenroth and Francis Mercury van Helmont when they compiled the *Kabbala denudata* at the end of the seventeenth century, echoed by Éliphas Lévi and his mid-nineteenth-century Jewish compatriots Adolphe Franck, Adolphe Crémieux, and Elie Soloweyczyk, and articulated in the late nineteenth and early twentieth centuries by occultists such as William Wynn Westcott and Israel Regardie. Berg offers two explanations for why the Kabbalah enjoys continuing popularity in the twenty-first century:

> The first reason is that Kabbalah works. When people apply the wisdom and tools of Kabbalah to their lives, they experience positive results. The second reason why so many people of different faiths become connected to Kabbalah is that it is a way of life that can enhance any religious practice. Christians, Hindus, Buddhists, Muslims, and Jews use Kabbalah to improve their spiritual experience.[8]

Berg's statement that the Kabbalah 'was never meant for a specific sect' is highly questionable and, not surprisingly, the Kabbalah Center's apparent universalism and dissociation from Judaism has generated fierce opposition in more conservative Jewish religious and academic circles.[9] Among the Kabbalistically inclined members of the Israeli *haredi*

Modernity, 259–81, on p. 259. For 'postmodern Kabbalah', see also Boaz Huss, 'The New Age of Kabbalah: Contemporary Kabbalah, the New Age and Postmodern Spirituality', *JMJS* 6:2 (2007), 107–25.

[7] See Idel, *Messianic Mystics*, 58–100. For Abulafia's efforts to reconcile Christians, Jews, and Muslims through encouraging them to learn the proper (Kabbalistic) way to read the Hebrew Scriptures, see also Harvey J. Hames, *Like Angels on Jacob's Ladder: Abraham Abulafia, the Franciscans and Joachimism* (New York: State University of New York Press, 2007).

[8] http://www.kabbalah.com. See n. 4 above.

[9] For the Kabbalah Center's 'determination to transcend cultural and religious boundaries', see Véronique Altglas, 'Yoga and Kabbalah as World Religions? A Comparative Perspective on Globalization of Religious Resources', in Boaz Huss (ed.), *Kabbalah and Contemporary Spiritual Revival* (Beer-Sheva: Ben-Gurion University of the Negev Press, 2011), 233–50.

community,[10] R. Yaakov Moshe Hillel, leader of the elitist
Yeshivat Hevrat Ahavat Shalom of Jerusalem, has demanded
that Berg's books be burned, and calls the Kabbalah Center
'the Cult of Counterfeit Kabbalists'.[11] As well as antagonising
Kabbalists amongst the orthodox, the 'populism' of the
Kabbalah Center infuriates scholars such as Joseph Dan,
who, echoing Scholem's rejection of 'occultist' Kabbalah as
'charlatanry', views non-academic engagement with the
Kabbalah in non-traditional circles as a serious distortion of
Jewish spirituality,[12] and calls the Kabbalah Center a 'New
Age mishmash of nonsense'.[13] With a conviction similar to R.
Hillel's insistence that a true Kabbalist can be identified by
his command of traditional Jewish sources,[14] 'real' Kabbalah,
in Dan's view, has always involved 'a life filled with study of
Torah and observance of the commandments', and real
Kabbalists tend to keep their studies secret;[15] moreover, real
Kabbalists apparently do not contaminate their teachings
with astrology and alchemy, let alone magic of the kind
practiced by the adepts of the Golden Dawn.[16] Although the
Golden Dawn was originally created as a secret society that
never encouraged 'populism', Lévi and his heirs – Westcott,

---

[10] *Haredi* or *chareidi* ('orthodox') is the self-definition of the most
conservative form of Orthodox Judaism. For this current in
contemporary Judaism, see Samuel C. Heilman, *Defenders of the
Faith: Inside Ultra-Orthodox Jewry* (Berkeley, CA: University of
California Press, 2000); Nurit Stadler, 'Is Profane Work an Obstacle
to Salvation? The Case of Ultra Orthodox (*Haredi*) Jews in
Contemporary Israel', *SR* 63:4 (2002), 455–74; Kimmy Caplan,
'God's Voice: Audiotaped Sermons in Israeli *Haredi* Society', *MJ* 17:3
(1997), 253–80; Yosseph Shilhav, 'The *Haredi* Ghetto: The Theology
Behind the Geography', *CJ* 10:2 (1989), 51–64. For the Kabbalah in
the *haredi* community in Israel, see Jonathan Garb, 'Towards the
Study of the Spiritual-Mystical Renaissance in the Contemporary
Ashkenazi Haredi World in Israel', in Huss (ed.), *Kabbalah and
Contemporary Spiritual Revival*, 117–40.
[11] See Meir, 'Boundaries of the Kabbalah', 173. According to Meir,
the first Orthodox responses to Berg came as early as 1988, in a
work by Shimon Kazar-Arram published in Los Angeles and
entitled *An Essay on Subduing Sinners which Exposes the Face of a False
and Despicable Messiah in Our Generation*.
[12] See Huss, 'Authorized Guardians', 97.
[13] Dan (ed.), *Heart and the Fountain*, 285.
[14] See Meir, 'Boundaries of the Kabbalah', 174–75.
[15] Joseph Dan, 'From Belief in the Torah to Belief in Pious Man',
Ma'ariv 12 (February 1988), cited in Huss, 'Ask No Questions', 157.
[16] Dan (ed.), *Heart and the Fountain*, 48.

Mathers, Waite, Crowley, and Fortune – all published books and articles on the Kabbalah, and Crowley and Fortune both believed their rituals should be publicly accessible and acted on this belief, to the consternation of more elitist adepts such as Waite. The internal debate over whether to keep the Kabbalistic magic of the Golden Dawn restricted to initiates echoes a similar debate occurring in the thirteenth century between those Kabbalists who viewed their 'reception' as the property of an initiated elite and those who believed this esoteric knowledge should be made available to any serious person willing to take the time to study it and capable of understanding it.[17] The echoes still reverberate in the debate between *haredi* Kabbalists such as R. Hillel and the current growing involvement with Kabbalah on the part of non-observant Israeli Jews. There are important parallels between the motivations of thirteenth-century Jewish Kabbalists to reveal their doctrines in textual form and the motivations of nineteenth-century British occultists to do the same. Both tried to use the power of revealing esoteric secrets in order to generate social and religious change as well as individual self-transformation; both attempted to reconcile esoteric doctrines with the scientific advances of the day; and both were responding to a widespread cultural perception that some kind of eschaton, messianic advent, or 'New Age' transformation of consciousness was imminent. The purportedly modern nature of the occultists' concern to shift Kabbalistic study and practice from esoteric and particularist to exoteric and universalist may not be so modern after all.

The Kabbalah Center has been subjected to virulent criticism similar to the criticism of the Kabbalah of the British occult revival. Both are viewed as disrespectful distortions of the Jewish Kabbalah, although the Kabbalah Center was founded by a Hasidic rabbi and is still run by one and,

---

[17] For this debate among early Kabbalists, see, *inter alia*, Halbertal, *Concealment*, 69–113; Elliot R. Wolfson, 'Occultation of the Feminine and the Body of Secrecy', in Wolfson (ed.), *Rending the Veil*, 113–54, on pp. 118–19; Hames, 'Exotericism and Esotericism'; Yechiel Shalom Goldberg, 'Spiritual Leadership and the Popularization of Kabbalah in Medieval Spain', *JSSMJ* 2:2 (2009), 2–59; Lachter, 'Spreading Secrets'; Moshe Idel, 'Nachmanides: Kabbalah, Halakhah, and Spiritual Leadership', in Moshe Idel and Mortimer Ostow (eds.), *Jewish Mystical Leaders and Leadership in the 13th Century* (Northvale, NJ: Jason Aronson, 1998), 15–96.

despite its large non-Jewish membership,[18] cannot be accused of promulgating a 'Christian', 'occultist', or 'Hermetic' Kabbalah. As Véronique Altglas points out in her analysis of the universalist trend of the Center, the inner circle, despite claims of inclusiveness, remains predominantly Jewish, and the teachers and full-time volunteers lead an observant way of life.[19] Although Boaz Huss describes the Center's Kabbalah as 'a postmodern bricolage' and Anthony J. Elia refers to it as 'a New Age practice with a twist of Jewish Mysticism',[20] Berg's Kabbalah might, with equal justification, be defined as a 'vernacular' expression of this centuries-old esoteric lore,[21] which, in the view of scholars such as Dan, can never be more than shallow and inauthentic because it oversimplifies complex concepts and caters to a following ignorant of Jewish religious traditions and unable to read Hebrew. But 'vernacular' religion is, in Leonard Primiano's view, 'lived' religion as it is expressed in everyday life: 'Vernacular religion can highlight the creative interpretation present in even the most ardent, devout, and accepting religious life'.[22] Primiano further asserts that a pure 'official' religion does not, in fact, exist,[23] and this perspective may be extended to include the idea of a pure, 'official' Jewish Kabbalah – clearly distinguishable from 'Christian', 'occultist', 'Hermetic', and 'populist' Kabbalahs – which likewise may not exist. Creative interpretation lies at the heart of the Kabbalistic 'pluralistic hermeneutic', and reflects the intense individualism which Kabbalists have continuously exhibited, from the thirteenth-century circle who produced the *Zohar* and the fifteenth-century group who generated the *Sefer ha-Meshiv* to the Habad Hasidism of R. Dov Ber's eighteenth-century disciples and the twenty-first-century Kabbalists of Beit El and the

---

[18] According to the Center's teachers, around half are non-Jewish. See Altglas, 'Yoga and Kabbalah', 243.

[19] Altglas, 'Yoga and Kabbalah', 246–47.

[20] Huss, 'All You Need is LAV', 619; Elia, 'An Historical Assessment', 20.

[21] For 'vernacular' religious expressions, see Leonard Norman Primiano, 'Vernacular Religion and the Search for Method in Religious Folklife', *WF* 54:1 (1995), 37–56; Don Yoder, 'Toward a Definition of Folk Religion', *WF* 33:1 (1974), 2–15.

[22] Primiano, 'Vernacular Religion', 47.

[23] Primiano, 'Vernacular Religion', 45.

Yeshivat Hevrat Ahavat Shalom.[24] While they may be 'vernacular' and couched in a language that appeals to non-Jews, the Kabbalah Center's teachings may also be viewed as no less 'real' Jewish Kabbalah than that of Isaac Luria or the Ba'al Shem Tov, who both applied creative interpretation to older Kabbalistic texts; and the same may be said of the Kabbalah of the British occult revival.

Even if Dan's assertions are accepted as definitive, British occultists did not popularise Kabbalistic theosophy and practice; Waite's *Holy Kabbalah* is sufficiently erudite to have earned even Scholem's reluctant approval, while Fortune's sophisticated exegesis in *The Mystical Qabalah*, praised by Joshua Abelson, may be seen as equal in clarity and understanding, if not in historical and religious sensibility, to many scholarly introductions to the Kabbalah published today. Boaz Huss refers to the Kabbalah Center's 'postmodern bricolage' as a cultural product that 'blurs...the traditional boundaries between elite and mass culture'.[25] However, Jewish esoteric traditions have never been the sole property of a rabbinic elite,[26] but have also been expressed in vernacular forms over many centuries. The recently discovered mid-eighteenth-century diary of the wandering Kabbalistic magician called Hillel Ba'al Shem, who was neither a learned rabbi nor a rabbinical scholar, reveals the daily life of a 'practical' Kabbalist who used the Divine Names as well as astrology, chiromancy, and astral magic to perform exorcisms and heal dizziness, headache, diarrhoea, and other mundane ills as he travelled from village to village, selling his services for food, money, lodgings, and the well-wishing prayers of his hosts.[27] Hillel's poignant complaints about the stiff competition in the marketplace indicate that he was not unique in his perambulations on the roads of eastern and central Poland.[28] Wandering Kabbalistic magicians like Hillel did not question their identity as

---

[24] For Beit El, see Giller, *Shalom Shar'abi*; Pinchas Giller, 'Leadership and Charisma Among Mizrahi Modern Kabbalists: In the Footsteps of Shar-abi – Contemporary Kabbalistic Prayer', *JSSMJ* 1:2 (2007), 21–41.

[25] Huss, 'All You Need is LAV', 619.

[26] See, for example, the hypothesis of the non-rabbinic milieu of the late antique *heikhalot* mystics discussed in Halperin, *Faces of the Chariot*, 447–55.

[27] See Petrovsky-Shtern, 'Master of an Evil Name'.

[28] Petrovsky-Shtern, 'Master of an Evil Name', 231–35.

Kabbalists, nor did the recipients of their services. British occultists, predominantly middle-class and usually ignorant or even contemptuous of Jewish religious traditions, were neither a rabbinic elite nor a troupe of travelling wonder-workers, although Waite's exceptional erudition and Crowley's often outrageous public performances might be seen to encompass both ends of the spectrum. But on closer inspection, the apparently impenetrable boundary between the Kabbalah practiced in the British occult revival and the Kabbalah practiced by Jewish Kabbalists over the centuries wavers and blurs to the point where it begins to look suspiciously like an artificially imposed academic construct.

Defining the Kabbalah

Attempts by contemporary scholars to define the Kabbalah continue without resolution. Moshe Hallamish wisely observes: 'It is difficult to formulate an inclusive definition that will exhaust the whole range of phenomena and currents populating the world of Kabbalah'.[29] Arthur Green points out that, within the currents of the Kabbalistic tradition, 'we do not have before us a single linear development of a particular type of mysticism, but rather a variety of mysticisms'.[30] Elliot Wolfson suggests that the variegated textures of Kabbalah are best classified as 'Jewish esotericism' rather than as 'Jewish mysticism', although mystical currents can be discerned as a particular dimension of esotericism in some Kabbalistic texts and practices.[31] Joseph Dan, more precise in his views, asserts that the Jewish Kabbalah is identified by both its practitioners and its scholars as 'an esoteric tradition which is centered around a group of symbols representing the ten manifestations of God, the sefirot'.[32] If this divine anatomy does indeed distinguish the Jewish Kabbalah from other esoteric literature, the Kabbalah of the British occult revival must also be considered Jewish Kabbalah because it too has budded from the sturdy trunk of the sefirotic Tree,

---

[29] Moshe Hallamish, *An Introduction to the Kabbalah*, trans. Ruth Bar-Ilan and Ora Wiskind-Elper (Albany, NY: State University of New York Press, 1999), 3.
[30] Arthur Green, *A Guide to the Zohar* (Stanford, CA: Stanford University Press, 2004), 7.
[31] Wolfson, *Abraham Abulafia*, 9–38; Wolfson, 'Beyond the Spoken Word', 168–70.
[32] Dan, 'Kabbalah of Johannes Reuchlin', 64.

and the Jewishness or non-Jewishness of the practitioner is irrelevant. 'Hermetic' and Platonic interpretations are common to many Jewish Kabbalistic texts; Abraham Cohen de Herrera's *Puerta del Cielo* ('Gate of Heaven'), included in a Latin translation in the *Kabbala denudata*, is a prime example of a Platonic orientation in Kabbalistic literature,[33] and Yohanan Alemanno's talismanic magic, discussed in Chapter Three, is a characteristic expression of the blend of Kabbalah and Hermetic-Neoplatonic currents common to many Jewish Kabbalists in the late fifteenth century.

Moshe Idel suggests that there are other ways of defining Kabbalah, found as early as the eleventh century and comprising 'an esoteric tradition concerning the divine names'.[34] Abraham Abulafia, to whom Idel has devoted a number of scholarly works, focused almost exclusively on the Divine Names and their magical and mystical potencies, and considered the 'way of the *sefirot*' to be a 'lower' type of Kabbalah.[35] Elliot Wolfson points out that 'the essence of the kabbalistic tradition has to do with knowledge of the divine name'.[36] If the linguo-theosophy of the Divine Names provides the distinguishing feature of what might be identified as Jewish Kabbalah, then, once again, the work of the British occultists must also be viewed as Jewish Kabbalah, because it invariably includes invocations and explanations of the powers of the Names and their angelic emanations. Westcott, Mathers, and Crowley were fond of Kabbalistic hermeneutics; Waite and Fortune, like Lévi before them, preferred to focus on the powerful symbol of the sefirotic Tree and, probably wisely, did not attempt *gematria*, *temurah*, or *notarikon*. But Kabbalistic hermeneutics and the use of the Divine Names, although often interwoven, are not identical. All the occultists discussed in this book, including the determinedly Christian mystic Waite, used the

---

[33] See de Herrera, *Gate of Heaven*; for an analysis of the philosophical content of this text, see Alexander Altmann, 'Lurianic Kabbalah in a Platonic Key: Abraham Cohen Herrera's *Puerta del Cielo*', in Isadore Twersky and Bernard Septimus (eds.), *Jewish Thought in the Seventeenth Century* (Cambridge, MA: Harvard University Press, 1987), 1–37.

[34] Idel, 'Introduction to the Bison Book Edition', in Reuchlin, *De arte cabalistica*, v–xxix, on p. v.

[35] Idel, *Kabbalah*, xi–xii.

[36] Wolfson, 'Beyond the Spoken Word', 180. See also Wald, *Doctrine of the Divine Name*, 3–31.

Divine Names in their explications of Kabbalistic ideas, and accepted the ontic reality of the powers they were invoking; and the rituals which these practitioners adapted or designed unfailingly relied on the traditional Jewish adjuration of the Tetragrammaton, the holiest of the Names.

In the early sixteenth century, Johann Reuchlin offered his own method of differentiating a 'real' practitioner of the Kabbalah:

> Kabbalah is a matter of divine revelation handed down to further the contemplation of the distinct Forms and of God, contemplation bringing salvation; Kabbalah is the receiving of this through symbols. Those who are given this by the breath of heaven are known as Kabbalics; their pupils we will call Kabbalaeans; and those who attempt the imitation of these are properly called Kabbalists.[37]

These terms have no equivalent in Hebrew,[38] but Reuchlin appears to be differentiating between those who have experienced direct 'reception' through revelation and those who learn the doctrines by rote with only an intellectual grasp of the mysteries they pursue. It is difficult to assess the nature of the 'reception' involved in the Kabbalistic literature produced by modern occultists. Lévi, Mathers, Waite, Crowley, and Fortune all claimed to have experienced what are now understood as RASCs ('religiously altered states of consciousness') in the development of their ideas.[39] Mathers, Crowley, and Fortune were explicit in their reliance on the angelic guides known in Jewish traditions as *maggidim*, and in describing the chief method through which they achieved their 'reception': focused meditation or *kavvanah*, the staple diet of every Jewish Kabbalist over the centuries who has sought direct experience of the godhead rather than contentedly absorbing intellectual formulae that explain it. Although the attribution of the knowledge gained through these 'altered states' to ontically objective supernal entities

---

[37] Reuchlin, *De arte cabalistica*, 1.63.

[38] See Reuchlin, *De arte cabalistica*, n. 9, 371.

[39] For this term and its alternative, RISCs ('religiously interpreted states of consciousness'), both regularly used in psychological literature concerned with religious experience, see Segal, *Life After Death*, 322–50 and references in n. 15; Alan F. Segal, 'Text Translation as a Prelude for Soul Translation', in Paula G. Rubel and Abraham Rosman (eds.), *Translating Cultures: Perspectives on Translation and Anthropology* (Oxford: Berg, 2003) 213–48.

belongs to the domains of theological and psychological discourse rather than historical research, these occultists are nevertheless entitled to be seen as 'Kabbalics' according to Reuchlin's definition because they built their understanding of the Kabbalah not only on textual sources and oral teachings handed down from adept to disciple, but also on some form of personal experience involving altered states of awareness. Even Westcott, who was more cautious about claiming such an intimate relationship with the supernal realms, may well have enjoyed his share of such states in the many rituals in which he participated.

Philip Beitchman suggests that the 'outsider quality' which permeates the Jewish Kabbalah has a special affinity with literature, 'with which it shares qualities of rootlessness, search, and movement'.[40] The adepts of the Golden Dawn and its offshoots demonstrated this affinity in the large number of works of poetry and fiction inspired by the Kabbalah which they produced over the decades – some, like Blackwood's *Human Chord*, unabashedly mediocre, and some, like Yeats' *A Vision*, viewed as great literature.[41] A number of recent papers have stressed the transformative power of the literary dimension of the *Zohar*; as with Dion Fortune's 'occult' novels, the reading of the *Zohar* seems to have been itself intended as an initiatory experience.[42] Rachel Elior places the Kabbalah and its magic firmly in the domain of art and literature, but categorically dismisses any ontic reality in its practices.[43] It has not been the purpose of this book to determine whether the Kabbalah of the British occult revival can provide empiric proof of its own validity. Like Jewish Kabbalists over the centuries, British occultists believed it did, and assumed that its efficacy depended on an understanding of the 'secret dynamic processes within the divine pleroma',[44] as well as on the correct application of Jewish linguo-theosophy in ritual practice.

---

[40] Beitchman, *Alchemy of the Word*, 35.
[41] William Butler Yeats, *A Vision* (London: Macmillan, 1937; repr. New York, NY: Macmillan/Collier, 1966).
[42] See, for example, Haskell, 'Metaphor, Transformation, and Transcendence'; Fishbane, 'The Scent of the Rose'; Idel, 'White Letters'. See also Wolfson, *Language, Eros, Being*, 38–39.
[43] Rachel Elior, 'Review of Yigal Arikha, *Practical Kabbalah*', *Yedi'ot Aharonot* 19 (June 1998), cited in Huss, 'Ask No Questions', 148.
[44] Dan, 'Kabbalah of Johannes Reuchlin', 82.

Among British occultists, only Waite could lay claim to
being any sort of Kabbalistic scholar, although he had little
knowledge of Hebrew and worked almost entirely from
translated texts. Westcott stands alone as the only British
occultist among those discussed who displayed a genuine
empathy toward the Jews, although Lévi evidenced a similar
empathy unusual in his cultural milieu. Practitioners such as
Fortune and Crowley were not interested in either
Kabbalistic scholarship or Jewish culture and history; they
wanted to exploit the Kabbalah's magical possibilities for
both personal and collective ends. That Waite, Fortune, and
Crowley were hostile toward Jews is clearly evident in their
writings, and their antisemitism, however 'gentlemanly' in
the case of the former two, reflects one of the more
unattractive elements in this remarkable cultural current in
fin-de-siècle Britain – although it was endemic in the British
society of the time and was not unique to occultists, nor has
it vanished from occult circles in the present day. But despite
the antipathy toward Jews displayed by these individuals,
their understanding of the Jewish Kabbalah deserves to be
considered, not as mere 'charlatanry' or as a modern
reinvention of an older tradition, but as a genuine and
sometimes successful effort to preserve the continuity of a
vigorous living tradition in the context of the cultural
currents of their times. The work of the occultists explored in
this book demonstrates that the Kabbalah of the British occult
revival has not been remade, reinvented, or newly created;
only the languages used to explain it reflect 'modernity'. It
remains Jewish Kabbalah, an esoteric lore shaped by
historical circumstances unique in the history of Western
religions, and apparently able to speak across the centuries to
particular individuals of varying religious persuasions who
have experienced that state of exile which awaits those who
cannot abandon their religiosity but who have been
wrenched, physically, emotionally, or intellectually, from a
secure and stable religion of 'there' and impelled into an
interiorised and imaginal religion of 'anywhere'. Beitchman
suggests that the Kabbalah's literature is directly related to
an exile that is 'metaphysically structural, for it is not only of
a people, but also one within the Godhead, from itself'.[45] It is
this state of disillusionment, fragmentation, and interior
homelessness, generated by the dramatically changing

---

[45] Beitchman, *Alchemy of the Word*, 20.

religious, scientific, and social paradigms of the late nineteeth and early twentieth centuries, which may have contributed so powerfully to the importance of the Kabbalah in the British occult revival.

While early nineteenth-century British clergymen dreamed of using the Kabbalah to convert Jews, non-Jewish practitioners of the Kabbalah today do not seem to share this motivation. However, the tendency to deny the Jewishness of the Kabbalah and 'reclaim' it as a different entity rooted in Platonic or Greco-Egyptian doctrines is still current, and appears to have first taken root during the late nineteenth and early twentieth centuries. Blavatsky offered an excellent late nineteenth-century example of the occultist tendency to assert that the Jews 'lost' their Kabbalah over the centuries, and that only non-Jewish occultists were able to rediscover it and truly understand its revelations; Charles Stansfield Jones, a disciple of Crowley, reiterated this argument in the early twentieth century.[46] Twenty-first-century versions, apparently more benign but still disturbing in their implications, continue to circulate in certain occult milieux. Jan Swanson attempts to differentiate between the Jewish Kabbalah and Mathers' 'Hermetic Qabalah', disregarding the many 'Hermetic', magical, and syncretic currents within the Jewish Kabbalah and the contributions of Jewish scholars and Kabbalists, both directly and through their written work, to the development of the Kabbalah of the Golden Dawn.[47] Michael T. Walton subdivides the Kabbalah into Jewish Kabbalah, Christian Kabbalah (such as that of Reuchlin and Postel, who 'used Cabala as a weapon to bolster Christian theology'), and Hermetic Kabbalah (such as that of John Dee, who 'approached Cabala as a tool to be applied in understanding nature').[48] As many Jewish Kabbalists, including Luria and his followers, utilised Kabbalistic ideas and practices to 'understand nature' as well as the nature of the godhead, Walton's distinction seems spurious. Colin Low

---

[46] Frater Achad [Charles Stansfield Jones], *The Anatomy of the Body of God, Being the Supreme Revelation of Cosmic Consciousness* (Chicago: Collegium ad Spiritum Sanctum, 1925), i–ii.

[47] Jan Swanson, 'The Qabalistic Tree', <http://www.kheper.net/topics/Hermeticism/Qabalah.htm>.

[48] Michael T. Walton, 'Hermetic Cabala in the *Monas Hieroglyphica* and the *Mosaicall Philosophy*' (1981), <http://homepages.ihug.com.au/~panopus/essentia/essentiaii2.htm#monas>.

declares that the Jewish Kabbalah is 'an extension and elaboration of Judaism', while 'Hermetic' Kabbalah 'derives from the philosophic notions of the divine in Plato and Plotinus, and in the related theosophy of the *Corpus Hermeticum*'.[49] Low further states that this 'new' Kabbalah is 'less connected with religious dogma and more with open and individual exploration'. The Jewish Kabbalah absorbed a number of Platonic and Neoplatonic ideas as well as Hermetic doctrines in the course of its travels, and the Hermetic philosophy of both late antiquity and the Renaissance in turn absorbed Jewish esoteric themes, as discussed in Chapter Three; and many Kabbalistic texts, particularly those emerging from Abraham Abulafia's thirteenth-century 'ecstatic' Kabbalistic current, are far more concerned with 'open and individual exploration' and individual spiritual transformation than they are with 'religious dogma'. The chief emphasis in Abulafia's work, which exercised a decisive influence on Pico's so-called 'Christian' Kabbalah as well as on modern Hasidism, is, according to Moshe Idel, focused on 'the path to self-transformation, to apotheosis (namely the mystic's becoming a god-like figure), and to self-redemption'.[50] Low's distinctions seem to reflect a personal agenda rather than historical evidence. But some scholars of Western esotericism still appear to accept such distinctions as though they were 'empiric'.

THE 'PLURALISTIC HERMENEUTIC'

This book has examined the Kabbalahs of five British occultists and their progenitor, Éliphas Lévi, who is credited with introducing the term 'occultism' into modern vocabularies. These six individuals were highly influential in the trajectory of the Kabbalah from the *fin-de-siécle* to contemporary spiritualities because they published works specifically intended to explain the Kabbalah to aspiring adepts. But every thinking practitioner of the occult revival, from Frederick Hockley to William Butler Yeats, developed his or her own understanding of the Kabbalah, just as Jewish

---

[49] Colin Low, 'Emanation and Ascent in Hermetic Kabbalah' (2003), <http://www.digital-brilliance.com/kab/essays/Emanation%20Ascent.pdf>.
[50] Idel, 'Inner Peace through Inner Struggle', 76.

Kabbalists expressed highly individualistic understandings of the Kabbalah's 'pluralistic hermeneutic' over the centuries. The Kabbalah of the occult revival is a multifaceted Kabbalah which reflects the individual predilections of each occultist as well as the specific cultural background within which he or she lived and the changes in religious, social, and scientific perspectives that occurred during the eighty years covered by this book. But the fundamentals of each of their Kabbalahs are all fully represented in Jewish Kabbalistic sources.

The newness of Lévi's 'modern' Kabbalah – the 'Great Secret' founded on the belief that divinity lies in the human soul and can be cultivated by the application of the human will – lies only in the specific vocabularies Lévi appropriated from Mesmer and the Romantic currents of his time. His Kabbalah expresses not only the esoteric dreams of post-Revolution France, but also his own artistic inclinations. The complex applications of *gematria*, *temurah*, and *notarikon* baffled him, but he excelled in responding creatively to the linguistic magic of the *Sefer Yetsirah* and the imagery presented both verbally and visually in Kabbalistic manuscripts, and developed innovative interpretations and interconnections that made full use of the rich imaginal resources of Jewish texts. Westcott, although more of a pedant than a poet, nevertheless recognised, through his tireless studies of Kabbalistic texts and his discourse with the Ashkenazi community of north London, the family resemblances between the Jewish Kabbalah and early modern alchemical, Masonic, and Rosicrucian currents; he helped to create rituals based on a textual legacy that represents far more than an attempt to impose the 'esoteric method' on history, and draws on historical routes of transmission that still await fuller examination. Westcott's 'Rosicrucian' Kabbalah, which amalgamates 'Hermetic' alchemy with Jewish theosophical and magical currents embedded in British occultism from John Dee's time onward, is no more newly invented than Lévi's.

Mathers recognised in the medieval grimoires the syncretic but unmistakably Jewish traditions of angel magic, alive and well in a nominally Christian framework, and he incorporated this 'practical' Kabbalah, and the mystico-magical traditions of the modern Hasidim, in the rituals of the Golden Dawn. Mathers' belief that ritual is the most effective means of engaging with, and even coercing, the supernal intermediaries, is evident in the Jewish *heikhalot* literature of late antiquity, and even the highly imaginative admixture of deities in Mathers' rituals has precedents in the *Sefer ha-Razim* and other early Jewish magical texts – which Jewish Kabbalists themselves, like Mathers, identified as 'practical' Kabbalah. Waite's understanding of the Kabbalah as a mystical path is hardly a new invention, since *heikhalot* adepts had been attempting the ascent of the soul to the *unio mystica* since late antiquity, and the medieval Kabbalah, no less than modern Hasidism, is fuelled by this quest for a direct encounter with the divine. Waite, steeped in the Christian mystical tradition, nevertheless used the sefirotic Tree as the basis for his meditations and rituals, incorporating the ancient Jewish practice of *kavvanah* to achieve his spiritual goals, and focusing on the Zoharic image of sacramental sexuality to express and facilitate his own vision of 'divine union'.

Crowley, apparently the most 'modern' of the British occultists in his use of the Kabbalah as an intellectual filing system, nevertheless reverted to the Kabbalistic adjuration of supernal powers to invoke his *maggid* and promote his eschatological revelations, and offered theories and practices of sexual magic that have their antecedents in the sacred eroticism of the *Zohar* and the more extreme Lurianic derivatives that emerged in the Jewish messianic movements of the seventeenth and eighteenth centuries. And Fortune's interiorised 'psychological' Kabbalah stands firmly on the shoulders not only of Freud and Jung, but of Abraham Abulafia, who formulated the idea in the thirteenth century that the ten *sefirot* exist as internal states and stages within the human being, and that the Holy Guardian Angel is a mirror-image, manifested in imaginal form, of the individual's own 'higher self'. While Fortune adopted the new psychologies to embed her Kabbalah in a cultural milieu increasingly drawn to self-examination after the Great War, she recognised the morphology of the Kabbalah in the work of both Freud and Jung, as well as the precociously psychological perspectives of medieval Kabbalistic theosophy and magic. However diverse the Kabbalahs of these occult practitioners, the elements stipulated by Kabbalistic scholars as a means of defining Jewish Kabbalah – the divine infrastructure of the ten *sefirot* and the lingo-theosophy of the Divine Names – remain consistent in the Kabbalah of the British occult revival. Mathers' addiction to ritual magic mirrors the ritual practices of the Kabbalistic circle that produced the *Sefer ha-Meshiv*; Waite's magico-mystical path reflects the sexual mysticism of the *Zohar* and the magico-mystical soul-journey of the Hasidic *Tanya*; Crowley's sexual 'magick' echoes the holiness of sin promulgated by Sabbatai Zevi and his followers. And Fortune's psychologised Kabbalah, the most modern 'occultist' Kabbalah in terms of its date, might be viewed as the least modern of all in its seamless synthesis of magic, mysticism, science, theosophy, and eroticism, and its interiorisation of a godhead recognisable under a multiplicity of names.

No empiric evidence has yet been found of a primal revealed Kabbalistic 'ur-religion' passed down from initiate to initiate through the ages. Nor can such a perennialist vision be validated in historical research by the occultists' claim that no evidence *can* be found because the revelation has been kept deliberately secret. But there is ample textual evidence of the continuity of Jewish esoteric traditions, and the magic of the 'practical' Kabbalah has a long textual history beginning with the Torah and the Talmud and gathering shape in the apocalyptic and *heikhalot* literature of late antiquity. The precise sources of this magical tradition may never be fully untangled. Recognition of the mutual influences between Jewish, Gnostic, Platonic, Pythagorean, and Greco-Egyptian currents was already demonstrated by Jewish academics in the mid-nineteenth century, and by the time Jewish magic emerged full-blown in the *Sefer ha-Razim* and the *Harba de Moshe*, its syncretic aspects, although expressed within a specifically Jewish framework, make it impossible to discern who borrowed what from whom and when. But the Jewish magical-mystical-theosophical tradition – in company with the other two 'occult sciences' of late antiquity, astrology and alchemy – is not a perennialist fantasy, but is supported by the concrete reality of written documents. Jewish esoteric lore in the British occult revival, which the practitioners themselves understood as 'Kabbalah', is not an invented tradition, but a vigorous complex of ideas that still enjoys a continuing life in the contemporary world. Although the ideas are expressed differently according to the vicissitudes of history and the various cultures in which the Jews of the diaspora have found themselves, the fundamental components – an unknown transcendent divinity whose immanent creative potency can be discovered in Nature, language, and the patterns of history; an interconnected cosmos peopled with intermediaries between human and divine; a pluralistic yet single godhead discernible within the human soul and body as well as in the world; and the capacity of the human will to engage with, and even transform, deity as well as the world – have remained consistent in both Jewish esoteric lore and the British occult revival. That all these components fulfil Faivre's definitions of 'Western esotericism' merely emphasises my conclusion that arbitrarily locating the origins of Western esotericism in the non-Jewish currents of the Renaissance and early modern period may reflect a highly questionable scholarly agenda.

Relatively few medieval and early modern Jewish Kabbalistic texts have been published to date, and even fewer have been translated into modern languages; and the same applies to Jewish magical literature, as only a small proportion of the texts of the Cairo Genizah has been edited and published,[51] in addition to the *Sefer ha-Razim*, the *Harbe de Moshe*, and the *Sefer ha-Raziel*. Kabbalistic manuscripts are constantly being unearthed in obscure libraries and private collections throughout Eastern Europe and Russia. While many of these documents do little more than reiterate the continuity of central concepts such as the ten *sefirot* and the potency of the Divine Names, they are all highly individual in their interpretations. Some, like the diary of Hillel Ba'al Shem and the private recipe-book of spells and amulets compiled by an obscure late eighteenth-century Italian Ashkenazi Jew called Signor Tranquillo,[52] reveal 'vernacular' aspects of the Kabbalah and its applications that challenge many of the assumptions of modern scholarship about the 'elite' nature of this lore. Kabbalistic scholarship has changed dramatically since Gershom Scholem's time, and the importance of magic in the Kabbalah is no longer as attenuated as it once was. As there is little, apart from language, in the conceptual structures of the Kabbalah of

---

[51] For a recent discussion of the state of research into the texts of the Cairo Genizah, see Gideon Bohak, 'The Magical Rotuli from the Cairo Genizah', in Bohak, Harari, and Shaked (eds.), *Continuity and Innovation in the Magical Tradition*, 321–40, and references on p. 321 n. 1 and 2.

[52] For this magical recipe-book, see Mark Verman, 'Signor Tranquillo's Magic Notebook', in Joseph Dan and Klaus Hermann (eds.), *Studies in Jewish Manuscripts* (Tübingen: Mohr Siebeck, 1998), 231–37.

British occultism that cannot be found in the Jewish esoteric literature developed over two millennia, it may be entirely inappropriate to view 'occultist' Kabbalah as anything other than the continuation of a stable tradition that, paradoxically, embraces at its core the practice of creative innovation.

The two academic communities most concerned with the study of the Kabbalah – Jewish Kabbalistic scholarship, focused primarily within Israeli and American universities, and the new academic discipline of the history of Western esotericism, focused primarily within the universities of northern Europe – have generated an immensely valuable body of work in recent years. Although the ongoing venture of Jewish Kabbalistic scholars has become increasingly sophisticated with each passing decade as academic paradigms change and connections are made between different disciplines and different expressions of Jewish culture, the unwillingness of many of these scholars to consider that the Kabbalah of the occult revival might merit being explored as a legitimate form of Jewish Kabbalah has helped to generate an unfortunate chasm which bars the inclusion of their exceptional expertise from research into non-Jewish spheres of Western culture such as Victorian, Edwardian, and inter-war occultism. Scholars of Western esotericism, in turn, have recognised the central importance of Kabbalistic doctrines within Western esoteric currents, but their determined reluctance to acknowledge that these doctrines have been and may still be considered Jewish, and that they may represent something far older and more resilient than a newly invented 'programmatic syncretism', has made the chasm even wider, making any real understanding of the Kabbalah of the occult revival difficult to achieve.

The various factors that may have contributed to the perpetuation of this chasm – the sensitive issue of religious identity, the long history of antisemitism within as well as outside academic circles, and the territorial tendencies and lack of reflexivity that can afflict academics as frequently as they do any other sort of animal – are entirely understandable, and some of these factors might even merit considerable sympathy. But a deeper and more prolonged investigation into the Kabbalah of the occult revival is an important dimension of research into the history of British religious currents in the modern world – an investigation that deserves a broader scope than the limitations of those

Procrustean beds built on an intractable insistence on one 'true' methodology or one 'true' Kabbalah. This book, based on evidence provided by both the practitioners of the British occult revival and Jewish Kabbalists across the centuries, is an attempt to build a small footbridge across the chasm.

GLOSSARY OF SOME HEBREW TERMS USED IN THIS BOOK

Adam Kadmon: 'primal earth', the scheme and substance of creation comprised of the ten *sefirot* and also the prototype of the human being. The organs and limbs of Adam Kadmon are the internal organs and limbs of the godhead, each of which, in the Lurianic Kabbalah, contains groups of incarnating souls with special attributes and functions as well as specific kingdoms of Nature. Adam Kadmon is thus simultaneously the anthropomorphised image of the godhead, the archetype of earthly creation, and the prototype of the inner and outer form of the human being.

ba'al shem: a 'Master of the Name', an individual who is knowledgeable in the magical use of the Divine and angelic Names to perform extraordinary acts, healings, blessings, and exorcisms.

berashit: 'in the beginning', used as the opening phrase of Genesis; also transliterated as *bereshit* or *be-reshit*. Crowley used the term as the title of a privately published work.

Binah: 'understanding', the third *sefira* to emerge from the unknown transcendent godhead, usually represented as feminine and often associated with the symbolism of the mother of the messiah as well as the 'lower' *sefirot*.

devekut: 'cleaving', a direct experience of deity. This may be represented in Jewish esoteric literature as a vision of God, a sense of closeness, encounter, or dialogue with divinity, or a full *unio mystica*.

dybbuk: a disincarnate entity with malefic propensities, either a disembodied human soul or a demonic being with an inclination to possess the body of a living human.

En Soph: the unknown transcendent deity beyond any human capacity to understand or articulate. The emanated cosmos, beginning with the primal light and the ten *sefirot*, emerges from the primordial oneness/nothingness of *En Soph*.

galut: exile, used in reference to the *galut ha-Shekhinah*, the 'exile of the *Shekhinah*' which represents the fracturing of the godhead and the dissociation of human beings from their source in divinity. *Galut* also refers to the historical exile of the Jews from their homeland.

Geburah: 'severity' or 'stern judgement', the fifth *sefira* to emerge from the unknown transcendent godhead, usually represented as feminine and associated with both necessary restrictions and, if unchecked by the balancing power of compassion (*Hesed*), with violence and destructiveness.

genizah: a secret cache or hiding-place for sacred documents, usually found in a synagogue.

gilgul (plural, *gilgulim*): literally 'rolling over' or 'revolution', used to describe the transmigration of the human soul from incarnation to incarnation.

Hasidei Ashkenaz: 'German Pietists', referring to a group of religious devotees living in the area of the Rhineland and northern France during the eleventh and twelfth centuries who produced a distinctive corpus of proto-Kabbalistic literature concerned with mystical speculations and magical formulae. The *Hasidei Ashkenaz* are seen as the predecessors of the modern eastern European Hasidim ('Pious Ones'), as their literature and doctrines moved north into Poland, Lithuania, and Russia as well as into Italy and Spain, where they influenced the early Kabbalah.

heikhalot (sing. *heikhal*): 'palaces', referring to the divine palaces in the seven heavens, the ultimate of which contains the divine Throne. The late antique corpus of literature referred to as *heikhalot* comprises many treatises describing the ascent of the soul to the vision of God on his Throne.

Hesed: 'mercy' or 'compassion', the fourth *sefira* to emerge from the unknown transcendent godhead, usually represented as masculine and associated with the qualities of mercy which, unless balanced and contained by judgement (*Geburah*), lead to indulgence, passivity, and chaos.

Hod: 'splendour', the eighth *sefira* to emerge from the unknown transcendent godhead, usually perceived as feminine and associated with the practical expression of *Geburah* in the world: justice imposed on society and individuals which is motivated by firmness but also tempered by mercy.

Hokhmah: 'wisdom', the second *sefira* to emerge from the unknown transcendent godhead, associated with gnosis and a direct understanding of the nature of divinity and the scheme of creation. *Hokhmah* is also used as a term to describe a form of knowledge or hermeneutics that was originally divinely revealed, such as *hokhmah ha-tseruf*, the 'wisdom of combination'.

ibbur: 'impregnation', referring to a higher soul or an angelic or demonic being who inhabits a living individual's body simultaneously with the person's own soul.

kavvanah: meditation with intent; a focused form of prayer which can involve visualisation, silent recitation of the Divine Names, and other formulae intended to facilitate a *unio mystica* or a direct prophetic revelation.

Keter: 'crown', the first of the ten *sefirot* to emerge from the unknown transcendent deity, representing the first differentiated emanation of the deity from which all the other *sefirot* come forth.

ma'aseh: a folk-tale, usually used to describe the homiletic stories emerging as a distinctive genre among the *Hasidei Ashkenaz* during the Middle Ages.

maggid (plural *maggidim*): a disincarnate sage or angelic mentor who communicates through dreams, visions, scrying, or automatic writing.

malakh (plural *malakhim*): an angel. Agrippa, in *Occult Philosophy*, 3.30, uses the term *malachim* to describe one of his 'angelic' alphabets; see Chapter Four, Fig. 12.

mazik: a demon, usually represented as mischievous, clever, and ingenious rather than purely evil.

merkabah: 'chariot', referring in Jewish esoteric literature to the chariot-throne found in the seventh heaven, which is the seat of deity. The *heikhalot* mystics of late antiquity are sometimes described as '*merkabah* mystics'.

Nezach: 'victory', the seventh *sefira* to emerge from the unknown transcendent godhead, usually perceived as masculine and associated with the practical expression of *Hesed* in the world: fortitude, patience, and leadership tempered with mercy but also disciplined by judgement.

'or kadmon: 'primal light', the first substance to stream from the unknown transcendent godhead, out of which both the Hebrew letters and the ten *sefirot* are formed.

qlipot (always plural): the 'shells' or detritus of the lower realms, generated through the process of creation, and viewed as demonic because they partake of the blind destructiveness and stasis of *Geburah* without the tempering of *Hesed*.

sar (plural, *sarim*): a prince or captain, used as a title for both angels and demonic entities who command groups or cohorts of supernal or demonic powers. Examples are the *Sar ha-Panim* ('Prince of the Presence'), the *Sar ha-Torah* ('Prince of the Torah'), and the *Sar ha-Halom* ('Prince of the Dream').

sefira (plural *sefirot*): one of the ten Kabbalistic emanations or aspects of deity, from which the entire cosmos has emerged and through which it is sustained. The sefirotic Tree is an image of the internal structure and dynamics of both the godhead and creation.

Shekhinah: the feminine aspect of the godhead, sometimes represented as God's presence, at other times his spouse; often equated with Nature, the manifest world, and either the third of the ten *sefirot*, *Binah*, or the last *sefira*, *Malkuth*.

Shem ha-Mephorasch: the 72-letter Divine Name (also sometimes referred to as the 72 names of God), each letter having the value of a name in itself. This Divine Name has been part of the Jewish magical tradition since late antiquity and may have origins in the decan system of Egyptian astrology, which divided each of the twelve constellations into three sections of $10°$ and associated each of these sections with an astral daimon. Invoking the *Shem ha-Mephorasch* is, in effect, invoking the entire array of the powers of the godhead embodied in the heavens.

Shem Kaf Bet: the 22-letter Divine Name, each letter being associated with an angel and an attribute of divinity embodied in that letter.

Talmud ('instruction', 'learning'): the seminal text of rabbinic discussions pertaining to Jewish law, ethics, customs, and history. The Talmud comprises two parts, the *Mishnah* (*c.* 200 CE), the first written redaction of ancient Jewish oral traditions, and the *Gemara* (*c.* 500 CE), a series of rabbinic commentaries on the *Mishnah*. Two versions of the Talmud exist: the Jerusalem Talmud or *Talmud Yerushalmi*, written in Aramaic and compiled in the 4th c. CE, and the Babylonian Talmud or *Talmud Bavli*, written in both Aramaic and Hebrew and compiled *c.* 500 CE. The latter is the text usually referred to as 'Talmud'.

tefillin: phylacteries or ritual objects, a set of small cubic black leather boxes containing passages from the Torah and worn during weekday morning prayers. They are placed on the forehead and wrapped around the arm with leather straps, and are meant to provide both protection and a constant reminder of the Exodus from Egypt.

Tiferet: 'Beauty', the sixth *sefira* to emerge from the unknown transcendent godhead, and the first *sefira* placed centrally on the 'pillar of equilibrium' of the sefirotic Tree. Tiferet is usually represented as masculine, and is seen as both the bridegroom of Malkuth, the last *sefira*, and the point of integration between the two polarised *sefirot* of Geburah ('stern judgement') and Hesed ('compassion'). Tiferet is also seen as the 'child' of the 'higher' *sefirot* Hokmah ('wisdom') and Binah ('understanding'), and is therefore the supernal prototype of the messiah; this *sefira* was therefore associated by Christian Kabbalists with Christ.

tikkun (plural *tikkunim*): restitution or reintegration, referring to the restoration of cosmic harmony; it can also refer to a specific practice intended to precipitate a personal experience of restitution, i.e. a *unio mystica*. The verb *tkn* appears in the late Biblical text *Kohelet* (*Ecclesiastes*), meaning 'to straighten' or 'to repair'. It is also used to emphasise the central role of the human being in repairing spiritual damage, rectifying sin, and completing God's work of creation.

Yesod: 'foundation', the ninth *sefira* to emerge from the unknown transcendent deity, usually represented as masculine and associated with distinctly phallic imagery. Yesod is the phallic potency which channels the power of the other *sefirot* into Malkuth and fertilises this last, feminine *sefira* to bring forth material manifestation.

zaddik (plural *zaddikim*): a sage or holy man, used in modern Hasidism to describe a religious leader with miraculous powers.

BIBLIOGRAPHY

PRIMARY SOURCES:

Abelson, Joshua, 'The Talmud and Theosophy', *Theosophical Review*, 37:1 (1905), 9–27
———, 'Maimonides on the Jewish Creed', *Jewish Quarterly Review*, 19:1 (1906), 24–58
———, *The Immanence of God in Rabbinical Literature* (London: Macmillan, 1912; repr. New York: Hermon Press, 1969)
———, *Jewish Mysticism: An Introduction to the Kabbalah* (London: G. Bell & Sons, 1913; repr. Mineola, NY: Dover Publications, 2001)
———, 'Occult Thought in Jewish Literature', *Jewish Chronicle Supplement* (28 January 1921), v–vi
———, 'A Garment of Divers Sorts', *Jewish Chronicle Supplement* (25 August 1922), v–vi
———, 'Review of Israel Regardie, *The Tree of Life: A Study in Magic'*, *Jewish Chronicle* (12 May 1933), 21
———, 'Jewish Magic', in *The Friday Night Book: A Jewish Miscellany* (London: Soncino Press, 1933), 45–69
———, 'Introduction', in Harry Sperling and Maurice Simon (trans.), *The Zohar*, 5 volumes (New York/London: Soncino Press, 1934), 1:ix–xxx
———, 'Review of Dion Fortune, *The Mystical Qabalah'*, *Jewish Chronicle* (24 May 1935), 26
Allen, P. M. (ed.), *A Christian Rosenkreutz Anthology* (Blauvelt, NY: Rudolf Steiner Publications, 1968)
'A Man We'd Like to Hang', *John Bull* (19 May 1923)
Anz, Wilhelm, *Zur Frage nach dem Ursprung des Gnostizismus: Ein Religionsgeschichtlicher Versuch* (Leipzig: A. Preis, 1897)
Ashmole, Elias, *Theatrum Chemicum Britannicum. Containing Severall Poetical Pieces of our Famous English Philosophers, who have written the Hermetique Mysteries in their owne Ancient Language. Faithfully Collected into one Volume, with Annotations thereon, by Elias Ashmole, Esq. Qui est Mercuriophilus Anglicus* (London: Nathaniel Brook, 1652)
Atwood, Mary Anne South, *A Suggestive Inquiry into 'The Hermetic Mystery', with a Dissertation on the More Celebrated Alchemical Philosophers* (London: Trelawney Saunders, 1850; repr. New York: Julian Press, 1960)
'A Wizard of Wickedness', *John Bull* (17 March 1923)
Banister, Joseph, *England under the Jews* (London: private publication, 1901; repr. Boston, MA: Adamant Media Corporation, 2001)
Barrett, Francis, *The Magus, or Celestial Intelligencer; Being a Complete System of Occult Philosophy* (London: Lackington, Allen & Co., 1801; repr. York Beach, ME: WeiserBooks, 2000)
Ben Nathan, Keleph [Marc Philippe Dutoit-Mambrini], *La philosophie divine, appliquée aux lumières naturelle, magique, astrale, surnaturelle, céleste et divine* (Lyon: self-published, 1793)
Besant, Annie, *Man and His Bodies* (Los Angeles, CA: Theosophical Publishing House, 1914)
———, *Theosophy and the New Psychology* (London/Benares: Theosophical Publishing Society, 1904)
———, 'Lord Lytton: A Great Occultist', *Theosophical Review*, 44 (February 1923), 448.
Besterman, Theodore, *Crystal-Gazing* (London: Rider & Co., 1924)

Blackwood, Algernon, 'Smith: An Episode in a Lodging-House', in Algernon
Blackwood, *The Empty House and Other Ghost Stories* (London: Evelyn
Nash, 1906; repr. in Algernon Blackwood, *Ancient Sorceries and Other
Weird Stories*, ed. S. T. Joshi, London: Penguin, 2002), 1–16

———, 'The Nemesis of Fire', in Algernon Blackwood, *John Silence, Physician
Extraordinary* (London: Evelyn Nash, 1908); repr. in *The Complete John
Silence Stories*, ed. S. T. Joshi (Mineola, NY: Dover, 1997), 84–143

———, *John Silence, Physician Extraordinary* (London: Evelyn Nash, 1908);
repr. in *The Complete John Silence Stories*, ed. S. T. Joshi (Mineola, NY:
Dover, 1997)

———, *The Human Chord* (London: Macmillan & Co., 1910; repr. Rockville,
MD: Wildside Press, 2005)

———, *Best Ghost Stories of Algernon Blackwood*, ed. E. F. Bleiler (New York:
Dover Publications, 1973)

———, *The Lost Valley and The Wolves of God*, ed. Simon Clark (Eureka, CA:
Stark House Press, 2003)

Blavatsky, H. P., *Isis Unveiled*, 2 volumes (London: Theosophical Publishing
Company, 1875)

———, 'Madame Blavatsky on Indian Metaphysics', *The Spiritualist* (22
March 1878), 140–41

———, 'A Posthumous Publication', *Theosophist*, 2:10 (1881), 211–12

———, 'Notice', *Theosophist*, 3:1 (1881), 1

———, 'Stray Thoughts on Death and Satan', *Theosophist*, 3:1 (1881), 12

———, 'Western "Adepts" and Eastern Theosophists', *Theosophist*, 3:2 (1881),
4–6

———,, 'Mr. Joseph Wallace', *Theosophist*, 4:2 (1882), 6–7, repr. in Blavatsky,
CW4, 44–48

———, 'Editorial', *Theosophist*, 4:2 (1882), 43

———, 'The Signs of the Times', *Lucifer*, 1:2 (1887), 83–89

———, 'Thoughts on the Elementals', *Lucifer*, 6:33 (1890), 177–88, repr. in
Blavatsky, CW12, 187–205

———, 'My Books', *Lucifer*, 8:45 (1891), repr. in Blavatsky, CW13, 191–202

———, *The Secret Doctrine: The Synthesis of Science, Religion, and Philosophy*, 2
volumes (London: Theosophical Publishing Company, 1888)

———, 'Astral Bodies, or Doppelgängers', *Lucifer*, 3:16 (1888), 328–33 repr. in
Blavatsky, CW10, 217–26

———, 'Elementals', *Lucifer*, 12:72 (1893), 537–48; *Lucifer*, 13:73–74 (1893), 30–
39, 111–21; repr. in Blavatsky, CW6, 184–201

———, *Kabala and Kabalism* (Los Angeles, CA: Theosophy Company, 1912)

———, CW3: *Collected Writings, Vol. III, 1881* (Wheaton, IL: Theosophical
Publishing House, 1985)

———, CW4: *Collected Writings, Vol. IV, 1882–1883* (Wheaton, IL:
Theosophical Publishing House, 1985)

———, CW6: *Collected Writings, Vol. VI, 1883–1884–1885* (Wheaton, IL:
Theosophical Publishing House, 1977)

———, CW10: *Collected Writings, Vol. X, 1888–1889* (Wheaton, IL:
Theosophical Publishing House, 1985)

———, CW12: *Collected Writings, Vol. XII, 1889–1990* (Wheaton, IL:
Theosophical Publishing House, 1985)

———, CW13: *Collected Writings, Vol. XIII, 1890–1891* (Wheaton, IL:
Theosophical Publishing House, 1985)

———, CW14: *Collected Writings, Vol. XIV, Miscellaneous* (Wheaton, IL:
Theosophical Publishing House, 1985)

———, *Studies in Occultism* (Pasadena, CA: Theosophical University Press,
1998).

Bosman, L. A., *The Mysteries of the Qabalah* (London: Dharma Press, 1913; repr. Kila, MT: Kessinger Publishing, 2003)

Bousset, Wilhelm, 'Die Himmelreise der Seele', *Archiv für Religionswissenschaft*, 4 (1901), 136–69, 229–73

Braid, James, *Satanic Agency and Mesmerism* (Manchester: Sims and Dinham, Galt and Anderson, 1842)

———, *Magic, Witchcraft, Animal Magnetism, Hypnotism, and Electrobiology* (London: John Churchill, 1852)

Brodie-Innes, J. W., *The Devil's Mistress* (London: William Rider & Son, 1915)

———, 'The Tarot Cards', *Occult Review*, 29:2 (1919), 90–98

———, 'MacGregor Mathers, some personal reminiscences', *Occult Review*, 29:5 (1919), 284–86

———, 'Essay on Clairvoyance and Travelling in the Spirit Vision', Flying Roll XXV, in Francis King (ed.), *Astral Projection, Ritual Magic, and Alchemy: Golden Dawn Material by S. L. MacGregor Mathers and Others* (Rochester, VT: Destiny Books, 1987), 85–89

———, 'Knowledge Lectures', in J. W. Brodie-Innes *et al.*, *The Astrology of the Golden Dawn*, ed. Darcy Küntz (Sequim, WA: Holmes Publishing Group, 1996), 7–24

Brodie-Innes, J. W. *et al.*, *The Astrology of the Golden Dawn*, ed. Darcy Küntz (Sequim, WA: Holmes Publishing Group, 1996)

Bullock, Percy ['L. O.'], 'Introduction', in William Wynn Westcott, (ed.), *Collectanea Hermetica*, 9 volumes (London: Theosophical Publishing Society, 1893–96), 6:7–22

Bulwer-Lytton, Edward, *Zanoni* (London: Saunders & Otley, 1842)

———, *A Strange Story: An Alchemical Novel* (London: George Routledge & Sons, 1861)

———, *The Coming Race* (London: William Blackwood & Sons, 1871)

Campbell, John McLeod, *The Nature of Atonement and Its Relation to Remission of Sins and Eternal Life* (Cambridge: Macmillan & Co., 1856)

Carpenter, Edward, *The Intermediate Sex* (London: Swan Sonnenschien & Co., 1908)

Carpenter, William, *The Israelites Found in the Anglo-Saxons. The Ten Tribes Supposed to Have Been Lost, Traced From the Land of Their Captivity to Their Occupation of the Isles of the Sea: With An Exhibition of Those Traits of Character and National Characteristics Assigned to Israel in the Books of the Hebrew Prophets* (London: George Kenning, 1873)

Casaubon, Meric, *A True & Faithful Relation of What passed For Many Yeers Between Dr. John Dee and Some Spirits,* British Museum MSS Cotton Appendix XLVI (London: T. Garthwait, 1659; repr. Berkeley, CA: Golem Media, 2008)

Caubet, Charles, *Souvenirs 1860–1889* (Paris: Cerf, 1893)

Chacornac, Paul, *Éliphas Lévi: Rénovateur de l'occultisme en France (1810–1875)* (Paris: Chacornac Frères, 1926)

Clymer, R. Swynburne, *Dr. Paschal Beverly Randolph and the Supreme Grand Dome of the Rosicrucians in France* (Quakertown, PA: Philosophical Publishing, 1929)

———, *The Book of Rosicruciae*, 3 volumes (Quakertown, PA: Philosophical Publishing, 1946)

———, *Higher Race Development: A Course of Instructions on the Right Use of Sex* (Quakertown, PA: Philosophical Publishing, 1950)

———, *The Rosy Cross, Its Teachings* (Quakertown, PA: Beverly Hall Corporation, 1965)

Coleman, William Emmette, 'The Sources of Madame Blavatsky's Writings', in Vsevolod Sergyeevich Solovyoff, *A Modern Priestess of Isis* (London: Longmans, Green & Co., 1895), 353–66

Coleridge, Samuel Taylor, *The Complete Works of Samuel Taylor Coleridge, With an Introductory Essay Upon his Philosophical and Theological Opinions*, 7 volumes, ed. W. G. T. Shedd (New York: Harper & Brothers, 1884)

Constant, Alphonse-Louis [Éliphas Lévi], *L'Assomption de la femme* (Paris: Le Gallois, 1841)

——, *La Mère de Dieu, épopée religieuse et humanitaire* (Paris: Charles Gosselin, 1844)

——, *Les trois harmonies: chansons et poésies* (Paris: Fellens et Dufour, 1845)

——, *Le livre des larmes ou le Christ consolateur: essai de conciliation entre l'église catholique et la philosophie moderne* (Paris: Paulier, 1845)

——, *Le deuil de Pologne: protestations de la démocratie française et du socialisme universel* (Paris: Le Gallois, 1847)

Cook, Arthur B., *Zeus: A Study in Ancient Religion*, 3 volumes (Cambridge: Cambridge University Press, 1914–1925)

Cornford, Francis M., *From Religion to Philosophy: A Study in the Origins of Western Speculation* (Cambridge: Cambridge University Press, 1912)

Court de Gébelin, Antoine, *Monde primitif, analysé et comparé avec le monde moderne, considéré dans divers objets concernant l'histoire, le blason, les monnaies, les jeux, les voyages des phéniciens autour du monde, les langues américaines, etc.*, 9 vols (Paris: M. Robinet, 1772–83)

——, *Le Tarot, présenté et commenté par Jean-Marie Lhôte* (Vol. 8 of Court de Gébelin, *Monde primitif*, ed. Jean-Marie Lhôte) (Paris: Berg International, 1983)

Crowe, Catherine, *The Night Side of Nature, Or: Ghosts and Ghost Seers*, 2 volumes (London: T. C. Newby, 1848)

Crowley, Aleister, *Aceldama, A Place to Bury Strangers in. A Philosophical Poem. By a Gentleman of the University of Cambridge* (London: Mandrake Press, 1898)

——, *White Stains* (Amsterdam: Leonard Smithers, 1898)

——, 'The Initiated Interpretations of Ceremonial Magic', in S. L. MacGregor Mathers (trans.), *The Goetia: The Lesser Key of Solomon the King* (London: private publication, 1904), 15–20

——, בראשת [*Berashit*]: *An Essay in Ontology, by Abhavananda* (Paris: private publication, 1907; Yorke Collection FBH 929 B26 C.1, Warburg Institute, London)

——, 'The Herb Dangerous', *Equinox*, 1:2 (1909), 31–89

——, 'Review of A E. Waite, *A Book of Mystery and Vision*', *Equinox*, 1:3 (1910), 113

——, 'The Temple of Solomon the King', *Equinox*, 1:5 (1911), 65–120

——, "My Crapulous Contemporaries: Wisdom While You Waite': Review of A. E. Waite, *The Book of Ceremonial Magic*', *Equinox*, 1:5 (1911), 133–41

——, *The Book of the Law (technically called Liber AL vel Legis Sub Figura CCXX, As Delivered by XCIII = 418 to DCLXVI)*, *The Equinox*, 1:7 (1912) (repr. London: OTO, 1921)

——, *777 and Other Qabalistic Writings of Aleister Crowley*, ed. Israel Regardie (London: Ordo Templi Orientis, 1912; repr. York Beach, ME: Samuel Weiser, 1973)

——, 'The Jewish Problem Restated, by a Gentile', *English Review* (July 1922), 28–37

——, *Moonchild* (London: Mandrake Press, 1929; repr. New York: Samuel Weiser, 1970)

——, *Magick in Theory and Practice* (Paris: Lecram Press, 1929; repr. Secaucus, NJ: Castle Books, 1991)

————, *The Confessions of Aleister Crowley: An Autohagiography*, eds. John Symonds and Kenneth Grant (Paris: Mandrake Press, 1929; repr. New York: Bantam, 1971)

————, *The Book of Thoth by the Master Therion* (London, self-published, 1944; repr. New York: Samuel Weiser, 1969)

————, *Magick Without Tears*, ed. Karl J. Germer (New York: Ordo Templi Orientis, 1954), reissued by Bill Heidrick for the OTO (1988), <http://danbartlett.co.uk/AC_MWT.pdf>

————, *De Arte Magica: Secundum ritum Gradus Nonae O.T.O.*, XVI, private publication, repr. in Francis King (ed.), *Crowley on Christ* (London: C. W. Daniel, 1974), 213–32

————, *The Revival of Magick and Other Essays* (Las Vegas: Falcon/O.T.O., 1998)

Cuthbert, Arthur A., *The Life and World-Work of Thomas Lake Harris* (Glasgow: private publication, 1908)

Daiches, Samuel, *Babylonian Oil Magic in the Talmud and in the Later Jewish Literature* (London: Oxford University Press/Jews' College, 1913)

Dee, John, *A True & Faithful Relation of what passed for many Yeers Between Dr John Dee...and Some Spirits*, ed. Meric Casaubon (London: 1659; repr. London: Askin Publishers, 1974)

De Montfaucon de Villars, Abbé Nicolas-Pierre-Henri, *Le Comte de Gabalis, ou Entretiens sur les Science Secrètes* (Paris: Claude Barbin, 1670)

De Pauly, Jean (trans.), *Moses de Leon. Le livre du Zohar. Pages traduites du Chaldaïque par Jean de Pauly*, 6 volumes (Paris: Lafuma-Giraud, 1906–1911)

De Quincey, Thomas ['XYZ'], 'Historico-Critical Inquiry Into the Origin of the Rosicrucians and the Free-Masons', *London Magazine* (January/February/March 1824), 5–13, 140–51, 256–61

Dobson, Roger, Godfrey Brangham, and R. A. Gilbert (eds.), *Arthur Machen: Selected Letters: The Private Writings of the Master of the Macabre* (Wellingborough: Aquarian Press, 1988)

Dunning, Edward (ed.), *A. E. Waite: Selected Masonic Papers* (Wellingborough: Aquarian Press, 1988)

————, 'Foreword', in E. J. Langford Garstin, *Theurgy, or the Hermetic Practice: A Treatise on Spiritual Alchemy* (London: Rider, 1930; repr. York Beach, ME: Nicolas-Hays, 2004), v–xvi

'E. J.', 'Review of W. H. B. Stoddart, *Mind and Its Disorders*', *International Journal of Psychoanalysis*, 3 (1922), 84

Eliot, T. S., 'The Waste Land', in *The Complete Poems and Plays of T. S. Eliot* (London: Faber & Faber, 1978), 59–75

————, *The Complete Poems and Plays of T. S. Eliot* (London: Faber & Faber, 1978)

Ellis, Havelock and John Addington Symonds, *Sexual Inversion* (London: Wilson & Macmillan, 1897)

Ellis, Havelock, *Studies in the Psychology of Sex*, 8 volumes (Philadelphia, PA: F. A. Davis, 1910)

Erdan, Alexander, *La France mystique*, 2 volumes (Amsterdam: R. C. Meyer, 1858)

Etteilla, *L'astrologie du Livre de Thot (1785), suivie de Recherches sur l'histoire de l'astrologie et du Tarot par Jacques Halbronn* (Paris: Guy Trédaniel, 1993)

Fabre d'Olivet, Antoine, *Lettres à Sophie sur l'histoire*, 2 volumes (Paris: Lavillette et Cie, 1801)

————, *La langue hébraïque réstituté* (Paris: private publication, 1815)

Farr, Florence, *The Dancing Faun* (London: Matthews and Lane, 1894)

Findlay, Arthur, *On the Edge of the Etheric* (London: Psychic Press, 1931)

Firth, Violet M. [Dion Fortune], *The Machinery of the Mind* (London: George Allen & Unwin, 1922)

Flamel, Hortensius, *Le livre rouge. Resumé du magisme, des sciences occultes et de la philosophie hermétique d'après Hermes Trismegiste, Pytagore, Cléopatre, Artephins, Marie-l'Egyptienne, Albert-le-Grand, Paracelse, Cornelius Agrippa, Cardan, Mesmer, Charles Fourrier, etc.* (Paris: Lavigne, 1841)

Fortune, Dion, *The Esoteric Philosophy of Love and Marriage* (London: Rider, 1923)

——, 'The Man Who Sought', in Dion Fortune, *The Secrets of Dr. Taverner* (London: Noel Douglas, 1926; repr. Ashcroft, BC: Ash-Tree Press, 2000), 29–38

——, 'The Soul That Would Not Be Born', in Dion Fortune, *The Secrets of Dr. Taverner* (London: Noel Douglas, 1926; repr. Ashcroft, BC: Ash-Tree Press, 2000), 39–47

——, 'A Daughter of Pan', in Dion Fortune, *The Secrets of Dr. Taverner* (London: Noel Douglas, 1926; repr. Ashcroft, BC: Ash-Tree Press, 2000), 75–91

——, 'A Son of the Night', in Dion Fortune, *The Secrets of Dr. Taverner* (London: Noel Douglas, 1926; repr. Ashcroft, BC: Ash-Tree Press, 2000), 145–62

——, *The Secrets of Dr. Taverner* (London: Noel Douglas, 1926; repr. Ashcroft, BC: Ash-Tree Press, 2000)

——, *The Demon Lover* (London: Douglas, 1927)

——, *The Esoteric Orders and Their Work* (London: Rider & Co., 1928)

——, *Sane Occultism* (London: Rider & Co., 1929)

——, 'The Literature of Illuminism', *Inner Light Magazine* (July 1929–September 1930), repr. in Dion Fortune and Gareth Knight, *Practical Occultism* (Loughborough: Thoth Publications, 2002), 140–74

——, *Mystical Meditations on the Collects* (London: Rider, 1930)

——, *Psychic Self-Defence* (London: Rider & Co., 1931)

——, 'Ceremonial Magic Unveiled', *Occult Review*, 57:1 (1933), 13–24

——, *Avalon of the Heart* (London: Muller, 1934)

——, *The Mystical Qabalah* (London: Ernest Benn, 1935)

——, *The Winged Bull* (London: Norgate, 1935)

——, *The Goat-Foot God* (London: Norgate, 1936)

——, 'The Paths Upon the Tree', *Inner Light Magazine*, 9:11; 9:12; 10:1 (1936), available at the Societas Rosicruciana in America, <http://www.sria.org/paths_tree.htm>

——, *The Sea Priestess* (London: Inner Light, 1938)

——, *The Cosmic Doctrine* (London: Inner Light, 1949; repr. York Beach, ME: WeiserBooks, 2000)

——, *Moon Magic* (Wellingborough: Aquarian Press, 1956)

——, *Aspects of Occultism* (Wellingborough: Aquarian Press, 1962)

——, *Applied Magic* and *Aspects of Occultism* (London: Thorsons/Society of the Inner Light, 1985)

——, 'Types of Mind Working', in Dion Fortune and Gareth Knight, *An Introduction to Ritual Magic* (Loughborough: Thoth Publications, 1997), 13–23

——, 'Mind Training', in Dion Fortune and Gareth Knight, *An Introduction to Ritual Magic* (Loughborough: Thoth Publications, 1997), 32–39

——, 'The Reality of the Subtle Planes', in Dion Fortune and Gareth Knight, *An Introduction to Ritual Magic* (Loughborough: Thoth Publications, 1997), 92–98

——, 'The Use of Ritual', in Dion Fortune and Gareth Knight, *An Introduction to Ritual Magic* (Loughborough: Thoth Publications, 1997), 48–53

——, 'Psychic Perception', in Dion Fortune and Gareth Knight, *An Introduction to Ritual Magic* (Loughborough: Thoth Publications, 1997), 62–69

——, 'Talismanic Magic', in Dion Fortune and Gareth Knight, *An Introduction to Ritual Magic* (Loughborough: Thoth Publications, 1997), 168–73

——, 'The Inhabitants of the Unseen', in Dion Fortune and Gareth Knight, *Spiritualism and Occultism* (Loughborough: Thoth Publications, 1999)

Fortune, Dion and Gareth Knight, *An Introduction to Ritual Magic* (Loughborough: Thoth Publications, 1997; originally published as separate articles by Dion Fortune in *The Inner Light Magazine*)

Fortune, Dion and Gareth Knight, *Spiritualism and Occultism* (Loughborough: Thoth Publications, 1999)

Fortune, Dion and Gareth Knight, *Practical Occultism* (Loughborough: Thoth Publications, 2002)

Franck, Adolphe, *La Kabbale, ou la philosophie religieuse des Hébreux* (Paris: Librairie de I. Hachette, 1843)

——, *Dictionnaire des sciences philosophiques* (Paris: Librairie de I. Hachette, 1855), available from Philo 19, Bibliographical Database of Nineteenth Century French Philosophy, <http://www.textesrares.com/philo19/franck.php>

——, *La philosophie mystique en France à la fin du XVIII-e siècle: Saint-Martin et son maître Martinez Pasqualis* (Paris: Germer Baillière, 1866; repr. Paris: Elibron Classics, 2005)

——, *The Kabbalah: The Religious Philosophy of the Hebrews*, trans. I. Sossnitz (New York: The Kabbalah Publishing Company, 1926)

Frater Achad [Charles Stansfield Jones], *Crystal Vision through Crystal Gazing, or The Crystal as a Stepping-Stone to Clear Vision* (Chicago: Yogi Publication Society, 1923)

——, *The Anatomy of the Body of God, Being the Supreme Revelation of Cosmic Consciousness* (Chicago: Collegium ad Spiritum Sanctum, 1925)

Frazer, James, *The Golden Bough: A Study in Comparative Religion*, 12 volumes (London: Macmillan, 1890–1915)

——, *Adonis, Attis, Osiris: Studies in the History of Oriental Religion*, 2 volumes (London: Macmillan, 1906)

Freehof, Solomon B., 'Review: Jewish Mystic Lore, *The Holy Kabbalah* by A. E. Waite', *Journal of Religion*, 10:2 (1930), 269–70

Fuller, J. C. F., *The Star in the West: A Critical Essay Upon the Works of Aleister Crowley* (New York: Walter Scott, 1907)

——, *The Secret Wisdom of the Qabalah: A Study in Jewish Mystical Thought* (London: Rider, 1937)

Gardner, Frederick Leigh, *Bibliotheca Rosicruciana: A Catalogue Raisonné of Works on the Occult Sciences, With an Introduction by William Wynn Westcott* (London: private publication, 1903)

——, *Bibliotheca Astrologica: A Catalogue Raisonné of Works on the Occult Sciences, Vol. II: Astrological Books, With a Sketch of the History of Astrology by Dr. William Wynn Westcott* (London: private publication, 1911; Yorke Collection FAI 25, Warburg Institute, London)

Garstin, E. J. Langford, *Theurgy, or the Hermetic Practice: A Treatise on Spiritual Alchemy* (London: Rider, 1930; repr. York Beach, ME: Nicolas-Hays, 2004)

Gaster, Moses, 'The Origin of the Kabbala', in Moses Gaster, *Judith "Montefiore" College Report for the Year, 1893–1894* (Ramsgate: The Judith "Montefiore" College, 1894), 15–28

——, *Judith "Montefiore" College Report for the Year, 1893–1894* (Ramsgate: The Judith "Montefiore" College, 1894)

—— (ed. and trans.), *Sword of Moses: An Ancient Book of Magic* (London: D. Nutt, 1896)

—— (ed. and trans.), 'The Wisdom of the Chaldeans: An Ancient Hebrew Astrological and Magical Treatise', *Proceedings of the Society of Biblical Archaeology* (20 December 1900), 329–51, repr. in Moses Gaster, *Studies and Texts in Folklore, Magic, Mediaeval Romance, Hebrew Apocrypha, and Samaritan Archaeology*, 3 volumes (London: Maggs Brothers, 1925–1928; repr. New York: Ktav Publishing, 1971), 1:338–55

——, 'The Logos Ebraikos in the Magical Papyrus of Paris, and the Book of Enoch', *Journal of the Royal Asiatic Society*, 33 (1901), 109–17, repr. in Moses Gaster, *Studies and Texts in Folklore, Magic, Mediaeval Romance, Hebrew Apocrypha, and Samaritan Archaeology*, 3 volumes (London: Maggs Brothers, 1925–1928; repr. New York: Ktav Publishing, 1971), 1:356–364

——, 'A Gnostic Text in the *Zohar*', paper given to the Quest Society (8 February 1923), repr. in Moses Gaster, *Studies and Texts in Folklore, Magic, Mediaeval Romance, Hebrew Apocrypha, and Samaritan Archaeology*, 3 volumes (London: Maggs Brothers, 1925–1928; repr. New York: Ktav Publishing, 1971), 1:369–86.

——, *Studies and Texts in Folklore, Magic, Mediaeval Romance, Hebrew Apocrypha, and Samaritan Archaeology*, 3 volumes (London: Maggs Brothers, 1925–1928; repr. New York: Ktav Publishing, 1971)

——, *Conjurations and the Ancient Mysteries*, Presidential Address to The Search Society 1931–32 (London: The Search Publishing Co., 1932)

—— (ed. and trans.), *Ma'aseh Book: Book of Jewish Tales and Legends Translated from the Judeo-German*, 2 volumes (Philadelphia, PA: Jewish Publication Society of America, 1934)

——, *The Gaster papers: a collection of letters, documents, etc. of the late Haham Dr. Moses Gaster (1856–1939), compiled by Trude Levi* (University College Library, London, 1976, MS 30217017796628)

Gaster, Theodore, 'Prolegomenon', in Moses Gaster, *Studies and Texts in Folklore, Magic, Mediaeval Romance, Hebrew Apocrypha, and Samaritan Archaeology*, 3 volumes (London: Maggs Brothers, 1925–1928; repr. New York: Ktav Publishing, 1971), 1:xv–xxxix

Gilbert, R. A. (ed.), *The Sorcerer and His Apprentice: Unknown Hermetic Writings of S. L. MacGregor Mathers and J. W. Brodie-Innes* (Wellingborough: Aquarian Press, 1983)

—— (ed.), *The Magical Mason: Forgotten Hermetic Writings of William Wynn Westcott, Physician and Magus* (Wellingborough: Aquarian Press, 1983)

—— (ed.), *Hermetic Papers of A. E. Waite: The Unknown Writings of a Modern Mystic* (Wellingborough: Aquarian Press, 1987)

Ginsburg, Christian D., *The Kabbalah: Its Doctrines, Development and Literature* (London: Longmans, Green & Co., 1863)

——, 'Kabbalah', *Encyclopedia Britannica* (1902), 15:620–23

——, *Letters and photographs of members of the Old Testament Revision Company*, c. 1870–85, Cambridge University Library: British and Foreign Bible Society's Library, GBR/0374/BSMS 651

Gollancz, Hermann, *Clavicula Salomonis: A Hebrew Manuscript* (London: D. Nutt, 1903)

Gougenot des Mousseaux, Henri-Roger, *La magie au dix-neuvième siècle. Ses agents, ses vérités, ses mensonges* (Paris: Dentu, 1860)

——, *Les Hauts phénomènes de la magie, précédés du spiritisme antique* (Paris: Plon, 1864)

——, *Le Juif, le judaïsme et le judaïsation des peuples chrétiens* (Paris: Plons, 1869)

Gould, Robert Freake, *A History of Freemasonry: Its Antiquities, Symbols, Constitutions, Customs, etc., Embracing an Investigation of the Records of the Fraternity in England, Scotland, Ireland, British Colonies, France, Germany and the United States; Derived from Official Sources*, 3 volumes (London: Caxton, 1884)

Greene, William B., *The Blazing Star; with an appendix treating of the Jewish Kabbala, also a tract on the Philosophy of Mr. Herbert Spencer and one on New England Transcendentalism* (Boston: A. Williams & Co., 1872)

Hamill, John (ed.), *The Rosicrucian Seer: Magical Writings of Frederick Hockley* (Wellingborough: Aquarian Press, 1986)

Harris, Thomas Lake, *A Lyric of the Morning Land* (New York: Partridge & Brittan, 1854)

——, *An Epic of the Starry Heaven* (New York: Partridge & Brittan, 1855)

——, *The Song of Theos. A Trilogy* (Glasgow: private publication, 1903)

Harrison, Jane, *Prolegomena to the Study of Greek Religion* (Cambridge: Cambridge University Press, 1903)

——, *Themis: A Study of the Social Origins of Greek Religion* (Cambridge: Cambridge University Press, 1912)

Heckethorn, Charles William, *The Secret Societies of All Ages and Countries* (London: Richard Bentley & Son, 1875)

Heindl, Max, *The Rosicrucian Cosmo-Conception, or Christian Occult Science: An Elementary Treatise on Man's Past Evolution, Present Constitution and Future Development* (Chicago: Donahue & Co., 1909)

Heydon, John, *The Holy-Guide: Leading the Way to The Golden Treasures of Nature* (London: 'T. M.', 1662)

Higgins, Godfrey, *Anacalypsis: An Attempt to Draw Aside the Veil of the Saitic Isis; or an Inquiry into the Origin of Languages, Nations, and Religions*, 2 volumes (London: private publication, 1833–36)

Hill, J. Arthur, *Spiritualism, Its History, Phenomena, and Doctrine* (London: Cassell, 1910)

Hindle, Beatrice M., 'Introduction', in C. G. Jung, *The Psychology of the Unconscious. A Study of the Transformations and Symbolisms of the Libido. A Contribution to the History of the Evolution of Thought*, trans. Beatrice M. Hinkle (London: Kegan Paul, 1917)

Hirsch, Samuel Abraham, 'Jewish Philosophy of Religion and Samson Raphael Hirsch', *Jewish Quarterly Review*, 2:2 (1890), 109–38; repr. in Samuel Abraham Hirsch, *A Book of Essays* (London: Jewish Historical Society of England/Macmillan & Co., 1905), 167–218

——, *A Book of Essays* (London: Jewish Historical Society of England/Macmillan & Co., 1905)

——, 'Jewish Mystics: An Appreciation', *Jewish Quarterly Review*, 20:1 (1907), 50–73

Hitchcock, Ethan Allen, *Remarks upon Alchemy and the Alchemists, Indicating a Method Discovering the True Nature of Hermetic Philosophy* (Boston, MA: Crosby, Nichols, 1857; repr. New York: Arno Press, 1976)

Hockley, Frederick, 'On the Ancient Magic Crystal, and its Probable Connexion with Mesmerism', *The Zoist: A Journal of Cerebral Physiology and Mesmerism*, 8 (1849), 251–66, repr. in *Theosophical Siftings: A Collection of Essays*, 7 volumes (London: Theosophical Publishing Society, 1888–95), Vol. 4 (1891–92), 9–22

Howe, Ellic (ed.), *The Alchemist of the Golden Dawn: The Letters of the Revd. W. A. Ayton to F. L. Gardner and Others 1886–1905* (Wellingborough: Aquarian Press, 1985)

Huysmans, J.-K., *Là-bas* (Paris: L'Echo de Paris, in successive chapters from February 1891; repr. Paris: Garnier-Flammarion, 1978)

Inge, William Ralph, *Christian Mysticism* (London: Methuen & Co., 1889)

James, William, *The Varieties of Religious Experience: A Study of Human Nature* (New York: Longmans Green, 1902; repr. New York: Viking Penguin, 1982)

Jay, Mike and Michael Neve (eds.), *1900: A Fin-de-siècle Reader* (London: Penguin, 1999)

Jennings, Hargrave, *The Rosicrucians: Their Rites and Mysteries, With Chapters on the Ancient Fire and Serpent-Worshippers, and Explanations of the Mystic Symbols Represented in the Monuments and Talismans of the Primeval Philosophers* (London: Chatto and Windus, 1870)

Joyce, James, *Finnegans Wake* (London: Faber & Faber, 1939)

King, Francis (ed.), *Crowley on Christ* (London: C. W. Daniel, 1974)

——— (ed.), *Astral Projection, Ritual Magic, and Alchemy: Golden Dawn Material by S. L. MacGregor Mathers and Others* (Rochester, VT: Destiny Books, 1987)

'King of Depravity Arrives', *John Bull* (11 April 1923)

Kingsford, Anna Bonus and Edward Maitland, *The Perfect Way; or, The Finding of Christ* (London: Field & Tuer, 1882; repr. New York: Cosimo Classics, 2007)

Kingsford, Anna Bonus, *Clothed With the Sun* (London: John M. Watkins, 1889)

Klein, Melanie, *Love, Guilt, and Reparation and Other Works 1921–1945* (London: Hogarth Press/Institute of Psycho-Analysis, 1981)

Knorr von Rosenroth, Christian, *Kabbala denudata, seu, Doctrina Hebraeorum transcendentalis et metaphysica atque theologica: opus antiquissimae philosophiae barbaricae... in quo, ante ipsam translationem libri...cui nomen Sohar tam veteris quam recentis, ejusque tikkunim...praemittitur apparatus [pars 1–4]*, 3 volumes (Sulzbach/Frankfurt: Abraham Lichtenthal, 1677–1684)

Kohn, Julius [J. K.], *The Real Black Magic Revealed Without Mystery* (Wellcome Institute Historical Medical Library, London, 1921, MS3126)

———, *The Secret of Anaxagoras: A Great Mystery Revealed by J. K.* (Wellcome Institute Historical Medical Library, London, no date, MS 3125)

Khunrath, Heinrich, *Amphitheatrum Sapientiae aeternae solius verae, christiano-kabalisticum, divino-magicum nec non-physico-chymicum, tertriunum catholicon* (Hanover: Giulielmus Antonius, 1609)

Küntz, Darcy (ed.), *The Golden Dawn Court Cards, as drawn by W. W. Westcott and Moïna Mathers* (Edmonds, WA: Holmes Publishing Group, 1996)

Kuranides: *The Magic of Kirani, King of Persia, and of Harpocration* (London: 1655, repr. Renaissance Astrology, 2005)

Leadbeater, C. W. *Man Visible and Invisible* (Wheaten, IL: Theosophical Publishing House, 1902)

———, *Life After Death* (Adyar: Theosophical Publishing House, 1912)

Leo, Alan, *How to Judge a Nativity* (London: Modern Astrology, 1903)

———, *Astrology for All* (London: Modern Astrology, 1904)

———, *The Key to Your Own Nativity* (London: Modern Astrology, 1910)

———, *Esoteric Astrology* (London: Modern Astrology, 1913)

Leo, Bessie, *The Life and Work of Alan Leo, Theosophist — Astrologer — Mason* (London: Fowler, 1919)

Lévi, Éliphas, *Dogme et rituel de la haute magie*, 2 volumes (Paris: Germer Baillière, 1855–56; repr. as one volume, Paris: Éditions Niclaus, 1972)

———, *Histoire de la magie, avec une exposition claire et précise de ses procédés, de ses rites et de ses mystères* (Paris: Germer Baillière, 1860; repr. Paris: Éditions de la Maisnie, 1974)

———, *Clefs majeures et clavicules de Salomon* (MS dated 1860; Paris: L. Chamuel, 1895; repr. Paris: Chacornac Frères, 1926)

—————, *Le clef des grand mystères, suivant Hénoch, Abraham, Hermès Trismégiste et Salomon* (Paris: Germer Baillière, 1861; repr. La Roche-sur-Yon: Éditions de la Maisnie, 1974)

—————, *La science des esprits: Révelation du dogme secret des Kabbalistes, esprit occulte des évangiles, appréciation des doctrines et des phénomènes spirits* (Paris: Germer-Baillière, 1865; repr. Paris: Elibron Classics, 2005)

—————, 'Cabale', in Pierre Larousse, *Grand dictionnaire universel du XIXe siècle français, historique géographique, mythologique, bibliographique, littéraire, artistique, scientifique,* 17 volumes (Paris: Administration du Grand Dictionnaire Universel, 1866–1890), Vol. 3 (1867), 4–6

—————, 'A Suicide's After-State', *Theosophist*, 2:10 (1881), 212

—————, 'The Magical Evocation of Apollonius of Tyana', *Theosophist*, 4:3 (1882), 58–60

—————, 'The Magisterium of the Sun', *Theosophist*, 4:4 (1883), 84

—————, *Paradoxes of the Highest Science, In Which the Most Advanced Truths of Occultism Are For the First Time Revealed (In Order to Reconcile the Future Developments of Science and Philosophy With the Eternal Religion)*, trans. 'A Master of the Wisdom', in *Theosophical Miscellany* (Calcutta: Calcutta Central Press Co., 1883; repr. Adyar: Madras Theosophical Publishing House, 1922)

—————, 'The Eggregores', *Theosophist* 5:6 (1884), 136–37

—————, 'What is Necessary to Become Initiated', *Theosophist* 5:7 (1884), 60–61

—————, *Le livre des splendeurs, contenant le soleil judaïque — la gloire chrétienne et le étoile flamboyant: études sur les origines de la Kabbale, avec des recherches sur les mystères de la franc-maçonnerie suivies de la profession de foi et des éléments de Kabbale* (Paris: Chamuel, 1894)

—————, *Letters to a Disciple: Letters from Eliphas Lévi Zahed to Baron Nicolas-Joseph Spedalieri on magic, numerology and the Tarot*, trans. Bertram Keightley (*Lucifer*, 14:79 (1894) to 17:100 (1895); repr. in one volume, Wellingborough: Aquarian Press, 1980)

—————, *Transcendental Magic*, trans. A. E. Waite (London: George Redway, 1896; repr. York Beach, ME: WeiserBooks, 1972)

—————, *The Magical Ritual of the Sanctum Regnum*, trans. William Wynn Westcott (private publication, 1896; repr. Sequim, WA: Holmes Publishing, 2006)

—————, *Le grand arcane, ou l'occultisme dévoilé* (Paris: Chamuel, 1898; repr. Paris: Elibron Classics, 2005)

—————, *Le livre des sages* (Paris: Chacornac Frères, 1912; repr. Le Tremblay: Diffusion Rosicrucienne, 1995)

—————, *The History of Magic*, trans. A. E. Waite (London: William Rider & Son, 1913; repr. York Beach, ME: Samuel Weiser, Inc., 2001)

—————, *Les mystères de la Kabbale, ou l'harmonie occulte des deux Testaments contenus dans la prophétie d'Ézéchiel et l'Apocalypse de Saint-Jean, d'après le manuscrit autographie d'Éliphas Lévi, 1861* (Paris: Émile Nourry, 1920)

—————, *Cours de philosophie occulte: Lettres au baron Spédalieri, de la Kabbale et de la science des nombres*, 2 volumes (Paris: Chacornac Frères, 1932–33; repr. Paris: Guy Trédaniel, 1977)

—————, *The Key of the Mysteries*, trans. Aleister Crowley (London: Rider & Co., 1959; repr. York Beach, ME: WeiserBooks, 2002)

Lilly, William *Christian Astrology* (London: John Macock, 1659)

'Literary Arrivals', *The Leeds Mercury* (29 August 1887)

Low, Barbara, 'Review of Violet M. Firth, *The Machinery of the Mind*', *International Journal of Psychoanalysis*, 5 (1924), 388–89

Ludendorff, Erich Friedrich Wilhelm, *Vernichtung der Freimauerei durch Enthüllung ihrer Geheimnisse* (Munich: self-published, 1927; English translation, *Destruction of Freemasonry Through Revelation of Their Secrets*, Newport Beach, CA: Noontide Press, 1977)

Machen, 'The Great God Pan', in *The Great God Pan and The Inmost Light* (London: John Lane, 1894); repr. in Arthur Machen, *Tales of Horror and the Supernatural* (London: John Baker, 1964), 61–115

———, *Things Near and Far* (London: Martin Secker, 1926)

Machen, Arthur and Arthur Edward Waite, *The House of the Hidden Light, Manifested and Set Forth in Certain Letters Communicated from a Lodge of the Adepts by the High Fratres Filius Aquarum and Elias Artista* (London: private publication, 1904; Warburg Institute, London, Yorke Collection FBH 904.H58)

Mackenzie, Kenneth, 'An account of what passed between Eliphas Lévi Zahed (Abbé Constant), Occult Philosopher, and Baphometus (Kenneth R. Mackenzie), Astrologer and Spiritualist, in the City of Paris, December 1861' (Warburg Institute, London, Yorke Collection, G.D. MSS V12, NS68(2), repr. as 'Philosophical and Cabbalistic Magic', *Rosicrucian and Red Cross*, 2 (April 1873), 28–34; repr. in Christopher McIntosh, *Eliphas Lévi and the French Occult Revival*, London: Rider, 1972, 117–22; repr. in Francis King, *Modern Ritual Magic: The Rise of Western Occultism*, Bridport: Prism Press, 1989), 28–38

———, 'Philosophical and Cabbalistic Magic', *Rosicrucian and Red Cross*, 2 (April 1873), 28–34

———, *The Royal Masonic Cyclopaedia of History, Rites, Symbolism and Biography* (London: John Hogg, 1877)

Mackey, Albert G., *A Lexicon of Freemasonry* (Philadelphia, PA: Moss, Brother, 1858)

———, *The Symbolism of Freemasonry, Illustrating and Explaining Its Science and Philosophy, Its Legends, Myths, and Symbols* (New York: Clark & Maynard, 1882)

Maitland, Edward, *The Life of Anna Kingsford*, 2 volumes (London: George Redway, 1896; repr. as *Anna Kingsford: Her Life, Letters, Diary and Work*, London: John M. Watkins, 1913)

Marsden, Victor E. (trans.), *Protocols of the Meetings of the Learned Elders of Zion* (London: The Britons Publishing Society, 1923)

Martindale, William Harrison and William Wynn Westcott, *The Extra Pharmocopoeia of Unofficial Drugs and Chemical and Pharmaceutical Preparations* (London: H. K. Lewis, 1883; repr. London: The Pharmaceutical Press, 2008)

Martinès de Pasqually, *Traité de la réintegration des êtres dans leur premières propriétés, vertus et puissances spirituelles et divines* (Paris: Bibliothèque Chacornac, 1899; repr. Paris: Éditions Traditionelles, 1988)

———, 'Discours d'instruction à un nouveau reçu sur les trois grades d'apprenti compagnon et maître symboliques', Bibliothèque municipale de Lyon, Fonds Willermoz, MS 5919–12, <http://www.Philosophe-inconnu.com>

Mathers, Moïna Bergson, 'Preface', in S. L. MacGregor Mathers (ed. and trans.), *The Kabbalah Unveiled: Containing the following Books of the Zohar: The Book of Concealed Mystery, The Greater Holy Assembly, The Lesser Holy Assembly, Translated into English from the Latin version of Knorr von Rosenroth, and collated with the original Chaldee and Hebrew text* (London: George Redway, 1887; revised edition, London: Routledge & Kegan Paul, 1926), vii–xiii

Mathers, S. L. MacGregor (ed. and trans.), *The Kabbalah Unveiled: Containing the following Books of the Zohar: The Book of Concealed Mystery, The Greater Holy Assembly, The Lesser Holy Assembly, Translated into English from the Latin version of Knorr von Rosenroth, and collated with the original Chaldee and Hebrew text* (London: George Redway, 1887; revised edition, London: Routledge & Kegan Paul, 1926)

——, 'Letter to the Editor', *Jewish Chronicle*, 22 September 1887, 6

—— (trans.), *The Key of Solomon (Clavicula Salomonis)* (London: George Redway, 1889; repr. San Francisco, CA: Red Wheel/Weiser, 2000)

——, 'Talismanic Magic: Saturn, The Occult Signification of his Square, Seal, and Sigils', *Lucifer*, 2:7 (1888), 9–14

——, *Fortune Telling Cards. The Tarot, its occult signification, use in fortune-telling, and method of play, etc.* (London: George Redway, 1888)

——, *The Symbolism of the 4 Ancients* (Clavicula II, Societas Rosicrucianae in Anglia, 1888; Yorke Collection FDD 805, Warburg Institute; reprinted in R. A. Gilbert (ed.), *The Sorcerer and His Apprentice: Unknown Hermetic Writings of S. L. MacGregor Mathers and J. W. Brodie-Innes* (Wellingborough: Aquarian Press, 1983), 19–22

——, (trans.), *The Book of the Sacred Magic of Abramelin the Mage*, London: John M. Watkins, 1900; repr. New York: Dover Publications, 1975)

——, 'The Qliphoth of the Qabalah', Golden Dawn Instructional Paper (c. 1900), in R. A. Gilbert (ed.), *The Sorcerer and His Apprentice: Unknown Hermetic Writings of S. L. MacGregor Mathers and J. W. Brodie-Innes* (Wellingborough: Aquarian Press, 1983), 23–29

—— (trans.), *The Goetia: The Lesser Key of Solomon the King* (London: private publication, 1904)

——, 'On the Tarot Trumps', Golden Dawn Instructional Paper (c. 1910), in R. A. Gilbert (ed.), *The Sorcerer and His Apprentice: Unknown Hermetic Writings of S. L. MacGregor Mathers and J. W. Brodie-Innes* (Wellingborough: Aquarian Press, 1983), 79–80

——, 'The Azoth Lecture', Golden Dawn Instructional Paper (c. 1910), in R. A. Gilbert (ed.), *The Sorcerer and His Apprentice: Unknown Hermetic Writings of S. L. MacGregor Mathers and J. W. Brodie-Innes* (Wellingborough: Aquarian Press, 1983), 30–39

—— (ed. and trans.), *The Grimoire of Almadel* (London: Routledge & Kegan Paul, 1980; repr. San Francisco, CA: Red Wheel/Weiser, 2001)

——, 'Clairvoyance', Flying Roll XI, in Francis King (ed.), *Astral Projection, Ritual Magic, and Alchemy: Golden Dawn Material by S. L. MacGregor Mathers and Others* (Rochester, VT: Destiny Books, 1987), 75–83

Maudsley, Henry, *Natural Causes and Supernatural Seemings* (London: Kegan Paul & Trench, 1886)

——, 'Lessons of Materialism', in *A Selection of Letters Delivered Before the Sunday Lecture Society, Fourth Selection* (London: Sunday Lecture Society, 1886)

——, 'Materialism and Spiritualism', *Journal of Mental Science*, 63:263 (1917), 494–506

Maugham, W. Somerset, *The Magician* (London: William Heinemann, 1908)

McBryde, J. M., Jr., 'The Sator-Acrostic', *Modern Language Notes*, 22:8 (1907), 245–49

Mead, G. R. S., 'Some Notes on the Gnostics', *Nineteenth Century and After*, 52:309 (1902), 822–35

—— (ed. and trans.), *Thrice-Greatest Hermes: Studies in Hellenistic Theosophy and Gnosis*, 3 volumes (London: Theosophical Publishing Society, 1906)

Mentor, 'Missions to Jews', *Jewish Chronicle*, 25 March 1927, 13

——, 'Two Matters', *Jewish Chronicle*, 24 February 1928, 9

Michelspacher, Steffan, *Cabala, Spiegel der Kunst und Natur: in Alchymia* (Augsburg: David Francken, 1616)

Mickiewicz, Adam, *Les Slaves: Cours professé au Collège de France (1842–44)* (Paris: Musée Adam Mickiewicz, 1914)

Mordell, Phineas, *The Origins of the Letters and Numerals According to the Sefer Yetzirah* (Philadelphia, PA: Dropsie College, 1914; repr. New York: Samuel Weiser, 1975)

——, 'Review: Notes on the *Sepher Yezirah*', *Jewish Quarterly Review*, 19:1 (1928), 79–80

——, 'The Beginning and Development of Hebrew Punctuation', *Jewish Quarterly Review*, 24:2 (1933), 137–49

Müller, Friedrich Max, *Introduction to the Science of Religion* (London: Longmans, Green & Co., 1873)

Munk, Salomon, *Palestine: déscription géographique, historique et archéologique* (Paris: Firmin Didot Frères, 1845)

——, *Mélanges de philosophie juive et arabe* (Paris: Librairie A. Franck, 1853)

Murray, Gilbert, *Four Stages of Greek Religion: Studies Based on a Course of Lectures Delivered in April 1912 at Columbia University* (New York: Columbia University, 1912)

Myer, Isaac, *Qabbalah: The Philosophical Writings of Solomon Ben Yehudah Ibn Gebirol or Avicebron, and their Connection with the Hebrew Qabbalah and Sepher ha-Zohar* (Philadelphia, PA: private publication, 1888; repr. New York: Samuel Weiser, 1970)

——, Papers, New York Public Library Rare Books and Manuscripts Division, No. 86M22, <http://www.nypl.org/research/chss/spe/rbk/faids/myeri.pdf>

Neubauer, A., 'The *Bahir* and the *Zohar*', *Jewish Quarterly Review*, 4:3 (1892), 357–68

Nilus, Sergei, *Velikoe v malom ili Antikhrist kak blizkaia politchkeskaia vozmoshnost* ('The Great in the Small, or the Antichrist as an Approaching Political Possibility') (Sergiev Posad, 1902)

Nizida [Louise Off], 'Nature-Spirits or Elementals', *Theosophical Siftings*, 1:10 (1888), 1–14

——, *The Astral Light: An Attempted Exposition of Certain Occult Principles in Nature With Some Remarks Upon Modern Spiritism* (London: Theosophical Publishing Co., 1889)

Olcott, Henry Steel, *Old Diary Leaves, First Series, 1874–1878* (London: Theosophical Publishing House, 1895)

——, *Old Diary Leaves, Third Series, 1883–1887* (London: Theosopical Publishing House, 1895)

'One of Them', 'With the Children of the Ghetto', *Jewish Chronicle*, 20 March 1914, 5

Oxlee, John, *The Christian Doctrines of the Trinity and Incarnation, considered and maintained on the Principles of Judaism*, 3 volumes (London: Hatchards, 1815/1820/1850)

——, *Three Letters, humbly addressed to the Lord Archbishop of Canterbury, on the inexpediency and futility of any attempt to convert the Jews to the Christian Faith, in the way and manner hitherto practised. Being a General Discussion of the whole Jewish Question* (private publication: London, 1842, repr. Philadelphia, PA: Abraham Collins, 1843)

Papus, *Traité méthodique de science occulte* (Paris: G. Carré, 1891)

——, *La Cabbale: tradition secrète de l'occident* (Paris: G. Carré, 1892)

Paracelsus, *Liber de Nymphis, Sylphis, Pygmaeis et Salamandris et de caeteris Spiritibus* (Basel, 1566), ed. Robert Blaser (Bern: A. Francke, 1960)

Paskauskas, R.. Andrew (ed.), *The Complete Correspondence of Sigmund Freud and Ernest Jones, 1908–1939* (Cambridge, MA: Harvard University Press, 1993)

Pike, Albert, *Morals and Dogma of the Ancient and Accepted Scottish Rite Freemasonry*, 2 volumes (privately published, 1871; repr. Charleston, NC: L. H. Jenkins, 1949)

Plummer, George Winslow, *Principles and Practice for Rosicrucians* (New York: Society of Rosicrucians, 1947)

Podmore, Frank, *Modern Spiritualism: A History and a Criticism*, 2 volumes (London: Methuen, 1902)

Postel, Guillaume, *Abrahami Patriarchae liber Jezirah sive formationis mundi, patribus quidem, Abrahami tempora praecedentibus revelatus, sed ab ipso etiam Abrahamo expositus Isaaco, et per prophetarum manus posteritati conservatus, ipsis autem LXXII Mosis auditoribus in secondu divinae veritatis loco, hoc est in Ratione, quae est posterior authorite, habitus. Vertebat ex Hebraeis et commentariis illustrabat 1551, ad Babylonis ruinam et corrupti mundi finem, Gulielmus Postellus, Restitutur* (Paris, 1552)

Randolph, Paschal Beverly, *P. B. Randolph: The "Learned Pundit" and "Man with Two Souls", His Curious Life, Works, and Career: The Great Free-Love Trial* (Boston, MA: self-published, 1872)

——, *Eulis! The History of Love: Its Wondrous Magic, Chemistry, Rules, Laws, Modes, Moods and Rationale; Being the Third Revelation of Soul and Sex* (Toledo, OH: Randolph Publishing, 1874)

——, *The Ansairetic Mystery: A New Revelation Concerning Sex! A Private Letter, Printed, but not Published; it being Sacred and Confidential* (Toledo, OH: privately printed, Toledo Sun Liberal Printing House, 1874)

——, *Sexual Magic*, ed. and trans. Robert North (New York: Magickal Childe, 1988)

'Review of Francis Barrett, *The Magus, or, Celestial Intelligencer'*, Art. VII, *Critical Review*, 34 (April 1802), 406

Regardie, Israel, *The Tree of Life: An Illustrated Study in Magic* (Chicago, IL: Aries Press, 1932; repr. Chic Cicero and Sandra Tabatha Cicero (eds.), Woodbury, MN: Llewellyn Publications, 2001)

——, *A Garden of Pomegranates: Skrying on the Tree of Life* (London: Rider, 1932; repr. Chic Cicero and Sandra Tabatha Cicero (eds.), Woodbury, MN: Llewellyn Publications, 2005)

——, *An Account of the Teachings, Rites and Ceremonies of the Order of the Golden Dawn*, 4 volumes (Chicago, IL: Aries Press, 1937–1940; repr. as *The Original Account of the Teachings, Rites and Ceremonies of the Hermetic Order of the Golden Dawn*, St. Paul, MN: Llewellyn, 1989)

Reuss, Theodor and Aleister Crowley, *O.T.O. Rituals and Sex Magick*, ed. Peter-R. Koenig (Thame: I-H-O Books, 1999)

'Review of *Sub-Mundanes; or, the Elementaries of the Cabala'*, *Book-lore* (May 1886), 180

'Review of *The Israelites Found in the Anglo-Saxons. The Ten Tribes Supposed to Have Been Lost, Traced From the Land of Their Captivity to Their Occupation of the Isles of the Sea: With an Exhibition of Those Traits of Character and National Characteristics Assigned to Israel in the Books of the Hebrew Prophets'*, *Jewish Chronicle* (17 January 1873), 587

Robertson, James, *Spiritualism: The Open Door to the Unseen Universe. Being Thirty Years of Personal Observation and Experience Concerning Intercourse between the Material and Spiritual Worlds* (London: L. N. Fowler, 1908)

Rudd, Thomas, *A Treatise on Angel Magic*, ed. Adam McLean (London: Phanes Press, 1989; repr. York Beach, ME: WeiserBooks, 2006)

Ruland, Martin, *A Lexicon of Alchemy or Alchemical Dictionary, Containing a Full and Plain Explanation of All Obscure Words, Hermetic Subjects, and Arcane Phrases of Paracelsus (Lexicon alchemiae sive dictionarium alchemistarum*, Frankfurt: Zachariah Palthenus, 1612), trans. A. E. Waite (London: John Watkins, 1893; repr. York Beach, ME: Samuel Weiser, 1984)

Sampson, Holden E., 'My Occult Experiences', *Occult Review*, 18:5 (1913), 273–79

————, *The True Mystic: Three Lectures on Mysticism* (London: Rider & Son, 1914)

————, *How to Read the Crystal; or Crystal and Seer; With a Concise Dictionary of Astrological Terms* (London: Foulsham & Co., 1922)

Shanks, George, *The Jewish Peril. Protocols of the Learned Elders of Zion* (London: Eyre & Spottiswoode, 1920)

Solovyoff, Vsevolod Sergyeevich, *A Modern Priestess of Isis* (London: Longmans, Green & Co., 1895)

Soloweyczyk, Elie [Eliyahu], *Kol Kore (Vox Clamantis): La Bible, le Talmud et l'Évangile*, 2 volumes, trans. from the Hebrew by Lazare Wogue (Vol. 1, Paris: Imprimèrie de E. Brière, 1870; Vol. 2, Paris: *Les Archives Israélites*, 1870)

Stewart, C. Nelson, *Bulwer Lytton as Occultist* (London: Theosophical Publishing House, 1927)

Stirling, William, *The Canon: An Exposition of the Pagan Mystery Perpetuated in the Cabala as the Rule of All the Arts* (London: Elkin Mathews, 1897)

Stoddart, Christina M. ['Inquire Within'], *Light-Bearers of Darkness* (London: Boswell, 1930)

———— ['Inquire Within'], *The Trail of the Serpent* (London: Boswell, 1936)

Stoddart, W. H. B., *Mind and Its Disorders* (London: H. K. Lewis, 1908)

Stoker, Bram, *Dracula* (London: A. Constable & Co., 1897)

Sub-mundanes: or, the Elementaries of the Cabala: being the history of spirits, reprinted from the text of the abbe de Villars, Physio-Astro-Mystic, wherein is asserted that there are in existence on earth rational creatures besides man (Bath: Robert H. Fryer, 1886)

Tennant, F. R., *The Concept of Sin* (Cambridge: Cambridge University Press, 1912)

The Editor, 'Review of William Carpenter, *The Israelites Found in the Anglo-Saxons*, *The Jewish Chronicle*, 17 January 1873, 587.

————, 'Review of Samuel Liddell MacGregor Mathers, *The Kabbalah Unveiled*', *The Jewish Chronicle*, 9 September 1887, 12

————, 'Cohanim as Jurymen', Jewish Chronicle, 21 September 1900, 15

'The Kabbalah', Art. IV, *Eclectic Review*, 11 (February 1856), 141–57

'The Wickedest Man in the World', *John Bull* (24 March 1923)

Theosophical Siftings: A Collection of Essays, 1888–1895, 7 volumes (London: Theosophical Publishing Society, 1888–95)

Underhill, Evelyn, 'A Defence of Magic', originally published in *The Fortnightly Review*, 82:491 (1907), 754–65; repr. in Dana Greene (ed.), *Evelyn Underhill: Modern Guide to the Ancient Quest for the Holy* (Albany, NY: State University of New York Press, 1988), 33–46

————, *Evelyn Underhill: Modern Guide to the Ancient Quest for the Holy*, ed. Dana Greene (Albany, NY: State University of New York Press, 1988)

Vaughan, Thomas [Eugenius Philalethes], *The Fame and Confession of the Fraternity of R. C. Commonly of the Rosie Cross* (London: Giles Calvert, 1652)

Viatte, Auguste, *Les Sources occultes du Romantisme: Illuminisme et Théosophie (1770–1820)*, 2 volumes (Paris: Librairie Ancienne Honoré Champion, 1928)

Von Krafft-Ebing, Richard, *Psychopathia Sexualis, With Especial Reference to the Antipathic Sexual Instinct: A Medico-Forensic Study* (London: F. A. Davis, 1892; original German publication, *Psychopathia Sexualis. Mit besonderer Berücksichtigung der konträren Sexualempfindung. Eine medizinisch-gerichtliche Studie für Ärtzte und Juristen*, 1886)

Waite, A. E. (ed. and trans.), *Mysteries of Magic: A Digest of the Writings of Eliphas Lévi* (London: George Redway, 1886)

——, 'Biographical and Critical Essay on the Life of Alphonse Louis Constant and Notes on the Mysteries of Magic as expounded in the Occult Philosophy of Eliphas Lévi', in A. E. Waite, ed., *Mysteries of Magic: A Digest of the Writings of Eliphas Lévi, with Biographical and Critical Essay* (London: George Redway, 1886), 1–41

——, *The Book of Black Magic: Including the Rites and Mysteries of Goëtic Theurgy, Sorcery, and Infernal Necromancy* (London: George Redway, 1886; reissued as *The Book of Ceremonial Magic*, London: William Rider & Son, 1911; repr. San Francisco, CA: WeiserBooks, 2006)

——, *The Real History of the Rosicrucians: Founded on Their Own Manifestoes, and On Facts and Documents Collected From the Writings of Initiated Brethren* (London: George Redway, 1887; repr. Blauvelt, NY: Steinerbooks, 1977)

——, 'The Rosicrucian Brotherhood', *Gentleman's Magazine*, 263 (1887), 598–607

——, *The Occult Sciences: A Compendium of Transcendental Doctrine and Experiment, Embracing an Account of Magical Practices; of Secret Sciences in Connection with Magic; of the Professors of Magical Arts; and of Modern Spiritualism, Mesmerism and Theosophy* (London: Kegan Paul, Trench, Trübner & Co., 1891)

——, *Azoth or The Star in the East: Embracing the First Matter of the Magnum Opus, the Evolution of Aphrodite-Urania, the Supernatural Generation of the Son of the Sun, and the Alchemical Transfiguration of Humanity* (London: Theosophical Publishing Society, 1893; repr. Secaucus, NJ: University Books, 1973)

——, 'What is Alchemy?', *The Unknown World*, 1:1 (1894), 7–11

——, 'Biographical Preface', in Éliphas Lévi, *Transcendental Magic*, trans. A. E. Waite (London: Rider, 1896), xix–xxxi

——, *The Life of Louis Claude de Saint-Martin, The Unknown Philosopher, and the Substance of His Transcendental Doctrine* (London: Philip Wellby, 1901; repr. London: William Rider & Son, 1910)

——, *The Doctrine and Literature of the Kabbalah* (London: Theosophical Publishing Society, 1902)

——, *A Book of Mystery and Vision* (London: Philip Welby & Son, 1902)

——, 'The Holy Graal in the Light of the Celtic Church', *Occult Review*, 5:6 (1907), 334–45

——, 'Mystic Aspects of the Grail Legend', *The Occult Review*, 6:2 (1907), 35–44

——, 'Notes on the Grail Tradition', *Occult Review*, 6:3 (1907), 121–25

——, 'A Message of Saint-Martin', *Seeker*, 5:17 (1909), 43–58, repr. in R. A. Gilbert (ed.), *Hermetic Papers of A. E. Waite: The Unknown Writings of a Modern Mystic* (Wellingborough: Aquarian Press, 1987), 205–14

——, 'The Tarot — A Wheel of Fortune', *Occult Review*, 10:12 (1909), 307–17

——, *The Hidden Church of the Holy Graal, Its Legends and Symbolism: Considered in their Affinity with Certain Mysteries of Initiation and other Traces of a Secret Tradition in Christian Times* (London: Rebman Ltd., 1909)

——, *The Key to the Tarot: Being Fragments of a Secret Tradition under the Veil of Divination* (London: William Rider & Son, 1910)

——, *The Pictorial Key to the Tarot* (London: Rider, 1910)

——, 'The Viaticum of Daily Life on the Way of the Homeward Quest' (unpublished typescript, 1910), repr. in R. A. Gilbert (ed.), *Hermetic Papers of A. E. Waite: The Unknown Writings of a Modern Mystic* (Wellingborough: Aquarian Press, 1987), 252–56

——, *The Secret Tradition in Freemasonry*, 2 volumes (London: Rebman Ltd., 1911)

——, *The Secret Doctrine of Israel: A Study of the Zohar and Its Connections* (London: William Rider & Son, 1913)

——, *The Way of Divine Union: Being a Doctrine of Experience in the Life of Sanctity, Considered on the Faith of Its Testimonies and Interpreted After a New Manner* (London: William Rider & Son, 1915; repr. Berkeley, CA: Golem Media, 2007)

——, 'Some Deeper Aspects of Masonic Symbolism', *The Builders* (1915), repr. in Edward Dunning (ed.), *A. E. Waite: Selected Masonic Papers* (Wellingborough: Aquarian Press, 1988), 153–70

——, 'A Lodge of Magic', *Occult Review*, 26:6 (1917), 228–34

——, 'The Tarot and Secret Tradition', *Occult Review*, 29:3 (1919), 157–61

——, 'Obituary for Samuel Liddell MacGregor Mathers', *Occult Review*, 29:4 (1919), 197–99

—— (ed.), *The Works of Thomas Vaughan: Eugenius Philalethes* (London: Theosophical Publishing House, 1919)

——, *The Book of the Holy Graal* (London: Watkins, 1921)

——, *A New Encyclopaedia of Freemasonry*, 2 volumes (London: Rider, 1921)

——, 'Masonic Tradition and the Royal Arch', *Transactions of the Somerset Masters' Lodge No. 3746* (1921), repr. in Edward Dunning (ed.), *A. E. Waite: Selected Masonic Papers* (Wellingborough: Aquarian Press, 1988), 19–29

——, *St. Martin: The French Mystic and the Story of Modern Martinism* (London: William Rider & Son, 1922; repr. in *Three Famous Mystics*, London: William Rider & Son, 1939)

——, 'Introduction', in Knut Stenring (trans.), *The Book of Formation (Sepher Yetzirah) by Rabbi Akiba ben Joseph, including the 32 Paths of Wisdom, their correspondences with the Hebrew alphabet and the Tarot symbols* (New York: Ktav Publishing House, 1923), 3–14

——, *The Brotherhood of the Rosy Cross: Being Records of the House of the Holy Spirit in Its Inward and Outward History* (London: William Rider & Son, 1924; repr. New Hyde Park, NY: University Books, 1961)

——, 'Periodical Literature', *Occult Review*, 41:5 (1925), 326–27

——, 'The Great Symbols of the Tarot', *Occult Review*, 43:1 (1926), 11–19

——, *The Secret Tradition in Alchemy* (London: Kegan Paul, 1926)

——, *The Holy Kabbalah: A Study of the Secret Tradition in Israel as Unfolded by Sons of the Doctrine for the Benefit and Consolation of the Elect Dispersed Through the Lands and Ages of the Greater Exile* (London: Williams & Norgate, 1929)

——, *The Holy Grail, Its Legends and Symbolism: An Explanatory Survey of Their Embodiment in Romance Literature and a Critical Study of the Interpretations Placed Thereon* (London: Rider & Co., 1933)

——, 'The Spiritual Symbolism of Freemasonry', in A. E. Waite (trans.), *The Liturgy of the Rite of the Strict Observance* (privately printed, 1934), repr. in Edward Dunning (ed.), *A. E. Waite: Selected Masonic Papers* (Wellingborough: Aquarian Press, 1988), 123–52

——, *Shadows of Life and Thought: A Retrospective Review in the Form of Memoirs* (London: Selwyn and Blount, 1938)

——, 'The Interior Life from the Standpoint of the Mystics', *Light*, 10:521 (1890), repr. in R. A. Gilbert (ed.), *Hermetic Papers of A. E. Waite: The Unknown Writings of a Modern Mystic* (Wellingborough: Aquarian Press, 1987), 195–204

——, 'On Intimations Concerning the Interior Church in Schools of Christian Mysticism', in I. V. Lopukhin, *Some Characteristics of the Interior Church* (London: Theosophical Publishing Society, 1912), repr.

in R. A. Gilbert (ed.), *Hermetic Papers of A. E. Waite: The Unknown Writings of a Modern Mystic* (Wellingborough: Aquarian Press, 1987), 215–51

—— (ed.), *The Harmonial Philosophy: A Compendium and Digest of the Works of Andrew Jackson Davis*, the Seer of Poughkeepsie (London: William Rider & Son, 1917)

Wakefield, H. Russell, *They Return at Evening* (London: Phillip Allen, 1928)

Webster, Nesta H., *Secret Societies and Subversive Movements* (London: Boswell, 1924)

Westcott, William Wynn, *A Therapeutic Index of Diseases and Symptoms* (London: H. K. Lewis, 1884)

——, *Suicide: Its History, Literature, Jurisprudence, Causation and Prevention* (London: H. K. Lewis, 1885)

—— (trans.), *Sepher Yetzirah: The Book of Formation and the Thirty-Two Paths of Wisdom* (Bath: Robert H. Fryar, 1887)

——, *Tabula Bembina sive Mensa Isiaca. The Isiac Tablet of Cardinal Bembo. Its History and occult Significance* (Bath: Robert H. Fryar, 1887)

——, 'The Religion of Freemasonry Illuminated by the Kabbalah', *Ars Quatuor Coronatorum*, 1 (1886–88), 55–58, reprinted in R. A. Gilbert (ed.), *The Magical Mason: Forgotten Hermetic Writings of William Wynn Westcott, Physician and Magus* (Wellingborough: Aquarian Press, 1983), 114–23

——, 'Historical Lecture for Neophytes', c. 1888, rewritten c. 1891, repr. in Francis King, *Modern Ritual Magic: The Rise of Western Occultism* (London: Neville Spearman, 1970; repr. Bridport: Prism Press, 1989), 212–17; also repr. in Israel Regardie, *An Account of the Teachings, Rites and Ceremonies of the Order of the Golden Dawn*, 4 volumes (Chicago, IL: Aries Press, 1937–1940; repr. as *The Original Account of the Teachings, Rites and Ceremonies of the Hermetic Order of the Golden Dawn*, St. Paul, MN: Llewellyn, 1989), 15–16

——, 'The Shamfer (Shamir) of King Solomon' (unpublished MS, London, 1888; recopied 1910; Grand Lodge Library and Museum of Freemasonry MS A180WES)

——, 'A Society of Kabbalists', *Notes and Queries*, 9 February 1889, 116

——, 'The Mandrake', *British Medical Journal*, 1:1524 (1890), 620–21

——, *Numbers, Their Occult Power and Mystic Virtues* (London: Theosophical Publishing Society, 1890; repr. *The Occult Power of Numbers*, North Hollywood, CA: Newcastle Publishing Co., 1984)

——, 'The Kabalah', paper delivered to the Blavatsky Lodge of the Theosophical Society in 1891, in *Lucifer*, 8:48 (1891), 465–69 and 9:49 (1891), 27–32, repr. in R. A. Gilbert (ed.), *The Magical Mason: Forgotten Hermetic Writings of William Wynn Westcott, Physician and Magus* (Wellingborough: Aquarian Press, 1983), 81–94

——, 'A Lecture to Enquirers into Theosophy and Practical Occultism', *Theosophical Siftings: A Collection of Essays*, 7 volumes (London: Theosophical Publishing Society, 1888–95), Vol. 3 (1891), 5–13

——, 'Catalogue of the Westcott Hermetic Library', unpublished MS, London, 1891, Grand Lodge Library and Museum of Freemasonry MS 1390WES

——, 'Death', paper delivered at the Adelphi Theosophical Society Lodge (6 February 1893), repr. in *Theosophical Siftings: A Collection of Essays*, 7 volumes (London: Theosophical Publishing Society, 1888–95), Vol. 6 (1893), 3–12

——, 'A Further Glance at the Kabalah', *Lucifer*, 12:68–69 (1893), 147–53 and 203–08, reprinted in R. A. Gilbert (ed.), *The Magical Mason:*

Forgotten Hermetic Writings of William Wynn Westcott, Physician and Magus (Wellingborough: Aquarian Press, 1983), 95–109.

———— (ed.), *Collectanea Hermetica*, 9 volumes (London: Theosophical Publishing Society, 1893–96)

———— (ed.), *The Chaldean Oracles Attributed to Zoroaster, Collectanea Hermetica*, Vol. 6 (London: Theosophical Publishing Society, 1895; repr. Sequim, WA: Holmes Publishing Group, 2008; original English translation by Thomas Taylor, *Collection of the Chaldean Oracles*, 1817)

————, *History of the Societas Rosicruciana in Anglia* (London: private publication, 1900)

————, 'Inebriety, Its Causes and Cure', *British Journal of Psychiatry*, 46:195 (1900), 653–73

————, 'Magic: Does It Exist?' (privately published, c. 1900, Gerald Yorke Collection FBF135, Warburg Institute, London)

————, 'An Address on the Coroner and His Relations with the Medical Examiner and Death Certification', *British Medical Journal*, 2:2188 (1902), 1756–759

————, 'The Devil, and Evil Spirits According to the Bible', SRIA, *Transactions of the Metropolitan College* (1902), 17–21, repr. in R. A. Gilbert (ed.), *The Magical Mason: Forgotten Hermetic Writings of William Wynn Westcott, Physician and Magus* (Wellingborough: Aquarian Press, 1983), 131–38

————, 'In Memory of Robert Fludd', address to the SRIA (14 September 1907), repr. in SRIA, *Transactions of the Metropolitan College* (1907), 7–11, repr. in R. A. Gilbert (ed.), *The Magical Mason: Forgotten Hermetic Writings of William Wynn Westcott, Physician and Magus* (Wellingborough: Aquarian Press, 1983), 48–53

————, *An Introduction to the Study of the Kabbalah, With Eight Diagrams* (London: Watkins, 1910)

————, 'The Rosicrucians, Past and Present, At Home and Abroad', privately printed, 1913; repr. in R. A. Gilbert (ed.), *The Magical Mason: Forgotten Hermetic Writings of William Wynn Westcott, Physician and Magus* (Wellingborough: Aquarian Press, 1983), 40–47

————, 'Data of the History of the Rosicrucians' (printed for the S.R.I.A., London: 1916; reprinted in R. A. Gilbert (ed.), *The Magical Mason: Forgotten Hermetic Writings of William Wynn Westcott, Physician and Magus* (Wellingborough: Aquarian Press, 1983), 28–39

————, 'Magic: Does It Exist?', privately published pamphlet, n.d., Gerald Yorke Collection FBF135, Warburg Institute, London

————, 'A Subject for Contemplation', Flying Roll II, Part 1, in Francis King (ed.), *Astral Projection, Ritual Magic, and Alchemy: Golden Dawn Material by S. L. MacGregor Mathers and Others* (Rochester, VT: Destiny Books, 1987), 55

Williams, Charles, *The Greater Trumps* (London: Victor Gollancz, 1932)

————, *All Hallows Eve* (London: Faber & Faber, 1948)

Wilson, John, *Our Israelitish Origin: Lectures on Ancient Israel, and the Israelitish Origin of the Modern Nations of Europe* (London: James Nisbet, 1840)

Yarker, John, *The Arcane Schools: A Review of their Origin and Antiquity; with a History of Freemasonry and its Relation to the Theosophic, Scientific, and Philosophic Mysteries* (Belfast: William Tait, 1909)

Yeats, William Butler, *Collected Poems of W. B. Yeats* (London: Macmillan, 1933)

————, *A Vision* (London: Macmillan, 1937; repr. New York: Macmillan/Collier, 1966)

————, *The Autobiography of William Butler Yeats* (New York: Macmillan, 1953)

———, *Essays and Introductions* (New York: Macmillan, 1961)

TRANSLATED PRIMARY SOURCES:

Abraham, Hilda C. and Ernst L. Freud (eds. and trans.), *The Letters of Sigmund Freud and Karl Abraham, 1907–1926* (New York: Basic Books, 1965)

Abulafia, Abraham, *Sheva Netivot Ha-Torah: The Seven Paths of Torah*, trans. Fabrizio Lanza, Kathryn Smith, and Talib Din (Monfalcone: Everburning Light/Providence University, 2006)

———, *Sefer Ha-Ot: The Book of the Sign*, trans. Fabrizio Lanza, Kathryn Smith, and Talib Din (Monfalcone: Everburning Light/Providence University, 2006)

———, *Get Ha-Shemot: Divorce of the Names*, trans. Fabrizio Lanza, Kathryn Smith, and Talib Din (Monfalcone: EverBurning Light/Providence University, 2007)

Agrippa, Henry Cornelius, *Three Books of Occult Philosophy* (*De occulta philosophia*), ed. Donald Tyson, trans. James Freake (St. Paul, MN: Llewellyn Publications, 2004 [1993]; first complete publication, Cologne: Soter and Hetorpius, 1533; first English translation, James Freake, London: Gregory Moule, 1651)

———, *The Vanity of Arts and Sciences* (*De incertitudine et vanitate scientiarum*), trans. Roger L'Estrange (London: Samuel Speed, 1676)

Al-Kindi, *On the Stellar Rays*, trans. Robert Zoller (Berkeley Springs, WV: Golden Hind Press, 1993)

Anonymous, *Aesch Mezareph, or Purifying Fire: A Chymico-Kabalistic Treatise Collected from the Kabala Denudata of Knorr von Rosenroth*, ed.William Wynn Westcott, Vol. 4 of *Collectanea Hermetica* (London: Theosophical Publishing Society, 1894)

Atallah, Hashem (trans.), *Picatrix: The Goal of the Wise*, (Seattle, WA: Ouroboros Press, 2002)

Augustine, *City of God, Books VIII–XVI*, ed. Vernon J. Bourke, trans. Gerald G. Walsh, Demetrius B. Zema, Grace Monohan, and Daniel J. Honan, in *Writings of St. Augustine*, Vol. 7 (Washington, D. C.: Catholic University of America Press, 1963)

Ayres, P. (trans.), *The Count of Gabalis, or the extravagant Mysteries of the Cabalists* (London: Cabalistical Society of the Sages, at the Sign of the Rosy-Crucian, 1680)

Berg, Philip S. and Yehuda Ashlag (eds. and trans.), *Ten Luminous Emanations*, 2 volumes (Jerusalem: Research Centre of Kabbalah, 1969–73)

Bar Chaim, Yitzchak (trans.), *Shaar HaGilgulim: The Gates of Reincarnation by Rabbi Isaac Luria and Rabbi Chaim Vital* (Malibu, CA: Thirty Seven Books Publishing, 2003)

Betz, Hans Dieter (ed. and trans.), *The Greek Magical Papyri in Translation, Including the Demotic Spells* (Chicago, IL: University of Chicago Press, 1986; revised second edition, University of Chicago Press, 1992)

———, 'Jewish Magic in the Greek Magical Papyri (*PGM* VII.260–71)', in Peter Schäfer and Hans G. Kippenberg (eds.), *Envisioning Magic: A Princeton Seminar and Symposium* (Leiden: Brill, 1997)

———, *The "Mithras Liturgy": Text, Translation, and Commentary* (Tübingen, Mohr-Siebeck, 2003)

Bonatti, Guido, *Liber Astronomiae*, trans. Robert Zoller (Berkeley Springs, WV: Golden Hind Press, 1994)

Campanini, Saverio (ed. and trans.), *The Book of Bahir: Flavius Mithridates' Latin Translation, the Hebrew Text, and an English Variation* (Torino: Nino Aragno Editore, 2005)

Charles, Robert Henry, *The Book of Enoch* (Oxford: Clarendon Press, 1893; repr. San Diego, CA: The Book Tree, 2006)

Charlesworth, James H. (ed.), *The Old Testament Pseudepigrapha*, 2 volumes (Garden City, NY: Doubleday, 1983)

Cicero, M. Tullius, *On Divination*, in M. Tullius Cicero, *Old Age, On Friendship, On Divination*, trans. W. A. Falconer (Cambridge, MA: Harvard University Press, 1970), 223–539

Clement, *Stromata*, trans. W. L. Alexander, in Alexander Roberts, James Donaldson, Philip Schaff, and Henry Wace (eds.), *The Ante-Nicene Fathers: Translations of the Writings of the Fathers Down to A.D. 325*, 10 volumes (Peabody, MA: Hendrickson, 1994), 2:299–568

Clementine Homilies, trans. Philip Schaff, in Alexander Roberts, James Donaldson, Philip Schaff, and Henry Wace (eds.), *The Ante-Nicene Fathers: Translations of the Writings of the Fathers Down to A.D. 325*, 10 volumes (Peabody, MA: Hendrickson, 1994), 8:213–346

Cole, Peter (trans.), *Selected Poems of Solomon ibn Gabirol* (Princeton, NJ: Princeton University Press, 2001)

Coneybeare, F. C. (trans.), 'The Testament of Solomon', *Jewish Quarterly Review*, 11 (1898), 1–45

Copenhaver, Brian (ed. and trans.), *Hermetica: The Greek* Corpus Hermeticum *and the Latin* Asclepius *in a new English translation with notes and introduction* (Cambridge: Cambridge University Press, 1992)

Cordovero, Moshe, *Pardes Rimonim: Orchard of Pomegranates, Parts 1–4*, trans. Elyakim Getz (Monfalcone: Providence University, 2007)

———, *The Palm Tree of Devorah*, trans. Moshe Miller (Southfield, MI: Targum Press, 1993)

———, *Moses Cordovero's Introduction to Kabbalah: An Annotated Translation of His* Or Ne'erav, trans. Ira Robinson (Hoboken, NJ: Ktav Publishing, 1994)

Dan, Joseph (ed. and trans.), *The Heart and the Fountain: An Anthology of Jewish Mystical Experiences* (Oxford: Oxford University Press, 2002)

De Herrera, Abraham Cohen, *Gate of Heaven*, trans. Kenneth Krabbenhoft (Leiden: Brill, 2002)

De Manhar, Nurho (trans.) *Zohar (Bereshith-Genesis): An Expository Translation from Hebrew* (serialised in *The Word*, ed. H. W. Percival, New York: Theosophical Publishing Society, 1900–1914; repr. San Diego, CA: Wizards Bookshelf, 1985)

Devereux, George (ed.), *Psychoanalysis and the Occult* (New York: International Universities Press, 1953)

Dodds, E. R., 'Theurgy and its Relationship to Neoplatonism', *Journal of Roman Studies*, 37 (1947), 55–69

———, 'The Astral Body in Neoplatonism', in E. R. Dodds (trans.), *Proclus: The Elements of Theology* (Oxford: Oxford University Press, 1963)

——— (trans.), *Proclus: The Elements of Theology* (Oxford: Oxford University Press, 1963)

Dorotheus Sidonius, *Carmen Astrologicum*, trans. David Pingree (Munich: K. G. Saur, 1976)

Duling, D. C. (trans.), 'Testament of Solomon', in James H. Charlesworth (ed.), *The Old Testament Pseudepigrapha*, 2 volumes (Garden City, NY: Doubleday, 1983), 1:935–87

Dunn, James David (ed.), *Window of the Soul: The Kabbalah of Rabbi Isaac Luria (1534–1572)*, trans. Nathan Snyder (San Francisco, CA: Red Wheel/Weiser, 2008)

Faierstein, Morris M., trans., *Jewish Mystical Autobiographies: Book of Visions and Book of Secrets* (Mahwah, NJ: Paulist Press, 1999)

Fine, Lawrence (ed. and trans.), *Safed Spirituality: Rules of Mystical Piety, The Beginning of Wisdom* (Mahwah, NJ: Paulist Press, 1984)

Finkel, Avraham Yaakov (ed. and trans.), *Sefer Chasidim: The Book of the Pious* (Northvale, NJ: Jason Aronson, 1997)

—— (ed. and trans.), *Kabbalah: Selections from Classic Kabbalistic Works from Raziel HaMalach to the Present Day* (Southfield, MI: Targum Press, 2002)

Fludd, Robert, *Mosaicall Philosophy* (London: Humphrey Moseley, 1659)

Frank, Jacob, *The Collection of the Words of the Lord*, ed. and trans. Harris Lenowitz (2004), <http://www.languages.utah.edu/kabbalah/protected/dicta_frank_le nowitz.pdf>

Freud, Sigmund, *Jokes in Relation to the Unconscious*, in *The Standard Edition of the Collected Works of Sigmund Freud*, trans. James Strachey, Vol. 8 (London: Hogarth Press/Institute of Psychoanalysis, 1960 [1905])

——, 'The Sexual Aberrations', first published in English in 1910, repr. in Freud, SE7

——, *The Interpretation of Dreams*, trans. A. A. Brill (London: George Allen & Unwin, 1913; repr. Freud, SE4–5)

——, *The Psychopathology of Everyday Life*, trans. A. A. Brill (London: T. Fisher Unwin, 1914; repr. Freud, SE6)

——, 'Dreams and Telepathy', trans. C. J. M. Hubback, *Imago*, Vol. 8 (1922), 1–22, repr. in Sigmund Freud, *Collected Papers*, 4 volumes, trans. C. J. M. Hubback and Joan Riviere (London: Hogarth Press, 1924–1925), 4:408–35

——, 'The Occult Significance of Dreams', in George Devereux (ed.), *Psychoanalysis and the Occult* (New York: International Universities Press, 1953), 87–90

——, 'Dreams and the Occult', in Sigmund Freud, *New Introductory Lectures in Psychoanalysis* (New York: Norton, 1933), 257–75, repr. in George Devereux (ed.), *Psychoanalysis and the Occult* (New York: International Universities Press, 1953), 91–109

——, *Collected Papers*, 4 volumes, trans. C. J. M. Hubback and Joan Riviere (London: Hogarth Press, 1924–1925)

——, 'Psychoanalysis and Telepathy', in Sigmund Freud, *Beyond the Pleasure Principle, Group Psychology, and Other Works*, trans. James Strachey, Vol. 18, *The Standard Edition of the Complete Psychological Works of Sigmund Freud* (London: Hogarth Press, 1961), 177–94

——, SE4: *The Interpretation of Dreams, Part One*, trans. James Strachey, Vol. 4, *The Standard Edition of the Complete Psychological Works of Sigmund Freud*, 24 volumes (London: Hogarth Press, 1961)

——, SE5: *The Interpretation of Dreams, Part Two*, trans. James Strachey, Vol. 5, *The Standard Edition of the Complete Psychological Works of Sigmund Freud*, 24 volumes (London: Hogarth Press, 1961)

——, SE6: *The Psychopathology of Everyday Life*, trans. A. A. Brill (London: T. Fisher Unwin, 1914; repr. trans. James Strachey, Vol. 6, *The Standard Edition of the Complete Psychological Works of Sigmund Freud*, 24 volumes (London: Hogarth Press, 1961)

——, SE7: *On Sexuality: Three Essays on the Theory of Sexuality and Other Works*, trans. James Strachey, Vol. 7, *The Standard Edition of the Complete Psychological Works of Sigmund Freud*, 24 volumes (London: Hogarth Press, 1961)

——, SE18: *Beyond the Pleasure Principle*, trans. C. J. M. Hubback (London: International Psycho-Analytical Press, 1922; repr. in *Beyond the Pleasure Principle, Group Psychology, and Other Works*, trans. James Strachey, Vol.

18, *The Standard Edition of the Complete Psychological Works of Sigmund Freud*, 24 volumes (London: Hogarth Press, 1961)

Gikatilla, R. Joseph, *Gates of Light: Sha'are Orah*, trans. Avi Weinstein, Bronfman Library of Jewish Classics (New York/Oxford: Rowan & Littlefield, 1994)

Godwin, Joscelyn (trans.), *Salomon Trismosin's Splendor Solis* (Grand Rapids, MI: Phanes Press, 1991)

Gollancz, Hermann (trans.), *Sepher Maphtea Shelomoh (Book of the Key of Solomon): An exact facsimile of an original book of magic in Hebrew with illustrations* (Oxford: Oxford University Press, 1914)

Greer, John Michael and Christopher Warnock (trans.), *The Latin Picatrix, Books I & II* (Raleigh, NC: Renaissance Astrology, 2009)

Hall, Manley Palmer (ed. and trans.), *Paracelsus: His Mystical and Medical Philosophy* (Los Angeles, CA: Philosophical Research Society, 1964)

Hayman, A. Peter (ed. and trans.), *Sefer Yesira: Edition, Translation and Text-Critical Commentary* (Tübingen: Mohr Sieback, 2004)

Huffman, William H., *Robert Fludd: Essential Readings* (London: Aquarian Press, 1992)

Ibn Ezra, Abraham, *The Beginning of Wisdom*, trans. Meira B. Epstein (Reston, VA: Archive for the Retrieval of Historical Astrological Texts, 1998)

———, *The Book of Reasons*, trans. Shlomo Sela (Leiden: Brill, 2007)

———, *The Book of Nativities and Revolutions*, trans. Meira B. Epstein (Reston, VA: Archive for the Retrieval of Historical Astrological Texts, 2008)

Irenaeus, *Adversus Haereses*, in Alexander Roberts, James Donaldson, and Philip Schaff (eds.), *The Ante-Nicene Fathers: Translations of the Writings of the Fathers Down to A.D. 325*, 10 volumes (Peabody, MA: Hendrickson, 1994), 1:309–567

Jacobi, Jolande, *The Psychology of C. G. Jung*, trans. K. W. Bash (London: Kegan Paul, Trench, Trubner & Co., 1942)

Jacobs, Louis (ed. and trans.), *The Jewish Mystics* (London: Kyle Cathie, 1990)

'J. K.' [Julius Kohn] (ed. and trans.),Trismosin, Solomon, Splendor Solis: Alchemical Treatises of Solomon Trismosin, Adept and Teacher of Paracelsus, Including 22 Allegorical Pictures Reproduced from the Original Paintings in the Unique Manuscript on Vellum, dated 1582, in the British Museum. With Introduction, Elucidation of the Paintings, aiding the Interpretation of their Occult meaning, Trismosin's Autobiographical Account of his Travels in Search of the Philosopher's Stone, a Summary of his Alchemical Process called "The Red Lion", and Explanatory Notes (London: Kegan Paul, Trench, Trubner & Co., 1920)

Jung, C. G., *The Psychology of the Unconscious. A Study of the Transformations and Symbolisms of the Libido. A Contribution to the History of the Evolution of Thought* trans. Beatrice M. Hinkle (London: Kegan Paul, 1917); repr. as CW5, *Symbols of Transformation*, trans. R. F. C. Hull (London: Routledge & Kegan Paul, 1956)

———, 'The Spiritual Problem of Modern Man', in C. G. Jung, *Modern Man in Search of a Soul*, trans. W. S. Dell and Cary F. Baynes (London: Kegan Paul, Trench, Trubner & Co., 1933), 226–54; repr. in Jung, CW10, *Civilization in Transition*, trans. R. F. C. Hull (London: Routledge & Kegan Paul, 1964), 74–94

———, *The Integration of the Personality*, trans. Stanley Dell (NY: Farrar & Rinehart, 1939; London: Routledge & Kegan Paul, 1940)

———, CW6: *Psychological Types*, trans. H. G. Baynes (London: Kegan Paul, 1923); repr. trans. R. F. C. Hull (London: Routledge & Kegan Paul, 1971)

———, CW8: *The Structure and Dynamics of the Psyche*, trans. R. F. C. Hull (London: Routledge & Kegan Paul, 1960)

———, CW9i: *The Archetypes and the Collective Unconscious*, trans. R. F. C. Hull (London: Routledge & Kegan Paul, 1959)

———, CW9ii: *Aion*, trans. R. F. C. Hull (London: Routledge & Kegan Paul, 1959)

———, CW10: *Civilization in Transition*, trans. R. F. C. Hull (London: Routledge & Kegan Paul, 1964)

———, CW11: *Psychology and Religion*, trans. R. F. C. Hull (London: Routledge & Kegan Paul, 1958)

———, CW12: *Psychology and Alchemy*, trans. R. F. C. Hull (London: Routledge & Kegan Paul, 1953)

———, CW13: *Alchemical Studies*, trans. R. F. C. Hull (London: Routledge & Kegan Paul, 1967)

———, CW14: *Mysterium Coniunctionis*, trans. R. F. C. Hull (London: Routledge & Kegan Paul, 1963)

———, CW16: *The Practice of Psychotherapy*, trans. R. F. C. Hull (London: Routledge & Kegan Paul, 1954)

———, CW18: *The Symbolic Life*, trans. R. F. C. Hull (London: Routledge & Kegan Paul, 1977)

———, CW20: General Index (London: Routledge & Kegan Paul, 1979)

———, *Memories, Dreams, Reflections*, trans. Richard and Clara Winston (London: Routledge & Kegan Paul, 1963; repr. London: HarperCollins/Fontana, 1995)

———, 'The Two Sources of Knowledge: the Light of Nature and the Light of Revelation', in *Alchemical Studies*, CW13, trans. R. F. C. Hull (London: Routledge & Kegan Paul, 1967), 111–32

———, *C. G. Jung Letters*, 2 volumes, ed. Gerhard Adler, trans. R. F. C. Hull (London: Routledge & Kegan Paul, 1976)

Kalisch, Isadore (ed. and trans.), *Sepher Yezirah. A Book on Creation; or, the Jewish Metaphysics of Remote Antiquity*, New York: L. H. Frank, 1877)

Kaplan, Aryeh (ed. and trans.), *The Bahir* (York Beach, ME: Red Wheel/Weiser, 1979)

——— (ed. and trans.), *Sefer Yetzirah: The Book of Creation, in Theory and Practice* (York Beach, ME: Samuel Weiser, 1997)

Karr, Don (ed.), *Liber Salomonis: Cephar Raziel* (1995), <http://www.digital-brilliance.com/kab/karr/Solomon/LibSal.pdf>

Klein, Eliahu (ed. and trans.), *Kabbalah of Creation: Isaac Luria's Earlier Mysticism* (Northvale, NJ: Jason Aronson, 2000)

Loewe, Raphael (ed. and trans.), *Meshal ha-kadmoni: Fables from the Distant Past* (Oxford: Littman Library of Jewish Civilization, 2004)

Maimonides, Moses, *The Guide of the Perplexed*, trans. Shlomo Pines, 2 volumes (Chicago, IL: University of Chicago Press, 1963)

Matt, Daniel C. (trans.), *The Zohar: Pritzker Edition*, 4 volumes (Stanford, CA: Stanford University Press, 2004–2007)

McGinn, Bernard (trans.), *Apocalyptic Spirituality: Treatises and Letters of Lactantius, Adso of Montier-en-Der, Joachim of Fiore, the Franciscan Spirituals, Savanarola* (New York: Paulist Press, 1979)

McGuire, William (ed.), *The Freud-Jung Letters*, trans. Ralph Manheim and R. F. C. Hull (London: Hogarth Press/Routledge & Kegan Paul, 1977)

——— (ed.), *Dream Analysis: Notes of the Seminar Given in 1928–1930 by C. G. Jung* (London: Routledge & Kegan Paul, 1984)

McGuire, William and R. F. C. Hull (eds.), *C. G. Jung Speaking: Interviews and Encounters* (Princeton, NJ: Princeton University Press, 1993)

Mead, G. R. S. (trans.), *Pistis Sophia* (London: J. M. Watkins, 1921)

Menzi, Donald Wilder and Zwe Padeh (trans.), *The Tree of Life: Chayyim Vital's Introduction to the Kabbalah of Isaac Luria, Vol. 1: The Palace of Adam Kadmon* (Northvale, NJ: Jason Aronson, 1999)

Mesmer, Franz Anton, *Mesmerism: A Translation of the Original Medical and Scientific Writings of F. A. Mesmer, M. D.*, ed. and trans. George J. Bloch (Los Altos, CA: William Kaufmann, 1980)

Meyrink, Gustav, *Der Golem* (original German publication serialised in *Die weissen Blätter*, 1913–14; published in complete form, Leipzig: Kurt Wolff, 1915; first English translation, New York: Houghton Mifflin, 1928; reissued, trans. Madge Pemberton, New York: Dover Publications, 1976)

Morgan, Michael A. (trans.), *Sepher ha-Razim: The Book of the Mysteries* (Chico, CA: Scholars Press, 1983)

Origen, *Against Celsus*, trans. F. Crombie and W. H. Cairns, in *The Anti-Nicene Fathers*, IV, ed. Alexander Roberts and James Donaldson (New York: Charles Scribner's Sons, 1899)

Paracelsus, *Selected Writings*, ed. Jolande Jacobi, trans. Norbert Guterman, Bollingen Series XXVIII (New York: Pantheon, 1958)

Pico della Mirandola, Giovanni, *Heptaplus*, trans. Douglas Carmichael, in *Giovanni Pico della Mirandola, On the Dignity of Man, On Being and the One, Heptaplus* (New York: Macmillan, 1985 [1940]), 63–174

——, *On the Dignity of Man*, trans. Charles Glenn Wallis, in *Giovanni Pico della Mirandola, On the Dignity of Man, On Being and the One, Heptaplus* (New York: Macmillan, 1985), 1–34

——, *On the Dignity of Man, On Being and the One, Heptaplus* (New York: Macmillan, 1985)

Pingree, David (ed.), *The Latin Version of the Ghayat al-hakim* (London: Studies of the Warburg Institute, 1986)

Placidus de Titis, *Primum Mobile*, trans. John Cooper (Bromley: Institute for the Study of Cycles in World Affairs, 1983)

Plato, *Timaeus*, trans. Benjamin Jowett, in Edith Hamilton and Huntington Cairns (eds.), *Plato: Collected Dialogues* (Princeton, NJ: Princeton University Press, 1961), 1151–1211

——, *Symposium*, trans. Michael Joyce, in Edith Hamilton and Huntington Cairns (eds.), *Plato: Collected Dialogues* (Princeton, NJ: Princeton University Press, 1961), 526–74

——, *Plato: Collected Dialogues*, eds. Edith Hamilton and Huntington Cairns (Princeton, NJ: Princeton University Press, 1961)

Plotinus, *The Enneads*, trans. Stephen MacKenna, Burdett, NY: Larson Publications, 1992)

——, *Commentary on Plato's Timaeus, Vol. 3: Proclus on the World's Body*, ed. and trans. Dirk Baltzly (Cambridge: Cambridge University Press, 2006)

Ptolemy, Claudius, *Tetrabiblos*, trans. F. E. Robbins (Cambridge, MA: Harvard University Press, 1971)

Reuchlin, Johannes, *On the Art of the Kabbalah* (*De arte cabalistica libri tres*), trans. Martin and Sarah Goodman (Lincoln, NE: University of Nebraska Press, 1983)

——, *Recommendation Whether to Confiscate, Destroy, and Burn All Jewish Books*, ed. and trans. Peter Wortman (Mahwah, NJ: Paulist Press, 2000)

Roberts, Alexander, James Donaldson, and Philip Schaff (eds.), *The Ante-Nicene Fathers: Translations of the Writings of the Fathers Down to A.D. 325*, 10 volumes (Peabody, MA: Hendrickson, 1994)

Robinson, James M. (ed.), *The Nag Hammadi Library in English* (Leiden: Brill, 1977)

Rosenberg, Roy A. (trans.), *The Anatomy of God: The Book of Concealment, the Great Holy Assembly and the Lesser Holy Assembly of the Zohar with the Assembly of the Tabernacle* (New York: Ktav Publishing House, 1973)

Savedow, Steve (ed. and trans.), *Sepher Rezial Hemelach: The Book of the Angel Rezial* (York Beach, ME: Samuel Weiser, 2000)

Sibly, Ebenezer and Frederick Hockley (trans.), *The Clavis or Key to the Magic of Solomon* (Lake Worth, FLA: Ibis Press, 2009)

Sigrist, Henry E. (ed.), *Paracelsus: Four Treatises*, trans. C. Lilian Temkin, George Rosen, Gregory Zilgoorg, and Henry E. Sigerist (Baltimore, MD: Johns Hopkins University Press, 1996)

Sperling, Harry and Maurice Simon (trans.), *The Zohar*, 5 volumes (New York/London: Soncino Press, 1934)

Stenring, Knut (trans.), *The Book of Formation (Sepher Yetzirah) by Rabbi Akiba ben Joseph, including the 32 Paths of Wisdom, their correspondences with the Hebrew alphabet and the Tarot symbols* (New York: Ktav Publishing House, 1923)

Swedenborg, Emanuel, *An Hieroglyphic Key to Natural and Spiritual Mysteries by Way of Representations and Correspondences*, ed. and trans. Robert Hindmarsh (London: Thomas Goyder, 1826)

———, *Emanuel Swedenborg's Journal of Dreams*, ed. W. R. Woofenden, trans. J. J. Garth Wilkinson (New York: Swedenborg Foundation, 1986)

Themanlys, Pascal (ed. and trans.), *Visions of the Eternal Present: Selections from the Cosmic Works of Max Theon* (Jerusalem: Argaman, 1991)

Tishby, Isaiah and David Goldstein (eds. and trans.), *The Wisdom of the Zohar: An Anthology of Texts*, 3 volumes (Portland, OR: Littman Library of Jewish Civilization/Oxford University Press, 1989)

Turner, Robert (trans.), *Henry Cornelius Agrippa his Fourth Book of Occult Philosophy* (London: John Harrison, 1655; repr. Berwick ME: Ibis Press, 2005)

——— (trans.), *Ars Notoria: The Magical Art of Solomon, Showing the Cabalistical Key of Magical Operations*, ed. Darcy Küntz (London: John Harrison, 1656; repr. Sequim, WA: Holmes Publishing Group, 2006)

Vital, Chayyim, *Window of the Soul: The Kabbalah of Rabbi Isaac Luria (1534–1572)*, ed. David Sunn, trans. Nathan Snyder (San Francisco, CA: Red Wheel/Weiser, 2008)

Wexelman, David M. (ed. and trans.), *The Jewish Concept of Reincarnation and Creation: Based on the Writings of Rabbi Chaim Vital* (Northvale, NJ: Jason Aronson, 1999)

Wolfson, Elliot R. (ed.), *The Book of the Pomegranate: Moses De Leon's Sefer Ha-Rimmon* (Atlanta, GA: Scholars Press, 1988)

Zoller, Robert (trans.), *Liber Hermetis*, ed. Robert Hand (Berkeley Springs, WV: Golden Hind Press, 1993)

SECONDARY WORKS:

Aakhus, Patricia, 'Astral Magic in the Renaissance', *Magic, Ritual, and Witchcraft* (Winter 2008), 185–206

Abrams, Daniel, 'From Germany to Spain: Numerology as a Mystical Technique', *Journal of Jewish Studies*, 47 (1996), 85–101

———, 'Presenting and Representing Gershom Scholem: A Review Essay', *Modern Judaism*, 20:2 (2000), 226–43

Abrams, Daniel and Avraham Elqayam (eds.), *Kabbalah: Journal for the Study of Jewish Mystical Texts*, Vol. 13 (Los Angeles, CA: Cherub Press, 2005)

Adams, George, *Physical and Ethereal Spaces* (London: Rudolf Steiner Press, 1965)

Adams, James Eli, *Dandies and Desert Saints: Styles of Victorian Manhood* (Ithaca, NY: Cornell University Press, 1995)

Adler, Hermann, 'Dr. Falk: The Baal Shem from London', *Transactions of the Jewish Historical Society of England, 1902–1905* (London, 1908), 57–60

Adkins, Lesley, *Empires of the Plain: Henry Rawlinson and the Lost Languages of Babylon* (London: HarperCollins, 2003)

Adrian, Jack, 'Introduction', in Dion Fortune, *The Secrets of Dr. Taverner* (Ashcroft, BC: Ash-Tree Press, 2000), ix–xxvi

Afterman, Adam, 'Letter Permutation Techniques, Kavannah and Prayer in Jewish Mysticism', *Journal for the Study of Religions and Ideologies*, 6:18 (2007), 52–78

Ages, Arnold, 'Lamennais and the Jews', *Jewish Quarterly Review*, 63:2 (1972), 158–70

Albert, Phillis Cohen, *The Modernization of French Jewry: Consistory and Community in the Nineteenth Century* (Hanover, NH: Brandeis University Press, 1977)

Alexander, Philip S., 'The Historical Setting of the Hebrew Book of Enoch', *Journal of Jewish Studies*, 28 (1977), 156–80

——, '3 (Hebrew Apocalypse of) Enoch', in James H. Charlesworth (ed.), *The Old Testament Pseudepigrapha*, 2 volumes (Garden City, NY: Doubleday, 1983), 1:223–315

——, '*Sefer ha-Razim* and the Problem of Black Magic in Early Judaism', in Todd E. Klutz (ed.), *Magic in the Biblical World: From the Rod of Aaron to the Ring of Solomon* (London: T & T Clark International, 2003), 170–90

Algeo, John, 'The Integrated Alien: Magic in the Fiction of Dion Fortune', in Olena H. Saciuk, ed., *The Shape of the Fantastic: Selected Essays from the Seventh International Conference on the Fantastic in the Arts* (New York: Greenwood Press, 1990), 211–18

Allen, James Smith, *Popular French Romanticism: Authors, Readers, and Books in the 19th Century* (Syracuse, NY: Syracuse University Press, 1981)

Allen, Michael J. B. and Valery Rees (eds.), *Marsilio Ficino: His Theology, His Philosophy, His Legacy* (Leiden: Brill, 2002)

Altglas, Véronique, 'Yoga and Kabbalah as World Religions? A Comparative Perspective on Globalization of Religious Resources', in Boaz Huss (ed.), *Kabbalah and Contemporary Spiritual Revival* (Beer-Sheva: Ben-Gurion University of the Negev Press, 2011), 233–50

Altmann, Alexander (ed.), *Biblical and Other Studies* (Cambridge, MA: Harvard University Press, 1963)

—— (ed.), *Jewish Medieval and Renaissance Studies* (Cambridge, MA: Harvard University Press, 1967)

——, *Essays in Jewish Intellectual History* (Hanover, NH: University Press of New England, 1981)

——, 'Lurianic Kabbalah in a Platonic Key: Abraham Cohen Herrera's *Puerta del Cielo*', in Isadore Twersky and Bernard Septimus (eds.), *Jewish Thought in the Seventeenth Century* (Cambridge, MA: Harvard University Press, 1987), 1–37

——, 'Eternality of Punishment: A Theological Controversy', in Lawrence Fine (ed.), *Essential Papers on Kabbalah* (New York: New York University Press, 1995), 270–87

Ancien Tarot de Marseilles (Paris: Cartomanche Grimaud, 1977)

Andresen, Jensene (ed.), *Religion in Mind: Cognitive Perspectives on Religious Belief, Ritual, and Experience* (Cambridge: Cambridge University Press, 2001)

Andrews, Naomi J., '"La Mère Humanité": Femininity in the Romantic Socialism of Pierre Leroux and the Abbé A.-L. Constant', *Journal of the History of Ideas*, 63:4 (2002), 697–716

——, 'Utopian Androgyny: Romantic Socialists Confront Individualism in July Monarchy France', *French Historical Studies*, 26:3 (2003), 437–57

——, *Socialism's Muse: Gender in the Intellectual Landscape of French Romantic Socialism* (Lanham, MD: Lexington Books, 2006)

Andriano, Joseph, *Feminine Demonology in Male Gothic Fiction* (University Park, PA: Pennsylvania State University Press, 1985)

Anonymous, 'Why Freemasonry Has Enemies' (27 May 1949), posted on the website of the Masonic Service Association of the United States in 2008 as 'The Short Talk Bulletin', <http://www.freemasoninformation.com>

Antes, Peter, Armin W. Geertz, and Randi R. Warne (eds.), *New Approaches to the Study of Religion, Vol. 1: Regional, Critical, and Historical Approaches* (Berlin/New York: Walter de Gruyter, 2004)

Aptekman, Marina, 'Kabbalah, Judeo-Masonic Myth, and Post-Soviet Literary Discourse: From Political Tool to Virtual Parody', *Russian Review*, 65:4 (2006), 657–81

Arbel, Vita Daphna, *Beholders of Divine Secrets: Mysticism and Myth in the Hekhalot and Merkavah Literature* (Albany, NY: State University of New York Press, 2003)

——, '"Seal of Resemblance, Full of Wisdom, and Perfect in Beauty": The Enoch/Metatron Narrative of 3 Enoch and Ezekiel 28', *Harvard Theological Review*, 98:2 (2005), 121–42

Aron, Willy, 'Notes on Sigmund Freud's Ancestry and Jewish Contacts', *YIVO Annual of Jewish Social Science*, 11 (1956–1957), 286–95

Aronson, Irwin Michael, *Troubled Waters: The Origins of the 1881 Anti-Jewish Pogroms in Russia* (Pittsburgh, PA: University of Pittsburgh Press, 1990)

Arvidsson, Stefan, 'Aryan Mythology As Science and Ideology', *Journal of the American Academy of Religion*, 67:2 (1999), 327–54

Arzy, Shahar, Moshe Idel, Theodor Landis, and Olaf Blanke, 'Speaking With One's Self: Autoscopic Phenomena in Writings from the Ecstatic Kabbalah', *Journal of Consciousness Studies*, 12:11 (2005), 4–30

Ashlag, Rav Yehuda, *Kabbalah for the Student*, trans. Michael Laitman (Toronto: Laitman Kabbalah Publishers, 2009)

Ashley, Mike, *Algernon Blackwood: A Bio-Bibliography* (New York: Greenwood Press, 1987)

Asprem, Egil, '*Kabbalah Recreata*: Reception and Adaptation of Kabbalah in Modern Occultism', *Pomegranate*, 9:2 (2007), 132–53

——, 'Magic Naturalized? Negotiating Science and Occult Experience in Aleister Crowley's Scientific Illuminism', *Aries*, 8 (2008), 139–65

——, 'False, Lying Spirits and Angels of Light: Ambiguous Mediation in Dr. Rudd's Seventeenth-Century Treatise on Angel Magic', *Magic, Ritual, and Witchcraft* (Summer 2008), 54–80

Assman, Jan, 'The Mosaic Distinction: Israel, Egypt, and the Invention of Paganism', *Representations*, 56 (Autumn 1996), 48–67

——, *Moses the Egyptian: The Memory of Egypt in Western Monotheism* (Cambridge, MA: Harvard University Press, 1997)

Atton, Christopher and Stephen Dziklewicz, *Kabbalistic Diagrams of Rosenroth* (London: The Hermetic Research Trust, 1987)

Atzmon, Leslie, 'A visual analysis of anthropomorphism in the Kabbalah: dissecting the Hebrew alphabet and Sephirotic diagram', *Visual Communication*, 2:97 (2003), 97–114

Austin, Kenneth, *From Judaism to Calvinism: The Life and Writings of Immanuel Tremellius (c. 1510–1580)* (Aldershot: Ashgate, 2007)

Auty, Robert and J. L. I. Fennell (eds.), *Oxford Slavonic Papers, New Series, Vol. 1* (Oxford: Clarendon Press, 1968)

Avery-Peck, Alan J. and Jacob Neusner (eds.), *Judaism in Late Antiquity, Part 4: Death, Life-After-Death, Resurrection and the World-to-Come in the Judaisms of Antiquity* (Leiden: Brill, 2000)

Ayres, Brenda, *Silent Voices: Forgotten Novels by Victorian Women Writers* (Westport, CT: Greenwood Publishing Group, 2003)

Badham, Paul, *The Contemporary Challenge of Modernist Theology* (Cardiff: University of Wales Press, 1998)

Bakan, David, *Sigmund Freud and the Jewish Mystical Tradition* (Princeton, NJ: D. Van Nostrand, 1958; repr. Boston: Beacon Press, 1975)

Barabashev, A. G., 'On the Impact of the World Outlook on Mathematical Creativity', *Philosophia Mathematica*, 2–3:1 (1988), 1–20

Barker, Eileen and Margit Warburg (eds.), *New Religions and New Religiosity* (Aarhus: Aarhus University Press, 1998)

Baron, Salo W., 'The Revolution of 1848 and Jewish Scholarship: Part I: France, the United States and Italy', *Proceedings of the American Academy for Jewish Research*, 18 (1948–49), 1–66

Barrow, Logic, *Independent Spirits: Spiritualism and the English Plebeians, 1850–1910* (London: Routledge & Kegan Paul, 1986)

Bartal, Israel, *The Jews of Eastern Europe, 1772–1881*, trans. Chaya Naor (Philadelphia, PA: University of Pennsylvania Press, 2005)

Barton, Tamsyn, *Ancient Astrology* (London: Routledge, 1994)

Baskind, Samantha, 'Distinguishing the Distinction: Picturing Ashkenazi and Sephardic Jews in Seventeenth- and Eighteenth-Century Amsterdam', *Journal for the Study of Sephardic and Mizrahi Jewry*, 1:1 (2007), 1–13

Bates, David, 'The Mystery of Truth: Louis-Claude de Saint-Martin's Enlightened Mysticism', *Journal of the History of Ideas*, 61:4 (2000), 635–55

Beck, Roger, *Planetary Gods and Planetary Orders in the Mysteries of Mithras* (Leiden: Brill, 1988)

———, Roger Beck, *The Religion of the Mithras Cult in the Roman Empire* (Oxford: Oxford University Press, 2006)

Beguin, Albert, 'Poetry and Occultism', trans. Robert G. Cohn, *Yale French Studies*, 4 (1949), 12–25

Beitchman, Philip, *Alchemy of the Word: Cabala of the Renaissance* (Albany, NY. State University of New York Press, 1998)

Benavides, Gustavo, 'Modernity', in Mark C. Taylor (ed.), *Critical Terms for Religious Studies* (Chicago, IL: University of Chicago Press, 1998), 186–204

Benz, Ernst, *Christian Kabbalah: Neglected Child of Theology*, trans. Kenneth W. Wesche, St. Paul, MN: Grailstone Press, 2004)

———, *The Mystical Sources of German Romantic Philosophy*, trans. Blair R. Reynolds and Eunice M. Paul (Eugene, OR: Pickwick Publications, 1983)

Beresiner, Yasha, 'Some Judaic Aspects of Freemasonry: Dermott's *Ahiman Rezon*', *Pietre-Stones Review of Freemasonry*, <http://www.freemasons-freemasonry.com/beresiner5.html> (18 December 2007); repr. from *Haboreh Hahofshi [The Israeli Freemason]*)

Berke, Joseph H., 'Psychoanalysis and Kabbalah', *Psychoanalytic Review*, 83 (1996), 849–63

Berke, Joseph H. and Stanley Schneider, 'Repairing Worlds: An Exploration of the Psychoanalytical and Kabbalistic Concepts of Reparation and Tikkun', *Psychoanalytic Review*, 90 (2003), 723–49

Berke, Joseph H. and Stanley Schneider, *Centers of Power: The Convergence of Psychoanalysis and Kabbalah* (New York, NY: Jason Aronson, 2008)

Berkovitz, Jay R., *The Shaping of Jewish Identity in Nineteenth-century France* (Detroit, MI: Wayne State University Press, 1989)

———, 'The French Revolution and the Jews: Assessing the Cultural Impact', *AJS Review*, 20:1 (1995), 25–86

Betegh, Gábor, *The Derveni Papyrus: Cosmology, Theology and Interpretation* (Cambridge: Cambridge University Press, 2004)

Bevir, Mark, 'The West Turns East: Madame Blavatsky and the Transformation of the Occult Tradition', *Journal of the American Academy of Religion*, 62:3 (1994), 747–67

Biale, David, *Gershom Scholem: Kabbalah and Counter-History* (Cambridge, MA: Harvard University Press, 1979)

Bilski, Emily D. (ed.), *Golem! Danger, Deliverance and Art* (New York: The Jewish Museum, 1988)

Bilu, Yoram, 'Pondering "The Princes of the Oil": New Light on an Old Phenomenon', *Journal of Anthropological Research*, 37:3 (1981), 269–78

———, 'Dybbuk and Maggid: Two Cultural Patterns of Altered Consciousness in Judaism', *AJS Review*, 21:2 (1996), 341–66

Bingham, Adrian, *Gender, Modernity, and the Popular Press in Inter-War Britain* (Oxford: Oxford University Press, 2004)

Black, Crofton, 'From Kabbalah to Psychology: The Allegorizing *Isagoge* of Paulus Riccius, 1509–41', *Magic, Ritual, and Witchcraft*, 2:2, (2007), 136–73

Black, Eugene C., 'A Typological Study of English Zionists', *Jewish Social Studies*, 9:3 (2003), 20–55

Blau, Joseph Leon, *The Christian Interpretation of the Cabala in the Renaissance* (New York: Columbia University Press, 1944)

Blau, Joshua and Stefan C. Reif (eds.), *Genizah Research after Ninety Years: The Case of Judaeo-Arabic* (Cambridge: Cambridge University Press, 1992)

Bleiler, E. F., 'Introduction', in *Best Ghost Stories of Algernon Blackwood* (New York: Dover Publications, 1973), v–x

Bloom, Harold, *Kabbalah and Criticism* (New York: Seabury Press, 1975)

Bloom, Maureen, *Jewish Mysticism and Magic: An Anthropological Perspective* (London: Routledge, 2007)

Bogdan, Henrik, *Western Esotericism and Rituals of Initiation* (Albany, NY: State University of New York Press, 2007)

———, 'Secret Societies and Western Esotericism', in R. A. Gilbert (ed.), *Seeking the Light: Freemasonry and Initiatic Traditions*, Canonbury Papers, Vol. 4 (Hersham: Lewis Masonic, 2007), 21–29

Bohak, Gideon, 'Hebrew, Hebrew Everywhere? Notes on the Interpretation of *Voces Magicae*', in Scott Noegel, Joel Walker, and Brannon Wheeler (eds.), *Prayer, Magic, and the Stars in the Ancient and Late Antique World* (University Park, PA: University of Pennsylvania Press, 2003), 69–82

———, *Ancient Jewish Magic: A History* (Cambridge: Cambridge University Press, 2008)

———, 'The Magical Rotuli from the Cairo Genizah', in Gideon Bohak, Yuva Harari, and Shaul Shaked (eds.), *Continuity and Innovation in the Magical Tradition* (Leiden: Brill, 2011), 321–40

Bohak, Gideon, Yuva Harari, and Shaul Shaked (eds.), *Continuity and Innovation in the Magical Tradition* (Leiden: Brill, 2011)

Bonardel, Françoise, 'Alchemical Esotericism and the Hermeneutics of Culture', in Antoine Faivre and Jacob Needleman (eds.), *Modern Esoteric Spirituality* (New York: Crossroad, 1992), 71–100

Bonner, Campbell, *Studies in Magical Amulets, Chiefly Greco-Egyptian* (Ann Arbor: University of Michigan Press, 1950)

Booth, Martin, *A Magick Life: A Biography of Aleister Crowley* (London: Hodder & Stoughton, 2000)

Borchardt, Frank L., 'The Magus as Renaissance Man', *Sixteenth Century Journal*, 21:1 (1990), 57–76

Borella, Jean, 'René Guénon and the Traditionalist School', in Antoine Faivre and Jacob Needleman (eds.), *Modern Esoteric Spirituality* (New York: Crossroad, 1992), 330–58

Boss, Gerrit, 'Hayyim Vital's *Kabbalah Ma'asit we-Alkhimiyah* ("Practical Kabbalah and Alchemy"): A 17th-Century Book of Secrets', *JJTP* 4 (1994), 55–112

Boustan, Ra'anan S., 'The Study of Heikhalot Literature: Between Mystical Experience and Textual Artifact', *Currents in Biblical Research*, 6:1 (2007), 130–60

Boustan, Ra'anan S. and Annette Yoshiko Reed (eds.), *Heavenly Realms and Earthly Realities in Late Antique Religions* (Cambridge: Cambridge University Press, 2004)

Bouwsma, William J., 'Postel and the Significance of Renaissance Cabalism', *Journal of the History of Ideas*, 15:2 (1954), 218–32

Bouyer, Louis, 'Understanding Mysticism: An Essay on the History of the Word', in Richard Woods (ed.), *Understanding Mysticism* (Garden City, NY: Doubleday/Image, 1980), 42–55

Bowman, Frank Paul, *Eliphas Lévi, visionnaire romantique* (Paris: Presses Universitaires de France, 1969)

———, 'Illuminism, Utopia, Mythology', in D. G. Charlton (ed.), *The French Romantics*, 2 volumes (Cambridge: Cambridge University Press, 1984), 1:76–112

———, *French Romanticism: Intertextual and Interdisciplinary Readings* (Baltimore, MD: Johns Hopkins University Press, 1990)

Boyer, Pascal (ed.), *Cognitive Aspects of Religious Symbolism* (Cambridge: Cambridge University Press, 1993)

Brach, Jean-Pierre, 'Magic IV: Renaissance — 17th Century', in Wouter J. Hanegraaff, ed., *Dictionary of Gnosis and Western Hermeticism* (Leiden: Brill, 2006), 731–38

Brainard, F. Samuel, 'Defining "Mystical Experience"', *Journal of the American Academy of Religion*, 64:2 (1996), 359–93

Brandon, Ruth, *The Spiritualists: The Passion for the Occult in the Nineteenth and Twentieth Centuries* (London: Weidenfeld and Nicolson, 1983)

Brann, Noel L., 'The Conflict Between Reason and Magic in Seventeenth-Century England: A Case Study of the Vaughan-More Debate', *Huntington Library Quarterly*, 43:2 (1980), 103–26

———, *Trithemius and Magical Theology: A Chapter in the Controversy Over Occult Studies in Early Modern Europe* (Albany, NY: State University of New York Press, 1999)

Braud, William and Rosemarie Anderson, *Transpersonal Research Methods for the Social Sciences: Honoring Human Experience* (London: Sage Publications, 1998)

Breckman, Warren, 'Politics in a Symbolic Key: Pierre Laroux, Romantic Socialism, and the Schelling Affair', *Modern Intellectual History*, 2:1 (2005), 61–86

Bremmer, Jan N., 'The Birth of the Term "Magic"', in Jan N. Bremmer and Jan R. Veenstra (eds.), *The Metamorphosis of Magic: from Late Antiquity to the Early Modern Period* (Leuven: Peeters, 2002), 1–11

Bremmer, Jan N. and Jan R. Veenstra (eds.), *The Metamorphosis of Magic: From Late Antiquity to the Early Modern Period* (Leuven: Peeters, 2002)

Brendon, Piers, 'The Devil's Decade': Review of Martin Pugh, *A Social History of Britain Between the Wars*, *The Guardian*, 5 July 2008, 9

Brenner, Michael, 'Gnosis and History: Polemics of German-Jewish Identity from Graetz to Scholem', *New German Critique*, 77 (1999), 45–60

Broughton, Trev Lynn, *Men of Letters, Writing Lives: Masculinity and Literary Auto/Biography in the Late Victorian Period* (London: Routledge, 1999)

Brown, Callum G., *The Death of Christian Britain: Understanding secularisation, 1800–2000* (London: Routledge, 2001)

Brown, J. F., 'Aleister Crowley's "Rites of Eleusis"', *Drama Review*, 22:2 (1978), 3–26

Brown, Mark, 'The Comité Franco-Polonais and the French reaction to the Polish uprising of November 1830', *English Historical Review*, 93:369 (1978), 774–93

Brown, Stuart, 'F. M. van Helmont: His Philosophical Connections and the Reception of His Later Cabbalistic Philosophy', in M. A. Stewart (ed.), *Studies in Seventeenth-Century European Philosophy* (Oxford: Clarendon Press, 1997), 97–116

Brustein, William I., *Roots of Hate: Anti-Semitism in Europe Before the Holocaust* (Cambridge: Cambridge University Press, 2003)

Bryman, Alan, *Quantity and Quality in Social Research* (London: Routledge, 1988)

Buber, Martin, *Tales of the Hasidim* (New York: Schocken Books, 1991; originally published in two volumes, *Tales of the Hasidim: The Early Masters* and *Tales of the Hasidim: The Later Masters*, New York: Schocken Books, 1947)

Büchler, Adolph, *Studies in Sin and Atonement in the Rabbinic Literature of the First Century* (London: Oxford University Press / Jews College, 1928)

Buisset, Christiane, *Eliphas Lévi: Sa vie, son oeuvre, ses pensées* (Paris: Guy Trédaniel / Éditions de la Maisnie, 1984)

Burkle, William Steve, 'Masonic Allusion and Symbolism in the Figures and Interpretations of the Major Arcana of the Tarot by Arthur Edward Waite' (23 September 2008), Pietre-Stones Review of Freemasonry, <http://www.freemasons-freemasonry.com/major_arcana_tarot.html>

Burmistrov, Konstantin, 'The Interpretation of Kabbalah in Early 20th-Century Russian Philosophy', *East European Jewish Affairs*, 37:2 (2007), 157–87

Burmistrov, Konstantin and Maria Endel, 'The Place of Kabbalah in the Doctrine of Russian Freemasons', *Aries*, 4:1 (2004), 27–68

Burnett, Charles S. F., 'The Legend of the Three Hermes and Abu Ma'shar's *Kitab al-Uluf* in the Latin Middle Ages', *Journal of the Warburg and Courtauld Institutes*, 39 (1976), 231–34

Burnett, Charles and W. F. Ryan (eds.), *Magic and the Classical Tradition* (London / Turin: Warburg Institute / Nino Aragno Editore, 2006)

Burstein, Sona Rosa, 'Moses Gaster and Folklore', *Folklore*, 68:1 (1957), 288–90

Bushaw, D., 'Wronski's Canons of Logarithms', *Mathematics Magazine*, 56:2 (1983), 91–97

Busi, Frederick A., 'Faith and Race: Gougenot des Mousseaux and the Development of Antisemitism in France', in L. Erlich, S. Bolzky, R. Rothstein, M. Schwartz, J. Berkovitz, and J. Young (eds.), *Textures and Meaning: Thirty Years of Judaic Studies at the University of Amherst* (2004), 119–39, <http://www.umass.edu/judaic/anniversaryvolume/articles/09-B2-Busi.pdf>

Busi, Giulio, *Qabalah Visiva* (Torino: Giulio Einaudi, 2005)

Butler, Alison, 'Magical Beginnings: The Intellectual Origins of the Victorian Occult Revival', *Limina*, 9 (2003), 78–95

———, 'Beyond Attribution: The Importance of Barrett's Magus', *Journal for the Academic Study of Magic*, 1 (2003), 7–33

———, *Victorian Occultism and the Making of Modern Magic: Invoking Tradition* (Basingstoke: Palgrave Macmillan, 2011)

Butler, E. M., *The Myth of the Magus* (Cambridge: Cambridge University Press, 1948)

———, *Ritual Magic* (Cambridge: Cambridge University Press, 1949

————, *The Fortunes of Faust* (Cambridge: Cambridge University Press, 1952)

Cahnmann, Werner J., 'Schelling and the New Thinking of Judaism', *Proceedings of the American Academy for Jewish Research*, 48 (1981), 1–56

Calkins, Mary Whiton, 'Henri Bergson: Personalist', *Philosophical Review*, 21:6 (1912), 666–75

Camille, Michel, 'Visual Art in Two Manuscripts of the Ars Notoria', in Claire Fanger (ed.), *Conjuring Spirits: Texts and Traditions of Medieval Ritual Magic* (University Park, PA: Pennsylvania State University Press, 1998), 110–39

Campanini, Saverio, 'Recent Literature on Christian Kabbalah', *European Association for Jewish Studies Newsletter*, 11 (October 2001–March 2002), <http://www.lzz.uni-halle.de/publikationen/essays/nl11_campanini.pdf>

Campbell, Bruce, *Ancient Wisdom Revived: A History of the Theosophical Movement* (Berkeley, CA: University of California Press, 1980)

Campion, Nicholas, *The Dawn of Astrology: A Cultural History of Western Astrology, Vol. 1: The Ancient and Classical Worlds* (London: Hambledon Continuum, 2008)

————, *A History of Western Astrology, Vol. 2: The Medieval and Modern Worlds* (London: Hambledon Continuum, 2009)

Caper, Robert, *Immaterial Facts: Freud's Discovery of Psychic Reality and Klein's Development of His Work* (London: Routledge, 1999)

Caplan, Kimmy, 'God's Voice: Audiotaped Sermons in Israeli Haredi Society', *Modern Judaism* 17:3 (1997), 253–80

Carey, Juanita S., *E. W. Bullinger: A Biography* (Grand Rapids, MI: Kregel Christian Books and Resources, 2000)

————, 'Two Amens That Delayed the Redemption: Jewish Messianism and Popular Spirituality in the Post-Sabbatian Century', *Jewish Quarterly Review*, 82 (1992), 208–16

Carlson, Maria, 'Fashionable Occultism: Spiritualism, Theosophy, Freemasonry, and Hermeticism in Fin-de-Siècle Russia', in Bernice Glatzer Rosenthal (ed.), *The Occult in Russian and Soviet Culture* (Ithaca, NY: Cornell University Press, 1997), 135–52

Casson, Stanley, *The Discovery of Man* (New York: Harper and Brothers, 1939)

Cellier, Léon, *L'Épopée Romantique* (Paris: Presses Universitaires de France, 1954)

Chadwick, Owen, *The Secularization of the European Mind in the 19th Century* (Cambridge: Cambridge University Press, 1975)

Chajes, J. H., *Between Worlds: Dybbuks, Exorcists, and Early Modern Judaism* (Philadelphia, PA: University of Pennsylvania Press, 2003)

————, 'He Said She Said: Hearing the Voices of Pneumatic Early Modern Jewish Women', *Nashim* 10 (2006), 99–125

Chapman, Janine, *Quest for Dion Fortune* (York Beach, ME: Samuel Weiser Inc., 1993)

Cherry, Shai, 'Three Twentieth-Century Jewish Responses to Evolutionary Theory', *Aleph: Historical Studies in Science and Judaism*, 3 (2003), 247–90

Chidester, David, *Salvation and Suicide: An Interpretation of Jim Jones, the Peoples Temple, and Jonestown* (Bloomington, IN: Indiana University Press, 2003)

Chishty-Mujahid, Nadya Q., *An Introduction to Western Esotericism: Essays in the Hidden Meaning of Literature, Groups, and Games* (Lampeter: Edwin Mellen Press, 2008)

Chodorow, Joan (ed.), *Jung on Active Imagination* (Princeton, NJ: Princeton University Press, 1997)

Chrostowski, Waldemar, 'The Suffering, Chosenness and Mission of the Polish Nation', *Religion in Eastern Europe*, 9:4 (1991), 1–14

Cicero, Chic and Sandra Tabatha Cicero (eds.), *The Golden Dawn Journal, Book II: Qabalah: Theory and Magic* (St. Paul, MN: Llewellyn, 1994)

———, 'Introduction to the Third Edition', in Israel Regardie, *The Tree of Life: An Illustrated Study in Magic* (Woodbury, MN: Llewellyn, 2001), xxiii–xxxii

Churton, Tobias, 'The First Rosicrucians', in *Seeking the Light: Freemasonry and Initiatic Traditions*, Canonbury Papers 4 (Hersham: Lewis Masonic, 2007), 72–79

Clark, Simon, 'Introduction', in Algernon Blackwood, *The Lost Valley and The Wolves of God* (Eureka, CA: Stark House Press, 2003), 7–12

Clifton, Chas S., 'A Goddess Arrives: The Novels of Dion Fortune and the Development of Gardnerian Witchcraft', *Gnosis*, 9 (Fall 1988), 20–30

Clifton, Chas S. and Graham Harvey (eds.), *The Paganism Reader* (London: Routledge, 2004)

Clucas, Stephen (ed.), *John Dee: Interdisciplinary Studies in English Renaissance Thought* (Dordrecht: Kluwer Academic Publishers, 2006)

Clulee, Nicholas H., *John Dee's Natural Philosophy: Between Science and Religion* (London: Routledge, 1988)

Cohen, Jeremy (ed.), *Essential Papers on Judaism and Christianity in Conflict: From Late Antiquity to the Reformation* (New York: New York University Press, 1991)

Cohn, Norman, *The Pursuit of the Millennium: Revolutionary Millenarians and Mystical Anarchists of the Middle Ages* (London: Secker and Warburg, 1957)

———, *Warrant for Genocide: The Myth of the Jewish World-Conspiracy and the Protocols of the Elders of Zion* (London: Eyre & Spottiswoode, 1967)

Cohn-Sherbok, Dan, *Fifty Key Jewiush Thinkers* (London: Routledge, 2007)

Collie, Michael, *Henry Maudsley: Victorian Psychiatrist. A Bibliographical Study* (Winchester: St. Paul's Bibliographies, 1988)

Collins, Adela Y., 'The Seven Heavens in Jewish and Christian Apocalypses', in John J. Collins and Michael Fishbane (eds.), *Death, Ecstasy, and Other Worldly Journeys* (Albany, NY: State University of New York Press, 1995), 57–92

Collins, John J. (ed.), *Apocalypse: The Morphology of a Genre* (Atlanta, GA: Society of Biblical Literature, 1979)

Collins, John J. and Michael Fishbane (eds.), *Death, Ecstasy, and Other Worldly Journeys* (Albany, NY: State University of New York Press, 1995)

Colquhoun, Ithell, *Sword of Wisdom: MacGregor Mathers and "The Golden Dawn"* (New York: G. P. Putnam's Sons, 1975)

Compton, Madonna, 'The Sacred Feminine on the Tree: Mother of Magic and Mystery', in Chic Cicero and Sandra Tabatha Cicero, *The Golden Dawn Journal, Book 2: Qabalah: Theory and Magic* (St. Paul, MN: Llewellyn, 1994), 233–52

Cooperman, Bernard Dov (ed.), *Jewish Thought in the Sixteenth Century* (Cambridge, MA: Harvard University Press, 1983)

Copenhaver, Brian P., 'Jewish Theologies of Space in the Scientific Revolution: Henry More, Joseph Raphson, Isaac Newton and their Predecessors', *AS*, 37 (1980), 489–548

———, 'The Secret of Pico's *Oration*: Cabala and Renaissance Philosophy', *Midwest Studies in Philosophy*, 26 (2002), 56–81

Coudert, Allison P., 'A Cambridge Platonist's Kabbalist Nightmare', *Journal of the History of Ideas*, 36:4 (1975), 633–52

———, *Alchemy: The Philosopher's Stone* (London: Wildwood House, 1980)

————, 'The *Kabbala Denudata*: Converting Jews or Seducing Christians', in Richard H. Popkin and Gordon M. Weiner (eds.), *Jewish Christians and Christian Jews: From the Renaissance to the Enlightenment* (Dordrecht: Kluwer Academic Publishers, 1994), 73–96

————, 'Isaac Luria and the Lurianic Kabbalah', in Richard H. Popkin (ed.), *The Columbia History of Western Philosophy* (New York: Columbia University Press, 1995), 213–15

————, *The Impact of the Kabbalah in the Seventeenth Century: The Life and Thought of Francis Mercury van Helmont (1614–1698)* (Leiden: Brill, 1999)

————, 'Five Seventeeht-Century Christian Hebraists', in Allison P. Coudert and Jeffrey S. Shoulson (eds.), *Hebraica Veritas? Christian Hebraists and the Study of Judaism in Early Modern Europe* (Philadelphia, PA: University of Pennsylvania Press, 2004), 286–308

————, 'Angel in the House or Idol of Perversity?: Women in Nineteenth Century Esotericism', *Esoterica*, 9 (2007), 8–48

Coudert, Allison P. and Jeffrey S. Shoulson (eds.), *Hebraica Veritas? Christian Hebraists and the Study of Judaism in Early Modern Europe* (Philadelphia, PA: University of Pennsylvania Press, 2004)

Couliano, Ioan P., *Psychanodia I: A Survey of the Evidence Concerning the Ascension of the Soul and Its Relevance* (Leiden: Brill, 1983)

————, *The Tree of Gnosis: Gnostic Mythology from Early Christianity to Modern Nihilism* (New York: Harper Collins, 1992)

Cox, James L., 'Religion Without God: Methodological Agnosticism and the Future of Religious Studies', (13 April 2003), <http://www.thehibberttrust.org.uk/documents/hibbert_lecture_2003.pdf>

Cox, Robert S., *Body and Soul: A Sympathetic History of American Spiritualism* (Charlottesville, VA: University of Virginia Press, 2003)

Crabtree, Adam, *From Mesmer to Freud: Magnetic Sleep and the Roots of Psychological Healing* (New Haven, CT: Yale University Press, 1993)

Craven, J. B., *Count Michael Maier, Doctor of Philosophy and of Medicine, Alchemist, Rosicrucian, Mystic, 1568–1622: Life and Writings* (Kirkwall: William Peace & Son, 1910; repr. Berwick, ME: Ibis Press, 2003)

Crowley, John, *Ægypt* (London: Victor Gollancz, 1987)

Crozier, Ivan, 'William Acton and the history of sexuality: the medical and professional context', *Journal of Victorian Culture*, 5:1 (2000), 1–27

Curry, Patrick, 'Magic vs. Enchantment', *Journal of Contemporary Religion*, 14:3 (1999), 401–12

————, *A Confusion of Prophets: Victorian and Edwardian Astrology* (London: Collins & Brown, 1999)

————, 'Astrology', in Kelly Boyd (ed.), *The Encyclopedia of Historians and Historical Writing* (London: Fitzroy Dearborn, 1999), 55–57

————, 'Nature Post-Nature', *New Formations* 64 (April 2008), 51–64

Dachez, Roger, 'Freemasonry', in Wouter J. Hanegraaff (ed.), *Dictionary of Gnosis and Western Hermeticism* (Leiden: Brill, 2006), 382–88

Daly, Mary, *Beyond God the Father: Toward a Philosophy of Women's Liberation* (Boston: Beacon Press, 1973)

Dan, Joseph and J. Hacker (eds.), *Jewish Mysticism, Philosophy and Ethical Literature* (Jerusalem: Magnes Press, 1986)

Dan, Joseph and Klaus Herrmann (eds.), *Studies in Jewish Manuscripts* (Tübingen: Mohr Siebeck, 1998)

Dan, Joseph, 'Joseph della Reina', in *Encyclopaedia Judaica*, 16 volumes (Jerusalem: Keter Publishing, 1971), 10:240–41

————, 'Maggid', in *Encyclopaedia Judaica*, 16 volumes (Jerusalem: Keter Publishing, 1971), 11:698–701

——, 'Magic', in *Encyclopaedia Judaica*, 16 volumes (Jerusalem: Keter Publishing, 1971), 11:703–15

——, 'Book of Raziel', in *Encyclopaedia Judaica*, 16 volumes (Jerusalem: Keter Publishing, 1971), 13:1591–593

——, 'Samael, Lilith, and the Concept of Evil in Early Kabbalah', *AJS Review*, 5 (1980), 17–40

——, 'The Seventy Names of Metatron', *Proceedings of the Eighth World Congress of Jewish Studies*, Division C (Jerusalem, 1982), 19–23

——, 'Gershom Scholem's Reconstruction of Early Kabbalah', *Modern Judaism*, 5:1 (1985), 39–66

—— (ed.), *The Early Kabbalah* (Mahwah, NJ: Paulist Press, 1986)

——, *Gershom Scholem and the Mystical Dimension of Jewish History* (New York: New York University Press, 1987)

——, 'A Bow to Frumkinian Hasidism', *Modern Judaism*, 11:2 (1991), 175–94

——, 'Scholem's View of Jewish Messianism', *Modern Judaism*, 12:2 (1992), 117–28

——, *The Revelation of the Secret of the World: The Beginning of Jewish Mysticism in Late Antiquity* (Providence, RI: Brown University Judaic Studies Series No. 2, 1992)

——, 'Jewish Gnosticism?', *Jewish Studies Quarterly*, 2 (1995), 309–28

——, 'Review of Wout Jac van Bekkum, *A Hebrew Alexander Romance according to MS London, Jews College 145'*, *Jewish Quarterly Review*, 86:3–4 (1996), 435–438

——, *Jewish Mysticism, Vol. 1: Late Antiquity* (Northvale, NJ: Jason Aronson, 1998)

——, 'In Quest of a Historical Definition of Mysticism: The Contingental Approach', in Joseph Dan, *Jewish Mysticism, Vol. 3: The Modern Period* (Northvale, NJ: Jason Aronson, 1999), 1–46

——, *Jewish Mysticism, Vol. 3: The Modern Period* (Northvale, NJ: Jason Aronson, 1999)

——, 'The Name of God, the Name of the Rose, and the Concept of Language in Jewish Mysticism', *Medieval Encounters*, 2:3 (1996), 228–48

—— (ed.), *The Christian Kabbalah: Jewish Mystical Books and Their Christian Interpreters* (Cambridge, MA: Harvard College Library, 1997)

——, 'The Kabbalah of Johannes Reuchlin and Its Historical Significance', in Joseph Dan, *The Christian Kabbalah: Jewish Mystical Books and Their Christian Interpreters* (Cambridge, MA: Harvard College Library, 1997), 55–95

——, 'Christian Kabbalah: From Mysticism to Esotericism', in Antoine Faivre and Wouter J. Hanegraaff (eds.), *Western Esotericism and the Science of Religion* (Leuven: Peeters, 1998), 131–44

——, 'Medieval Jewish Influences on Renaissance Concepts of "Harmonia Mundi"', *Aries*, 1:2 (2001), 135–52

——, *Kabbalah: A Very Short Introduction* (Oxford: Oxford University Press, 2006)

Danilewicz, M. L., '"The King of the New Israel": Thaddeus Grabianka (1740–1807)', in Robert Auty and J. L. I. Fennell (eds.), *Oxford Slavonic Papers*, New Series, Vol. 1 (Oxford: Clarendon Press, 1968), 49–73

Darby, Robert, *A Surgical Temptation: The Demonization of the Foreskin and the Rise of Circumcision in Britain* (Chicago: University of Chicago Press, 2005)

Darnton, Robert, *Mesmerism and the End of the Enlightenment in France* (Cambridge, MA: Harvard University Press, 1968)

Dau, Duc, 'Perfect Chastity: Celibacy and Virgin Marriage in Tractarian Poetry', *Victorian Poetry*, 44:1 (2006), 77–92

Daunton, Martin and Bernhard Rieger (eds.), *Meanings of Modernity: Britain from the Late-Victorian Era to World War II* (Oxford: Berg, 2001)

Davies, Charlotte Aull, *Reflexive Ethnography: A Guide to Researching Selves and Others* (London: Routledge, 1999)

Davies, Owen, *Witchcraft, Magic and Culture 1736–1951* (Manchester: Manchester University Press, 1999)

———, *Popular Magic: Cunning-folk in English History* (London: Hambledon Continuum, 2003)

———, *Grimoires: A History of Magic Books* (Oxford: Oxford University Press, 2009)

Davila, James R., 'The Hekhalot Literature and Shamanism', in *Society of Biblical Literature 1994 Seminar Papers*, SBLSP No. 33 (Atlanta, GA: Scholars Press, 1994), 767–89

De Blécourt, William, Ronald Hutton, and Jean la Fontaine, *Witchcraft and Magic in Europe, Vol. 6: The Twentieth Century* (London: Athlone Pres, 1999)

Debus, Allen G., *The English Paracelsians* (London: Oldbourne Book Co. Ltd., 1965)

———, *The Chemical Philosophy: Paracelsian Science and Medicine in the Sixteenth and Seventeenth Centuries*, 2 volumes (New York: Science History Publications/Neale Watson Academic Publications, 1977; repr. Mineola, NY: Dover Publications, 2002)

———, *Robert Fludd and His Philosophical Key* (Sagamore Beach, MA: Watson Publishing International, 1979)

———, 'Alchemy in an Age of Reason: The Chemical Philosophers in Early Eighteenth-Century France', in Ingrid Merkel and Allen G. Debus (eds.), *Hermeticism and the Renaissance: Intellectual History and the Occult in Early Modern Europe* (London: Associated University Presses, 1988), 231–50

——— (ed.), *Alchemy and Early Modern Chemistry: Papers from Ambix* (London: Jeremy Mills/Society for the History of Alchemy and Chemistry, 2004), 178–85

Decker, Ronald and Michael Dummett, *A History of the Occult Tarot 1870–1970* (London: Duckworth, 2002)

Decker, Ronald, Thierry Depaulis and Michael Dummett, *A Wicked Pack of Cards: The Origins of the Occult Tarot* (London: Duckworth, 1996)

Deghaye, Pierre, 'Jacob Boehme and His Followers', in Antoine Faivre and Jacob Needleman (eds.), *Modern Esoteric Spirituality* (New York: Crossroad, 1992), 210–47

De Léon-Jones, Karen Silvia, *Giordano Bruno and the Kabbalah: Prophets, Magicians, and Rabbis* (New Haven, CT: Yale University Press, 1997)

———, 'John Dee and the Kabbalah', in Stephen Clucas (ed.), *John Dee: Interdisciplinary Studies in English Renaissance Thought* (Dordrecht: Kluwer Academic Publishers, 2006), 143–58

Del Valle, Carlos, 'Abraham Ibn Ezra's Mathematical Speculations on the Divine Name', in R. A. Herrera (ed.), *Mystics of the Book: Themes, Topics and Typologies* (New York: Peter Lang, 1993), 159–76

Dennis, Geoffrey W., 'The Use of Water as a Medium for Altered States of Consciousness in Early Jewish Mysticism: A Cross-Disciplinary Analysis', *Anthropology of Consciousness*, 19:1 (2008), 84–106

Den Otter, Sandra M., *British Idealism and Social Explanation: A Study in Late Victorian Thought* (Oxford: Clarendon Press, 1996)

De Rola, Stanislas Klossowski, *The Golden Game: Alchemical Engravings of the Seventeenth Century* (London: Thames and Hudson, 1988)

Derrida, Jacques, *Dissemination*, trans. Barbara Johnson (Chicago, IL: University of Chicago Press, 1981)

Deutsch, Nathaniel, *Guardians of the Gate: Angelic Vice Regency in Late Antiquity* (Leiden: Brill, 1999)

Deveney, John Patrick, *Paschal Beverly Randolph: A Nineteenth-Century Black American Spiritualist, Rosicrucian, and Sex Magician* (Albany, NY: State University of New York Press, 1996)

———, 'Paschal Beverly Randolph and Sexual Magic', in Wouter J. Hanegraaff and Jeffrey J. Kripal (eds.), *Hidden Intercourse: Eros and Sexuality in the History of Western Esotericism* (Leiden: Brill, 2008), 355–67

Dickson, Donald R., 'Johann Valentin Andreae's Utopian Brotherhoods', *Renaissance Quarterly*, 49:4 (1996), 760–802

Dillon, John, *The Middle Platonists: A Study of Platonism, 80 B.C. to A.D. 220* (London: Duckworth, 1977)

Dillon, John M., 'Solomon Ibn Gabirol's Doctrine of Intelligible Matter', in Lenn E. Goodman (ed.), *Neoplatonism and Jewish Thought* (Albany, NY: State University of New York Press, 1992), 43–59

Dixon, Joy, *Divine Feminine: Theosophy and Feminism in England* (Baltimore, MD: Johns Hopkins University Press, 2001)

Dobbin, Joel C., *Kabbalistic Astrology: The Sacred Tradition of the Hebrew Sages* (Rochester, VT: Inner Traditions, 1999)

Dodds, E. R., *The Greeks and the Irrational* (Cambridge: Cambridge University Press, 1951)

———, 'Theurgy and its Relationship to Neoplatonism', *Journal of Roman Studies*, 37 (1947), 55–69

———, 'The Astral Body in Neoplatonism', in Proclus, *The Elements of Theology: A Revised Text with Translation, Introduction, and Commentary*, trans. E. R. Dodds (Oxford: Oxford University Press, 1963), 313–22

———, *The Ancient Concept of Progress and Other Essays on Greek Literature and Belief* (Oxford: Clarendon Press, 1973)

Dossey, Larry, 'Mind-Body Medicine: Whose Mind and Whose Body?', at <http://www.heartmdinstitute.com/heart-healthy-lifestyles/mindbody-connection/whose-mind-body>

Dowling, Linda C., *Hellenism and Homosexuality in Victorian Oxford* (Ithaca, NY: Cornell University Press, 1994)

Dreifuss, Gustav, 'The Union of Opposites in the Kabbalah', *Journal of Jungian Theory and Practice*, 7:1 (2005), 65–71

Dresner, Samuel H., *The Zaddik: The Doctrine of the Zaddik According to the Writings of Rabbi Yaakov Yosef of Polnoy* (London: Abelard-Schuman, 1960)

Drob, Sanford L., 'Jung and the Kabbalah', *History of Psychology*, 2:2 (1999), 102–18

———, 'Towards a Kabbalistic Psychology: C. G. Jung and the Jewish Foundations of Alchemy', *Journal of Jungian Theory and Practice*, 5:2 (2003), 77–100

———, 'Jung's Kabbalistic Visions', *Journal of Jungian Theory and Practice*, 7:1 (2005), 33–54

———, '"This is Gold": Freud, Psychotherapy and the Lurianic Kabbalah' (1998–2006), <http://www.newkabbalah.com>

Drury, Nevill, *Stealing Fire from Heaven: The Rise of Modern Western Magic* (Oxford: Oxford University Press, 2011)

Duker, Abraham G., 'Mickiewicz and the Jewish Problem', in Manfred Kridl (ed.), *Adam Mickiewicz, Poet of Poland* (New York: Columbia University Press, 1951), 108–25

———, 'The Polish Political Emigrés and the Jews in 1848', *Proceedings of the American Academy for Jewish Research*, 24 (1955), 69–102

————, 'Jewish Emancipation and the Polish Insurrection of 1863: Jan Czynski's Letter of 1862 to Ludwik Królikowski', *Proceedings of the American Academy for Jewish Research*, 46 (1979–80), 87–103

Dumà, Giovanangelo, 'Max Théon e il Movimento Cosmique', *Lex Aurea: Libera Rivista di Formazione Esoterica*, 19 (2006), 14–18

Dumville, D. M., 'Biblical Apocrypha and the Early Irish: A Preliminary Investigation', *Proceedings of the Royal Irish Academy*, 73:8 (1973), 318–19

Dundes, Alan (ed.), *The Blood Libel Legend: A Casebook in Anti-Semitic Folklore* (Madison, WI: University of Wisconsin Press, 1991)

Dupré, Louis, 'Unio mystica: The State and the Experience', in Moshe Idel and Bernard McGinn (eds.), *Mystical Union and Monotheistic Faith: An Ecumenical Dialogue* (New York: Macmillan, 1989), 3–23

DuQuette, Lon Milo, *Understanding Aleister Crowley's Thoth Tarot: An Authoritative Examination of the World's Most Fascinating and Magical Tarot Cards* (York Beach, ME: Red Wheel/Weiser, 2003)

Durov, Victoria, 'Codicological Notes on the Text of a Hebrew Magic Manual: A New Perspective?', *Societas Magica Newsletter*, 19 (Spring 2008), 1–7

Dynner, Glenn, 'Merchant Princes and Tsadikim: The Patronage of Polish Hasidism', *Jewish Social Studies*, 12:1 (2005), 64–110

————, *Men of Silk: The Hasidic Conquest of Polish Jewish Society* (Oxford: Oxford University Press, 2006)

Eco, Umberto, *Foucault's Pendulum*, trans. William Weaver (New York: Harcourt Brace Jovanovich, 1987)

Edighoffer, Roland, 'Rosicrucianism: From the Seventeenth to the Twentieth Century', in Antoine Faivre, Antoine and Jacob Needleman (eds.), *Modern Esoteric Spirituality* (New York: Crossroad, 1992), 186–209

————, 'Hermeticism in Early Rosicrucianism', in Roelof van den Broek and Wouter J. Hanegraaff (eds.), *Gnosis and Hermeticism: From Antiquity to Modern Times* (Albany, NY: State University of New York Press, 1998), 197–215

————, 'Rosicrucianism', in Wouter J. Hanegraaff (ed.), *Dictionary of Gnosis and Western Hermeticism* (Leiden: Brill, 2006), 1009–1020

Edwards, Lawrence, *Projective Geometry: An Approach to the Secrets of Space From the Standpoint of Artistic and Imaginative Thought* (Phoenixville, PA: Rudolf Steiner Institute, 1985)

Ehrman, James F., 'Pragmatics and Translation: the Problem of Presupposition', *TTR: traduction, terminologie, rédaction*, 6:1 (1993), 149–70

Eilberg-Schwartz, Howard (ed.), *People of the Body: Jews and Judaism from an Embodied Perspective* (Albany, NY: State University of New York Press, 1992)

Elia, Anthony J., 'An Historical Assessment of the Narrative Uses of the Words "Kabbalah", "Cabala", and "Qabala/h": Discerning the Differences for Theological Libraries', *Theological Librarianship*, 2:2 (2009), 11–23

Eliade, Mircea, *The Forge and the Crucible: The Origins and Structures of Alchemy*, trans. Stephen Corrin (Chicago, IL: University of Chicago Press, 1956)

Elior, Rachel, 'The Concept of God in Hekhalot Literature', in Joseph Dan (ed.), *Binah: Studies in Jewish History, Thought, and Culture*, Vol. 2 (NY: Praeger, 1989), 108–10

————, *The Paradoxical Ascent to God: The Kabbalistic Theosophy of Habad Hasidism*, trans. Jeffrey M. Green (Albany, NY: State University of New York Press, 1993)

————, 'Mysticism, Magic, and Angelology: The Perception of Angels in Hekhalot Litereature', *Jewish Studies Quarterly*, 1 (1993), 3–53

————, 'The Doctrine of Transmigration in *Galya Raza*', in Lawrence Fine (ed.), *Essential Papers on Kabbalah* (New York: New York University Press, 1995), 243–69

————, 'From Earthly Temple to Heavenly Shrines: Prayer and Sacred Song in the Hekhalot Literature and Its Relations to Temple Traditions', *Jewish Studies Quarterly*, 4:3 (1997), 217–67

————, *The Three Temples: On the Emergence of Jewish Mysticism*, trans. David Louvish (Oxford: The Littman Library of Jewish Civilization, 2004)

————, *The Mystical Origins of Hasidism* (Oxford: Littman Library of Jewish Civilization, 2006)

————, 'Early Forms of Jewish Mysticism', in Steven T. Katz (ed.), *The Cambridge History of Judaism, Vol. 4: The Late Roman-Rabbinic Period* (Cambridge: Cambridge University Press, 2006), 749–91

Ellenberger, Henri, *The Discovery of the Unconscious* (New York: Basic Books, 1970)

Elman, Yaakov and Israel Gershoni (eds.), *Transmitting Jewish Traditions: Orality, Textuality and Cultural Diffusion* (New Haven, CT: Yale University Press, 2000)

Elukin, Jonathan M., 'A New Essenism: Heinrich Graetz and Mysticism', *Journal of the History of Ideas*, 59:1 (1998), 135–48

Encyclopaedia Judaica, 16 volumes (Jerusalem: Keter Publishing, 1971)

Endelman, Todd M., 'The Checkered Career of "Jew" King: A Study in Anglo-Jewish Social History', *AJS Review*, 7 (1982), 69–100

————, 'The Englishness of Jewish Modernity in England', in Jacob Katz (ed.), *Towards Modernity: The European Jewish Model* (New Brunswick, NJ: Transaction Books, 1987), 225–46

————, 'English Jewish History', *Modern Judaism*, 11:1 (1991), 91–109

Engler, Steven and Gregory P. Grieve (eds.), *Historicizing "Tradition" in the Study of Religion* (Berlin/New York: Walter de Gruyter, 2005)

Etkes, Immanuel, *The Besht: Magician, Mystic, and Leader* (Waltham, MA: Brandeis University Press, 2005)

Eylon, Dina Ripsman, *Reincarnation in Jewish Mysticism and Gnosticism* (Lampeter: Edwin Mellen Press, 2003)

Faierstein, Morris M., 'Hasidism: The Last Decade in Research', *Modern Judaism*, 11:1 (1991), 111–24

Faivre, Antoine and Jacob Needleman (eds.), *Modern Esoteric Spirituality* (New York: Crossroad, 1992)

Faivre, Antoine and Karen-Claire Voss, 'Western Esotericism and the Science of Religion', *Numen*, 42:1 (1995), 48–77

Faivre, Antoine and Wouter J. Hanegraaff (eds.), *Western Esotericism and the Science of Religion* (Leuven: Peeters, 1998)

Faivre, Antoine, 'What is Occultism?', in Lawrence E. Sullivan (ed.), *Hidden Truths: Magic, Alchemy, and the Occult* (New York/London: Macmillan & Collier, 1987), 3–9

————, 'Introduction 1', in Antoine Faivre and Jacob Needleman (eds.), *Modern Esoteric Spirituality* (New York: Crossroad, 1992), xv–xx

————, *Access to Western Esotericism* (Albany, NY: State University of New York Press, 1994)

————, *The Eternal Hermes: From Greek God to Alchemical Magus*, trans. Joscelyn Godwin (Grand Rapids, MI: Phanes Press, 1995)

————, 'Questions of Terminology Proper to the Study of Esoteric Currents in Modern and Contemporary Europe', in Antoine Faivre and Wouter J. Hanegraaff (eds.), *Western Esotericism and the Science of Religion* (Leuven: Peeters, 1998), 1–10

508 Magi and *Maggidim*

————, 'The Notions of Concealment and Secrecy in Modern Esoteric Currents since the Renaissance (A Methodological Approach)', in Elliot R. Wolfson (ed.), *Rending the Veil: Concealment and Secrecy in the History of Religions* (New York: Seven Bridges Press, 1999), 155–76

————, 'Histoire de la notion moderne de tradition dans ses rapports avec les courants ésotériques (XVe–XX3 siècles)', in *Symboles et Mythes dans les mouvements initiatiques et ésotériques, XVIIIe–XXe siècles: Filiations et emprunts* (Paris: Archè/La Table d'Émeraude, 1999), 9–12

————, *Symboles et Mythes dans les mouvements initiatiques et ésotériques, XVIIIe–XXe siècles: Filiations et emprunts* (Paris: Archè/La Table d'Émeraude, 1999)

————, *Theosophy, Imagination, Tradition: Studies in Western Esotericism*, trans. Christine Rhone (Albany, NY: State University of New York Press, 2000)

————, 'Elie Artiste, ou le Messie des Philosophes de la Nature', Part 1, *Aries*, 2:2 (2002), 120–52; Part 2, *Aries*, 3:1 (2003), 25–54

————, 'Asiatic Brethren', in Wouter J. Hanegraaff (ed.), *Dictionary of Gnosis and Western Esotericism* (Leiden: Brill, 2006), 107–09

————, *L'esoterisme* (Paris: Presses Universitaires de France, 2007)

Fanger, Claire, 'Medieval Ritual Magic: What It Is and Why We Need to Know More About It', in Claire Fanger (ed.), *Conjuring Spirits: Texts and Traditions of Medieval Ritual Magic* (University Park, PA: Pennsylvania State University Press, 1998), vii–xviii

———— (ed.), *Conjuring Spirits: Texts and Traditions of Medieval Ritual Magic* (University Park, PA: Pennsylvania State University Press, 1998)

————, 'Mirror Mask and Anti-self: Forces of Literary Creation in Dion Fortune and W. B. Yeats', in Arthur Versluis, Lee Irwin, John Richards, and Melina Weinstein (eds.), *Esotericism, Art, and Imagination* (East Lansing, MI: Michigan State University Press, 2008), 161–82

Faraone, Christopher A., *Ancient Greek Love Magic* (Cambridge, MA: Harvard University Press, 1999)

Faraone, Christopher A. and Dirk Obbink (eds.), *Magika Hiera: Ancient Greek Magic and Religion* (Oxford: Oxford University Press, 1991)

Farley, Helen, *A Cultural History of the Tarot: From Entertainment to Esotericism* (London: I. B. Tauris, 2009)

Farmer, S. A., *Syncretism in the West: Pico's 900 Theses (1486)* (Tempe, AR: Medieval & Renaissance Texts & Studies, 1998)

Farnell, Kim, *The Astral Tramp* (London: Ascella, 1998)

Feldman, David, *Englishmen and Jews: Social Relations and Political Culture, 1840–1914* (New Haven, CT: Yale University Press, 1994)

Ferreiro, Alberto and Moshe Sharon (eds.), *Studies in Modern Religions, Religious Movements and the Babi-Baha'i Faiths* (Leiden: Brill, 2004)

Fielding, Charles and Carr Collins, *The Story of Dion Fortune* (Loughborough: Thoth Publications, 1998)

Finamore, John F., *Iamblichus and the Theory of the Vehicle of the Soul* (Chico, CA: Scholars Press, 1985)

Findlen, Paula K. (ed.), *Athanasius Kircher: The Last Man Who Knew Everything* (London: Routledge, 2004)

Fine, Lawrence, 'The Art of Metoposcopy: A Study in Isaac Luria's "Charismatic Knowledge", *AJS Review*, 11:1 (1986), 79–101

————, 'Purifying the Body in the Name of the Soul: The Problem of the Body in Sixteenth-Century Kabbalah', in Howard Eilberg-Schwartz (ed.), *People of the Body: Jews and Judaism from an Embodied Perspective* (Albany, NY: State University of New York Press, 1992), 117–42

———— (ed.), *Essential Papers on Kabbalah* (New York: New York University Press, 1995)

———, 'The Contemplative Practice of Yihudim in Lurianic Kabbalah', in Arthur Green (ed.), *Jewish Spirituality, Volume 2: From the Sixteenth-Century Revival to the Present* (New York: Crossroad, 1997), 64–98

———, *Physician of the Soul, Healer of the Cosmos: Isaac Luria and His Kabbalistic Fellowship* (Stanford, CA: Stanford University Press, 2003)

Fishbane, Eitan, 'Tears of Disclosure: The Role of Weeping in Zoharic Narrative', *Journal of Jewish Thought and Philosophy*, 11:1 (2002), 25–47

———, 'Authority, Tradition, and the Creation of Meaning in Medieval Kabbalah: Isaac of Acre's *Illumination of the Eyes*', *Journal of the American Academy of Religion*, 72:1 (2004), 59–95

———, 'The Speech of Being, the Voice of God: Phonetic Mysticism in the Kabbalah of Asher ben David and His Contemporaries', *Jewish Quarterly Review*, 98:4 (2008), 485–521

———, 'The Scent of the Rose: Drama, Fiction, and Narrative Form in the Zohar', *Prooftexts*, 29 (2009), 324–61

Fishbane, Michael, *The Kiss of God: Spiritual and Mystical Death in Judaism* (Seattle, WA: University of Washington Press, 1994)

Fishman, David E., *Russia's First Modern Jews: The Jews of Shklov* (New York: New York University Press, 1995)

Fleming, Anthony, 'Introductory Notes', in Darcy Küntz (ed.), *The Golden Dawn Court Cards, as drawn by W. W. Westcott and Moïna Mathers* (Edmonds, WA: Holmes Publishing Group, 1996), 3

Florence, Ronald, *Blood Libel: The Damascus Affair of 1840* (Madison, WI: University of Wisconsin Press, 2004)

Flusser, David and Shua Amorai-Stark, 'The Goddess Thermutis, Moses, and Artapanus', *Jewish Studies Quarterly*, 1 (1993–94), 217–33

Forshaw, Peter J., 'The Early Alchemical Reception of John Dee's *Monas Hieroglyphica*', *Ambix*, 52:3 (2005), 247–69

Forster, E. S. and D. J. Furley (trans.), *Aristotle III: On Sophistical Refutations; On Coming-to-be and Passing Away; On the Cosmos* (Cambridge, MA: Loeb Classical Library, Harvard University Press, 1955)

Fowden, Garth, *The Egyptian Hermes: A Historical Approach to the Late Pagan Mind* (Cambridge: Cambridge University Press, 1986)

Fox, Adam, *Dean Inge (1860–1954)* (London: John Murray, 1960)

Frank, Daniel H. and Oliver Leaman (eds.), *The Cambridge Companion to Medieval Jewish Philosophy* (Cambridge: Cambridge University Press, 2003)

Frankel, Jonathan, *Prophecy and Politics: Socialism, Nationalism, and the Russian Jews, 1862–1917* (Cambridge: Cambridge University Press, 1984)

———, 'Crisis as a Factor in Modern Jewish Politics, 1840 and 1881–82', in Jehudah Reinharz (ed.), *Living with Antisemitism: Modern Jewish Responses* (Lebanon, NH: Brandeis University Press/University Press of New England, 1987), 42–58

Frankfurter, David, 'Narrating Power: The Theory and Practice of the Magical *Historiolae* in Ritual Spells', in Marvin Meyer and Paul Mirecki (eds.), *Ancient Magic and Ritual Power* (Leiden: Brill, 2001), 457–76

Freedman, David Noel, Allen C Meyers, and Astrid B. Beck (eds.), *Eerdmans Dictionary of the Bible* (Grand Rapids, MI: Eerdmans Publishing, 2000)

Freedman, Daphne, 'Shem Tov ibn Shem Tov on "Sefer Yesirah"', *Journal of Jewish Studies*, 58:2 (2007), 303–13

Freeman, Nicholas, 'The Shrineless God: Paganism, Literature and Art in Forties' Britain', *Pomegranate* 6.2 (2004), 157–74

———, '"Nothing of the Wild Wood"? Pan, Paganism, and Spiritual Confusion in E. F. Benson's "The Man Who Went Too Far"', *Literature and Theology*, 19:1 (2005), 22–33

French, Peter, *John Dee: The World of an Elizabethan Magus* (London: Routledge & Kegan Paul, 1972)

Friedman, Harris, 'Methodolatry and Graphicacy', *American Psychologist* 58:10 (2003), 817–18

Friedman, O. Michael, *Origins of the British Israelites: the Lost Tribes* (Lewiston, NY: Edwin Mellen Press, 1993)

Gager, John G., *Moses in Greco-Roman Paganism* (Atlanta, GA: Society of Biblical Literature, 1972)

———, *Curse Tablets and Binding Spells from the Ancient World* (Oxford: Oxford University Press, 1992)

Ganz, Timothy, *Early Greek Myth: A Guide to Literary and Artistic Sources* (Baltimore, MD: Johns Hopkins University Press, 1993)

Garb, Jonathan, 'Rabbi Kook and his Sources: From Kabbalistic Historiosophy to National Mysticism', in Moshe Sharon (ed.), *Studies in Modern Religions, Religious Movements and the Babi-Bahai Faiths* (Brill: Leiden, 2004), 77–96

———, 'The Cult of the Saints in Lurianic Kabbalah', *Jewish Quarterly Review*, 98:2 (2008), 203–29

———, 'The Modernization of Kabbalah: A Case Study', *Modern Judaism* 30:1 (2010), 1–22

———, 'Towards the Study of the Spiritual-Mystical Renaissance in the Contemporary Ashkenazi Haredi World in Israel', in Boaz Huss (ed.), *Kabbalah and Contemporary Spiritual Revival* (Beer-Sheva: Ben-Gurion University of the Negev Press, 2011), 117–40

Gartner, Lloyd P., 'Emancipation, Social Change and Communal Reconstruction in Anglo-Jewry 1789–1881', *Proceedings of the American Academy for Jewish Research*, 54 (1987), 73–116

Gaster, Moses, 'Magen David', *Rimon/Milgroim* 3 (1923)

Gauld, Alan, *A History of Hypnotism* (Cambridge: Cambridge University Press, 1992)

Gay, Peter, *A Godless Jew: Freud, Atheism, and the Making of Psychoanalysis* (New Haven, CT: Yale University Press, 1987)

Geller, Mark J., 'Deconstructing Talmudic Magic', in Charles Burnett and W. F. Ryan (eds.), *Magic and the Classical Tradition* (London/Turin: Warburg Institute/Nino Aragno Editore, 2006), 1–18

Geller, Mark J. and Dan Levene, 'Magical Texts From the Genizah', *Journal of Jewish Studies*, 49:2 (1998), 334–40

Gerth, H. H. and C. Mills Wright (eds. and trans.), *From Max Weber: Essays in Sociology* (Oxford: Oxford University Press, 1958)

Gezundhajt, Henriette, 'An Evolution of the Historical Origins of Hypnotism Prior to the Twentieth Century: Between Spirituality and Subconscious', *Contemporary Hypnosis*, British Society of Experimental and Clinical Hypnosis, 24:4 (2007), 178–94

Gibbons, B. J., *Spirituality and the Occult: From the Renaissance to the Modern Age* (London: Routledge, 2001)

Giegerich, Wolfgang, 'Response to Sanford Drob', *Journal of Jungian Theory and Practice*, 7:1 (2005), 55–58

Gilbert, R. A., *The Golden Dawn Scrapbook: The Rise and Fall of a Magical Order* (Slough: Quantum, 1997)

———, *A. E. Waite: A Bibliography* (Wellingborough: Aquarian Press, 1983)

———, 'Introduction', in John Hamill (ed.), *The Rosicrucian Seer: Magical Writings of Frederick Hockley* (Wellingborough: Aquarian Press, 1986), 11–25

———, 'Secret Writing: The Magical Manuscripts of Frederick Hockley', in John Hamill (ed.), *The Rosicrucian Seer: Magical Writings of Frederick Hockley* (Wellingborough: Aquarian Press, 1986), 26–33

————, *A. E. Waite: Magician of Many Parts* (Wellingborough: Crucible, 1987)

————, 'William Wynn Westcott and the Esoteric School of Masonic Research', *Ars Quatuor Coronatorum*, 100 (1987), 6–20

————, 'Chaos Out of Order: The Rise and Fall of the Swedenborgian Rite', *Ars Quatuor Coronatorum*, 108 (1995), 122–49

————, 'Two Circles to Gain and Two Squares to Lose": The Golden Dawn in Popular Fiction', in Marie Mulvey Roberts and Hugh Ormsby-Lennon (eds.), *Secret Texts: The Literature of Secret Societies* (New York: AMS Press, 1995), 303–21

————, 'Foreword', in S. L. MacGregor Mathers (trans.), *The Key of Solomon the King (Clavicula Salomonis)* (London: George Redway, 1889; repr. San Francisco, CA: Red Wheel/Weiser, 2000), v–viii

———— (ed.), *Seeking the Light: Freemasonry and Initiatic Traditions*, Canonbury Papers Vol. 4 (Hersham/London: Lewis Masonic/Canonbury Masonic Research Centre, 2007)

Gilhus, Ingvild Saelid, 'Gnosticism: A Study in Liminal Symbolism', *Numen*, 31:1 (1984), 106–28

Giller, Pinchas, 'Between Poland and Jerusalem: Kabbalistic Prayer in Early Modernity', *Modern Judaism*, 24:3 (2004), 226–50

————, 'Leadership and Charisma Among Mizrahi Modern Kabbalists: In the Footsteps of Shar-abi — Contemporary Kabbalistic Prayer', *Journal for the Study of Sephardic and Mizrahi Jewry*, 1:2 (2007), 21–41

————, *Shalom Shar'abi and the Kabbalists of Beit El* (Oxford: Oxford University Press, 2008)

Ginzberg, Louis and Kaufmann Kohler, 'Cabala', in *The Jewish Encyclopedia* (1901–06), <http://www.jewishencyclopedia.com>

Ginzberg, Louis, *Legends of the Jews*, 7 volumes, trans. Henrietta Szold (Philadelphia, PA: Jewish Publication Society, 1909–1938; repr. in 4 volumes, Baltimore, MD: Johns Hopkins University Press, 1998)

Godwin, Joscelyn, *Athanasius Kircher: A Late Renaissance Philosopher and Scientist* (London: Thames and Hudson, 1979)

————, *Robert Fludd: Hermetic Philosopher and Surveyor of Two Worlds* (London: Thames & Hudson, 1979)

————, *The Theosophical Enlightenment* (Albany, NY: State University of New York Press, 1994)

Godwin, Joscelyn, Christian Chanel, and John P. Deveney, *The Hermetic Brotherhood of Luxor: Initiatic and Historical Documents of an Order of Practical Occultism* (York Beach, ME: Samuel Weiser, 1995)

Golb, Norman, 'Aspects of the Historical Background of Jewish Life in Medieval Egypt', in Alexander Altmann (ed.), *Jewish Medieval and Renaissance Studies* (Cambridge, MA: Harvard University Press, 1967), 1–18

Goldberg, Stuart, 'Konrad and Jacob: A Hypothetical Kabbalistic Subtext in Adam Mickiewicz's *Forefathers' Eve*, Part III', *Slavic and East European Journal*, 45:4 (2001), 695–715

Goldberg, Yechiel Shalom, 'Spiritual Leadership and the Popularization of Kabbalah in Medieval Spain', *Journal for the Study of Sephardic and Mizrahi Jewry*, 2:2 (2009), 2–59

Goldish, Matt, *The Sabbatean Prophets* (Cambridge, MA: Harvard University Press, 2004)

Goldish, Matt (ed.), *Spirit Possession in Judaism: Cases and Contexts from the Middle Ages to the Present* (Detroit, MI: Wayne State University Press, 2003)

Goldish, Matt and Richard H. Popkin (eds.), *Millenarianism and Messianism in Early Modern European Culture, Vol. 1: Jewish Messianism in the Early Modern World* (Dordrecht: Kluwer Academic Publishers, 2001)

Goldman, Steven Louis, 'On the Interpretation of Symbols and the Christian Origins of Modern Science', *Journal of Religion*, 62:1 (1982), 1–20

Gombrich, Ernst H., '*Icones Symbolicae*: The Visual Image in Neo-Platonic Thought', *Journal of the Warburg and Courtauld Institutes*, 11 (1948), 163–92

Gomel, Elana, '"Spirits in the Material World": Spiritualism and Identity in the Fin de Siècle', *Victorian Literature and Culture*, 35 (2007), 189–213

Goldsmith, Margaret, *Franz Anton Mesmer: The History of an Idea* (London: Arthur Barker, 1934)

Goodenough, Erwin R., *By Light, Light: The Mystic Gospel of Hellenistic Judaism* (New Haven, CT: Yale University Press, 1935)

Goodman, Lenn E. (ed.), *Neoplatonism and Jewish Thought* (Albany, NY: State University of New York Press, 1992)

Goodrick-Clarke, Clare and Nicholas Goodrick-Clarke (eds.), *G. R. S. Mead and the Gnostic Quest* (Berkeley, CA: North Atlantic Books, 2005)

Graetz, Heinrich, *History of the Jews*, ed. and trans. Bella Löwy, 5 volumes (London: Jewish Chronicle Office, 1901)

Graetz, Michael, *The Jews in Nineteenth-Century France: From the French Revolution to the Alliance Israélite Universelle* (Stanford, CA: Stanford University Press, 1996)

Graf, Fritz, *Magic in the Ancient World*, trans. Franklin Philip (Cambridge, MA: Harvard University Press, 1997)

Graf, Susan Johnston, 'The Occult Novels of Dion Fortune', *Journal of Gender Studies*, 16:1 (2007), 47–56

Green, Arthur, *Menahem Nahum of Chernobyl: Upright Practices, The Light of the Eyes* (New York: Paulist Press, 1982)

—— (ed.), *Jewish Spirituality, Vol. 2: From the Sixteenth Century Revival to the Present* (New York: Crossroad, 1987)

——, 'Typologies of Leadership and the Hasidic Zaddiq', in Arthur Green (ed.), *Jewish Spirituality, Vol. 2: From the Sixteenth Century Revival to the Present* (New York: Crossroad, 1987), 127–56

——, 'The Zaddiq as Axis Mundi in Later Judaism', in Lawrence Fine (ed.), *Essential Papers on Kabbalah* (New York: New York University Press, 1995), 291–314

——, *Keter: The Crown of God in Early Jewish Mysticism* (Princeton, NJ: Princeton University Press, 1997)

——, 'Shekhinah, the Virgin Mary, and the Song of Songs: Reflections on a Kabbalistic Symbol in Its Historical Context', *AJS Review*, 26:1 (2002), 1–52

——, *A Guide to the Zohar* (Stanford, CA: Stanford University Press, 2004)

Greenberg, Louis M., 'Bergson and Durkheim as Sons and Assimilators: The Early Years', *French Historical Studies*, 9:4 (1976), 619–34

Greenfield, Allen H., *The Roots of Modern Magick: Glimpses of the Authentic Tradition From 1700 to 2000* (self-published, 2004)

Greenfield, Jonas C. and Michael E. Stone, 'The Books of Enoch and the Traditions of Enoch', *Numen*, 26:1 (1979), 89–103

Greenwood, Susan, *Magic, Witchcraft and the Otherworld: An Anthropology* (Oxford: Berg, 2000)

Greer, John Michael, *Paths of Wisdom: Principles and Practice of the Magical Cabala in the Western Tradition* (St Paul, MN: Llewellyn Publications, 1996)

——, *Circles of Power: Ritual Magic in the Western Tradition* (St. Paul, MN: Llewellyn Publications, 1997)

Greer, Mary K., *Women of the Golden Dawn: Rebels and Priestesses* (Rochester, VT: Park Street Press, 1995)

Greer, Mary K. and Darcy Kuntz, *The Chronology of the Golden Dawn: Being a Chronological History of a Magical Order, 1378–1994* (Edmonds, WA: Holmes Publishing Group, 1999)

Grözinger, Karl Erich and Joseph Dan (eds.), *Mysticism, Magic and Kabbalah in Ashkenazi Judaism*, (Berlin: Walter de Gruyter, 1995)

Gruenwald, Ithamar, 'Reflections on the Nature and Origins of Jewish Mysticism', in Peter Schäfer and Joseph Dan (eds.), *Gershom Scholem's Major Trends in Jewish Mysticism: 50 Years After* (Tubingen: Mohr Siebeck, 1993), 25–48

———, 'When Magical Techniques and Mystical Practices Become Neighbors: Methodological Considerations', in Gideon Bohak, Yuval Harari, and Shaul Shaked (eds.), *Continuity and Innovation in the Magical Tradition* (Leiden: Brill, 2011), 159–86

Guinsberg, A. M., 'Henry More, Thomas Vaughan and the Late Renaissance Magical Tradition', *Ambix*, 27 (1980), 36–58

Gunn, Joshua, *Modern Occult Rhetoric: Mass Media and the Drama of Secrecy in the Twentieth Century* (Tuscaloosa, AL: University of Alabama Press, 2005)

Hadot, Pierre, *The Veil of Isis: An Essay on the History of the Idea of Nature*, trans. Michael Chase (Cambridge, MA: Harvard University Press, 2008)

Halbertal, Moshe, *Concealment and Revelation: Esotericism in Jewish Thought and Its Philosophical Implications*, trans. Jackie Feldman (Princeton, NJ: Princeton University Press, 2007)

Haley, Bruce, *The Healthy Body and Victorian Culture* (Cambridge: Cambridge University Press, 1978)

Hallamish, Moshe, *An Introduction to the Kabbalah*, trans. Ruth Bar-Ilan and Ora Wiskind-Elper (Albany, NY: State University of New York Press, 1999)

Halperin, David Joel, *The Faces of the Chariot: Early Jewish Responses to Ezekiel's Vision* (Tübingen: Mohr Siebeck, 1988)

———, *Sabbatai Zevi: Testimonies to a Fallen Messiah* (Oxford: Littman Library of Jewish Civilization, 2007)

Hames, Harvey J., *The Art of Conversion: Christianity and Kabbalah in the Thirteenth Century* (Leiden: Brill, 2000)

———, 'Exotericism and Esotericism in Thirteenth Century Kabbalah', *Esoterica*, 6 (2004), 102–12

———, 'A Seal Within a Seal: The Imprint of Sufism in Abraham Abulafia's Teachings', *Medieval Encounters*, 12:2 (2006), 153–72

———, *Like Angels on Jacob's Ladder: Abraham Abulafia, the Franciscans and Joachimism* (New York, NY: State University of New York Press, 2007)

Hammer, Olav, *Claiming Knowledge: Strategies of Epistemology from Theosophy to the New Age* (Leiden: Brill, 2004)

Hammer, Olav and Kocku von Stuckrad, 'Introduction: Western Esotericism and Polemics', in Olav Hammer and Kocku von Stuckrad (eds.), *Polemical Encounters: Esoteric Discourse and Its Others* (Leiden: Brill, 2007), vi–xxii

——— (eds.), *Polemical Encounters: Esoteric Discourse and Its Others* (Leiden: Brill, 2007)

Handelman, Susan A., 'Interpretation as Devotion: Freud's Relation to Rabbinic Hermeneutics', *Psychoanalytic Review*, 68 (1981), 201–18

———, *The Slayers of Moses: The Emergence of Rabbinic Interpretation in Modern Literary Theory* (Albany, NY: State University of New York Press, 1982)

Hanegraaff, Wouter J., *New Age Religion and Western Culture: Esotericism in the Mirror of Secular Thought* (Leiden: Brill, 1996)

——, 'On the Construction of "Esoteric Traditions"', in Antoine Faivre and Wouter J. Hanegraaff (eds.), *Western Esotericism and the Science of Religion* (Leuven: Peeters, 1998), 11–62

——, 'New Age Religion and Secularization', *Numen*, 47:3 (2000), 288–312

——, 'How magic survived the disenchantment of the world', *Religion*, 33 (2003), 357–80

——, 'The Study of Western Esotericism: New Approaches to Christian and Secular Culture', in Peter Antes, Armin W. Geertz, and Randi R. Warne (eds.), *New Approaches to the Study of Religion, Vol. 1: Regional, Critical, and Historical Approaches* (Berlin/New York: Walter de Gruyter, 2004), 489–519

——, 'Emanuel Swedenborg, the Jews, and Jewish Traditions', in Peter Schäfer and Irina Wandrey (eds.), *Reuchlin und Seine Erben* (Ostfildern: Jan Thorbecke Verlag, 2005), 135–54

—— (ed.), *Dictionary of Gnosis and Western Hermeticism* (Leiden: Brill, 2006)

——, 'Jewish Influences V: Occultist Kabbalah', in Wouter J. Hanegraaff (ed.), *Dictionary of Gnosis and Western Hermeticism* (Leiden: Brill, 2006), 644–47

——, 'Tradition', in Wouter J. Hanegraaff (ed.), *Dictionary of Gnosis and Western Hermeticism* (Leiden: Brill, 2006), 1132–134

——, 'Magic V: 18th–20th Century', in Wouter J. Hanegraaff, ed., *Dictionary of Gnosis and Western Hermeticism* (Leiden: Brill, 2006), 738–44

——, 'The Beginnings of Occultist Kabbalah: Adolphe Franck and Eliphas Lévi', in Boaz Huss, Marco Pasi, and Kocku von Stuckrad (eds.), *Kabbalah and Modernity: Interpretations, Transformations, Adaptations* (Leiden: Brill, 2010)

——, *Esotericism and the Academy: Rejected Knowledge in Western Culture* (Cambridge: Cambridge University Press, 2011)

——, 'Kabbalah in *Gnosis* Magazine (1985–1999), in Boaz Huss (ed.), *Kabbalah and Contemporary Spiritual Revival* (Beer-Sheva: Ben-Gurion University of theNegev Press, 2011), 251–66

Hanegraaff, Wouter J. and Jeffrey J. Kripal (eds.), *Hidden Intercourse: Eros and Sexuality in the History of Western Esotericism* (Leiden: Brill, 2008)

Harari, Yuval, 'What Is a Magical Text? Methodological Reflections Aimed at Redefining Early Jewish Magic', in Shaul Shaked, ed., *Officina Magica: Essays on the Practice of Magic in Antiquity* (Leiden: Brill, 2005), 91–124

——, 'Moses, the Sword, and *The Sword of Moses*: Between Rabbinical and Magical Traditions', *Jewish Studies Quarterly*, 12 (2005), 293–329

Harding, James and Loveday Alexander, 'Dating the Testament of Solomon', University of St. Andrews School of Divinity, 28 May 1999, www.st-andrews.ac.uk/divinity/rt/otp/guestlectures/harding/

Harkness, Deborah E., *John Dee's Conversations with Angels: Cabala, Alchemy, and the End of Nature* (Cambridge: Cambridge University Press, 1999)

——, 'Shows in the Showstone: A Theater of Alchemy and Apocalypse in the Angel Conversations of John Dee (1527–1698/9)', *Renaissance Quarterly*, 49 (1996), 707–37

Harper, George Mills, *Yeats's Golden Dawn: The Influence of the Hermetic Order of the Golden Dawn on the Life and Art of W. B. Yeats* (London: Macmillan, 1974)

Hartman, David, *Maimonides: Torah and Philosophic Quest* (Philadelphia, PA: Jewish Publication Society, 1976)

Harvey, David Allen, 'Beyond Enlightenment: Occultism, Politics, and Culture in France from the Old Regime to the *Fin-de-Siècle*', *The Historian*, 65:3 (2003), 665–94

——, *Beyond Enlightenment: Occultism and Politics in Modern France* (Dekalb, IL: Northern Illinois University Press, 2005)

Hary, B. H., J. L. Hayes, and F. Astern (eds.), *Judaism and Islam: Boundaries, Communication and Interaction* (Leiden: Brill, 2000)

Hasdai, Yaacov, 'The Origins of the Conflict Between Hasidim and Mitnagdim', in Bezalel Safran (ed.), *Hasidism: Continuity or Innovation?* (Cambridge, MA: Harvard University Press, 1988), 27–45

Haskell, Ellen, 'Metaphor, Transformation, and Transcendence: Toward an Understanding of Kabbalistic Imagery in *Sefer hazohar*', *Prooftexts*, 28 (2008), 335–62

Hattersley, Roy, *Borrowed Time: The Story of Britain Between the Wars* (London: Little, Brown, 2007)

Haus, Jeffrey, 'How much Latin should a rabbi know? State finance and rabbinical education in nineteenth-century France', *Jewish History*, 15 (2001), 59–86

Haynes, Renée, *The Society for Psychical Research 1882–1982: A History* (London: MacDonald, 1982)

Hayward, Rhodri, 'Demonology, Neurology, and Medicine in Edwardian Britain', *Bulletin of the History of Medicine*, 78 (2004), 37–58

Hazelgrove, Jenny, *Spiritualism and British Society Between the Wars* (Manchester: Manchester University Press, 2000)

Heelas, Paul, *The New Age Movement: the Celebration of the Self and the Sacralization of Modernity* (Oxford: Blackwell, 1996)

Heilman, Samuel C., *Defenders of the Faith: Inside Ultra-Orthodox Jewry* (Berkeley, CA: University of California Press, 2000)

Helfland, Jonathan I., 'Passports and Piety: Apostasy in Nineteenth Century France', *Jewish History*, 3:2 (1988), 59–83

Helm, Robert M., *The Gloomy Dean: The Thought of William Ralph Inge* (Winston-Salem, NC: John F. Blair, 1962)

Henriques, Ursula R. Q., 'The Jewish Emancipation Controversy in Nineteenth-Century Britain', *Past and Present*, 40 (1968), 126–46

Henderson, James L., *A Bridge Across Time: An Assessment of Historical Archetypes* (London: Turnstone Books, 1975)

Henderson, Joseph L. and Dyane N. Sherwood, *Transformation of the Psyche: The Symbolic Alchemy of the Splendor Solis* (London: Routledge, 2003)

Herboulet, Marie-Louise, *La loi de Wronski appliquée à l'astrologie* (Garches: Éditions du Nouvel Humanisme, 1949)

Herrera, R. A. (ed.), *Mystics of the Book: Themes, Topics and Typologies* (New York: Peter Lang, 1993), 159–76

Herrero de Jáuregui, Miguel, *Orphism and Christianity in Late Antiquity* (Berlin: Walter de Gruyter, 2010)

Herzberg, Arthur, *The French Enlightenment and the Jews: The Origins of Modern Antisemitism* (New York: Columbia University Press, 1968)

Heschel, Abraham J., *The Circle of the Baal Shem Tov: Studies in Hasidism* (Chicago, IL: University of Chicago Press, 1985)

Hillman, James (ed.), *Timeless Documents of the Soul* (Evanston, IL: Northwestern University Press, 1952/1968)

Himmelfarb, Martha, *Ascent to Heaven in Jewish and Christian Apocalypses* (Oxford: Oxford University Press, 1993)

Hinshelwood, R. D., 'Psychoanalysis in Britain: Points of Cultural Access, 1893–1918', *International Journal of Psycho-Analysis*, 76 (February 1995), 135–51

Hjelm, Titus, 'Tradition as Legitimation in New Religious Movements', in Steven Engler and Gregory P. Grieve (eds.), *Historicizing "Tradition" in the Study of Religion* (Berlin/New York: Walter de Gruyter, 2005), 109–23

Hobsbawm, Eric, 'Inventing Traditions', in Eric Hobsbawm and Terence Ranger (eds.), *The Invention of Tradition* (Cambridge: Cambridge University Press, 1983), 1–14

Hobsbawm, Eric and Terence Ranger (eds.), *The Invention of Tradition* (Cambridge: Cambridge University Press, 1983)

Holmes, Colin, *Anti-Semitism in British Society, 1876–1939* (London: Edward Arnold Ltd., 1979)

Hood, Ralph W., Jr., 'The Construction and Preliminary Validation of a Measure of Reported Mystical Experience', *Journal for the Scientific Study of Religion*, 14 (1975), 29–41

——, 'Sin and Guilt in Faith Traditions: Issues for Self-Esteem', in John F. Schumaker (ed.), *Religion and Mental Health* (Oxford: Oxford University Press, 1992), 110–21

Hornung, Erik, *The Secret Lore of Egypt: Its Impact On the West*, trans. David Lorton (Ithaca, NY: Cornell University Press, 2001)

Horodezky, S. A., 'Gematria', in *Encyclopaedia Judaica*, VII:170–79

Horowitz, Asher and Terry Maley (eds.), *The Barbarism of Reason: Max Weber and the Twilight of Enlightenment* (Toronto/London: University of Toronto Press, 1994)

Howe, Ellic, *The Magicians of the Golden Dawn: A Documentary History of a Magical Order 1887–1923* (London: Routledge & Kegan Paul, 1972)

——, 'Fringe Masonry in England, 1870–85', *Ars Quatuor Coronatorum*, 85 (1972), 242–80

Howe, Ellic and Helmut Moller, 'Theodor Reuss: Irregular Freemasonry in Germany, 1900–23', *Ars Quatuor Coronatorum*, 91 (1978), <http://freemasonry.bcy.ca/aqc/reuss/reuss/html>

Huffman, William H., *Robert Fludd and the End of the Renaissance* (London: Routledge, 1988)

Hughes, R. T. L., 'The Powers and Properties of Numbers in Rosicrucian Metaphysics', Bishop Wilkins College No. 58, SRIA, <http://www.bishopwilkins.co.uk/Powers_and_Properties_of_Numbers_in_Rosicrucian_Metaph_.pdf>

Hurley, Kelly, *The Gothic Body: Sexuality, Materialism, and Degeneration at the Fin de Siècle* (Cambridge: Cambridge University Press, 1997)

Hurwitz, Siegmund, 'Psychological Aspects in Early Hasidic Literature', trans. H. Nagel, in James Hillman (ed.), *Timeless Documents of the Soul* (Evanston, IL: Northwestern University Press, 1952/1968), 151–239

Huson, Paul, *Mystical Origins of the Tarot: From Ancient Roots to Modern Usage* (Rochester, VT: Destiny Books, 2004)

Huss, Boaz, 'Ask No Questions: Gershom Scholem and the Study of Contemporary Jewish Mysticism', *Modern Judaism*, 25:2 (2005), 141–58

——, 'All You Need Is LAV: Madonna and Postmodern Kabbalah', *The Jewish Quarterly Review*, 95:4 (2005), 611–24

——, 'Jewish Mysticism in the University: Academic Study or Theological Practice?' (lecture given as part of the programme, 'The Academy and Spirituality: Can They Go Together?', Van Leer Institute, Jerusalem (30 May 2006), <http://www.zeek.net/712academy>

——, '"Authorized Guardians": The Polemics of Academic Scholars of Jewish Mysticism Against Kabbalah Practitioners', in Kocku von Stuckrad and Olav Hammer (eds.), *Polemical Encounters: Esoteric Discourse and Its Others* (Leiden: Brill, 2007), 81–103

——, 'The Sufis from America: Kabbalah and Theosophy in Puna in the Late 19th Century', in Boaz Huss, Marco Pasi, and Kocku von Stuckrad (eds.), *Kabbalah and Modernity: Interpretations, Transformations, Adaptations* (Leiden: Brill, 2010)

———, 'The New Age of Kabbalah: Contemporary Kabbalah, the New Age and Postmodern Spirituality', *Journal of Modern Jewish Studies*, 6:2 (2007), 107–25

———, 'Martin Buber's Introduction to *The Tales of Rabbi Nachman* and the Early 20th Century Construction of 'Jewish Mysticism' (2008), Ben-Gurion University of the Negev, <http://hsf.bgu.ac.il/cjt/files/electures/Buber1.htm>

———, 'The Mystification of the Kabbalah and the Modern Construction of Jewish Mysticism', trans. Elana Lutsky, *Ben Gurion University of the Negev Review* (Summer 2008), originally published in Hebrew in *Pe'anim* 110 (2007), 9–30, <http://web.bgu.ac.il/Eng/Centers/review/summer2008/Mysticism.htm>

——— (ed.), *Kabbalah and Contemporary Spiritual Revival* (Beer-Sheva: Ben-Gurion University of the Negev Press, 2011)

Huss, Boaz, Marco Pasi, and Kocku von Stuckrad (eds.), *Kabbalah and Modernity: Interpretations, Transformations, Adaptations* (Leiden: Brill, 2010)

Hutchinson, Roger, *Aleister Crowley: The Beast Demystified* (Edinburgh: Mainstream Publishing, 1998)

Huttler, Miriam, 'Jewish Origins of Freud's Interpretations of Dreams', *Journal of Psychology and Judaism*, 23:1 (1999), 5–48

Hutton, Ronald, *The Triumph of the Moon: A History of Modern Pagan Witchcraft* (Oxford: Oxford University Press, 1999)

———, 'Modern Pagan Witchcraft', in William de Blécourt, Ronald Hutton, and Jean la Fontaine, *Witchcraft and Magic in Europe, Vol. 6: The Twentieth Century* (London: Athlone Pres, 1999), 1–79

———, *Witches, Druids and King Arthur* (London: Hambledon Continuum, 2003)

———, 'Astral Magic: The Acceptable Face of Paganism', in Nicholas Campion, Patrick Curry, and Michael York (eds.), *Astrology and the Academy: Papers from the Inaugural Conference of the Sophia Centre, Bath Spa University, 13–14 June 2003* (Bristol: Cinnabar Books, 2004), 10–24

———, 'Writing the History of Witchcraft: A Personal View', *The Pomegranate* 12:2 (2010), 239–62

Idel, Moshe, 'The Magical and Neoplatonic Interpretations of the Kabbalah in the Renaissance', in Bernard Dov Cooperman (ed.), *Jewish Thought in the Sixteenth Century* (Cambridge, MA: Harvard University Press, 1983), 186–242

———, 'The World of Angels in Human Shape', in Joseph Dan and J. Hacker (eds.), *Jewish Mysticism, Philosophy and Ethical Literature* (Jerusalem: Magnes Press, 1986), 1–66

———, 'The Origin of Alchemy According to Zosimos and a Hebrew Parallel', *Revue des Études Juives*, 145:1–2 (1986), 117–24

———, *Kabbalah: New Perspectives* (New Haven, CT: Yale University Press, 1988)

———, 'Ramon Lull and Ecstatic Kabbalah: A Preliminary Observation', *Journal of the Warburg and Courtauld Institutes*, 51 (1988), 170–74

———, 'Hermeticism and Judaism', in Merkel, Ingrid and Allen G. Debus (eds.), *Hermeticism and the Renaissance: Intellectual History and the Occult in Early Modern Europe* (London: Associated University Presses, 1988), 59–76

———, *Studies in Ecstatic Kabbalah* (Albany, NY: State University of New York Press, 1988)

———, 'The Anthropology of Yohanan Alemanno: Sources and Influences', *Topoi*, 7 (1988), 201–10

———, 'The Golem in Jewish Magic and Mysticism', in Emily D. Bilski (ed.), *Golem! Danger, Deliverance and Art* (New York: Jewish Museum, 1988), 15–35

———, *The Mystical Experience in Abraham Abulafia*, trans. Jonathan Chipman (Albany, NY: State University of New York Press, 1988)

———, 'L'attitude envers le christianisme du Sefer ha-Mechiv', *Pardes*, 76 (1988), 77–93

———, 'Kabbalistic Prayer and Color', in David R. Blumenthal (ed.), *Approaches to Judaism in Medieval Times*, Vol. 3 (Chico, CA: Scholar's Press, 1988), 17–28

———, 'An Anonymous Kabbalistic Commentary on *Shir ha-Yihud*', in Karl Erich Grözinger and Joseph Dan (eds.), *Mysticism, Magic and Kabbalah in Ashkenazi Judaism*, ed. (Berlin: Walter de Gruyter, 1995), 139–54

———, *Language, Torah, and Hermeneutics in Abraham Abulafia* (Albany, NY: State University of New York Press, 1989)

———, 'Jewish Magic from the Renaissance Period to Early Hasidism', in Jacob Neusner, Ernest S. Frerichs, and Paul Virgil McCracken Flesher (eds.), *Religion, Science, and Magic: In Concert and in Conflict* (Oxford: Oxford University Press, 1989), 82–117

———, 'Sexual Metaphors and Praxis in the Kabbalah', in David Kraemer (ed.), *The Jewish Family: Metaphor and Memory* (Oxford: Oxford University Press, 1989), 197–224

———, ''Universalization and Integration: Two Conceptions of Mystical Union in Jewish Mysticism', in Idel, Moshe and Bernard McGinn (eds.), *Mystical Union and Monotheistic Faith: An Ecumenical Dialogue* (New York: Macmillan, 1989), 27–57

———, *Golem: Jewish Magical and Mystical Traditions On the Artificial Anthropoid* (Albany, NY: State University of New York Press, 1990)

———, 'Rabbinism Versus Kabbalism: On G. Scholem's Phenomenology of Judaism', *Modern Judaism*, 11:3 (1991), 281–96

———, 'Major Currents in Italian Kabbalah between 1560 and 1660', in David B. Ruderman (ed.), *Essential Papers on Jewish Culture in Renaissance and Baroque Italy* (New York: New York University Press, 1992), 345–68

———, '"One from a Town, Two from a Clan" — The Diffusion of Lurianic Kabbala and Sabbateanism: A Re-Examination', *Jewish History*, 7:2 (1993), 79–104

———, 'Introduction to the Bison Book Edition', in Johann Reuchlin, *De arte cabalistica: On the Art of the Kabbalah*, trans. Martin and Sarah Goodman (Lincoln, NE: University of Nebraska Press, 1993), v–xxix.

———, 'Defining Kabbalah: The Kabbalah of the Divine Names', in R. A. Herrera, ed., *Mystics of the Book: Themes, Topics and Typologies* (New York: Peter Lang, 1993), 97–122

———, 'Magic and Kabbalah in the *Book of the Responding Entity*', in Mayer I. Gruber (ed.), *The Solomon Goldman Lectures, Vol. VI* (Chicago, IL: Spertus College of Judaica Press, 1993), 125–38

———, 'Historical Introduction', in Joseph Gikatilia, *Gates of Light (Sha'are Orah)*, trans. Avi Weinstein, ed. Kerry Brown and Sima Sharma (Walnut Creek, CA: Bronfman Library of Jewish Classics, Alta Mira Press, 1994), xxiii–xxxi

———, 'Jewish Mysticism in Spain: Some Cultural Observations', *Espacio, Tiempo y Forma* 7 (1994), 289–314

———, *Hasidism: Between Ecstasy and Magic* (Albany, NY: State University of New York Press, 1995)

——, 'Mystical Techniques', in Lawrence Fine (ed.), *Essential Papers on Kabbalah* (New York: New York University Press, 1995), 483–94

——, 'On Talismanic Language in Jewish Mysticism', *Diogenes*, 43:2 (1995), 23–41

——, 'On Judaism, Jewish Mysticism and Magic', in Peter Schäfer and Hans G. Kippenberg (eds.), *Envisioning Magic: A Princeton Seminar and Symposium* (Leiden: Brill, 1997), 195–214

——, *Messianic Mystics* (New Haven, CT: Yale University Press, 1998)

——, 'Nachmanides: Kabbalah, Halakhah, and Spiritual Leadership', in Moshe Idel and Mortimer Ostow (eds.), *Jewish Mystical Leaders and Leadership in the 13th Century* (Northvale, NJ: Jason Aronson, 1998), 15–96

——, 'Saturn and Sabbatai Tzevi: A New Approach to Sabbateanism', in Peter Schäfer and Mark R. Cohen (eds.), *Toward the Millennium: Messianic Expectations from the Bible to Waco* (Leiden: Brill, 1998), 173–202

——, 'Transmission in Thirteenth-Century Kabbalah', in Yaakov Elman and Israel Gershoni (eds.), *Transmitting Jewish Traditions: Orality, Textuality and Cultural Diffusion* (New Haven, CT: Yale University Press, 2000), 138–65

——, 'Prisca Theologia in Marsilio Ficino and in Some Jewish Treatments', in Michael J. B. Allen and Valery Rees (eds.), *Marsilio Ficino: His Theology, His Philosophy, His Legacy* (Leiden: Brill, 2002), 137–58

——, *Absorbing Perfections: Kabbalah and Interpretation* (New Haven, CT: Yale University Press, 2002)

——, 'Maimonides' Guide of the Perplexed and the Kabbalah', *Jewish History*, 18 (2004), 197–226

——, 'On Prophecy and Early Hasidism', in Alberto Ferreiro and Moshe Sharon (eds.), *Studies in Modern Religions, Religious Movements and the Babi-Baha'i Faiths* (Leiden: Brill, 2004), 41–75

——, *Kabbalah and Eros* (New Haven, CT: Yale University Press, 2005)

——, *Ascensions on High in Jewish Mysticism: Pillars, Lines, Ladders* (Budapest: Central European University Press, 2005)

——, 'Androgyny and Equality in the Theosophico-Theurgical Kabbalah', *Diogenes*, 208 (2005), 27–38

——, *Enchanted Chains: Techniques and Rituals in Jewish Mysticism* (Los Angeles, CA: Cherub Press, 2005)

——, 'Some Forlorn Writings of a Forgotten Ashkenazi Prophet', *Jewish Quarterly Review*, 95:1 (2005), 183–96

——, 'On European Cultural Renaissances and Jewish Mysticism', in Daniel Abrams and Avraham Elqayam (eds.), *Kabbalah: Journal for the Study of Jewish Mystical Texts*, Vol. 13 (Los Angeles, CA: Cherub Press, 2005), 43–78

——, 'White Letters: From R. Levi Isaac of Berditchev's Views to Postmodern Hermeneutics', *Modern Judaism*, 26:2 (2006), 169–92

——, 'A Unique Manuscript of an Untitled Treatise of Abraham Abulafia', *Kabbalah: Journal for the Study of Jewish Mystical Texts*, 17 (2008), 7–28

——, 'Ta'anug: Erotic Delights from Kabbalah to Hasidism', in Wouter J. Hanegraaff and Jeffrey J. Kripal (eds.), *Hidden Intercourse: Eros and Sexuality in the History of Western Esotericism* (Leiden: Brill, 2008), 111–51

——, 'Johannes Reuchlin: Kabbalah, Pythagorean Philosophy and Modern Scholarship', *Studia Judaica*, 16 (2008), 30–55

——, 'Inner Peace through Inner Struggle in Abraham Abulafia's Ecstatic Kabbalah', *Journal for the Study of Sephardic and Mizrahi Jewry*, 2:2 (2009), 62–96

——, *Old Worlds, New Mirrors: On Jewish Mysticism and Twentieth-Century Thought* (Philadelphia, PA: University of Pennsylvania Press, 2010).

――, *Kabbalah in Italy, 1280-1510* (New Haven, CT: Yale University Press, 2011)

――, *Saturn's Jews: On the Witches' Sabbath and Sabbateanism* (London: Continuum, 2011)

Idel, Moshe and Bernard McGinn (eds.), *Mystical Union and Monotheistic Faith: An Ecumenical Dialogue* (New York: Macmillan, 1989)

Idel, Moshe and Mortimer Ostow (eds.), *Jewish Mystical Leaders and Leadership in the 13th Century* (Northvale, NJ: Jason Aronson, 1998)

Ingram, Brannon, 'René Guénon and the Traditionalist Polemic', in Olav Hammer and Kocku von Stuckrad (eds.), *Polemical Encounters: Esoteric Discourse and Its Others* (Leiden: Brill, 2007), 201–26

Ivakhiv, Adrian, 'The Resurgence of Magical Religion as a Response to the Crisis of Modernity: A Postmodern Depth Psychological Perspective', in James R. Lewis (ed.), *Magical Religion and Modern Witchcraft* (Albany, NY: State University of New York Press, 1996), 237–65

Jackson, Holbrook, *The Eighteen Nineties: A Review of Art and Ideas at the Close of the Nineteenth Century* (London: Penguin, 1913; repr. London: Penguin/Pelican, 1939)

Jacobs, Janet Liebman, 'Freud as Other: Antisemitism and the Development of Psychoanalysis', in Janet Liebman Jacobs and Donald Capps (eds.), *Religion, Society, and Psychoanalysis: Readings in Contemporary Theory* (Boulder, CO: Westview Press, 1997), 11–22

Jacobs, Janet Liebman and Donald Capps (eds.), *Religion, Society, and Psychoanalysis: Readings in Contemporary Theory* (Boulder, CO: Westview Press, 1997)

Jacobs, Louis, *A Jewish Theology* (Springfield, NJ: Behrman House, 1973)

――, 'Uplifting the Sparks in Later Jewish Mysticism', in Arthur Green (ed.), *Jewish Spirituality, Vol. 2: From the Sixteenth Century Revival to the Present* (New York: Crossroad, 1987), 99–126

――, 'The *Maggid* of Rabbi Moses Hayyim Luzzato', in Louis Jacobs (ed. and trans.), *The Jewish Mystics* (London: Kyle Cathie, 1990), 136–47

Jacobson, Eric, 'The Future of the Kabbalah: On the Dislocation of Past Primacy, the Problem of Evil, and the Future of Illusions', in Boaz Huss, Marco Pasi, and Kocku von Stuckrad (eds.), *Kabbalah and Modernity: Interpretations, Adaptations, Transformations* (Leiden: Brill, 2010), 47–75

Jacobson, Yoram, 'The Aspect of the "Feminine" in the Lurianic Kabbalah', in Peter Schäfer and Joseph Dan (eds.), *Gershom Scholem's* Major Trends in Jewish Mysticism *50 Years After* (Tübingen: Mohr-Siebeck, 1993), 239–55

James, Geoffrey, *The Enochian Evocation of Dr. John Dee* (Gillette, NJ: Heptangle Books, 1984)

Janowitz, Naomi, *The Poetics of Ascent: Theories of Language in a Rabbinic Ascent Text* (Albany, NY: State University of New York Press, 1989)

Jenkins, Edward, *Haverholme, or the Apotheosis of Jingo: A Satire* (London: William Mullan & Son, 1878)

Jensen, K. Frank, *The Story of the Waite-Smith Tarot* (Melbourne: Association for Tarot Studies, 2006)

Johannisson, Karen, 'Magic, Science, and Institutionalization in the Seventeenth and Eighteenth Centuries', in Ingrid Merkel and Allen G. Debus (eds.), *Hermeticism and the Renaissance: Intellectual History and the Occult in Early Modern Europe* (London: Associated University Presses, 1988), 251–61

Johnson, John, 'Henry Maudsley on Swedenborg's Messianic Psychosis', *British Journal of Psychiatry*, 165 (1994), 690–91

Johnson, K. Paul, *The Masters Revealed: Madame Blavatsky and the Myth of the Great White Lodge* (Albany, NY: State University of New York Press, 1994)

Johnston, Sarah Iles, *Hekate Soteira: A Study of Hekate's Roles in the Chaldean Oracles and Related Literature* (Oxford: Oxford University Press, 2000)

——, 'The Testament of Solomon: from Late Antiquity to the Renaissance', in Jan N. Bremmer and Jan R. Veenstra (eds.), *The Metamorphosis of Magic: from Late Antiquity to the Early Modern Period* (Leuven: Peeters, 2002), 35–49

——, 'Introduction: Divining Divination', in Sarah Iles Johnston and Peter T. Struck (eds.), *Mantikê: Studies in Ancient Divination* (Leiden: Brill, 2005), 1–28

Johnston, Sarah Iles and Peter T. Struck (eds.), *Mantikê: Studies in Ancient Divination* (Leiden: Brill, 2005)

Johnston, Sarah Iles, John G. Gager, Martha Himmelfarb, Marvin Meyer, Brian Schmidt, David Frankfurter, and Fritz Graf, 'Panel Discussion: *Magic in the Ancient World* by Fritz Graf', *Numen*, 46:3 (1999), 291–325

Jonas, Hans, *The Gnostic Religion: The Message of the Alien God and the Beginnings of Christianity* (Boston, MA: Beacon Press, 1963)

——, 'Myth and Mysticism: A Study of Objectification and Interiorization in Religious Thought', *Journal of Religion*, 49:4 (1969), 315–29

Jones, Ernest, 'Reminiscent Notes on the Early History of Psycho-Analysis in English-Speaking Countries', *International Journal of Psycho-Analysis*, 26 (1945), 8-10

——, *Free Associations: Memories of a Psycho-Analyst* (London: Hogarth Press, 1959)

Joseph, Steven M., 'Jung and Kabbalah: imaginal and noetic aspects', *Journal of Analytical Psychology*, 52 (2007), 321–41

Joshti, S. T., 'Introduction', in Algernon Blackwood, *The Complete John Silence Stories* (Mineola, NY: Dover, 1997), v–x

Kaczynski, Richard, *Perdurabo: The Life of Aleister Crowley* (Tempe, AR: New Falcon Publications, 2002)

Kahn, Didier, 'The Rosicrucian Hoax in France', in William R. Newman and Anthony Grafton (eds.), *Secrets of Nature: Astrology and Alchemy in Early Modern Europe* (Cambridge, MA: MIT Press, 2001), 235–344

Kallus, Menachem, 'Pneumatic Mystical Possession and the Eschatology of the Soul in Lurianic Kabbalah', in Matt Goldish (ed.), *Spirit Possession in Judaism: Cases and Contexts from the Middle Ages to the Present* (Detroit, MI: Wayne State University Press, 2003), 159–85

Kanarfogel, Ephraim, *'Peering Through the Lattices': Mystical, Magical, and Pietistic Dimensions in the Tosafist Period* (Detroit, MI: Wayne State University Press, 2000)

Kaplan, Aryeh, *Meditation and Kabbalah* (York Beach, ME: WeiserBooks, 1982)

Kaplan, Fred, '"The Mesmeric Mania": The Early Victorians and Animal Magnetism', *Journal of the History of Ideas*, 35:4 (1974), 691–702

Karr, Don, 'Notes on the Study of Later Kabbalah in English: The Safed Period and Lurianic Kabbalah', in Don Karr, *Collected Articles on the Kabbalah*, Vol. 2 (Ithaca, NY: KoM, No. 6, 1985), 23–31

——, *Collected Articles on the Kabbalah*, Vol. 2 (Ithaca, NY: KoM, No. 6, 1985)

——, 'Notes on Editions of *Sefer Yetzirah* in English' (2001–07), <http://www.digital-brilliance.com/kab/karr/syie.pdf>

——, 'The Study of Christian Cabala in English: Addenda' (1995–2006), 77–86, <http://www.digital-brilliance.com/kab/karr/ccineb.pdf>

——, 'The Study of Solomonic Magic in English' (2007), <http://www.digital-brilliance.com/kab/karr/tssmie.pdf>

——, *The Jews in the History of England, 1485–1850* (Oxford: Oxford University Press, 1997)

——, *The Occult Tradition: From the Renaissance to the Present Day* (London: Jonathan Cape, 2005)

Katz, Jacob, *Jews and Freemasons in Europe 1723–1939*, trans. Leonard Oschry (Cambridge, MA: Harvard University Press, 1970)

—— (ed.), *Towards Modernity: The European Jewish Model* (New Brunswick, NJ: Transaction Books, 1987)

Katz, Steven T., 'Language, Epistemology, and Mysticism', in Steven T. Katz (ed.), *Mysticism and Philosophical Analysis* (London: Sheldon Press, 1978), 22–74

—— (ed.), *Mysticism and Philosophical Analysis* (London: Sheldon Press, 1978)

—— (ed.), *Mysticism and Religious Traditions* (Oxford: Oxford University Press, 1983)

—— (ed.), *The Cambridge History of Judaism, Vol. 4: The Late Roman-Rabbinic Period* (Cambridge: Cambridge University Press, 2006)

Keane, Lloyd Kenton, *Routes of Wholeness: Jungian and Post-Jungian Dialogues with the Western Esoteric Tradition* (unpublished PhD dissertation, Centre for Psychoanalytic Studies, University of Essex, 2007)

Kellner, Menachem, *Maimonides' Confrontation with Mysticism* (Oxford: Littman Library of Jewish Civilization, 2006)

Kenton, Warren (Z'ev ben Shimon Halevi), *The Anatomy of Fate: Kabbalistic Astrology* (London: Rider, 1978)

——, *Kabbalah and Exodus* (York Beach, ME: WeiserBooks, 1988)

——, *Adam and the Kabbalistic Tree* (York Beach, ME: WeiserBooks, 1990)

——, *Introduction to the Cabala: Tree of Life* (York Beach, ME: WeiserBooks, 1991)

——, 'The House of the Psyche', *Inner Light Journal*, 24:4 (2004), <http://www.innerlight.org.uk/journals/Vol24No4/house.pdf>

——, 'Interview', <http://www.skyscript.co.uk/kenton.html>

Kern-Ulmer, Brigitte, 'The Depiction of Magic in Rabbinic Texts: The Rabbinic and the Greek Concept of Magic', *Journal for the Study of Judaism*, 27:3 (1998), 289–303

Kieckhefer, Richard, 'The Specific Rationality of Medieval Magic', *American Historical Review*, 99:3 (1994), 813–36

——, *Forbidden Rites: A Necromancer's Manual of the Fifteenth Century* (University Park, PA: Pennsylvania State University Press, 1997)

——, 'The Devil's Contemplatives: the *Liber Iuratus*, the *Liber Visionum*, and Christian Appropriation of Jewish Occultism', in Claire Fanger (ed.), *Conjuring Spirits: Texts and Traditions of Medieval Ritual Magic* (University Park, PA: Pennsylvania State University Press, 1998), 250–65

Kiessling, Nicolas, *The Incubus in English Literature: Provenance and Progeny* (Spokane, WA: Washington State University Press, 1977)

Kieval, Hillel J., 'Pursuing the Golem of Prague: Jewish Culture and the Invention of a Tradition', *Modern Judaism*, 17 (1997), 1–23

Kilcher, Andreas B., *Die Sprachtheorie der Kabbala als ästhetisches Paradigma: die Konstruktion einer ästhetischen Kabbala seit der frühen Neuzeit* (Stuttgart: Metzler, 1998)

——, 'Kabbala und Moderne: Gershom Scholems Geschichte und Metaphysik des Judentums', in Joachim Valentin and Saskia Wendel (eds.), *Jüdische Traditionen in der Philosophie des 20. Jahrhunderts* (Darmstadt: Primus Verlag, 2000), 86–99

——, 'The Moses of Sinai and the Moses of Egypt: Moses as Magician in Jewish Literature and Western Esotericism', *Aries*, 4:2 (2004), 148–70

———, 'Verhüllung und Enthüllung des Gehimnisses: Die *Kabbala Denudata* im Okkultismus der Moderne', in Andreas B. Kilcher (ed.), *Morgen-Glantz: Zeitschrift der Christian Knorr von Rosenroth-Gesellschaft*, 16 (2006), 343–83

———, ed., *Morgen-Glantz: Zeitschrift der Christian Knorr von Rosenroth-Gesellschaft*, Vol. 16 (2006)

King, Francis, *The Secret Rituals of the O.T.O.* (York Beach, ME: Samuel Weiser, 1973)

———, *The Flying Sorcerer: Being the Magical and Aeronautical Adventures of Francis Barrett, Author of The Magus* (Oxford: Mandrake Press, 1986)

———, *Modern Ritual Magic: The Rise of Western Occultism* (Bridport: Prism Press, 1989)

King, Sallie B., 'Two Epistemological Models for the Interpretation of Mysticism', *Journal of the American Academy of Religion*, 56:2 (1988), 257–79

King, Richard, *Orientalism and Religion: Postcolonial Theory, India, and 'The Mystic East'* (London: Routledge, 1999)

Kissling, Robert Christian, 'The *Ochêma-Pneuma* of the Neo-Platonists and the *De Insomniis* of Synesius of Cyrene, *American Journal of Philology* 43:4 (1922), 318–30

Klaassen, Frank, 'Medieval Magic in the Renaissance', *Aries*, 3:2 (2003), 166–99

Klawans, Jonathan, *Impurity and Sin in Ancient Judaism* (Oxford: Oxford University Press, 2000)

Klein, D. B., *Jewish Origins of the Psychoanalytic Movement* (New York: Praeger, 1981)

Klein-Braslavy, Sara, 'Maimonides' Exoteric and Esoteric Biblical Interpretations in the Guide of the Perplexed', in Howard Kreisel (ed.), *Study and Knowledge in Jewish Thought, Vol. 1* (Beer Sheva: Ben Gurion University of the Negev Press, 2006), 137–64.

Klier, John D. and Shlomo Lambroza, *Pogroms: Anti-Jewish Violence in Modern Russian History* (Cambridge: Cambridge University Press, 1992)

Klutz, Todd E. (ed.), *Magic in the Biblical World: From the Rod of Aaron to the Ring of Solomon* (London: T & T Clark International, 2003)

———, *Rewriting the Testament of Solomon: Tradition, Conflict and Identity in a Late Antique Pseudepigraphon* (London: T & T Clark International, 2005)

Kluveld, Amanda, 'Anna Bonus Kingsford', in Wouter J. Hanegraaff (ed.), *Dictionary of Gnosis and Western Esotericism* (Leiden: Brill, 2006), 663–65

Knepper, Paul, 'British Jews and the Racialisation of Crime in the Age of Empire', *British Journal of Criminology*, 47: (2007), 61–79

Knight, Gareth, *Dion Fortune and the Inner Light* (Loughborough: Thoth Publications, 2000)

———, *A Practical Guide to Qabalistic Symbolism* (York Beach, ME: WeiserBooks, 2002)

———, 'The Magical World of Dion Fortune', *Inner Light Journal*, 24:1 (2003), <http://www.innerlight.org.uk/journals/Vol24No1/magwrld.pdf>

———, *The Occult Fiction of Dion Fortune* (Loughborough: Thoth Publications, 2007)

Kontos, Alkis, 'The World Disenchanted, and the Return of Gods and Demons', in Asher Horowitz and Terry Maley (eds.), *The Barbarism of Reason: Max Weber and the Twilight of Enlightenment* (Toronto: University of Toronto Press, 1994), 223–47

Kraemer, David (ed.), *The Jewish Family: Metaphor and Memory* (Oxford: Oxford University Press, 1989)

Kreisel, Howard, 'Esotericism to Exotericism: From Maimonides to Gersonides', in Howard Kreisel (ed.), *Study and Knowledge in Jewish*

Thought, Vol. 1 (Beer Sheva: Ben Gurion University of the Negev Press, 2006), 165–83
———— (ed.), *Study and Knowledge in Jewish Thought, Vol. 1* (Beer Sheva: Ben Gurion University of the Negev Press, 2006)
Kridl, Manfred, 'Two Champions of a New Christianity: Lammenais and Mickiewicz', *Comparative Literature*, 4:3 (1952), 239–67
———— (ed.), *Adam Mickiewicz, Poet of Poland* (New York: Greenwood Press, 1951)
Kristeller, Paul Oskar, 'Giovanni Pico della Mirandola and His Sources', in *L'Opera e il Pensiero di Giovanni Pico della Mirandola nella Storia dell'Umanesimo, Vol. 1* (Firenze: Istituto Nazionale di Studi sul Rinascimento, 1965), 35–142
Kristeva, Julia, *Desire in Language: A Semiotic Approach to Literature and Art*, ed. Léon Roudiez, trans. Alice Jardine, Thomas Gora, and Léon Roudiez (New York: Columbia University Press, 1980)
Kupperman, Jeffrey S., 'Towards a Definition of Initiation: Emic and Etic Views of Initiation in the Western Mystery Tradition', *Esoterica*, 6 (2004), 67–80
Kzutsu, Toshihiko, *The Concept of Belief in Islamic Theology: A Semantic Analysis of Iman and Islam* (Selangor, Malasia: Islamic Book Trust/The Other Press, 2001)
Laarss, R. H., *Eliphas Lévi: Der Grosse Kabbalist und Seine Magischen Werke* (Vienna/Berlin: Rikola Verlag, 1922)
Lachter, Hartley, 'Spreading Secrets: Kabbalah and Esotericism in Isaac ibn Sahula's *Meshal ha-kadmoni*', *Jewish Quarterly Review*, 100:1 (2010), 111–38
Laenen, J. H., *Jewish Mysticism: An Introduction*, trans. David E. Orton (Louisville, KY: Westminster/John Knox Press, 2001)
LaFleur, William R., 'Body', in Mark C. Taylor (ed.), *Critical Terms for Religious Studies* (Chicago, IL: University of Chicago Press, 1998), 36–54
Laks, André and Glenn W. Most, *Studies on the Derveni Papyrus* (Oxford: Clarendon Press, 1997)
Láng, Benedek, *Unlocked Books: Manuscripts of Learned Magic in the Medieval Libraries of Central Europe* (University Park, PA: Penn State University Press, 2008)
Langermann, Y. Tzvi, 'Cosmology and Cosmogony in *Doresh Reshumoth*, a Thirteenth-Century Commentary on the Torah', *Harvard Theological Review*, 97:2 (2004), 199–227
Lankewish, Vincent A., 'Love Among the Ruins: the Catacombs, the Closet, and the Victorian "Early Christian Novel"', *Victorian Literature and Culture*, 28:2 (2000), 239–73
Laqueur, Thomas, 'Why the Margins Matter: Occultism and the Making of Modernity', *Modern Intellectual History*, 3:1 (2006), 111–35
Latimer, Bonnie, 'Alchemies of Satire: A History of the Sylphs in *The Rape of the Lock*', *Review of English Studies*, 57:232 (2006), 684–700
Laycock, Donald C., *The Complete Enochian Dictionary: A Dictionary of the Angelic Language as Revealed to Dr. John Dee and Edward Kelley* (London: Askin Publishers, 1978; repr. San Francisco, CA: Weiserbooks, 2001)
Laurant, Jean-Pierre, 'Esotericism in Freemasonry: The Example of François-Nicolas Noël's *La Géometrie du Maçon* (1812), in Antoine Faivre and Wouter J. Hanegraaff (eds.), *Western Esotericism and the Science of Religion* (Leuven: Peeters, 1998), 191–200
————, 'Eliphas Lévi' in Wouter J. Hanegraaff (ed.), *Dictionary of Gnosis and Western Esotericism* (Leiden: Brill, 2006), 689–91
Laybourn, Keith (ed.), *Modern Britain Since 1906 — A Reader* (London: I. B. Tauris, 1999)

Le Forestier, René, *La Franc-Maçonnerie Templière et Occultiste aux XVIIIe et XIXe Siècles* (Paris: Aubier-Montaigne, 1970)

Le Hir, Yves, *Lamennais écrivain* (Paris: P. A. Colin, 1948)

Lebzelter, Gisela C., *Political Anti-Semitism in England 1918–1939* (London: Macmillan, 1978)

Lednicki, W., 'Mickiewicz at the Collège de France, 1840–1940', *Slavonic Year-Book, American Series*, Vol. 1 (1941), 149–72

Lehrich, Christopher I., *The Language of Demons and Angels: Cornelius Agrippa's Occult Philosophy*, (Leiden: Brill, 2003)

Lehrmann, Chanan, *Bergsonisme et Judaïsme: Cours professé à l'Université de Lausanne* (Geneva: Éditions Union, 1937)

Leitch, Aaron, *Secrets of the Magical Grimoires: The Classical Texts of Magick Deciphered* (Woodbury, MN: Llewellyn Publications, 2005)

Lelli, Fabrizio, '"Prisca Philosophia" and "Docta Religio": The Boundaries of Rational Knowledge in Jewish and Christian Humanist Thought', *Jewish Quarterly Review*, 91:1/2 (2000), 53–99

——, 'Hermes Among the Jews: *Hermetica* as *Hebraica* from Antiquity to the Renaissance', *Magic, Ritual, and Witchcraft*, 2:2 (2007), 111–35

Lenowitz, Harris, *The Jewish Messiahs: From the Galilee to Crown Heights* (Oxford: Oxford University Press, 1998)

——, 'The Charlatan at the *Gottes Haus* in Offenbach', in Matt Goldish and Richard H. Popkin, (eds.), *Millenarianism and Messianism in Early Modern European Culture, Vol. I: Jewish Messianism in the Early Modern World* (Dordrecht: Kluwer Academic Publishers, 2001), 189–202

Leopold, Joan, 'The Aryan Theory of Race', *Indian Economic and Social History Review*, 7 (1970), 271–97

Levine, Lee I., *Judaism and Hellenism in Antiquity: Confict or Confluence?* (Seattle, WA: University of Washington Press, 1998)

Lévy, Tony and Charles Burnett, '*Sefer ha-Middot*: A Mid-Twelfth-Century Text on Arithmetic and Geometry Atrributed to Abraham Ibn Ezra', *Aleph*, 6 (2006), 57–238

Lewis, James R. (ed.), *Magical Religion and Modern Witchcraft* (Albany, NY: State University of New York Press, 1996)

Lewy, Hans, *The Chaldaean Oracles and Theurgy: Mysticism, Magic and Platonism in the Later Roman Empire*, ed. Michel Tardieu (Paris: Études Augustiniennes, 1978)

Lesses, Rebecca Macy, 'Speaking with Angels: Jewish and Greco-Egyptian Revelatory Adjurations', *Harvard Theological Review*, 89:1 (1996), 41–60

——, *Ritual Practices to Gain Power: Angels, Incantations, and Revelation in Early Jewish Mysticism* (Harrisburg, PA: Trinity Press International, 1998)

——, 'The Adjuration of the Prince of the Presence: Performative Utterance in a Jewish Ritual', in Marvin Meyer and Paul Mirecki (eds.), *Ancient Magic and Ritual Power* (Leiden: Brill, 2001), 185–206

Lewis, H. S., 'Maimonides on Superstition', *Jewish Quarterly Review*, 17:3 (1905), 475–88

Lewis, H. Spencer, *Rosicrucian Questions and Answers with Complete Answers* (San Jose, CA: Supreme Grand Lodge of AMORC, 1969)

Liberles, Robert, 'The Origins of the Jewish Reform Movement in England', *AJS Review*, 1 (1976), 121–50

Lidaka, Juris G., '*The Book of Angels, Rings, Characters and Images of the Planets*: Attributed to Osbern Bokenham', in Claire Fanger (ed.), *Conjuring Spirits: Texts and Traditions of Medieval Ritual Magic* (University Park, PA: Pennsylvania State University Press, 1998), 32–75

Liebes, Yehuda, *Studies in Jewish Myth and Jewish Messianism*, trans. Batya Stein (Albany, NY: State University of New York Press, 1993)

————, *Studies in the Zohar*, trans. Arnold Schwartz, Stephanie Nakache, and Penina Peli (Albany, NY: State University of New York Press, 1993)

————, '*Zohar* and Iamblichus', *Journal for the Study of Religions and Ideologies*, 18:18 (2007), 95–100

Liljegren, S. B., *Bulwer-Lytton's Novels and Isis Unveiled* (Cambridge, MA: Harvard University Press, 1957)

Linden, Stanton J., *The Alchemy Reader: From Hermes Trismegistus to Isaac Newton* (Cambridge: Cambridge University Press, 2003)

Lindsay, Jack, *The Origins of Alchemy in Greco-Roman Egypt* (London: Frederick Muller, 1970)

————, *Origins of Astrology* (London: Frederick Muller, 1971)

Linehan, Thomas P., *British Fascism, 1918–1939: Parties, Ideology and Culture* (Manchester: Manchester University Press, 2000)

Littlewood, Roland and Simon Dein, 'The Effectiveness of Words: Religion and Healing Among the Lubavich of Stamford Hill', *Culture, Medicine and Psychiatry*, 19 (1995), 339–83

Loewenthal, Naftali, *Communicating the Infinite: The Emergence of the Habad School* (Chicago, IL: University of Chicago Press, 1990)

————, 'Rabbi Shneur Zalman of Liadi's *Kitzur Likkutei Amarim*, British Library Or 10456', in Joseph Dan and Klaus Herrmann (eds.), *Studies in Jewish Manuscripts* (Tübingen: Mohr Siebeck, 1998), 89–138

Louth, Andrew, *The Origins of the Christian Mystical Tradition: From Plato to Denys* (Oxford: Clarendon Press, 1981)

Lovejoy, Arthur O., *The Great Chain of Being: A Study of the History of an Idea* (Cambridge, MA: Harvard University Press, 1936)

Low, Colin, 'Emanation and Ascent in Hermetic Kabbalah' (2003), <http://www.digital-brilliance.com/kab/essays/Emanation%20Ascent.pdf>

Luck, Georg, *Arcana Mundi: Magic and the Occult in the Greek and Roman Worlds* (Baltimore, MD: Johns Hopkins University Press, 1985)

Luhrmann, T. M., *Persuasions of the Witch's Craft: Ritual Magic in Contemporary England* (Cambridge, MA: Harvard University Press, 1989)

Lunn, Kenneth and Richard C. Thurlow (eds.), *British Fascism: Essays on the Radical Right in Inter-War Britain* (London: Croom Helm, 1980)

Lutzky, Harriet, 'Reparation and Tikkun: A Comparison of the Kleinian and Kabbalistic Concepts', *International Review of Psycho-Analysis*, 16 (1989), 449–58

Magid, Shaul, 'From Theosophy to Midrash: Lurianic Exegesis and the Garden of Eden', *AJS Review*, 22:1 (1997), 37–75

————, *From Metaphysics to Midrash: Myth, History, and the Interpretation of Scripture in Lurianic Kabbalah* (Bloomington, IN: Indiana University Press, 2008)

Mahler, Raphael, *Hasidism and the Jewish Enlightenment: Their Confrontation in Galicia and Poland in the First Half of the Nineteenth Century*, trans. Eugene Orenstein, Aaron Klein, and Jenny Machlowitz Klein (New York: The Jewish Publication Society of America, 1985)

Maidenbaum, Aryeh (ed.), *Jung and the Shadow of Anti-Semitism: Collected Essays* (Berwick, ME: Nicolas-Hays, 2002)

Maidenbaum, Aryeh and Stephen A. Martin (eds.), *Lingering Shadows: Jungians, Freudians, and Anti-Semitism* (Boston: Shambhala, 1991)

Maier, Johann, 'The Significance of Philosophy for the Kabbalah of Moshe Cordovero and Its Impact', *European Association for Jewish Studies Newsletter*, 13 (2003), <http://www.lzz.uni-halle.de/publikationen/essays/n/13_maier.pdf>

Majercik, Ruth, *The Chaldean Oracles* (Leiden: Brill, 1989)

Mandic, Maja, *The Keys of Arcana: Practical Handbook to Crowley's Tarot* (Belgrade: Arkona, 2008)

Marcus, Ivan G., 'The Recensions and Structure of "Sefer Hasidim"', *Proceedings of the American Academy for Jewish Research*, 45 (1978), 131–53

Marek, Edmond, *Destinées françaises de l'oeuvre messianique d'Adam Mickiewicz* (Fribourg: Galley et Cie, 1945)

———, *Quand toute la France devant polonaise: l'insurrection de novembre 1830 et l'opinion française* (Lille: Club Polonia-Nord, 1994)

Margoliouth, George, 'The Doctrine of the Ether in the Kabbalah', *Jewish Quarterly Review*, 20:4 (1908), 825–61

Martindale, Philippa, '"Against All Hushing Up and Stamping Down": The Medico-Psychological Clinic of London and the Novelist May Sinclair', *Psychoanalysis and History*, 6:2 (2004), 177–200

Marvin, Carolyn and David W. Ingle, 'Blood Sacrifice and the Nation: Revisiting Civil Religion', *Journal of the American Academy of Religion*, 64:4 (1996), 767–80

Mason, Michael, *The Making of Victorian Sexuality* (Oxford: Oxford University Press, 1995)

Masters, G. Mallary, 'Renaissance Kabbalah', in Antoine Faivre and Jacob Needleman (eds.), *Modern Esoteric Spirituality* (New York: Crossroad, 1992), 132–53

Mastrocinque, Attilio, *From Jewish Magic to Gnosticism* (Tübingen: Mohr Siebeck, 2005)

Mathiesen, Robert, 'A Thirteenth-Century Ritual to Attain the Beatific Vision From the Sworn Book of Honorius of Thebes', in Claire Fanger (ed.), *Conjuring Spirits: Texts and Traditions of Medieval Ritual Magic* (University Park, PA: Pennsylvania State University Press, 1998), 143–62

———, 'The Key of Solomon: Toward a Typology of the Manuscripts', *Societas Magica Newsletter*, 17 (Spring 2007), <http://brindedcow.umd.edu/socmag>

Matt, Daniel C., '*Ayin*: the Concept of Nothingness in Jewish Mysticism', in Lawrence Fine (ed.), *Essential Papers on Kabbalah* (New York: New York University Press, 1995), 67–108

———, *The Essential Kabbalah: The Heart of Jewish Mysticism* (Edison, NJ: Castle Books, 1997)

Mauss, Marcel, *A General Theory of Magic*, trans. Robert Brain (London: Routledge, 2001; original publication, Marcel Mauss and Henri Hubert, *Esquisse d'une théorie générale de la magie*, Paris, *l'Année sociologique*,1902–1903)

Mazet, Edmond, 'Freemasonry and Esotericism', in Antoine Faivre and Jacob Needleman (eds.), *Modern Esoteric Spirituality* (New York: Crossroad, 1992), 248–76

McCalla, Arthur, 'Illuminism and French Romantic Philosophies of History', in Antoine Faivre and Wouter J. Hanegraaff (eds.), *Western Esotericism and the Science of Religion* (Leuven: Peeters, 1998), 253–68

———, 'Romanticism', in Wouter J. Hanegraaff, ed., *Dictionary of Gnosis and Western Hermeticism* (Leiden: Brill, 2006), 1000–07

———, '"Eternal Sun/Black Sun": Illuminism and Disenchanted Romanticism', *Aries*, 7 (2007), 3–19

McCutcheon, Russell T. (ed.), *The Insider/Outsider Problem in the Study of Religion: A Reader* (London: Cassell, 1999)

McGinn, Bernard, 'Love, Knowledge, and Unio Mystica in the Western Christian Tradition', in Moshe Idel and Bernard McGinn (eds.), *Mystical Union and Monotheistic Faith: An Ecumenical Dialogue* (New York: Macmillan, 1989), 59–86

————, 'Cabalists and Christians: Reflections on Cabala in Medieval and Renaissance Thought', in Richard H. Popkin and Gordon M. Weiner (eds.), *Jewish Christians and Christian Jews: From the Renaissance to the Enlightenment* (Dordrecht: Kluwer Academic Publishers, 1994), 11–34
————, *The Foundations of Mysticism: Origins to the Fifth Century* (New York: Crossroad, 1991)
McIntosh, Christopher, *Eliphas Lévi and the French Occult Revival* (London: Rider, 1972)
————, *The Rose Cross and the Age of Reason: Eighteenth-Century Rosicrucianism in Central Europe and its Relationship to the Enlightenment* (Leiden: Brill, 1992)
————, *The Rosicrucians: The History, Mythology, and Rituals of an Esoteric Order* (York Beach, ME: Weiser Books, 1998)
McKeon, Michael, 'Sabbatai Sevi in England', *AJS Review*, 3 (1977), 131–69
McLean, Adam, 'Manuscripts of the "Key of Solomon" in English', <http://www.levity.com/alchemy/clav_eng.html>
Meir, Jonathan, 'The Boundaries of the Kabbalah: R . Yaakov Moshe Hillel and the Kabbalah in Jerusalem', in Boaz Huss (ed.), *Kabbalah and Contemporary Spiritual Revival* (Beer-Sheva: Ben-Gurion University of the Negev Press, 2011), 163–80
Meltzer, David (ed.), *The Secret Garden: An Anthology of the Kabbalah* (New York: Seabury Press, 1976)
Meltzer, Françoise, 'On Rimbaud's "Voyelles"', *Modern Philology*, 76:4 (1979), 344–54
Mendes-Flohr, Paul, 'Fin de Siècle Orientalism, the *Ostjuden*, and the aesthetics of Jewish self-affirmation', in Paul Mendes-Flohr, *Divided Passions: Jewish Intellectuals and the Experience of Modernity* (Detroit, MI: Wayne State University Press, 1991), 77–132
————, *Divided Passions: Jewish Intellectuals and the Experience of Modernity* (Detroit, MI: Wayne State University Press, 1991)
Merchavjah, Chen, 'Sefer ha-Razim', in *Encyclopaedia Judaica*, 16 volumes (Jerusalem: Keter Publishing, 1971), 13:1594–596
Mercier, Alain, *Éliphas Lévi et la pensée magique* (Paris: Seghers, 1974)
Merkel, Ingrid and Allen G. Debus (eds.), *Hermeticism and the Renaissance: Intellectual History and the Occult in Early Modern Europe* (London: Associated University Presses, 1988)
Merkur, Dan, 'Unitive Experiences and the State of Trance', in Moshe Idel and Bernard McGinn (eds.), *Mystical Union and Monotheistic Faith: An Ecumenical Dialogue* (New York: Macmillan, 1989), 125–53
————, *Gnosis: An Esoteric Tradition of Mystical Visions and Unions* (Albany, NY: State University of New York Press, 1993)
————, 'Freud and Hasidism', in Janet Liebman Jacobs and Donald Capps (eds.), *Religion, Society, and Psychoanalysis: Readings in Contemporary Theory* (Boulder, CO: Westview Press, 1997), 11–22
————, 'Stages of Ascension in Hermetic Rebirth', *Esoterica*, 1 (1999), 79–96
Meroz, Ronit, 'Zoharic Narratives and Their Adaptations', *Hispania Judaica Bulletin*, 3 (2000), 3–63
————, 'The Middle Eastern Origins of Kabbalah', *Journal for the Study of Sephardic and Mizrahi Jewry*, 1:1 (2007), 39–56
Mesguich, Sophie Kessler, 'Early Christian Hebraists', in Magne Saebø (ed.), *Hebrew Bible/Old Testament: The History of Its Interpretation, Vol. 2: From the Renaissance to the Enlightenment* (Göttingen: Vandenhoek & Ruprecht, 2008), 254–75
Meyer, Marvin W. and Richard Smith (eds.), *Ancient Christian Magic: Coptic Texts of Ritual Power* (Princeton: Princeton University Press, 1999)

Meyer, Marvin W. and Paul Mirecki (eds.), *Ancient Magic and Ritual Power* (Leiden: Brill, 2001)

Meyer, Michael A., 'The Emergence of Jewish Historiography: Motives and Motifs', *History and Theory*, 27:4 (1988), 160–75

———, 'Two Persistent Tensions Within *Wissenschaft des Judentums*', *Modern Judaism*, 24:2 (2004), 105–19

Micaninová, Mária, 'The Synthetic Thinking of Solomon ibn Gabirol', *Studia Judaica*, 11:2 (2008), 215–31

Mock, L., 'Oral Law, Oral Magic: Some Observations on Talmudic Magic', *Zutot*, 5:1 (2008), 9–14

Mohr, C., T. Landis, and P. Brugger, 'Lateralized semantic priming: modulation by levodopa, semantic distance, and participants' magical beliefs', *Neuropsychiatric Disease and Treatment*, 2 (2006), 71–84

Monastre, Chris and David Griffin, 'Israel Regardie, The Golden Dawn, and Psychotherapy', *Gnosis*, 37 (1995), 37–42

Moray-Jones, Christopher R. A., 'Paradise Revisited (2 Cor. 12:1–12): The Jewish Mystical Background of Paul's Apostolate, Part 2: Paul's Heavenly Ascent and Its Significance', *Harvard Theological Review*, 86:3 (1993), 265–92

Morrisson, Mark S., 'The Periodical Culture of the Occult Revival: Esoteric Wisdom, Modernity and Counter-Public Spheres', *Journal of Modern Literature*, 31:2 (2008), 1–22

Mort, Frank, *Dangerous Sexualities: Medico-Moral Politics in England since 1830* (London: Routledge & Kegan Paul, 1987)

Mowat, Charles Loch, *Britain Between the Wars, 1918–1940* (Chicago, IL: University of Chicago Press, 1955)

Myers, David, 'The Fall and Rise of Jewish Historicism: The Evolution of the *Akademie für die Wissenschaft des Judentums*', *Hebrew Union College Annual*, 63 (1992), 107–44

Myers, Jody, *Kabbalah and the Spiritual Quest: The Kabbalah Center in America* (Westport, CT: Praeger, 2007)

———, 'Marriage and Sexual Behavior in the Teachings of the Kabbalah Center', in Marco Pasi and Kocku von Stuckrad (eds.), *Kabbalah and Modernity* (Leiden: Brill, 2010), 259–81

Nathans, Benjamin, *Beyond the Pale: The Jewish Encounter with Late Imperial Russia* (Berkeley, CA: University of California Press, 2004)

Naveh, Joseph and Shaul Shaked, *Amulets and Magic Bowls: Aramaic Incantations of Late Antiquity* (Leiden: Brill, 1985)

———, *Magic Spells and Formulae: Aramaic Incantations of Late Antiquity* (Jerusalem: Magnes Press, 1993)

Nelson, Claudia, 'Sex and the Single Boy: Ideals of Manliness and Sexuality in Victorian Literature for Boys', *Victorian Studies*, 32:4 (1989), 525–50

Neusner, Jacob, Ernest S. Frerichs, and Paul Virgil McCracken Flesher (eds.), *Religion, Science, and Magic: In Concert and in Conflict* (Oxford: Oxford University Press, 1989)

Newman, William R. and Anthony Grafton (eds.), *Secrets of Nature: Astrology and Alchemy in Early Modern Europe* (Cambridge, MA: MIT Press, 2001)

Nigal, Gedalyah, *Magic, Mysticism, and Hasidism: The Supernatural in Jewish Thought* (Northvale, NJ: Jason Aronson, 1994)

Nock, A. D., 'Religious Symbols and Symbolism I', *Gnomon*, 27 (1955), 558–72

Noegel, Scott, Joel Walker, and Brannon Wheeler (eds.), *Prayer, Magic, and the Stars in the Ancient and Late Antique World* (University Park, PA: University of Pennsylvania Press, 2003)

Noll, Richard, *The Jung Cult: Origins of a Charismatic Movement* (Princeton: Princeton University Press, 1994)

Nord, Philip, 'Republicanism and Utopian Vision: French Freemasonry in the 1860s and 1870s', *Journal of Modern History*, 63:2 (1991), 213–29

Novak, B. C., 'Giovanni Pico della Mirandola and Jochanan Alemanno', *Journal of the Warburg and Courtauld Institutes*, 45 (1982), 125–47

Nowotny, Karl Anton, 'The Construction of Certain Seals and Characters in the Work of Agrippa of Nettesheim', *Journal of the Warburg and Courtauld Institutes*, 12 (1949), 46–57

Odeberg, Hugo, *The Hebrew Book of Enoch or Third Enoch* (Cambridge: Camrbridge University Press, 1928; repr. New York: Ktav Publishing, 1973)

Oppenheim, Janet, *The Other World: Spiritualism and Psychical Research in England, 1850–1914* (Cambridge: Cambridge University Press, 1985)

Orlov, Andrei A., 'On the Polemical Nature of 2 *(Slavonic) Enoch*', *Journal for the Study of Judaism*, 34:3 (2003), 274–303

———, *The Enoch-Metatron Tradition* (Tübingen: Mohr Siebeck, 2005)

Oron, Michal, 'Dr. Samuel Falk and the Eibeschütz-Emden Controversy', in Karl Erich Grözinger and Joseph Dan (eds.), *Mysticism, Magic and Kabbalah in Ashkenazi Judaism* (Berlin: Walter de Gruyter, 1995), 243–56

Orr, Mary, *Intertextuality: Debates and Contexts* (London:Wiley-Blackwell, 2003)

Otto, Rudolf, *Mysticism East and West: A Comparative Analysis of the Nature of Mysticism*, trans. Bertha L. Bracey and Richenda C. Payne (New York: Macmillan, 1932)

Overy, Richard, *The Morbid Age: Britain Between the Wars* (London: Allen Lane, 2009)

Owen, A. R. G., *Hysteria, Hypnosis and Healing: The Work of J.-M. Charcot* (London: Dennis Dobson, 1971)

Owen, Alex, *The Darkened Room: Women, Power, and Spiritualism in Late Victorian England* (Chicago, IL: University of Chicago Press, 1989)

———, 'The Sorcerer and His Apprentice: Aleister Crowley and the Magical Exploration of Edwardian Subjectivity', *The Journal of British Studies*, 36:1 (1997), 99–133

———, 'Occultism and the "Modern Self" in Fin-de-Siècle Britain', in Martin Daunton and Bernhard Rieger (eds.), *Meanings of Modernity: Britain from the Late-Victorian Era to World War II* (Oxford: Berg, 2001), 71–96

———, *The Place of Enchantment: British Occultism and the Culture of the Modern* (Chicago, IL: University of Chicago Press, 2004)

Page, Sophie, 'Uplifting Souls and Speaking with Spirits: The *Liber de essentia spirituum* and the *Liber Razielis*' (paper delivered at the conference 'Magie und Theurgie: Internationales Symposium an der Friedrich-Schiller-Universitaät Jena' (31 January–2 February 2002), <http://www.digital-brilliance.com/kab/karr/Solomon/LibSal.pdf>

———, *Magic in Medieval Manuscripts* (London: British Library, 2004)

Pagel, Walter, *Paracelsus: An Introduction to the Philosophical Medicine of the Renaissance* (Basel/New York: S. Karger, 1958)

———, 'Book Review', *Isis*, 53:4 (1962), 527–30

———, 'The Paracelsian Elias Artista and the Alchemical Tradition', *Medizinhistorisches Journal*, 16 (1981), 6–19

———, *From Paracelsus to Van Helmont: Studies in Renaissance Medicine and Science* (London: Variorum Reprints, 1986)

———, 'Paracelsus and the Neoplatonic and Gnostic Traditions', in Allen G. Debus (ed.), *Alchemy and Early Modern Chemistry: Papers from Ambix* (London: Jeremy Mills/Society for the History of Alchemy and Chemistry, 2004), 101–42

Parfitt, Tudor, *The Lost Tribes of Israel: The History of a Myth* (London: Weidenfeld & Nicolson, 2002)

Pasi, Marco, 'The Neverendingly Told Story: Recent Biographies of Aleister Crowley', *Aries*, 3:2 (2003), 224–45
——, *Aleister Crowley und die Versuchung der Politik*, trans. Ferdinand Leopold (Graz: Ares Verlag, 2006)
——, 'Arthur Machen's Panic Fears: Western Esotericism and the Irruption of Negative Epistemology', *Aries*, 7:1 (2007), 63–83
——, 'Oriental Kabbalah and the Parting of East and West in the Early Theosophical Society', in Boaz Huss, Marco Pasi, and Kocku von Stuckrad (eds.), *Kabbalah and Modernity: Interpretations, Transformations, Adaptations* (Leiden: Brill, 2010), 151–66
Patai, Raphael, 'Lilith', *Journal of American Folkore*, 77 (1964), 295–314
——, *The Hebrew Goddess* (New York: Ktav Publishing House, 1967)
——, *The Jewish Mind* (New York: Charles Scribner's Sons, 1977)
——, *The Jewish Alchemists: A History and Source Book* (Princeton, NJ: Princeton University Press, 1994)
Paul, Harry W., 'In Quest of Kerygma: Catholic Intellectual Life in Nineteenth-Century France', *American Historical Review*, 75:2 (1969), 387–423
Payne-Towler, Christine, *The Underground Stream: Esoteric Tarot Revealed* (Eugene, OR: Noreah Press, 1999)
Payne-Towler, Christine, 'The Continental Tarots',
    <http://www.tarot.com/pdf/continental.pdf>
Pearsall, Ronald, *The Worm in the Bud: The World of Victorian Sexuality* (London: Weidenfeld & Nicholson, 1969)
Pearson, Clive, Allan Davidson, and Peter Lineham, *Scholarship and Fierce Sincerity: Henry D. A. Major, The Face of Anglican Modernism* (Auckland: Polygraphia, 2006)
Pearson, Birger A., *Gnosticism, Judaism, and Egyptian Christianity* (Minneapolis, MN: Fortress Press, 1990)
——, 'Jewish Elements in *Corpus Hermeticum* I (Poimandres)', in Roelof van den Broek and M. J. Vermaseren (eds.), *Studies in Gnosticism and Hellenistic Religions* (Leiden: Brill, 1981), 336–348
Penner, Hans H., 'The Mystical Illusion', in Steven T. Katz (ed.), *Mysticism and Religious Traditions* (Oxford: Oxford University Press, 1983), 89–116
Pépin, Jean, 'Theories of Procession in Plotinus and the Gnostics', in Richard T. Wallis and Jay Bregman (eds.), *Neoplatonism and Gnosticism* (Albany, NY: State University of New York Press, 1992), 297–336
Perilman, Nathan A., *The Doctrine of Original Sin in Judaism* (unpublished PhD dissertation, Hebrew Union College, 1932)
Pessin, Sarah, 'Jewish Neoplatonism: Being Above Being and Divine Emanations in Solomon ibn Gabirol and Isaac Israeli', in Daniel H. Frank and Oliver Leaman (eds.), *The Cambridge Companion to Medieval Jewish Philosophy* (Cambridge: Cambridge University Press, 2003), 91–110
Peterson, Gregory R., 'Demarcation and the Scientistic Fallacy', *Zygon: Journal of Religion and Science*, 38:4 (2003), 751–61
Petrie, Yvonne, *Gender, Kabbalah and the Reformation: The Mystical Theology of Guillaume Postel* (Leiden: Brill, 2004)
Petrovsky-Shtem, Yohanan, 'The Master of an Evil Name: Hillel Ba'al Shem and His *Sefer ha-Heshek*', *AJS Review*, 28:2 (2004), 217–48
Pichois, Claude, 'Baudelaire en 1847', *Revue des sciences humaines* (January–March 1958), 121–38
Pieper, Joseph, *The Concept of Sin* (South Bend, IN: St. Augustine's Press, 2001)
Pingree, David, *The Thousands of Abu Ma'shar* (London: Studies of the Warburg Institute, No. 30, 1968)

————, 'Some of the Sources of the *Ghayat al-Hakim*', *Journal of the Warburg and Courtauld Institutes*, 43 (1980), 1–15

Poliakov, Léon, *The Aryan Myth: A History of Racist and Nationalist Ideas in Europe*, trans. Edmund Howard (New York: Basic Books, 1971)

Popkin, Richard H., 'Christian Jews and Jewish Christians in the 17th Century', in Richard H. Popkin and Gordon M. Weiner (eds.), *Jewish Christians and Christian Jews: From the Renaissance to the Enlightenment* (Dordrecht: Kluwer Academic Publishers, 1994), 57–72

————, 'Three English Tellings of the Sabbatai Zevi Story', *Jewish History*, 8 (1994), 43–54

———— (ed.), *The Columbia History of Western Philosophy* (New York, NY: Columbia University Press, 1995)

————, 'Christian Interest and Concerns About Sabbatai Zevi', in Matt Goldish and Richard H. Popkin (eds.), *Millenarianism and Messianism in Early Modern European Culture, Vol. 1: Jewish Messianism in the Early Modern World* (Dordrecht: Kluwer Academic Publishers, 2001), 91–106

Popkin, Richard H. and Gordon M. Weiner (eds.), *Jewish Christians and Christian Jews: From the Renaissance to the Enlightenment* (Dordrecht: Kluwer Academic Publishers, 1994)

Posener, S., *Adolphe Crémieux (1796–1880)*, 2 volumes (Paris: Félix Alcan, 1933–34)

Potter, David, *Prophets and Emperors: Human and Divine Authority from Augustus to Theodosius* (Cambridge, MA: Harvard University Press, 1994)

Price, David H., 'Christian Humanism and the Representation of Judaism: Johannes Reuchlin and the Discovery of Hebrew', *Arthuriana*, 19:3 (2009), 80–96

Primiano, Leonard Norman, 'Vernacular Religion and the Search for Method in Religious Folklife', *Western Folklore*, 54:1 (1995), 37–56

Prophet, Elizabeth Clare, *Fallen Angels and the Origin of Evil* (Corwin Springs, MT: Summit University Press, 2000)

Proudfoot, Wayne, *Religious Experience* (Berkeley: University of California Press, 1985)

Quispel, Gilles, 'Hermes Trismegistus and the Origins of Gnosticism', in Roelof van den Broek and Cis van Heertum (eds.), *From Poimandres to Jacob Böhme: Gnosis, Hermetism, and the Christian Tradition* (Amsterdam: Im de Pelikaan, 2000), 145–66

————, 'Transformation through Vision in Jewish Gnosticism and the Cologne Mani Codex', in Roelof van den Broek and Cis van Heertum (eds.), *From Poimandres to Jacob Böhme: Gnosis, Hermetism, and the Christian Tradition* (Amsterdam: Im de Pelikaan, 2000), 265–69

Raff, Jeffrey, *Jung and the Alchemical Imagination* (York Beach, ME: Nicolas-Hays, 2000)

Raia, Courtenay Grean, 'From Ether Theory to Ether Theology: Oliver Lodge and the Physics of Immortality', *Journal of the History of the Behavioral Sciences*, 43:1 (2007), 19–43

Raiders of the Lost Ark, directed by Steven Spielberg, written by George Lucas, with Harrison Ford and Karen Allen, Paramount Pictures, 1981

Rainbow, Jesse, 'The Song of Songs and the *Testament of Solomon*: Solomon's Love Poetry and Christian Magic', *Harvard Theological Review*, 100:3 (2007), 249–74

Raine, Kathleen, *Yeats, The Tarot and the Golden Dawn* (Dublin: Dolmen Press, 1972)

Raitt, Suzanne, *May Sinclair: A Modern Victorian* (Oxford: Oxford University Press, 2000)

——, 'Early British Psychoanalysis and the Medico-Psychological Clinic', *History Workshop Journal*, 58 (2004), 63–85

Ransom, Josephine, *A Short History of the Theosophical Society* (London: Theosophical Publishing House, 1992)

Rapoport-Albert, Ada, 'God and the Zaddik as the Two Focal Points of Hasidic Worship', *History of Religions*, 18:4 (1979), 296–325

Rapp, Dean, 'The Early Discovery of Freud by the British General Educated Public, 1912–1919', *Society for the Social History of Medicine*, 3 (August 1990), 217–43

Rappoport, Angelo S., *Myths and Legends of Ancient Israel*, 3 volumes (London: Gresham, 1928; repr. as *Ancient Israel: Myths and Legends*, London: Mystic Press, 1987)

Ray, Jonathan, 'New Approaches to the Jewish Diaspora: The Sephardim as a Sub-Ethnic Group', *Jewish Social Studies*, 15:1 (2008), 10–31

Reardon, Bernard, *Liberalism and Tradition: Aspects of Catholic Thought in Nineteenth-Century France* (Cambridge: Cambridge University Press, 1975)

Reed, Annette Yoshiko, 'Heavenly Ascent, Angelic Descent, and the Transmission of Knowledge in *1 Enoch* 6–16', in Ra'anan S. Boustan and Annette Yoshiko Reed (eds.), *Heavenly Realms and Earthly Realities in Late Antique Religions* (Cambridge: Cambridge University Press, 2004), 47–66

Reid, Donald Malcolm, *Whose Pharoahs?: Archaeology, Museums, and Egyptian National Identity from Napoleon to World War I* (Berkeley, CA: University of California Press, 2002)

Reinharz, Jehudah (ed.), *Living with Antisemitism: Modern Jewish Responses* (Lebanon, NH: Brandeis University Press/University Press of New England, 1987)

Riasanovsky, Nicholas V., 'On Lamennais, Chaadaev, and the Romantic Revolt in France and Russia', *American Historical Review*, 82:5 (1977), 1165–86

Rice, Emanuel, *Freud and Moses: The Long Journey Home* (Albany, NY: State University of New York Press, 1990)

Richardson, Alan, *The Magical Life of Dion Fortune: Priestess of the 20th Century* (Wellingborough: Aquarian Press, 1987)

Richer, Jean, *L'Alchimie du verbe de Rimbaud ou les jeux de Jean-Arthur* (Paris: Didier, 1972)

Ricoeur, Paul, *The Rule of Metaphor: Multi-Disciplinary Studies of the Creation of Meaning in Language,* trans. Robert Czerny (Toronto: University of Toronto Press, 1977)

Riffard, Pierre A., *L'Ésotérisme: Qu'est-ce que l'ésotérisme? Anthologie de l'ésotérisme occidental* (Paris: Robert Laffont, 1990)

——, 'The Esoteric Method', in Antoine Faivre and Wouter J. Hanegraaff (eds.), *Western Esotericism and the Science of Religion* (Leuven: Peeters, 1998), 63–74

Rizzuto, Ana-Maria, *Why Did Freud Reject God?* (New Haven, CT: Yale University Press, 1998)

Roazen, Paul, *Meeting Freud's Family* (Amherst, MA: University of Massachusetts Press, 1993)

Roberts, Marie Mulvey and Hugh Ormsby-Lennon (eds.), *Secret Texts: The Literature of Secret Societies* (New York: AMS Press, 1995)

Robinson, Ira, 'Kabbala and Science in "Sefer Ha-Berit": A Modernization Strategy for Orthodox Jews', *Modern Judaism*, 9:3 (1989), 275–88

Roling, Bernd, 'The Complete Nature of Christ: Sources and Structures of a Christological Theurgy in the Works of Johannes Reuchlin', in Jan N.

Bremmer and Jan R. Veenstra (eds.), *The Metamorphosis of Magic: From Late Antiquity to the Early Modern Period* (Leuven: Peeters, 2002), 231–66

Rosenthal, Bernice Glatzer (ed.), *The Occult in Russian and Soviet Culture* (Ithaca, NY: Cornell University Press, 1997)

Röstvig, Maren-Sofie, 'Renaissance Numerology: Acrostics or Criticism?', *Essays in Criticism*, 16:1 (1996), 6–21

———, *Benjamin Disraeli: Early of Beaconsfield* (New York: Philosophical Library, 1952)

———, 'The Medieval Conception of the Jew: A New Interpretation', in Jeremy Cohen (ed.), *Essential Papers on Judaism and Christianity in Conflict: From Late Antiquity to the Reformation* (New York: New York University Press, 1991), 298–309

Roth, Norman, 'The Theft of Philosophy by the Greeks from the Jews', *Classical Folia*, 32 (1978), 53–67

Rubel, Paula G. and Abraham Rosman (eds.), *Translating Cultures: Perspectives on Translation and Anthropology* (Oxford: Berg, 2003)

Ruderman, David B., *Kabbalah, Magic, and Science: The Cultural Universe of a Sixteenth-Century Jewish Physician* (Cambridge, MA: Harvard University Press, 1988)

——— (ed.), *Essential Papers on Jewish Culture in Renaissance and Baroque Italy* (New York: New York University Press, 1992)

———, *Jewish Enlightenment in an English Key: Anglo-Jewry's Construction of Modern Jewish Thought* (Oxford: Oxford University Press, 2000)

Rummel, Erika, *The Case Against Johann Reuchlin: Social and Religious Controversy in Sixteenth-Century Germany* (Toronto: University of Toronto Press, 2002)

Runyon, Carroll "Poke", *Secrets of the Golden Dawn Cypher Manuscript* (Silverado, CA: Church of the Hermetic Sciences, 1997)

Ryken, Leland, Jim Wilhoit, and Tremper Longman (eds.), *Dictionary of Biblical Imagery* (Westmont, IL: InterVarsity Press, 1998)

Saciuk, Olena H. (ed.), *The Shape of the Fantastic: Selected Essays from the Seventh International Conference on the Fantastic in the Arts* (New York: Greenwood Press, 1990)

Saebø, Magne (ed.), *Hebrew Bible/Old Testament: The History of Its Interpretation, Vol. 2: From the Renaissance to the Enlightenment* (Göttingen: Vandenhoek & Ruprecht, 2008)

Safran, Bezalel (ed.), *Hasidism: Continuity or Innovation?* (Center for Jewish Studies, Harvard Judaic Texts and Monographs, Vol. 5) (Cambridge, MA: Harvard University Press, 1988)

Said, Edward, *Orientalism* (New York: Pantheon, 1978)

Saposnik, Arieh Bruce, 'Europe and Its Orients in Zionist Culture Before the First World War', *Historical Journal*, 49:4 (2006), 1105–23

Saurat, Denis, 'Baudelaire, Rimbaud, la Cabale', *Nouvelle revue française*, 46:2 (1936), 258–61

Sausman, Justin, 'Science, Drugs and Occultism: Aleister Crowley, Henry Maudsley and Late-Nineteenth Century Degeneration Theories', *JLS*, 1:1 (2007), 40–54

Schäfer, Peter, 'Jewish Magic Literature in Late Antiquity and the Early Middle Ages', *Journal of Jewish Studies*, 41:1 (1990), 75–91

———, *The Hidden and Manifest God: Some Major Themes in Early Jewish Mysticism*, trans. Aubrey Pomerance (Albany, NY: State University of New York Press, 1992)

———, 'Merkavah Mysticism and Magic', in Peter Schäfer and Joseph Dan (eds.), *Gershom Scholem's* Major Trends in Jewish Mysticism *50 Years*

After: Proceedings of the Sixth International Conference on the History of Jewish Mysticism (Tübingen: Mohr-Siebeck, 1993), 59–78

——, 'Magic and Religion in Ancient Judaism', in Peter Schäfer and Hans G. Kippenberg (eds.), *Envisioning Magic: A Princeton Seminar and Symposium* (Leiden: Brill, 1997), 19–43

——, 'Daughter, Sister, Bride, and Mother: Images of the Femininity of God in the Early Kabbala', *Journal of the American Academy of Religion*, 68:2 (2000), 221–42

——, *Mirror of His Beauty: Feminine Images of God From the Bible to the Early Kabbalah* (Princeton: Princeton University Press, 2002)

Schäfer, Peter and Joseph Dan (eds.), *Gershom Scholem's Major Trends in Jewish Mysticism 50 Years After* (Tübingen: Mohr-Siebeck, 1993)

Schäfer, Peter and Hans G. Kippenberg (eds.), *Envisioning Magic: A Princeton Seminar and Symposium* (Leiden: Brill, 1997)

Schäfer, Peter and Irina Wandrey (eds.), *Reuchlin und Seine Erben* (Ostfildern: Jan Thorbecke Verlag, 2005)

Schäfer, Peter and Mark R. Cohen (eds.), *Toward the Millennium: Messianic Expectations from the Bible to Waco* (Leiden: Brill, 1998)

Scharfstein, Ben Ami, *Roots of Bergson's Philosophy* (New York: Columbia University Press, 1943)

Scheps, Samuel, *Adam Mickiewicz, ses affinités juives* (Paris: Nagel, 1964)

Schiffman, Lawrence H. and Michael D. Swarz, *Hebrew and Aramaic Incantation Texts from the Cairo Genizah* (Sheffield: Sheffield Academic Press, 1992)

Schimanowski, Gottfried, '"Connecting Heaven and Earth": The Function of the Hymns in Revelation 4–5', in Ra'anan S. Boustan and Annette Yoshiko Reed (eds.), *Heavenly Realms and Earthly Realities in Late Antique Religions* (Cambridge: Cambridge University Press, 2004), 67–84

Schindler, Bruno (ed.), *Gaster Centenary Publication* (London: Lund Humphries, 1958)

Schmidt, Leigh Eric, 'The Making of Modern "Mysticism"', *Journal of the American Academy of Religion*, 71:2 (2003), 273–302

Schmitt, Charles B., 'Perennial Philosophy: From Agostino Steuco to Leibniz', *Journal of the History of Ideas*, 27:4 (1966), 505–32

——, '*Prisca Theologia* e *Philosophia Perennis*: due temi del Rinascimento italiano e la loro fortuna', in Giovannagiola Tarugi (ed.), *Il pensiero italiano del Rinascimento e il tempo nostro* (Firenze: Olschki, 1968), 211–36

Schneider, Stanley and Joseph H. Berke, 'Sigmund Freud and the Lubavitcher Rebbe', *The Psychoanalytic Review*, 87 (2000), 39–59

——, 'The Oceanic Feeling, Mysticism and Kabbalah: Freud's Historical Roots', *Psychoanalytic Review*, 95:1 (2008), 131–56

Schneider, Stanley and Joseph H. Berke, 'Freud's Meeting with Rabbi Alexandre Safran', *Psychoanalysis and History* 12:1 (2010), 15–28

Schochet, Elijah, *The Hasidic Movement and the Gaon of Vilna* (Northvale, NJ: Jason Aronson, 1994)

Schochet, Jacob Immanuel, *The Great Maggid: The Life and Teachings of Rabbi Dov Ber of Mezhirech* (New York: Kehot Publication Society, 1974)

Scholem, Gershom, *Das Buch Bahir. Ein Schriftdenkmal aus der Frühzeit der Kabbala auf Grund der kritischen Neuausgabe* (Leipzig: W. Drugulin, 1923)

——, *Bibliographia Kabbalistica: Verzeichnis der Gedruckten; die jüdische Mystik (Gnosis, Kabbala, Sabbatianismus, Frankismus, Chassidismus) behandelnden Bücher und Aufsätze von Reuchlin bis zur Gegenwart* (Leipzig: W. Drugulin, 1927)

——, *Major Trends in Jewish Mysticism* (New York: Schocken Books, 1941; repr. 1961)

————, *Sabbatai Sevi: The Mystical Messiah* (Princeton, NJ: Princeton University Press, 1957)

————, *Jewish Gnosticism, Merkabah Mysticism, and Talmudic Tradition* (New York: Jewish Theological Seminary of America, 1960)

————, *On the Kabbalah and Its Symbolism*, trans. Ralph Manheim (New York: Schocken Books, 1969)

————, *The Messianic Idea in Judaism and Other Essays on Jewish Spirituality* (New York: Schocken Books, 1971)

————, 'Practical Kabbalah', in *Encyclopaedia Judaica*, 16 volumes (Jerusalem: Keter Publishing, 1971), 10:632–38

————, 'The Name of God and the Linguistic Theory of the Kabbala', trans. Simon Pleasance, *Diogenes*, Part 1, 20:79 (1972), 59–80, Part 2, 20:80 (1972), 164–94

————, *Kabbalah* (New York: Keter Publishing House, 1974)

————, 'Isaac Luria: A Central Figure in Jewish Mysticism', *Bulletin of the American Academy of Arts and Sciences*, 29:8 (1976), 8–13

————, 'Colors and Their Symbolism in Jewish Tradition and Mysticism', trans. Klaus Ottman, *Diogenes*, 109 (1980), 69–71

————, *Origins of the Kabbalah*, trans. Allan Arkush, ed. R. J. Zwi Werblowsky (Princeton, NJ: Princeton University Press, 1990)

————, *On the Mystical Shape of the Godhead: Basic Concepts in the Kaballah*, trans. Joachim Neugroschel, ed. Jonathan Chipman (New York: Schocken Books, 1991)

————, 'The beginnings of the Christian Kabbalah', in Joseph Dan (ed.), *The Christian Kabbalah: Jewish Mystical Books and Their Christian Interpreters* (Cambridge, MA: Harvard College Library, 1997), 17–51

————, *On the Possibility of Jewish Mysticism in Our Time and Other Essays*, ed. Avraham Shapira, trans. Jonathan Chipman (Philadelphia, PA: Jewish Publication Society, 1997)

————, *Alchemy and Kabbalah*, trans. Klaus Ottman (Putnam, CT: Spring Publications, 2006)

————, *Bibliography of the Writings of Gershom G. Scholem Presented to Gershom G. Scholem On the Occasion of his Eightieth Birthday by The Israel Academy of Sciences and Humanities* (Jerusalem: Magnes Press, 1977)

Schuchard, Marsha Keith, *Freemasonry, Secret Societies, and the Continuity of the Occult Tradition in English Literature* (unpublished PhD Dissertation, University of Texas at Austin, 1975)

————, 'Yeats and the "Unknown Superiors": Swedenborg, Falk and Cagliostro', in Roberts, Marie Mulvey and Hugh Ormsby-Lennon (eds.), *Secret Texts: The Literature of Secret Societies* (New York: AMS Press, 1995), 114–68

————, 'Emanuel Swedenborg: Deciphering the Codes of a Terrestrial and Celestial Intelligencer', in Elliot R. Wolfson (ed.), *Rending the Veil: Concealment and Secrecy in the History of Religions* (New York: Seven Bridges, 1999), 177–207

————, 'Why Mrs. Blake Cried: Swedenborg, Blake, and the Sexual Basis of Spiritual Vision', *Esoterica*, 2 (2000), 45–93

————, 'Dr. Samuel Jacob Falk: A Sabbatian Adventurer in the Masonic Underground', in Matt Goldish and Richard H. Popkin (eds.), *Millenarianism and Messianism in Early Modern European Culture, Vol. 1: Jewish Messianism in the Early Modern World* (Dordrecht: Kluwer Academic Publishers, 2001), 203–26

————, *Restoring the Temple of Vision: Cabalistic Freemasonry and Stuart Culture* (Leiden: Brill, 2002)

————, *Why Mrs. Blake Cried: William Blake and the Erotic Imagination* (London: Century, 2006)

Schumaker, John F. (ed.), *Religion and Mental Health* (Oxford: Oxford University Press, 1992)

Schwartz, Dov, *Studies on Astral Magic in Medieval Jewish Thought* (Leiden: Brill, 2005)

Schwartz, Sarah L., 'Reconsidering the Testament of Solomon', *Journal for the Study of the Pseudepigrapha*, 16:3 (2007), 203–37

Scribner, Robert W., 'The Reformation, Popular Magic, and the "Disenchantment of the World"', *Journal of Interdisciplinary History*, 23:3 (1993), 475–94

Secret, François, *Les Kabbalistes Chrétiens de la Renaissance* (La Haye-Paris: Mouton et Cie, 1964)

——, 'Sur quelques traductions du Sefer Raziel', *Revue des Études Juives*, 128 (1969), 223–45

——, *Hermétisme et Kabbale* (Napoli: Bibliopolis, 1972)

——, 'Eliphas Lévi et la Kabbale', *Charis: Archives de l'Unicorne*, 1 (Milan: Archè, 1988), 81–89

——, *I Cabbalisti Cristiani del Rinascimento* (Rome: Arkeios Edizioni, 2001)

Sedgwick, Martin, *Against the Modern World: Traditonalism and the Secret Intellectual History of the Twentieth Century* (Oxford: Oxford University Press, 2004)

Seeskin, Kenneth, *Maimonides on the Origin of the World* (Cambridge: Cambridge University Press, 2005)

Segal, Alan F., 'Hellenistic Magic: Some Questions of Definition', in Roelof van den Broek and M. J. Vermaseren (eds.), *Studies in Gnosticism and Hellenistic Religions* (Leiden: Brill, 1981), 349–75

——, *The Other Judaisms of Late Antiquity* (Atlanta, GA: Scholars Press, 1987)

——, *Two Powers in Heaven: Early Rabbinic Reports about Christianity and Gnosticism* (Leiden: Brill, 2002)

——, 'Text Translation as a Prelude for Soul Translation', in Paula G. Rubel and Abraham Rosman (eds.), *Translating Cultures: Perspectives on Translation and Anthropology* (Oxford: Berg, 2003) 213–48

——, *Life After Death: A History of the Afterlife in Western Religion* (New York: Doubleday, 2004)

Segal, Hannah, *Introduction to the Works of Melanie Klein* (London: Hogarth Press, 1975)

Sela, Shlomo, 'Abraham ibn Ezra's Scientific Corpus: Basic Constituents and General Characterization', *Arabic Sciences and Philosophy*, 11 (2001), 91–149

——, *Abraham Ibn Ezra and the Rise of Medieval Hebrew Science* (Leiden: Brill, 2003)

Selby, John, 'Key Figures in Twentieth Century Esoteric Kabbalah', *Inner Light Journal*, 23:1 (2005), <http://www.innerlight.org.uk/journals/Vol23No1/keyfig.htm>

——, *Dion Fortune and her Inner Plane Contacts: Intermediaries in the Western Esoteric Tradition* (unpublished PhD dissertation, Department of Theology, University of Exeter, 2008)

Shackelford, Jole R., *A Philosophical Path for Paracelsian Medicine: The Ideas, Intellectual Context, and Influence of Petrus Severinus (1540–1602)* (Copenhagen: Museum Tusculanum Press, 2004)

Shaftesley, John M., 'Jews in English Freemasonry in the 18th and 19th Centuries', *Ars Quatuor Coronatorum*, 92 (1979), 25–81

Shaked, Shaul, '"Peace Be Upon You, Exalted Angels": on Hekhalot, Liturgy and Incantation Bowls', *Jewish Studies Quarterly*, 2:3 (1995), 197–219

——, 'Form and Purpose in Aramaic Spells: Some Jewish Themes', in Shaul Shaked (ed.), *Officina Magica: Essays on the Practice of Magic in Antiquity* (Leiden: Brill, 2005), 1–30

—— (ed.), *Officina Magica: Essays on the Practice of Magic in Antiquity* (Leiden: Brill, 2005)

Sharon, Moshe (ed.), *Studies in Modern Religions, Religious Movements and the Babi-Bahai Faiths* (Brill: Leiden, 2004)

Sharot, Stephen, 'Hasidism and the Routinization of Charisma', *Journal for the Scientific Study of Religion*, 19:4 (1980), 325–36

——, *Messianism, Mysticism, and Magic: A Sociological Analysis of Jewish Religious Movements* (Chapel Hill, NC: University of North Carolina Press, 1982)

——, 'Medieval Jewish Magic in Relation to Islam: Theoretical Attitudes and Genres', in B. H. Hary, J. L. Hayes, and F. Astern (eds.), *Judaism and Islam: Boundaries, Communication and Interaction* (Leiden: Brill, 2000), 97–109

Shaw, Gregory, *Theurgy and the Soul: The Neoplatonism of Iamblichus* (University Park, PA: Penn State Press, 1971)

Shepard, Leslie, 'The *Anacalypsis* of Godfrey Higgins: Precursor of *Isis Unveiled* and *The Secret Doctrine*', *Theosophical History*, 1:3 (1985), 46–53

Sheppard, H. J., 'Gnosticism and Alchemy', *Ambix*, 6 (1957), 88–109

Shilhav, Yosseph, 'The Haredi Ghetto: The Theology Behind the Geography', *Contemporary Jewry* 10:2 (1989), 51–64

Shumaker, Wayne, *The Occult Sciences in the Renaissance* (Berkeley, CA: University of California Press, 1972)

Simon, Marcel, 'Christian Ant-Semitism', in Jeremy Cohen (ed.), *Essential Papers on Judaism and Christianity in Conflict: From Late Antiquity to the Reformation* (New York: New York University Press, 1991), 131–73

Singer, Isaac Bashevis, *Love and Exile* (New York: Doubleday, 1984)

Singer, Steven, 'Jewish Religious Thought in Early Victorian London', *AJS Review*, 10:2 (1985), 181–210

——, 'The Anglo-Jewish Ministry in Early Victorian London', *Modern Judaism*, 5 (1985), 279–299

Skinner, Stephen and David Rankine, *Practical Angel Magic of Dr. John Dee's Enochian Tables* (London: Golden Hoard Press, 2004)

—— (eds.), *The Goetia of Dr. Rudd* (London: Golden Hoard Press, 2007)

Smart, Ninian, *The Science of Religion and the Sociology of Knowledge* (Princeton, NJ: Princeton University Press, 1973)

Smith, Jonathan Z., 'Earth and Gods', *Journal of Religion*, 49:2 (1969), 103–127

——, 'Trading Places', in Marvin Meyer and Paul Mirecki (eds.), *Ancient Magic and Ritual Power* (Leiden: Brill, 1995), 13–27

——, 'Here, There, and Anywhere', in Scott Noegel, Joel Walker, and Brannon Wheeler (eds.), *Prayer, Magic, and the Stars in the Ancient and Late Antique World* (University Park, PA: Pennsylvania State University Press, 2003), 21–36

Smith, Morton, 'Observations on Hekhalot Rabbati', in Alexander Altmann (ed.), *Biblical and Other Studies* (Cambridge, MA: Harvard University Press, 1963), 142–60

Smith, Warren Sylvester, *The London Heretics 1870–1914* (New York: Dodd, Mead, 1968)

Snoek, Jan, 'On the Creation of Masonic Degrees: A Method and its Fruits', in Antoine Faivre and Wouter J. Hanegraaff (eds.), *Western Esotericism and the Science of Religion* (Leuven: Peeters, 1998), 145–90

Snuffin, Michael Osiris, *The Thoth Companion: The Key to the True Symbolic Meaning of the Thoth Tarot* (St. Paul, MN: Llewellyn Publications, 2007)

Sokolów, Nahum, 'Henri Bergson's Old-Warsaw Lineage', in Lucy Dawidowicz (ed.), *The Golden Tradition: Jewish Life and Thought in Eastern Europe* (New York: Holt, Rinehart and Winston, 1967), 349–59

Soloweitchik, Haym, 'Three Themes in the "Sefer Hasidim"', *AJS Review*, 1 (1976), 311–57

Sperber, Dan, 'Anthropology and psychology: towards an epidemiology of representations', *Man*, 20 (1985), 73–89

Stace, Walter T., *Mysticism and Philosophy* (Philadelphia, PA: Lippincott, 1960)

Stadler, Nurit, 'Is Profane Work an Obstacle to Salvation? The Case of Ultra Orthodox (*Haredi*) Jews in Contemporary Israel', *Sociology of Religion* 63:4 (2002), 455–74

Starr, Karen E., *Repair of the Soul: Metaphors of Transformation in Jewish Mysticism and Psychoanalysis* (London: Routledge 2008)

Staudenmeier, Peter, 'Occultism, Race and Politics in German-speaking Europe, 1880–1940: A Survey of the Historical Literature', *European Historical Quarterly*, 39:1 (2009), 47–70

Stearns, Carol Zisowitz and Peter N. Stearns, 'Victorian Sexuality: Can Historians Do It Better?', *Journal of Social History*, 18:4 (1985), 625–34

Steinsalz, Adin, *Opening the Tanya: Discovering the Moral and Mystical Teachings of a Classic Work of Kabbalah*, trans. Yaacov Tauber (San Francisco, CA: Josey-Bass, 2003)

Stephenson, Alan, *The Rise and Decline of English Modernism* (London: SPCK, 1984)

Stern, S. M., 'Rationalists and Kabbalists in Medieval Allegory', *Journal of Jewish Studies*, 6:2 (1956), 73–86

Stevenson, John and Chris Cook, *Britain in the Depression: Society and Politics, 1929–39* (London: Longman, 1994)

Stevenson, Peter Kenneth, *God in Our Nature: The Incarnational Theology of John McLeod Campbell* (Chester: Paternoster Press, 1969; repr. Eugene, OR: Wipf & Stock, 2006)

Stewart, M. A. (ed.), *Studies in Seventeenth–Century European Philosophy* (Oxford: Clarendon Press, 1997)

Stewart, Mary, *The Hollow Hills* (London: Hodder & Stoughton, 1973)

Stolzenberg, Daniel, *Egyptian Oedpius: Antiquarianism, Oriental Studies and Occult Philosophy in the Work of Athanasius Kircher* (unpublished PhD dissertation, Stanford University, 2004)

Stroumsa, Gedaliahu G., 'Form(s) of God: Some Notes on Metatron and Christ', *Harvard Theological Review*, 76:3 (1983), 269–88

——, 'Gnosis and Judaism in Nineteenth Century Christian Thought', in Eveline Goodman-Thau, Gert Mattenklott, and Christoph Schulte (eds.), *Kabbala und Romantik* (Tübingen: Max Niemeyer Verlag, 1994), 43–57

——, 'Mystical Descents', in John J. Collins and Michael Fishbane (eds.), *Death, Ecstasy, and Other Worldly Journeys* (Albany, NY: State University of New York Press, 1995), pp. 139–54

——, *Hidden Wisdom: Esoteric Traditions and the Roots of Christian Mysticism* (Leiden: Brill, 1996)

Struck, Peter T., *Birth of the Symbol: Ancient Readers at the Limits of Their Texts* (Princeton, NJ: Princeton University Press, 2004)

Sullivan, Lawrence E. (ed.), *Hidden Truths: Magic, Alchemy, and the Occult* (New York/London: Macmillan & Collier, 1987)

Summers, Montague, *Witchcraft and Black Magic* (London: Rider & Co., 1946; repr. Mineola, NY: Dover Publications, 2000)

Suster, Gerald, *The Legacy of the Beast: The Life, Work and Influence of Aleister Crowley* (London: Whallen, 1988)

————, *Crowley's Apprentice: The Life and Ideas of Israel Regardie* (London: Rider, 1989)

Sutcliffe, Adam, *Judaism and Enlightenment* (Cambridge: Cambridge University Press, 2003)

Sutcliffe, Steven and Marion Bowman (eds.), *Beyond New Age: Exploring Alternative Spirituality* (Edinburgh: Edinburgh University Press, 2000)

Sutin, Lawrence, *Do What Thou Wilt: A Life of Aleister Crowley* (New York: St. Martin's Press, 2000)

Swanson, Jan, 'The Qabalistic Tree', <http://www.kheper.net/topics/Hermeticism/Qabalah.htm>

Swartz, Michael D., 'Scribal Magic and Its Rhetoric: Formal Patterns in Medieval Hebrew and Aramaic Incantation Texts from the Cairo Genizah', *Harvard Theological Review*, 83:2 (1990), 163–80

————, *Mystical Prayer in Ancient Judaism: An Analysis of Ma'aseh Merkavah* (Tübingen: Mohr Siebeck, 1992)

————, '"Like the Ministering Angels": Ritual and Purity in Early Jewish Mysticism and Magic', *AJS Review*, 19:2, 1994, 135–67

————, *Scholastic Magic: Ritual and Revelation in Early Jewish Mysticism* (Princeton: Princeton University Press, 1996)

————, 'Divination and Its Discontents: Finding and Questioning Meaning in Ancient and Medieval Judaism', in Scott Noegel, Joel Walker, and Brannon Wheeler (eds.), *Prayer, Magic, and the Stars in the Ancient and Late Antique World* (University Park, PA: Pennsylvania State University Press, 2003), 155–66

Swatos, Richard H., 'Enchantment and Disenchantment in Modernity: The Significance of "Religion" as a Sociological Category', *SA*, 44:4 (1983), 321–37

Symonds, John, *The Great Beast: The Life of Aleister Crowley* (London: Rider & Co., 1951)

Szajkowski, Zosa, 'Notes on the Occupational Status of French Jews, 1800–1880', *Proceedings of the American Academy for Jewish Research*, 46:2 (1979–80), 531–54

Szónyi, György E., 'John Dee', in Wouter J. Hanegraaff (ed.), *Dictionary of Gnosis and Western Hermeticism* (Leiden: Brill, 2006), 301–09

————, 'Paracelsus, Scrying, and the *Lingua Adamica*: Contexts for John Dee's Angel Magic', in Clucas (ed.), *John Dee: Interdisciplinary Studies in Renaissance Thought* (Dordrecht: Kluwer Academic Publishers, 2006), 207–29

Szulakowska, Urszula, *The Alchemy of Light: Geometry and Optics in Late Renaissance Alchemical Illustration* (Leiden: Brill, 2000)

Tabor, James D., 'Patterns of the End: Textual Weaving from Qumran to Waco', in Peter Schäfer and Mark R. Cohen (eds.), *Toward the Millennium: Messianic Expectations from the Bible to Waco* (Leiden: Brill, 1998), 409–30

Talbot, Margaret, 'An Emancipated Voice: Flora Tristan and Utopian Allegory', *Feminist Studies*, 17:2 (1991), 219–39

Tarantino, P. C., *Tarot for the New Aeon: A Practical Guide to the Power and Wisdom of the Thoth Tarot* (Pebble Beach, CA: Alternative Insights Publishing, 2007)

Tarugi, Giovannagiola (ed.), *Il pensiero italiano del Rinascimento e il tempo nostro* (Firenze: Olschki, 1968)

Taylor, F. Sherwood, 'The Visons of Zosimos: Translation and Prefatory Note', *Ambix*, 1:1 (1937), 88–92

Taylor, Mark C. (ed.), *Critical Terms for Religious Studies* (Chicago, IL: University of Chicago Press, 1998)

Teboul, Margaret, 'Bergson, le temps et le judaïsme. Le débat des années 1960', *Archives juives*, 38:1 (2005), 56–78

Teller, Adam, 'Hasidism and the Challenge of Geography: The Polish Background to the Spread of the Hasidic Movement', *AJS Review*, 30:1 (2006), 1–29

Thalbourne, Michael A., 'A Note on the Greeley Measure of Mystical Experience', *International Journal for the Psychology of Religion*, 14:3 (2004), 215–22

Theisohn, Philipp, 'Zur Rezeption von Naphtali Herz Bacharachs *Sefer Emeq ha-Melech* in der *Kabbala Denudata*', in Andreas B. Kilcher (ed.), *Morgen-Glantz: Zeitschrift der Christian Knorr von Rosenroth-Gesellschaft*, 16 (2006), 221-241

The X-Files: 'Kaddish', written by Howard Gordon, directed by Kim Manners, with David Duchovny, Gillian Anderson, and Justine Miceli (Episode 15, Season 4, 20th Century Fox, 1994)

Thomas, Keith, *Religion and the Decline of Magic: Studies in Popular Beliefs in Sixteenth- and Seventeenth-Century England* (London: Weidenfeld & Nicolson, 1971)

Thomson, Mathew, 'Psychology and the "Consciousness of Modernity" in Early Twentieth-century Britain', in Martin Daunton and Bernhard Rieger (eds.), *Meanings of Modernity: Britain from the Late-Victorian Era to World War II* (Oxford: Berg, 2001), 97–115

Thorndike, Lynn, *A History of Magic and Experimental Science During the First Thirteen Centuries of Our Era* (New York: Columbia University Press, 1923)

Thrower, James, *Religion: The Classical Theories* (Edinburgh: Edinburgh University Press, 1999)

Tilton, Hereward, '*Regni Christi Frater*: Count Michael Maier and the Fraternity R.C.', *Aries*, 2:1 (2002), 3–33

———, *The Quest for the Phoenix: Spiritual Alchemy and Rosicrucianism in the Work of Count Michael Maier (1569–1622)* (Berlin/New York: Walter de Gruyter, 2003)

Timmerman, Anke, '"Pictures passing before the mind's eye": the Tarot, the Order of the Golden Dawn, and William Butler Yeats's Poetry', *Societas Magica Newsletter*, 15 (Spring 2006), 1–8

Tiryakian, Edward A., 'Toward the Sociology of Esoteric Culture', *American Journal of Sociology*, 78:3 (1972), 491–512

Tishby, Isaiah, 'General Introduction', in Isaiah Tishby (ed.), *The Wisdom of the Zohar: An Anthology of Texts*, 3 volumes, trans. David Goldstein (Portland, OR: Littman Library of Jewish Civilization/Oxford University Press, 1989)

Torijano, Pablo A., *Solomon the Esoteric King: From King to Magus, Development of a Tradition* (Leiden: Brill, 2002)

Trachtenberg, Joshua, *The Devil and the Jews: The Medieval Conception of the Jew and Its Relation to Modern Antisemitism* (New Haven, CT: Yale University Press, 1943)

———, *Jewish Magic and Superstition* (New York: Behrman's Jewish Book House, 1939; repr. Philadelphia, PA: University of Pennsylvania Press, 2004)

Trigger, Bruce G., *A History of Archaeological Thought* (Cambridge: Cambridge University Press, 1989)

Trosman, Harry, 'Freud's Cultural Background', *Annual of Psychoanalysis*, 1 (1973), 318–35

Tura, Adolfo, 'Un Codice Ebraico di Cabala Appartenuto a Egidio da Viterbo', *Bibliothèque d'Humanisme et Renaissance* 68:3 (2006), 535–43

Turner, Trevor H., 'Henry Maudsley: Psychiatrist, Philosopher and Entrepreneur', *Psychological Medicine*, 18 (1988), 551–74

Tuttle, George M., *John McLeod Campbell on Christian Atonement: So Rich a Soul* (Edinburgh: Handsel Press, 1986)

Twersky, Isadore and Bernard Septimus (eds.), *Jewish Thought in the Seventeenth Century* (Cambridge, MA: Harvard University Press, 1987)

Tylor, Edward Burnett, *Primitive Culture: Researches into the Development of Mythology, Philosophy, Religion, Language, Art and Custom*, 2 volumes (London: John Murray, 1871)

Ulansey, David, *The Origins of the Mithraic Mysteries: Cosmology and Salvation in the Ancient World* (Oxford: Oxford University Press, 1989)

Underhill, Karen C., '*Aux Grand Hommes de la Parole*: On the Verbal Messiah in Adam Mickiewicz's Paris Lectures', *Slavic and East European Journal*, 45:4 (2001), 716–31

Urban, Hugh, 'Unleashing the Beast: Aleister Crowley, Tantra and Sex Magic in Late Victorian England', *Esoterica*, 5 (2003), 138–92

———, *Magia Sexualis: Sex, Magic, and Liberation in Modern Western Esotericism* (Berkeley, CA: University of California Press, 2006)

———, 'The Yoga of Sex: Tantra, Orientalism, and Sex Magic in the Ordo Templi Orientis', in Wouter J. Hanegraaff and Jeffrey J. Kripal (eds.), *Hidden Intercourse: Eros and Sexuality in the History of Western Esotericism* (Leiden: Brill, 2008), 401–43

Uzzel, Robert L., *The Kabbalistic Thought of Eliphas Lévi and Its Influence on Modern Occultism in America* (PhD dissertation: Baylor University, 1995)

———, *Eliphas Lévi and the Kabbalah: The Masonic and French Connection of the American Mystery Tradition* (Lafayette, LA: Cornerstone, 2006)

Vagg, Jon and Tim Newburn (eds.), *The British Society of Criminology Conferences: Selected Proceedings, Vol. 1: Emerging Themes in Criminology* (London: British Society of Criminology, 1998)

Valiér, Claire, 'Psychoanalysis and Crime in Britain During the Inter-war Years', in Jon Vagg and Tim Newburn (eds.), *The British Society of Criminology Conferences: Selected Proceedings, Vol. 1: Emerging Themes in Criminology* (London: British Society of Criminology, 1998), 1–12

Van Bekkum, Wout Jac, *A Hebrew Alexander Romance according to MS London, Jews College 145* (Louvain: Peeters, 1992)

Van den Broek, Roelof, 'The Creation of Adam's Psychic Body in the Apocryphon of John', in Roelof van den Broek and M. J. Vermaseren (eds.), *Studies in Gnosticism and Hellenistic Religions* (Leiden: Brill, 1981), 38–57

Van den Broek, Roelof and M. J. Vermaseren (eds.), *Studies in Gnosticism and Hellenistic Religions* (Leiden: Brill, 1981)

Van den Broek, Roelof and Wouter J. Hanegraaff (eds.), *Gnosis and Hermeticism: From Antiquity to Modern Times* (Albany, NY: State University of New York Press, 1998)

Van den Broek, Roelof and Ciss van Heertum (eds.), *From Poimandres to Jacob Böhme: Gnosis, Hermetism and the Christian Tradition* (Amsterdam: Im de Pelikaan, 2000)

Van Egmond, Daniel, 'Western Esoteric Schools in the Late Nineteenth and Early Twentieth Centuries', in Roelof van den Broek and Wouter J. Hanegraaff (eds.), *Gnosis and Hermeticism: From Antiquity to Modern Times* (Albany, NY: State University of New York Press, 1998), 311–46

———, '"This Mysterious Individual, William Stirling": Unpublished Letters Relating to the Author of *The Canon* (1897)', *English Studies*, 88:5 (2007), 531–62

———, 'The alchemical and kabbalistic correspondence of Walter Pagel and Gershom Scholem', *Bibliotheca Philosophica Hermetica* (13 December 2007), <http://www.ritmanlibrary.nl/c/p/h/bel_34.html>

Van Kleeck, Justin Scott, 'The Art of the Law: Aleister Crowley's Use of Ritual and Drama', *Esoterica*, 5 (2003), 193–218

Van Rijnberk, Gérard, *Un thaumaturge au 18e siècle, Martinès de Pasqually, sa vie, son œuvre, son ordre*, 2 volumes (Lyon: Derain et Raclet, 1938)

Varner, Eric R., *Mutilation and Transformation: Damnatio Memoriae and Roman Imperial Portraiture* (Leiden: Brill, 2004)

Vaughan, Michael, 'Introduction: Henri Bergson's Creative Evolution', *SubStance*, 36:3 (2007), 7–24

Veenstra, Jan R., 'The Holy Almandel: Angels and the Intellectual Aims of Magic', in Bremmer, Jan N. and Jan R. Veenstra (eds.), *The Metamorphosis of Magic: From Late Antiquity to the Early Modern Period* (Leuven: Peeters, 2002), 189–230)

Veltri, Guiseppe, 'The Rabbis and Pliny the Elder: Jewish and Greco-Roman Attitudes toward Magic and Empirical Knowledge', *Poetics Today*, 19:1 (1998), 63–89

Verman, Mark, *The Books of Contemplation: Medieval Jewish Mystical Sources* (Albany, NY: State University of New York Press, 1992)

———, *The History and Varieties of Jewish Meditation* (Northvale, NJ: Jason Aronson, 1996)

———, 'Signor Tranquillo's Magic Notebook', in Joseph Dan and Klaus Herrmann (eds.), *Studies in Jewish Manuscripts* (Tübingen: Mohr Siebeck, 1998), 231–37

Verman, Mark and Shulamit H. Adler, 'Path Jumping in the Jewish Magical Tradition', *Jewish Studies Quarterly*, 1:2 (1993/94), 131–48

Vernon, Roland, *Star in the East: Krishnamurti, the Invention of a Messiah* (Boulder, CO: Sentient Publications, 2002)

Versluis, Arthur, 'Methods in the Study of Western Esotericism', Part 1, 'What is Esoteric?', *Esoterica*, 4 (2002), 1–15; Part 2, 'Mysticism and the Study of Esotericism', *Esoterica*, 5 (2003), 27–40

———, *Restoring Paradise: Western Esotericism, Literature, Art, and Consciousness* (Albany, NY: State University of New York Press, 2004)

———, 'Sexual Mysticisms in Nineteenth Century America: John Humphrey Noyes, Thomas Lake Harris, and Alice Bunker Stockham', in Wouter J. Hanegraaff and Jeffrey J. Kripal (eds.), *Hidden Intercourse: Eros and Sexuality in the History of Western Esotericism* (Leiden: Brill, 2008), 333–54

Versluis, Arthur, Lee Irwin, John Richards, and Melina Weinstein (eds.), *Esotericism, Art, and Imagination* (East Lansing, MI: Michigan State University Press, 2008)

Versnel, H. S., 'Some Reflections on the Relationship Magic-Religion', *Numen*, 38 (1991), 177–97

Verter, Bradford, *Dark Star Rising: The Emergence of Modern Occultism, 1800–1950* (PhD Dissertation, Princeton University, 1997)

Vickers, Brian (ed.), *Occult and Scientific Mentalities in the Renaissance* (Cambridge: Cambridge University Press, 1984)

Vitale, Alfred, '"The Method of Science, The Aim of Religion": A Systematic Model for the Academic Study of Modern Western Occultism', *Esoterica*, 6 (2004), 39–67

Volovici, Leon, 'A Jewish European Modern Intellectual', *Eastern European Jewish Affairs*, 28:2 (1998–1999), 109–11

Von Engelhardt, Dietrich, 'Natural Science in the Age of Romanticism', in Antoine Faivre and Jacob Needleman (eds.), *Modern Esoteric Spirituality* (New York: Crossroad, 1992), 101–31

Von Franz, Marie-Louise, *Alchemical Active Imagination* (Irving, TX: Spring Publications, 1979; repr. New York: Shambhala, 1997)

Von Stuckrad, Kocku, 'Western esotericism: Towards an integrative model of interpretation', *Religion*, 35 (2005), 78–97

——, 'Whose Tradition? Conflicting Ideologies in Medieval and Early Modern Esotericism', in Steven Engler and Gregory P. Grieve (eds.), *Historicizing 'Tradition' in the Study of Religion* (Berlin / New York: Walter de Gruyter, 2005), 211–26

——, *Western Esotericism: A Brief History of Secret Knowledge* (London: Equinox, 2005)

——, Review of Marco Pasi, *Aleister Crowley und die Versuchung der Politik*, trans. Ferdinand Leopold, *Pomegranate*, 9:2 (2007), 194–96

——, 'Astral Magic in Ancient Jewish Discourse: Adoption, Transformation, Differentiation' (paper delivered at the Colloquium on Ancient Astrology, Warburg Institute, London, 16–17 February 2007)

Von Stuckrad, Kocku and Olav Hammer (eds.), *Polemical Encounters: Esoteric Discourse and Its Others* (Leiden: Brill, 2007)

Wakefield, Walter L. and Austin P. Evans (eds. and trans.), *Heresies of the High Middle Ages: Selected Sources Translated and Annotated* (New York: Columbia University Press, 1969)

Wald, Stephen G., *The Doctrine of the Divine Name: An Introduction to Classical Kabbalistic Theology* Brown (Atlanta, GA: Scholars Press, 1988)

Walker, D. P., 'The Prisca Theologia in France', Journal of the Warburg and Courtauld Institutes, 17:3/4 (1954), 204–59

——, 'The Astral Body in Renaissance Medicine', *Journal of the Warburg and Courtauld Institutes*, 21:1/2 (1958), 119–33

——, *The Ancient Theology: Studies in Christian Platonism from the Fifteenth to the Eighteenth Century* (London: Duckworth, 1972)

——, *Spiritual and Demonic Magic: From Ficino to Campanella* (London: University of Notre Dame Press, 1975)

Wallis, Richard T. and Jay Bregman (eds.), *Neoplatonism and Gnosticism* (Albany, NY: State University of New York Press, 1992)

Walters, Jennifer, *Magical Revival: Occultism and the Culture of Regeneration in Britain, c. 1880–1929* (PhD dissertation, University of Stirling, 2007)

Walton, Michael T., 'Hermetic Cabala in the *Monas Hieroglyphica* and the *Mosaicall Philosophy*' (1981), <http://www.greylodge.org/occultreview/glor_009/hermetic_cabala.htm>

——, 'John Dee's *Monas Hieroglyphica*: Geometrical Cabala', in Allen G. Debus, ed., *Alchemy and Early Modern Chemistry: Papers from Ambix* (London: Jeremy Mills/Society for the History of Alchemy and Chemistry, 2004), 178–85

Wang, Robert, *An Introduction to the Golden Dawn Tarot: Including the Original Documents on Tarot from the Order of the Golden Dawn with Explanatory Notes* (Wellingborough: Aquarian Press, 1978)

Wasserstrom, Steven M., 'The Magical Texts in the Cairo Genizah', in Joshua Blau and Stefan C. Reif (eds.), *Genizah Research after Ninety Years: The Case of Judaeo-Arabic* (Cambridge: Cambridge University Press, 1992), 160–66

——, *Religion After Religion: Gershom Scholem, Mircea Eliade, and Henry Corbin at Eranos* (Princeton, NJ: Princeton University Press, 1999)

——, 'Further Thoughts on the Origins of "Sefer Yesirah"', *Aleph*, 2 (2002), 201–21

Waterfield, Robin, *Hidden Depths: The Story of Hypnosis* (London: Macmillan, 2002)

Webb, James, *The Flight from Reason* (London: Macdonald, 1971; repr. as *The Occult Underground*, La Salle, IL: Open Court Publishing, 1974)
———, *The Occult Establishment* (London: Richard Drew Publishing, 1981)
Weber, Eugen, 'Religion and Superstition in Nineteenth-Century France', *Historical Journal*, 31:2 (1988), 399–423
Weber, Max, *The Protestant Ethic and the Spirit of Capitalism,* trans. Talcott Parsons (New York: Charles Scribner & Sons, 1958)
———, *The Sociology of Religion*, trans. Ephraim Fischoff (Boston, MA: Beacon Press, 1963)
———, *Economy and Society: An Outline of Interpretive Sociology*, ed. Guenther Roth and Claus Witich, trans. Ephraim Fischoff (Berkeley, CA: University of California Press, 1978)
Weber, Thomas, 'Anti-Semitism and Philo-Semitism among the British and German Elites: Oxford and Heidelberg before the First World War', *English Historical Review*, 118:475 (2003), 86–119
Webster, Charles, 'Paracelsus, Paracelsianism, and the Secularization of the Worldview', *Science in Context*, 15:1 (2002), 9–27
Weiss, Joseph, *Studies in Eastern European Jewish Mysticism*, ed. David Goldstein (Oxford: Oxford University Press, 1985)
Werblowsky, R. J. Zvi, 'Mystical and Magical Contemplation: The Kabbalists in Sixteenth-Century Safed', *History of Religions*, 1:1 (1961), 9–36
———, *Joseph Karo: Lawyer and Mystic* (Philadelphia, PA: The Jewish Publication Society of America/Oxford University Press, 1977)
———, 'The Safed Revival and Its Aftermath', in Arthur Green (ed.), *Jewish Spirituality, Volume 2: From the Sixteenth-Century Revival to the Present* (New York: Crossroad, 1997), 7–33
Whicher, Olive, *Projective Geometry: Creative Polarities in Space and Time* (London: Rudolf Steiner Press, 1971)
White, Hayden, *Metahistory: The Historical Imagination in Nineteenth-Century Europe* (Baltimore, MD: Johns Hopkins University Press, 1973)
Wilkinson, Lynn, *The Dream of an Absolute Language: Emanuel Swedenborg and French Literary Culture* (Albany, NY: State University of New York Press, 1996)
Wilkinson, R. J., *Orientalism, Aramaic and Kabbalah in the Catholic Reformation: The First Printing of the Syriac New Testament* (Leiden: Brill, 2007)
Willard, Thomas, 'Acts of the Companions: A. E. Waite's Fellowship and the Novels of Charles Williams', in Marie Mulvey Roberts and Hugh Ormsby-Lennon (eds.), *Secret Texts: The Literature of Secret Societies* (New York: AMS Press, 1995), 269–302
Williams, Thomas A., *Eliphas Lévi: Master of the Cabala, the Tarot and the Secret Doctrines* (Tuscaloosa, AL: University of Alabama Press, 1975)
Willis, Roy and Patrick Curry, *Astrology, Science and Culture: Pulling Down the Moon* (Oxford: Berg, 2004)
Winslade, J. Lawton, 'Techno-Kabbalah: The Performative Language of Magick and the Production of Occult Knowledge', *The Drama Review*, 44:2 (2000), 84–100
Wirszubski, Chaim, *Pico della Mirandola's Encounter with Jewish Mysticism* (Cambridge, MA: Harvard University Press, 1989)
Wistrich, Robert S., 'Radical Antisemitism in France and Germany (1840–1880)', *Modern Judaism*, 15:2 (1995), 109–35
Wittgenstein, Ludwig, *Philosophical Investigations*, trans. G. E. M. Anscombe (London: Blackwell, 2001)
Wodzinski, Marcin, 'How Modern Is an Antimodernist Movement? The Emergence of Hasidic Politics in Congress Poland', *AJS Review*, 31:2 (2007), 221–40

Wohl, Anthony S., '"Dizzi-Ben-Dizzi": Disraeli as Alien', *The Journal of British Studies*, 34:3 (1995), 375–411

Wolfson, Elliot R., 'The Theosophy of Shabbetai Donnolo, with Special Emphasis on the Doctrine of *Sefirot* in His *Sefer Hakhmoni*', *Jewish History*, 6:1–2 (1992), 281–316

——, 'Forms of Visionary Ascent as Ecstatic Experience in the Zoharic Literature', in Peter Schäfer and Joseph Dan (eds.), *Gershom Scholem's Major Trends in Jewish Mysticism: 50 Years After* (Tubingen: Mohr Siebeck, 1993), 209–35

——, *Circle in the Square: Studies in the Use of Gender in Kabbalistic Symbolism* (Albany, NY: State University of New York Press, 1995)

——, 'Metatron and Shi'ur Qomah in the Writings of Haside Ashkenaz', in Karl E. Grözinger and Joseph Dan (eds.), *Mysticism, Magic and Kabbalah in Ashkenazi Judaism* (Berlin: Walter de Gruyter, 1995), 60–92

——, 'Weeping, Death, and Spiritual Ascent in Sixteenth-Century Jewish Mysticism', in John J. Collins and Michael Fishbane (eds.), *Death, Ecstasy, and Other Worldly Journeys* (Albany, NY: State University of New York Press, 1995), 209–47

——, *Through a Speculum That Shines: Vision and Imagination in Medieval Jewish Mysticism* (Princeton, NJ: Princeton University Press, 1997)

——, 'Hebraic and Hellenic Conceptions of Wisdom in *Sefer ha-Bahir*', *PT*, 19:1 (1998), 147–76

——, 'Occultation of the Feminine and the Body of Secrecy', in Elliot R. Wolfson, ed., *Rending the Veil: Concealment and Secrecy in the History of Religions* (New York: Seven Bridges Press, 1999), 155–76

—— (ed.), *Rending the Veil: Concealment and Secrecy in the History of Religions* (New York: Seven Bridges Press, 1999)

——, *Abraham Abulafia – Kabbalist and Prophet: Hermeneutics, Theosophy and Theurgy* (Los Angeles, CA: Cherub Press, 2000)

——, 'Beyond the Spoken Word: Oral Tradition and Written Transmission in Medieval Jewish Mysticism', in Yaakov Elman and Israel Gershoni (eds.), *Transmitting Jewish Traditions: Orality, Textuality and Cultural Diffusion* (New Haven, CT: Yale University Press, 2000), 167–224

——, 'Phantasmagoria: The Image of the Image in Jewish Magic from Late Antiquity to the Early Middle Ages', *Review of Rabbinic Judaism*, 4:1 (2001), 78–120

——, 'Assaulting the Border: Kabbalistic Traces in the Margins of Derrida', *Journal of the American Academy of Religion*, 70:3 (2002), 475–514

——, *Language, Eros, Being: Kabbalistic Hermeneutics and Poetic Imagination* (New York: Fordham University Press, 2005)

——, 'Language, Secrecy, and the Mysteries of the Law: Theurgy and the Christian Kabbalah of Johannes Reuchlin', in Daniel Abrams and Avraham Elqayam (eds.), *Kabbalah: Journal for the Study of Jewish Mystical Texts*, Vol. 13 (Los Angeles, CA: Cherub Press, 2005), 7–41

——, *Alef, Mem, Tau: Kabbalistic Musings on Time, Truth, and Death* (Berkeley, CA: University of California Press, 2006)

——, *Luminal Darkness: Imaginal Gleanings from Zoharic Literature* (Oxford: Oneworld, 2007)

——, 'Structure, Innovation, and Diremptive Temporality: The Use of Models to Study Continuity and Discontinuity in Kabbalistic Tradition', *Journal for the Study of Religions and Ideologies*, 6:18 (2007), 143–67

——, 'Murmuring Secrets: Eroticism and Esotericism in Medieval Kabbalah', in Wouter J. Hanegraaff and Jeffrey J. Kripal (eds.), *Hidden Intercourse: Eros and Sexuality in the History of Western Esotericism* (Leiden: Brill, 2008), 65–109

————, *A Dream Interpreted Within a Dream: Oneiropoiesis and the Prism of Imagination* (New York, NY: Zone, 2011)

Wolfson, H. A., *Philo: Foundations of Religious Philosophy in Judaism, Christianity, and Islam*, 2 volumes (Cambridge, MA: Harvard University Press, 1947)

Wood, Juliette, 'The Celtic Tarot and the Secret Tradition: A Study in Modern Legend Making', *Folklore*, 109 (1998), 15–24

Woods, Richard (ed.), *Understanding Mysticism* (Garden City, NY: Doubleday/Image, 1980)

Wright, J. Edward, *The Early History of Heaven* (Oxford: Oxford University Press, 2000)

Yates, Frances A., *Giordano Bruno and the Hermetic Tradition* (London: Routledge & Kegan Paul, 1964)

————, 'Giovanni Pico della Mirandola and magic', in *L'opera e il pensiero di Giovanni Pico della Mirandola nella storia dell'umanismo, Vol. 1* (Firenze: Istituto Nazionale di Studi sul Rinascimento, 1965), 159–204

————, *The Art of Memory* (London: Routledge & Kegan Paul, 1966)

————, *Theatre of the World* (London: Routledge & Kegan Paul, 1969)

————, *The Rosicrucian Enlightenment* (London: Routledge & Kegan Paul, 1972)

————, *The Occult Philosophy in the Elizabethan Age* (London: Routledge & Kegan Paul, 1979)

————, *Lull and Bruno: Collected Essays, Vol. 1* (London: Routledge & Kegan Paul, 1982)

Yerushalmi, Yosef Hayim, *Freud's Moses: Judaism Terminable and Interminable* (New Haven, CT: Yale University Press, 1991)

Yoder, Don, 'Toward a Definition of Folk Religion', *Western Folklore*, 33:1 (1974), 2–15

Yorke, Gerald, 'Foreword', in Ellic Howe, *The Magicians of the Golden Dawn: A Documentary History of a Magical Order 1887–1923* (London: Routledge & Kegan Paul, 1972), ix–xix

Zaleski, Carol, *Otherworld Journeys: Accounts of Near-Death Experiences in Medieval and Modern Times* (Oxford: Oxford University Press, 1987)

————, *Inner Order Teachings of the Golden Dawn* (Loughborough: Thoth Publications, 2006)

Zalewski, Pat, *Kabbalah of the Golden Dawn* (St. Paul, MN: Llewellyn, 1993)

————, *Inner Order Teachings of the Golden Dawn* (Loughborough: Thoth Publications, 2006)

Zielonka, Anthony, *Alphonse Esquiros (1812–1876): Choix de lettres: Textes réunis, présentés et annotés par Anthony Zielonka* (Paris: Champion-Slatkine, 1990)

Zika, Charles, 'Reuchlin's *De Verbo Mirifico* and the Magic Debate of the Late Fifteenth Century', *Journal of the Warburg and Courtauld Institutes*, 39 (1976), 104–38

Zimmels, H. J., *Ashkenazim and Sephardim: Their Relations, Differences, and Problems as Reflected in the Rabbinical Responsa* (Oxford: Oxford University Press, 1958)

Zweig, Janet, '*Ars Combinatoria*: Mystical Systems, Procedural Art, and the Computer', *Art Journal*, 56:3 (1997), 20–29

WEBSITES

Aeclectic Tarot
<http://www.aeclectic.net/tarot>

Alchemy
<http://www.levity.com/alchemy>

Bibliotheca Philosophica Hermetica
<http://www.ritmanlibrary.nl>

Bishop Wilkins College No. 58, SRIA
<http://www.bishopwilkins.co.uk>

Confraternity of the Rosy Cross
<http://www.crcsite.org >

Economic Expert
<http://www.economicexpert.com>

European Association for Jewish Studies Newsletter
<http://www.lzz.uni-halle.de/publikationen/essays>

Fraternitas Rosae Crucis
<http://www.soul.org>

Hermetic Kabbalah
<http://digital-brilliance.com/kab/index.htm>

Kabbalah Center
<http://www.kabbalah.com>

Kabbala denudata
<http://www.billheidrick.com/Orpd/KRKD/index.htm>

Kabbalah Society
<http://www.kabbalahsociety.org>

Ordo Templi Orientis
<http://www.oto-uk.org> (Grand Lodge of Great Britain and Northern Ireland)
<http://oto-usa.org> (United States Grand Lodge)

Oxford Dictionary of National Biography
<http://www.oxforddnb.com>

Philo 19: Bibliographical Database of Nineteenth Century French Philosophy
<http://www.textesrares.com/philo19>

Pietre-Stones Review of Freemasonry
<http://www.freemasons-freemasonry.com>

Rosicrucian Fellowship
<http://www.rosicrucian.com>

Society for the Inner Light Journal
<http://www.innerlight.org.uk/journals>

Societas Magica Newsletter
<http://brindedcow.umd.edu/socmag>

Societas Rosicruciana in America
<http://www.sria.org>

Societas Rosicruciana in Anglia
<http://www.sria.info>

Stanford University Encyclopedia of Philosophy
<http://plato.stanford.edu>

Tarot.com
<http://www/tarot.com>

'The Short Talk Bulletin'
<http://www.freemasoninformation.com>

Wiktionary
<http://en.wiktionary.org>

Lightning Source UK Ltd.
Milton Keynes UK
UKOW06f1807310816

281936UK00014B/309/P